# INTRODUCTION TO P☉LICING

EDITION **3**

STEVEN M. COX ▪ SUSAN MARCHIONNA ▪ BRIAN D. FITCH

An **accessible** and **engaging** writing style with **stories from the field** to make policing concepts and practices easy for your students to **understand** and **apply**.

Focusing on the thought-provoking, contemporary issues that underscore the challenging and rewarding world of policing, Steven M. Cox, Susan Marchionna, and experienced law enforcement officer Brian D. Fitch balance theory, research, and practice to give students a comprehensive, yet concise, overview of both the foundations of policing and the expanded role of today's police officers.

Unique coverage of policing in multicultural communities, the impact of technology on policing, and extensive coverage of policing strategies and procedures—such as those that detail the use of force—make this bestselling book a must-have for policing courses.

"*I would* **absolutely** *recommend this book. It is current, comprehensive, and relatable, and has a balanced presentation of research and practice. It is well-written and won't bore students with what can be fairly dry subjects by providing anecdotes and insight.*"

—**Melanie Norwood,**
*University of Illinois–Chicago*

# Stories From Real-World Policing

Police Stories use first-person vignettes drawn from the experiences of the authors and other law enforcement officers to bring policing dilemmas to life.

> The police stories I read were good, and students can relate to this more personal level of insight, that is, from looking over the shoulders of working cops.
>
> —**James Chriss**, *Cleveland State University*

**POLICE ⬡ STORIES** 12.1

### Connie Koski, Professor and Former Police Officer

It wasn't until I retired and took the time to study the history of the mistreatment of minorities at the hands of law enforcement officers that I fully understood the root causes of minority mistrust and conflict with the police.

This became clear to me one evening, when I was working the night shift without a partner or nearby backup, and I attempted to arrest an African American man on the street who had multiple felony warrants. He began to resist, assaulting me in an attempt to get away. A crowd began to gather around us, and both the man and the crowd began to chant, "Rodney King, Rodney King!" I was concerned for my safety, as the crowd grew more adamant, shouting that I was a racist and was unnecessarily harassing this man because he was Black. This was a common occurrence in the city in which I worked, and I, a White female from a middle-class background, would always become enraged that people seemed to continuously "pull the race card." I deeply resented being accused of being racist and was often angry about it.

What I did not understand at the time was the significance of the historical context surrounding the long-standing mistreatment of African Americans and other minorities across this country, including similar past practices by former officers of my own department. Looking back, I believe that this significantly impeded my ability to understand many of the citizens I dealt with on a daily basis. Historical context is rarely taught in police in-service "multicultural human relations" classes, and students often rush through chapters to get to what they perceive to be the real "nuts and bolts" of policing. Upon reflection, I wish I had paid more attention to the relevance of history and how the past affects today. Arguably, a fuller understanding of U.S. police history would assist officers in serving the minority members of their communities more empathetically and help them more fully understand the potential consequences of their actions.

---

# Thought-Provoking Features

You Decide boxes present realistic dilemmas and include new material, plus suggested responses for discussion and critical thinking on the Student Study Site.

> I'm a fan of the *Case in Point* and *You Decide* exercises.
>
> —**Michael S. Penrod**, *Kirkwood Community College*

> These encourage critical thinking, and application of the readings which are useful learning tools.
>
> —**Amy Stutzenberger**, *Western Oregon University*

> This is an excellent feature that I hope instructors will use. I thought your examples were thoughtful and could promote a great discussion with a willing class. It opens a great opportunity to get the students involved and thinking and encourages the use of the Socratic method of teaching.
>
> —**Paul Brent Foushee**, *University of North Carolina at Charlotte*

**YOU ??? DECIDE** 6.1

Police officers are now wearing a type of body camera on their uniforms and, in some cases, also equipping stun guns with cameras. Janesville, Wisconsin, police record all interactions with residents. "The video cameras are about the size of a Bic lighter and clip onto an officer's uniform." They turn off and on by touch and are "downloaded at the end of the shift or on to laptops immediately after an incident."

Police officers in Janesville have found the tiny video cameras to be particularly useful for the arrest of intoxicated drivers. "It's hard to write notes about a field sobriety test when you have to watch someone attempt the test and count the number of steps he or she is taking. In the past, officers had to juggle a flashlight and a clipboard while never taking their eyes off the suspected drunk driver".

In the wake of high-profile and lethal police shootings of citizens in Missouri and New York in 2014, President Barack Obama convened the Task Force on 21st Century Policing to explore ways to help repair public confidence in the nation's police forces. The task force issued many justice-related recommendations, some of which pertain to technology. The task force stopped short of specifically recommending the use of body cameras on the police, calling it a complex issue and noting the difficulties in implementing it. In addition, the task force acknowledged that there is a difficult balance between monitoring the police, protecting privacy rights of citizens, and the temptation to rely too heavily on the video as a source of infallible information. Obama himself cautioned that cameras would not be a "panacea."

The hope of many is that the cameras will serve a tempering influence on the police. In any case, the use of body cameras is likely to increase. As it does, each state will have to grapple with the fine points of using such monitoring devices. According to Wisconsin statutes, police are not required to inform a person that they are recording an interview or a traffic stop.

1. Should police officers be required to use tiny video cameras to record actions of all persons they encounter? Why or why not?

2. Do you believe public knowledge that police are recording all interactions with the public has an effect on police–citizen interactions? If so, explain.

3. Under what circumstances should officers be required or allowed to turn cameras off?

*Sources:* "Janesville police officers see benefit in body cameras," by Ann Marie Ames, 2012. *Janesville Extra*. Retrieved May 2012 from http://gazettextra.com; "Obama task force urges independent probes of police killings," by David Jackson, March 2, 2015. *USA Today*. Retrieved from http://www.usatoday.com/story/news/nation/2015/03/02/obama-task-force-on-21st-century-policing-ferguson/24258019/

## Computer Hacking

16.1

Law enforcement officials at all levels are in the position of having to play "catch up" with technologically sophisticated criminals, whose very motive is to stay a step ahead.

In July 2015, the U.S. government revealed a data breach of staggering proportions at its Office of Personnel Management (OPM). Highly personal information obtained by conducting background checks for security clearances included State Department posts, Social Security numbers, addresses, medical histories, criminal background information, drug use profiles, and romantic histories. The fear was that hackers could use the information for the purposes of blackmail or any number of nefarious purposes.

Far exceeding original estimates, the hackers accessed data on 22.1 million current, former, and prospective government employees and contractors, and their friends and family members, which is approximately 7% of the nation's population.[5]

The incident was considered one of the most damaging to date, given the number of people affected and the sensitivity of the information the hackers obtained. Katherine Archuleta headed the organization and expressed an intention to remain in place as the agency's leader, despite calls for her resignation. The White House National Security Council stopped short of an official accusation, but investigators told the news service that a team with links to China's ministry of state security was a suspect in the hacking incident. The data were not encrypted, and parts of the agency's computer system were likely outdated. Hackers appeared to have used malicious software to carry out the "cyber intrusion," considered by some to be an "aggressive act of espionage."[6] It was not yet known how the information would be put to use. Some of the individuals whose personal data was stolen received information from the government about containing and responding to the incident, such as a promise of three years of credit monitoring; others have received scant information.

1. Discuss how this incident could exemplify the need for effective public/private law enforcement partnerships.

2. How can federal and local law enforcement most effectively respond to the hacking of personal information?

# Unique & Diverse Coverage of Current Topics

Current topics include coverage on Ferguson events, the most recent U.S. Supreme court decisions that affect the police, technological developments in policing, and much more.

> This feature assists students in seeing how textbook knowledge translates into real-world situations. Additionally, *Case In Point* boxes help illustrate difficult concepts in ways in which an instructor or professor may not be particularly knowledgeable, and thus this only furthers their usefulness to the student.
>
> —**Connie Koski**, *Longwood University*

7.1

## Community Police in Nepal for Security and Justice

Policing is a vital part of the security institution in Nepal, and efforts have been made to mobilize the police to meet the needs of society. Established in 2004, community police in Nepal have been working to achieve security, justice, and public order. To achieve these goals, community police have coordinated with several social institutions in the community to work on problems such as household violence, children's issues, drugs, and other social ills. In addition, community police focus more on improvement than on punishment.

Apart from security, justice, and public order, community police are involved in humanitarian tasks as well. For example, the community police unit in Chitwan assists in providing shelters for street children and female victims of war and domestic abuse. Community police have also been providing scholarships and stationery to deserving students from poor economic backgrounds in coordination with various educational institutions. Head Constable of Community Policing Gokarna Prasad Dhakal noted, "We give counseling to school and college children for their mistakes rather than taking direct actions on them because in the long run it might have a negative impact on the future of these children. Therefore, if they are caught doing anything wrong, we bring [in] their parents and give counseling together."

There are still a number of obstacles to successful community policing in Nepal, including a lack of resources and budget and the difficulty of establishing coordination and cooperation with the community. On the positive side, Dhakal says, "Since the community is involved, information is delivered very quickly because of which our actions can be prompt."

Dhakal has been involved with community policing as an officer for three years and says, "I am very satisfied with my job . . . It gives me a feeling of self-contentment to be able to build the society. Now I am directed toward doing something for the society and [helping] the society transform itself as well."

1. Skeptics of Nepal's community policing efforts would argue that law enforcement officers should be fighting crime, not providing counseling to school and college children. What would justify these efforts as the best use of the Security Institution's limited resources?

2. The community police have shifted their focus in many cases from punishment to improvement. Do you believe that these efforts are effective at fighting crime?

3. Is there anything that U.S. law enforcement can learn from Nepal's efforts?

*Source:* Pradhan, P. (2012, February 10). Community police in Nepal for security and justice. *Xinhua News Agency*; Dateline: CHITWAN, Nepal. Record Number: ChkhaeE000047_20120210_GWTFN1_fake. COPYRIGHT 2012 Xinhua News Agency.

# Global Perspectives

Around the World boxes highlight relevant topics in other nations to afford readers the opportunity to consider, from a global perspective, what they might otherwise view as problems unique to U.S. police agencies.

> *Around the World* is also definitely beneficial to my students. My students, just like students across the nation, need more understanding of what is going outside the United States.
>
> —**Emmanuel N. Amadi**, *Mississippi Valley State University*

# SAGE Original Video

An extensive video package, available in the SAGE edge online resources and within the Interactive eBook, includes original SAGE videos, including interviews with:

- Brian Fitch, author, LA County Sheriff's Department
- Jeri Williams, Chief of Police with the Oxnard Police Department
- Kevin Wilmott, Police Officer in Southern California

# Interactive eBook Tools

**Audio Links** from programs, like NPR.

**Web Links** to informative sites, including the Department of Justice.

**Video Links** to relevant sources, such as PBS and Police One.

**SAGE Journal Articles** from journals, like *Police Quarterly* and *Criminal Justice and Behavior*.

**Author Videos** feature Brian Fitch and his career with the LA County Sheriff's Department.

***Policing in Practice* Videos** were filmed specifically for this text. These SAGE original videos feature Oxnard Chief of Police Jeri Williams and Police Officer Kevin Wilmott's experiences in policing. The videos also include a collection of interviews with professionals in the policing field.

# Experienced Author Team

### Steven M. Cox, Ph.D., Western Illinois University

Dr. Cox was a member of the Law Enforcement and Justice Administration faculty at Western Illinois University from 1975 to 2007. For the past 45 years he has served as trainer and consultant to numerous criminal justice agencies in the United States and abroad and has worked with several universities in the area of course development.

### Susan Marchionna, Criminal Justice Communications Consultant

Susan Marchionna is a Criminal Justice Communications Consultant with a varied background in writing, publications, and communications. She has consulted with the Earl Warren Institute on Law and Social Policy at UC Berkeley, the MOSS Group on publications projects related to PREA compliance and sexual safety in institutions, and the Nation Partnership for Juvenile Services in conjunction with OJJDP. Prior to her current consulting work, Susan was the Director of Communication at the National Council on Crime and Delinquency (NCCD).

### Brian D. Fitch, Los Angeles County Sheriff's Department

Brian D. Fitch, Ph.D., is a lieutenant and a 33-year veteran of the Los Angeles County Sheriff's Department. He has worked assignments in custody, field operations, investigations, and training throughout the United States, as well as internationally in Canada, Oman, Qatar, Saudi Arabia, and the United Arab Emirates, in leadership and communication skills. He holds faculty positions at California State University, Long Beach and Woodbury University.

# INTRODUCTION TO
# PLICING

EDITION
3

*I would like to dedicate this third edition to William P. McCamey and Gene L. Scaramella, co-authors of the first and second editions, who both lost their battles with cancer. Both Bill and Gene were close friends and colleagues. I miss them more than words can say. Memories made over many years remain fresh in my mind.*

—Steve Cox

*I would like to dedicate my work on this book to the original three authors, Steven M. Cox, William P. McCamey, and Gene L. Scaramella, whom I never had the good fortune to meet in person, and whose work established a firm platform for me from which to spring.*

*I also dedicate this volume to my mother, Sara, who nursed me through an illness that occurred just as I approached a critical deadline. She instilled in me the values of hard work, honesty, and perseverance, all of which have proven to be qualities indispensible in arriving at the completed third edition of* Introduction to Policing.

*Lastly, I would like to acknowledge the men and women who dedicate themselves to public service in police organizations across the nation and who perform their difficult jobs with integrity and a balanced sense of justice. We all depend on them.*

—Susan Marchionna

# INTRODUCTION TO
# POLICING

EDITION
3

## STEVEN M. COX
Western Illinois University

## SUSAN MARCHIONNA
Criminal Justice Communications Consultant

## BRIAN D. FITCH
Los Angeles County Sheriff's Department
Woodbury University

Los Angeles | London | New Delhi
Singapore | Washington DC

Los Angeles | London | New Delhi
Singapore | Washington DC

FOR INFORMATION:

SAGE Publications, Inc.
2455 Teller Road
Thousand Oaks, California 91320
E-mail: order@sagepub.com

SAGE Publications Ltd.
1 Oliver's Yard
55 City Road
London EC1Y 1SP
United Kingdom

SAGE Publications India Pvt. Ltd.
B 1/I 1 Mohan Cooperative Industrial Area
Mathura Road, New Delhi 110 044
India

SAGE Publications Asia-Pacific Pte. Ltd.
3 Church Street
#10-04 Samsung Hub
Singapore 049483

Printed in the United States of America

*Library of Congress Cataloging-in-Publication Data*

Names: Cox, Steven M. | Marchionna, Susan. | Fitch, Brian D.

Title: Introduction to policing / Steven M. Cox, Susan Marchionna, Brian D. Fitch.

Description: Third Edition. | Thousand Oaks : SAGE Publications, Inc., 2016. | ?2017 | Revised edition of Introduction to policing, 2014. | Includes bibliographical references and index.

Identifiers: LCCN 2015038734 | ISBN 978-1-5063-0754-1 (pbk. : alk. paper)

Subjects: LCSH: Police—United States. | Community policing—United States.

Classification: LCC HV8139 .C69 2016 | DDC 363.20973—dc23 LC record available at http://lccn.loc.gov/2015038734

Acquisitions Editor:   Jerry Westby
Associate Editor:   Jessica Miller
Editorial Assistant:   Laura Kirkhuff
eLearning Editor:   Nicole Mangona
Production Editor:   Libby Larson
Copy Editor:   Melinda Masson
Typesetter:   C&M Digitals (P) Ltd.
Proofreader:   Eleni Georgiou
Indexer:   Will Ragsdale
Cover Designer:   Janet Kiesel
Marketing Manager:   Terra Schultz

This book is printed on acid-free paper.

SUSTAINABLE FORESTRY INITIATIVE
Certified Chain of Custody
Promoting Sustainable Forestry
www.sfiprogram.org
SFI-01268
SFI label applies to text stock

16 17 18 19 20 10 9 8 7 6 5 4 3 2

## BRIEF CONTENTS

# ■■■■■ DETAILED CONTENTS

REUTERS/Jim Youn

AP Photo/Julio Cortez

# PART IV. CONTEMPORARY ISSUES IN POLICING    277

istockphoto.com/Bastiaan Slabber

## Chapter 13. Technology and the Police — 312

## Chapter 14. Organized Crime, Homeland Security, and Global Issues — 342

## Chapter 15. Private Police — 362

P olice in the United States must operate in the face of a climate that is constantly changing—politically, economically, socially, and legally.

As the 21st century unfolds, police officers must continue to perform traditional tasks related to law enforcement and order maintenance. At the same time, they must find innovative ways to be problem solvers and community organizers. The public expects them to perform all of these diverse tasks wisely and ethically.

The nation's police also have had to come to terms with the global nature of crime. The conditions that exist throughout the world increasingly complicate the organizational and functional dynamics of the police community. Police executives must think and plan globally in a spirit of interagency cooperation now more than at any point in history.

A series of controversial and high-profile events have given rise to a new wave of public attention on the police, especially in regards to the use of force and race.

Standing in relief among several other similar events, the deaths of Eric Garner in New York, Walter Scott in North Charleston, South Carolina, and—perhaps most symbolically—Michael Brown in Ferguson, Missouri, have galvanized a wave of protests against police practices that much of the public perceives as unjust. Communities are scrutinizing police behavior and accountability, as has occurred in other eras. However, today, almost everyone is carrying a video camera around in his or her pocket or purse. Video footage of police interactions with the public appears instantly online.

Many consider the issues surrounding police use of force, especially in communities of color, to be the most important civil rights cause of our current day.

There is clearly a vast gulf in understanding between the police and the community that these events illuminate. In some communities, the public and the police have squared off and are maintaining polar positions. Men and women in uniform have become the targets of angry and violent retaliation, while police departments across the nation struggle to defend their policies and practices.

In many ways, Ferguson has become a lightning rod for these critical policing issues. The U.S. Department of Justice (DOJ) reported in March 2015 that the Ferguson Police Department's law enforcement efforts were focused on generating revenue rather than ensuring public safety. The DOJ also reported that the department's practices violated the 1st, 4th, and 14th Amendments; caused significant harm to individual members of the community; and undermined the public trust. The report applauded the efforts of many of the department's and the city's employees who "perform their duties lawfully and with respect for all members of the Ferguson community."[1] Finally, the DOJ recommended a host of changes to police practices and court procedures. Primary among these recommendations is that Ferguson implement a robust program of community policing, which includes some of the following points—that it fundamentally change the way it conducts stops and searches, issues citations and summonses, and makes arrests; that it increase its data collection and analysis; that it change its use-of-force policies and practices to encourage de-escalation; and that it retrain its officers to improve interaction with vulnerable people. At the same time, the DOJ analyzed the shooting in detail, cleared Officer Darren Wilson of willfully violating Brown's civil rights, and stated that Wilson's use of force was defensible. Also, many of the media accounts contained erroneous information about Brown's actions immediately prior to the shooting, according to the report.[2]

To the extent that these issues resonate in other of the nation's police departments, the lessons of Ferguson will prove to have enormous value. Thus, the public and the police both are coming to realize, once again, that a basic requirement for effective and efficient civil policing is a meaningful community partnership. Only when such a partnership exists can the police perform all of their tasks as problem solvers, service providers, and law enforcers. Only then will the public provide the support and resources necessary for the successful performance of these tasks. This partnership must be based on open, two-way communication, trust, and mutual respect.

This text attempts to shed light on the complex world of policing and to help bridge the gulf of understanding. Although the chapters examine a variety of topics separately, all of the subject matter is interrelated and is best considered as a totality. Changes in any one area have repercussions in other areas. Examining the relationships among the issues facing the police helps to bring some much-needed clarity to this dynamic and multifaceted world.

## ■ THE ORGANIZATION

This text consists of five sections and 16 chapters, providing readers with thought-provoking and contemporary issues that underscore today's challenging world of policing. The text begins with a discussion of past and current policing strategies. Part I, Foundations of Policing, encompasses Chapters 1, 2, and 3 and provides context for subsequent chapter topics by introducing the general subject of the police, its history in the United States, and how the police are organized and administered.

Part II, Police Operations, includes Chapters 4 through 7, which focus on the human dynamics that affect policing: the recruitment, selection, and promotion of police officers; training and education; the operations and functions of police work; and contemporary strategies that take into account the public perceptions of police and various strategies such as community-based policing and intelligence-led policing.

Part III, Police Conduct, includes Chapters 8 through 11, which examine the police subculture that often determines individual and group decision making; the institutional and organizational structures and processes that pertain to the law; the social, political, and economic forces that affect the field; discretion and ethics; and police misconduct and accountability.

Part IV, Contemporary Issues in Policing, includes Chapters 12 through 15 and deals with complex factors that affect the field of policing, including issues such as social diversity, the use of rapidly advancing technology, the impact of global issues such as terrorism and transnational organized crime, and the increasingly significant role of the private security industry.

The book concludes with Part V (Chapter 16), Looking Ahead, which takes a view toward the future of policing in the United States.

## ■ KEY FEATURES OF THE TEXT

Each chapter contains a variety of thought-provoking exercises, highlights, and supplemental materials. These unique features include the following:

*Around the World* highlights relevant topics in other nations to afford readers the opportunity to consider, from a worldwide perspective, what they might otherwise view as problems unique to U.S. police agencies. The feature also suggests resources for further exploration.

*You Decide* presents students with realistic dilemmas that might be encountered during a career in policing. Students are encouraged to consider possible solutions to these dilemmas using information from the text, other sources, or personal experiences. This feature should help promote spirited classroom discussions.

*Case in Point* includes real-life examples from current and past events to emphasize one or more of the major issues associated with the chapter topic. This feature also includes thought-provoking discussion questions.

*Police Stories* bring in personal experiences from the field of policing. They are firsthand accounts that share with students actual incidents from the past that serve as meaningful learning experiences. Students can reflect on and discuss what they would do under similar circumstances.

*Exhibits* are brief supplemental pieces that relate to and enhance the text and provide additional insight and depth.

Beyond these features, each chapter also includes a set of learning objectives, key terms and phrases, discussion questions based on the learning objectives, and two to three Internet exercises.

We hope that these key features will make this text even more useful as students develop a deeper understanding of the complex and dynamic field of policing.

## ■ NEW TO THIS EDITION

Each chapter of the third edition has been reorganized and presents the subject in a more streamlined and direct writing style. Throughout, this edition incorporates issues of ethnicity and race, including practices and outcomes.

In addition to these overall changes, this third edition:

- Contains the most recent U.S. Supreme Court decisions that affect the police.
- Includes the most important technological developments in policing.
- Provides up-to-date coverage of current issues, emerging trends, and innovations in the areas of technology, use of force, diversity, and police–community relations.

Plus:

- Research, statistics, and data have been updated to provide an accurate snapshot of policing today.
- Ten new Police Stories have been added to include a wider range of officer voices.
- Exhibit boxes have been added that provide concrete examples to help students make real-world connections.
- The number of figures included in the text has been quadrupled to provide a more visual display of information.
- Over half of the You Decide boxes have been updated to present new scenarios.
- Seven new Case in Point boxes have been added to highlight recent events.
- The organization and writing style of each chapter has been enhanced to increase student engagement, comprehension, and retention of the information.
- Questions have been added to the Case in Point and Around the World boxes to further engage students and encourage critical thinking.

## ■ ANCILLARIES

**SAGE edge** offers a robust online environment featuring an impressive array of tools and resources for review, study, and further exploration, keeping both instructors and students on the cutting edge of teaching and learning. SAGE edge content is open access and available on demand. Learning and teaching have never been easier!

**SAGE edge for Instructors** supports teaching by making it easy to integrate quality content and create a rich learning environment for students.

**edge.sagepub.com/coxpolicing3e**

- **Test banks** provide a diverse range of prewritten options as well as the opportunity to edit any

question and/or insert personalized questions to effectively assess students' progress and understanding.

- **Sample course syllabi** for semester and quarter courses provide suggested models for structuring one's course.
- Editable, chapter-specific **PowerPoint®️ slides** offer complete flexibility for creating a multimedia presentation for the course.
- EXCLUSIVE! Full-text **SAGE journal articles** have been carefully selected to support and expand on the concepts presented in each chapter to encourage students to think critically.
- **Video and audio links** includes original SAGE videos that appeal to students with different learning styles.
- **Lecture notes** summarize key concepts by chapter to ease preparation for lectures and class discussions.
- **Web resources** extend and reinforce learning and allow for further research on important chapter topics

**SAGE edge for Students** provides a personalized approach to help students accomplish their coursework goals in an easy-to-use learning environment.

- Mobile-friendly **eFlashcards** strengthen understanding of key terms and concepts.
- Mobile-friendly practice **quizzes** allow for independent assessment by students of their mastery of course material.
- **Video and audio links** enhance classroom-based exploration of key topics.
- A customized online **action plan** includes tips and feedback on progress through the course and materials, which allows students to individualize their learning experience.
- **Learning objectives** reinforce the most important material.
- **Web resources** and **web exercises** allow for further research on important chapter topics
- EXCLUSIVE! Full-text **SAGE journal articles** have been carefully selected to support and expand on the concepts presented in each chapter.

# ■ ACKNOWLEDGMENTS

Thanks to Professors Richard Ward, Paul Ilsley, Michael Hazlett, John Wade, Matthew Lippman, David Harpool, Bob Fischer, Giri Raj Gupta, Denny Bliss, Terry Campbell, Sandy Yeh, Bill Lin, Jennifer Allen, John Conrad, John Song, Stan Cunningham, and Don Bytner for their friendship, guidance, encouragement, and contributions to the book. Thanks also to the many police officers who shared their experiences with us over the years, including O. J. Clark, Jerry Bratcher, Mark Fleischhauer, Brian Howerton, Jerry Friend, Bill Hedeen, Bob Elliott, Donna Cox, Michael Holub, Dwight Baird, John Harris, William Lansdowne, Michael Ruth, Anthony Abbate, Timothy Bolger, and Richard Williams. And thanks to Judges John D. Tourtelot, Edward R. Danner, and Thomas J. Homer.

The third edition authors wish to also thank the first and second edition authors, Steven M. Cox, William P. McCamey, and Gene L. Scaramella. Thanks go as well to current and former police officers Connie Koski, Dan Kroenig, and John Crombach for their insights and contributions.

Finally, we offer a huge debt of gratitude to Jerry Westby, Jessica Miller, Laura Kirkhuff, Libby Larson, and Melinda Masson of SAGE Publications for making this book a reality. Your guidance and patience is of untold value.

The authors and SAGE gratefully acknowledge the contributions of the reviewers who provided feedback on the manuscript.

For the first edition, we thank Earl Ballou, Palo Alto College; Lorenzo Boyd, Fayetteville State University; Obie Clayton, Morehouse College; Jennifer Estis-Sumerel, Itawamba Community College–Tupelo; Arthur Hayden, Kentucky State University; Daniel Howard, Rutgers University; Richard Kania, Jacksonville State University; Connie Koski, University of Nebraska at Omaha; Douglas Larkins, Arkansas State University–Beebe; Thomas O'Connor, Austin Peay State University; Jeffrey Rush, Austin Peay State University; and Rupendra Simlot, Richard Stockton College.

For the second edition, we thank George Coroian, Penn State Wilkes-Barre; Michele W. Covington, Georgia Southern University; Doris L. Edmonds, Norfolk State University; Michael Freeman, Mountain View College; Todd Lough, Western Illinois University; Alison Marganski, Virginia Wesleyan College; Thomas S. Mosley, University of Maryland Eastern Shore; Melanie B. Norwood, University of Illinois–Chicago; Dorothy M. Schulz, John Jay College of Criminal Justice; and Rupendra Simlot, Richard Stockton College.

For the third edition, we thank Emmanuel N. Amadi, Mississippi Valley State University; Marcel F. Beausoleil Jr., Fitchburg State University; Heidi S. Bonner, East Carolina University; James J. Chriss, Cleveland State University; Amber L. Ciccanti, Willingboro Police Department/Burlington County College; Michele W. Covington, University of South Carolina–Upstate; Mengyan Dai, Old Dominion University; Jean Dawson, Franklin Pierce University; Paul Brent Foushee, University of North Carolina at Charlotte; Jon W. Glassford, University of Louisville; David Keys, New Mexico State University; Connie M. Koski, Longwood University; Keith Gregory Logan, Kutztown University of Pennsylvania; Kenneth Ryan, California State University, Fresno; Michael R. Ramon, Missouri State University; Steven Ruffatto, Harrisburg Area Community College; Shawn Schwaner, Miami Dade College; Amy Stutzenberger, Western Oregon University; and Carol L. S. Trent, University of Pittsburgh.

We would also like to extend our sincere gratitude to the contributors and filming participants who have helped make this edition better than ever.

Thank you to Connie Kosiki, Dan Koenig, and John Crombach for their exceptional contributions to the Police Stories feature. Thank you to Coy Johnston for his help in revising many of the You Decides. Thank you to Connie Koski for her invaluable assistance providing current research for this new edition.

To our filming participants, thank you for your time, candor, and expertise: Jeri Williams, Oxnard Chief of Police; Kevin Wilmott, Southern California Police Officer; and Brian Fitch, author and retired LA Country Sheriff's Lieutenant.

As always, your comments and concerns are welcomed.

—S. M.
*smarchioness@hotmail.com*

—B. F.
*Brian.Fitch@Woodbury.edu*

**Steven M. Cox** earned his BS in psychology, MA in sociology, and PhD in sociology at the University of Illinois in Urbana–Champaign. Dr. Cox was a member of the Law Enforcement and Justice Administration faculty at Western Illinois University from 1975 to 2007. For the past 45 years, he has served as trainer and consultant to numerous criminal justice agencies in the United States and abroad and has worked with several universities in the area of course development. In addition, Dr. Cox has authored and co-authored numerous successful textbooks and articles.

**Susan Marchionna** has a varied background in writing, publications, and communications in the criminal justice field. She has consulted with the Earl Warren Institute on Law and Social Policy at the University of California, Berkeley, on a number of projects, such as developing evidence-based policy and procedures for the San Francisco Adult Probation Department. Other Warren projects include evaluations of probation caseloads, the Juvenile Detention Alternatives Initiative (JDAI), and policing and crime in California cities. Susan has worked with the Moss Group on reports related to Prison Rape Elimination Act (PREA) compliance and sexual safety in institutions. She served as the technical editor for the *Desktop Guide to Quality Practice for Working with Youth* produced by the National Partnership for Juvenile Services (NPJS) and the Office of Juvenile Justice and Delinquency Prevention (OJJDP) and served as editor on a National Institute of Corrections (NIC) policy review for lesbian, gay, bisexual, transgender, and questioning (LGBTQ) individuals in custody. Prior to her current consulting work, Susan was the director of communication at the National Council on Crime and Delinquency (NCCD). There, she developed various agency publications. Susan is a graduate of the University of California, Santa Cruz, and a longtime resident of the San Francisco Bay Area.

**Brian D. Fitch**, PhD, is an associate professor of public safety administration at Woodbury University. Prior to joining Woodbury, he served for 33 years with the Los Angeles County Sheriff's Department before retiring as a lieutenant. He has worked assignments in field operations, narcotics, forgery and fraud, advanced officer training, professional development, custody, and correctional services. Dr. Fitch has trained more than 10,000 law enforcement officers throughout the United States, as well as internationally in Canada, Oman, Qatar, Saudi Arabia, and the United Arab Emirates, in leadership, decision making, and communication skills. He has held positions at California State University–Long Beach, Southwestern University School of Law, Cerritos College, Riverside College, and East Los Angeles College. Dr. Fitch teaches in the leadership development programs sponsored by the Los Angeles Police Department, Los Angeles Fire Department, and Los Angeles County Sheriff's Department. Dr. Fitch has published two prior books with Sage, *Law Enforcement Ethics: Classic and Contemporary Issues* (2013) and *Law Enforcement Interpersonal Communication and Conflict Management: The IMPACT Model*. Dr. Fitch lives in Orange County, California, with his wife Monica.

© REUTERS/Jim Young

# FOUNDATIONS OF POLICING

PART

1

# POLICING IN THE UNITED STATES

## CHAPTER LEARNING OBJECTIVES:

1. Discuss the concepts and mandate of the police in U.S. society

2. Describe the difficulty associated with attempting to make generalizations about law enforcement and the scope of the functions they perform

3. Identify the various levels and types of policing in the United States

4. Discuss some of the current concerns of police in the United States

5. Summarize the additional types of police and the functions they perform

Even in its most basic form, policing is a difficult and complex task. Any time one group of people is given power and authority to control the behavior of others, human nature will insert variety and intricacy into the equation. By definition, then, law enforcement is a complex and difficult profession. Unless one has been a police officer, it is difficult to fully grasp what that life is like. One of the goals of this text is to shed light on the reality of policing.

Today, police officers are under ever-increasing levels of public scrutiny. The actions that a police officer takes can save a life or produce a string of lasting, catastrophic effects. Although most police officers perform their duties honorably, ethically, and professionally, the actions of a single officer can tarnish the profession.

The mid-2010s have seen a series of incidents that the media have amplified, that have sparked sometimes fierce reactions from all sides, and that challenge the serious among us with a quest for solutions. Although these incidents represent a small fraction of the tens of thousands of police interactions that occur every day, when things go wrong, the consequences can be momentous.

After a nationwide drop in crime that lasted two decades starting in the mid 1990s, cities such as New York, Baltimore, Los Angeles, St. Louis, and Milwaukee began experiencing a spike in homicides and shootings of 30%–60% over the year before.[1] This occurred in the wake of a series of racially charged incidents involving unarmed young Black men dying in confrontations with the police, rekindling a smoldering social tension over disproportionate treatment of minorities by law enforcement and the criminal justice system. One pivotal event was the death of Eric Garner in July 2014, after an officer put Garner in a chokehold during a confrontation on the street. In August 2014, Michael Brown was fatally shot by a police officer in Ferguson, Missouri, a town neighboring St. Louis. In April 2015, Freddie Gray died of spinal cord injuries he sustained while in custody of the Baltimore police. Police–community relations have deteriorated in the wake of these incidents; communities have sporadically erupted in protests, some ending in more violence. Politicians and police union representatives are caught up in the fray as well, with all parties demanding protection and justice.

This emotionally charged atmosphere has also led to increased dangers for the police. In December 2014, two Brooklyn police officers—Rafael Ramos and Wenjian Liu—were shot and killed assassination style as they sat in their patrol car. A review of his social media comments revealed that the shooter intended to retaliate for the killings of Eric Garner and Michael Brown.[2] Two Las Vegas police officers—Igor Soldo and Alyn Beck—were ambushed in a restaurant in June 2014 by a couple who appeared to hold a confused set of political views on government oppression and White supremacy. A gunman whom authorities characterized as an "anti-law enforcement survivalist" ambushed and killed Pennsylvania State Trooper Bryon Dickson in September 2014.[3]

Some observers are calling the violent crime spike "the Ferguson effect" and are suggesting that the police may be holding back on their discretionary law enforcement duties due to a reticence to open themselves up to legal and disciplinary risks, beyond the physical risks they take every day.[4] In addition, some fear that the crime spike will compel police departments to abandon progress they have made in their community-policing efforts and send them back into a more combative style of law enforcement.[5]

Although the average rate for violent crime is still well below the 1995 level, spikes in crime are alarming to the public and the police alike. Everyone wants answers, but the causes of crime are complex and dynamic. Factors such as gang activity, domestic violence, a curtailment of stop-and-frisk strategies, and even changes in sentencing laws may have an influence on crime. Others believe that the rise in crime began before the Ferguson incident and point out that a sudden increase does not necessarily indicate a reversal of the 20-year downward trend. It is simply too soon to say.

Law enforcement is only a portion of the duties of the police, who provide many additional services, such as order maintenance and crime prevention. Here an officer directs traffic at a crowded Manhattan intersection.

This situation points to several key issues current in the larger arena of policing today that are explored throughout this text—including the complex causes of fluctuations in crime rates. The issue of public trust raises the question of the basis upon which the police claim to have legitimate authority over other citizens. In turn, the police and public both must scrutinize police policy and strategy and the methods used to accomplish those strategies, especially within the limits of the resources that departments have at their disposal. The use of force in particular must be scrutinized, especially in the face of the persistent issue of racial disproportion in law enforcement and the criminal justice system. This, of course, is in turn related to the question of how to hold the police accountable and what are the best measures of police performance. Meaningful measurement is reliant on accurate and complete data, and achieving that is a constant concern and an area with much room for improvement. Indeed, without accurate statistics, it is nearly impossible to know the truth about how the police are doing, especially when high-profile cases and emotionally charged issues dominate the conversation. True data could reveal that the police are assaulted even more often than they assault, or it could be the opposite. The data that could allow for an objective assessment of violence involving the police are simply not available.

Changes in technology and the militarization of the police are also salient issues, as are the attempts to steer police culture to a model more focused on community linkages and partnerships, on the health and welfare of the police officer, and on recruiting and hiring the personnel best suited to participate in a new paradigm. Additionally, terrorism and globalization are tied to the notion of a broader police mandate, resulting in the need for increased cooperation across police jurisdictions.

## ■ THE CONCEPT AND MANDATE OF THE POLICE

Every society needs citizens who serve as mediators and arbitrators to settle disputes among its members. The term **police** is derived from the Greek words *polis* and *politeuein*, which refer to being a citizen who participates in the affairs of a city or state. The contemporary police officer is just that—a citizen actively involved in the affairs of the state, in the broad sense of the word.

In all modern societies, specially designated citizens (police officers) are appointed to apprehend those who appear to have violated the rights of others and to bring them before other specially designated citizens (prosecutors, judges) who have the authority to sanction undesirable behavior.

■ **Police:** Derived from the Greek words *polis* and *politeuein*, which refer to being a citizen who participates in the affairs of a city or state

Societies experience a tension between the needs of order and liberty, which often results in a paradox involving the need for police and the need for protection from the police.

The police in civilian society can impose or force solutions on citizens when problems or emergencies arise—such as making arrests, on the one hand, and providing services for the physically or mentally ill, on the other. The police are responsible for protecting individual rights and ensuring an orderly society. To help accomplish the latter, police officers frequently intervene in the daily affairs of private citizens, for example when enforcing traffic laws or dealing with domestic violence. Individuals want the protection of the police when they are threatened or harmed, but—especially in the United States—they do not want the police to interfere in their activities and lives. Many early settlers came to this country precisely because they did not want government intervention in, and regulation of, their daily activities.[6]

This often places individual police officers in difficult positions; both intervention and a lack of intervention may lead to public criticism. Some types of police agents are far more likely to intervene in the daily affairs of citizens than others; local police officers (municipal and county) are more likely than state or federal officers to investigate domestic violence, simple burglaries, and disorderly complaints.

State troopers are more likely to stop speeding motorists on highways, and local officers are more likely to perform traffic details within city or county limits. Federal officers generally avoid such incidents altogether, but run investigations into federal crimes.

Regardless of the type of agent, police officers are influenced by the expectations of police administrators, courts, residents of the community, other officers in the department, and even their own perceptions, each of which entails expectations of moral and ethical behavior and accountability.

However, the job of a police officer is much more complex than most people realize. Societies expect police to achieve a variety of outcomes defined by the police mission and mandate.

- Reduce crime and maintain order.
- Reduce the fear of crime.
- Solve neighborhood problems and improve the quality of life.
- Develop greater community cohesion.

To achieve these outcomes, maintain order, and enforce the law, police do intervene in the daily affairs of private citizens. Regulation of morals, enforcement of traffic laws, mediation of domestic disputes, administration of juveniles, and many other police activities require such intervention. Neither police training nor the law addresses every conflict or intervention. Police officers exercise discretion—warn some individuals, arrest or ticket others, or refer parties in a dispute to a private attorney or professional

**Audio Link:**
Be Guardians, Not Warriors: Training a New Generation of Police

**Police Officer:** A specially designated citizen whose functions include order maintenance, provision of services, and law enforcement

**Law Enforcement Officer:** A specially designated citizen who focuses on enforcing laws through detection and apprehension

## Exhibit 1.1

### Policing Activities Versus Enforcement of the Law

The terms **police officer** and **law enforcement officer** are sometimes viewed as interchangeable. In fact, the term *law enforcement officer* describes very little of what police officers do. The police in the United States are primarily providers of services. Among the services they provide are law enforcement, order maintenance, and crime prevention.

Police activities in the area of law enforcement tend to be more visible in the media and interesting to the general public. We often evaluate the police in this area rather than on order maintenance and service, on which they spend much more of their time; police provide far more than law enforcement to the communities they serve and devote a relatively small portion of the day to law enforcement activities.

### Commander Dan Koenig, LAPD Retired

It was a strange call: "See the man looking for information." But, when the dispatcher sends you a call, you go. So my partner and I drove to the house and walked up to the door. There we were met by a middle-aged African American man and his wife. Standing with them was a neatly dressed young man who appeared to be about 16 or 17 years old. Just inside the house stood a young girl who looked to be about the same age as the young man. "Good afternoon, Sir, how can we help you?" we inquired of the man. He explained to us that the young man wanted to take their daughter to a movie, and he would appreciate it if we would "check him out." We could see clearly that this was a fine young man, but we went through the motions anyway. He walked with us over to our police car, and we chatted for a few minutes. His family had moved only recently to a house a few blocks away. He went to school with the young lady in question, and he attended Sunday church with his family regularly. We all returned to the front porch where we assured the girl's parents that he came from a good family, and we believed it would be safe for their daughter to accompany him to the movies. After agreeing to a reasonable curfew, the young couple left. The parents thanked us for our service, and we left with waves to them and the small gathering of neighbors that had formed.

As police officers, we have a pretty good idea of what our job is, or at least what it should be. But the community that pays our salaries and that we are meant to serve often has a much different idea. Law enforcement has a history of being asked to look the other way on more minor crimes such as gambling, prostitution, and "soft" drugs. But we're part of the executive branch, so we don't get to decide which laws to enforce. We certainly can prioritize, but we can't legalize through inaction. While we can't violate our ethics or the principles that guide us, we are in the business of "protecting and serving," and that can take many forms throughout a career.

mediator. Almost all police officers practice some form of discretion with their actions. However, police must also follow department policies that in some cases remove officer discretion and require enforcement—for example, that all persons not wearing a seat belt be ticketed—or mandate the arrest of any persons they observe committing a serious felony.

The police officer's job involves inherently problematic positions. A brief overview of the history of American policing may help us understand the origins and consequences of some of the issues encountered by police officers in a democratic society.

The police are also expected to share in a number of social service functions that require intervention in cases such as domestic violence, mentally ill and emotionally disturbed individuals, and child and elder abuse.[8] This type of police responsibility is occurring at a time when some police have begun "severely limiting the types of calls that result in direct face-to-face responses by officers."[9]

**Video Link:**
The Miranda rights
are established

### ■ SCOPE OF THE LAW ENFORCEMENT SECTOR

Every day, tens of thousands of American citizens don uniforms, pin on badges and name tags, and strap on equipment belts that may carry a firearm and Taser, extra ammunition, handcuffs, pepper spray, and a baton. These citizens assemble at distinctively marked locations and disperse from these locations carrying radios and cell phones in clearly marked and equipped vehicles designed to make them easily identifiable. They go forth as police officers providing services, maintaining order, and enforcing the law in large metropolitan, suburban, and rural areas as well as on college campuses, on the borders between the United States and other countries, in airports and harbors, and in dozens of other settings.

At the same time, thousands of others cover their badges and firearms with street or business attire and assemble at distinctively marked locations, both in and out of the United States, to work on current investigations through the use of phones and computers or to disperse from these locations in unmarked vehicles to conduct surveillance, to conduct interviews, and to make arrests.

Others conceal their identities as police officers and attempt to pass themselves off as members of criminal groups to obtain information that will lead to arrests.

Other privately employed citizens don uniforms and badges more or less similar to those of the police; arm themselves with firearms, pepper spray, Tasers, and handcuffs; and proceed in marked vehicles to work in gated communities, shopping malls, industrial areas, and a wide variety of other locations to provide security for people and property.

Simultaneously, thousands of others go to work in police agencies of all types and sizes as nonsworn technicians, as communications personnel, as administrative assistants, and in dozens of other capacities.

**Policing in Practice Video:**
Why is policing difficult in a democratic society?

## Levels of Policing

American police personnel are employed at the international, federal, state, county, and municipal levels. The federal Bureau of Justice Statistics (BJS) conducts comprehensive and detailed surveys of police agencies in the United States. There is one census for state and local agencies and another for federal agencies. In both cases, the most recent BJS data are from 2008. At that time, there were over 1.1 million police personnel employed full-time at the state and local (city, county, suburban) levels in approximately 18,000 agencies. Of those employees, 765,000 were sworn full-time officers, and 369,000 were nonsworn full-time; another 100,000 were part-time, both sworn and nonsworn.[10]

These state and local officers worked in agencies ranging in personnel size from 36,000 (New York City) to one (some 2,125 agencies with only one sworn officer were reported in 2008). Some agencies have no full-time sworn personnel, and instead hire a number of part-time officers or contract with outside agencies to provide their police services. See Table 1.1 for statistics on police personnel.

### Table 1.1 ■ Police Personnel Statistics

| Type of Agency | Number of Agencies | Number of Full-Time Sworn Officers |
|---|---|---|
| All state and local | 17,985 | 765,246 |
| Local police* | 12,326 | 477,317 |
| Sheriff* | 3,012 | 188,952 |
| Primary state* | 50 | 58,421 |
| Special jurisdiction | 1,733 | 56,968 |
| Constable/marshal | 638 | 3,464 |
| Federal** | 73 | 120,000 |

*Source:* Reaves, 2015 (http://www.bjs.gov/content/pub/pdf/lpd13ppp.pdf), and Reaves, 2011 (http://www.bjs.gov/content/pub/pdf/csllea08.pdf).

*Note:* *Data on local police, sheriff, and primary state are from Reaves, 2015.

**Nonmilitary federal officers authorized to carry firearms and make arrests. Data on federal law enforcement officers are from Reaves, 2012.

This photo shows a nontraditional view of police officers. Here, rural county sheriff's department officers travel by all-terrain vehicles in search of meth labs that have sprouted in hard-to-reach locales.

© AP Photo/Darron Cumming

Video Link:
A Day in the Life

The Federal Bureau of Investigation (FBI)—which uses a different methodology from the Bureau of Justice Statistics—also keeps statistics on law enforcement employment. The most recent FBI data available (from 2011) report 14,633 city and county agencies that employ over 1 million sworn, nonsworn, and civilian staff members.[11] In addition, there are approximately 106,000 state police employees.[12]

### State Police

All states have some type of state police agency. In addition to their basic tasks, many of these agencies provide statewide communications or computer systems, assist in crime-scene analysis and multijurisdictional investigations, provide training for other police agencies, and collect, analyze, and disseminate information on crime patterns in the state. Also, many state police agencies have expanded their services to include aircraft support, underwater search and rescue, and canine assistance. State police agencies may also be responsible for state park security (park police or rangers), security of state property and state officials, and regulation of liquor- and gambling-related activities.

State police agencies have the responsibility for traffic enforcement on highways, particularly in areas outside the city or township limits. Some agencies focus almost exclusively on traffic control (highway patrol departments), and others maintain more general enforcement powers (state police investigation departments).[13] Typically, the state police are empowered to provide law enforcement service anywhere in the state, while the highway patrol officers have limited authority based on their specific duty assignment, type of offense, or jurisdiction.

### Federal Law Enforcement

At the federal level, in 1789, U.S. marshals were the first police established for the purpose of enforcing directives of the federal courts. The U.S. Secret Service was founded in 1865 as a branch of the U.S. Treasury Department. It was originally created to combat the counterfeiting of U.S. currency—a serious problem at the time. Later, in 1901, following the assassination of President William McKinley, the Secret Service was tasked with its second mission: the protection of the president. Today, the Secret Service's mission is twofold: (1) protect the president, vice president, and others; and (2) investigate crimes against the financial infrastructure of the United States.

According to the International Association of Chiefs of Police, police are expected to achieve the following outcomes:

- Reduce crime and disorder

- Reduce the fear of crime

- Solve neighborhood problems and improving the quality of life

- Develop greater community cohesion

To achieve these outcomes, police intervene in the daily affairs of private citizens. This includes asking or telling citizens not to move, where to stand, what to do, how to behave, and when they are free to leave. When citizens refuse to cooperate, police have the authority to force citizens to comply if necessary.

Police are most often called upon to stop some act of violence, unwanted behavior, or threats to public safety. In these situations, the use of unnecessary force by police can lead to negative consequences, including avoidable injuries or death, community complaints, distrust of the police, civil liability, civil unrest, and federal injunctive orders. On the other hand, insufficient use of force exposes officers to their own harm or death, negatively affects an officer's ability to enforce the law, and may increase the danger to public safety. Fyfe (1987) concludes that unnecessary force "could be avoided by measures such as better training, officer selection, and other use-of-force options."

1. Should police officers be permitted to use force when unarmed citizens refuse to comply?

2. What do you think would be a viable alternative to use of force in situations where citizens will not comply?

3. Which poses a greater risk to the community, unnecessary use of force, or insufficient use of force?

*Suggestions for addressing these questions can be found on the Student Study Site:* **edge.sagepub.com/ coxpolicing3e**

Customs and Border Protection is part of the **Department of Homeland Security (DHS)**. The responsibilities of the DHS are as follows:

- Prevention of terrorism and enhancement of security, management of national borders, administration of immigration laws, security of cyberspace, and ensuring disaster resilience.

- Security of the nation's air, land, and sea borders to prevent illegal activity, and facilitation of lawful travel and trade.

- Coordination of police activities among agencies at a variety of levels, and provision of training, grants, and resources.

Other federal agencies that employ law enforcement officers include the Drug Enforcement Administration (DEA), the U.S. Marshals Service, the Bureau of Alcohol, Tobacco, Firearms and Explosives (ATF), the U.S. Supreme Court, the Environmental Protection Agency (EPA), Amtrak, and the Library of Congress, among many others.

Other federal agencies employed more than 104,000 full-time sworn personnel in 2008.[14] For the most part, they do not engage in the activities that local and county police normally provide. Relatively few federal officers (usually referred to as *agents*) are uniformed, and their primary duties involve investigation and control of federal crimes, such as bank robberies, illegal immigration, and interstate crimes. They are also responsible for protecting federal property and federal officials. At times, federal agencies provide

**Department of Homeland Security (DHS):** Federal agency responsible for a unified national effort to secure the country and preserve freedom

| Table 1.2 ■ The Five Largest Federal Agencies With Authority for Firearms and Arrest, 2008* | | |
|---|---|---|
| Agency | Number of Full-Time Officers | Agency Responsibility |
| Customs and Border Protection | 36,863 | Enforcement of controlled substance laws. |
| Federal Bureau of Prisons (BOP) | 16,835 | Custody and care of federal inmates. |
| Federal Bureau of Investigation (FBI) | 12,760 | Investigation of violations of federal criminal law in a variety of areas (e.g., civil rights, terrorism, espionage, cyber-based attacks, public corruption, white-collar crime, and violent crime). |
| Immigration and Customs Enforcement (ICE) | 12,446 | Promotion of homeland security and public safety through the criminal and civil enforcement of federal laws governing border control, customs, trade, and immigration. |
| Secret Service | 5,213 | Investigation of violent crimes, criminal organizations, illegal use and storage of explosives, acts of arson and bombings, acts of terrorism, and the illegal diversion of alcohol and tobacco products. |

*Source:* Reaves, 2012.
*Most recent data available

training and logistical support for state and local police. Although each agency has a set of specific duties, there is still some overlap and duplication among them. See Table 1.2 for a description of the five largest federal agencies with authority for firearms and arrest.

## ■ A CHANGING LANDSCAPE

Police agencies vary in many ways beyond mere numbers. Many agencies use modern technological equipment, while others lack advanced equipment. Some officers are well trained; others receive very little training. Some routinely intervene in the daily lives of their fellow citizens; others do not. Some departments are keen to adopt new or promising strategies; others are more resistant to change. Some are held in high regard by their fellow citizens; others are not. The chapters of this text will discuss these and many other variations among police departments.

Regardless of their status as public or private, full-time or part-time, sworn or nonsworn, police personnel currently find themselves operating in a rapidly changing environment. For example, the use of unmanned aerial vehicles for crime-scene mapping, traffic control, and border monitoring is slowly increasing, as is the use of global positioning systems (GPS) and sophisticated video surveillance.[15] At the same time, the USA PATRIOT (Uniting and Strengthening America by Providing Appropriate Tools Required to Intercept and Obstruct Terrorism) Act extended government authority to tap phones and computers, which requires the police to process huge amounts of information.

**Web Link:**
Future Trends in Policing

All of these changes have been happening at a time when many municipalities are facing declining tax revenues and increasing tax burdens for middle-class citizens, leaving city officials struggling to balance public safety needs with other infrastructure needs.

Partly or mostly as a result of the economic downturn starting in 2008, the number of police officers started to decline in some areas. For example, in 25 of California's cities that have a population greater than 140,000 people, the number of sworn police officers declined from 23,355 to 22,129 between 2009 and 2011.[16] During the same period, an estimated 53% of counties were working with fewer staff in 2011 than in the prior year,

### Racketeering, Drug Conspiracy Charges for 27 in Schenectady, New York

[In April 2012,] United States Attorney Richard S. Hartunian announced the unsealing of two indictments returned by a federal grand jury for the Northern District of New York in Albany, New York[,] which, in total, charged 27 with a federal racketeering conspiracy and/or federal drug felonies. . . .

Hartunian praised the outstanding cooperative efforts of the federal, state, and local law enforcement agencies that participated in this investigation and emphasized that his office will continue to work closely with authorities at all levels to prosecute gang members and narcotics traffickers. . . .

[Police agencies involved in the investigation included the Federal Bureau of Investigation, the Drug Enforcement Administration, the New York State Police, the Schenectady Police Department, and the Schenectady County Sheriff's Office.]

New York State Police Superintendent Joseph A. D'Amico said, "This multi-agency investigation and subsequent arrests extinguished an organized criminal network responsible for infusing illegal narcotics into the Schenectady community. This is a solid example of how collaborative law enforcement efforts work to make our communities safer."

1.  Despite the considerable resources directed at the "war on drugs," narcotics continue to flow into this country. What kinds of improvements should justify a continuation of the war on drugs?

2.  If you were a local police chief, how would you address the growing problems of gangs and narcotics in your city?

3.  What would be the advantages and disadvantages of legalizing drugs in the United States?

*Source:* Racketeering, drug conspiracy charges for 27 in Schenectady, New York. Targeted News Service (USA)—Friday, April 6, 2012. Record Number: 3833234. Copyright (c) 2012 Targeted News Service. All rights reserved.

© AP Photo/ Mark Wilson

Federal agencies exercise police powers regarding a specific set of duties. For example, the Drug Enforcement Administration is tasked with enforcing controlled substance laws.

## Making Lives Safer—A Cop's Career on the Thin Blue Line

One incident in the career of Sergeant Greg Donaldson stands out as he reflects over his 23 years as a police officer in Australia.

"When I was a dog handler there was a young nine-year-old girl who was abducted by a convicted murderer and I turned up to Mount Druitt and had to drive up to the Queensland border as soon as I could," he said.

"With the help of two Aboriginal trackers, we tracked for the next 12 hours overnight and recovered the girl safe and well. Given the guy's form there is no doubt in my mind she would have been killed at some time and we saved her life that night."

Sergeant Donaldson joined the police force because he has a good sense of what's right and wrong and he stayed on because he enjoys the diversity of police work. Over the years, Donaldson has been a street cop, an undercover officer, and a dog handler. He notes that in private business you can change employment to enjoy different experiences, while in policing you can do a variety of things while remaining a police officer. "You don't have to change supers and you accumulate your long service leave. It's good."

Donaldson concludes, "No two days are the same, no two jobs are the same, and the mates you make, the blokes who cover your back and back you up and sit by you for hours, there are not many jobs that build those friendships and trust."

1. Considering the negative press surrounding law enforcement, what can police agencies do to interest the right kinds of people in a law enforcement career?

2. Police officers are often forced to work long hours doing a thankless job. What can law enforcement agencies do to keep their officers interested and motivated?

*Source:* Sharples, S. (2012, February 29). Making lives safer—A cop's career on the thin blue line. *Parramatta Advertiser*. Sydney, Australia. Edition: 1—Main Book, Section: Features, Page: 099. Record Number: PAG_T-20120229-1-099-823321. Copyright, 2012, Nationwide News Pty Limited.

and more than one-third of the agencies that applied for federal funding reported a drop of at least 5% in their operating budget.[17]

One set of projections suggests that approximately "12,000 police officers and sheriffs' deputies [were] laid off in 2011; approximately 30,000 law enforcement positions [went] unfilled; and approximately 28,000 sworn personnel faced work furloughs of at least one week."[18] Many communities are asking themselves how much protection can they afford or afford to be without.

## ■ ADDITIONAL TYPES OF POLICE

### Private Police

Estimates of private security and contract personnel indicated that between 11,000 and 15,000 companies employed at least 1.2 million private security personnel in a number of different occupations ranging from private security or contract guards, to executive protection, to private investigators, to industrial security, to contract employees for the military.[19] (See Chapter 15.)

### Special Jurisdiction Police

Special jurisdictions include college and university police, public and private school police, and agencies that serve transportation systems and facilities.[20] In many cases, special jurisdiction police are both sworn and nonsworn police officers assigned to a specific geographic jurisdiction.

University police officers respond to requests for service that cannot be fulfilled by local police. As an example, the University of Illinois at Urbana–Champaign provides specific class training in the following areas: active threat training, safe walk programs, crime prevention classes, rape aggression defense classes, and courses related to intolerance/hate crime prevention.[21]

## Sheriffs and Deputy Sheriffs

Sheriff's departments provide police services to counties, and sheriffs are one of the only elected law enforcement officials still in existence today. A majority of sheriff's deputies perform duties similar to those of municipal police officers: routine patrol, criminal investigations, traffic control, and accident investigation. Additional duties and responsibilities of a sheriff include maintaining the safety and security of courthouses, which often involves sheriff's employees serving as bailiffs. Sheriffs are also responsible for the security of jurors when they are outside the courtroom, serve court papers, extradite prisoners, and perform other court functions.[22] Likewise, in most counties, the sheriff is responsible for the jail, the supervision of inmates, and the transportation of inmates to court.

## Auxiliary/Reserve/Special Police

Auxiliary, reserve, and special police assist regular police officers. They usually work part-time; they can be armed or unarmed and either paid for their services or volunteer. The extent of training varies in many cases based on the duties assigned, but the training is usually very similar to that completed by full-time sworn police officers. This type of officer may be assigned to vehicle, foot, or bicycle patrol. Table 1.3 includes a list of some of these special tasks and the percentage of departments that designate personnel to perform each task.

**SAGE Journal Article:** A Sheriff's Office as a Learning Organization

## Conservation Police Officers, Game Wardens

These types of police officers usually have full police authority and statewide or federal jurisdiction. The enforcement duties of Illinois officers, for example, include enforcement in state parks of criminal laws, vehicle laws, drug laws, fish and wildlife laws, timber transportation laws, endangered species laws, and snowmobile operation; as well as patrolling Illinois lakes and rivers to check boating safety equipment and watercraft registration.[23]

## Tribal Police Officers

As of 2008, American Indian tribes operated 178 law enforcement agencies. A majority of these police departments are general-purpose police agencies, and the others are special jurisdiction agencies that enforce natural resource laws.[24]

These agencies provided a broad range of police services on tribal lands, including "responding to calls for service, investigating crimes, enforcing traffic laws, executing search warrants, serving process, providing court security, and conducting search and rescue operations."[25]

| Table 1.3 ■ Personnel designated to perform special operational tasks in local police departments, by size of department, 2013 | | |
|---|---|---|
| Problem or Task | Departments Employing 100 Officers or More | Departments Employing 99 Officers or Fewer |
| | Total | Total |
| Bomb/explosive disposal | 41% | 6% |
| Fugitives/warrants | 68 | 24 |
| Re-entry surveillance | 21 | 8 |
| Tactical operations [e.g., SWAT] | 95 | 31 |
| Terrorism homeland security | 71 | 16 |

*Source:* Reaves, 2015 (http://www.bjs.gov/content/pub/pdf/lpd13ppp.pdf).

A County sheriff bailiff separates women after a confrontation broke out in the court. Court security is one of the key areas of responsibility of sheriff's deputies.

© ZUMA Press, Inc / Alamy Stock Photo

**Policing in Practice Video:** Tension between serving and protecting but enforcing the laws

Given the diversity and breadth of police services in the United States, there is a great deal of jurisdictional overlap. Thus, for example, a college student may be subject to the jurisdiction of the campus police, the city police, the county police, the state police, and a variety of federal police agencies all at the same time. In point of fact, which of these agencies is likely to become involved depends on the type and location of the offense in question and the existence of formal and informal agreements among the agencies. Although each agency has its unique qualities, all agencies face many of the same issues. The extent to which American police are prepared to perform their jobs varies from agency to agency.

## CHAPTER SUMMARY

The term *police* is derived from the Greek words *polis* and *politeuein* and refers to a citizen who participates in the affairs of a city or state. This is an excellent way of describing the role of the contemporary police officer—he or she is a citizen who is actively involved in the affairs of a city or state. Thus, a police officer is a specially designated citizen appointed to apprehend those who appear to have violated the rights of others and to bring them before other specially designated citizens such as prosecutors and judges who determine whether further action is justified.

To maintain order and enforce the law, the police are granted the right to intervene in the daily affairs of private citizens. Yet some kinds of police intervention generate suspicion and hostility toward the police. Citizens want the police to address their concerns and to solve the problems they bring to the attention of the police, but would otherwise prefer to be left alone. Therefore, police officers occupy inherently problematic positions in our society.

American police agencies operate at the local, state, and federal levels and come in a variety of sizes in both the public and private sectors. Especially when considering private police and their relationships with public police, the disparities in size and jurisdiction often make it difficult to comprehensively define the nature of the police, the relationships between officers and agencies, and the policies and practices of departments. Nonetheless, there are commonalities and shared challenges among these agencies.

In a democratic nation, we expect the police to operate within the framework of our defining principles— equal treatment, respect for individual liberty, and accountability. When police reflect these principles, they play an important role in social control and the overall well-being of society, which results in a more willing and cooperative public.

Ongoing social tensions point to the complex issues that departments are grappling with on a daily basis—appropriate policy and procedure, officer recruitment and training, policing strategies and operations, police performance, officer safety, optimal use of technology, and many others.

## KEY TERMS

- Police  4
- Police officer  5
- Law enforcement officer  5
- Department of Homeland Security (DHS)  9

**SAGE edge™**
Review key terms with eFlashcards.

**SAGE edge™**
Test your understanding of chapter content. Take the practice quiz.

## DISCUSSION QUESTIONS

1. Why is it so difficult to discuss and generalize about the police in the United States?

2. Describe and discuss the various levels of public police in the United States.

3. What are some of the contradictions and tensions inherent in policing?

4. What are some of the issues currently confronting police in the United States?

## INTERNET EXERCISES

1. Using your browser, locate information on public police agencies in your state. What is the size and jurisdiction of the largest agency? What information can you locate about your local or county agency?

2. Search for information online concerning private police in your home state.

3. Using your browser, see what you can discover about order maintenance and law enforcement as police functions.

## STUDENT STUDY SITE

**SAGE edge™**  edge.sagepub.com/coxpolicing3e

**Sharpen your skills with SAGE edge!**

SAGE edge for Students provides a personalized approach to help you accomplish your coursework goals in an easy-to-use learning environment. You'll find action plans, mobile-friendly eFlashcards, and quizzes as well as videos, web resources, and links to SAGE journal articles to support and expand on the concepts presented in this chapter.

Chapter 1: Policing in the United States  ■  15

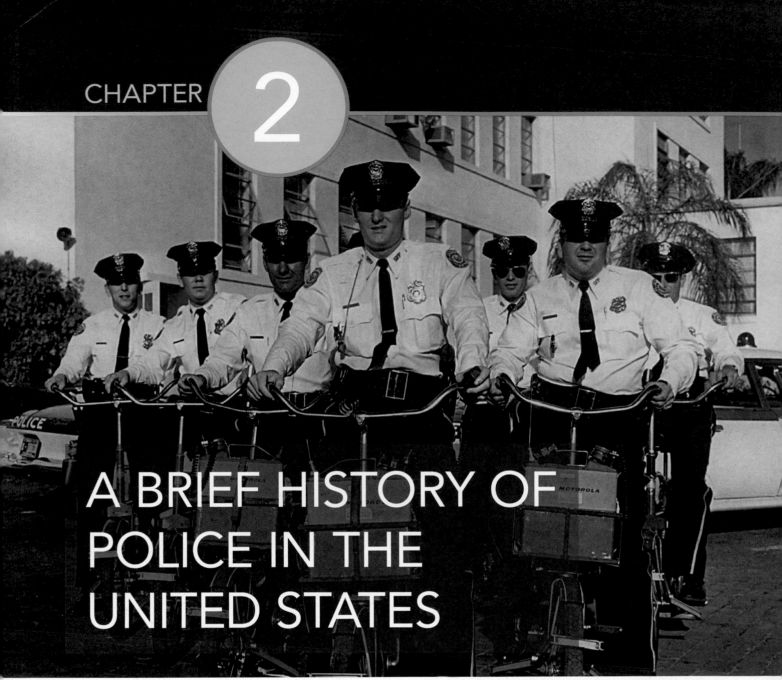

CHAPTER 2

# A BRIEF HISTORY OF POLICE IN THE UNITED STATES

© iStockphoto.com/HultonArchive

## CHAPTER LEARNING OBJECTIVES:

1. Identify the influence of English roots of policing on U.S. policing

2. Describe the influence of technology on the evolution of early U.S. policing

3. Summarize the issues facing policing during the Political Era

4. Explain the effect on policing of the changes implemented during the Reform Era

5. Describe the relationship between the social upheaval of the 1960s and 1970s and the increased emphasis on research on police effectiveness

6. Identify aspects of the community policing model and problem-oriented policing

7. Evaluate at least three contemporary policing strategies in terms of their effectiveness

8. Describe the challenges facing contemporary police departments

P olice in the United States provide an extremely wide range of services, many of which may have little to do with crime or law enforcement. There is a great deal of variation among police agencies with respect to size, degree of specialization, and officer discretion, for example. This variation creates a striking complexity. Still, police agencies share many common issues and challenges. Historical analysis reveals the roots of many current issues in policing—such as **professionalism**, discretion, inefficiency, and corruption—and helps to clarify the complexities and variations of police operations in the United States today.

## ■ ENGLISH ROOTS OF POLICING

The origins of policing date back to ancient empires around the world such as the Greeks, Romans, Egyptians, Spartans, Israelis, and Chinese. Throughout medieval times to the present, Europeans had forms of policing to enforce laws and maintain order. Although policing has an international history, the roots of policing in the United States can be traced back to England.

> Our English police system . . . rests on foundations designed with the full approval of the people . . . and has been slowly molded by the careful hand of experience, developing as a rule along the line of least resistance, now in advance of the general intelligence of the country, now lagging far behind, but always in the long run adjusting itself to the popular temper, always consistent with local self government. . . .[1]

Although the quote above is about the development of the police in England, it is applicable to policing in the United States as well.

Early settlers to America from England brought with them a **night watch system** that required able-bodied males to donate their time to help protect the cities. As was the case in England, those who could afford to do so often hired others to serve their shifts, and those who served were not particularly effective. During the 1700s, citizens often resolved disputes among themselves. Such resolutions involved intergenerational blood feuds, eye-gouging, gunfights, and duels.[2] As the nation's cities grew larger and more diverse, voluntary citizen participation in law enforcement and order maintenance became increasingly less effective, and some other system was needed to replace it. In 1749, residents of Philadelphia convinced legislators to pass a law creating the position of warden. The warden was authorized to hire as many watchmen as needed, the powers of the watchmen expanded,

© Heritage Images/Corbis

■ **Professionalism:** An end state that is largely based on ethical practice and other related characteristics such as good personal character, personal and organizational accountability, a commitment to higher education and continuous training, and intolerance for misconduct

■ **Night Watch System:** Early policing system that required able-bodied males to donate their time to help protect cities

The origins of U.S. policing can be traced back to England where a night watch system was employed to help protect cities.

© Library of Congress, Prints & Photographs Division, photograph by Harris & Ewing, LC-DIG-hec-42115

SAGE Journal Article: The Study of Policing

and the city paid selected individuals from taxes. Other cities soon adopted similar plans.[3] The wardens and their watchmen served warrants, acted as detectives, and patrolled the streets.[4] But these wardens were not widely respected and were considered inefficient, corrupt, and susceptible to political interference.[5]

By the 1800s, with the rapid growth of cities, crime and mob violence had become problems in British and U.S. cities alike. In response, **Sir Robert Peel**, who was then home secretary in London, developed municipal policing. Peel believed that the police should be organized along military lines and under government control. He also thought police officers should be men of quiet demeanor and good appearance and should be familiar with the neighborhoods where they were to police. In addition, he supported a territorial strategy of policing in which officers would walk prescribed beats to prevent and deal with crime. Peel and **Patrick Colquhoun** (superintending magistrate of the Thames River Police, a forerunner of the Metropolitan Police, and author of works on metropolitan policing) put many of these principles into practice in establishing the London Metropolitan Police. By 1870, Peel's territorial strategy, at least, had spread to every major city in the United States.[6]

## ■ THE EVOLUTION OF EARLY U.S. POLICING

In the United States in the early to middle 1800s, day watch systems were established in U.S. cities (Philadelphia, 1833; Boston, 1838; New York, 1844; San Francisco, 1850; Los Angeles, 1851). By the 1850s, day and night watch systems were consolidated to provide 24-hour protection to city dwellers.[7]

Also by this time, the main structural elements of U.S. municipal policing had emerged. Watch and ward systems had been replaced—in the cities at least—by centralized, government-supported police agencies whose tasks included crime prevention, provision of a wide variety of services to the public, enforcement of "morality," and the apprehension of criminals. A large force of uniformed police walked regular beats, had the power to arrest without a warrant, and began to carry revolvers in the late 1850s.[8] The concept of preventive policing included maintenance of order functions such as searching for missing children, mediating quarrels, and helping at fire scenes. Both municipal police and county sheriffs performed these tasks. State and federal agencies arose to supplement the work of the police.[9] One such agency, the Federal Bureau of Investigation (FBI), was established in 1908, when a number of Department of Justice (DOJ) investigators were taken on as special agents. The new agency was formally named in 1909. The FBI has since developed into a worldwide investigative agency with international offices located in 60 U.S. embassies.[10]

■ **Sir Robert Peel:** The founder of modern territorial policing (London Metropolitan Police) in 1829 in London

■ **Patrick Colquhoun:** Superintending magistrate of the Thames River Police, a forerunner of the Metropolitan Police and author of works on metropolitan policing

## Exhibit 2.1

### Peel's Principles of Policing

1: The basic mission for which the police exist is to prevent crime and disorder.

2: The ability of the police to perform their duties is dependent upon public approval of police actions.

3: Police must secure the willing cooperation of the public in voluntary observance of the law to be able to secure and maintain the respect of the public.

4: The degree of cooperation of the public that can be secured diminishes proportionately to the necessity of the use of physical force.

5: Police seek and preserve public favor not by catering to the public opinion but by constantly demonstrating absolute impartial service to the law.

6: Police use physical force to the extent necessary to secure observance of the law or to restore order only when the exercise of persuasion, advice and warning is found to be insufficient.

7: Police, at all times, should maintain a relationship with the public that gives reality to the historic tradition that the police are the public and the public are the police; the police being only members of the public who are paid to give full-time attention to duties which are incumbent on every citizen in the interests of community welfare and existence.

8: Police should always direct their action strictly towards their functions and never appear to usurp the powers of the judiciary.

9: The test of police efficiency is the absence of crime and disorder, not the visible evidence of police action in dealing with it.

Meanwhile, police in the United States began to take advantage of technology; the use of call boxes, telegraphs, teletypes, two-way radios, and patrol cars grew rapidly. For example, in 1871, the central headquarters of the Boston Police Department was connected to all other station houses by telegraph. Prior to this, the only communication among these locations was by messenger. In 1878, the first telephones were installed in the department. And, in 1903, the nation's first motor patrol was established in Boston, with a Stanley Steamer automobile. A civilian chauffeur drove the vehicle, allowing police officers to sit on a high seat in the rear so they could look over high backyard fences. By 1906, the Boston Police Department owned five automobiles.[11] Another example of technological progress occurred in the 1920s in St. Louis, Missouri, when the department deployed a system to enable the police chief to alert a local public radio station about a major crime, and news of the crime was broadcast over the airwaves both to the public and to the police in squad cars. In 1929, Chicago announced that all squad cars of the Chicago Police Department Detective Division were equipped with radio receiving sets. Chicago's early one-way radio system was supported by the *Chicago Tribune*, which operated station WGN. The following year, St. Louis had installed its own transmitting station, which could send messages to squad cars and police stations equipped with receivers using a dedicated frequency.[12]

## ■ THE POLITICAL ERA

While technological progress in policing was occurring around the country, political considerations continued to play an important role in policing. Although they adopted a good many practices from their British counterparts, U.S. police lacked the central

This photo depicts an early police radio used by the Chicago Police Department, which enabled the police to send messages from the field to headquarters.

© Bettmann/Corbis

**Web Link:**
How Katrina Sparked
Reform in a Troubled
Police Department

authority of the Crown to establish a legitimate mandate for their actions. Small departments acted independently within their jurisdictions. Large departments were divided into precincts that often operated more as small, individual departments than as branches of the same organization.[13] Police officers more often represented the local political party in power than the legal system.[14]

Patrol officers were often required to enforce unpopular laws in immigrant neighborhoods whose norms they did not understand. In their own neighborhoods, their personal relationships made them vulnerable to bribes for lax enforcement or nonenforcement.[15] In addition, the police found themselves in frequent conflict with rioters, union workers and their management counterparts, and looters. As a result of such conflicts, the public questioned whether the police could remain impartial in administering the law.

> Expectations that the police would be disinterested public servants ran afoul of the realities of urban social and political life. Heterogeneity made it more difficult to determine what behavior was acceptable and what was unacceptable. Moreover, urban diversity encouraged a political life based upon racial and ethnic cleavages as well as clashes of economic interests. Democratic control of police assured that heterogeneous cities would have constant conflicts over police organization and shifts of emphasis depending upon which groups controlled the political machinery at any one time.[16]

Consequently, in some cities such as New York, political corruption and manipulation were built into policing. New York police officers in the 1830s were hired and fired by elected officials who expected those they hired to support them politically and fired those who did not. "The late nineteenth century policeman had a difficult job. He had to maintain order, cope with vice and crime, provide service to people in trouble, and keep his nose clean politically."[17] The police became involved in party politics, which included granting immunity from arrest to those in power.[18] Corruption and extortion became traditions in some departments, and discipline and professional pride were largely absent from many departments. Police spent most of their time providing services to local supporters, maintaining a reasonable level of social order necessary for the city and local businesses to operate smoothly, and seeking out every opportunity available to them to make money.[19]

The U.S. brand of local self-government gave professional politicians considerable influence in policing.

> The need to respond to the diverse, often conflicting demands of various constituencies has given American policing a unique character which affects its efficiency as well as its reputation. However one views the police today, it is essential to understand how the theory and practice of politics influenced the nature, successes, and problems of law enforcement.[20]

Some attempts to address corruption and related issues began in the late 1800s such as the **Pendleton Act**, which required that government jobs be awarded on the basis of merit rather than on the basis of friendship or political favor. But old traditions and perceptions died hard—and, in some cases, not at all. One such example of old traditions is the **sheriff**, who remains a political figure charged with police duties.

Throughout most of the 19th century and into the 20th, the basic qualification for becoming a police officer was a political connection rather than a demonstrated ability to perform the job.[21] Police agencies hired men with no education, with criminal records, and with health problems.[22] Training was practically nonexistent, with most new officers being handed equipment and an assignment area and told to "hit the streets." Officers were expected to handle whatever problems they encountered while patrolling their beats, not simply to enforce the law. They provided a range of services, including basic medical care, babysitting at the police station, helping people find employment, and feeding the homeless.

The police were a part of the political machinery, and politicians were seldom interested in impartial justice. The police became a mechanism that permitted politicians to solidify their power by controlling political adversaries and assisting friends and allies.[23] Arrests were of little importance; the primary mission of the police was to provide services to citizens and garner votes for politicians. "For the patrolman, unless he was exceptionally stubborn or a notoriously slow learner, the moral was clear: if you want to get along, go along."[24]

The lack of a strong central administration, the influence of politicians, and the neighborhood ties between the police and the people ensured a partisan style of policing and led to fragmented police services, inconsistency, confusion, and eventually

**Pendleton Act:** Required that government jobs be awarded on the basis of merit rather than on the basis of friendship or political favor

**Sheriff:** Typically, an elected official responsible for county law enforcement and, in many instances, the county jail

---

### Exhibit 2.2

### Origin of the Term *Sheriff*

The term *sheriff* stems from 12th-century England and is a contraction of the term *shire reeve*, which referred to an official appointed by the king with the responsibility for keeping the peace and collecting taxes throughout a shire or county. Today, the sheriff is still typically an elected official and the chief law enforcement officer in the county in which he or she serves.

a call for reform.[25] With no accountability for either the politicians or the police, corruption, graft, and bribery reached a new level. Not infrequently, police promotions and assignments were auctioned to the highest bidder, and illegal operations, including gambling halls and brothels, made monthly contributions to police officers. While some improvements resulted from reform efforts, political motivations continued to plague the selection of both officers and chiefs. "Too many chiefs were simply fifty-five-year-old patrolmen."[26]

**Web Link:**
President's Task Force on 21st Century Policing Recommendations

The tradition of political involvement in policing continues today, despite the attempts to remove certain elements of political action and is, indeed, still deep-rooted in policing. In New Orleans, for example, the police department has long been criticized as "a cesspool of corruption and violence."[27] In 2014, ex-mayor Ray Nagin was convicted on 20 criminal counts, including bribery and money laundering during his terms as mayor, for which he was sentenced to 10 years in prison. The police department entered into one of the most far-reaching consent decrees to date with the DOJ because of long-standing police abuses, racist policing tactics, and widespread violations of the Constitution.[28]

These and other efforts have been mounted to reform the New Orleans Police Department. Yet, it is a slow process that many fear is superficial at best.

Reform is "a core element in improving police–community relations for a department that has become notorious for political interference, corruption, racial insensitivity and civil-service rigidities."[29]

Chicago is also plagued by continuing problems with political corruption and has been called "the most corrupt city in the country . . . The crimes include ghost payrolls, bogus contracts, city official thefts, bribes, and the likely most publicized of bad behaviors in recent times—police brutality."[30]

## CASE IN POINT 2.1

For nearly two centuries, Tammany Hall in New York City was a social organization that exerted a powerful political influence over elections, the courts, and the police. The eventual vice president under Thomas Jefferson, Aaron Burr, recognized and developed Tammany Hall as a political tool. One of its most notorious leaders was William "Boss" Tweed, an infamously corrupt figure who held the reins during the mid-1800s, who later spent time in prison for graft and corruption. The power of the political machinery of Tammany grew in part due to its help for poor immigrants such as getting them jobs, supporting widows with children, and helping immigrants make their way through the naturalization process. This base was then beholden to cast its votes in support of Tammany Hall. The Hall played a major role in fostering economic growth and benefits for its constituents, even while it exploited its influence with police administrators and judges.

In all that time, Tammany Hall's leadership and power went through many changes and challenges from reformers, but at its strongest, the established machinery ensured that its candidates were elected, that its members were protected in the courts, and that its loyal members enjoyed leniency from the police.

1. Do you believe the good done by the Hall justifies the ways it exploited its members for political gains?

2. Does society have sufficient protections in place for new immigrants and other underprivileged members of society? Why or why not?

*Sources:* Burrows, E. G., & Wallace, M. (1999). *Gotham: A history of New York City to 1898*. New York: Oxford University Press; Connable, A., & Silberfarb, E. (1967). *Tigers of Tammany: Nine men who ran New York*. New York: Holt, Rinehart & Winston; NPR. (2014, March 5). "The case for Tammany Hall being on the right side of history." Retrieved from http://www.npr.org/2014/03/05/286218423/the-case-for-tammany-hall-being-on-the-right-side-of-history.

**Police Accountability**

With accompanying changes in the political leadership, the hiring and firing of police chiefs in different communities continues, as do attempts on behalf of politicians to influence the daily activity of police officers, chiefs, and sheriffs.[31] Such attempts to control the police raise the issues of how to control the police in a democratic society, how to hold them accountable in ways that are not politically motivated, and how to ensure that they are responsive to the concerns of the citizens they are meant to serve and not beholden to the interests of politicians. (These issues are explored in more depth in Chapters 10 and 11.)

> The suggestion that police agencies be directly supervised by elected municipal executives conjures up the image of police administrators beholden to various interests—including criminal elements—on whose continued support the elected mayor, their boss, may depend . . . is this not one of the costs of operating under our system of government?[32]

# ■ THE REFORM ERA

Serious attempts to reform and professionalize the police began to materialize in the late 1800s and early 1900s, ushering in the **Reform Era**, or **Reform Movement**. The Reform Era involved radical reorganization, including strong centralized administrative bureaucracy, highly specialized units, and substantial increases in the number of officers. Police professionalization was recognized as an important issue at least as early as 1909 by the father of modern police management systems, August Vollmer, who served as chief of police in Berkeley, California, from 1905 to 1932. In part because of the Depression, policing as a profession became more attractive to young men who in better times might have sought other employment, thus making it possible to recruit and select qualified police officers. Positive results began to show due to the efforts of Vollmer, Arthur Niederhoffer, William Parker, and O. W. Wilson, among others, to promote professionalism and higher education for police officers.

■ **Reform Era (Reform Movement):** Involved radical reorganization of police agencies, including strong centralized administrative bureaucracy, hiring and promotion based on merit, highly specialized units, and application of science to crime through improved record keeping, fingerprinting, serology, and criminal investigation

Various reform movements were under way also, the goal of which was to centralize police administration, improve the quality of police personnel, and destroy the power of the political bosses.[33] As reformers attempted to define policing as a profession, the service role of the police changed into more of a crime-fighting role. The passage of the 18th Amendment in 1920 and the onset of the Great Depression in 1929 placed the police under a new public mandate for crime control and public safety. As a result, police stopped providing a wide range of services, including assisting the homeless, babysitting, and helping people locate employment.

Concern about the police reached a national level with the appointment by

August Vollmer, the father of modern police management systems.

President Hoover of the Wickersham Commission in 1931. The commission was formed to investigate rising crime rates, and it directed police away from the service role, challenging them to become law enforcers and to reduce the crime rate.

Reformers adopted military customs and created specialized units, including vice, juvenile, and traffic divisions.[34] The historical development of large, bureaucratically organized police departments can be attributed in part to a larger movement by government to obtain legitimacy for their agencies by adopting the rational–legal formal structure that placed more emphasis on impersonal rules, laws, and discipline.[35] Reformers rapidly infused more technological advances into policing through improved record keeping, fingerprinting, serology, and criminal investigation. Training academies to teach these and other subjects became more common, and agencies emphasized promotion and selection based on merit (often through the use of civil service testing).

The onset of World War II and the Korean War made recruitment of well-qualified officers more difficult during the 1940s and 1950s. During this period, observers of the police, and sometimes the police themselves, seemed to equate technological advances and improved administration with professionalism.

## ■ THE ERA OF SOCIAL UPHEAVAL (1960s AND 1970s)

The 1960s proved to be one of the most challenging eras in U.S. policing. The crime rate per 100,000 persons doubled, the civil rights movement began, and antiwar sentiment and urban riots brought police to the center of the maelstrom.[36]

At the same time, the social disorder of this period produced fear among the public, because it appeared that family, church, and the police were losing their grip on society.[37] One result of this fear was that legislators began to pass laws that provided substantial resources to police agencies. In the 1960s and into the 1970s, there was a rapid development of two- and four-year college degree programs in law enforcement and an increased emphasis on training. These changes were in large part due to the 1967 report of the President's Commission on Law Enforcement and Administration of Justice, which was partially responsible for Congress passing the Omnibus Crime Control and Safe Streets Act of 1968. This act established the **Law Enforcement Assistance Administration (LEAA)** and provided a billion dollars each year to improve and strengthen criminal justice agencies. With funding available, social scientists began to test the traditional methods of police deployment, employee selection, and education and training and to question the appearance of racial discrimination in arrests and the use of deadly force.[38]

Federal and state funding was available to police officers who sought to further their educations, and potential police officers began to see some advantage in taking at least some college-level courses. Although there were vast differences in the quality of college programs, they did create a pool of relatively well-qualified applicants for both supervisory and entry-level positions. These developments—coupled with improvements in police training, salaries and benefits, and equipment—helped to create a more professional image of the police. At the same time, police came under increasing scrutiny as a result of their roles in the urban disorders of the late 1960s and early 1970s. Challenges to both authority and procedure were common, and public criticism continued into the 1980s. The police were seen as partially responsible for continued high crime rates and civil unrest, and the number of complaints and civil actions brought against the police skyrocketed.

It is becoming ever clearer that underlying social and economic conditions are spawning crime and that society's unwillingness to do anything meaningful about them has really sealed the fate of the police effort to cope with the symptoms. Society

**Video Link:**
Can police reform happen in Philadelphia?

**Audio Link:**
Vietnam War Protests Speeches and Audios

■ **Law Enforcement Assistance Administration (LEAA):** During the 1960s and 1970s, provided a billion dollars each year to improve and strengthen criminal justice agencies

wants to fight crime with more cops, tougher judges, and bigger jails, not through such scorned "liberal" schemes as social welfare programs. . . . Police executives believe that today's unattended problems, concentrated in our urban centers, will only get worse, eventually resulting in riots and heightened violence.[39]

There is clearly a discrepancy between what the public assumes the police can accomplish and what the police can *actually* accomplish. Although the expectation may be that *more* police will solve the problems referred to in the quote above, the reality is that merely increasing the numbers of police officers will not produce the desired result. The discrepancy was highly problematic and impacted not only police administrators' decisions concerning operations, but also the type of personnel who applied for police positions and the type of preparations for the jobs they received. At the same time, collective bargaining and unionization in police departments considerably changed the complexion of relationships between police administrators and rank-and-file officers. Though police unions have undoubtedly helped improve police salaries and working conditions, they remain controversial because of their emphasis on seniority and their opposition to reform.

### Research on Police Effectiveness

This period saw a wave of bureaucratic responses, fueled in part by research on the police, the amount and quality of which improved drastically beginning in the 1960s. The 1967 **President's Commission on Law Enforcement and Administration of Justice**, the **National Advisory Commission on Civil Disorders** in the same year, and the 1973 **National Advisory Commission on Criminal Justice Standards and Goals** represented major efforts to better understand styles of policing, police–community relations, and police selection and training.[40] Many other private and government-funded research projects contributed to the field. However, police still carry the burden of over 180 years of conflict and attempts at reform. Most chiefs continue to be selected against a political backdrop, which may be good or bad for the agency, as we have seen.

■ **President's Commission on Law Enforcement and Administration of Justice (1967):** Represented a major effort to better understand styles of policing, police–community relations, and police selection and training

■ **National Advisory Commission on Civil Disorders (1967):** Another major effort to better understand styles of policing, police–community relations, and police selection and training

■ **National Advisory Commission on Criminal Justice Standards and Goals (1973):** Another attempt to better understand styles of policing, police–community relations, and police selection and training

© Bettmann/CORBIS

Officers should show restraint even when their personal beliefs differ from those of the citizens they serve. Of course, as illustrated here, not all officers act in accordance with that philosophy.

## Exhibit 2.3

### Commission on Accreditation for Law Enforcement Agencies

A noteworthy development in policing occurred in 1979. In response to repeated calls for police professionalism, the **Commission on Accreditation for Law Enforcement Agencies (CALEA)** was established, through the efforts of the International Association of Chiefs of Police, the National Organization of Black Law Enforcement Executives, the National Sheriffs' Association, and the Police Executive Research Forum. CALEA became operational in 1983 and accepted applications for accreditation, conducted evaluations based on specific standards for law enforcement agencies, and granted accreditation. By 2012, one-quarter of law enforcement officers in the United States worked for agencies that have CALEA accreditation. Most states have their own agencies to oversee law enforcement standards. California is among the most professional and formalized of such agencies. Many police departments have now been through a reaccreditation process, and numerous others are awaiting either accreditation or reaccreditation.

There has been some consolidation and standardization of services, but not a great deal. In general, the U.S. police appear to have become more concerned about social responsibility, but they still have difficulties interacting with some segments of society. Diversity remains the key characteristic of municipal police and local control the key to such diversity. Progress in policing has been made on many fronts. Progressive police chiefs, concerned academics, and other involved citizens have helped push the boundaries of traditional policing and shared their thoughts and findings at both national and international levels by publishing, teaching or training, and promoting exchange programs. Research on and by the police has increased dramatically in the past several years.

> [P]olice leaders have been under considerable pressure to manage personnel and operations as efficiently as possible. This pressure may help explain why police administrators have apparently been even more willing than leadership in other criminal justice areas to question traditional assumptions and methods, to entertain the conclusions of research, and to test research recommendations.[41]

"Essentially, what the [police] literature describes about the policing role in the United States is that it is unsettled, subject to ongoing societal change, and continually evolving."[42] A panel of experts found that "the boundaries of the police are shifting on a number of dimensions."[43] Those shifts were perceived to be in terms of intelligence and privacy, jurisdiction, engagement with other criminal justice agencies, cultural and normative dimensions, and reach of social control. In all of these areas, the shift was perceived in terms of an expansion of the police function. One of the major challenges confronting the police in the 21st century involves dealing with these changes.

### ■ THE COMMUNITY-POLICING ERA (1980–2000)

The 1980s ushered in numerous technological advances in policing. Increased use of computers enabled departments to institute crime analysis programs to track crime incidents, analyze their common factors, make predictions concerning crime trends, and develop strategies to apprehend offenders.[44] Also during this time, departments began to use newly developed record management systems to store and retrieve information in addition to computer-aided dispatch and 911 systems. Together, these advances enabled communications personnel to receive calls for service, determine and

■ **Commission on Accreditation for Law Enforcement Agencies (CALEA):** Established in 1979 (operational in 1983), the commission conducts evaluations based on specific standards for law enforcement agencies and accredits agencies meeting the criteria

dispatch the closest police officer, and inform the officer who was answering the call. As the use of computers and wireless communications grew, mobile data terminals allowed officers to immediately access information that the communication center had received and relayed.[45]

Police administrators in the second half of the 1900s attempted to maximize the use of this technology, increase specialization, provide better training, and expand educational opportunities in an attempt to enhance the image of the police and create a more effective police force. However, in doing so, they created some unanticipated problems, including increasing the proverbial gap between officers and the other citizens they served. One obvious example of this was the use of patrol officers who policed the streets in vehicles that served as offices on wheels. Patrol cars effectively isolated the officers from the public, and community members often did not know the officers patrolling their neighborhoods. Although understanding the need for speed and mobility, many citizens preferred to have recognizable officers walking the beat. Research on foot patrol suggested that it contributed to city life, reduced fear among citizens, increased citizen satisfaction with the police, improved police attitudes toward citizens, and increased the morale and job satisfaction of police officers.[46]

**Community relations programs**, developed in the 1960s, were initially an experiment in bridging the gap between the police and the community. Such programs were later to become a revolution in policing.

Speaking at community centers and in schools was one of the first attempts to improve community relations. These programs eventually expanded to include neighborhood storefront offices, ride-along programs, fear-reduction programs, police academies for citizens, cultural diversity training, police–community athletic programs, and **Drug Abuse Resistance Education (DARE)**.[47]

■ **Community Relations Programs:** Programs sponsored by police agencies that attempt to improve police–community relations

■ **Drug Abuse Resistance Education (DARE):** Educational programs presented by police officers in cooperation with school authorities in an attempt to prevent abuse of drugs by youth

## POLICE ✪ STORIES 2.1

### Commander Dan Koenig, LAPD Retired

For decades, the Hollenbeck area of Los Angeles was home to most of the city's Mexican American community. Many of its residents were undocumented immigrants who avoided contact with the police at any cost. Hollenbeck also had four public housing developments where many of the community's gang members lived. Officers had always suspected that the gang members were victimizing the immigrants, but there was no way to know for sure the extent to which it was occurring.

In 1968, Captain Rudy DeLeon was assigned as the Hollenbeck commanding officer. Rudy had grown up there and was well aware of the problems facing the law-abiding, albeit undocumented, community. Rudy soon opened up a storefront on Brooklyn Avenue, which was the community's main thoroughfare. He named the storefront Estofadores and staffed it with officers fluent in Spanish. Soon, members of the immigrant community began stopping in to report crimes, which allowed us to address their crime problems. But Rudy wasn't willing to settle for that success. Soon he decided to assign foot beats to each of the housing developments. The foot beats were not well received by the gangs, who believed they "owned" the developments, and there were several violent confrontations. But after a while, the officers could walk the beats safely and eventually became welcome members of the communities they served.

This was the first time a "walk in" satellite police station had been tried in a major U.S. city, with the goal of encouraging undocumented immigrants to report crime. From this flowed a policy at the Los Angeles Police Department not to inquire into a person's immigration status when he or she is reporting a crime. That was a big deal when it was adopted in Los Angeles. Because it was effective, most major cities soon followed suit.

By the early 1980s, there was a gradual movement away from the crime-fighting model and toward a **community-policing** model. By the mid-1980s, it was clear that the police by themselves were unable to deal with increasing crime and violence. Recognizing that performance in the areas of crime control and order maintenance could only improve with public cooperation, progressive police administrators turned to community-oriented or community-based policing as a possible solution to their problems. Community policing was intended to counter enhanced technology, specialization, and paramilitary organization and restore relationships that the police had lost with the citizenry they were sworn to serve and protect.[48] This move represented a return to the principles of policing originally specified by Sir Robert Peel. However, embedded in the more modern version of Peel's principles was enhanced professionalism and better communication with neighborhood residents.

**Audio Link:**
Wisconsin City
Serves as Model for
Community Policing

At the same time, **problem-oriented policing** began to attract increased attention. This approach to policing emphasized the interrelationships among what might otherwise appear to be disparate events. For example, police officers often report that the same families continue to account for many crimes over the years and across generations. Rather than dealing with all of these calls as separate incidents to be handled before clearing the calls and going on to other calls, problem-oriented policing focuses attention on the underlying difficulties that create patterns of incidents.[49] It allows officers to take a holistic approach, working with other citizens and other agency representatives to find more permanent solutions to a variety of police and neighborhood problems. Both community-oriented and problem-oriented policing emphasize the importance of the police–community relationship and the fact that police work consists in large measure of order maintenance through the use of negotiations among the police and other citizens. Police education programs should emphasize the consideration of value choices and ethical dilemmas in policing and should "include comprehensive treatment of the most commonly performed police work, which falls outside of the criminal justice system."[50]

> Policing organized around perspectives that not only emphasize crime control and order-maintenance, but also emphasize more diverse approaches such as crime prevention, proactive policing, community problem-solving, improvement of police–community relations by reducing the social distance between the police and the public through increased police accountability and improved service to the public, empowerment of front-line officers, and a flatter organizational power structure that promotes team work and a collectivist spirit among all.[51]

In a study of some 281 municipal departments that serve populations of 25,000 or more, researchers found that police departments that prioritize homeland security planning are associated with fewer officers devoted solely to community policing and smaller or static departmental budgets.[52] Nonetheless, homeland security planning was positively associated with community-policing programs and activities. And, police departments that emphasize community policing are more likely to have a website, to exhibit greater transparency in the display of data, and to provide more opportunities for citizen input.[53] Not all observers of the police see a continuing role for community policing. Some predict a return to the professional model of policing driven by centralization, technology, and sophisticated surveillance.[54] Even though some argue that community policing has taken a backseat to other policing strategies, it continues to play an important role. Many of the more recent strategies in policing could not be effective without strong police–community partnerships.

**■ Community
Policing:** A model
of policing based on
establishing partnerships
among police and other
citizens in an attempt to
improve quality of life
through crime prevention,
information sharing, and
mutual understanding

**■ Problem-Oriented
Policing:** Encourages
officers to take a holistic
approach, working with
other citizens and other
agency representatives
to find long-term
solutions to a variety of
recurrent problems

## ■ THE HOMELAND SECURITY ERA (2001–PRESENT)

The terrorist attacks of September 11, 2001, set in motion a new era of policing in the United States called "the era of homeland security."[55] The nation responded to 9/11 by launching a "war on terrorism" and enacting the USA PATRIOT Act (discussed in Chapters 9 and 14). Many other countries also strengthened their antiterrorism legislation and expanded law enforcement powers.

Police in the era of homeland security have to be more familiar with information technology and the gathering, processing, and disseminating of information. The police also need enhanced skills that pertain to weapons of mass destruction (nuclear, chemical, and biological weapons), events involving mass casualties, and methods of preventing terrorism.[56]

Although all law enforcement agencies have a more heightened awareness of homeland security in this new era, it is mostly federal law enforcement agencies and police in larger metropolitan areas that have concentrated their investigative efforts and resources on homeland security. It is debatable whether such investigations—and the interrogations and detention that sometimes result—are the most effective means of protecting the country from further terrorist attacks. It is certain, however, that infringing inappropriately on the civil rights of certain target groups can lead to hostility among those groups, whose assistance with developing intelligence concerning possible terrorists is essential. Collecting intelligence was a standard aspect of local policing that disappeared in most respects during the 1960s and 1970s, largely as a result of the fear of abuse of powers by the police. Bringing back this intelligence-gathering component means that safeguards need to be put in place to protect against the abuse of authority. It was for this very reason that intelligence gathering was eliminated. Undoubtedly, the risk to civil liberties still exists, and safeguards are necessary to protect against such abuse.

**Video Link:**
Are We Safer?

It is therefore critical that police officers treat targeted groups with respect, help ensure that their liberties are not unduly trampled on, and help them to maintain their sense of dignity.[57] Community-oriented policing efforts that develop partnerships with diverse groups in the community represent perhaps the best way of accomplishing these goals. Communication between police administrators and line officers, lateral communication between the police and other governmental agencies, and communication among local, state, and federal agencies is critical in this new era of policing.

A summary of these four eras is included in Table 2.1.

**Table 2.1 ■ The Four Eras of Policing**

| Elements | Political Era | Reform Era | Community Era | Homeland Security Era |
|---|---|---|---|---|
| **Authorization** | Politics and law | Law and professionalism | Community support (political), law, professionalism | National/international threats (politics), law (intergovernmental), professionalism |
| **Function** | Broad social services | Crime control | Broad, provision of service | Crime control, antiterrorism/counterterrorism, intelligence gathering |
| **Organizational Design** | Decentralized | Centralized, classical | Decentralized, task forces, matrices | Centralized decision making, decentralized execution |
| **Relationship to Environment** | Intimate | Professionally remote | Intimate | Professional |
| **Demand** | Decentralized, to patrol and politicians | Centralized | Decentralized | Centralized |
| **Tactics and Technology** | Foot patrol | Preventive patrol and rapid response to calls for service | Foot patrol, problem solving, and the like | Risk assessment, police operations centers, information systems |
| **Desired Outcome** | Citizen political satisfaction | Crime control | Quality of life and citizen satisfaction | Citizen safety, crime control, antiterrorism |

*Source:* National Institute of Justice

# ■ SOME CONTEMPORARY POLICING STRATEGIES

As the review of the history of policing indicates, policing is dynamic and constantly changing. Based on analysis of the effectiveness of past police practices, numerous contemporary strategies have emerged. Time and evaluation will help determine the relative effectiveness of each of these strategies, which are briefly mentioned here and discussed in more detail in Chapter 7.

## Intelligence-Led or Intelligence-Based Policing

**Intelligence-led or intelligence-based policing** is a policing model that originated in Britain and focuses on risk assessment and risk management. The approach involves identifying risks or patterns associated with groups, individuals, and locations to predict when and where crime is likely to occur. Many agencies now conduct crime analyses on a regular basis, thus identifying reported crime patterns. An effective records management system allows frontline officers to easily obtain this information on a timely basis prior to or while responding to a call. This may assist officers in proactively identifying and anticipating problems they may encounter rather than reacting to them at the scene. The approach has gained momentum globally following the September 11 terrorist attacks on the United States.[58]

## Terrorism-Oriented Policing

As previously mentioned, the events of 9/11 led to new duties and strategies for police at all levels in the United States. Now, in contrast to much of the history of policing, some of the public wants to trust the government and the police as agents of government to protect them from criminals both domestic and foreign. Terrorism and homeland security are among many important issues that currently face police agencies, but homeland security issues are of such extreme concern that agencies must question whether their existing strategies are adequate to the task.[59] What might be termed **terrorism-oriented policing** requires changes at all levels of policing, most of which add new duties and strategies to existing ones.

For example, "the workload of already busy departments has significantly expanded to include identifying potential terrorists, protecting vulnerable targets, and coordinating

---

**■ Intelligence-Led or Intelligence-Based Policing:** A policing model that originated in Britain and focuses on risk assessment and risk management. Involves identifying risks or patterns associated with groups, individuals, and locations to predict when and where crime is likely to occur; builds on community policing and problem-oriented policing and includes an information gathering process that allows police agencies to better understand their crime problems and take a measure of resources available to be able to decide on enforcement and prevention strategies

**■ Terrorism-Oriented Policing:** Adds new duties to those already assumed by the police in an attempt to detect and prevent terrorist acts

---

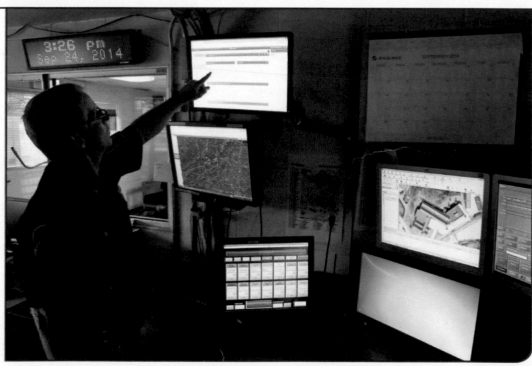

Today, police have found that crime mapping and other technology-based methods have a significant impact on the prevention and investigation of crime.

© AP Photo / Matt Gentry

In March 2009, the Peoria Police Department launched a crime-mapping program known as "CrimeView Community." The service, developed by The Omega Group, is billed as "intelligence-led policing." CrimeView enables law enforcement agencies to map and analyze their own data for a more informed approach to police functions such as investigations, deployment of officers, and emergency management. It allows public web users to check crime trends for 90-day periods in user-designated areas of the city. Such programs are already in hundreds of departments and in most states.

It is believed that the program will help the public make educated decisions about crime in the areas in which they live, work, go to school, and shop. When users log on to CrimeView in Peoria, they will be able to search 16 different types of crime by location within the city. The website is scheduled to be updated daily.

1. What are the advantages and disadvantages to "CrimeView Community" and other programs that map and analyze neighborhood crime data?

2. Do you think that access to crime data may cause citizens to be unnecessarily fearful of becoming crime victims?

3. Is it possible for criminals to use programs like "CrimeView Community" to their benefit? How?

*Source:* From "Tool tracks city crime," by G. Childs, 2009, *Journal Star*, pp. A1, A8.

---

first response."[60] In addition, whether the police are operating in a small town or a large city, it is now their "responsibility to ensure that plans are in place to prevent attack and to respond quickly should an attack occur."[61]

Some observers insist that partnerships with citizens and problem-solving principles are essential to successful and sustainable crime-reduction and terrorism-prevention strategies that are consistent with U.S. democratic values. Community partnership

## Exhibit 2.4

## How the Long Beach Police Department Has Adapted to the Terrorism Threat

- Created a counterterrorism unit and appointed terrorist liaison officers.

- Reassigned officers to assess and protect critical infrastructure, such as the port, airport, and water treatment facilities.

- Sent officers to train in new skills, such as WMD [weapons of mass destruction] response and recognizing signs of terrorism.

- Established a port police unit equipped with small boats.

- Reassigned officers to respond to areas with high population growth.

- Increased visibility and response times by switching officers from two- to one-person cars.

- Reduced staffing on lower priority programs, such as Drug Abuse Resistance Education (DARE).

- Reduced foot patrols and staffing in the narcotics division.

- Requested additional resources to cover demand, both from the city for local needs and from the federal government for national needs.

*Source:* Raymond, B., Hickman, L., Miller, L., and Wong, J. (2005). *Police personnel challenges after September 11: Anticipating expanded duties and a changing labor pool.* Santa Monica, CA: RAND Corporation.

and problem solving in policing are as relevant and modern as the war on terror.[62] In addition, terrorists often commit ordinary crimes such as robbery, drug dealing, and fraud to sustain themselves. Thus, "from a policing point of view, there is much to be said for regarding terrorists as criminals with political motives."[63]

"Local police can identify potential terrorists living or operating in their jurisdictions, they can help protect vulnerable targets, and they can coordinate the first response to terror attacks. These are heavy new responsibilities that significantly expand the workload of already busy departments."[64] However, "counterterrorism has to be woven into the everyday workings of every department. It should be included on the agenda of every meeting, and this new role must be imparted to officers on the street so that terrorism prevention becomes part of their everyday thinking."[65]

The potential for loss of life from a terrorist attack makes prevention a critical goal. Consequently, the police have had to increase security at major events and increase patrols at ports, bridges, and other potential targets. They might also need to conduct security surveys or to give advice for protecting vulnerable sites.[66] Undoubtedly, this requires additional and appropriate training.

## ■ POLICING IN THE PAST, PRESENT, AND FUTURE

History has shown us that policing has evolved and adapted over time as the police attempt to meet the needs of society. In earlier times, police personnel could be recruited from almost any walk of life, because the nature of crime did not generally require great technical police expertise. In the new millennium, communication is instantaneous, crime can be global in scope, and technology continues to increase in sophistication. Effective policing demands that police expertise be sufficiently sophisticated as well to deter and apprehend (for example) individuals who are involved in transnational crime, who use the most advanced technologies to prey on their victims, who traffic in human beings across borders, and who threaten to spread terror and chaos.

All of these and other activities often require direct intervention into the lives of citizens. The debate rages over the balance between the needs of law enforcement for information and the public's democratic right to privacy. Democracy represents consensus, freedom,

### Police Bolster Attack on Cybercrime

British police, in a response to the growing threat of online attacks, are bolstering their campaign against cyber criminals with the formation of three new regional e-crime control centers.

These centers are designed to "provide an enhanced ability to investigate this fast growing area of crime and provide an improved internet investigation capability."

"Cyber crime has been identified by law enforcement agencies as a 'tier-one' national security threat, putting it on a par with international terrorism, an international military crisis, or a natural disaster."

1. How much freedom should the government be given to "spy" on private emails, text messages, and phone records to detect and to prevent threats to national security?

2. Would you be willing to subject your personal emails, text messages, and phone records to government scrutiny in the name of "safety"?

*Source:* Warrell, H. (2012, Feb. 7). Police bolster attack on cyber crime. *Financial Times* (London, England). Retrieved from FT.com. Record Number: 13CCD7F5AD08C730.

participation, and equality; the police represent restriction and the imposition of authority of government on the individual.[67] The police and the community must share in controlling crime. In exchange for greater legal leeway to do so, the police may need to be more transparent and raise their standard for accountability. Community service may require better training in the theory and practice of total crime prevention.[68]

Policing has changed immensely over the past 50 years in response to the demands imposed on it by an increasingly diverse, technological, urbanized, globalized, mobile, sophisticated, rights-conscious, and knowledge-based society."[69] Agencies must decide how best to use their limited budgets. They must determine how much specialized training they should require of officers to be effective in the complex world of international terrorist conspiracies and rapidly changing technologically sophisticated crimes, all on a finite budget. They must balance a centralized and sophisticated organization with the need to have close ties with the community, while maintaining accountability, transparency, and respect for individual rights.

### Exhibit 2.5

### Contemporary Police Issues

- New strategies in policing
- Concerns with continuing education and training
- Recruitment and selection of officers
- Police accountability
- Exercise of discretion
- Ethical issues
- Police misconduct
- Policing in a multicultural society
- Police officer stress
- Changing technology and cybercrime
- Globalization, terrorism, immigration, and homeland security
- Privatization

## CHAPTER SUMMARY

The manner in which organized and professional police agencies operate today has been influenced greatly by their historical development from English origins over the last 200 years. Police officers of the early days had little to no training, and there were no formal educational requirements. The system of night watchmen over time evolved into a more militarily organized system of police under government control. The close ties of officers to the communities they served gave them great problem-solving abilities, but also left the door open to bribery and corruption. There was considerable political influence on police officers, some of which was unprofessional at best, including unethical and unlawful acts at the behest of the politicians who controlled them. Although politics still play an important role in policing, there are many other and perhaps more pressing and complicated influences.

Important technological advances gave the police more options in fighting crime, but changes in standards, development of ethical codes, education and training provided by those outside policing, and other indicators of professionalism were largely lacking. To be sure, some important changes had occurred. Reformers had identified inappropriate political involvement as a major problem in U.S. policing. Civil service successfully removed some of the patronage and ward influences from police officers. Law and professionalism were established as the bases of police legitimacy. Under these circumstances, policing became a legal and technical matter left to the discretion of professional police executives. Eliminating all political influence from policing is unlikely and, if we wish to maintain civilian control of the police, perhaps undesirable.

The political and social environment of each decade has had its influence on how the police operate, the degree of the connection they have with their communities, and how the public perceives them. Numerous policing strategies have been implemented and tested over the years in an attempt to satisfy the goals of various segments of the U.S. public. Inattention to the will of diverse minorities has often been the basis of strained police–community relations.

During the last three decades, the police began to reconsider their fundamental mission, as well as the nature of the core strategies of policing, and the nature of their relationships with the communities they serve.[70] In spite of numerous innovative programs initiated in recent years and the research needed to evaluate them, the evidence related to police performance and implementation associated with these innovations on crime reduction and community satisfaction is limited.[71]

Some of the newest policing strategies are based on the tenets of community- and problem-oriented policing and operate in response to various global issues that now affect local police operations. The increasing complexities of policing, coupled with the technology-based nature of the world in which we live and work, demand vigilant, cooperative, and proactive forms of policing to effectively address a wide variety of issues.

**⑤SAGE edge™**

Review key terms with eFlashcards.

## KEY TERMS

- Professionalism  17
- Night watch system  17
- Sir Robert Peel  18
- Patrick Colquhoun  18
- Pendleton Act  21
- Sheriff  21
- Reform Era (Reform Movement)  23
- Law Enforcement Assistance Administration (LEAA)  24

- Commission on Accreditation for Law Enforcement Agencies (CALEA)  26
- President's Commission on Law Enforcement and Administration of Justice (1967)  25
- National Advisory Commission on Civil Disorders (1967)  25
- National Advisory Commission on Criminal Justice Standards and Goals (1973)  25

- Community relations programs  27
- Drug Abuse Resistance Education (DARE)  27
- Community policing  28
- Problem-oriented policing  28
- Intelligence-led or intelligence-based policing  30
- Terrorism-oriented policing  30

**⑤SAGE edge™**

Test your understanding of chapter content. Take the practice quiz.

## DISCUSSION QUESTIONS

1. Briefly discuss the evolution of the U.S. police and the problems they currently confront.

2. How did the need for police arise?

3. What problems confronting the police are inherent in democratic societies?

4. What are the positive and negative effects of the interaction between politics and the police in our society?

5. Discuss some of the most recent policing strategies and their potential effectiveness.

## INTERNET EXERCISES

1. Using your favorite search engine, go online and see what you can find out about the history of policing. What two or three websites did you find most interesting? What kinds of information did these websites contain?

2. Go to the Internet and search for articles dealing with current police corruption. In light of the articles you found, do you believe there is still a need for reform in policing? If so, what types of reform would you like to see?

Accreditation is briefly introduced here in chapter 2 and is discussed again in chapter 3. An accredited law enforcement agency is officially recognized as meeting essential requirements set forth by the Commission on Accreditation for Law Enforcement (CALEA). Without knowing what these essential requirements are, one might not be impressed by the credentials.

According to the CALEA Standards Manual (1999), the goals of law enforcement accreditation are to: "(a) improve crime prevention and control capabilities, (b) formalize management procedures, (c) establish fair and non-discriminatory personnel practices, (d) improve service delivery, (e) improve inter-agency cooperation and coordination, and (f) increase confidence in the law enforcement agency" (CALEA, 1999, xiii).

1. If you could implement one standard or rule that police agencies had to follow, what would that be?

2. In general, do you trust officers from an accredited agency more than those working for one that is not accredited? Why or why not?

*Suggestions for addressing these questions can be found on the Student Study Site:* **edge.sagepub.com/ coxpolicing3e**

## STUDENT STUDY SITE

**$SAGE edge™** edge.sagepub.com/coxpolicing3e

**Sharpen your skills with SAGE edge!**

SAGE edge for Students provides a personalized approach to help you accomplish your coursework goals in an easy-to-use learning environment. You'll find action plans, mobile-friendly eFlashcards, and quizzes as well as videos, web resources, and links to SAGE journal articles to support and expand on the concepts presented in this chapter.

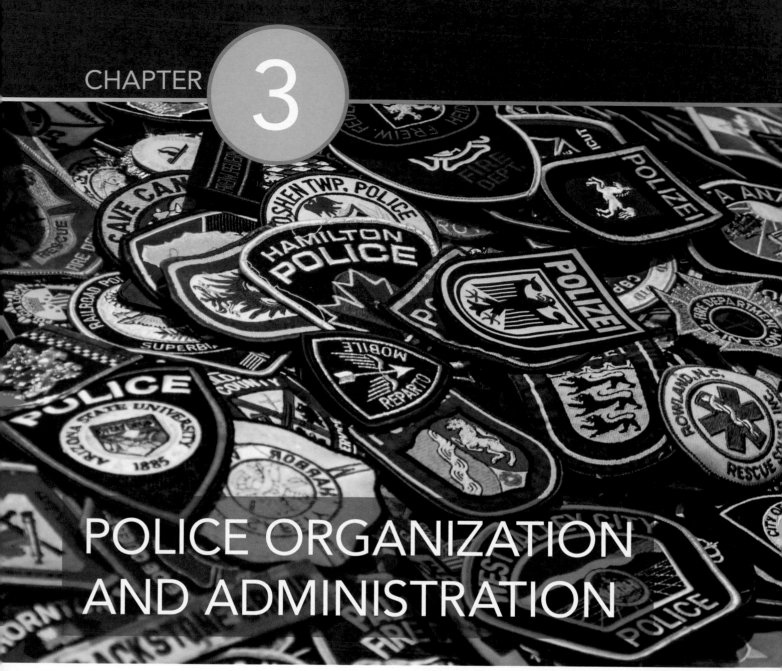

© iStockphoto.com/Vilches

# CHAPTER 3

# POLICE ORGANIZATION AND ADMINISTRATION

## CHAPTER LEARNING OBJECTIVES:

1. Explain the importance of organizational structures in police departments

2. List the duties typically associated with the operations division

3. Describe the influence of organizational substructures, such as geography and scheduling, on the operations of police departments

4. Explain a few strategies police organizations can use to handle change favorably

5. Evaluate the extent to which police departments have become "militarized" and the implications of this

6. Identify the pros and cons of collective bargaining in police organizations

7. Describe the purported advantages of accreditation in the field of policing

P olice agencies must perform a variety of functions. This includes responding to routine and emergency calls for service, enforcing traffic laws, conducting investigations, processing evidence, working with community groups, and accomplishing other specialized functions. Police departments have developed a variety of organizational structures to effectively and efficiently perform these functions. Effective organizations accomplish their goals, and efficient organizations make optimum use of resources. The best police agencies are both effective and efficient.

Police organizations are dynamic in nature. People are coming and going and often under stress, and priorities may shift at any moment due to both internal (e.g., number, quality, dedication of personnel) and external (e.g., legal, political, financial) factors. All of the normal operations require planning, organizing, staffing, directing, and controlling, and these activities are performed by personnel who occupy positions at different levels within the agency.

Administrators of both small and large organizations must perform a wide range of tasks:

- Planning what the organization needs to accomplish
- Organizing a formal structure to accomplish the organization's mission
- Staffing the organization through recruitment, selection, and training
- Directing the decision-making process and developing rules, policies, and procedures
- Coordinating groups to work together toward a common mission
- Reporting, keeping records, and communicating
- Budgeting and fiscal management of organization resources

Depending on the structure of an organization, these tasks can be divided up in several ways among all of the administrators. Planning and organizing functions are typically considerations for upper-level managers, while managers at lower levels likely spend more time directing and coordinating everyday activities. In police organizations, the chief of police and his or her immediate staff are likely to be involved in budgeting and policy making, while shift and field supervisors are more concerned with the day-to-day operations of directing other staff members. Nonetheless, personnel at all ranks in an organization might perform any of these functions from time to time. A police sergeant and police captain both engage in some level of planning, though at different scales. The chief of a small police agency may perform all the tasks associated with planning, coordinating, reporting, and directly supervising employees.

## ■ ORGANIZATIONAL STRUCTURES

The organizational structures of police departments differ considerably depending on the style of policing and other interdependent variables, such as the size of the community, the size of the police force, and the available resources. The functions police officers perform depend to a considerable extent on the type of organization and the position officers occupy within the **organization**. Organizational structures range from the small, single-person department—where the chief of police performs all functions related to policing—to those involving thousands of police personnel and dozens of specializations. The largest police departments exhibit a wide variety in their organizational structures; some have 4 or 5 rank levels, whereas others have 10 to 12 different ranks.[1] In addition, certain police departments operate from a single headquarters, whereas others have many different substations. The structure of police organizations helps to determine productivity, the manner in which goals are achieved, and the influence of individual variations on the organization. Police organizations exist in certain contexts—they possess different histories and traditions, and approach policing in many different ways.[2] Current and future organizational structures for the

**Policing In Practice Video:**
How do you and your department communicate efficiently in this structured environment?

■ **Organization:**
A rational, efficient form of grouping people

**Policing in Practice Video:**
Policing in Practice Video: Police Captain

■ **Hierarchies:** Organizational structures that take the shape of a pyramid, with many employees at the bottom and a few management personnel at the top

■ **Line Personnel:** Perform actual police work and include patrol officers and investigators

■ **Unity of Command:** Each member of the organization has an immediate supervisor

■ **Rank Structure:** Chain of command that identifies who communicates with whom and identifies lines of authority

■ **Span of Control:** Ratio of supervisors to subordinates

police must strike a balance between inclusiveness and the need for rapid response and efficiency, especially in emergency situations. And, they need to do this with consideration to the factors of a changing world, such as terrorism, homeland security, and performance-based standards.

## Police Hierarchy

Through the years, police leaders have explored a variety of organizational structures, but most police organizations are **hierarchies**. Most hierarchical organizational charts resemble pyramids, as illustrated in Figure 3.1, with numerous employees at the bottom of the pyramid and a few management personnel at the top.

The base of the police hierarchy consists of those who do the actual police work in the organization—**line personnel**, such as patrol officers and investigators. In most organizations, the position in the hierarchy dictates the type of responsibility for the rank. Thus, chief executives have a different set of responsibilities than middle managers, who have different responsibilities than lower-level employees. However, in policing, the amount of actual "police work" a person performs is usually inversely related to his or her position in the organization. In other words, lower-ranking police officers on the street have more policing responsibilities than administrators.

There are three important characteristics of a hierarchical structure: unity of command, rank structure, and span of control. The principle of **unity of command** means that every member of the police organization reports to an immediate superior. Thus, patrol officers in a police agency are typically responsible to a field supervisor (e.g., a sergeant); the field supervisor is typically responsible to a shift administrator (e.g., lieutenant), who is responsible to a division commander; and so on.

**Rank structure**, or chain of command, identifies who communicates with and gives orders to whom and clearly and precisely identifies lines of authority. The complexity of the chain of command and the number of ranks depends in part on the size of the police department. Small departments tend to have fewer ranks and often operate informally yet still have a chain of command. In almost all cases, the chain of command and rank structure in a police department is indicated by different colors of uniforms or caps, different brass accessories, or different types of striping on the uniforms.

The chain of command of a police organization may be confusing, because it often involves multiple hierarchies, such as an authority hierarchy and a status hierarchy. For example, a police commander with 15 years of experience holds a higher rank in the department than a shift sergeant with 25 years of experience. However, in the seniority hierarchy, the sergeant occupies a higher position than the police commander.

The final important characteristic of a hierarchy is the **span of control**, or the ratio of supervisors to subordinates. The span of control differs from one rank layer in the hierarchy to the next, and the ratio of supervisors to police officers is usually smaller near the top of the departmental hierarchy compared to the bottom.

### Hierarchy and Communication

Hierarchical organizational structures have certain advantages. For example, the division of authority is clear-cut and well understood, ensures clear responsibility and accountability for tasks, and clarifies a supervisor's span of control. However, hierarchies tend to suffer from a variety of communication problems, including the top-down, one-way flow of information and a lack of feedback. Top administrators communicate explicit orders and directives downward, but there are few provisions for upward communication from lower ranks—the ones who must carry out orders, whether they agree with them or not. Because of this, there are few opportunities for

Figure 3.1 ■ Pyramid Structure

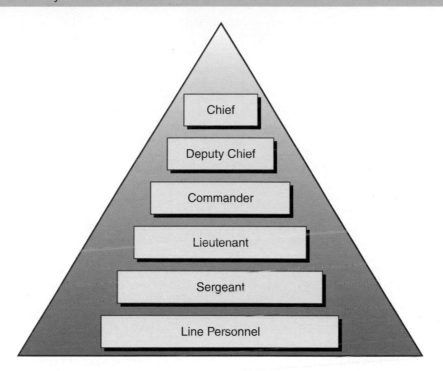

**Video Link:**
Law Enforcement
Supervisors Job Overview

## Exhibit 3.1

### Incident Command System (ICS)

Emergency situations, such as natural disasters or civil disturbances, require rapid and accurate communication. To overcome some of the communication problems common to hierarchies, many agencies have adopted an **Incident Command System (ICS)** for use in emergency situations.

Depending on the nature of the incident, the operation and staffing of an ICS may require a different location, dedicated phone lines, or other infrastructure that is separate from those required for normal, day-to-day operations. It may also involve multiple agencies working together and pooling their resources, especially during large-scale incidents, such as riots, fires, earthquakes, floods, or other natural disasters.

According to the U.S. Department of Labor, an ICS addresses the following problems:

- Too many people reporting to one supervisor
- Different emergency response organizational structures
- Lack of reliable incident information
- Inadequate and incompatible communications
- Lack of structure for coordinated planning among agencies
- Unclear lines of authority
- Terminology differences among agencies
- Unclear or unspecified incident objectives[3]

■ **Incident Command System (ICS):** Coordinates police personnel, allocates resources, and allows emergency responders to adopt and integrate organization structure; attempts to achieve effective coordination of police personnel while ensuring appropriate allocation of resources and providing emergency responders an integrated organizational structure unhindered by jurisdictional boundaries

The paramilitary
model is frequently
employed in
police paramilitary
units including
SWAT teams.

**SAGE Journal Article:**
Police Academy
Socialization:
Understanding Lessons
Learned in a Paramilitary-
Bureaucratic Organization

low-ranking staff to provide valuable feedback on the effectiveness of organizational policies or procedures. Feedback from line officers is increasingly important as today's police organizations reexamine their existing policies and procedures to meet a myriad of challenges, including court-ordered training mandates, budget and staffing shortages, changing laws, and new technologies.

### The Paramilitary Structure

Early police organizations developed a close relationship with the public and were focused on resolving problems. The typical police organizational structure prior to 1900 was very informal. The police and the public developed a close relationship, and the police were involved in assisting people with all types of social problems. However, this informality also bred a lack of accountability, training, and supervision. With their power and authority, accusations of graft, corruption, abuse of authority, and other violations were perhaps inevitable—especially since local politicians controlled, promoted, and hired the police. During the professional era (1950–1980), police administrators wanted to distance officers from the public in an effort to minimize corruption and wanted to achieve increasing levels of efficiency in their operations.[4] Therefore, they placed more emphasis on centralization and control of the police. The resulting organizational structure resembled that of the military, with its focus on accountability and its rigid structure.[5]

The result was "top-down management," which involves decision making by "top" central managers who impose policies down through the department ranks. Under the paramilitary model, police agencies focused on enforcing the law and fighting crime rather than attempting to solve community and citizen problems. The intent of the structure was to improve the efficiency of operations, provide fast responses to emergency situations, use criminal investigations, and attempt to ensure the fair and impartial enforcement of the law.[6]

As a result of the focus on centralized control, accountability, and rigidity, the classical principles of management through a paramilitary structure took a stronghold in police agencies. The typical characteristics associated with this paramilitary model include the following:

- Central command structure
- Rigid differences among ranks
- Terminology similar to that of the military
- Frequent use of commands and orders
- Strong enforcement of rules, regulations, and discipline
- Discouragement of individual creativity
- Resistance of system to change[7]

There are times in policing (and in the military) when a highly centralized, authoritarian command structure has these and other advantages. For example, there is little time to call a committee meeting to decide what to do when riotous protesters are threatening the police station or when there is an armed robbery in progress.

The paramilitary structure also has some distinct disadvantages. As noted previously, these organizational structures often fail to promote communication horizontally and from the bottom up. They frequently fail to encourage employee commitment through participation. Because of its emphasis on strict obedience, the top-down structure tends to hinder discretion and critical thinking.

Partially due to the inflexibility of the paramilitary structure, change in police organizations can be slow. Administrators and managers interested in creating change often pursue it in informal ways. For example, a lieutenant interested in formally changing long-standing procedures would normally be required to go to the patrol commander, who would then have to approach the assistant chief, who would finally seek the chief's approval. Instead, the lieutenant might see the chief after duty to gain support. Similarly, individual patrol officers and detectives may meet informally to discuss a case and share intelligence that their immediate supervisor may not wish to share as a result of internal rivalries. The changes that take place in most police organizations are often the result of both traditional and nontraditional methods.

Despite the long-standing practices of employing a quasi-military structure, police agencies are increasingly recognizing its inherent limitations, including the restrictions on personal freedoms, poor communication, and a lack of flexibility and a narrowness of job descriptions. The authoritarian paramilitary command structure is even more problematic when applied to the 21st-century demands and expectations of a community.[8]

Most police departments borrow rank names from the military. Officers are promoted to the level of the field supervisor (typically at the rank of sergeant), shift or watch

**Police Paramilitary Unit:** A highly specialized police unit such as a special response team

## Exhibit 3.2

## Specialized Paramilitary Units

Many police organizations have adopted the paramilitary model in highly specialized police units, called **police paramilitary units (PPUs)**. PPUs include such units as SWAT (special weapons and tactics), SRTs (special response teams), and ERUs (emergency response units). Well before September 11, 2001, police departments were adopting military tactics in patrol operations and in their response to and management of crime. In the aftermath of al-Qaeda's attacks, paramilitary policing increased faster than at any other time in history.[10] However, most police work is not of this nature. In fact, many are concerned that a terrorist-oriented mission will accelerate the militarization of police rather than bring the police closer to the community.[11]

These concerns raise questions about how much militarization is necessary or desirable and what value it has to the police and to society. Agency budgets are finite, so choosing military-style equipment, for instance, means that resources are not devoted to other aspects of policing.

commander (typically at the rank of lieutenant or commander), and division commander (typically with the rank of captain or above).

However, despite a number of superficial similarities (e.g., rank structure and uniforms), the police role in society is actually quite different from the military's role. Strict rules and orders are rarely required, due to the nature of the work and the fact that police are often on the street out of view of supervisors.[9] In addition, many believe that the best job performance requires a great amount of initiative and discretion.

### Decentralized and Proactive Organizations

Based on the limitations of existing designs and the need to adapt to a changing environment, many police agencies are experimenting with more decentralized organizational structures. Community policing has been one catalyst for organizational change toward decentralized structures and decreased formalization in police organizations; some police departments have modified the traditional paramilitary style of policing, sharing decision making with patrol officers.[12] Much of the literature related to community policing also called for "flatter" organizations, or police departments with few ranks, but this change may be problematic for unionized departments. In addition, community policing encourages the development of police officers as generalists to serve the diverse needs and different problems in a community instead of focusing only on crime control.

If the traits of the paramilitary model were ever conducive to effective policing, they are considerably less so with the transition to better-educated, better-trained officers. Although some police chiefs reflect on the "good old days" when officers simply did what they were told by an officer of superior rank and seldom questioned orders and directives, most chiefs realize that current conditions require officers who can think critically, question, understand, and explain the rationale for the directives they follow and exercise discretion wisely.

This more proactive police work in contemporary society calls for organizations that achieve the following:

1. Support of the exercise of initiative and discretion at all levels
2. Control through the use of guidance techniques, coaching, and counseling
3. Communication that flows both horizontally and vertically in both directions
4. Positive reinforcement (as opposed to punishment) to motivate personnel
5. Flexibility in operations
6. More decentralization
7. Decision making encouraged at the lowest possible level
8. Participatory management
9. Change regarded as an indicator of organizational health
10. Guidelines that delineate organizational expectations and evaluation of personnel in terms of these guidelines[13]

Another example of an option to the traditional organizational designs is the matrix structure. A **matrix structure** is based on multiple support systems and authority relationships, whereby some employees report to two superiors rather than one—a clear departure from the typical chain of command. The formation of a drug task force is an example of a matrix structure. Task forces are intended to reduce the reliance on the resources of a single unit or department and share that responsibility. Each agency brings a different perspective and different tools, expertise, strategies, and intelligence. Different agencies may even be governed by different laws. The Federal Bureau of Investigation (FBI), for instance, is a federal agency that adheres to federal law. The drug task force supervisor directs task force operations. Officers assigned to the task force are selected based on their expertise and their ability to contribute to the group. They may come

**Matrix Structure:** Involves multiple support systems and authority relationships often found in a drug task force

## CompStat

Today's need for innovative organizational designs has produced a number of tools. One such innovation is CompStat—a management philosophy and organizational management tool that alters some aspects of the organizational department structure by delegating decision making and authority to police commanders or middle managers.

CompStat (computerized statistics) originated in New York City; today most medium and large police agencies employ some form of management tool similar to CompStat. CompStat relies on capturing, mapping, compiling, and analyzing complaint and arrest data that police administrators can use to discern trends, distinguish anomalies, and develop crime control strategies. The data can also be used to hold staff accountable for their performance. CompStat has been credited with helping agencies reduce crime by significant margins.

from different units and may still be required to report to the supervisors of those units or departments. Reporting to multiple supervisors can cause confusion for the officers involved or proprietary feelings among the various supervisors. Nonetheless, because a task force assignment is often temporary, the personnel involved eventually return to their regular duties and regular supervisors after a specific period or after the task force has completed its goal.

### Police Organizations in Context

It is important to note that police organizations do not exist in a vacuum, nor are police functions determined totally or even largely by the police themselves. The police always operate in a political arena under public scrutiny (though a good many try to minimize such scrutiny). The municipal police chief heads the police department, but he or she is also responsible to a city manager, mayor, police commissioner, and city council.

Police departments draw resources from and provide services to their communities. How much a department has to work with and what level of service the police can provide is largely controlled by external factors. Further, police departments are only one component of the criminal justice network that sets the operating parameters for the police. The courts, for example, frequently intervene in police practices ranging from search and seizure, to interrogation, to hiring and promotion.

When city government regards the separate public service agencies as consumer oriented, chief executive officers are viewed as part of a cooperative team, with responsibilities to one another as well. Thus, the chief of police may request new equipment monies one year but defer to the fire chief the next. Further, in the vast majority of police agencies, hiring, disciplining (beyond a limited amount), termination, award of benefits, and so on are governed not by the police chief but by fire and police commissions or civil service merit boards.

## ■ OPERATIONS DIVISION

The operations division is usually the largest division, in terms of number of personnel and other resources, and it typically consists of two main subdivisions—patrol and investigations.

### Patrol

The patrol division is responsible for providing continuous police service and some degree of visibility. Patrol officers are responsible for responding to calls, making initial contact with crime victims, making arrests, gathering evidence, completing incident reports, and at times processing a crime scene.

It was long assumed that patrol operations were a crime deterrent and increased citizen satisfaction. However, some research indicates otherwise causing police administrators to reconsider whether traditional patrol is the best use of resources.

© iStockphoto.com/DnHolm

Patrol operations have long been regarded as the backbone of the police organization. Patrol is typically the largest division in a police department, with as many as 6 of every 10 officers assigned to patrol duties.[14] However, the proportion of police officers responding to 911 calls ranges from 6 in 10 among departments serving 100,000 or more residents to about 9 in 10 among police departments serving fewer than 100,000 residents.

In the past, patrol operations were assumed to deter crime, and many police administrators still believe that patrol serves a deterrent function and enhances citizen satisfaction. A number of patrol studies suggest that routine patrol does not perform either of these functions.[15] Still, many police administrators continue to operate as if patrol were the most effective approach to public safety.

An increasing number of police administrators, recognizing that routine patrol may not pay good dividends, are experimenting with other types of patrol. This is not to say that patrol officers have no impact on other citizens. Patrol officers respond to calls for service in their zones, beats, or districts, and they patrol the streets in their assigned areas when they are not responding to calls or completing their reports. The majority of patrol work is reactive, although patrol officers do at times arrive at a crime in progress. They also often use patrol to initiate contact based on traffic violations, and patrol officers are generally responsible for securing crime scenes and conducting preliminary investigations as first responders.

Once a crime scene has been secured, patrol officers often turn further responsibilities over to the investigative or detective division, although in some departments, patrol officers maintain responsibility for such investigations. In addition to their involvement in crime control, in smaller departments, patrol officers are also responsible for traffic control and investigating traffic accidents. Larger departments often have separate traffic and accident investigation units within the operations division. Some departments use watercraft, aircraft, bicycle, and canine-assisted patrols; others use civilian volunteers to patrol specific areas, under the supervision of police officers.

### Investigations

The investigations bureau is a subdivision of the operations division and is basically responsible for obtaining and processing evidence and making arrests based on that evidence. The evidence involved may be tangible (physical evidence collected at a crime scene or at the residence of a suspect) or intangible (accounts from witnesses or informants). This division is often regarded as the "glamour division"; it tends to be glorified on television and in the media, because it is thought to involve "real" police work and solving crime. However, contrary to popular belief, investigators are not particularly likely to solve crimes unless a witness steps forward to identify the offender.[16]

**Video Link:**
Cleveland Patrol Officers Recount Finding Missing Women

In 2012, the Huntington Beach Police Department announced its plans to reduce its patrol officers, respond to fewer accident calls, and refer residents to file minor crime reports online as part of a department reorganization to make up for budget cuts and a lack of overtime funding.

Previously, Huntington Beach made several changes to police patrol, including moving investigators to patrol and no longer investigating certain minor financial and property types of crimes. One supervisor in the department does not believe crime will increase, but does admit it will take longer to apprehend certain criminals. "The reduction of the number of officers on patrol means that not every accident or crime will be investigated," since the department will no longer respond to accidents in which there are no injuries.

The department lists the following criteria for filing reports online:

- There are *no* known suspects, or suspect description.
- There is no evidence to be collected.
- This is not an ongoing problem.
- The crime occurred within the Huntington Beach city limits.

The department will also implement an Internet crime reporting site, which will allow residents "who are not able to get an officer to take a crime report for vandalism or other petty crime" to make their own online report. These online reports will not be addressed by a police officer but do allow residents of Huntington Beach to "track" minor crimes.

1. Do police departments have a responsibility to respond to all calls for service, regardless of their nature?
2. Should cities fund their police departments, including overtime, at the expense of other services, such as maintaining parks and roadways?
3. Should private citizens be allowed to make their own online crime reports?
4. How can police departments ensure that online citizen reports are complete and accurate?

*Source:* "Police to reduce patrol officers' responses," by Mona Shadia, 2012, *Huntington Beach Independent* (http://infoweb. newsbank.com).

Investigators spend a good deal of time documenting crime scenes; locating, reinterviewing, and interrogating suspects and witnesses; analyzing records and reports; authoring search warrants; making arrests; and preparing cases and testifying in court. Crime scene investigators are involved in photographing, collecting, and analyzing DNA and fingerprints and processing other materials that may contain relevant leads to specific crimes. Once evidence has been obtained, investigators are responsible for establishing a **chain of custody**, which governs the storage, transmission, and protection of the evidence. Investigators are also responsible for conducting undercover operations and developing informants (though many patrol officers also have informants), often in connection with investigations related to vice or drugs.

Investigations bureaus often also include a juvenile unit. Among these juvenile unit officers are specialists in gang intelligence, physical and sexual abuse of children, and crime prevention among youth. Other officers specialize as school liaisons or resource officers; serve as counselors, facilitators, and coordinators for youth; and represent other service agencies and schools. In an increasing number of states, youth officers must be specially trained or certified, because they deal with laws relating to juvenile or family court acts, which are often considerably different from criminal statutes in terms of their procedural requirements.

**Policing in Practice Video:**
Policing in Practice Video: Federal Agent

■ **Chain of Custody:** The chronological documentation that shows the seizure, custody, control, transfer, analysis, and disposition of physical or electronic evidence

### Commander Dan Koenig, LAPD Retired

My first assignment upon being promoted to lieutenant was to serve as the night shift watch commander in the Rampart area of Los Angeles. Eight sergeants were assigned to that shift along with 125 officers. At that time, gang crime was rampant, and shootings were common—often two or three per night. To compound matters, the average tenure of the officers was about 2.4 years. The only way to deal with the violence and be a leader for a very young and inexperienced patrol force was for the lieutenant to be "larger than life." I had to be strict, but encourage people to take risks; give them room to make decisions, but make sure they learned from their mistakes; and encourage teamwork, but hold supervisors accountable for the outcomes.

My next assignment was as the officer in charge of Hollywood vice. There, the work was much less violent, and the workforce was much more mature, with an average tenure of about 10 years. This environment required a complete shift in management styles. Participative decision making became much more common, and the leadership style that worked was one of facilitator. There is nothing particularly "scientific" about police work especially when conducting vice investigations; it's more of an art. There are usually several ways to do the same thing, and the challenge is to find the one that works best for the particular situation and people involved. As a facilitator, you set out the parameters for the mission—we have only so many people and only so much money—and let the officers and their supervisors come up with a plan. Then you review it, make any adjustments that are needed, and send them off to execute the plan. That type of participative management style would not work in the day-to-day environment at Rampart, because patrol's job was to handle radio calls, which requires little if any follow-up. In that department, detectives do follow up, not patrol.

No single management style or organizational structure works in every department or even in the same department at different times. Good leaders and managers need to be adept at using all the variations and, most importantly, making sure the style they select fits the needs of the organization and the community it serves.

Criminal investigators spend time collecting and processing evidence from crime scenes, but are also frequently called on to testify in court about evidence.

© REUTERS/Robert Sorbo

## Administrative or Staff Services Division

The other division found commonly in a police department is the administrative or staff services division. The primary functions of this division include record keeping, communication, research and planning, training and education, and logistics. Although many of these functions are performed by sworn officers, there is a trend toward employing civilian personnel to perform a majority of the staff services tasks. The administrative services division may include several subdivisions:

- Personnel
- Research and planning
- Budgeting
- Data collection/crime analysis/computers
- Training
- Counseling services
- Maintenance
- Communications/records
- Civilian employees
- Legal advisors
- Internal affairs

Staff in the administrative division are often specialists. They typically work outside the normal law enforcement chain of command, although the rank structure may be the same as in other divisions. Administrative staff provide information and advice to the

No single management style or organizational structure works in every department or even in the same department at different times. Good leaders and managers need to be adept at using all the variations and, most importantly, making sure the style they select fits the needs of the organization and the community it serves.

—Dan Koenig

### Exhibit 3.4

### Civilian Staff

Police departments employ both sworn and nonsworn (civilian) personnel. One of the major trends accompanying community policing in the past decade has been to employ more civilians. The vast majority of the nation's 25 largest cities employ civilians, and the trend appears to be toward civilianization.[17] Civilianization has allowed police agencies to offload routine tasks from sworn police officers (crossing guards, dispatchers, data entry clerks), fill new specialist positions (computer technicians, forensics), and staff community policing programs (community coordinators, domestic violence specialists, and crime prevention planners).[18] Many police departments are using civilians in administration, research, technologies, human resources, finance, grant writing, and crime analysis.[19]

Adding civilian employees has a financial advantage as well. Civilians are generally paid less, have less generous retirement plans, need less equipment, and are subject to less mandatory training than sworn police personnel.[20] However, police unions may raise objections if they perceive a loss of police jobs, and less educated officers may resist accepting their more highly educated fellow officers.

Another advantage is an increase in the diversity of police agencies. Employing women, minorities, older citizens, and persons with disabilities is often easier to accomplish in civilian positions than in sworn positions.[21] In addition, many feel that the professional reputation of the police can only be strengthened if more police staff have higher education and better critical thinking skills.

Unfortunately, in recent years, many police departments have been forced to significantly reduce their budgets and (in some cases) eliminate civilian employees. Some caution that cutbacks can result in removing police officers from the street to cover the work previously done by civilians.

Another strategy for stretching resources is to outsource certain tasks to private organizations that may be better suited to perform the work, such as financial investigations, forensic accounting investigations, computer forensic services, and chain of custody documentation.

chief and other supervisors concerning a wide variety of topics and process the massive amounts of information that police organizations have to deal with.

# ■ ORGANIZATIONAL SUBSTRUCTURES

## Functional Design

A **functional organizational design** involves the creation of positions and departments on the basis of specialized activities. The functional design is one of the most widely used methods of organizing police agencies and involves identifying and consolidating common tasks (functions) and areas of work. The functional design is based on the tasks performed by all police departments, but varies according to department size. In large departments, it can be efficient and cost effective to establish a specific unit for a specific task. For example, the operations function could be divided into patrol, traffic, burglary, narcotics, juvenile, vice, and many other specialized areas.

A typical functional design organizational chart for a small police department is shown in Figure 3.2. In larger police organizations, the number of specializations within each division increases, leading to an organizational structure such as Figure 3.3.

One advantage to this type of organization is that responsibility and accountability for the completion of work is clearly understood by employees assigned to each unit. A disadvantage is that the functional method fosters a limited point of view in which employees often lose sight of the functions of the organization as a whole.[22] In addition, the functional organization design has minimal application to small police departments, which lack the staffing and funding to establish specialized units. In the case of smaller departments, officers are expected to possess multiple skills and broad knowledge concerning the police role. For example, in a small department, a single officer may handle in one day a traffic problem, then a juvenile issue, and then a major burglary, which requires crime scene search skills.

Because no one officer can readily accumulate all the sophisticated skills associated with all of the functions performed by police officers, numerous small departments have developed alternatives. Many agencies have begun to contract for specialized services with other law enforcement agencies, created mutual aid agreements, or consolidated services in regional crime laboratories.[23]

Departments with a sufficient number of personnel tend to organize by function by creating at least two divisions with distinct, if somewhat overlapping, responsibilities. These divisions are operations and administrative or staff services. Each of these typically includes several subdivisions. As the number of subdivisions grows, coordinating the various functions becomes a more complex task.

In larger, more complex departments, officers may not know all the other officers who work on their shifts or in their divisions. Further, only designated officers may be permitted to handle cases in their specialization. That is, an officer working in burglary may not handle a robbery or some other type of theft. Officers may become so specialized that they handle only one particular type of crime (e.g., computer theft). Patrol officers may be limited by departmental policy as to their involvement in investigations, in part because they lack the specialized training required to handle certain types of investigations.

## Geography

**Place design** involves establishing an organization's primary units geographically while retaining significant aspects of functional design. For example, patrol divisions are responsible for all geographic areas within city limits. The city is typically divided into beats, zones, districts, or areas. Patrol officers perform their basic functions mostly within the assigned geographic areas. In large cities, beats may be combined to form

**Author Video:**
What do you believe are important topics in police organizations and administrations?

■ **Functional Organization Design:** Creation of positions and departments in an organization based on specialized activities

■ **Place Design:** Geographical establishment of primary units in an organization, including assignment of personnel to beats, zones, districts, and areas

Figure 3.2 ■ Oswego Police Department

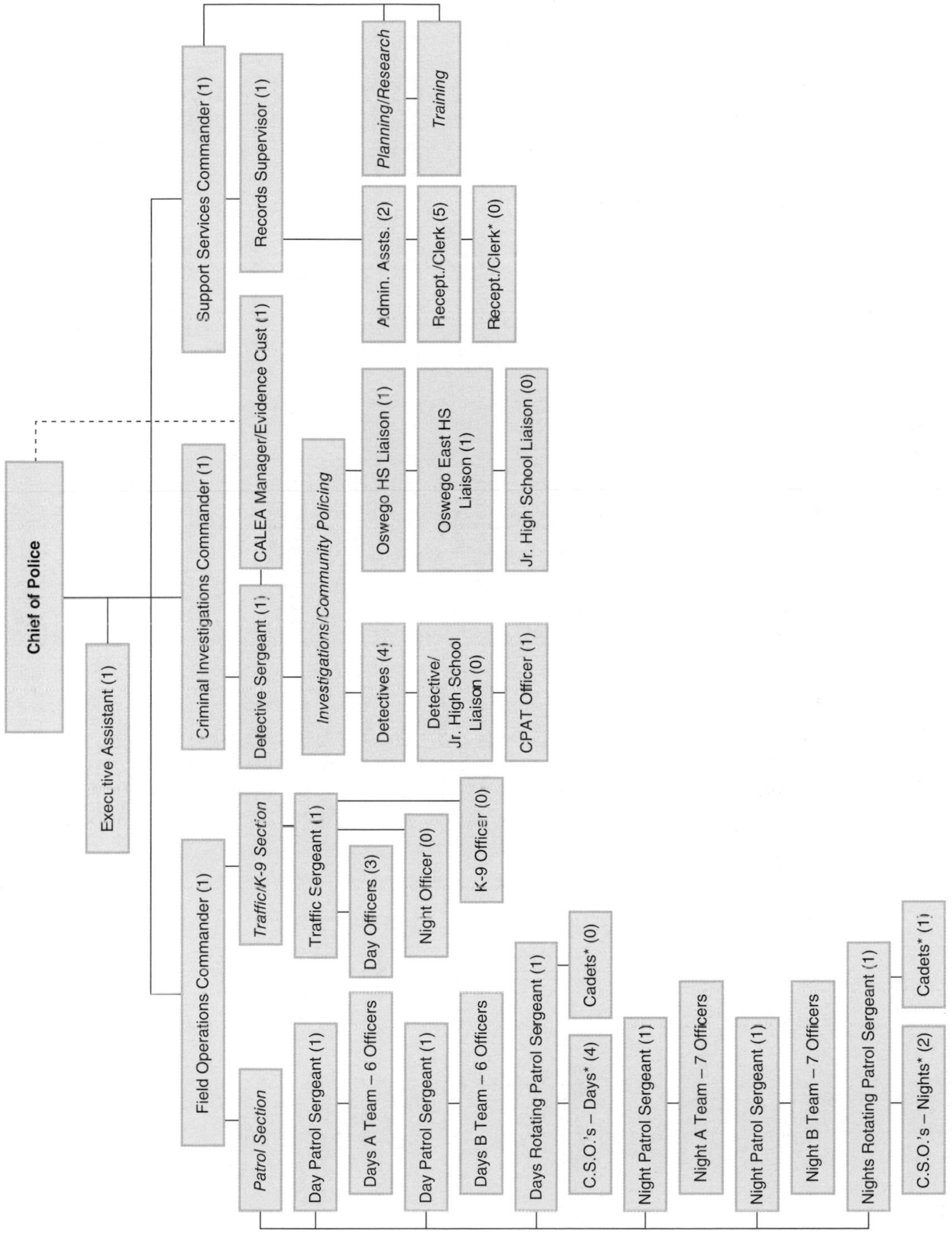

Source: Courtesy of Village of Oswego, Illinois, Police Department

Figure 3.3 ■ San Diego Police Department

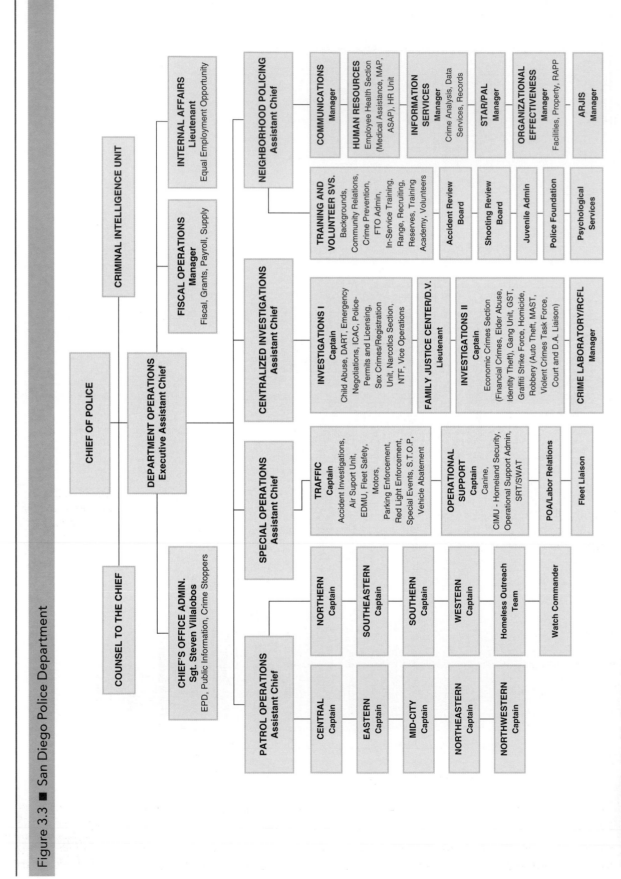

CHIEF OF POLICE

COUNSEL TO THE CHIEF

CRIMINAL INTELLIGENCE UNIT

DEPARTMENT OPERATIONS
Executive Assistant Chief

INTERNAL AFFAIRS
Lieutenant
Equal Employment Opportunity

FISCAL OPERATIONS
Manager
Fiscal, Grants, Payroll, Supply

CHIEF'S OFFICE ADMIN.
Sgt. Steven Villalobos
EPD, Public Information, Crime Stoppers

NEIGHBORHOOD POLICING
Assistant Chief

COMMUNICATIONS
Manager

HUMAN RESOURCES
Employee Health Section
(Medical Assistance, MAP,
ASAP), HR Unit

INFORMATION
SERVICES
Manager
Crime Analysis, Data
Services, Records

STAR/PAL
Manager

ORGANIZATIONAL
EFFECTIVENESS
Manager
Facilities, Property, RAPP

ARJIS
Manager

TRAINING AND
VOLUNTEER SVS.
Backgrounds,
Community Relations,
Crime Prevention,
FTO Admin,
In-Service Training,
Range, Recruiting,
Reserves, Training
Academy, Volunteers

Accident Review
Board

Shooting Review
Board

Juvenile Admin

Police Foundation

Psychological
Services

CENTRALIZED INVESTIGATIONS
Assistant Chief

INVESTIGATIONS I
Captain
Child Abuse, DART, Emergency
Negotiations, ICAC, Police-
Permits and Licensing,
Sex Crimes/Registration
Unit, Narcotics Section,
NTF, Vice Operations

FAMILY JUSTICE CENTER/D.V.
Lieutenant

INVESTIGATIONS II
Captain
Economic Crimes Section
(Financial Crimes, Elder Abuse,
Identity Theft), Gang Unit, GST,
Graffiti Strike Force, Homicide,
Robbery (Auto Theft, MAST,
Violent Crimes Task Force,
Court and D.A. Liaison)

CRIME LABORATORY/RCFL
Manager

SPECIAL OPERATIONS
Assistant Chief

TRAFFIC
Captain
Accident Investigations,
Air Suport Unit,
EDMU, Fleet Safety,
Motors,
Parking Enforcement,
Red Light Enforcement,
Special Events, S.T.O.P,
Vehicle Abatement

OPERATIONAL
SUPPORT
Captain
Canine,
CIMU - Homeland Security,
Operational Support Admin,
SRT/SWAT

POA/Labor Relations

Fleet Liaison

PATROL OPERATIONS
Assistant Chief

CENTRAL
Captain

NORTHERN
Captain

EASTERN
Captain

SOUTHEASTERN
Captain

MID-CITY
Captain

SOUTHERN
Captain

NORTHEASTERN
Captain

WESTERN
Captain

NORTHWESTERN
Captain

Homeless Outreach
Team

Watch Commander

Source: Courtesy of the San Diego Police Department.

sectors, which are administered by a sergeant or a lieutenant, or both. In the largest cities, sectors may be combined to form precincts. Precinct houses are distributed geographically, and each may be viewed, to some extent, as a separate department with ties to central headquarters. For example, the New York Police Department has approximately 34,500 police officers, distributed among 76 police precincts, plus additional officers assigned to transit districts and housing service areas.[24] As with the functional design, the place design can increase coordination problems, depending on the number and location of beats, zones, districts, areas, sectors, or precincts.

### Scheduling

Another organizational consideration involves **time design**. The patrol division may be divided into three watches, tours, or shifts to provide 24-hour coverage. Typically, the day shift often operates from 8 a.m. to 4 p.m., the afternoon or evening shift from 4 p.m. to midnight, and the night shift from midnight until 8 a.m. Some departments employ power or overlap shifts, which typically involve assigning additional personnel to cover part of the evening and part of the night shift (e.g., adding additional personnel who work from 8 p.m. until 4 a.m.).

Although officers have traditionally been assigned to 8-hour shifts five days per week, with two days off, some departments schedule officers for 10-hour shifts. However, a 24-hour period requires three 10-hour shifts, creating significant overlap between the shifts. Depending on conditions, some overlap can be useful, but much of the overlap is wasted. Other agencies divide the 24-hour required coverage into 12-hour shifts and thus require only two shifts rather than the typical three shifts. The 12-hour shift schedule results in an 84-hour schedule over a two-week period, increasing the number of hours worked by police officers by 104 per year, while at the same time providing an extra 26 days off.[25] These additional hours mean additional police officers on the street. Departments must balance their shift coverage, hiring of new staff, and use of overtime, with an eye toward the relative strain on agency budgets.

## ■ HANDLING CHANGE IN POLICE ORGANIZATIONS

Author Video:
The supervisor's role
In law enforcement
administration

The way an organization deals with change tells us a great deal about its effectiveness and efficiency. Change is a given in all organizations; personnel retire, resign, and are injured, recruited, and promoted. Resources fluctuate with the state of the economy and the political power of the organization. Laws change, department policies and procedures change, and new leadership can usher in changes in department mission or culture. Realistically, police personnel must be willing to accept change as a normal part of their occupational world, and police supervisors must be prepared to administer change.

But change is very challenging for most organizations, and even more so for those with long-standing institutional traditions. The reactive, paramilitary structure of many departments reinforces the tendency among police personnel to resist change.

> Innovation is stifled in the traditional organization; members of traditional organizations tend to resist changes which challenge the old ways of operating. . . . Members of traditional organizations are also exposed to a conflicting set of expectations—one moment they must make on-the-spot life-and-death decisions, and the next they are treated like children who are not permitted to decide which uniform to wear when the weather changes.[26]

In any case, if changes are sudden or drastic, they often elicit negative reactions from the people they affect.

When change occurs in organizations that are flexible, encourage initiative, and allow for the exercise of discretion in implementing change, the results can be favorable. Change

**Time Design:** An organizational design that involves assignment of personnel based on watches, tours, or shifts

can be accomplished smoothly if employees are involved in the decision-making process, are knowledgeable about the consequences of the change, and feel as though a need has been fulfilled by the change.[27]

As police administrators adopt less rigid, less hierarchical structures and encourage more participation on the part of personnel at all levels, the police might be able to handle change as a healthy organizational function rather than a crisis. That said, most police chiefs serve at the pleasure of the city council, mayor, or city manager (at state and federal levels, they also serve at the pleasure of political bodies).

Although they are key figures in implementing successful change, chiefs must also respond to external pressure, have minimal job security, and may be indebted to politicians for their tenure in office. Without job security, and lacking the necessary political cover, the ability of a chief to implement broad changes in the department may be extremely limited. The average tenure of municipal police chiefs is slightly more than five years.[28] Health concerns, stress, politics, and personal issues are related to the short tenures of chiefs; therefore, the position of chief of police in major cities and small towns is a virtual revolving door. This can be another destabilizing change as well as a significant expense for departments.

## ■ POLICE MILITARIZATION

The separation between the police and the military is a fundamental underpinning of democracy. That separation was established in this nation during the Civil War, but has become less distinct in recent years. During Reconstruction after the Civil War, the Posse Comitatus Act of 1878 (updated in 1956 and in 1981) was intended to limit federal government powers in using military personnel for domestic law enforcement.

Modern police militarization began with the advent of the SWAT team. The development of the SWAT team is credited to former Los Angeles police chief Daryl F. Gates in 1966. SWAT originally stood for special weapons attack team but was later changed to special weapons and tactics, because the word *attack* seemed inappropriate to some city officials for a civilian police force.[29] Chief Gates needed a strategy to effectively respond to guerrilla tactics that were being used against the police in Watts. Thus, the original intent of the SWAT team was to handle extraordinary and dangerous situations with a specially trained force. SWAT raids are violent events, with typically 20 officers, armed with assault rifles and grenades, breaking down doors and using weapons such as stun or flashbang grenades, designed to disorient the target with loud noise and blinding light.

**Web Link:**
Ferguson and the militarization of America's police

In part, due to high-profile SWAT team deployments against the Black Panther Party and the Symbionese Liberation Army, the idea of the SWAT team caught on, and less than 10 years later, approximately 500 police agencies across the nation had established such forces.[30] The SWAT team made an impression on the public imagination as well, becoming a subject for television and children's toys.

During that same period, then-president Richard Nixon was escalating the so-called war on drugs. Although the issue was strenuously debated, Congress authorized a "no-knock" raid policy for federal narcotics agencies, eliminating the traditional knock and announce procedural requirement for the police.[31] Rhetoric from the White House that dehumanized drug offenders helped to create an atmosphere of support for these federal raids, many of which agents conducted without warrants.

Since 1980, the SWAT team and the drug war have converged. President Ronald Reagan declared drugs to be a threat to national security. President George H. W. Bush created Department of Defense task forces that linked soldiers and police officers for drug interdiction. Police agencies increasingly used special tactics as a strategy to search the homes of drug offenders. This practice has persisted, despite an ongoing controversy over militarization. Proponents defend the need for its use, citing officer safety and the presumed dangerousness of the typical drug trafficker and drug user. Since 9/11, military operations are not confined to theaters of war but are carried out among civilians in densely populated areas. This has contributed to the blurring of the lines between war and law enforcement.

The critics of militarization argue that neighborhoods should not be war zones, and local police departments should not be convenient markets for surplus military equipment. Further, it is dangerous for the police to view fellow citizens as enemies. They maintain that the force of military operations is unnecessarily violent for carrying out domestic drug investigations, that there is very little policy or standards to guide the use of military equipment, that there is virtually no entity responsible for overseeing the use of such equipment, and that there are no requirements to collect reliable and consistent data for properly evaluating military-style operations.

Militarization has gone beyond the SWAT team. In 1991, Congress created a program to "reutilize" military equipment by making it available to police departments. Estimates are that 500 police departments have Mine Resistant Ambush Protected (MRAP) vehicles built to "withstand armor piercing roadside bombs."[32] Many of these have used federal grants to purchase these and other military weapons include assault rifles, grenade launchers, and even aircraft.[33] Even small towns with lower-than-average crime rates have received tanks and M16s.

The drug war is largely considered a failure; the public mandate for continuing military policing is waning. Some states are beginning to pass legislation to prevent excessive police militarization, and in 2013 the attorney general stated the intention of the White House to support criminal justice reforms and widespread basis.

## ■ POLICE UNIONS AND COLLECTIVE BARGAINING

The history of police labor disputes in the United States dates back to the 1800s. Generally, public-sector unionization in the past lagged behind that of the private sector by at least 25 to 30 years, partly because the government had legal mechanisms not available to the private sector that effectively squelched labor movements.[35] Also, public opinion opposed strikes by police and firefighters whose duties were to protect people and property. Historically, the public has been strongly opposed to the use of work stoppages by the police, and the courts are generally willing to issue injunctions to bring them to

An armored police vehicle takes position on the street in Benton Harbor, Michigan, June 18, 2003. Police ordered a 10 p.m. curfew on the town following two nights of rioting that left five houses and five vehicles burned. Tension erupted after a motorcycle rider was killed following a police chase.

© Reuters Photographer

**Audio Link:**
Collective Bargaining Curbs Spread Across the U.S.

a halt in a relatively short time. Many police officers share this public rejection of any police work stoppage and view collective action as self-defeating, because it may result in hostility on the part of the public, the police chief, or others in positions of power.

Unionization of police personnel gained importance in the 1960s and 1970s, when many began to recognize the increasing complexity of policing. Police officers began to demand compensation commensurate with the task and the private sector.[36] Union representatives began to recognize the tremendous potential for growth in the expanding public sector and began to explore this new market. Coupled with police dissatisfaction with wages, working conditions, and level of public support, these changes resulted in a wave of union activities in police agencies. Furthermore, police administrators had seen the results of well-organized, concerted action among other groups and reasoned that such actions could succeed among police officers.

Unlike many other governmental occupations, there currently is no national police officers' union. However, there is national recognition of the Fraternal Order of Police, police benevolent associations, and police officers' associations. In 2011, public-sector workers had a significantly higher union membership rate (37%) than private-sector workers (7%).[37]

Most states and local governments engage in **collective bargaining** with police officers. Although such negotiations affect a substantial portion of state and local budgets, they often occur away from the public view.

Collective bargaining often involves an adversarial relationship between the union and management, and negotiations are required to bridge the gap between the interests of the union and those of management (see Figure 3.4). Police unions negotiate with management for salary, insurance, vacation and sick days, pensions, longevity pay, compensatory time or pay, hiring standards, assignment policies, discipline and grievance procedures, promotions, layoffs, productivity, and the procedural rights of officers; negotiations cover the entire range of working conditions of officers and management rights to determine the level of and the manner in which activities are conducted, managed, and administered.

■ **Collective Bargaining:** Negotiations between an employer and groups of employees to determine conditions of employment

© Rick Friedman/Corbis

When good-faith bargaining and arbitration fail, unions may choose to strike to try to reach a contract agreement. This happened in 2004 when members of the police union in Boston picketed outside the convention center to delay preparations for the upcoming Democratic National Convention. However, most police unions are denied strike privileges.

The use of force, including the use of deadly force, is an important concern for police officers and agencies. Some states (e.g., Illinois) prohibit collective bargaining related to the circumstances in which a police officer is permitted to use force.[38]

If union negotiations fail to lead to an agreement, the possibility of a work stoppage exists in unionized police departments. As indicated previously, for the most part, police strikes are prohibited by law, but police officers occasionally use **job actions** involving "blue flu," work slowdowns, or work speedups. The final product of collective bargaining

Figure 3.4 ■ Status of Collective Bargaining Agreements for Sworn Personnel in Local Police Departments, 2013

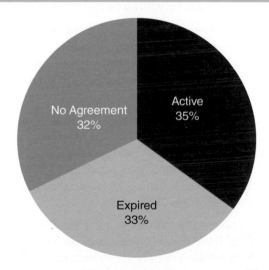

No Agreement
32%

Active
35%

Expired
33%

*Source: Local police departments, 2013: Personnel, policies, and practices, by Brian A. Reaves, May 2015. Bureau of Justice Statistics*

■ **Job Action:** Occurs when negotiations fail to lead to an agreement and can include "blue flu", work slowdowns, and work speedups

## AROUND THE WORLD 3.1

Compared to the United States, other nations around the world are much more accustomed to work stoppages and strikes by those who provide vital services. Votes to strike by police in Rio de Janeiro and the threat of work stoppages by police "have kept regions of the country on edge." The issue involves police salaries, and federal authorities have decided to ready soldiers and national police officers to maintain order if a strike occurs. Salaries for police officers in Bahia are "about $1,250 a month" and approximately "$1,170 per month in Rio de Janeiro."

"Authorities registered at least 142 homicides during the strike in Salvador, more than double the number in the same period last year." Intercepted cell phone conversations involving certain leaders of the police strike "suggested that rebellious police officers were plotting acts of vandalism and were trying to extend the strike to other states." The judiciary is divided concerning the strike by police. Some judges believe it is lawful for police officers to strike. However, other judges described the strike by police as an "aggression against the democratic rule of law."

1. Do you believe that police officers and other safety employees (i.e., ambulance drivers and firefighters) should have the same rights to strike as private citizens?

2. How do you feel about tying police salaries to a national financial index as a way of ensuring that law enforcement officers across the nation receive a fair wage?

3. If police officers are not allowed to strike, do you believe it is reasonable for officers to take other measures, such as work slowdowns or the "blue flu" (large number of officers calling in sick) to secure pay raises?

"Police strike by Brazilians makes holiday seem a threat," by Simon Romero, February 2012. *The New York Times*. Available online at http://www.nytimes.com

negotiations is a contract that covers specific areas of employer–employee relations and that binds both parties legally and morally to abide by its provisions during a specified time period.

### Police Unions and Professionalism

Collective bargaining typically results in highly formalized rules that delineate the rights and obligations of both parties. The formal nature of such rules makes it difficult to bend them, even though both parties may be willing to cooperate.

In clarifying the relationships between police administrators and line officers, union contracts may have the effect of limiting discretion on both sides. For example, a contract that limits the amount of overtime an officer is allowed to work may be an obstacle to an officer who is willing to work and is needed on a particular shift.

The principle of rewards based on merit is often compromised in the process of unionization, so that those who perform best can be rewarded no more than those who perform at minimum levels. Some argue that unions promote mediocrity by requiring only minimal performance levels and by failing to allow rewards for those who exceed these levels. Those who are self-motivated, dedicated, and interested in advancing their careers and aiding the organization are not encouraged to do so, and those who contribute little to the organization are protected.

In addition, unions tend to take on lives of their own, resulting in union leaders sometimes representing their own or the union's interests rather than those of the involved officers. Union representatives may view these union positions as more important than their positions as police officers, and police administrators may view union representatives as adversaries rather than employees. Unions and management need not be adversaries. Both can work toward the betterment of the organization and its police employees, and this sometimes happens.

## ■ POLICE PROFESSIONALISM

Professionalism involves belonging to a profession, achieving a level of mastery and specialized knowledge, and behaving in a way that is consistent with professional standards. Furthermore, a **profession** usually requires some form of accreditation, certification, or licensing and has a code of ethics that guides members and helps hold them accountable.

An overriding value that affects all police operations is professionalism, which became a goal of policing during the Reform Era (see Chapter 2) and continues to be so.

However, early on, society had yet to clearly decide the proper role of the police, and the resulting ambiguity concerning the police role seriously hampered these efforts to increase police professionalism. In addition, the term means different things to different people, making consensus about the requirements for a professional police force difficult to achieve. Some police administrators refer to tangible improvements such as computers, the latest weaponry or communications, or advances in crime lab equipment as signs of professionalism. In fact, a department may have all of these tangible indicators but still be unprofessional if officers fail to meet certain requirements.

■ **Profession:** Occupation often requiring some form of accreditation, certification, or licensing and usually includes a code of ethics

As police agencies became more bureaucratic, relied more on civil services rules and regulations, and became more unionized, officer discretion tended to be more restricted. That is, officer autonomy was increasingly curtailed—yet autonomy is highly valued by most professionals. The distinguishing feature of professional work is the freedom to make decisions according to professional norms of conduct without having to temper every decision by bureaucratic constraint.[39]

Characteristics of a profession include the following:

1. A body of professional literature

2. Research

3. A code of ethics

4. Membership in professional associations

5. Dedication to self-improvement

6. The existence of a unique, identifiable academic field of knowledge attainable through higher education

## Professional Literature and Research

There is a growing body of professional literature on the police. Journals such as *Police Quarterly* and *Policing: An International Journal of Police Strategies and Management* contain reports of police research (the second criterion). Periodicals such as *Police Chief*, the *FBI Law Enforcement Bulletin*, and a rapidly expanding number of government reports and texts on the police contribute additional information on police operations, organizations, and programs. In addition, there are literally hundreds of master's theses and doctoral dissertations concerning the police. Much of the information contained in these publications was collected using legitimate research techniques, and as grant monies from a variety of sources have become available, the body of literature based on police research has expanded dramatically in recent years.

## Code of Ethics

The International Association of Chiefs of Police developed and later modified a **code of ethics** (conduct) for police. It is difficult to determine the extent to which police officers are familiar with these documents.

## Professional Associations

There are a number of professional police associations, mostly for chief executive officers. Organizations such as the Fraternal Order of Police are oriented toward rank-and-file officers as well, but they may serve mainly as social organizations as collective-bargaining agents. Associations for staff personnel and field supervisors have traditionally been far less common. In recent years, there has been some expansion of professional organizations among police planners, investigators, and those assigned to the accreditation process.

## Self-Improvement

The evidence is mixed when it comes to dedication to self-improvement. There are as yet no national minimum standards for either departments or police personnel. Many states do not even mandate ongoing training after an officer completes the basic-training program. Among more progressive police personnel, there is an increasing interest in accreditation in establishing police officer standards. To the extent that both rank-and-file and middle-management personnel view their jobs as blue-collar shift work involving little need for advanced education, dedication to self-improvement may be minimal. To some extent, this view is encouraged by both the paramilitary nature of police organizations and the police subculture, which often regards police work as

**Code of Ethics:**
A set of principles that guide decision making and behavior for police officers, both on and off duty; the code defines the standards for professionalism, which is key to the integrity of police officers and their credibility with the public

piecework—a certain number of traffic citations, responses to service requests, and arrests equals a good day's work. To be fair, some police administrations encourage this view as well.

## Academic Field

A unique, identifiable field of study in police science has emerged. As we have seen, there are hundreds of college-level academic programs in policing and criminal justice. The quality of these programs varies tremendously. In addition, there is no consensus on precisely what topics should be included in these programs. Still, some officers are earning both undergraduate and graduate degrees in police science, law enforcement, and criminal justice programs. These achievements notwithstanding, police professionalism remains an elusive goal for a variety of reasons. Some police executives are dedicated to the attainment of professional standards, while others pay only lip service to it. Still others have no dedication to professionalism. Even though presidential commissions have recommended a higher education requirement, police have failed to keep pace with many other service professions. By far, the most common educational requirement in policing is still a high school education. In fact, some departments that required a four-year college degree subsequently eased their hiring requirements and began accepting applicants with two years of college or three years of service in the military.[40] These professional requirements will help determine the nature of the police for many years to come.

## Accreditation

Through the combined efforts of the International Association of Chiefs of Police (IACP), the National Organization of Black Law Enforcement Executives, the National Sheriffs' Association, and the Police Executive Research Forum, the Commission on Accreditation for Law Enforcement Agencies (CALEA) was established in 1979. The foundation of **accreditation**, a significant professional achievement, lies in the development of standards that articulate a clear statement of professional objectives.[41] Participating law enforcement agencies conduct a self-analysis to determine how existing operations can be adapted to meet the objectives developed by CALEA. When the procedures are in place, a team of trained assessors verifies that the application standards have been successfully implemented, which then results in accreditation for the agency.[42]

**SAGE Journal Article:** Assessing Professionalism: Street-Level Attitudes and Agency Accreditation

The commission developed a voluntary accreditation process wherein law enforcement agencies at the state, county, and municipal levels are evaluated in terms of the defined standards. The current edition of the process includes over 400 standards that cover nine law enforcement areas. Ultimately, the CALEA standards are designed to assist law enforcement agencies concerning six goals:

1. Strengthen crime prevention and control capabilities

2. Formalize essential management procedures

3. Establish fair and nondiscriminatory personnel practices

4. Improve service delivery

5. Solidify interagency cooperation and coordination

6. Increase community and staff confidence in the agency[43]

To remain accredited, agencies must maintain compliance with applicable standards. Many states have police accrediting organizations, and many police departments have attained accreditation at the state level.

Although professionalism has proven an elusive goal for the police, and while there are still pockets of resistance to meeting the requirements of a profession, a growing number of police personnel appear to be committed to that goal. Enlightened police administrators and unions should participate as partners in the search for professionalism.

**Accreditation:** Development of standards containing a clear statement of professional objectives

## CHAPTER SUMMARY

In general, organizational structure is often influenced by the size of the organization, tradition, function, degree of professionalism, receptiveness to change, and style of leadership. Today's police agencies implement organizational structures that vary depending on the style of policing, the size of the community, and the resources available to the agency. In addition, the size of the organization depends on the surrounding environment; on whether the police agency is a municipal, county, state, or federal organization; and on political and economic considerations.

Most police organizations have a form of hierarchical structure that involves the principles of unity of command, rank, structure, and span of control. Agencies consider function, geography, and scheduling in designing their organizations. Many departments have implemented and experimented with more decentralized organizational structures. This has been in part based on community-oriented policing, which calls for flatter organizations, fewer ranks, and the development of police officers as generalists.

During the earliest politics-controlled era, police were generalists who maintained close contact with the citizens they served as well as with politicians.[44] During the professional era, in an attempt to eradicate the corruption and patronage abuses endemic to the previous era, police operated as specialists in crime control and distanced themselves from citizens and heavy-handed political influence.[45] To address contemporary problems, community-oriented policing research called for police to once again become more involved in solving problems and providing service to the community.

Major concerns of police unions in negotiations with management include issues of salary, insurance, vacation and sick days, pension, longevity, compensation time, discipline, and grievance procedures. However, departments retain certain management rights including the right to determine the mission of the police department, standard of service, and procedures for selection and promotion. In most cases, if negotiations fail between the police union and management, strikes are prohibited by law. Resolution of stalled negotiations between the union and police management usually involves a form of mediation, fact finding, or arbitration. Professionalism and professional standards for the police are enhanced through a code of ethics, higher education, and agency accreditation, among other things.

## KEY TERMS

**§SAGE edge™**
Review key terms with eFlashcards.

- Organizations  37
- Hierarchies  38
- Unity of Command  38
- Rank Structure  38
- Span of Control  38
- Incident Command System (ICS)  39

- Line Personnel  38
- Police Paramilitary Unit  41
- Chain of Custody  45
- Functional Organizational Design  48
- Matrix Structure  42
- Place Design  48

- Time Design  51
- Collective Bargaining  54
- Job Action  55
- Profession  57
- Code of Ethics  58
- Accreditation  59

## DISCUSSION QUESTIONS

**§SAGE edge™**
Test your understanding of chapter content. Take the practice quiz.

1. What are the interconnections among police discretionary practices, police organizational structures, and police functions?

2. Describe the traditional police organizational structure. Discuss its strengths and weaknesses.

3. Compare and contrast the advantages of small (fewer than 10 personnel) and large police agencies from the perspective of the public, the officers involved, and the chief executive officer.

4. Compare and contrast the function, place, and time organizational designs.

5. Discuss the context in which police organizations operate and the importance of the environment to the police.

6. Assess the current state of police leadership in your community, using whatever sources are available (interviews with police supervisors, the media, etc.).

7. What are the characteristics of a profession? To what extent are these characteristics currently found among police personnel?

8. Are police unions and police professionalism compatible? Why or why not?

9. What are the relationships between police professionalism and accreditation? What is the rationale behind police accreditation?

## INTERNET EXERCISES

Look up your local or campus police department online.

1. Does the department provide information or a chart describing the agency's organizational structure?

2. What forms of organizational design does the department use? Explain how it is organized by function, place, and time.

## STUDENT STUDY SITE

 **$SAGE edge™** edgc.sagepub.com/coxpolicing3e

**Sharpen your skills with SAGE edge!**

SAGE edge for Students provides a personalized approach to help you accomplish your coursework goals in an easy-to-use learning environment. You'll find action plans, mobile-friendly eFlashcards, and quizzes as well as videos, web resources, and links to SAGE journal articles to support and expand on the concepts presented in this chapter.

# REVIEW » PRACTICE » IMPROVE

▶ edge.sagepub.com/coxpolicing3e

HEAD TO THE STUDY SITE WHERE YOU'LL FIND:

- An online **action plan that includes tips and feedback** on progress through the course and materials

- **Chapter summaries with learning objectives** that reinforce the key concepts in each chapter

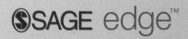

© AP Photo/Julio Cortez

# POLICE OPERATIONS

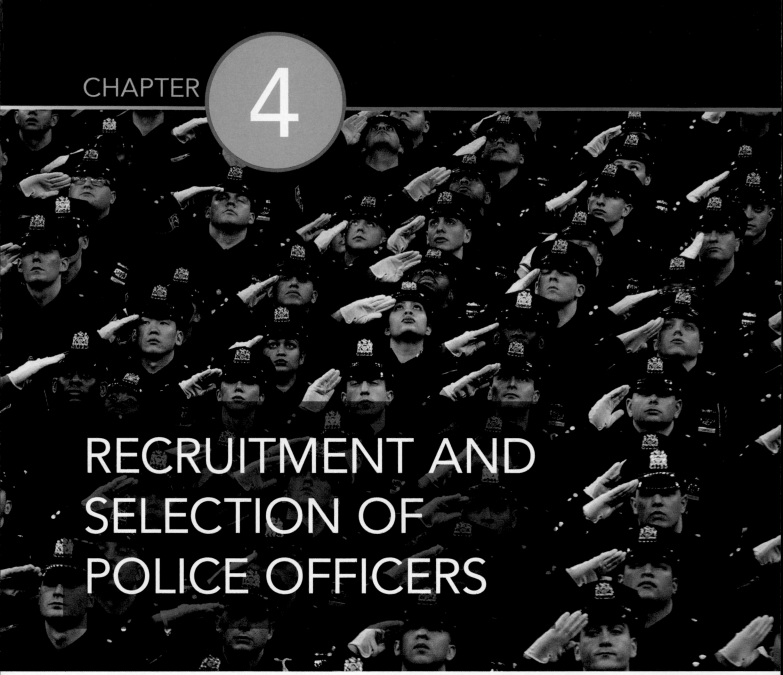

# CHAPTER 4

© AP Photo/John Minchillo

# RECRUITMENT AND SELECTION OF POLICE OFFICERS

## CHAPTER LEARNING OBJECTIVES:

1. Explain the importance of recruiting and selecting officers in a dynamic cultural context

2. Discuss some of the laws and regulations that affect the recruitment and hiring processes of police organizations

3. Evaluate strategies police organizations use to recruit qualified and diverse entry-level applicants

4. Describe the five areas police organizations test to screen applicants

5. Summarize the processes police organizations use to fill supervisory positions

6. Identify the skills and requirements for police chiefs

Every police department must recruit and select personnel to fill its positions and the complex roles involved in policing. There are three basic personnel levels: the entry level, the supervisory level, and the chief level. The prolonged economic downturn of the 2000s has resulted in a greater number of high-caliber candidates looking for jobs.[1] This is a reversal from other periods when police agencies struggled to locate qualified recruits. Observers agree that this increase is largely based on the reduction in corporate organizations; police chiefs expect that those victims of corporate reductions should be well suited for public safety positions, because many have experience in the workforce, worked as a part of a team, and are more mature about the world of work in general.[2] Recruitment and selection are critical to the success of any agency.

A large percentage of promotions in police agencies are internal, but some agencies hire from outside at all levels. Either way, it is imperative that police administrators attract qualified applicants, especially with respect to women and minorities, an issue that is addressed in detail in Chapter 12. Police agencies must all grapple with how they define the traits that characterize the ideal police officer, police supervisor, and police chief. They must decide which of the desired traits a candidate must have at the outset and which can be developed through training. Then, agencies must develop the most effective strategies for locating, attracting, and hiring those desirable candidates.

## ■ THE IMPORTANCE OF RECRUITMENT AND SELECTION

Recruiting and selecting personnel is enormously important for police departments, which rely on every officer to maintain high performance and a good reputation. Personnel is also a department's main expense, roughly 85%.

Productive recruitment and selection procedures are critical at every level of a police organization. Poor recruitment and selection procedures result in hiring or promoting personnel who cannot or will not perform well and according to agency standards, for example, communicating effectively with diverse populations or exercising appropriate discretion. Even in the 21st century, questions still exist about whether current preemployment screening techniques accurately identify the candidates who can successfully complete the training academy and perform well on the job.[3]

**Video Link:**
Officers wanted: Police departments struggle with recruiting

---

### Exhibit 4.1

### Traits and Principles of an Effective Police Officer

The following is a list some of the traits necessary to be an effective police officer.

- Honesty
- Trustworthiness
- Leadership
- Confidentiality
- Acceptance of responsibility for self and others
- Acceptance of criticism
- Acceptance of extra responsibility without compensation
- Analytical, without tendency to jump to conclusions

- Readiness to lend assistance
- Ability to compromise for greater good
- Ability to challenge unlawful orders or authority
- Obedience to lawful and reasonable orders
- Perspective
- Intolerance of corruption
- Teamwork
- Rejection of unearned personal praise

*Source:* From "Sixteen traits recruiters are looking for," by P. Patti, 2009, *Police Link: The Nation's Law Enforcement Community*

Members of the June 2014 graduating class of the New York City Police Academy embrace during their graduation ceremony at Madison Square Garden in New York.

© REUTERS/Shannon Stapleton

**Policing in Practice Video:**
What do you find as the most enjoyable aspect of being a police officer?

### Generational Issues

There are generational differences among these groups based on their experiences and the social context in which they matured.[4] Although generation gaps are not new, they are much more complex today than those previously experienced.[5] Generational differences can create conflicts in values between the veteran officers and their younger counterparts. Many sociologists who study the workforce predict that there will be stiff competition for dedicated and skilled workers in the future. They also project that by 2020, the majority of police officers will be Millennials.[6] In many departments, Generation X police officers are now supervising baby-boomer officers. To the extent that the younger generation of police professionals is characterized by a feeling of entitlement to personal time or upward mobility, this may pose a conflict for police organizations.[7] Policing is 24/7 and often requires personnel to continue to work overtime, to replace missing personnel, or to be recalled to duty because of an emergency. Police work is rigorous and constant and often calls for service outside of a 9–5 schedule.

---

### Exhibit 4.2

### Boomers to Generation Z

In most police departments, several generations work side by side. According to one demographic model, the current generations are popularly referred to as follows:

- "Baby boomers" (born between 1946 and 1964)
- "Generation X" (born between 1961 and 1984)
- "Millennials" or "Generation Y" (born between 1982 and 2002)
- "Generation Z" (born between 2003 and present day)

---

Many baby-boomer police officers served in the military and became used to discipline and a hierarchy of authority. They had the ability to cope with stress in the crucible of military training and service and fit readily into the hierarchical structures that typically define police organizations.[8] However, younger recruits have been exposed to modern liberalism, the passage of affirmative-action laws, increased civil disobedience, and changes in both family and authority structures.

Generation X came of age when the world was less welcoming and concerned about children than the atmosphere for raising the subsequent generation. A context characterized by zero population growth and institutional day care helped foster a generation marked by self-centeredness and a fierce sense of independence.

The Millennials have a different work ethic, are influenced by the digital media, regard the threat of terrorism as a fact of life, and live in a global community that is constantly connected.[9] As employees, this generation is confident, idealistic, eager, and passionate about their quality of life.[10]

Sociologists are paying considerable attention to the effect on a new generation of workers of coming of age with video games. Some argue that the result is a generation with a systematically different way of working.[11] Some believe that the traits associated with video games, for example, will have a positive effect on policing and will allow those agencies that recruit and retain these new-generation officers to thrive. Specifically, the following characteristics may be associated with Millennial police applicants:

- Work in teams
- Perform work of significance
- Have flexibility in their daily environment
- Engage in activities consistent with heroism[12]

**Policing in Practice Video:**
Policing in Practice Video: In consideration of your new status as a young police officer, do you find there are any generation gaps in your department?

Both Gen X and the Millennials are technoliterate and skilled at multitasking. Technoliteracy is the highly refined level of understanding and skill in manipulating the various technologies present in today's workplace.

Forward-thinking leaders in police departments recognize that they must begin planning, especially for recruiting high-quality leaders. Weak leadership leads to more of the same; thus, today's efforts to understand and address generational differences will set the stage for leadership succession far into the future. Unfortunately, many departments have neglected planning at the agency level, and have certainly failed to consider how the transition from one generation to the next affects the change of leadership. Understanding the generational differences in characteristics and attitudes will be crucial for the Generation X peers, supervisors, and managers who will be training and mentoring members of the millennial generation in the future.[13]

The strong tradition of service by the police to the community could be a powerful motivator for the new generation of police officers. Many police agencies have been slow to recognize the generational distinctions that accompany today's police applicant. However, as police agency culture and values evolve with the times, many agencies are recruiting a new type of candidate to fit with their mission and expanding community partnerships.[14] Members of the new generation of police officers need to feel they will be included in decision making, will be recognized for their achievements, and will work for an organization with high moral values. In addition, they may crave a dynamic environment and not have the patience for bureaucracy.[15] Police agencies are applying marketing strategies in recruiting to law enforcement by characterizing it as an exciting profession that offers adventure and an opportunity to be of service.[16] They realize more and more that the competition for qualified workers means convincing them that law enforcement offers an important and fulfilling career.

> Members of the new generation of police officers need to feel they will be included in decision making, will be recognized for their achievements, and will work for an organization with high moral values.

**Policing in Practice Video:**
Police Chief's recruitment and interview tips for students interested in policing careers

**Policing in Practice Video:**
Police Officer's advice for students interested in policing careers

**Immutable Characteristics:** Characteristics determined at birth or characteristics individuals should not be asked to change

**Discrimination:** Treating people differently because of their race, gender, religion, or national origin; involves behavior that, in its negative form, excludes all members of a certain group from some rights, opportunities, or privileges

**Disparate Impact:** Involves an employment policy or practice that, although seemingly neutral, adversely impacts a person or group

### The Process

In many cases, much of the recruitment and selection of police personnel is conducted by civilians with varying degrees of input from police administrators. That is, police and fire commissioners, personnel departments, or civil service board members often determine who is eligible for hiring, and police officials may select officers from among those on the eligibility list. The former also have a good deal of input in the case of promotions. Assessment teams, city managers, mayors, and council members typically determine the selection of chief.

Depending on the trajectory of an officer's career, he or she is subject to parts of the recruitment and selection process on a recurring basis. Once selected for an entry-level position by a specific department, the officer is likely to be screened for promotions or training programs for different assignments (detective, juvenile officer, crime technician, patrol officer) or a different rank. Some may ultimately be selected as chief.

Some officers make a conscious choice to remain patrol officers and to not seek opportunities for promotion. These officers choose to serve their careers "working the line," specializing, or doing traditional police work (e.g., handling calls for service and conducting investigations). In contrast, other officers are more focused on administration and opportunities for promotion. They spend the majority of their careers working a variety of supervisory and managerial positions. Because of differences in career goals and experiences, the groups may have conflicting views about the organization's mission and goals. Career patrol officers must learn to work with career administrators and vice versa.

## ■ ANTIDISCRIMINATION LEGISLATION

The various requirements of recruitment reveal some of the difficulties involved in selecting personnel who will meet situation-specific needs. It is important to understand the legal context in which such processes occur. Federal antidiscrimination laws are of particular interest to police agencies.

### Equal Employment Opportunity and Affirmative Action

For most of our history, U.S. employers, both public and private, have been relatively free to establish their own criteria for hiring, promoting, denying employment to, or firing staff, even though the U.S. Constitution—in the 1st, 5th, and 14th Amendments—prohibits deprivation of employment rights without due process of law. Further, the Civil Rights Acts of 1866, 1870, and 1871 prohibited racial discrimination in hiring and placement as well as deprivation of equal employment rights under the cover of state law.[17]

Still, it wasn't until 1964 and the passage of the Civil Rights Act of that year—specifically Title VII—that many employers began to take equal employment rights seriously. Discrimination on the basis of an **immutable characteristic** associated with race—such as skin color, hair texture, or certain facial features—violated Title VII. The protection was conceived in this way even though not all members of a race share the same characteristics.[18] In addition, the Office of Personnel Management has included a prohibition against discrimination based on sexual orientation. In fact, certain personnel actions cannot be based on attributes or conduct—such as marital status or political affiliation—that does not adversely affect employee performance.[19] The Equal Employment Opportunity Act (EEOA) established the Equal Employment Opportunity Commission (EEOC) to investigate complaints of discrimination. Following these changes in federal law, states also began passing such laws in the form of fair employment statutes.[20]

In general terms, these laws hold that **discrimination** occurs when requirements for hiring and promotion are not *bona fide* (they are not actually related to the job) and when a **disparate impact** occurs to members of a minority group.[21] Federal legislation requires that all employers with more than 15 employees refrain from policies and procedures that discriminate against specified categories of individuals.[22] The burden of demonstrating that requirements for hire are job-related falls on the employer, while the burden of showing a disparate impact of those requirements falls on the complainant. For a complainant to successfully sue an employer for discrimination, the court must find both conditions in favor of the complainant. That is, it is possible to have job requirements that have a disparate impact but are nonetheless valid. For example, if it could be demonstrated that police officers routinely had to remove accident victims from vehicles to avoid the possibility of further injury due to fire or explosion, and if this job requirement also eliminated from policing women or other categories of applicants, the requirement *would not* be discriminatory under the law. If, however, these actions were seldom if ever required of police officers, the requirement *would* be discriminatory.

It is important to understand the context within which charges of discrimination are filed and decided. Government agencies, including police departments, have gradually realized the combined impact of equal employment opportunity laws and executive orders. Prior to the early 1970s, most police departments employed predominantly White men, a practice that became the focus of numerous legal challenges. These challenges came in the form of court actions and as complaints to the EEOC alleging discrimination on the part of employers.

During this same period, the concept of **affirmative action** gained prominence. Affirmative-action programs are intended to prevent discrimination in current hiring and promotional practices. They are also meant to actively correct imbalances in the racial proportions of employee populations so that those more accurately reflect their respective communities and more equitably distribute opportunity.

Some employers voluntarily establish affirmative-action programs, because they recognize the importance of hiring without regard to race, creed, or ethnicity. Other employers implement such programs only when threatened with legal action based on alleged discrimination. Some employers fight charges of discrimination in the courts. If employers are found to be in violation, they stand to lose federal financial support; they often agree to develop and implement affirmative-action programs to prevent this loss. Such cases often involve a **consent decree** that is designed to achieve some sort of

Web Link:
Nottinghamshire Police, Policy for Equal Opportunities for Employment

■ **Affirmative Action:** Programs that are ntended to prevent discrimination in present hiring and promotion practices and to actively promote proportional representation and equitable opportunity

■ **Consent Decree:** Agreement related to an employer achieving a balance in terms of race, ethnicity, and gender in the workforce

© Richard B. Levine/Newscom

A billboard recruiting employment for the Seattle Police Dept. appears on the West Side of Manhattan. Pay in Seattle starts at $47,334 a year and rises to its maximum base pay of $67,045 after six years. NYPD recruits start at $25,100 jumping to $32,800 after graduation and reaching $59,588 after seven years.

balance in terms of race, ethnicity, or gender in the workforce. In other cases, the courts impose plans and timetables on employers and can impose severe sanctions, such as fines, if the agency fails to meet the goals of the plans within the specified time period.

The use of consent decrees has led to a good deal of confusion and widespread ill feelings among employers and White male employees. On the one hand, the EEOA prohibits discrimination based on race, creed, religion, sex, or national origin and states that employers will not be forced to hire less qualified candidates over more qualified candidates. On the other hand, as part of a consent decree or out-of-court settlement, quotas have been used as a remedy in discrimination lawsuits.[23] In most cases, there must be a compelling state interest to justify a quota, which is often only applied when no other policy is likely to work.[24]

The shift away from discriminatory employment practices in policing, as well as in many other areas, has been slow and sometimes painful, yet it is necessary to maximize the number of qualified applicants and to make police agencies representative of the communities they serve. The police will not be viewed as understanding community problems unless they have employees who reflect the community's population and perspective.[28] Many agencies have tried and are still trying to hire and promote minority group members for the obvious advantages that result.

> The police will not be viewed as understanding community problems unless they have employees who reflect the community's population and perspective.

The following list illustrates that certain requirements must be met to avoid charges of discrimination in employment.

- Job requirements must be valid.
- Job requirements must be reliable.
- Testing must be consistent.
- Testing must accurately reflect the job.
- Rating errors and bias must be monitored.[29]

### Title VII of the Civil Rights Act of 1964

Title VII prohibits job discrimination based on specific characteristics of a person that are determined at birth and other characteristics that applicants should not be expected to alter (race, gender, age, national origin, disability, religion). Besides these characteristics, a number of employer practices can also become violations of Title VII. For example, it is illegal to discriminate against an individual because of birthplace,

### Exhibit 4.3

### *Ricci v. DeStefano*

In the case of *Ricci v. DeStefano,* the U.S. Supreme Court found that employment law only rarely permits quotas to remedy racial imbalance.[25] The case involved 58 White, 23 African American, and 19 Hispanic firefighters who tested to determine eligibility for promotion to captain and lieutenant in the city of New Haven, Connecticut. The civil service board refused to certify the results, denying promotions to those who had earned them. The tests generated a disparate impact, since the results of the African American and Hispanic applicants were below those of the White candidates for the open positions.[26] The Court ruled that the New Haven civil service board violated Title VII of the 1964 Civil Rights Act. The case of *Ricci v. DeStefano* indicates that employers should carefully evaluate whether a test (or any method of selection) may have disproportionate or adverse effects on certain groups, whether a less discriminatory method of testing or selection is available, and how accurately the test or method of selection is in correctly selecting those employees who are "best able to perform the required duties and responsibilities of the relevant job."[27] This is particularly important for police agencies that require applicants to perform a variety of testing procedures prior to appointment as a police officer.

ancestry, culture, or linguistic characteristics common to a specific ethnic group.[30] In addition, requiring that employees speak only English on the job may violate Title VII unless the organization shows that the requirement is necessary to conduct business. Most police departments require English; many have also established minimum competency levels for Spanish.

With respect to religion under Title VII, employers are required to reasonably accommodate the religious beliefs of an employee or prospective employee, unless doing so would impose an undue hardship on the organization.[31]

Title VII also involves a number of broad prohibitions concerning sex discrimination. Agencies must ensure that pregnant applicants and employees are afforded the full protection of the law, policies, and practices with respect to evaluating applicants for positions within the department.[32]

## The Age Discrimination in Employment Act

The Age Discrimination in Employment Act (ADEA) provides for a broad ban concerning age discrimination. An age limit may only be specified in the rare circumstance where age has been proven to be a **bona fide occupational qualification (BFOQ)**—a necessity for the normal operation of an organization.[33] As an example, Elk Grove Village, Illinois, only hired police officers who at the time of application were between ages 21 and 35, or up to age 40 if the applicant was already certified as a full-time police officer. In most cases, police agencies are allowed to restrict the age of applicants if they pass the two-step test for analyzing BFOQs that pertain to certain age groups. In other words, "an employer must show that there is either (1) a substantial basis for believing that all or nearly all the employees above a certain age lack the qualifications for the position in question; or (2) that reliance on an age classification is necessary because it is highly impractical for the employer to insure by individual testing that its employees will have the necessary qualifications for the job."[34] In most cases, the approach involved in restricting the age for police applicants or setting a mandatory retirement age requires the employer to "show a relationship, usually empirical, between age and increased risk to public safety; age and physical ability, agility, or decline; or age and risk of personal injury or trauma."[35]

## The Americans with Disabilities Act

The Americans with Disabilities Act (ADA) was enacted in 1990. There is little doubt that many police agencies could be vulnerable to litigation as a result of the act. The ADA makes it illegal to discriminate against persons with certain categories of disabilities, limits blanket exclusions, and requires that the selection process deal with individuals on a case-by-case basis. To be protected under the ADA, the individual must have a disability or physical or mental impairment, must have a record of such disability, or must be regarded as having such a disability, and must be otherwise qualified for the position in question. In cases of a **qualified individual with a disability**, the employer may be required to provide a **reasonable accommodation** for the employee with a disability.

In most cases, the ADA applies to persons who have impairments that substantially limit major life activities defined as seeing, hearing, speaking, walking, breathing, performing manual tasks, learning, caring for oneself, and working.[36] For example, the Illinois State Police agreed to eliminate a policy that automatically excluded police cadet applicants who used assistive devices such as hearing aids to attenuate hearing loss or insulin pumps to control diabetes.[37] The state agreed to individually assess such applicants to determine their eligibility for hiring. Additionally, a person with epilepsy, paralysis, HIV infection, AIDS, or a substantial learning disability is covered, but an individual with a minor, nonchronic condition of short duration such as a sprain, a broken arm, or the flu is not covered. Examples of accommodation include building ramps to provide access to buildings or work sites, designating parking spaces for those with disabilities, installing elevators, or redesigning work stations or restrooms.

■ **Bona Fide Occupational Qualification (BFOQ):** An exception to the prohibition against basing hiring decisions on religion, race, sex, age, or national origin, if such basis is shown to be a requirement necessary to the specific functions of the job

■ **Qualified Individual With a Disability:** Interpreted to mean the job applicant must be able to perform the essential elements of the job with or without reasonable accommodation

■ **Reasonable Accommodation:** Refers to new construction or modification of existing facilities and work schedules, as long as the modification does not cause the agency undue hardship, such as significant expense or difficulty

The ADA divides the employment process into three phases: (1) the application/interview phase, (2) the postconditional offer stage, and (3) the working stage.[38] During the first phase, the ADA limits inquiries to nondisability qualifications of applicants. Employers may not ask about prior drug addiction, for example, because that is covered under the ADA. They may ask about *current* illegal drug use, because that is not covered under the ADA.

The ADA protects those with mental impairments who are otherwise qualified for the job. A psychological examination could violate the ADA if it is used to uncover recognized mental disorders and is viewed as part of the medical examination. In such cases, the psychological test, like the medical examination, should be delayed until the second stage—after an employment offer is made. However, if a psychological test deals with characteristics such as honesty, taste, or habits, it is not considered a medical examination and may be used at the application or interview stage.[39]

**Author Video:**
Hiring process

Once a conditional offer of employment has been made, employers may ask about disabilities or may require a medical examination to determine whether accommodation is necessary and reasonable. If it is, the employer must generally provide such accommodation. In most cases, police departments can administer tests that measure an applicant's ability to perform job-related tasks or physical fitness before any job offer is made.[40] These tests are not considered to be medical exams. Additionally, any test that screens out a police applicant with disabilities must be job related and consistent with business necessity. Also, it is not a violation of the ADA to ask a police applicant to provide a certification from a medical doctor that he or she can safely perform the physical agility test. Following employment—during the third stage—the ADA requires that disability-related inquiries be made only if they are job related, and reasonable accommodation is again required.

## ■ ENTRY-LEVEL RECRUITMENT AND SELECTION

One important personnel expense for any organization, including police departments, is the cost associated with attracting qualified applicants, such as advertising. The objective of the recruitment process is to select candidates who can meet entry-level requirements and who can successfully complete the training academy and the probationary period and become high-performing officers who stay with the job.

### Costs of Outreach

**Policing in Practice Video:**
Challenging aspects of the recruitment and selection processes

The objective of outreach is to attract from the total pool of potential applicants for police work those—and only those—who are both qualified and seriously interested in policing. The more applicants who do not meet both of these requirements, the more expensive the recruiting process. Let us assume, hypothetically, that the cost of processing one police recruit from application to placement on the eligibility list is $1,000. Suppose the agency attracts 50 applicants for one available vacancy. And suppose that 40 of the 50 applicants pass all the tests given in the early stages of the selection process. When the agency conducts background investigations on the 40, however, it discovers that 10 of them have prior felony convictions. The municipality has wasted the money spent on processing these individuals, because in most jurisdictions, they cannot be hired as police officers, regardless of their performance on the tests. Suppose that 10 more applicants have no interest in police work once they discover something about its nature and would not accept a police position if it were offered. Now there are 20 applicants remaining, but the agency has only one vacancy. As you can see, the cost of recruiting the one individual can run into tens of thousands of dollars. To some extent, these difficulties are inherent in the recruitment and selection processes. But the expense involved compels agencies to be as smart as possible with their recruiting strategies.

There are several ways for agencies to reduce some of their recruitment costs, for instance recruiting and selecting for multiple positions at once. Some departments have found that charging a nominal fee for the application eliminates some applicants who might simply be testing the waters. However, in today's tight market, charging an application fee—especially when not all agencies do so—may not be in a department's best interests. Detailed application forms that request specific information probably also eliminate some who are using narcotics, some who have prior felony convictions, and so on. The more of these applicants eliminated at this stage, the less costly the recruiting process.

Costs also may be reduced, however, by developing an advertising campaign that clearly states the requirements of the position and describes the duties to be performed as accurately as possible. Thus, a statement that those with prior felony convictions need not apply might be part of the advertisement. This may not guarantee that such persons will not apply, but it may discourage those who have no chance of being hired. The point is that the more accurately the qualities sought are described, the less likely it is that large numbers of unqualified people will apply, thus helping to keep recruiting costs as low as possible. At the same time, however, advertisements must be designed to attract as many qualified applicants as possible. Basic logic in human resources would recommend improving pay and benefits, recruiting officers with the right skills for community policing, allowing or encouraging changes in job roles to enhance officers' satisfaction, improving career development, changing residency requirements, and creating incentives for retirement-eligible officers to remain with the agency.[41]

## Targeted Recruiting

Targeted recruiting strategies are intended to attract the most qualified, eligible, and interested candidates, which, in turn, can reduce department personnel costs. Departments need to understand the ways their applicants learn about opportunities. For example, younger applicants increasingly use the Internet to assist them in their job searches. Therefore, police agencies must be attuned to the goals and communication methods of potential recruits to recruit effectively. Recruits are most likely to be interested in a good salary and a good benefits package. They also may assess the state of departmental technology, opportunities for advancement, and available equipment before they make a career choice. Recruiting efforts may be directed at college campuses, high schools, and minority neighborhoods. Conducting orientation sessions for applicants that provide a realistic picture of police work in the different departments is another valuable tool in "selecting out" unsuitable applicants.

Many police departments use the Internet to advertise vacancies, and some allow applications over the Internet. Those seeking jobs as police officers can also use the web to learn how to take entry-level tests.[42]

## Diversity

Outreach efforts should also indicate that the police department is an equal opportunity employer and women and minorities are invited to apply. Including these statements is especially necessary in police recruitment, because police departments have traditionally been viewed by both minorities and women as White male domains. Advertising campaigns must take this fact into account, and advertisements should be placed beyond the more traditional professional journals and newspapers and should appear in magazines and on Internet sites that are most likely to reach women and minorities. If departments want to accurately represent their communities and provide the best-possible services, they must find ways to attract the best-qualified candidates.

One strategy for increasing diversity is to ensure that women and members of minority groups are part of the hiring process. In addition, women and minorities need to be part of the group that evaluates the hiring process. (See Chapter 12 for more information on diversity in policing.)

**Policing in Practice Video:**
Experience as a dispatcher

**Policing in Practice Video:**
What are some challenges of achieving diversity in the police force?

### Monitoring and Evaluating

For departments to clearly understand the effects of their recruiting efforts, they must continually monitor, evaluate, and adjust their strategies. For example, if a department collects data from candidates about how they heard about the job opportunity and what made them decide to apply, the collected data can be used to analyze whether strategies are having their intended effect and where they can be adjusted to improve. This is especially true in regards to recruiting women and minorities—groups that may be overlooked or excluded in police recruiting. In the case of women, administrators can analyze where along the selection process women are being disqualified or rated lower than men. They can make deliberate attempts to remove the obstacles that prevent women from succeeding, when possible. In addition, they can examine their entire recruitment and selection process and analyze it for gender bias.[43] One part of the process that has come under specific scrutiny is testing for physical agility and strength. As mentioned elsewhere, such tests need to be specifically related to the requirements of the job.

### Recruiting and Retaining Women Officers

The successful recruitment and retention of women entails challenges worthy of special attention. In today's economy, law enforcement agencies face enormous obstacles in recruiting qualified candidates, yet traditional strategies for recruitment frequently overlook women as a pool of qualified applicants. Departments that make the decision to hire women need to adequately express their commitment to doing so in their outreach efforts.

As time passes, fewer people question the need for women in all professions. In policing, the qualities that women can bring to the field are more widely recognized and accepted than ever. The National Center for Women and Policing (NCWP) cited a number of advantages for police agencies that hire and retain women:

- Enlarging the pool of competent candidates
- Reducing the likelihood of the use of excessive force by officers
- Assistance in implementing community-oriented policing
- Improving law enforcement's response to violence against women
- Reducing the incidence of sex discrimination and sexual harassment claims
- Bringing about beneficial changes in policy for all officers[44]

---

### Exhibit 4.4

### Recruiting Female Officers

Police departments can counteract the negative messages women receive about policing careers with strong positive messages (when they are true), such as the following:

- We have women officers who are role models in the department.
- We want women to apply.
- We welcome women.
- Women are leaders in the department, and upward career paths are available.
- Women have career opportunities in all areas of the agency, including special operations.
- Law enforcement offers a good salary and benefits.[45]

The question is more how to break down entrenched obstacles and achieve gender equity. Recruitment strategies need to maximize media attention through websites, publications that have a large female readership, career fairs, strategic marketing, and communications that address the job considerations of likely candidates. Some are borrowing from the recruiting strategies of the corporate world, which have always invested in understanding the preferences and attitudes of their potential clients.[46] Recruitment efforts to attract women candidates need to focus on positive images of female officers and should be conducted in places women frequent, such as job centers that focus on women. Having female officers serve as recruiters is another strategy. Reaching out to girls in high school may help to encourage women to consider policing as a possible career. Designing and employing more female-friendly equipment and uniforms may boost job satisfaction among women officers. Emphasis on programs designed to accommodate work and family issues, such as pregnancy leave and assistance allowances for child care, can have an enormous impact on recruiting efforts, as does the value of insurance and retirement programs. In addition, departments can look to their civilian employees, as many of these are women. They can make specific efforts to groom such women to take on sworn positions.

Attracting female applicants may be less difficult than retaining them once hired. One way of helping retain women officers is to establish a formal mentoring program. Often, this program may begin even before the new recruit begins her job, when a veteran officer contacts her and lets her know what to expect at the workplace. The mentor then continues to serve as an information resource and confidant.

Groups such as the NCWP, the National Association of Women Law Enforcement Executives, and the International Association of Women Police are available to provide guidance on recruitment and retention efforts. Still, even if a police administrator uses all of these strategies and greatly increases the number of female applicants, the applicants may not follow through with the hiring process or might leave the job after a short time if they find that there is sexism or sexual harassment in the work environment. As Figure 4.1 shows, while there has been an increase in the number of female law enforcement employees, the majority of sworn law enforcement officers are still male.

Figure 4.1 ■ Percentage of Male Versus Female Law Enforcement Employees, 1995 and 2013

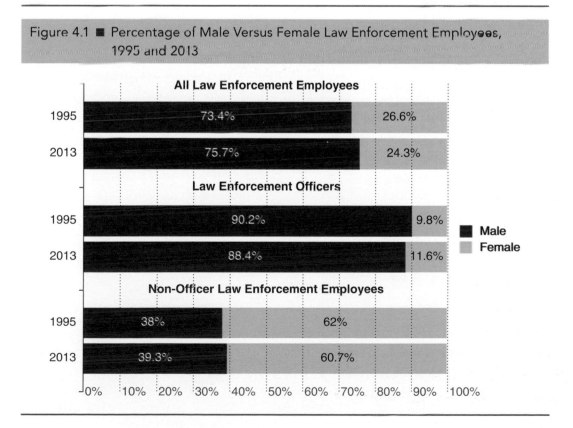

To increase equity for women already on the police force, performance evaluations must clearly evaluate the desired and actual behaviors and skills of the job. Performance evaluations are often used as the basis for special assignments, transfers, and promotions—the main avenues toward new challenges, broader experience, and better compensation.

### Women and Promotions

A 2008 study concluded that, despite early occupational experiences of sexual harassment, discrimination, and disrespect, after long tenures, female officers do achieve acceptance in police work and that female officers are increasingly occupying higher ranks in police agencies.[47] Still, barriers remain when it comes to women advancing through the ranks.[48] With very few exceptions, women are virtually absent from decision-making ranks and positions of authority. In 2008, less than 1% of police chiefs in the United States were women.[49] Women have been chiefs in Detroit, San Francisco, and Washington, but most small and rural agencies do not have any women in top command positions. Discriminating on the basis of gender when hiring or promoting police officers is illegal.

### Recruiting and Retaining Officers of Color

Blacks first served as police officers prior to the Civil War.[50] Their numbers remained low until World War II, when they began to increase gradually. These early Black officers were largely confined to Black neighborhoods, and their powers of arrest did not extend to Whites. In some cities, restrictions on the powers of Black officers remained in place until the 1960s.[51] In the mid-1960s, only 22 law enforcement agencies employed Blacks in positions above the level of patrol officers.[52] A 1971 report of the Commission on Civil Rights affirmed the need to bring minority officers into law enforcement.[53] Litigation involving discrimination in hiring and promotion followed in the 1970s and 1980s; consent decrees frequently resulted, leading to the hiring of more minorities, particularly Black officers.

---

### Exhibit 4.5

## Commission on Peace Officer Standards and Training (POST)

In 1959, the California legislature established the Commission on Peace Officer Standards and Training (POST) to set minimum selection and training standards for California law enforcement.

POST is funded largely through criminal penalty fees. Agencies volunteer to adhere to your standards, and the motivation is to enhance their reputation and professionalism.

The program has other benefits for participating agencies, such as the following:

- Job-related assessment tools
- Research into improved officer selection standards
- Management counseling services
- The development of new training courses
- Reimbursement for training
- Quality leadership training programs

The Commission on POST views itself as a partner with law enforcement and an advocate for law enforcement with the public. Its values include service, respect, cooperation, accountability, and diversity.

*Source:* Commission on POST: Peace Officer Standards and Training, "About POST"

Promotions of Black officers appear to be problematic in many departments. There is a general consensus that officers of all minority groups are greatly underrepresented above the patrol level.[54] This may be due, in part, to **institutional discrimination** (e.g., biased testing procedures, job assignments, and educational requirements) and to the fact that federal agencies that wish to satisfy affirmative-action requirements often recruit minorities from the ranks of municipal departments. The increasing number of Black politicians occupying positions as mayors and chiefs of police may, over time, help alleviate the promotional dilemma.

The rationale for recruiting Hispanic officers is much the same as for recruiting women and Blacks, with the additional consideration of being bilingual and, ideally perhaps, bicultural. Police officers who serve in heavily Hispanic areas need to speak at least basic Spanish to render assistance as well as to engage in order maintenance and law enforcement functions. Further, a basic understanding of Hispanic culture is likely to make the officer who polices in Hispanic neighborhoods more comfortable with his or her surroundings and more understanding of the cultural norms.

With changing physical requirements; greater emphasis on unbiased, job-related tests; and affirmative-action programs, opportunities for Hispanics in policing have increased. What we know suggests that Hispanics seek police positions for the same reasons as officers from all other racial and ethnic groups and share basically the same problems, including the double marginality and discrimination in promotions and assignments discussed previously with respect to Black police officers. In 1988, for example, a U.S. district court judge found that hundreds of Latino agents had been victims of discrimination by the Federal Bureau of Investigation (FBI). The judge found that Hispanics were often given unpleasant assignments that were rarely meted out to their White counterparts. "A frequent complaint supported by the preponderance of the evidence is that an Hispanic agent with five years of Bureau tenure who has ridden the 'Taco Circuit' may not have the experience of an Anglo on duty for two years."[55] The obvious result of such discrimination can be seen in terms of promotions, which often depend on a variety of different police experiences as well as other factors.

Reasons for failure to recruit more Hispanics continue to include a history of negative stereotypes of the police in Hispanic communities, lack of interest in law enforcement careers among young Hispanics, misdirected recruitment efforts, and a lack of role models.[56]

As is the case with recruitment efforts aimed at women, minority recruitment efforts must overcome a number of obstacles. First, of course, members of minorities must be reached, and many conventional efforts fail to do so. Use of minority publications, recruitment efforts directed at colleges and universities, and recruitment efforts aimed at recognizing and supporting high school students who have an interest in law enforcement have all shown positive results. Enlisting the aid of national organizations such as the NAACP (National Association for the Advancement of Colored People), NOBLE (National Organization of Black Law Enforcement Executives), NAPOA (National Asian Peace Officers' Association), HAPCOA (Hispanic American Police Command Officers Association), IAWP (International Association of Women Police), local church leaders, and civic and local leaders who are members of minority groups also may prove beneficial. It is crucial to address the issues confronting minorities entering policing and moving to new communities with the help of the resources mentioned above. Questions concerning establishment of a comfort level at work and in the community should be addressed. If the new officer is the first Black, Asian, or Hispanic officer hired by the agency, he or she is bound to have concerns about acceptance, both in the agency and in the larger community. These questions may extend to family members and their acceptance within the new community. Civic and religious leaders may help to answer some of these questions.

Recruitment teams that include women or minorities may also help in minority recruitment. Some departments have instituted incentive pay for successful

**Video Link:**
Why it's so difficult to retain a diverse police force

■ **Institutional Discrimination:** Unfair testing procedures, hiring practices, job assignments, and educational requirements

recruitment.[57] Other departments have found that developing citizen police academies to familiarize the public with police activities is a beneficial strategy. Community speaking engagements by officers reflecting diversity and interest in minority recruitment, development of linkages with the military, and formation of partnerships with the media are also worthwhile minority recruitment activities.[58]

## ■ TESTING OF CANDIDATES

When the application deadline indicated in the advertisements has been reached, the applications that have been submitted must be analyzed. The better the application form, the easier the analysis. The form might request information on prior experience in policing, prior criminal convictions, educational background, reasons for the interest in police work, prior drug and alcohol use, and other information considered pertinent by specific departments. It should also provide some indication of the applicant's writing ability.

In recent years, the **multiple-hurdle procedure** has become more common.[59] The term refers to a battery of tests or hurdles that must be completed in succession before a recruit can become a police officer. Each assessment hurdle is scored as pass-fail, and only applicants who pass may proceed to the next hurdle. Failure to pass a hurdle results in the applicant being dropped from further consideration.

The multiple-hurdle approach is distinct from a compensatory approach, in which all candidates complete all selection tests, and the agency compiles and ranks the final scores of all the tests for all the candidates.

Multiple hurdles are generally favored when the following are true about the job:

- Training is long, complex, and expensive.
- An essential skill cannot be compensated for by high skill levels in other areas.
- The consequences of error in hiring are high (e.g., airline pilots, air traffic controllers, nuclear engineers).[60]

Multiple-hurdle tests are generally divided into the following categories:

1. Status tests
2. Physical tests
3. Mental tests
4. Tests of morality
5. Tests of ability to communicate

### Status Tests

**Status tests** have to do with changeable factors such as U.S. citizenship, possession of or ability to obtain a driver's license, residency, service in the military, educational level, and age. Whether the applicant meets the status requirements can be determined largely from the application form.

#### U.S. Citizenship

Police officers are required to be U.S. citizens in most cases, although there have been court challenges to this requirement. Is citizenship a *bona fide* job requirement? For instance, can a citizen perform police functions better than a permanent resident who has passed a test covering the U.S. and state constitutions? As an example, to become an FBI officer, you must be a citizen of the United States or the Northern Mariana Islands.[61] And to serve as a Los Angeles police officer, a candidate is required to be a U.S.

**Policing in Practice Video:**
Experience of the recruitment and selection processes

■ **Multiple-Hurdle Procedure:** A battery of tests or hurdles that must be completed before a recruit can become a police officer; the failure to pass any of the sequential hurdles disqualifies the candidate

■ **Status Test:** Related to an applicant's citizenship, possession of or ability to obtain a driver's license, residency requirement, and age and education level

citizen or a permanent resident alien who is eligible for and has applied for citizenship.[62] These requirements are consistent with the Immigration Reform and Control Act, which requires employers to ensure that employees are legally authorized to work in the United States.[63] The requirement that the applicant has or is able to obtain a driver's license seems likely to be upheld for obvious reasons. Some municipalities and states require that newly hired personnel be residents (or be willing to become residents) of the jurisdiction involved. This requirement has also been tested in court, resulting in a majority of jurisdictions changing the requirement.[64]

### Preference Points

Questions concerning prior military service arise, because bonus points (veterans' preference points) may be added to the test scores of applicants if they have such prior service. For instance, the Philadelphia Police Department will add 10 points to the raw score of a veteran's entrance examination.[65] Most departments have minimum educational standards that applicants must meet—typically possession of a high school diploma or its equivalent—and these standards have been upheld by the courts. Many departments use preference points to recognize education level. For example, the Philadelphia Police Department will add one point to the final test score if the applicant attained an associate's degree, two points for a bachelor's degree, and three points for a master's degree.[66] As departments change, they may not see military service as a reason for an advantage in hiring.

### Age

Finally, the vast majority of departments require that applicants be adults (the age of majority) at the time of employment and not be more than age 36–40 at the time of initial employment in policing. The minimum age requirement makes sense in terms of maturity and meeting statutory requirements for entering certain types of establishments. The upper age limit has been called into question as a result of the Age Discrimination in Employment Act of 1990, which prohibits age discrimination with respect to those over age 40. Consequently, the Memphis Police Department's minimum age for applicants is 21; however, there is no maximum age limit.[67]

## Physical Tests

Physical tests include physical agility tests, height-weight proportionate tests, vision tests, and medical examinations.

### Physical Agility Tests

Physical agility tests are used by about 80% of police agencies to determine whether applicants demonstrate appropriate agility, conditioning, strength, and endurance to perform police work.[68] These tests must be job related, and many have been eliminated as a result of court challenges. Tests of coordination and actual agility can typically be shown to be job related, whereas tests based on sheer strength are more difficult to validate. Departments may need to revisit physical standards to ensure that they are still appropriate in the context of new technologies and changes in job expectations.[69] Formerly, many departments require that applicants complete a precise number of pull-ups or push-ups in a specified time period. It is difficult to justify such tests on the basis of job relatedness, however. How often does a police officer have to do pull-ups in the performance of his duty? It could be that "candidates (male or female) who lack sufficient upper body strength to pass the tests on the basis of strength alone may be taught techniques by which the same objectives can be accomplished by relying on lower body strength and/or better techniques."[70]

All testing of police applicants should be valid, reliable, and consistent, and should accurately reflect the required duties of the police officer. However, when police agencies

The physical test is just one of many that recruits must pass at the academy.

© iStockphoto.com/laflor

conduct research to validate a protocol for physical agility testing, they usually employ job analysis techniques that suffer from validity problems.[71] "Research that documents what an officer does on the job does not tell us anything about whether the officer should have done it, what happens when the officer decides not to do it, and whether it could have been done with the assistance of another officer."[72]

Many police departments require applicants to complete a **simulation or work sample test**. These tests measure job skills by examining behavior under realistic job-like conditions."[73] Police officer applicants often complete these tests, which involve pushing a police vehicle a required distance, firing an unloaded firearm a certain number of times, or searching a mock crime scene. However, in some cases, these types of tests have been found deficient due to lack of adequate job analysis, lack of relationship between the job and test performance, and the arbitrary nature of the cutoff score.[74] Currently in police applicant testing, those standards that prove to be job related, to be consistent with a business necessity, and to represent the least discriminatory alternative for selection are likely to be upheld by courts.[75]

### Height-Weight Proportion Tests

Height–weight proportion tests have replaced traditional height requirements, which eliminated most women and many minority group members from policing. Such tests make sense in the context of police work and the previously discussed agility requirements. As originally employed, these tests seemed largely superfluous, because few departments required that proportionate height and weight be maintained after initial employment, but many, if not most, departments now test for proportionate height and weight on a regular basis. As an example, the New York State Police Recruitment Center provides a chart of height and weight requirements by gender, and those who do not fall within the acceptable limits must submit to a fat content test using a skin caliper.[76]

■ **Simulation or Work Sample Test:** Measures job skills of an applicant using samples of behavior under realistic job-like conditions

### Vision Requirements

Vision requirements vary greatly among departments and are also controversial, especially for uncorrected vision. Most departments have established corrected vision requirements that may be justified on the basis of driving ability, ability to identify license plates or persons, or qualifications to carry weapons.[77] In a related study, researchers concluded that police must be able to perform two essential tasks when visually incapacitated: identifying a weapon in a typical room and finding spectacles that have been dislodged.[78] In reality, few police departments have performed a systematic study of the critical vision task required for police officer job performance, and even fewer have validated their vision requirements to ensure they comply with the ADA.[79] The point is that agencies are not certain about what level of visual acuity is required to adequately perform specific job duties.

Because technology has provided a variety of alternatives for vision correction not mentioned in earlier studies, many police departments have adapted their vision requirements. Many are concerned that the visual acuity requirements are implemented at the time of hire but only enforced in the most extreme cases. However, visual acuity changes with age, and some police officers with more than 20 years of service may experience a reduction in uncorrected vision. Currently, few departments address these issues and enforce vision requirements for police applicants, even though new recruits and officers with over 20 years of service perform the same duties involving weapons, driving, and identifying license plates.

### Medical Examinations

From the point of view of a police department, the medical examination is a critical part of the testing process. Physical well-being must be established to the extent that physical condition is related specifically to job performance. Certainly, a physically fit staff is advantageous to efficient police operations. Another practical consideration for agencies is that officers who become disabled as a result of injury or illness are often eligible for lifelong disability payments.

To detect conditions that may lead to illnesses or injuries, virtually all police agencies require a medical examination that is intended to detect problems of the heart, back, legs, and feet, among others. These conditions may be aggravated by police work, and the department prefers to eliminate from consideration any applicants with such medical problems. As an example, the Pittsburgh Department of Personnel and Civil Service Commission uses a "combined cardiovascular-pulmonary test (treadmill test), hearing test, vision test and blood test."[80] Due consideration must be given to the requirements of the ADA, which states that an employer may only ask about an applicant's disability or administer a medical examination after the employer has made a job offer. In most cases, police departments make passing the medical exam a condition to the job offer.

> Due consideration must be given to the requirements of the ADA, which states that an employer may only ask about an applicant's disability or administer a medical examination after the employer has made a job offer.

## Mental Tests

Mental tests fall into two categories: (1) those designed to measure intelligence, knowledge, or aptitude and (2) those designed to evaluate psychological fitness.

### Tests of Intelligence, Knowledge, or Aptitude

A majority of police agencies use written tests, in both paper and computerized forms. These tests are intended to measure a variety of things. To be of merit, they must deal with job-related issues and must have predictive value; as with other evaluation tools, these tests should be able to predict whether an applicant has the ability to perform police work well. The International Public Management Association for Human Resources (IPMA-HR) is a common resource for entry-level police tests. IPMA-HR assesses critical abilities of entry-level police applicants in the following areas:

- Ability to learn and apply police information
- Ability to observe and remember details
- Ability to follow directions
- Ability to use judgment and logic[81]

These written tests have historically eliminated most minority group members. Millions of dollars have been spent in attempts to develop "culture fair" tests to avoid this bias, but with only moderate success.[82] And perhaps for lack of a better screening device and in spite of their obvious inadequacies, the vast majority of departments continue to use written tests. In most cases, they are scored on a point system, and the score obtained becomes a part of the overall point total used to determine who makes it to the eligibility list. Therefore, differences of one or two points might make the difference between hiring one applicant and hiring another, even though differences of five to ten points probably indicate minor differences between candidates. There are many different tests and forms of tests available but no consensus about which is best.

Although it is difficult to evaluate written entry-level tests, such research is essential to developing a test with truly predictive capability. This research method would presumably require a department to hire applicants regardless of their scores on the test (including those who failed), keep the test results secret from those who evaluate the officers' performance over a period of time (preferably at least 18 months to two years), and then compare performance evaluations with initial test scores. If those who scored high on the written test were also the best performers on the job, the validity of the test would be demonstrated, all other factors being equal (which they seldom are). Questions of liability exist for a department choosing to participate in such research. What happens, for instance, if an applicant who failed the test is hired and performs so badly that someone is injured or killed as a result? In addition, the time period involved is quite long, and many agencies and test constructors are unwilling to wait the required time to obtain meaningful results.

Research has shown that screening of applicants for police positions should go beyond simply using standardized intelligence tests and should include other measures and screening procedures.[83]

Some agencies use **integrity tests**, which are used to assess a candidate's honesty and propensity for counterproductive behavior on the job, such as drug use or theft. Psychological evaluation and **polygraph** tests screen for similar characteristics, unlike cognitive ability tests.[84] If administered early in the selection process, an integrity test could disqualify applicants likely to fail a polygraph or psychological test, thus saving the agency the costs of administering these two tests.

### Psychological Tests

The challenges of policing make it especially important to select candidates who are emotionally fit for duty. Officers are in constant contact with all different kinds of people and are often involved in volatile or stressful situations. The stress of the job can often contribute to complex problems such as police corruption and abuse of power, and psychological testing is meant to assist in predicting, controlling, and preventing corruption and abuse.[85] The task of determining whether a candidate has the requisite psychological stability—for hire as well as the duration of a police officer's career—is a formidable one. The use of psychological tests has steadily increased over the years in selecting police officers; in 1967, the President's Commission on Law Enforcement and Administration of Justice recommended that such tests be used by all police departments to determine the emotional stability of police recruits.[86] Since then, other commissions have supported the idea as well.[87]

However, psychological tests present even more difficulties than written tests of intelligence, aptitude, or knowledge. The psychological characteristics of the ideal police officer have not been identified—and perhaps cannot be. Attempts to discover a particular type of personality best suited for policing are inconclusive. In reality, policing attracts a wide spectrum of personalities, most of which do a commendable job across a wide range of tasks and responsibilities.[88] Furthermore, psychological tests must be administered in compliance with the ADA.

**Video Link:**
Investigating police psychological exams as 30 cadets graduate from the academy

**Policing in Practice Video:**
What competencies of new police force candidates do you feel need improvement?

**■ Integrity Test:**
Test used to assess a candidate's honesty and propensity for counterproductive behavior on the job, such as drug use or theft

**■ Polygraph:**
Psychological evaluation and polygraph tests screen for similar characteristics, unlike cognitive ability tests.

Nevertheless, in spite of their weaknesses, psychological tests are still part of screening. For one thing, departments can be held liable by the courts if they hire police officers *without* the use of such tests. In addition, many police administrators believe that the tests at least screen out applicants who are clearly emotionally unfit for police work.

Some experts have observed that 90% of police departments require some form of psychological evaluation of applicants.[89] The most frequently used personality measures are the revised Minnesota Multiphasic Personality Inventory (71.6%), the California Psychological Inventory (24.5%), the Sixteen Personality Factor (16PF) Questionnaire (18.7%), and the Inwald Personality Inventory (11.6%).[90] In most cases, preemployment psychological evaluations include medical (e.g., substance abuse and disabling mental conditions) and nonmedical matters (e.g., judgment, resilience, and integrity).[91]

One researcher discussed the extent to which psychological tests can select out police applicants who are either unstable or unsuitable (or both) and concluded,

> It matters little that the field of psychology is only marginally capable of predicting "bad" officer candidates. Psychologists and psychiatrists are expected, not only, to screen out the "bad" but be able to screen in the "good." Unfortunately, consensus definitions of "good" or "suitable" have not been developed either among the professionals or members of the lay public.[92]

Other research indicated that psychological tests can make a contribution to the selection process but should not replace other methods or be used as a sole method. Many recommend that the psychological evaluation of police candidates include a face-to-face interview. Topics typically covered in the interview include the following areas:

- Educational history
- Employment history
- Compliance with laws and regulations
- Recent illegal substance use
- Interpersonal and familial interactions
- Financial difficulties
- Self-perceived strengths and weaknesses
- Reasons for wanting to work in a public safety position
- Professional goals
- Psychologically relevant medical history (any psychological or psychiatric treatment and medication history, alcohol use and abuse, legal and illegal drug use, trauma history, sexual misconduct, domestic violence, and suicidal ideation or attempts)[93]

The literature on psychological testing of police recruits is inconclusive. Despite the variety of assessment techniques and personality inventories, it remains unknown whether they predict on-the-job law enforcement performance in any reliable way.[94] Predictive tests must undergo continual evaluation and monitoring to improve their usefulness and accuracy. Evaluation should answer some of the following questions:

- Does the test accurately evaluate and relate to job performance?
- Does the test underrepresent or have a bias against women or minorities?
- Does the test elicit responses related to protected topics such as sexual orientation or religion?

It remains to researchers to help determine whether psychological testing done only prior to employment can ever be an accurate predictor, especially of longer-term police officer behavior. One result of serving as a police officer can be the onset of new psychological problems.[95]

## Tests of Morality

Tests of morality include background investigations, drug tests, and polygraph examinations. We refer to these requirements as tests of morality, because they are used to evaluate the moral character of police applicants.

### Background Investigations

The background investigation represents an attempt to select only those candidates with good moral character. Background investigations are used by almost all police agencies, but the extent and intensiveness of these investigations vary considerably (see Table 4.1). In some cases, department hiring managers simply check listed references by phone, while in other cases, they expend a good deal of time and money to verify the character of the applicant. In the latter cases, the investigation normally includes the types of information listed below, which are often public records created by government agencies. However, it is important to note that school records, bankruptcy reports, medical records, and workers' compensation records are often confidential and require written consent of the applicant or require that the information is relevant to the duties of the position.[96]

A major purpose of the background investigation is to determine the applicant's honesty as reflected by the information on the application form and in subsequent communications. Departments tend to emphasize the background investigation, because an intensive background check helps to ensure that departments hire only the most qualified applicants. The check can also indicate an individual's competency, motivation, and personal ethics.[97] Background investigations may exclude or highlight for further inquiry those applicants with prior felony convictions or currently wanted by the police; those with a history of serious employment, family, or financial problems; those dishonorably discharged from the military; and those determined to have lied during the application process. In addition, the reference check provides an opportunity to discover prior and current use of alcohol or other drugs. Several types of incidents are alarms for employment screening: child abuse and abduction, terrorist acts, and false and inflated information supplied by applicants. Furthermore, there are computer databases that contain volumes of personal information.[98] The rationale for excluding or further investigating applicants with problems in these areas is relatively clear. It makes little sense to hire an individual who has serious drug-related problems; in virtually all jurisdictions, those with prior felony convictions are excluded from policing by statute. Applicants with histories of domestic violence or bankruptcy also present problems, because they may be corruptible or prone to the use of force in their positions as police officers.

### Drug Tests

The possession, manufacture, distribution, and sale of illegal drugs are all serious problems in our society, and applicants for police work are not immune to these problematic behaviors. However, many police departments have modified their

### Table 4.1 ■ Information Included in a Background Check

| Public Records | Legal Records | Personal Information | Financial Information |
|---|---|---|---|
| Driving records | Court records | Education records | Bankruptcy |
| Social Security number | State licensing records | Character references | Property ownership |
| Vehicle registration | Incarceration records | Personal references | Past employers |
| Military records | Criminal records | Medical records | Credit records |
| Workers' compensation | Drug test records | Neighbor interviews | Sex offender lists |

Source: From "Employment background checks: A jobseeker's guide," by Privacy Rights Clearinghouse, 2011

zero-tolerance policy that disqualified all applicants who had previously used any type of drug. It is now more often the use of drugs rather than the impact of the drugs on the physical well-being of the applicant that is of primary concern. Due to increasing difficulties in recruiting, there is

> a growing tendency to tolerate some history of drug use or criminal activity by recruit candidates. . . . Many agencies now take into consideration the type and amount of drugs used, the length of time since the last use, and the nature of the offense. Those who have merely "experimented during high school or college" are often allowed to join the force.[99]

As an example, the Santa Rosa Police Department in California considers the following factors when there is evidence of past abuse of controlled substances: patterns of use, how the drug was obtained, type of drug used, circumstances of the start of the drug use, and discontinuance and nature of treatment and prognosis.[100] (See Table 4.2.)

Although the issue of drug testing, usually accomplished through urinalysis, has led to a great deal of litigation, it appears that when such testing is done according to a schedule (as opposed to random testing), and when it is done in a reasonable fashion and on reasonable grounds, the courts allow the testing as it relates to policing and

**Policing in Practice Video:**
How do applicants' possible use of drugs and social media play roles in recruitment?

## Table 4.2 ■ Illegal Drug Use Guidelines

| Substance | Minimum Years Since Last Use | Maximum Number of Times Used |
|---|---|---|
| Marijuana | 3 | 50 |
| Hash/Hash Oil | 3 | 20 |
| Amphetamine | 5 | 5 |
| Methamphetamine | 5 | 5 |
| Cocaine (powder) | 5 | 5 |
| Crack Cocaine (rock) | Any use is automatically disqualifying | |
| CNS Depressants (Barbiturates) | 5 | 5 |
| Quaaludes | 5 | 5 |
| Heroin | Any use is automatically disqualifying | |
| Opiates (or derivative) | Any use is automatically disqualfiying | |
| Methadone | Any use is automatically disqualifying | |
| LSD | 5 | 2 |
| Mushrooms (Psilocybin) | 5 | 2 |
| Mescaline/Peyote | 5 | 2 |
| Toluene or other solvents/inhalants | 5 | 5 |
| Nitrous Oxide | 5 | 5 |
| Amyl Nitrate (Poppers) | 5 | 5 |
| Synthetic Based Designer Drugs | 5 | 5 |
| PCP | Any use is automatically disqualifying | |
| Steroids | 5 | 5 cycles |

*Source:* From "Illegal drug use guidelines," by the Santa Rosa Police Department, 2009

public safety. Departments must guard against the possibility of a drug-impaired police officer injuring a colleague or another person, whether due to a vehicle accident, firearm discharge, or use of excessive force. Thus, drug testing is likely to become even more prevalent among police agencies than it is now, because courts and legislatures are clarifying the legal requirements for such testing.

Another drug use issue addressed by many police departments involves the restriction of the use of anabolic steroids by police applicants. Anabolic steroids may appeal to police officers who desire a tactical edge or an intimidating appearance to improve their performance.[101] Testing for performance-enhancing substances presents a myriad of challenges and is not as straightforward as discovering heroin in an applicant's drug screen.[102]

### Polygraph Examinations

Polygraph examinations are employed by many police agencies in the United States, although changes in federal legislation have already greatly restricted their use in the private sector and may eventually have the same impact on the public sector. Currently, a police agency can conduct a polygraph before a conditional offer of employment but must avoid asking any prohibited disability-related inquires in administering the pre-offer exam.[103]

The rationale behind the use of the polygraph for recruitment and selection appears to be twofold. First, the results of the examination are used as one indicator of the honesty of the job applicant. Second, the results are used to eliminate applicants whose

**Author Video:**
How do law enforcement look at recruits' drug use and past drug use?

---

After completion of contract negotiations, the city of Portland, Oregon, began random drug testing on its police officers. The testing involved five different types of drugs: marijuana, cocaine, opiates, phencyclidine (PCP), and amphetamines. If a police officer tested positive for less than .08 blood-alcohol content; marijuana; or illegally used drugs, for a first offense, the officer could seek treatment, face a suspension, or assume a desk job with restricted police authority.

The city decided not to test for steroids, because the department decided that testing was too expensive. However, a police commander from Phoenix believes "it's steroids that police are more likely to abuse," and "other police agencies have been able to establish standards for steroid testing with local labs." One physician at Oregon Health and Science University reported, "steroid testing to me is more important than PCP. It is expensive. However, with steroids you can have uncontrolled aggression, and these guys have Tasers and guns. A lawsuit is expensive too." Many police departments test police officers for steroids or other drugs based on a reasonable suspicion the officer is using a prohibited drug.

As marijuana laws are relaxed in some states, especially for medical use, police recruiters feel that their job will be that much harder. It is already difficult to find qualified candidates who make it all the way through the recruiting and hiring process and the academy, and go on to become excellent officers. With marijuana use being more widely accepted, some agencies may feel they need to have more lenient standards for screening for past marijuana use among recruits.

1. Should police departments prioritize testing for steroids, despite the cost?

2. What criteria would you use to determine whether an officer's drug use—as it was determined by testing—is severe enough to warrant treatment, discipline, or termination?

3. Should police departments change their drug use standards to attract more recruits?

*Source:* From "Police face random drug tests," by Maxine Bernstein, 2011, The Oregonian

responses are not acceptable to the police agency in question, regardless of the honesty of the applicant. As an example, during the polygraph exam, police applicants are often questioned about a variety of prior experiences.

Either or both of these reasons for the exam may be justified, but there is, and always has been, considerable controversy over the accuracy of polygraph tests, which raises the problem of rejecting some qualified applicants while accepting others who are deceitful.[104] Numerous websites offer advice on how to beat the polygraph using deliberate attempts to alter the data through the use of physiological changes with body movements.[105] In response to this type of information, the polygraph profession has added a fourth parameter, which involves monitoring body movements associated with countermeasures. This change is in addition to the three basic physiological functions monitored today: blood volume and pressure, respiration, and sweating.[106] Research has explored a new generation of lie detection technology using functional magnetic resonance imaging (fMRI), electroencephalography (EEG), near-infrared light, and other devices that permit access to brain function.[107] The problem with polygraph tests is not with the machine, which simply measures heart rate, rate of breathing, and **galvanic skin response** (changes in electrical resistance in the skin) over time. The interpretation of the results and the way in which the test is administered depend on the polygraph examiner. The training, skills, and competence of polygraph examiners vary widely, and the conditions (anxiety and nervousness on behalf of applicants) under which employment and promotional polygraph interviews are conducted are less than ideal for ensuring accurate results.

**Galvanic Skin Response:** Changes in electrical resistance in the skin over time

Police officers may undergo polygraph examinations as part of the selection process for being hired as a police officer.

© iStockphoto.com/Sprootnick

**Author Video:**
How do law enforcement look at recruits' use of social media?

### Tests of Ability to Communicate

As indicated earlier, many of the recruitment and selection procedures used by the police overlap. This interdependence of procedures is perhaps best illustrated by the tests of an applicant's ability to communicate. The oral interview or *oral board,* as it is often called, is both possible and desirable for evaluating the written communications skills of applicants by requiring them to write a job history or autobiographical statement; a large measure of police work involves writing reports that demand accuracy and comprehensiveness. While a misspelled word or two is probably no cause for concern, serious defects in the ability to communicate in writing indicate, at the very minimum, the need for some remedial work in this area.

### *The Oral Board*

Most agencies use oral interviews of police applicants. These interviews, or boards, are typically conducted by members of the fire and police or civil service commission or by the personnel department in larger police agencies, often in conjunction with representatives of the police agency. In some cases, the latter actually participate in the interview, while in others, they simply observe. The number of interviewers varies, but three to five is typical.

## POLICE ✪ STORIES 4.1

### Gene L. Scaramella, Former Police Officer, Author, and Educator

Most police hiring processes involve numerous activities. For example, the specific elements of the physical agility test are no secret and allow a police applicant to prepare for the test through running, lifting weights, or engaging in other forms of exercise. In addition, in most cases, applicants have taken multiple-choice tests in school and are prepared for the challenge of a department's written exam. However, as a merit commissioner for a sheriff's department, I have observed many applicants encounter problems at the oral board interview. The oral interview is stressful, and many applicants are eliminated from the hiring process based on their performance.

- To be successful at the oral board, I tell students to dress professionally, leave cell phones in the car, and arrive early to locate the building, designated parking, and the specific room. I encourage them, upon entering the interview room, to introduce themselves to members of the board by shaking hands.

- I indicate to students that there may well be questions concerning ethics, such as those related to arresting off-duty police officers or city officials who have openly committed criminal acts. I tell them I hope they will respond by indicating they would do the right thing and that I'm sure they know what the "right thing" involves.

- I believe applicants should know as much as possible about the department to which they are applying. At the conclusion of the interview, board members will often ask if the interviewee has any questions. Questions concerning the department and the community might be appropriate, but questions such as "What is the starting salary?" are generally unnecessary, since this information is readily available on most police departments' websites.

- Police applicants can expect questions from the board about background, future goals, and current police issues in the form of hypothetical scenarios. Finally, the board might conclude the interview by asking, "Why should we hire you over all the other applicants?" This is the applicant's chance to hit a home run and convince the members of the board that he or she is one of the top applicants immediately before they begin the process of calculating final scores. I also tell students to remember that the more oral board interviews they participate in by applying to different departments, the more comfortable they will become with the process.

The expressed purpose of the oral board is to select a suitable applicant to fill the existing police vacancy. Suitability includes the "type of person." In addition to the skills necessary to fill the formal organizational position, interviewers might consider the applicant's loyalty to the department, trustworthiness with respect to other police officers, and (although legally and formally forbidden) his or her race, gender, and general presentation of self.[108] Although interviewers make efforts to reduce the amount of subjectivity in oral interviews by using such things as standardized questions and independent evaluation, it is equally true that the way a candidate looks (dress, skin color, gender, etc.) and acts (eye contact, handshake, degree of self-confidence expressed) affects the impression he or she makes.[109] It is possible that factors that are expressly forbidden from consideration, in terms of equal employment opportunity guidelines, can affect the judgment of interviewers in subtle, if not obvious, ways.

**Audio Link:**
Have American Police Become More Cautious?

The interview format varies a good deal. In most cases, it will include general questions about the applicant's background, experiences, education, prior training, and interest in police work in general and in the specific department. These questions may be followed by a series of questions to test the applicant's knowledge of some legal, moral, and ethical issues related to police work. For example, the applicant may be asked how he or she would respond to the apparent corruption of another officer, what response would be appropriate if a traffic violator turned out to be the mayor, or how much force is justified in a certain type of incident.

Candidates are often nervous about the oral interview. Interviewers may ask questions slowly, with follow-up questions, or in other ways that create stress for the interviewee.[110] The raters independently evaluate the respondent's answers and attempt to reach consensus in the event of a wide difference of opinion.

The final scores for the oral board are added to the other test scores to establish an eligibility list from which the chief of police or personnel department may select candidates to fill existing and future vacancies.

Although the selection process today is conducted to maximize objectivity—including sending written tests elsewhere for scoring, scoring by identification numbers as opposed to names, rating interviewees independently, and calculating scores to the nearest point or fraction of a point—the chief of police will choose those candidates from the eligibility list that best meet the needs of the department.

## Exhibit 4.7

## Typical Performance Dimensions

- Problem solving
- Judgment and reasoning
- Decision making
- Teamwork orientation
- Interpersonal skills
- Oral communications and presentation skills
- Honesty and integrity
- Self-motivation and initiative
- Stress tolerance and composure

*Source:* From *Master the police officer examination,* by F. M. Rafilson and T. DeAngelis, 2008, Georgetown, CT: ARCO Publishing.

In 2014, Indonesia launched a massive effort to hire women police officers, resulting in 7,000 new recruits, despite the stringent requirements. Female candidates for the Indonesian police force must be between ages 17.5 and 22, must have completed high school, must not be or ever have been married, must not need glasses, and must be at least 65 inches tall. The most controversial requirement by far, however, is that all recruits must be virgins. Human Rights Watch (HRW) has condemned this requirement as discriminatory and degrading, and many women object to it, but despite the efforts of even high-level women to ban its use, the decades-old tradition remains in place.

HRW conducted interviews with women who described learning about the test just minutes before it was to take place. They understood that they would disqualify themselves from employment if they refused the test, which required them to undress in front of other candidates and allow testers to insert their fingers into the women's vaginas. Some of the women feared that the test would deprive them of their virginity.

Among officials in Indonesia, virginity is still seen as a sign of purity and moral and physical fitness. The test is not limited to the police. Women recruits for the army or those who want to marry a police officer or member of the army must also undergo this misogynistic screening.

1. In the United States, only about 15% of law enforcement officers are female, while females make up approximately 51% of the general population. Why do you believe this disparity exists?

2. Do you believe that females are suited for every type of law enforcement function? Are there certain jobs that should be reserved exclusively for men?

3. Should women be held to a different hiring standard than men?

4. Can you identify any law enforcement functions where you would expect women to outperform men?

*Source:* "Indonesia subjects female police applicants to virginity tests," by M. Dhumieres, *Global Post*, November 17, 2014 (http://www.globalpost.com/dispatch/news/regions/asia-pacific/indonesia/141117/indonesia-female-police-virginity-tests).

What is most important is to identify as specifically as possible what the job requirements are for each specific position. The processes for hiring and promotion have been legally scrutinized and have been affected by the resulting litigation over the disparate impact on different groups of people, the validity of measures, and job relevant functions.

The recruitment and selection process does not end with the eligibility list. Rather, it continues as those selected for hiring go to the training academy, as they return to the department to serve their probationary period, and as they proceed through their careers in policing.

## ■ SUPERVISORY RECRUITMENT AND SELECTION

As indicated earlier, the recruitment and selection process is ongoing, as some individuals are promoted to supervisory positions and special assignments. It is important to promote carefully to ensure that those who supervise new recruits are well prepared to do so. Most departments can improve in this area.

> Individual police agencies must do a better job of providing structured career development programs for future leaders. Historically, law enforcement organizations focus well on the task of serving their respective communities but tend to neglect internal personnel development needs due to logistical or budgetary reasons. As a result, police organizations risk promoting weak or inexperienced leaders.[111]

Most supervisors are promoted from within the ranks. In larger departments, field supervisors, typically holding the rank of sergeant, are selected based on years of experience (a minimum of two to three years may be required to even test for the position), performance evaluations in patrol or investigative work, written examinations, and oral interviews. Unfortunately, neither years of service nor performance in investigative or patrol functions necessarily indicates an ability to succeed as a supervisor. Mistakes made in promotions at this level are likely perpetuated, because those promoted to the rank of shift supervisor (typically lieutenants) are generally selected from a pool of sergeants with a specified minimum level of experience. Similarly, division commanders (captains) are selected from the ranks of shift commanders based on the criteria mentioned previously. Lateral entry at any of these levels is rare, although exempt rank positions (particularly at the upper ranks) are becoming more popular.

**SAGE Journal Article:** Supervisory Recruitment and Selection

Efforts to recruit supervisor candidates typically consist of position vacancy announcements posted within the police agency. Smaller agencies more often open up their searches to other agencies for lieutenants and sergeants. Outside advertisement sometimes extends to other agencies that employ city workers. This practice has both advantages and disadvantages. Wherever they appear, the vacancy announcements should clearly state the qualifications for the positions and indicate how interested parties can apply.

Simple longevity in the department is not necessarily the best qualification for supervisory positions. A long-term employee does not always make a good supervisor. But when a supervisor is well trained and makes good decisions, he or she earns the respect of fellow officers. Mutual respect helps create a good working environment, which is one of the best recruiting tools a department can have.

The same equal employment and affirmative-action rules discussed previously apply to the selection and recruitment of police supervisors, including chiefs. The vast majority of police supervisors are promoted from within the ranks of the department (with the exception of police chiefs); lateral entry is the exception rather than the rule in U.S. policing.

In larger departments, officers may also be promoted to a host of specialized assignments, such as juvenile, burglary, fraud, and vice.

Individuals who apply for these positions are required to pass status tests similar to those discussed for entry-level employees, with the additional stipulation that they have served a specified number of years in policing or are at the level immediately below the one for which they are applying. In other words, to become a lieutenant, an officer has to meet the basic status requirements of the department and, in addition, might be required to have served three years at the rank of sergeant.

## Grooming Supervisors

There are two ways of shaping supervisory talent: formal education—such as postgraduate degrees—and on-the-job training. Either way, a skilled supervisor needs a wide variety of experiences and assignments. Police culture largely downplays the importance of theories of management and a liberal arts education. An officer builds credibility through his or her real experience, lending special importance to on-the-job training. However, an officer on track for promotion may have valuable skills and may have "specialized" within the department. A narrow focus can make it difficult to understand the broader police picture. A lack of expertise in important areas may lead to scorn on behalf of line officers. Further, the testing procedure itself is almost always suspect from the perspective of both those applying for advancement and those who have a new supervisor. If the promotion process is handled poorly, staff tend to believe that it is *who* you know rather than *what* you know that leads to promotion.

### Testing Candidates

Typically, agencies do not use physical tests in the selection of supervisors. The assumption may be that they already passed the tests that the department requires or that the position to which they aspire does not require the same degree of physical agility required of line officers. Neither of these assumptions is entirely justified, however, and some measures of physical fitness appear to be appropriate. At a minimum, a thorough medical examination should be required.

### Assessment Centers

Assessment centers are usually an important part of the process for police promotion. Although the assessment center is costly to develop and implement, its record of validity and legal defensibility has justified the costs, and its use has spread.[112]

The **assessment center** had its origins in the 1920s and was used by the military in World War II. The concept was furthered in the 1950s in private industry.[113] An assessment center is not a specific location, but a formal process that involves a series of exercises designed to test how well a candidate would perform in a job using task simulations and role players to replicate real, on-the-job situations.[114] Prior to the 1970s, many police departments promoted people because they had influential contacts, or did well in objective written tests, or impressed a civil service board.[115]

Such promotions often resulted in ineffective supervisors, because they were based on an inaccurate picture of the duties and responsibilities of the position or otherwise were ill aligned with the mission of the department. The results of traditional promotional tools such as interviews and written tests highlight the problems in identifying suitable candidates for promotion. As a result, police agencies are exploring more nontraditional methods including the use of assessment centers and job analysis.

■ **Assessment Center:** A formal process that involves a series of exercises (simulation and role playing) designed to test how well a candidate would perform in a job

To use the assessment center, first there must be a comprehensive and accurate job description for the position. Second, a group of trained observers from outside the department, usually three to five in number, must observe the candidates for the position as they go through a number of job-related activities. A multiple-exercise process allows candidates who may not perform well in one exercise (e.g., an interview) to excel in

Today, many police agencies use sophisticated processes to select personnel, particularly with those seeking promotion to the supervisory ranks.

another exercise (e.g., an analysis and presentation exercise).[116] This is a more objective process in which the assessors rate the applicants individually on each of the tasks assigned over a one- or two-day period. Examples of multiple exercises used in a typical assessment center include the following:

- **In-basket exercises** measure the person's administrative and decision-making abilities through day-to-day administrative activities.
- **Written problem solving** tests the candidate's ability to perceive a problem and gather sufficient data to document a solution.
- **Group discussion** involves candidates in a timed group discussion in which they attempt to reach a joint solution to one or more problems.
- **Oral presentation** requires candidates to present ideas or tasks to the group with or without prior preparation.
- **Counseling session** is an interview simulation that involves assessment of an applicant's ability to "motivate work performance, correct misbehavior, provide key information, direct actions towards an appropriate solution, develop an effective working relation, demonstrate flexibility, analyze problems and demonstrate effective oral communication."[117]

In some cases, applicant performances are videotaped so the assessors can review them at their convenience.

Assessors interview candidates using a standardized format that provides latitude for assessors to raise questions concerning issues brought to light by the various exercises in which the candidates have engaged. Most assessors evaluate candidates based on oral communications, command presence, technical and professional knowledge, decision making, judgment, planning and organization, work perspective, and problem analysis.[118] Tests of ability to communicate are incorporated into the assessment center or evaluated by an oral board in a manner similar to that discussed for entry-level personnel.

Polygraph, drug, and psychological tests, as well as an updated background investigation, may also be required for promotion. Evaluations based on past performance are also frequently used when considering applicants for promotion. The usefulness of these measures remains to be established, because they are typically based on behaviors relevant to the current position of the applicant that may or may not be related to the position for which she or he is applying. That is, excellent performance as a street officer may be largely unrelated to performance as a supervisor. Nonetheless, in many departments, these evaluations account for 20% to 30% of the total score considered for promotion.

Usually under the direction of a team leader, the assessors meet to discuss their impressions of the applicants and their scores. Each assessor must be prepared to defend his or her scores, and discrepant scores often become topics of heated debate. In the ideal case, differences can be resolved through discussion, and the applicants are then listed in order of the assessors' preferences. The final selection is accomplished by the personnel department, police chief, city manager, mayor, or council, or some combination of those individuals.

### Strengths of the Assessment Center

Assessment center success in predicting good performance has been high, and when measured against the costs of making a bad appointment, the costs are less imposing than they might seem. Many police departments use assessment centers not only to determine who should be hired for top-ranking positions, but also as a promotional process and a way to identify strengths and weaknesses of an agency and its employees.[119] In most cases, assessment center participants can identify their shortcomings and learn how to improve their own job performance. The agency can learn about the training deficiencies of the individual as well as the organization.[120] An assessment center can also have a positive effect on morale if it is viewed as an objective, reliable, and fair process wherein the most qualified person is promoted.

## ■ RECRUITMENT AND SELECTION OF POLICE CHIEFS

**Policing in Practice Video:**
What do you find as the most enjoyable aspects of policing?

The skills required of a police chief are, in many instances, significantly different from those required of new recruits or lower-ranking supervisors. The chief not only maintains general control over the department, but also serves as a representative in dealing with other municipal agencies, other police agencies, and elected officials. In some very small departments, the police chief must perform patrol and investigative functions and has few supervisory responsibilities. However, in police agencies with more than four or five employees, administrative and supervisory responsibilities become more important than street work.

Those occupying the position of police chief run the gamut from "good old boys" who have worked their way through the ranks of the department to those who are highly skilled, trained, or educated professional managers. Although the most prevalent path to chief is the insider path, outsiders with police experience and advanced education are increasingly in demand in progressive agencies.

Outreach for police chiefs is generally accomplished through professional police organizations and news outlets. Recruitment for the position of chief may involve reaching outside the department, staying within the department, or a combination of the two.[121]

Thus, lateral entry from outside the agency, while seldom a possibility at other police ranks, *is* possible at the level of chief.

The status requirements discussed for other supervisory personnel typically apply when selecting a chief; however, the level and extent of police experience required varies across communities. The mayor, city manager, or city council are the parties primarily responsible for hiring the chief of police.[122] As is the case with other supervisory personnel, written tests related to administrative and supervisory tasks are often used. In addition, attempts may be made to assess the extent to which the candidates view themselves as part of a management team. Education and training requirements also vary considerably, ranging from high school graduation and basic police training to possession of a master's degree and attendance at one of the more prestigious police management schools (such as the FBI Academy or the Southern Police Institute).

Although many chiefs are hired based on interviews with officials of city government, performance on written tests, and background investigations, more and more are being processed through assessment centers designed to test their administrative skills. The vast majority of police chiefs come from the police ranks, and hiring those without prior police experience, though it does occasionally occur, is the exception. Unlike other police personnel, chiefs are seldom required to attend training academies after being hired, although the political and public relations skills required to be successful suggest the need for further training in many, if not most, cases.

Although this area has improved somewhat, promotion to the rank of chief from within undoubtedly contributes to continuing resistance to change in many police agencies. Some chiefs are basically contractors who serve for a specified period of time with periodic reviews. Others are essentially given tenure when hired, though almost all serve at the pleasure of the head of city government and the city council, and job security is often a major concern.[123] When the chief reports directly to the mayor or city council, political considerations often play an extremely important role. The city manager form of government provides some insulation from direct political ties; from the perspective of promoting a professional, a somewhat apolitical department is probably superior.

You have just been appointed as the chief of police of the Middletown Police Department (MPD). Middletown is a city of about 200,000 and has 260 sworn officers on its police force.

During the past several years, the MPD has been plagued with a significant increase in reported crime, citizen complaints against police, and poor officer morale. Members of the community and the local media are beginning to voice grave concerns about the ability of the MPD to effectively respond to the needs of the community.

The Middletown city manager told you that the primary reason she hired you was because of your reputation as a progressive police administrator. She has given you the green light, along with the needed resources, to improve the department on as many fronts as needed.

One of the first issues you must attend to is to prepare for the next police exam. Your new department has eight immediate openings for entry-level police officers, and it is anticipated that it will have 20 to 30 additional vacancies in the next two years.

Your administrative assistant asks you to prepare an announcement for the exam, along with all of the qualifications, so that these ads can be published in a timely fashion. The last ad, and all of the prior ads, posted the following requirements:

21 to 35 years of age

High school or GED equivalent

U.S. citizen

Pass written exam

Pass background investigation

Pass medical exam

If you were in charge of the department, what would you do to attract the most qualified and representative candidates while still controlling the costs of recruitment?

*Suggestions for addressing these questions can be found on the Student Study Site:* **edge.sagepub.com/ coxpolicing3e**

## CHAPTER SUMMARY

The recruitment and selection of entry-level police officers, supervisors, and chiefs of police is critical to the success of police agencies. The selection process for entry-level police officers involves many steps to ensure that the most qualified applicants who are seriously interested in a career in policing are selected for the training academy.

It is important that recruitment and selection are performed within the legal requirements established by the Equal Employment Opportunity Act, Title VII, the Americans with Disabilities Act, and the Age Discrimination in Employment Act.

Recruiting and hiring decisions are not easy, and the processes used to make these judgments can be quite expensive. Careful, thorough, and lawful hiring and promotion of qualified personnel should reduce the number of lawsuits, increase performance by personnel, and improve the overall professionalization of the agency.

Many factors influence recruitment and promotional practices, such as the use of valid and reliable test instruments and related materials, thorough background investigations, physical and psychological fitness tests, potential leadership capabilities assessments, and the implementation of proper performance evaluation techniques. Even so, it is difficult to evaluate assessment methods to determine if they accurately predict who will perform up to the professional standards of the department.

Police administrators must realize that, new demands are consistently being added to the list of police duties, and as such, new policies and shifts in philosophy regarding crime control and the overall functions and priorities of law enforcement agencies require a flexible organization. One significant issue that is germane to this organizational flexibility is the fact that there are three different generations working in police agencies: the baby boomers, who occupy the majority of high-ranking positions, and Generation X and Y officers. The motivations and actions of officers from each of these generations are quite different and challenging, requiring departments to find ways to effectively supervise and accommodate the legitimate needs of each group. Departments must also recognize that in a multicultural society, an effective outreach effort to minorities is necessary. Specific outreach strategies are required for women as well. Ignoring them only limits the departments and prevents them from taking advantage of entire pools of talent. Retaining new officers requires scrutiny and reevaluation of cultural norms, in many cases. Not making these efforts can result in poor morale, high turnover, and low overall performance, all elements that stymie the growth and development of any organization.

The hiring of police chiefs requires special considerations. Should the chief be promoted from within the existing ranks or selected from outside the department? What minimum criteria should be used regarding the background of applicants with respect to formal education, past administrative accomplishments, specialized training, and leadership ability?

Conducting careful and legitimate recruitment, selection, and promotional practices is a necessity in today's society.

## KEY TERMS

- Immutable characteristics  68
- Discrimination  68
- Disparate impact  68
- Affirmative action  69
- Consent decree  69
- Bona fide occupational qualification  71

- Qualified individual with a disability  71
- Reasonable accommodation  71
- Institutional discrimination  77
- Multiple-hurdle procedure  78
- Status test  78

- Simulation or work sample test  80
- Integrity test  82
- Polygraph  82
- Galvanic skin response  87
- Assessment center  92

## DISCUSSION QUESTIONS

1. Why are the costs of recruitment of police personnel so high? How can these costs reasonably be reduced?

2. Why is recruitment of qualified personnel so important to police agencies?

3. Discuss some of the changes in the selection of police officers that have occurred as a result of equal employment opportunity laws and affirmative-action programs. What are some of the positive and negative consequences of the Equal Employment Opportunity Act and affirmative-action programs?

4. List and discuss the five basic types of police officer selection requirements. How do such requirements apply to promotions?

5. What is an assessment center, why are such centers increasingly being used, and what, if any, disadvantages do they have?

6. What are the backgrounds of most police chiefs, and what implications do these backgrounds have for policing as a profession?

7. How do the provisions of the Americans with Disabilities Act affect the police?

8. How should police departments balance periodic, ongoing psychological testing of their officers with the practical difficulties and legal limitations of doing so?

1. Select one of the tests administered to police officer applicants discussed in the chapter (drug test, physical agility, polygraph, etc.). Go to the Internet and locate information about this test. How is the test administered? What method is used for scoring the test and interpreting the results? Is the test you selected a valid measure of a critical task performed by today's police officers? Why or why not?

2. Locate an advertisement for a police chief that discusses the selection requirements. How is the selection process for chiefs of police different from the process for the selection of police officers? Based on the advertisement, what knowledge, skills, and abilities should today's police chief possess?

## STUDENT STUDY SITE

 **SSAGE edge**™ edge.sagepub.com/coxpolicing3e

**Sharpen your skills with SAGE edge!**

SAGE edge for Students provides a personalized approach to help you accomplish your coursework goals in an easy-to-use learning environment. You'll find action plans, mobile-friendly eFlashcards, and quizzes as well as videos, web resources, and links to SAGE journal articles to support and expand on the concepts presented in this chapter.

# POLICE TRAINING AND EDUCATION

© REUTERS/Randall Benton/Sacramento Bee

## CHAPTER LEARNING OBJECTIVES:

1. Evaluate the pros and cons associated with higher education requirements for police officers

2. Appraise the results of research studies that examine the relationship between higher education and job performance

3. Identify the purposes of police training

4. Describe the three basic types of police training

5. Discuss some of the challenges related to training police organizations face as well as some strategies to address those challenges

olicing is a difficult and complex career. The police officer may be called on to play psychiatrist, doctor, lawyer, judge, jury, priest, counselor, fighter, or dogcatcher. The training required to become a police officer is also quite complex. The public expects the police to be experts in interpersonal communication, be capable and versed in crisis intervention, and be able to defuse volatile domestic disputes. Many agencies do not focus on training and evaluating officers' interpersonal skills, even though officers rely on them to competently perform tactical and legal tasks.[1] Since 1989, however, both the time necessary and the variety of topics covered in police training centers and universities throughout the nation have increased, although there are significant differences among the states.

There are many questions among professionals about both training and education. How much training should be done? Who should do it? What should the content of the training be? What form should it take? How can training and education be used to benefit officers and the citizens they serve? How effective is training and education? What are the optimum educational requirements for police? Answering these questions is not easy, but departments must wrestle with them if the goal is to develop highly trained, competent police officers.

The extent and nature of police training and education have been controversial since at least 1908, when August Vollmer began formal training for police officers and advocated for a baccalaureate degree as a requirement for entry-level police officers in the Berkeley (California) Police Department. The two issues are intimately interrelated, and yet distinct.

This distinction between training and education is a frequently debated issue. Although the two are interrelated, **training** has more to do with the basic and advanced skills necessary to do the job, and **education** the concepts and principles underlying the training. Thus, many think of training as more concrete and practical, and education as more abstract and theoretical. However, there is no absolute agreement concerning the distinctions. For example, a good deal of contemporary police training (e.g., cultural diversity, communications, and interpersonal skills) is based on scholarly theory and research.[2] However, the distinction in people's minds between training and education is not always clear, even though in practice, there is a wide separation between the more theoretical university criminal justice programs and practical police training.

■ **POLICE EDUCATION**

**Background**

Historically, the desired qualifications for police applicants were focused on physical assets.[3] The belief was that police officers should have an adequate level of physical strength to engage dangerous criminals. There was little attention paid to the concept that the police would need to draw on such skills as thoughtful and enlightened

**Training:** The provision of basic skills necessary to perform essential job functions

**Education:** The provision of familiarity with the theoretical concepts and principles underlying the training

© iStockphoto.com/Rich Legg

© iStockphoto.com/lisafx

Police work clearly requires a combination of effective, relevant training and higher education coursework.

communication, advanced decision making, and strategic tactics—skills that rest on intellectual capacity and develop through training and education.[4]

One of the most popular proposals for improving the quality of policing in the United States entailed higher education requirements for officers. Presidential commissions found that policing should become more like a profession and should require education beyond high school.[5] The idea that a college-educated police officer would be a better police officer spawned a federal program called the Law Enforcement Assistance Administration (LEAA, introduced in Chapter 2), which provided millions of dollars annually for such education and dramatically increased the number of related college programs and the number of police officers with at least some college education.[6] However, the conclusions formed by the commissions that education improved police officer performance were based mostly on anecdotes, and the debate over the importance of police education continues. Federal funding for police education has diminished considerably, new federal programs have been proposed, and there are continuing concerns over the content and quality of police education.

There is no doubt that the field of policing has advanced in professionalization over the past few decades. However, if the law enforcement community wishes to continue to advance, the public must perceive it more broadly as a profession, not just an occupation. Such a distinction requires the police to stay current by participating in continuing professional education (CPE) activities. In 2013, all local police departments serving a population of 100,000 or more, and nearly all departments in smaller jurisdictions, had a minimum education requirement for new officers. The breakdown of these requirements is listed in Figure 5.1. Although the majority require only a high school diploma, the number of agencies that require a two-year degree has doubled since 1993.

**Office of the Police Corps and Law Enforcement Education:** Created by the U.S. Department of Justice in 1999, the goal of this program was to weave a college education with state-of-the-art police training to produce highly qualified personnel who would be able to confront the demands and intricacies of 21st-century policing; unfortunately, funding for the program has been eliminated, and the Police Corps is no longer awarding scholarships or providing training

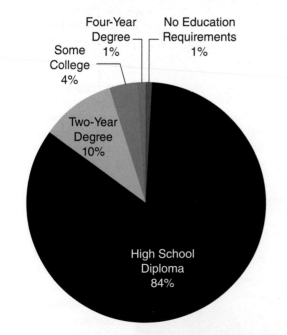

Figure 5.1 ■ Education Requirements for New Officers in Local Police Departments, 2013

Four-Year Degree
1%

No Education Requirements
1%

Some College
4%

Two-Year Degree
10%

High School Diploma
84%

*Source:* Local police departments, 2013: Personnel, policies, and practices, by Brian A. Reaves, May 2015. Bureau of Justice Statistics (http://www.bjs.gov/content/pub/pdf/lpd13ppp.pdf).

Some believe that liberal arts courses provide the best background for police officers in a multiethnic, multicultural society; others are convinced that specialized courses in criminal justice are preferable; and still others question the value of any college education for police officers. The number of programs in criminal justice and related areas increased dramatically in the 1970s. By 2015, there were 2,452 colleges and universities offering over 6,800 degree and certificate programs, ranging from the associate to the doctorate.[7] In addition, the growth of online degree programs has been exponential.

Still, the quality of these programs has been questioned since their inception. Data collected in 1985 indicated that many in academia still perceived criminal justice education as being basically technical or vocational training, often taught by faculty without proper credentials. Although this may have been true at the time, things are different now. Many believe that criminal justice education has flourished intellectually and broadened in scope. Most contemporary programs attempt to achieve a more structured balance between the academic and practical needs of their students.[8]

In response to some of these concerns, the U.S. Department of Justice created the **Office of the Police Corps and Law Enforcement Education** in 1999. The Police Corps was designed to address violent crime by helping police and sheriffs' departments increase the number of officers with advanced education and training assigned to community patrol. The program offered competitive college scholarships for students who agreed to work in a state or local police force for at least four years. Students accepted into the Police Corps received a yearly stipend to cover the expenses of a bachelor's or graduate degree.[9]

The goal of the program was to combine a college education with state-of-the-art police training to produce highly qualified personnel able to confront the demands and intricacies of contemporary policing. However, funding for the program was eventually eliminated, and the Police Corps is no longer awarding scholarships or providing training.

Highlights of the program were as follows:

**Policing in Practice Video:**
How did your education prepare you for your career in policing?

- Participants must possess the necessary mental and physical capabilities and emotional characteristics to be an effective law enforcement officer, be of good character, and demonstrate sincere motivation and dedication to law enforcement and public service.

- Participants can receive up to $3,750 per academic year, with a maximum per student total of $15,000.

- The student's service commitment must follow receipt of the baccalaureate degree or precede commencement of graduate studies funded by the Police Corps.

- A police agency whose size has declined by more than 5% since June 21, 1989, or which has members who have been laid off but not retired, cannot participate in the Police Corps program.[10]

## YOU ??? DECIDE  5.1

The education requirement for law enforcement has been the subject of debate in the U.S. since the early 1900s. Several national commissions have recommended that state and local police departments consider higher education as a requirement for employment. One reason for the push is to "professionalize" police forces and improve their public image. Another reason is that numerous studies have shown that officers with a four-year degree perform better than officers with just a high school diploma.

Most federal law enforcement agencies require either a bachelor's degree or related work experience or a combination of the two. However, according to a Bureau of Justice Statistics study from 2015, 84% of United States police agencies only required a high school diploma, with only 4% requiring some college. Only 1% of municipal police agencies required a four-year college degree and 10% require a 2-year degree.

1. With strong support for educated police officers, why do you think more local agencies have not mirrored the federal protocol in requiring a college degree?

2. Would you support a new standard of requiring a college degree for hiring at all local police departments? Why or why not?

*Suggestions for addressing these questions can be found on the Student Study Site:* **edge.sagepub.com/coxpolicing3e**

**Source:** Reaves, (2015). Local Police Departments, 2013: Personnel, Policies, and Practices. Bureau of Justice Statistics, Law Enforcement Management and Administrative Statistics (LEMAS) Survey. U.S. Department of Justice, Office of Justice Programs.

## Higher Education and the Police: A Debate

The debate about how much and what kind of education should be required for police personnel continues in spite of research results and the fact that virtually every national commission on the police over the past half-century has recommended such education.

The issue is complex. According to a renowned observer:

> Some argue that police work, especially at the local level, does not require a formal education beyond high school, because such tasks as directing traffic, writing parking tickets, conducting permit inspections, and performing clerical tasks do not require higher education.[11] Some have suggested that a highly intelligent and well-educated person would soon become bored with these mundane and repetitive tasks and either resign or remain and become either an ineffective member of the force or a malcontent. Others have argued that the complex role of policing a multiethnic, culturally diverse society requires nothing less than a college degree as a condition of initial employment for police officers.[12]

> We have come a long way from the commissions of nearly thirty years ago, when the issue was relatively simple—whether it made sense to require a college degree of police officers. . . . requiring a college education does not begin to meet the larger educational challenge the policing profession faces—how to prepare everyone in the department, from line officer to highest executive, to exercise an increasing degree of discretion in an increasingly complex world.[13]

### Arguments in Favor of Education

In an era of community-oriented policing, many police executives expect college-educated officers to be both more open-minded and more humanitarian than less educated officers.

Increased legal support for higher education of police officers, coupled with the changing role of the police in recent years, would appear to support increasingly higher standards for police training and education. In fact, an increasing body of legal evidence indicates that failure to train and educate police officers may lead to serious financial consequences for police agencies, agents, and municipalities alike.

According to the **Police Association for College Education (PACE)**, a professional organization dedicated to the professionalization of law enforcement, higher education is beneficial for a number of reasons:

- It develops a broader base of information for decision making.
- It provides additional years and experiences for increasing maturity.
- It inculcates responsibility in the individual through course requirements and achievements.
- It permits an individual to learn more about the history of the United States and the democratic process.[14]
- It leads to a more flexible value system.
- It improves attitudes toward minority groups.
- It cultivates a more aware attitude about culture and ethics.[15]

**■ Police Association for College Education (PACE):** Formerly known as the American Police Foundation, PACE is a professional organization dedicated to the professionalization of law enforcement through higher education

Although only a small proportion of police agencies now require college education for initial employment or promotion, informal discussions with police executives indicate that such education is of considerable importance and that increased education requirements are inevitable. A promising report in this regard, sponsored by the Bureau of Justice Statistics (BJS), is that by 2016 it is projected that 52% of police officers in this country will possess at least an associate degree and that 33% will hold a baccalaureate degree or higher on entrance to the field.[16]

However, the benefits of continuing education for police officers are not limited to course content. A good deal of benefit accrues from having police officers and other students share the same classroom, coming to know each other as individuals and hearing one another's perspectives on a variety of issues. This is perhaps particularly true when the class is diverse with respect to age, race and ethnicity, gender, size of hometown, and cultural background.

"The culture of a police department that successfully requires college degrees for officers differs from that of a department that does not. The former creates a culture of responsibility, the latter, of obedience."[17] It is obvious that the increasingly complex nature of crime and of requests for police services and the laws regulating activities in these areas support the need for better-educated and -trained police. To reach these goals, colleges and universities, as well as police training institutes and academies, must continually revise and update curricula while maintaining high standards.

> The culture of a police department that successfully requires college degrees for officers differs from that of a department that does not. The former creates a culture of responsibility, the latter, of obedience.

The transition to police officers with higher education has not, however, been smooth or easy. First of all, the question of whether higher education is necessary at all is far from settled. In addition, it is a practical challenge to hire more educated officers, as the requirement would severely limit the pool of candidates. Also, if agency leaders hold no such degrees, they are unlikely to hire officers who are more highly educated than they are themselves.

Some early studies of police education questioned the value of the requirement, suggesting that more highly educated officers held questionable attitudes about women on the force and negative perceptions of the public and maintained more authoritarianism, which contradicts other research results (see below).[18]

### What Do Agencies Require?

In spite of the calls for an education requirement for police officers, a large number of agencies continue to require only a high school education or equivalent. In the Police Executive Research Forum survey, only about 14% of the responding agencies required any college, and less than 1% required a bachelor's degree.[19] Similarly, a 2005 study found that approximately 1% of local police departments in the United States required a four-year college degree.[20]

Some departments that *do* require college education as a condition of initial employment have been challenged in the courts, which are willing to uphold college education as a requirement in at least some cases, which makes it possible to establish a "defensible college education entrance requirement for employment" (and, for that matter, for promotion) in law enforcement.[21]

Police agencies that desire to implement educational requirements must develop a policy that outlines the requirement and its rationale. There are cases in support of such a rationale, such as *Davis v. City of Dallas,* in which the U.S. Supreme Court allowed the Dallas Police Department's requirement of 45 semester-hours of college coursework for entry-level officers to stand.[22] In addition, the state of Minnesota was one of the first states to require a two-year law enforcement or criminal justice degree through a professional peace officer educational program.[23]

### What Do the Police Think?

The police themselves tend to ascribe advantages to higher education. A 2005 study used self-report surveys to poll the opinions of nearly 400 patrol officers regarding the perceived benefits of higher education in policing. The vast majority of respondents (82%) believed at least some higher education requirement to be necessary in today's policing environment. Ironically, although nearly 90% of the officers surveyed had some college education, 22% of them also reported that their respective agencies were not supportive of their educational pursuits. Moreover, 65% of the officers polled reported that their agencies had no formal policies linking higher education to promotion.[24]

The same study indicated a general doubt among the respondents that colleges and universities have curricula that meet the contemporary needs of law enforcement agencies. Although the respondents found that criminal justice graduates were very knowledgeable about the criminal justice system and policing in general, they were often "narrow in ideology" and lacked the broader understanding of divergent cultures and social issues that confront the police.

**Video Link:**
Criminal Justice
Professions

Another study attempted to assess the value that police officers with criminal justice degrees place on their personal educational experiences, while comparing those perceptions with officers educated in other academic disciplines.[25] The survey of 1,114 police officers concluded that officers with criminal justice degrees reported that the degree substantially improved their knowledge and abilities on a wide range of areas, from the criminal justice system to conceptual and managerial skills. Interestingly, responses did not differ significantly from officers educated in noncriminal justice academic disciplines. Thus, the respondents found the degrees to be useful, regardless of the academic specialty in question.

The criminal justice profession has responded to many concerns and recommendations voiced by law enforcement executives. The **Academy of Criminal Justice Sciences (ACJS)**—founded in 1963—is the largest professional organization dedicated to the advancement of knowledge in the criminal justice profession. ACJS promotes criminal justice education, research, and policy analysis for both educators and practitioners by providing curriculum guidelines and recommendations for colleges and universities that offer degree programs in criminal justice.[26] The recommended curricula for these criminal justice programs were developed via numerous working groups consisting of law enforcement executives, university professors, and many other actors within the criminal justice community. The ACJS also offers voluntary certification to colleges and universities.[27]

## ■ RESEARCH ON COLLEGE EDUCATION AND POLICE PERFORMANCE

Researchers have explored a variety of topics related to whether education improves police performance, testing the assumption that "a bachelor of arts degree emphasizes problem-solving from a variety of viewpoints, develops understanding of how perceptions influence behavior, increases a person's comfort level with ambiguity, and assumes that the things going on in the world are fluid and interrelated."[28]

The research topics in recent years that relate to the relationship between education and police performance are varied. Some have found a clear relationship, but others have not been able to detect a distinct correlation.[29] Research topics include the relationship between educational level and police use of deadly force[30] and the relationship between educational level and absenteeism.[31]

### Research Results
#### *Positive Results*

One study found an inverse relationship between educational levels of patrol officers and performance ratings, but a significant relationship between educational levels and job achievement.[32] A 1983 study examined police officer educational levels and differences in delivery of services and concluded that college graduates were more likely to explain the nature of complaints to offenders, talk with people to establish rapport, analyze and compare incidents for similarity of modus operandi, recruit confidential informants, and verify reliability and credibility of witnesses than were officers with only some college or high school education. However, the researcher was unwilling to attribute these performance differences solely to educational differences.[33] A 2015 report suggests that there is a positive correlation between higher education and officers' job satisfaction, views of top management, and role orientation.[34]

**■ Academy of Criminal Justice Sciences (ACJS):** One of the largest professional organizations in the world dedicated to the advancement of knowledge in the criminal justice profession

Many studies have found a positive correlation between education and desirable officer characteristics. For example, officers with the best performance evaluations also

1. have significantly higher education;[35]

2. are less authoritarian;[36]

3. have better communication skills, have fewer civilian complaints of verbal and physical abuse, and use less sick time;[37]

4. have better problem-solving and analytical abilities and require fewer disciplinary actions;[38-39] and

5. are less tolerant of abuse of authority.[40]

Additional studies noted that college-educated officers are more sensitive to community relations, and more understanding of human behavior, and hold higher ethical and service standards, than their peers.[41]

### Inconclusive Results

Other research was less conclusive about higher education being a significant advantage for new officers.[42] One study concluded that college education was weakly related to some police officer attitudes and unrelated to others and that officers' performance in police–citizen encounters, as measured by citizen evaluations, was largely unrelated to officer education.[43] Another concluded that officers with four-year degrees generated at least as many violations of departmental policy as those with two-year degrees.[44]

**SAGE Journal Article:** Impact of Police Academy Training on Recruits' Integrity

Other studies concerned the effect of police officer education on police decision-making points such as arrest, search, and use of force. One team reported that "higher education carries no influence over the probability of an arrest or search occurring in a police-suspect encounter."[45] However, the same researchers found that college education significantly reduced the likelihood of force occurring, which is important given the recent hotly debated issue of excessive use of force by the police.[46]

The ability to communicate with citizens of all ages, ethnicities, and educational levels is critical for police officers.

© Peter Casolino/Alamy

## Table 5.1 ■ Studies of Police Officers With College Degrees

| Author | Title | Year | Findings/Recommendations |
|---|---|---|---|
| President's Commission | Task Force Report | 1967 | Bachelor of science for entry-level police is needed to address complex social problems. |
| U.S. National Institute of Mental Health (Bittner) | The Functions of the Police in a Modern Society | 1970 | The report recommended a master's degree for entry-level police. |
| Rand Corporation (Cohen & Chaiken) | Police Background Characteristics . . . | 1972 | There is a strong correlation between level of education and citizen complaints. |
| American Bar Association (Goldstein & Krantz) | The Urban Police Function | 1973 | Traits such as those provided by higher education (intellectual curiosity, ability to synthesize information, etc.) are needed by police. |
| Finckenauer | Higher Education & Police Discretion | 1975 | Police recruits with a college education were more likely than those without to use discretion in a much more community-minded fashion. |
| Sanderson | Police Officers: Relationship of College Education to Job Performance | 1977 | The author shows strong correlation between college education and performance (i.e., lower absenteeism rate, fewer complaints, promoted more frequently). |
| Carter, Stephens, & Sapp | Effect of Higher Education on Police Liability . . . | 1989 | Police officers with college degrees received significantly fewer citizen complaints. A policy of a college degree was recommended to reduce agency liability. |
| Kappalar, Allen, Sapp, & Carter | Police Officer Higher Education, Citizen Complaints, and Department Rule | 1992 | Police officers with college degrees received significantly fewer citizen complaints than those officers without college degrees. |
| Tyre & Braunstein | Higher Education & Ethical Policing | 1992 | The authors concluded that officers with higher levels of education tended to select more ethical courses of action than their counterparts without a college degree. |
| Committee on Integrity: Report to Mayor Daley | Final Report: Volume 1: Corruption | 1997 | The report recommended an entrance requirement of a bachelor's degree for police officers to mitigate corrupt police practices. |
| Wilson | Post-Secondary Education of the Police Officer and Its Effect on the Frequency of Citizen Complaints | 1999 | The research showed that officers with college degrees received fewer citizen complaints than officers without a college degree. |
| Fullerton | Higher Education as a Prerequisite to Employment as a Law Enforcement Officer | 2002 | Fullerton summarized several research projects between 1967 and 1992 that addressed the issue of higher education and the police. Throughout the studies, several traits were associated more with college-educated officers, such as fewer citizen complaints, less authoritarianism, better decision making, and many others. |
| Aamodt | Research in Law Enforcement Selection | 2004 | From a review of more than 300 studies related to police officer selection policies, officers with a college education received better performance evaluations, received fewer citizen complaints, had less absenteeism, and tended to use less force than the officers without college degrees. |

*Source:* Reprinted with permission from Police Association for College Education (PACE).

### The Importance of Leadership in Education: What Are Leaders to Do?

Leaders who value both education and training know that the commitment to those should last an officer's entire career. Regardless of education level, continuing education courses can be challenging, motivating, and worthwhile. Such courses also are beneficial for officers who do not wish to pursue a college degree.

It is up to administrators to offer departmental incentives for becoming involved in continuing education, which indicate to officers that their efforts are appreciated. Such incentives may include tuition reimbursement, time off to attend classes (or allowing officers to attend class while on duty in an "on-call" status), reimbursement for the cost of books, and so on. In many departments that provide these incentives, there are also enhanced chances for promotion. As is the case with training, commitment to education and continuing education must come from the top.[47]

One survey of police departments that serve cities with populations of 50,000 or more found that about half of all police executives who responded prefer to hire officers who have majored in criminal justice.[48] The rest indicated no preference in college degrees or majors. Those who preferred criminal justice majors did so because of the graduates' knowledge of policing and criminal justice, while those stating no preference indicated they preferred a broader education to prepare officers to deal with a wide variety of situations.

These leaders do not want colleges and universities to teach police skills; they seek graduates who can integrate the duties of a police officer with an understanding of democratic values.[49] The consensus was that a liberal arts curriculum should be part and parcel of college and university criminal justice programs. There was general agreement that a quality education is needed, particularly in the areas of communication skills, critical thinking, decision making, research, the ability to integrate concepts, and an understanding of diverse cultures.

However, the majority (75%) of police executives indicated a lack of communication between colleges and universities and police agencies; they were never consulted about issues of common interest. The researchers concluded that "colleges and universities should be developing policies, changing and modifying curricula, and focusing on providing the educational background needed by students and society. Criminal justice educators must introspectively give detailed attention to curricula to ensure that today's curricula fit today's needs in law enforcement and other areas of the criminal justice system."[50]

### Evaluating Leaders

A study of police chief performance and leadership styles surveyed 205 city managers in Pennsylvania and asked them to rate the performance and leadership attributes of the police chief they supervised.[51] Chiefs with college educations were rated significantly higher than their high school graduate counterparts on 35 of 45 performance indicators. Perhaps the most significant finding in this study was that "those police chiefs with poor ratings were identified as those without college credit. Education was the only significant predictor of police chiefs being rated as bad or poor."[52]

## ■ POLICE TRAINING

### Purposes of Training

Training is increasingly recognized as a major aspect of the police role. A basic purpose of training is to keep police personnel current with respect to important changes in the profession. Police training should identify, instill, and help develop the core competencies that enable officers to do their jobs. Core competencies are the "non-negotiables," the things an officer absolutely must be competent at doing—for example, firearms, force, driving, report writing, first aid. Substantive topics may include things like interviewing witnesses or drug identification. Training should ensure that police personnel are knowledgeable about policy and procedure, relevant case law, and the skills and attitudes needed for them to perform at the highest level possible. In a larger sense, however, the purposes of training depend on the ways in which the role of the police is defined.

The 1960s and 1970s emphasized crime fighting and law enforcement, and to some extent, many officers still view these aspects of the police role as the most important part of police work. Notwithstanding incremental changes, police training today continues to reflect those influences.[53] As a result, training courses dealing with survival techniques, patrol techniques, criminal investigation, use of force, and the law are among the most popular courses.

**Audio Link:**
Simulation Technology
Trains Police Officers to
Face Real Life Situations

The importance of training cannot be overemphasized; "proper training boosts officer performance, reduces agency liability for poor performance, and mitigates community aversion to the presence of law enforcement."[54] Inadequate or inappropriate training can too often result in inaccurate assessments of situations and poor decision making, not to mention officers feeling a lack of self-confidence or even feeling overly confident.

One of the major purposes of police training is—or should be—to make better communicators of the public servants responsible for maintaining order.[55] Communication and negotiation is what police officers do most often. Some police officers have excellent skills in these areas, but others have practically none. Such officers are unlikely to get cooperation from a range of citizens, either because they alienate them by being authoritarian to compensate for their poor communication skills or because they cannot express clearly and convincingly what they want or need people to do. They receive little input from the public about crime or police performance. They routinely enforce the law and maintain order through arrests or becoming unnecessarily physical in encounters with the public.[56] In similar situations, their more skilled colleagues are able to achieve order without resorting to arrest. Furthermore, communication skills are critical during the training itself.[57]

Another purpose of training is to help agencies on the way to litigation. For the most part, CPE training is mandated as outcomes of litigation and normally pertains to areas associated with civil liability, such as the use of firearms, physical force, the handling of hazardous materials, and high-speed vehicle pursuits; there is very little elective training. Many agencies have no requirements for additional continuing education.[58]

Police agencies can improve their training in many ways, for instance, a focus on the less traditional aspects of policing (human relations, communication skills, community policing strategies, ethical decision making, responsible exercise of discretionary authority); administrators leading by example and assuming an active role in the training process; innovative training methods; and trainers qualified both as content experts and as experienced and knowledgeable educators. See Table 5.2 for a breakdown of how many police departments request recruits and in-service officers to receive community policing training.

The training in most larger law enforcement agencies is very well organized. It is often taught by officers who are well versed in adult-learning theory and experienced in their fields. Most police officers recognize the tremendous and ever-expanding liability associated with the job. Training may very well prevent an officer from facing litigation, an internal investigation, or criminal charges. Many of the subjects of training reoccur annually or semiannually and, in many cases, are mandated by laws or litigation.

### What Kind of Training and How Much?

All training is, or should be, interrelated. Also, training topics are not static but constantly changing, and what we knew to be true yesterday may turn out to be myth tomorrow.[59] Skilled communication is extremely relevant, whether an officer is investigating a crime (interviewing and interrogation skills), whether a department is defending a police action by a questioning public (public relations), whether orders or directives are involved (departmental policies must be understood to be effective), or whether evaluations

**Table 5.2 ■ Community Policing Training for Recruits and Officers in Local Police Departments, by Size of Population Served, 2013**

| Population Served | Recruits | | | In-service officers | | |
|---|---|---|---|---|---|---|
| | Total | All | Some | Total | All | Some |
| All sizes | 60% | 44% | 16% | 67% | 40% | 27% |
| 1,000,000 or more | 100 | 92 | 8 | 92 | 38 | 54 |
| 500,000–999,999 | 93 | 82 | 11 | 76 | 31 | 44 |
| 250,000–499,999 | 87 | 85 | 3 | 67 | 33 | 34 |
| 100,000–249,999 | 83 | 74 | 9 | 66 | 26 | 40 |
| 50,000–99,999 | 80 | 68 | 12 | 70 | 33 | 37 |
| 25,000–49,999 | 76 | 56 | 20 | 67 | 24 | 44 |
| 10,000–24,999 | 73 | 52 | 21 | 70 | 33 | 37 |
| 2,500–9,999 | 57 | 39 | 17 | 67 | 37 | 30 |
| 2,499 or fewer | 46 | 34 | 12 | 64 | 51 | 12 |

*Source:* Bureau of Justice Statistics, Law Enforcement Management and Administrative Statistics (LEMAS) Survey, 2013.

*Note:* Includes departments that provided 8 hours or more of community policing training. Detail may not sum to total because of rounding.

or promotions are involved (both require clear communication between those being evaluated or promoted and those doing the evaluating or promoting).

The content of police training, of course, varies with time, place, personnel involved, subject matter, and training goals. In general, however, it may be said that the content should be relevant to the needs of trainees, timely, well organized, and clearly presented. When these requirements are met, trainees can best appreciate the value of the training. It is imperative that the information conveyed in training sessions be current and accurate. The range of subjects that may be covered in training sessions is limited only by the imagination of planners and presenters. Further, a good deal of training can now be accomplished through Internet presentations and seminars, making training opportunities more widely available than ever before.

**Video Link:**
Police Training Aims
to Eliminate Biases

Courses dealing with both verbal and nonverbal communications should be required of all police personnel. It is also possible, however, to improve communication skills regardless of the specific content of the training. Topics that require feedback from the participants can be presented in an organized fashion and can help participants express themselves more clearly and become better listeners. Police officers trained to express themselves clearly and as good listeners are likely to be more effective in performing order maintenance and law enforcement.

Police officers can never have enough training; thus, training is a career-long commitment.

In a professional world that is changing constantly and rapidly, only proper training and education can help police officers stay current. We see this, for example, in the increased use of computers, forensics, and crime analysis.

But exactly what kinds of skills and how many hours of training should be required are questions that every agency must wrestle with. Every agency has to balance the needs of growing its capacity with the expense and time needed to accomplish that growth.

A number of states now mandate training both at the entry level and on a continuing basis. Peace Officer Standards and Training commissions now operate in all states—prescribing and supervising training for police officers. All states require initial training, and many also require ongoing training during an officer's career.

**Policing in Practice Video:**
Experience and importance of the training process

### *Department Support for Training*

The need for training is relevant at all levels of policing, including that of police chief. Unfortunately, police administrators sometimes fail to take advantage of training opportunities because of busy schedules, lack of interest, or the mistaken belief that they already know all there is to know. Officers often attend training not required of the chief. A frequently heard comment at patrol officer training sessions is, "I wish the chief could hear this." In some instances, the chief may fail to follow the lessons taught by the course that the officers have been exposed to. For example, officers might attend a course on the importance of communication, after which they realize that the chief has poor communication skills. A supervisor that lacks up-to-date training may hinder a subordinate officer or investigator from using newly acquired skills. A police administrator who wants a well-trained department must send the message that training is important in a variety of ways, including by his or her own occasional attendance at training sessions and continued openness to learning.

## ■ TYPES OF TRAINING

There are many kinds of training for police officers and supervisors. The most basic types are recruit training, field training, and ongoing in-service training. The specific subjects covered in training of all kinds vary significantly among all police agencies. As technology advances, agencies are adopting more training strategies, including use of the Internet and online training.

### Recruit Training

Most new police recruits attend police training institutes or academies. Such training is referred to as basic or **recruit training** and encompasses the following core competencies (roughly in order of the amount of time spent on each):

- Patrol techniques and officer safety
- Criminal investigation
- Force and weaponry
- Legal issues
- Administration
- Communication
- Criminal justice systems
- Human relations
- Emergency driving
- Crime scene management and evidence handling
- Court testimony
- Report writing

Additional skills may include the following

- Conflict resolution
- Policy and procedure
- Organizational philosophy and ethics
- Leadership
- Community-specific problems

■ **Recruit Training:** Also known as basic training, refers to the initial training successful police applicants are exposed to; training covers criminal law, traffic code enforcement, arrest techniques, firearm training, self-defense tactics, vehicle searches, and a host of similar topics; successful recruit training culminates in certification as a sworn police or peace officer

- Cultural diversity, special needs groups
- Individual rights
- Lifestyle stressors, self-awareness, and self-regulation

Training can be measured most directly in terms of the number of hours. As of the year 2000, the lowest number of mandatory training academy hours was 320; the highest was 1,118; and the mean number of training hours required of entry-level recruits was 516.[60] Almost none of these academies spend more than 10% of the time on human or community relations and ethical decision making—even though the vast majority of a police officer's time is spent in encounters and duties that require skills in these areas. The majority of training curricula teach police officers about things that take up only a small percentage of their time on the job.[61] Training priorities are a matter of time and money. It is tremendously expensive to put a recruit through an academy. A police agency may invest as much as $100,000 to recruit, hire, and train a new police officer. Until that recruit graduates, the agency sees no "return on its investment." From a practical and monetary standpoint, the time a recruit spends in the academy is necessarily limited. Police academies must focus on those topics with the highest degree of liability, thus the emphasis on force, firearms, and driving. A two-year basic academy is simply not practical. However, recruits are tested in each area of instruction, and to graduate, recruits must achieve a passing score in every training domain.

## AROUND THE WORLD 5.1

The Royal Canadian Mounted Police (RCMP) is a national police service that has approximately 26,000 employees, including sworn, civilian, and public service employees. Strategic priorities include organized crime, terrorism, youth, economic integrity, and serving Aboriginal communities. The RCMP is unique because it is a national, federal, provincial, and municipal policing body.

Cadet training involves a 24-week, basic training course and then a 6-month Field Coaching Program under the supervision of a field coach. The Cadet Training Program consists of 785 hours in the following areas:

- Applied police sciences: 373 hours
- Detachment visits, exams, etc.: 115 hours
- Police defensive tactics: 75 hours
- Police driving: 65 hours
- Firearms: 64 hours
- Drill, deportment, and tactics: 48 hours
- Fitness and lifestyle: 45 hours

The Capra Model is an operational application of the RCMP's vision and mission . . . and combines commitment to communities and clients, problem solving in partnership, and continuous learning. The acronym CAPRA stands for:

- C = Clients
- A = Acquiring and analyzing information
- P = Partnership
- R = Response
- A = Assessment for continuous improvement

*Source:* "Cadet training program brief overview," and "Corporate facts," *Royal Canadian Mounted Police*, 2011 (http://www.rcmp-grc.gc.ca).

We have come to recognize that, although law enforcement and crime fighting are critical parts of the police role, they are not the most important in terms of time spent or citizen satisfaction. As is commonly understood, police personnel spend the majority of their time negotiating settlements between spouses, lovers, or neighbors and providing other services that have little to do with law enforcement. As buffers between aggrieved parties, police personnel need to develop skills in this area. Successful intervention into the daily lives of citizens requires specific skills, as well as cooperation on the part of the individuals involved. Increasingly, communication skills (both verbal and nonverbal) and human, community, and cultural competency are emerging as among the most important assets of a skilled, effective police officer.

### Training and Community-Oriented Policing

Basic training curricula place little emphasis on these skills in the job setting. Recent research regarding this issue shows mixed results. Approximately 80% of police academies offer recruits at least some form of training in subjects related to community policing; however, the amount of time spent on those and similar issues is minimal in comparison to the more traditional subjects, such as firearms training, physical fitness, and the like.[62]

As policing evolved to become more community oriented, academies could have included more than the mechanical aspects of policing in their curricula.[63] Unfortunately, many never did, and now that community-oriented policing initiatives are no longer funded to the same extent they were during the late 1990s and early 2000s, the topic areas covered remain dominated by a concrete and practical approach. Thus, for example, the BJS reported the following statistics. Unlike the data cited in the above studies, this report examined police recruits attending all state, local, municipal, and college campus-based training academies, regardless of population.

- As of the end of 2006, there were 648 police training facilities offering basic recruit training.
- Basic training programs averaged 19 weeks in length.
- Topics with the most instruction included firearms, self-defense, health and fitness, patrol procedures, investigations, emergency vehicle operations, criminal law, and basic first aid.
- Of the approximately 57,000 police recruits who entered the basic training program in 2005, 86% (49,000) graduated from the academy.
- Academies with a predominantly academic orientation had a higher completion rate (89%) than academies with a predominantly paramilitary orientation (80%).
- Community policing instruction increased slightly, while sizeable increases were observed in terrorism-related training.[64]

Still, there are good arguments for maintaining a community-oriented policing focus in training recruits. A 2008 study compared traditional and community policing academy curricula and found that the newer model had a higher rate of recruit officer success in academy performance. Additionally, findings indicated that recruits who had higher levels of education and females performed better in this training model.[65]

1. What lessons can U.S. law enforcement agencies learn from the RCMP's model?

2. What types of unique challenges does the RCMP face? Do you see similar challenges faced by U.S. police agencies?

3. How might U.S. law enforcement agencies use the CAPRA model to solve problems, improve community-oriented policing outcomes, and reduce crime?

## Field Training

Although the information provided in basic training academies is crucial, there is often a considerable gap between the academy content and what actually occurs on the streets. In a very real sense, academy training is simply a preparatory step for OJT or **field training**. The same is true in many other professions; for example, doctors complete four years of medical training, but much of what they learn is theoretical. To be fully confident and competent, doctors require additional training through residency and internship. Their book learning is necessary preparation for the real world.

Field training is an opportunity for new officers to put to use what they learned in the classroom under the watchful eye of an experienced officer who can provide immediate feedback and mentoring. Additionally, it is impossible in the academy to provide training for every potential event an officer might encounter. Field training, when done correctly, should extend and build upon academy training.

The first opportunity for the rookie to practice what he or she has been taught comes during the first year or two of service, often referred to as the **probationary period**. Field training and the probationary period work hand in glove. Field training is typically conducted during the first six months of probation. The idea is to see how an officer performs on the job. During this period, the officer has very little in the way of civil service employee protections. Thus, if an officer is unable to perform satisfactorily during training, it is relatively simple for the agency to terminate the officer. This becomes exponentially more difficult at the conclusion of probation.

Normally, new officers are or should be involved in field training under the supervision of **field training officers (FTOs)** who have been selected and prepared to direct, evaluate, and correct the performance of recruits immediately after their basic academy training. Such programs have become widespread since they began in San Jose, California, in the early 1970s. They provide daily evaluation of a recruit's performance by two or more FTOs, as well as weekly or monthly evaluations by other supervisory personnel. The FTO programs are expected to achieve the following goals:

- Produce a competent police officer capable of working solo patrol assignments in a safe, skillful, productive, and professional manner.
- Provide standardized training to all newly assigned regular officers in the practical application of learned information.
- Provide clear standards for rating and evaluation, which give all trainees every reasonable opportunity to succeed.
- Enhance the professionalism, job skills, and ethical standards of the law enforcement community.[66]

If the recruit successfully completes field training and probation, she or he becomes a full-fledged and sworn police officer. If remedial training is required but still fails to produce the desired results, FTO evaluations may serve as a basis for terminating undesirable or ineffective personnel. This can pose a dilemma for administrators, because when FTOs and supervisory personnel determine or recommend that a recruit be terminated for unsatisfactory performance, many police executives remain reluctant to terminate the individual(s) in question, due to the significant costs already incurred during the hiring process. However, this economic shortsightedness could cost the agency more through the years than the cost of training—in terms of civil liability and strained community relations. It is sometimes necessary to terminate probationary officers who do not satisfy the demands placed on them during field training.

Formalized field training programs make it easier for both the FTOs and the recruits to assess progress. One researcher indicated, "FTOs are no longer macho types, although certain physical and survival skills remain important. Good FTOs teach their trainees

**SAGE Journal Article:** Field Training Officers, Their Trainees, and Allegations of Misconduct

**Field Training:** Occurs immediately following successful recruit training; during field training, new officers are paired with specially trained veterans and are evaluated on how they perform on the street, normally in the patrol division; field training programs normally last anywhere from six weeks to six months

**Probationary Period:** The period starting on the first day of recruit training, during which the performance of new officers is evaluated; this period ranges from six months to two years, depending on the agency; during probation, officers are "employees at will" and do not enjoy any of the employment protections (such as grievance procedures) granted to officers who have successfully completed their probationary periods

**Field Training Officers (FTOs):** Officers who have been selected and trained to direct, evaluate, and correct the performance of recruits immediately after their basic academy training

how to recognize and deal effectively with problems in ways other than the use of physical force. Trained FTOs know that an officer's verbalizations should be used to avoid problems rather than create them."[67]

Although the FTO program continues to be used today, the **Police Training Officer (PTO) program** is a more recent postacademy training program. The PTO program "provides a foundation of lifelong learning that prepares new officers for the complexities of policing."[68] A PTO program is different from the traditional methods often employed in policing training. Learners are presented with real-life problems and follow a pattern of discovery whereby they express ideas about solving a problem, list facts already known surrounding the problem, determine what they need to know and where to go for the answers, develop an action plan, and—finally—evaluate their outcomes.[69]

### Ongoing In-Service Training

**In-service training**, also known as **continuing professional education (CPE)**, is one of the cornerstones of professionalism.

Most police personnel receive periodic in-service training that is provided by department personnel, training consultants hired by the department, or regional or local training boards. Most law enforcement agencies require their officers to complete in-service training to maintain competency. From management's perspective, in-service training enhances efficiency and effectiveness and may be an important factor in work motivation.[70] Those with specialty skills need ongoing refreshers and can share their skills with others through in-service training.

Further, inadequate training could be a basis for liability under Section 1983 actions.[71] The U.S. Supreme Court, in deciding the case of *City of Canton v. Harris*, noted that inadequate police training may constitute a jurisdictional liability "if the failure to train amounts to deliberate indifference to the rights of persons with whom the police come into contact and the deficiency in the training program is closely related to the injury suffered."[72]

■ **Police Training Officer (PTO) Program:** Recently developed field training program that many researchers and police executives claim is effective at helping new officers entering the field develop problem-solving skills rarely seen at the early stages of their career; the PTO program involves two primary training areas: substantive topics and core competencies

■ **In-service Training:** Also known as **continuing professional education**, the intent is to keep professionals up to date with continuous changes that affect their practice

Although most departments offer occasional in-service training, many conduct it in a more random way, with no real plan or program in mind. It can be viewed as a somewhat necessary evil by both those conducting it and those being trained—rather than as a valuable means of keeping current in the field.

Video Link:
County Police Begin
Training to Patrol Camden

### Licensing

In some states, professional boards issue licenses to qualified individuals who are required to meet established qualifications. In many cases, this includes some form of in-service training. Licensure of professionals has served as a gate-keeping function by ensuring the proficiency of professionals who provide services to others, and it protects the profession itself by determining who can use the title.[73] This requires that the government create a governing body to regulate licensure and discipline those who violate their privileges or are found to be performing without a license. (See Case in Point 5.1 for an example of the license requirement for Missouri police officers.)

## Technological Advances and Online Training

Policing strategies and technological advances are closely and dynamically related. Radar changed the way the police enforced speeding laws. The advent of Tasers offers a new option in use-of-force situations. Global positioning systems (GPS) and electronic monitoring devices on probationers and parolees help keep real-time tabs on high-risk citizens.

In the world of training, online courses are promising to reach large numbers of officers and keep associated costs—which can be significant—to a minimum. Online education initially gained popularity more than 10 years ago and has been gaining popularity since then. Improved technology has produced sophisticated yet user-friendly online delivery platforms that make interaction between student and teacher as robust as that of a traditional training or education environment. Audiovisual capabilities, such as document viewing and sharing, animation, and interactive exercises, offer a wide range of training possibilities.

Online training is not suitable for some police training needs, such as emergency driving and firearms training. But, with the addition of computers in today's police cars, a good deal of online training can be done on the job. It can be used to teach and test things like knowledge of policy and law prior to conducting the "hands-on" portions. By breaking training courses into small modules, officers can complete one module a day (or week or month or whatever). The important point is that officers can continue to work their regular assignments. Why spend time covering recurring policy training when the student can complete the training in his or her patrol car, free of charge! This also provides the agency with a permanent record of the officer's test scores.

© AP Photo/The News-Item

Training officers mentor, observe, and evaluate probationary officers.

Continuing professional education is crucial to keeping officers' skills sharp. Here officers receive additional training on the proper use and safety procedures for Tasers.

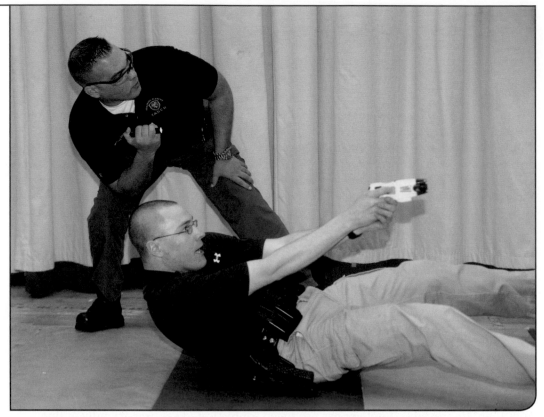

Steve Liss/The LIFE Images Collection/Getty Images

**CASE IN POINT** 5.1

The state of Missouri requires that all persons commissioned as peace officers possess a valid peace officer's license. The director of the Commission on Peace Officer Standards and Training establishes the "minimum age, citizenship, and general education requirements and may require a qualifying score on a certification examination as conditions of eligibility for a peace officer license."

The number of hours of basic training for licensure is a minimum of 470 and a maximum of 600. However, up to 1,000 hours may be required for license by state law enforcement agencies.

Peace officers in Missouri who make traffic stops are required to receive three hours of training within the law enforcement "continuing education three-year reporting period concerning the prohibition against racial profiling and such training shall promote understanding and respect for racial and cultural differences and the use of effective, noncombative methods for carrying out law enforcement duties in a racially and culturally diverse environment."

A peace officer's license can be suspended immediately if the officer is under indictment for, charged with, or convicted of a felony or if the officer is a clear and present danger to public health or safety.

1. Is three hours of training on racial profiling adequate?
2. What is more effective at eliminating racial bias from local police practice, leadership attitudes or training?
3. Discuss some circumstances under which police officers should be disciplined or terminated. Be specific.

*Source:* "Peace officers, selection, training and discipline," *Missouri Revised Statutes*, Chapter 590, Section 590.020 to 590.090, 2011.

## Exhibit 5.1

### Internet-Based Training Portal Topics

- *Terrorism awareness*
- *Hazardous materials*
- *Workplace harassment*
- *Federal firearm laws*
- *Search and seizure*
- *Dealing with people with mental retardation*
- *Cultural diversity*
- *Crime scene investigation*
- *Weapons of mass destruction*
- *Sexual assault*

*Source:* "Partnering for Progress: Maine Law Enforcement Online Training Initiative," by Schwartz, Rogers, and Plaisted, 2009. *The Police Chief, 76*(11), 1–7.

An additional example of alternative methods of police training is the **Use of Force Training Simulator (UFTS)**, which uses computer-generated images (CGI) and speech technology that enable variability in characters and scenarios and responses to user commands and conversation.[74] CGI allows the police trainer to incorporate an array of features such as character ethnicity, voice, gender, mood, and compliance, in addition to weather and time of day. The speech recognition capability of the UFTS enables the police trainee to converse with CGI characters, and the nature and the tone of the conversation from the trainee influence the character and scenario responses.[75] Using this technology, the trainee can attempt to gain the suspect's compliance by using less-than-lethal force. Alternatively, the officer can cause the suspect's level of resistance to the officer's commands to escalate.

Many law enforcement agencies use this new and interactive form of training. Perhaps one of the more innovative programs is one started and sponsored by a partnership between the Minnesota Chiefs of Police Association, the Minnesota Sheriffs' Association, and the League of Minnesota Cities Insurance Trust, known as **Peace officer Accredited TRaining OnLine (PATROL)**.[76] Dozens of training courses are now offered online and are available to any law enforcement agency in the state for a nominal fee per officer. The cost of online training is far less than for traditional teaching methods. The topics are varied and include the use of force, blood-borne pathogens, and current legal issues, to name a few. More agencies are turning to this easily accessible and relatively affordable form of training to reach more officers over longer distances. Approximately 92% of respondents rated the Maine Law Enforcement Online Training Initiative system as almost as effective as or better than traditional classroom training.[77]

### Who Should Conduct Police Training?

Police trainers often come from diverse backgrounds. Trainers may include police officers, physicians, computer experts, self-defense experts, college professors, and business leaders, to name a few. They may be men or women and may be racially or ethnically the same or different from their students. In general, the broader the spectrum of qualified trainers and the greater the exposure to different skills,

**Use of Force Training Simulator (UFTS):** Technology that employs computer-generated images (CGI) and speech technology that enable variability in characters and scenarios as well as character and scenario responses to user commands and conversation

**Peace officer Accredited TRaining OnLine (PATROL):** Innovative and inexpensive way to provide a myriad of in-service training opportunities to officers on a statewide basis; this asynchronous, online training initiative was formed by a partnership between the Minnesota Chiefs of Police Association, the Minnesota Sheriffs' Association, and the League of Minnesota Cities Insurance Trust

the better.[78] Some police officers make good trainers when they have both information to share and good communication skills to present their information. It is important to note that these are two separate, equally important requirements. It is not enough to be an expert if good communication skills are lacking. Similarly, it does little good to have expert communicators present out-of-date or irrelevant information. Unfortunately, both situations occur in police training. When in-service or retired officers meet both requirements of a successful trainer, they often have a significant advantage over other trainers. Although other trainers may be similarly qualified, a current or former police officer often has greater credibility among police personnel.

A related issue is the education requirements for police trainers. Only about two-thirds of police training facilities had an educational requirement for full-time trainers.[79] Of those, the most frequent requirement was a high school diploma or GED, and the least frequent requirement was a bachelor's degree.[80]

It is common in many police agencies to prepare officers for their role as an FTO by sending them to instructor development programs that teach differences in learning styles, adult learning theory, and communication skills. In fact, many agencies require that FTOs attend an instructor development school prior to their final appointment as FTOs.

It is essential, however, that police training also be conducted by those outside the profession, for two reasons. First, many of the skills required of trainers and educators are not frequently found among police officers, such as technical skills, ability to analyze trainee interactions, and disease prevention expertise. Many academies require their full-time trainers to have a certification as a subject matter expert and as a trainer.[81] Second, and perhaps most importantly, relying only on those within the profession for training typically leads to a myopic worldview, which serves to isolate members from the rest of society. Progressive thinking suggests that the police need to be more—not less—connected to their communities.

One shortcoming of police training is that there is not enough emphasis on the skills needed to deliver training effectively. Trainers need to establish a "three-dimensional" delivery environment.[82] First, the instructor must have the requisite knowledge to deliver accurate topical information. Second, the trainer must possess the facilitation skills needed to deliver information effectively. Third, the trainer must have the ability to accurately assess trainee retention.

Thus, the reasons for recruit failure are not always directly attributable to the shortcomings of the new officer. One example is a case involving the South San Francisco Police Department (SSFPD) in 2002. That year, the chief became concerned about the 50% failure rate of recruits in the FTO program. He had been to a conference that addressed the importance of acknowledging and responding to various adult learning styles in the training and education environment, so he set up a series of meetings with training personnel and professors from a local university. A review of their FTO program showed no consideration of different learning styles and concluded that this may have caused confusion among the recruits.[83] Key actions that led to the modification of the SSFPD's FTO program included the following:

- A more detailed understanding of adult learning principles and different learning styles, provided by the local professoriate
- Recognition of differences in generations and culture between FTOs and recruits (at the time, the FTOs were baby boomers, and the recruits were both Generation Xers—born between 1965 and 1980—and Millennials)
- Proper assessment of preferred learning styles among recruits
- Commensurate changes to the program[84]

The most significant program changes instituted as a result of this effort were as follows:

- Including a variety of approaches, taking audio, visual, and kinesthetic preferences into account
- Customizing training by facilitation through the integration of preferred learning styles, whenever possible or feasible
- Engaging recruits in more dialogue, so that the new information can be related to their past experiences
- Reinforcing learning by having recruits verbalize their understanding of what they have just learned[85]

Observers found this basically simple solution to a rather complex problem resulted in a greater success rate among recruits for a relatively low cost.[86]

Additional tips for a positive training experience include knowing the average skill level of attendees ahead of time and planning accordingly. This also includes the technical skills needed to operate any equipment. In addition, using real-life or job-related applications can emphasize and clearly demonstrate the benefits of the training at hand. When feasible, a hands-on approach for the learners is desirable, especially with technical equipment.[87]

Individuals who have a passion for training, a knowledge of the specific subject, a style that is conducive to interaction with students, and a willingness to learn and to teach are the best suited and most well prepared for the task.

There are eight general qualities of effective law enforcement trainers:

- Humility
- Honesty
- Dedication
- Passion
- Preparedness
- Inspiration
- Purposefulness
- Style[88]

## ■ CHALLENGES

Administrators face many challenges in their decisions around exactly what training to require of their officers and how to manage the time and financial burden that training demands.

One challenge with in-service training is its geographic availability. In response to this dilemma, some states have developed mobile training units that provide access to training within a specified geographic area to make attendance easier for police personnel from rural areas and small towns. Unfortunately, budget cuts and, in some instances, union contracts have made it increasingly difficult for departments to release personnel to attend such training.

In some instances, longer training courses are offered to senior-level personnel as a reward for longevity rather than to personnel who are in positions in which they could make active use of the information provided. In addition, much of the information provided during these courses remains in the minds of those who attend rather than being disseminated to others in the department through in-service training sessions. Still, a good deal of the information obtained from such courses has practical application.

**Author Video:**
What challenges do law enforcement face to meet training requirements?

## Funding for Training

Law enforcement agencies face a growing dilemma. They are confronting many new burdens, such as computer crimes, identity theft, the threat of terrorism, and the need for homeland defense. However, department resources are not growing as rapidly as the increased demand for police services. On the contrary, many agencies have experienced a decline in funding, and training often represents one of the first budget items cut. For training to gain and maintain a degree of importance, agencies must be confident that their resources are well spent and that training leads to positive results for both the police and the communities they serve.

> For training to gain and maintain a degree of importance, agencies must be confident that their resources are well spent and that training leads to positive results for both the police and the communities they serve.

Cost and convenience are huge factors. When an agency sends an officer to training, it has two choices: (1) run short that day (or night); do not hire an officer to work overtime to fill in, or (2) pay the overtime.

What happens when the number of hours or programs is cut? This is what often occurs in times of budgetary shortfalls. Approximately 70% of police agencies reduced or eliminated training programs in 2010 as a result of budget reductions.[89] These data were based on a survey of over 600 police agencies by the Police Executive Research Forum, whose report states, "When you cut training, not only are you no longer having to pay for the training, you're also not having to pull the officers off of the street and replace them with other officers who may be working overtime."[90] Attempts to offset the high costs of training have been implemented and actually show promise in this regard. For example, Mobile Team Training Unit (MTTU) IV provides law enforcement certification training to 39 municipal and sheriffs' police agencies in Illinois and Iowa.[91]

**Web Link:**
LAPD broke labor laws in requiring some officers to repay training costs, court rules

## Mandatory Versus Voluntary Training

Mandatory participation may adversely affect the quality of the learning experience. This is a difficult and controversial issue, one that most police agencies are fully aware of and struggle with daily. Training in communication, human relations, cultural competency, analysis of encounters, and negotiating is available and has become more widespread, but may still be poorly attended unless attendance is mandatory. There is a significant difference between "mandated" and "elective" training. Typically, officers who are forced to attend such training fail to see the benefits of the training.

Although officers often tolerate certain forms of mandated training, many of those same officers enjoy attending more advanced courses—especially, when there is a nexus to the job. It is safe to say that certain forms of training are more enjoyable than others, more highly sought after, and given to senior officers or administrators because of their tenure.

One problem is that something like a new court decision or litigation that was created by the actions of a small group of officers often results in department-wide training efforts to prevent similar events in the future, even when the chances of an officer encountering the situation in question are slim to none. Nonetheless, any time there is a new requirement, the whole agency is typically mandated, usually by law, to attend the training.

Researchers point to a variety of benefits associated with a policy of **mandatory continuing education (MCE)**, including the following:

- MCE serves to either eliminate the laggards from the ranks of the profession or revive their interest in learning.[92]
- By virtue of the very existence of MCE, the quantity and quality of its programs tend to increase.[93]
- Professionals view participation in MCE as being more acceptable to professionals than periodic reexamination for license renewal.[94]
- MCE protects the public from those who are unwilling to keep up with current developments in their field, thus increasing public confidence.[95]

**Mandatory Continuing Education (MCE):** Career-long training standards for police professionals to maintain and improve their professional competence

It is worth noting that, among many other professions and their related literature, participation in MCE is no longer a debate; rather, it has become accepted practice. Unfortunately, the field of policing has not consistently incorporated this educational philosophy.

## Training and Police Leadership

One way of determining the value that police supervisors attach to training is to examine the extent to which they participate themselves. Historically, many police supervisors (including chiefs) avoided training and rationalized their absences by pointing out the other demands on their time such as meetings, planning, administrative chores, and bureaucratic requirements. In reality, the absence of police supervisors from training sessions may have more to do with other factors.

Some police executives operate as if they have no need for additional information. Why should those at the top sacrifice their time and energy to attend training when those still striving for such positions may benefit more? Related to this may be doubts about how well they will perform in the classroom. What if they appear uninformed before their subordinates? What if their contributions to the training session are not appreciated or well received? What if their performance is exceeded by other, lower-ranking trainees? While these concerns are real, they are worth risking to demonstrate that training is not a frill or superficial symbol, but a valued, ongoing part of the organization's performance.

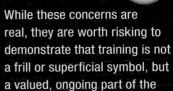

> While these concerns are real, they are worth risking to demonstrate that training is not a frill or superficial symbol, but a valued, ongoing part of the organization's performance.

However, it may be detrimental to the functioning or morale of an organization if leaders are less informed than officers. It is clearly frustrating to return from a period of training and education with an idea that seems ideal for implementation in one's own organization, only to be ignored by supervisors.

The sharing of training content is most effective when it includes supervisory personnel who may otherwise find the concepts disseminated difficult to understand and may continue to operate using outdated information. Again, the commitment to training must come from administrators, along with the recognition that training is one of the ways that police personnel can receive an acknowledgement. Merit-based selection for a specialized training course conducted at the department's expense is a rewarding experience, as is recognition of an officer's ability to train others. Without such recognition, training is more likely to be viewed in an unfavorable light.

Selected police personnel have the opportunity to participate in longer-term, specialized, or more intensive training offered by a variety of training institutes around the country. Among the more popular of these training groups are the Northwestern University Center for Public Safety, the Southern Police Institute, and the FBI National Academy, all of which offer courses lasting a week to several months. Courses offered by these institutions cover topics ranging from traffic investigation to executive management. In California, the Law Enforcement Command College began operation in 1984 with the mission of preparing "law enforcement leaders of today for the challenges of the future."[96] The program focuses on the following:

**Policing in Practice Video:** Challenging aspects of the training process

- Leadership principles needed to influence the future direction of the organization
- Strategies to identify emerging issues and provide a proactive response
- Skills and knowledge necessary to anticipate and prepare for the future
- Methods and benefits of sharing information
- Use of stakeholders in problem solving

The program emphasizes adult learning theories and holds students accountable for their participation.[97]

### Training Effectiveness

Many professions use sophisticated evaluation techniques to assess program effectiveness and relevancy and emphasize research that attempts to link training to job performance.[98] Proper evaluation helps determine whether training changes the way employees do their job and whether the change is what leaders want. One of the major problems that criminal justice training programs have encountered through the years is their lack of emphasis on evaluation with respect to the relevance and applicability of training.

Although training techniques continue to advance, many questions remain about the impact of training on the job. The effects of training are frequently improperly assessed by police agencies.

**Web Link:**
How Police Training
Contributes to
Avoidable Death

Police training has few easily measurable results, because training does not often result in clearly measurable end products. The impact of training is often measured in terms of the numbers of hours or programs attended annually. Clearly, such measurement fails to evaluate a program's quality or relevance. Policy agency leaders need to know if training provides useful information and if trainees understand the material. Leaders too often neglect even a simple evaluation because they *assume* that training is effective.

A reliable way to assess the value of training is to conduct routine evaluations, which would ideally include a pretest of and posttest of attendees' knowledge of the material. Vendors of police training are still analyzing program effectiveness by evaluating participants' attitudes only *after* instruction is completed. Research concerning CPE activities and their impact on relevancy, competency, and improved job performance suggests that evaluation efforts should concentrate on techniques such as practice audits and complex task analyses to achieve a positive relationship between participation in CPE activities and professional competency.[99]

Important research from the 1980s offered insight as to why some training programs are more effective than others in producing positive changes in job performance. The research analyzed eight studies that produced positive changes in performance by physicians after participation in CPE activities. The following five elements were common to all of the studies:

1. **Specified audience.** All of the participants expressed a desire to learn something.
2. **Identified learning needs.** All participants could identify a learning need and a gap between present and optimal performance.
3. **Clear goals and objectives.** It was clear to everyone involved what was to be learned.
4. **Relevant learning methods and emphasis on participation.** Learning was participative in nature, occurred in familiar surroundings, and involved small group discussions.
5. **Systematic effort to evaluate.** Assessment and evaluation procedures began the day the programs were developed, course development was based on clear definitions of learning needs, and a variety of evaluation techniques were employed.[100]

There are many reasons to question the effectiveness of CPE. The purpose and benefits of CPE and whether participation should be mandatory for professionals have been extensively discussed in the literature for nearly two decades, from the mid- or late 1970s to the early 1990s. It is not a given that participation in CPE activities keeps a police officer current in the field. Nor is it a certainty that police personnel participate in these activities at all.

Best practice, the technological revolution, and public accountability are some of the underlying and important reasons for professionals to consistently update their knowledge and skills. Experience shows us that government intervention often results when professional groups fail in their responsibility to maintain and improve their level of competence and professionalism. Imposing increased education and training standards from within policing is critical. The police must perceive participation in CPE activities as a natural extension of the job.

## SUMMARY

The underlying issues regarding police education and training, in all of its forms, have always assumed an aura of controversy. Questions such as the following continually arise: How much initial and continuing training is actually needed? What should be the minimum level of formal education required of police officers? Are training and higher education related to work performance? Who should conduct the education and training—academicians or police officers?

The two types of programs—training and education—can and must coexist; improved cooperation between proponents of each can only lead to more qualified police officers. Law enforcement agencies must recognize the changes that are taking place in policing. These changes include an increase in the educational level of citizens and the number of police programs based on increased police–citizen interactions. These two developments require a review of law enforcement educational policies. The main question could be not whether college education is necessary for police officers, but how much and how soon.

Other issues involving training and education are intimately related to organizational and individual civil liability issues. Agencies must be prepared to demonstrate to the courts that their officers have received proper training, such as in firearm proficiency, the use of force, constitutional issues germane to policing (search and seizure requirements, excessive use of force, etc.). The courts have also ruled that police agencies must be able to demonstrate that they utilize sound supervisory practices and that they do not retain personnel in a way that could be construed as negligent.

One form of training stressed in this chapter is of extreme importance: officers' initial field training received after successful completion of academy or basic training. The selection of the right officers to be field trainers is critical, because those individuals have tremendous influence on the subsequent behavior of the rookies they train. As such, these officers should be men and women committed to professional policing and the mission of their respective organizations. Appointing officers to these positions on the basis of seniority alone is an unwise policy and should be avoided.

Numerous studies conducted through the years have concluded that officers with higher levels of education tend to be more professional, receive fewer citizen complaints, possess more tolerance for diversity, possess better oral and written communication skills, and seem better suited for community-oriented policing strategies than their high school graduate counterparts. Still, there are those who maintain that street experience rather than higher education makes or breaks an officer. Most authorities, however, assert that higher education is a definite advantage to the individual officers, their respective agencies, and the profession.

## KEY TERMS

- Training 99
- Education 99
- Office of the Police Corps and Law Enforcement Education 100
- Police Association for College Education (PACE) 102
- Academy of Criminal Justice Sciences (ACJS) 104
- Recruit training 110
- Field training 113
- Probationary period 113
- Field training officers (FTOs) 113
- Police Training Officer (PTO) program 114
- In-service training 114
- Continuing professional education (CPE) 114
- Use of Force Training Simulator (UFTS) 117
- Peace officer Accredited TRaining OnLine (PATROL) 117
- Mandatory continuing education (MCE) 120

**$SAGE edge™**

Review key terms with eFlashcards.

## DISCUSSION QUESTIONS

1. Why is recurrent training so important to police personnel? What are some of the possible consequences of failure to train?

2. What types of topics should be included in police training? Who should conduct the training?

3. How would you evaluate the effectiveness of a police training program? Why is evaluation so important?

4. What is the relationship between education and training? Can one replace the other? Why or why not?

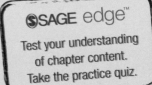

**$SAGE edge™**

Test your understanding of chapter content. Take the practice quiz.

5. Discuss the arguments for and against college education for police officers.

6. Is there legal justification for requiring some college for entry-level police officers? What are the legal issues involved with this requirement?

7. Has the relationship between college education and improved police performance been thoroughly evaluated?

## INTERNET EXERCISES

1. Use the web to locate the home pages of at least five different local police agencies. Find information pertaining to their entry-level requirements and compare and contrast those agencies to find significant differences. Explain which agency's requirements are the most applicable to the activities of police officers in today's society.

2. Regarding criminal justice curricula in higher education, go to the home page of the Academy of Criminal Justice Sciences (ACJS) and peruse the sections relevant to what ACJS refers to as its "curriculum standards." Do you agree with the ACJS recommendations? Why or why not?

3. Using the *FBI Law Enforcement Bulletin,* examine applicable journals from the issues generated during the past couple of years and identify the views of the Federal Bureau of Investigation on the importance of higher education for those working in law enforcement.

4. Use International Association of Chiefs of Police (IACP) website to determine its recommendations regarding higher education and in-service training in the field of policing.

## STUDENT STUDY SITE

**$SAGE edge™** edge.sagepub.com/coxpolicing3e

**Sharpen your skills with SAGE edge!**

SAGE edge for Students provides a personalized approach to help you accomplish your coursework goals in an easy-to-use learning environment. You'll find action plans, mobile-friendly eFlashcards, and quizzes as well as videos, web resources, and links to SAGE journal articles to support and expand on the concepts presented in this chapter.

# CHAPTER 6

## POLICE WORK: OPERATIONS AND FUNCTIONS

© REUTERS/Reuters Photography

## CHAPTER LEARNING OBJECTIVES:

1. Explain why the way that police view their role determines the nature of the functions they perform

2. List the priorities of the three main styles of policing

3. Describe how the three approaches to allocation are used to determine the appropriate number of police personnel for various jurisdictions

4. Evaluate the effectiveness of each of the four main forms of patrol

5. Discuss implications of the seminal Kansas City preventive patrol experiment and other similar research results

6. Describe the strategies to evaluate officer and agency performance

7. Identify how the relationship between the local police and the local media can either enhance or hinder police–community relations

U.S. police officers are expected to monitor public manners and morals, prevent crime by patrolling, apprehend criminals, recover stolen property, resolve domestic disputes, and accomplish dozens of additional tasks. Police performance in these and other areas is generally governed by the U.S. Constitution, related statutes, and court decisions, all of which outline the powers, duties, and limitations of police officers. City charters and ordinances further govern operations at the municipal level. The following state statute is an example of the unique powers granted to police officers.

> The *Illinois Compiled Statutes* (Illinois General Assembly, 2012) describe police officers as "conservators of the peace" with powers to (1) arrest or cause to be arrested, with or without process, all persons who break the peace or are found violating any municipal ordinance or any criminal law of the state; (2) commit arrested persons in custody overnight or on Sunday in any safe place, or until they can be brought before a proper court (65 ILCS 11-1-2).

Other states, of course, have similar statutes that serve to indicate some of the specific functions of the police (e.g., serving warrants, detaining persons), as well as some of the general ones (e.g., keeping the peace). As a check on police power, the Bill of Rights and civil rights legislation restrict police behavior by establishing, defining, and guaranteeing certain freedoms for all U.S. citizens (see Chapter 9). This means that police powers and actions must balance delicately with the rights of the individual to freedom of speech, religion, press, assembly, and security from unreasonable searches and seizures.

Police functions are performed through the processes of arrest and detention, investigation, and police–community relations programs. To help ensure that these processes are carried out successfully, the police must recruit, select, train, educate, evaluate, and promote officers capable of facing ever-increasing challenges. Some of the near-future challenges to law enforcement include "local and transnational criminals engaging in more elaborate schemes, the increased movement of money through sophisticated local and international communications systems, and the migration of criminal enterprises to terrorist-related activities."[1] The Michigan Commission on Law Enforcement Standards noted that the number of crimes associated with technology, such as identity theft, has dramatically expanded the responsibilities of police over the past 15 years.

An officer performing a frequent police function, a "routine" traffic stop.

# ■ BASIC POLICE FUNCTIONS

The three main basic police functions are crime prevention, law enforcement, and order maintenance. Though these purposes are generally the same across all agencies, there may be tremendous variation in the manner in which officers perform their tasks—even on the same shift, in the same division, and in the same department. Department organization and philosophy, the exercise of discretion by individual officers, training and education, and many other factors influence police performance, especially officers' encounters with other citizens.

**Policing in Practice Video:**
Experience of basic police functions and experience of patrolling

Frequently, newspapers, news magazines, and "reality" police programs on television show police officers reaching for their guns as they burst through the doors of an apartment in a housing project. In the background is a police car with flashing lights. A less dramatic scene shows a policewoman talking to a grateful mother whose lost child was returned. Which of these illustrations more accurately describes the police role? How frequently do these kinds of events occur? What percentage of police activity is violent and dangerous? Have police activities changed since the terrorist attacks on September 11, 2001, or since the devastation of Hurricane Katrina? What do police officers really do?

The answer to the last question is that officers spend a good deal of their time on routine matters, including taking statements, writing reports, running errands, and attending court. Traffic, social service, police-initiated events, and crimes against property account for most of the rest of a patrol officer's time. Only a small percentage of the officer's time is spent on serious crime.

Patrol officers' responsibilities in large municipal police departments include the following:

**Author Video:**
Police functions and duties

- Patrol
- Traffic enforcement
- Community relations
- Criminal investigation
- Warrant service and property control
- Narcotics investigation
- Identification
- Intervening in domestic violence situations
- Civil process
- Vice investigation
- Dispatching
- Bail/court officer and other duties[2]

The way the police view their role helps to determine the nature of the functions they perform and the manner in which they organize to perform these functions. Any list of police functions is likely to be incomplete, but the following police functions are common in many agencies:

- Preservation of public peace
- Protection of the rights of persons and property
- Prevention of crime
- Detection and arrest of those breaking the law
- Enforcement and prevention of violations of state laws and city ordinances
- Service of processes and notices in civil and criminal proceedings[3]

## Order Maintenance and Law Enforcement

It is difficult to arrive at a formal and universally accepted definition of the role of the police. Most authorities recognize the existence of a law enforcement role and an order maintenance component of policing.

The term *order maintenance* describes the police maintaining the status quo by using interventions with short-term effects to keep society stable and functioning by acceptable rules. Order maintenance can involve activity that is at the same time necessary and controversial. It is necessary because the community dislikes disorder and controversial because the police often use some form of coercion or force. The police can maintain order by settling a neighbor-versus-neighbor dispute, directing traffic at the scene of an accident, or calming an angry patron at a restaurant.

The distinction between law enforcement and order maintenance for certain activities is not always clear, especially when civil law gets involved, such as with landlord–tenant disputes or a customer refusing to pay for an auto repair bill because she is not happy with the work.

The on-scene objectives of the police and their preferred intervention techniques might be best represented as a continuum of responses, not as separate categories. For example, a theft involving acquaintances is often conflict management, while a lost child—which appears to be a public service/public safety problem—may evolve into a law enforcement issue (e.g., kidnapping, rape, or murder). Hence, the police often respond to a given situation with an assumed on-scene objective and with a preferred intervention technique, but both very often change as they obtain additional information.[4] Thus, it is clear that there are no mutually exclusive categories of police intervention techniques.

■ **Broken Windows Theory:** A theory stating that neighborhood social disorder causes a decline of the overall condition of the neighborhood, which leads to criminal activity

### Broken Windows and Zero Tolerance Policing

Order maintenance typically involves calls for service such as suspicious person complaints, intoxicated persons, or loud-music calls. Such relatively minor complaints are basic to an approach referred to as "broken windows." A major premise of **broken windows theory** is that neighborhood social disorder causes a decline of overall conditions and leads to more violent criminal activity.[5] Degraded conditions lead to more fearful residents who disengage and withdraw, which creates an environment where more serious crime can occur. This idea was introduced during the 1980s. To prevent serious criminal activity, police focus on order maintenance, most of which does not directly involve criminal behaviors. According to broken windows theory, "fighting the minor indicators of neighborhood decay and disorder—broken windows, graffiti, even litter— helps prevent major crimes."[6] Early studies supported the premise, but over the years, evaluations did not demonstrate a strong causal relationship between broken windows order maintenance and reductions in crime rates.[7] Broken windows has been criticized for being long on public popularity, but weak when rigorously evaluated. Its claims to crime reduction in New York City, for example, were discredited by those pointing to lower crime rates in other cities that did not implement broken windows and that the decline in crack cocaine use was far more of an influence in reducing crime rates.

According to the "broken windows" theory, addressing issues such as graffiti, vandalism, and littering in this neighborhood can help prevent the rise of violent crime.

**Video Link:**
Broken Windows'
Policing, Three
Decades On

Some argue, however, that broken windows–style order maintenance is valuable in improving community life even if it does not significantly affect serious crime rates—that improving public order has an intrinsic value separate from police officers' role in crime prevention.[8]

Order maintenance policing has also been associated with "**zero tolerance**," which implies that officers exercise little discretion when enforcing minor offenses and stick to the "letter of the law."[9] Most police organizations adopted this theory and began some form of broken windows policing in the 1980s.

Others have questioned the theory, arguing that broken windows policing has resulted in "mass stop-and-frisks, mass suspicionless searches of housing projects, prohibitions against loitering with known gang members, and aggressive, even repeated arrests of minor misdemeanants."[10] Still others have questioned the effectiveness of the broken windows theory in light of reported increases in some crime rates.

**Zero Tolerance:**
An aggressive policing strategy in which all violators are ticketed or arrested and which disregards extenuating circumstances

### Policing the Mentally Ill

Another way that the police maintain order is by assuming sole responsibility for dealing with mentally ill persons whose behavior warrants some form of intervention. Research has shown that the frequency of contact between police and persons with mental illness has increased significantly in the decades since deinstitutionalization.[11] Training in appropriate responses to the mentally ill has become a more critical skill for police officers. Similarly, public drunkenness often becomes the responsibility of the police; limited bed space and selective admission practices at detoxification centers hinder police attempts to find shelter and care for those who are taken into custody for being drunk in public. At the same time, of course, the use of jails to house public inebriates is deemed inappropriate, further limiting the alternatives available to the police. The police also are frequently called to remove the homeless from streets and parks, because these persons are perceived to have a negative impact on businesses, create an appearance of community neglect, and are often a danger to themselves

**Video Link:**
Memphis police take specialized approach to mental illness

Frequently, police are called on to remove the homeless from the streets, but often have very few options in terms of providing shelter and services.

Image: © epa european pressphoto agency b.v./Alamy

(especially in cold weather). Finding a suitable alternative for the homeless often becomes a difficult task for the police.

## Investigations and Forensic Science

Investigation is another basic function of the police, typically carried out by detectives who dress in plain clothes. Almost all calls to the police involve some type of investigation. Police investigate all types of incidents, from simple vandalism to homicide. Depending on such things as the strength of the evidence, the complexity of the case, and the seriousness of the crime, an initial investigation may result in further, more protracted investigation. Ultimately, the goal of the investigation is to identify, locate, and arrest the suspect for processing through the criminal justice system.

The duties and responsibilities associated with an investigation unit include the following:

- Determining whether a crime was committed
- Searching the crime scene
- Photographing and sketching the crime scene
- Collecting and processing physical evidence
- Interviewing victims and witnesses
- Interrogating suspects
- Maintaining field notes and writing preliminary, follow-up, and supplemental arrest reports
- Maintaining surveillance of suspects and known criminals
- Recovering stolen property
- Arresting suspects
- Preparing criminal cases for court
- Testifying[12]

The timing of investigation activities is often of great importance, as evidence can change, witnesses and suspects become harder to locate, and other opportunities for solving the crime can be lost. A longer-term investigation requires more planning and benefits from clearly defined objectives and strategies, and an analysis of the resources required to conduct the additional inquiry.[13]

There are far fewer personnel in investigations than in patrol. "About 15% of police personnel are assigned to it, much smaller than the 60% assigned to patrol."[14] A national study of detective work reported similar percentages and concluded that investigators account for 16% of all police agency personnel.

Early research by the RAND Corporation and the Police Executive Research Forum examined the efficiency of the criminal investigation process. The RAND study concluded that a substantial amount of an investigator's time is spent in nonproductive work and that investigators' expertise has little impact on the solving of cases. Furthermore, this study concluded that more than half of all serious crimes received no more than superficial attention from investigators and that half of all investigators could be eliminated without negatively influencing the crime clearance rate.[15] Many argue that the actions of patrol officers are extremely important if a criminal investigation is to be successful. Often, the single most important determinant of whether a case will be solved is the information a victim provides to the responding patrol officer. If information that uniquely identifies a perpetrator is not available when the crime is reported to the police, the perpetrator is often not identified.[16]

**Policing in Practice Video:**
Policing in Practice Video: Crime Scene Investigator

Many criminal investigation divisions have established cybercrime units because of the increasing frequency of such crime on the Internet, which includes online sexual predation, distribution of online child pornography, computer fraud, and online theft. Police investigators might assist in operations related to the Federal Bureau of Investigation's (FBI) national security priorities.[17] These include the following:

- Counterterrorism
- Counterintelligence
- Cybercrime
- Public corruption
- Civil rights
- Organized crime
- White-collar crime

### Investigations and Community-Oriented Policing

The adoption of a community-policing philosophy—in all its varieties—by many police departments has influenced investigative unit functions. Many departments reexamined the traditional method of permitting only specialists to conduct criminal investigations and have now trained patrol officers as generalists, permitting them to conduct follow-up investigations.

Rather than simply taking the initial report of the offense and forwarding it to detectives for follow-up, officers conduct follow-up, regardless of the type of crime. In larger departments, investigators usually specialize. For example, detective bureaus are divided among property crime investigators, domestic violence investigators, robbery-homicide investigators, gang investigators, narcotics investigators, and so forth. Using this model, the first officer to respond conducts the complete investigation. Therefore, there is no break in the investigation, and no information is lost.

### Forensics

Despite these changes, police work has remained relatively unchanged over the years. However, police departments have experienced major changes in the application of **forensic science** techniques to the increasing complexity of criminal investigations. Forensic science can be defined as any branch of science used in the resolution of legal disputes.[18] As an example, the West Virginia State Police Forensic Laboratory (2015) outlines forensic science examinations and functions. It covers the proper methods for collecting evidence and maintaining a chain of evidence related to such things as drugs and alcohol; paint, glass, and building materials; biological materials; firearms; fractured, cut, or torn items; and skin impressions.[19]

How have these techniques employed by the police affected criminal investigations? Some believe that technical advancements have resulted in a **CSI effect**, which refers to the television show *Crime Scene Investigation* and the increasing public awareness of advances in DNA testing and other forensic exams and the growing expectation on the part of jurors to see forensic evidence at criminal trials. The result, experts say, is that police are sending much more evidence to labs for testing than they used to.[20] However, one study of randomly summoned jurors revealed that, "although the CSI viewers had higher expectations for scientific evidence than non-CSI viewers, these expectations had little, if any, effect on the respondents' propensity to convict."[21]

DNA analysis *has* had some positive impacts on criminal investigations. One study found that, when conventional investigative techniques were used, a suspect was

**Policing in Practice Video:**
How does your department use social media to engage with the community and in investigations?

**Forensic Science:** Any branch of science used in the resolution of legal disputes

**CSI Effect:** Refers to the perception of scientific testing by television viewers

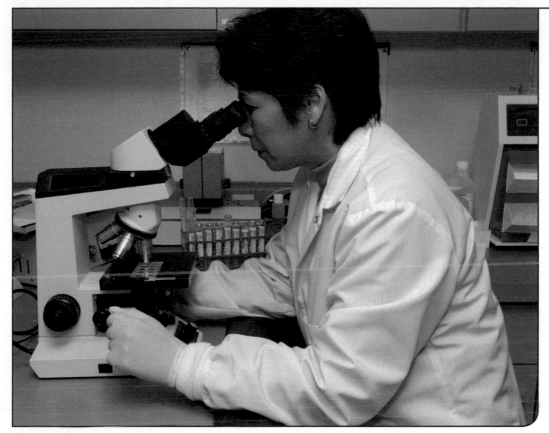

A forensic examiner from the crime lab at work using a comparison microscope on evidence retrieved from a crime scene.

identified 12% of the time, compared with 31% of the cases using DNA evidence. Additional findings of this study include the following:

- Property crime cases that involve the processing of DNA have twice as many suspects identified, arrested, and accepted for prosecution compared with traditional investigations.
- DNA is approximately five times as likely as fingerprints to result in the identification of a suspect.[22]

## ■ STYLES OF POLICING

### Watchman Style

James Q. Wilson identified three relatively distinct types of policing—the watchman style, the legalistic style, and the service style.[23] The **watchman style** involves the principal function as order maintenance rather than law enforcement in cases that do not involve serious crime. The police use the law more as a means of maintaining order than of regulating conduct and judge the seriousness of infractions less by what the law says about them than by their immediate and personal consequences. In other words, circumstances of person and situation are taken into account. Police officers are encouraged to follow the path of least resistance in carrying out their daily duties. Minor issues are to be ignored, but officers are to be "tough" when serious matters arise. This style of policing often occurs in departments with low-level educational requirements (high school education or less), relatively low wages, little formal training, considerable on-the-job training, and few formal policies. Such departments have few specialized personnel; thus, departmental transfers are rare. Officers are encouraged to take individual differences of citizens into account, both when communicating with them and when enforcing the law. Who the citizen is, other than in serious cases, is as important as what he or she has done.[24]

■ **Watchman Style:** Focuses on an order maintenance style of policing

In the legalistic style of policing, juveniles are more frequently detained, and misdemeanor arrests are more common.

©iStockphoto.com/Robert Ingelhart

### Legalistic Style

In police organizations that use a **legalistic style**, officers are encouraged to handle commonplace situations as if they were matters of law enforcement as opposed to order maintenance. Officers frequently issue traffic tickets, detain and arrest juveniles, and arrest for misdemeanors. These officers take action against illicit enterprises on a regular basis. They are under pressure to "produce" arrests and tickets and are expected to simply do their jobs as defined by an administration that views a high volume of traffic and other stops as simply a means of discovering more serious crimes and enhancing revenues.

The legalistic style values technical efficiency, and promotions are based on such efficiency. Administrators prefer middle-class officers with high school educations and emphasize a professional image (new buildings and equipment). The law is used to punish those perceived as deserving of punishment. Supervisors issue orders, and officers follow them, regardless of whether such orders seem appropriate.[25]

### Service Style

The **service style** of policing requires officers to intervene frequently but not formally, take all requests for service seriously, and find alternatives to arrest and other formal sanctions. Officers are encouraged to be consumer-oriented and to meet community needs. Officers are expected to be neat, courteous, and professional. Authority is less centralized, and community relations and public education are viewed as important aspects of policing. The service style values college education, rewards officers with good salaries, and encourages specialized expertise.[26]

■ **Legalistic Style:**
Focus is on law enforcement and arrests

■ **Service Style:**
Searches for alternatives to arrest and the uses of formal sanctions

One researcher proposed another array of police operational styles that focuses on individual officers rather than entire police organizations, suggesting four officer personality types.[27] Enforcers are concerned with the enforcement of laws versus protection of individual rights. Idealists place value on the individual rights of all citizens. Realists focus on neither enforcement of laws nor the protection of individual rights, and optimists are more service-oriented and value individual rights.[28]

Although most police organizations have characteristics of all four styles of policing, tendencies to emphasize one style over the others are often easily discernible. In fact, a community may become known for its emphasis on a specific style of policing. ("Don't speed in that town; they ticket everybody"; "That town lives off income from traffic citations"; or "You can get anything you want in that town as long as you don't rock the boat.") Many watchman and legalistic departments exist, but service-style organizations appear to represent the current trend in policing. This makes sense, given the trend toward community-oriented policing and cooperation between the police and other citizens in maintaining order and enforcing the law. An emphasis on community-oriented policing and problem solving has required police administrators to reexamine the abilities of current personnel to accomplish these initiatives.

**Web Link:** When Schooling Meets Policing

Although research supports the belief that police officers have certain general styles that influence their behaviors, it may be that other factors are more important.[29] These factors are personal characteristics (age, gender, education); situational characteristics (demeanor of the parties involved, seriousness of the offense); environmental characteristics (amount of perceived crime in the neighborhood, social disorganization); and organizational characteristics (department style, shift assignment, management support).[30] Furthermore, a police officer's style could change during his or her career, following the assignment to a different patrol shift or a special unit such as narcotics.

## YOU ??? DECIDE — 6.1

Police officers are now wearing a type of body camera on their uniforms and, in some cases, also equipping stun guns with cameras. Janesville, Wisconsin, police record all interactions with residents. "The video cameras are about the size of a Bic lighter and clip onto an officer's uniform." They turn off and on by touch and are "downloaded at the end of the shift or on to laptops immediately after an incident."

Police officers in Janesville have found the tiny video cameras to be particularly useful for the arrest of intoxicated drivers. "It's hard to write notes about a field sobriety test when you have to watch someone attempt the test and count the number of steps he or she is taking. In the past, officers had to juggle a flashlight and a clipboard while never taking their eyes off the suspected drunk driver."

In the wake of high-profile and lethal police shootings of citizens in Missouri and New York in 2014, President Barack Obama convened the Task Force on 21st Century Policing to explore ways to help repair public confidence in the nation's police forces. The task force issued many justice-related recommendations, some of which pertain to technology. The task force stopped short of specifically recommending the use of body cameras on the police, calling it a complex issue and noting the difficulties in implementing it. In addition, the task force acknowledged that there is a difficult balance between monitoring the police, protecting privacy rights of citizens, and the temptation to rely too heavily on the video as a source of infallible information. Obama himself cautioned that cameras would not be a "panacea."

The hope of many is that the cameras will serve a tempering influence on the police. In any case, the use of body cameras is likely to increase. As it does, each state will have to grapple with the fine points of using such monitoring devices. According to Wisconsin statutes, police are not required to inform a person that they are recording an interview or a traffic stop.

1. Should police officers be required to use tiny video cameras to record actions of all persons they encounter? Why or why not?

2. Do you believe public knowledge that police are recording all interactions with the public has an effect on police–citizen interactions? If so, explain.

3. Under what circumstances should officers be required or allowed to turn cameras off?

*Suggestions for addressing these questions can be found on the Student Study Site:* **edge.sagepub.com/ coxpolicing3e**

*Sources:* "Janesville police officers see benefit in body cameras," by Ann Marie Ames, 2012. *Janesville Extra.* Retrieved May 2012 from http://gazettextra.com; "Obama task force urges independent probes of police killings," by David Jackson, March 2, 2015. *USA Today.* Retrieved from http://www.usatoday.com/story/news/nation/2015/03/02/obama-task-force-on-21st-century-policing-ferguson/24258019/

## ■ PATROL STRENGTH AND ALLOCATION

Before determining the required number of patrol officers and their allocation, an agency must determine the desired outcomes of patrol. Patrol can be divided into three related outcomes.[31] First, the presence of patrol officers may frighten offenders away or influence them not to commit violations, at least until the police leave the area. There is sufficient evidence to conclude that these actions do not actually prevent crime, but rather simply displace or delay the criminal activity. Second, patrol provides police an opportunity to determine the probabilities of criminal behavior and, through preventive strategies, to reduce or eliminate those probabilities. Third, patrol provides police the opportunity to respond to calls for assistance in a timely manner.

**Policing in Practice Video:**
A day in the life of a police officer

Police patrol staffing has three performance measures: crime reduction, visibility, and political accountability. Leaders must consider these when determining how to achieve the desired results. No single component of policing stands alone as a clear measure of the outcomes of patrol; other factors, such as community support and cooperation, are also important in assessing the desired outcomes.[32]

Police administrators must consider not only the abilities of the officers they supervise, but also the number of officers when they are assigning various tasks. There is no exact standard for determining the required number of officers, but there is an expectation that police administrators can justify staffing levels, especially as staffing relates to response times. Determining the number and assignment of patrol officers is critical not only internally (to meet staffing needs), but also externally, when considering the impact of numbers on the type of police service that can be provided to the community.[33] Thus, two cities with very similar populations may have different numbers of patrol officers on the same shift. Population size is one factor that helps to determine the number of police officers needed to answer service requests. Additional factors to consider include the types of services provided (bomb disposal, underwater recovery, school-crossing services, search and rescue), whether the department has a community policing plan, available resources, and other variables. It should be noted that, beginning in 2008, many police departments' budgets were cut, and some small departments experienced difficulty in maintaining continuous patrol coverage. In some of these areas that lacked patrol coverage, other police agencies, such as the county sheriff's department or the state police, provided patrol and responded to calls.

**POLICE ✪ STORIES** | 6.1

*Patrol* is defined as moving about an area and observing or inspecting. While patrol can often be a monotonous and boring job, things can very quickly turn deadly. In the span of a few seconds, an officer can go from bored to fighting for his life. In one recent incident, a Morrisville, Pennsylvania, police officer and a suspect were injured during a confrontation at a local 7-Eleven. The officer was on routine patrol at about 5:30 a.m. on Valentine's Day, February 14, when he pulled into the store and noticed a vehicle with its motor running. A check of the vehicle's license plate revealed the vehicle had recently been stolen.

As the officer attempted to approach the vehicle, the driver put the car in reverse, hitting the officer and his patrol car. The suspect took off, but the officer fired two shots, striking the suspect in the chest. The suspect eventually crashed the car up an embankment with a bullet hole in the back door. The suspect was taken to St. Mary Medical Center in Langhorne, in critical but stable condition. He is now facing attempted murder charges.

The officer, who is a six-year veteran of the department, was treated at Aria Health Torresdale Campus and released.[34]

## Intuitive Approach

There is a variety of ways to determine the appropriate number of police personnel for any given jurisdiction—intuitively, comparatively, and by workload.[35] The **intuitive approach** involves little more than an educated guess and is often based on tradition, such as personnel numbers from previous years. This approach can be related to the number of crimes cleared or the total number of arrests; many administrators demand more police officers be hired as crime rates increase. However, some research has suggested that differences in crime rates should not be attributed to variations in the number of police.[36] Since World War II, increases in the number of police have closely paralleled increases in crime rates. Communities hire more police when crime rates rise, but some see this as a desperate game of catch-up that has no effect on the increase in crime.[37] Others attribute positive effects to hiring more police officers.

## Comparative Approach

The **comparative approach** uses the ratio of police officers (per 1,000 in the general population) to a certain number of residents or square miles to be policed.

If the comparison city has a higher ratio of police to citizens, it is assumed that an increase in personnel is justified to at least the level of the comparison city.[38]

For example, the city of Los Angeles has one of the lowest citizen-to-officer ratios in the country, about 400 residents to every 1 officer. New York is even worse, with 570 residents for every 1 officer. So, if the New York Police Department wanted to use the comparative approach, it would argue that the Los Angeles Police Department has a 400-to-1 ratio and that, because the cities are similar, the NYPD should hire enough officers to obtain a 400-to-1 ratio.

■ **Intuitive Approach:** Little more than an educated guess concerning the appropriate number of police personnel

■ **Comparative Approach:** Involves comparing the number of police officers between cities of similar characteristics or the ratio of police officers to population

## CASE IN POINT 6.1

Although the average crime rate in the United States has declined significantly since the early 1990s, a 2011 RAND Corporation report shows that a "10% increase in the size of a police force decreases the rate of homicide by 9%, robbery by 6% and vehicle theft by 4% each year. (The effect on rates of sexual assault is less clear.)"

The costs of crime are far reaching and include the costs associated with the various parts of the criminal justice system, including prosecution and corrections, to mention a few. Of course, costs also include the effects on victims, including fear, pain, and suffering.

The addition of 725 police officers to the Los Angeles Police Department costs approximately $110 million annually. "When Rand researchers factored in all serious crimes averted by adding those police officers, savings to citizens in the city came to $415 million a year, a 280% return on investment." The report suggested that small departments that have a large burden of crime could benefit from the investment of added police officers. However, "cities where police departments are big and crime rates relatively low might not see reductions that exceed the costs of new officers' training, salary and benefits."

1. List all of the types of costs that you can think of that would be associated with a homicide.

2. What are the average rates of person and property crimes in your city? How many police officers does your city have? How much does your city spend on its police force?

3. Given your answers from question 2, do you think your city should hire more police officers?

*Source:* "Save money—hire police," by Gregg Ridgeway and Paul Heaton, 2011. *Los Angeles Times.*

The exclusive use of this method to compute police personnel needs is not advisable, as it is too simplistic. Communities possess unique characteristics such as the size of the area served, miles of roads to be covered, crime rate, number of juveniles, economic strength, employment rates, the size of the elderly population, and special tourist attractions, all of which have an impact on the number of officers required to respond to requests for police service. There is no universal number or simple formula for determining a department's optimal staffing level.

### Workload Analysis

**Workload analysis** is an important tool for administrators, which requires an elaborate information system, standards of expected performance, well-defined community expectations, and the prioritization of police activities.[39] The workload analysis of patrol often involves the following:

- Documenting the total amount of patrol workload that occurs
- Determining the time it takes to handle that workload
- Translating the workload data into the number of patrol officers required to handle it
- Determining how many patrol officers are needed at different times of the day (allocation)
- Determining how many patrol officers are needed on different days of the week (scheduling)
- Determining how best to assign patrol officers to geographic areas (deployment)[40]

The actual computation of patrol workload is also complicated by the issue of uncommitted or discretionary time. During a typical shift, police officers may enjoy substantial amounts of unassigned or uncommitted time, during which they may initiate a wide range of tasks at their own discretion.[41] This self-initiation is often based on the individual officer's motivation and can be influenced by the department's desired style of policing.

Police work is incredibly unpredictable. One evening, an officer may drive around the city with nothing to do. The following week, the same officer on the same beat might be so busy he won't have time to handle all of the evening's assigned calls, which would need to be reassigned to other officers.

The RAND Corporation and the Center for Public Safety at Northwestern University developed some of the few existing workload approaches to patrol staffing—the Chaiken Patrol Allocation Methodology (1975) and the Patrol Allocation Model (1993), respectively. One of the more current models is the **Allocation Model for Patrol (AMP)** developed by Justex Systems Inc. The AMP projects the number of officers needed for patrol operations, using four primary performance objectives for patrol: "1) the visibility of officers, 2) meeting response time goals for Priority 1 calls, 3) meeting response time goals for Priority 2 calls, and 4) having an officer immediately available for Priority 1 calls."[42] Even though many workload analysis models have proven to be methodologically sound, few jurisdictions use them to compute patrol staffing. Most administrators cite the cost, the complexity of the formula, and extensive data collection as the reasons for not using a workload formula.

Whatever the method of arriving at staffing levels, the police administrator must determine the appropriate method for assigning personnel. The unique problems of each community prohibit the rote assignment of personnel across all shifts, districts, beats, or zones. The effective assignment of personnel involves a variety of factors that are ever changing as new problems develop and others are resolved.

As geographic information systems (GIS) and other computer systems improved, another method of effectively allocating patrol resources arose. *Operational analysis*, which relies on internal operational factors, began to achieve higher status in the

■ **Workload Analysis:**
Consists of an elaborate information system with defined levels of police performance for computing the number of appropriate police personnel

■ **Allocation Model for Patrol (AMP):**
A model involving several variables for estimating the number of required police personnel

Exhibit 6.1

## Patrol Staffing Requirements

The International Association of Chiefs of Police uses the following factors to define patrol staffing requirements. The organization noted that the process is complex, because the factors considered in patrol staffing are unique to each locality and police agency.

- Policing philosophy
- Cultural conditions
- Policing priorities
- Climate, especially seasonality
- Police policies and practices
- Policies of prosecutorial, judicial, correctional, and probation agencies
- Number of calls for service

- Citizen demands for crime control and non–crime control services
- Population size and density
- Crime-reporting practices of citizenry
- Composition of population, particularly age structure
- Municipal resources
- Stability and transiency of population
- Trend in foregoing areas

*Source:* "Patrol staffing and deployment study," International Association of Chiefs of Police.

literature. Computer-aided crime reporting modules track where, when, and possibly how crimes are occurring in a particular area, allowing a more precise response from the police. (See Chapter 13.)

The intent of various **deployment models**, such as the police district, zone, or area, is for police work to be channeled through dispatch so that the closest police personnel are assigned to calls. Some consider the fixed-grid form of deployment that is used by most police agencies to be problematic in practice.[43] For example, "You leave your district to answer a call in another district; while you are gone, another officer from

■ **Deployment Models:** The assignment of police personnel to districts, zones, and areas

As technology improves, police departments are relying more on geographic information systems to make decisions about deployment.

Alain Le Bot/Getty Images

another district is sent to answer a call in your assigned area. And so it begins, one call leading to another until, shortly, no officers are close to their assignments."[44] Thus, in response to the traditional district model, some departments have created a model that allows supervisors to deploy patrol officers to hot-spot areas. These deployments involve an incident-command model of dispatch using hot-spot technology. They entail dynamic and ongoing experience, and a patrol officer may be assigned to any number of deployments throughout a given workday. The paradigm has shifted, and an increasing number of police organizations are turning to geographic analysis and advanced technology to make decisions about the best use of police resources to address problems *as they develop*.[45] For example, Corona Solutions uses three complementary software applications for patrol staffing, scheduling, and redistricting.[46] One of these applications is GeoBalance, which helps distribute workload based on the level of activity.[47]

## ■ OTHER TYPES OF PATROL

Police use a variety of techniques to complete the tasks associated with patrol. Often, these variations depend on the size and individual needs of the local jurisdiction. The Law Enforcement Management and Administrative Statistics (LEMAS) survey reported that approximately 55% of local police departments employed scheduled foot patrol, and about 32% patrolled with bicycles.[48]

**Foot patrol** was the original form of patrol. Many agencies report that they routinely use foot patrol; a number employ this strategy for special occasions, such as festivals, concerts, sporting events, and parades. Foot patrol works extremely well where patrol officers on foot are in a one-on-one situation with other people who are also on foot, such as in shopping malls, multiple-family residential villages, parks, beaches, and recreational and amusement areas.[49] It is not simply the existence of foot patrol that improves police–community relations, but the actions of the officer.[50]

Significant studies to evaluate foot patrol were conducted in Newark, New Jersey, and Flint, Michigan. In Newark, foot patrol officers were assigned patrol beats in one of eight neighborhoods.[51] The results of one study suggested that increased foot patrol by police officers was not associated with reduced levels of crime, but it was noticed by citizens and appeared to reduce fear of crime and to increase public satisfaction with the police.[52] The Newark study showed that citizens felt more secure and had a more favorable opinion of the police compared with those residing in other areas.[53] Directed foot patrol (assigning the officer to a specific area) is the most popular form of foot patrol and is used in areas that allow the police to interact easily with large numbers of people. Departments that combine the positive elements of foot patrols with a data analysis of the time, location, and type of crime may use the findings to develop effective strategies to decrease crime and improve life in their communities.[54] Another form of foot patrol involves the "Park, Walk, and Talk" initiative, where "officers are required to get out of their patrol cars and conduct 30-minute foot patrols at least twice a shift."[55] This form of foot patrol is not directed at a specific area or crime problem. The intent of this program is to encourage communication between the police and the residents of the areas they patrol. Some communities are also using trained volunteers to walk neighborhood streets, parks, and schools to deter crime and report incidents and problems.[56]

**Bicycle patrol** is popular in many departments. Bicycle patrols do require additional training and special equipment. However, they have the advantage of low cost compared with automobiles. Officers are accessible to the public; they can silently approach a situation on specially designed bicycles. Officers can cover much more area than when they are on foot patrol, and bicycles can travel where automobiles are unable to patrol.[57] In Seattle, police department bicycle officers participate in night and day patrols and are involved in undercover and **on-view crimes** (crimes that the police officer actually observes while on patrol), drug enforcement, crowd control, and 911 calls.[58] In one study, bicycle patrols

**Video Link:**
Foot Patrols Lead to
Less Crime in Boston

■ **Foot Patrol:**
The original form of police patrol; often employed today at parades, concerts, and sporting events

■ **Bicycle Patrol:**
Police patrolling while riding bicycles; this is a popular form of patrol because of the low cost and possible coverage compared to foot patrol

■ **On-View Crimes:**
Crimes that the police officer actually observes while on patrol

reported more than double the number of contacts as automobile patrols—10.5 people contacted per hour from cars compared with 22.8 people per hour from bicycles.[59]

**Air patrol** involves support units consisting of fixed-wing aircraft and helicopters. Air support units often assist ground units with fleeing felons, high-speed pursuits, missing person searches, drug suppression, and general crime prevention. Although there is little question about its effectiveness, air support is by far the most expensive type of police patrol. Studies claim that helicopters have 15 times the surveillance capacity of a ground unit and that one helicopter can be as effective as 23 ground officers in terms of observation ability.[60]

**Mounted patrols**—police on horseback—are popular in larger departments with unique patrol requirements, including parks and lakefronts. Mounted patrols are involved in crime prevention, community interaction, and crowd control. The Chicago Police Department estimated that one mounted police officer has the effect of 10 to 20 police officers on foot.[61] However, with the addition of bicycles, more foot patrols, and all-terrain vehicles (ATVs), the number of mounted patrol units has been declining.

## ■ EVALUATING PATROL

Although the patrol division involves the largest number of personnel in a police department, little research into the effectiveness of this division was completed until 1960. Prior to this, patrol officers provided a wide range of services, dealing with almost any problem presented to them, with minimal accountability to administrators, the public, or the courts. This kind of patrol can be referred to as "**911 policing**," which involves allocating resources in a case-by-case fashion (incident-driven basis) as citizens demand them (reactively). "Under 911 policing, departments have invested in increasingly sophisticated systems to receive citizens' calls for service, to locate calls spatially, and to designate a patrol unit for rapid response."[62]

Various reform efforts and tensions between the police and citizens have led to the examination of several aspects of policing, including patrol. In 1972, the **Kansas City preventive patrol experiment** was one of the most comprehensive assessments of the

■ **Air Patrol:** Police patrolling from fixed-wing aircraft and helicopter

■ **Mounted Patrol:** Police patrolling on horseback

■ **911 Policing:** Allocation of police resources in a case-by-case fashion

■ **Kansas City Preventive Patrol Experiment:** One of the most comprehensive assessments of police patrol

©iStockphoto.com/shaunl

Bicycle patrol is low cost and allows officers more direct access to the public.

effectiveness of random police patrol. The experiment analyzed variations in the level of routine preventive patrol within Kansas City. In the reactive beats, routine preventive patrol was eliminated, and police officers only responded to calls for service. In the control beats, routine preventive patrol was maintained at its usual level. In the proactive beats, routine preventive patrol was intensified by two to three times its usual level by assigning additional patrol cars so that patrol cars were a frequent presence. The researchers concluded that decreasing or increasing routine preventive patrol in the areas tested had no measurable influence on crime, citizen fear of crime, community attitudes toward the police on the delivery of patrol services, police response time, or traffic accidents.[63]

The results of the Kansas City study had minimal effect on the primary strategy of police. Several decades after the Kansas City experiment, random, mobile, uniformed patrol is still the primary strategy used by police. The Kansas City preventive patrol research results "are generally accepted as being true; its research strategy is considered to be seriously flawed; it has never been replicated; it has not lessened appreciably the reliance of the police on random patrolling; but it has encouraged a rethinking of police purposes and methods."[64] In other words, the implications of the Kansas City study were that personnel normally allocated to preventive patrol could be assigned to more productive crime-control strategies. The results indicated that police deployment strategies could be based on targeted crime prevention and service goals rather than on routine preventive patrol (see Figure 6.1).[65]

Some suggest that **random preventive patrol** offers many opportunities for proactive activity on the part of individual officers.[66] Random preventive patrol is a way of doing police work that allows police officers to control their territories. Officers can decide to do what they want and where they want to do it, as long as they control what goes on in their territory. Police supervisory styles influence patrol officer behavior in the community. One study showed that patrol officers who were managed by an active supervisor were more likely to be proactive in their policing and to spend more time per shift engaged in problem solving and community-oriented activities.[67]

A 1991 study concluded that police spend roughly two-thirds of their work time on criminal matters, order maintenance assignments, service-related functions, traffic matters, medical assistance, and administrative matters.[68] Another reexamined the data from this study and found that the police spent approximately 50% of their time on criminal matters,

---

### Figure 6.1 ■ Results of Kansas City Preventive Patrol Experiment

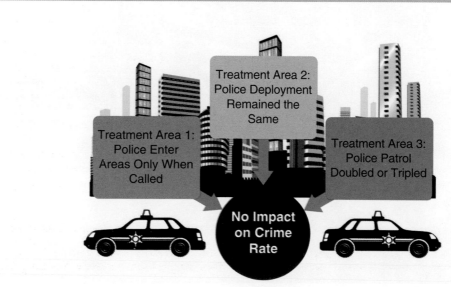

**Random Preventive Patrol:** Method of performing police work that permits officers to control their area

16% on order maintenance, 8% on service, 21% on traffic, and 4% on medical assistance; thus, about 47% of a police officer's time was not spent on actual assignments.[69] This is a reasonable amount of uncommitted time, because in reality most service organizations have limited numbers of contacts with their clients. An attempt to specify the desired amount of time police officers spend engaged in specific tasks was developed by the police department in Longmont, Colorado. According to its staffing study:

> There is some agreement among community policing departments that a patrol officer's day should be divided between reactive, coactive, and proactive policing. Though no nationally recognized standard exists, the Longmont Police Department strives for a benchmark where patrol officers, on a routine and daily schedule, spend at least 60 percent of an average day handling calls for service and report writing (reactive), 30 percent conducting proactive and coactive patrol, and 10 percent dedicated to administrative duties, such as briefing, court appearances, meal breaks, meetings, etc. Note that this time breakdown does not include training time. Training time is recognized as a necessary addition to every officer's on-duty obligation; however it is not an everyday event. When training is provided, it will reduce the percentage of time spent in the other three areas for that particular day or week.[70]

The results of these studies challenge police departments to examine their patrol operations and to develop alternative strategies for random mobile patrol. The police have responded by developing a number of new strategies, which are discussed in detail in Chapter 7.

**Audio Link:**
NYC Police Chief Calls Inspector General's Critical Report 'Grandstanding'

## ■ EVALUATING POLICE PERFORMANCE

Evaluation and measurement of employee performance are closely related to the delivery of an organization's services. "Without such measurement devices, we will not know when the organization needs improvement; we will not know what aspects of

### Report: London No Safer for All Its CCTV Cameras

"London is considered the most spied-on city in the world," but according to some reports, there has been little change in the crime rate since closed-circuit television (CCTV) cameras were widely installed in the 1980s.

A report from the British Security Industry Association (BSIA)—considered the most comprehensive study to date—estimates that there are close to 6 million CCTV cameras, or 1 for every 11 British citizens. Over 400,000 of those are in schools. In one half-mile stretch of a main road, there are approximately "70 cameras on display on lampposts, sides of buildings and in underground and mainline train stations."

Others disagree and believe that the CCTV cameras are important to preventing or solving crime. A BSIA spokesperson claimed that 95% of Scotland Yard murder cases used footage from the cameras as evidence. In addition, the cameras have other uses such as identifying locations of "traffic congestion and other ways like the time they helped rescue someone from the Thames when they had fallen in the river."

Critics of the camera system reject the invasion of privacy. A spokesperson for a civil rights and privacy watchdog organization called the surveillance "out of control." He added, "This report should be a wake up call that in modern Britain there are people in positions of responsibility who seem to think '1984' was an instruction manual."

*Sources:* "Report: London no safer for all its CCTV cameras," by Ian Evans, February 22, 2012. *The Christian Science Monitor.* Retrieved from http://www.csmonitor.com/World/Europe/2012/0222/Report-London-no-safer-for-all-its-CCTV-cameras; "One surveillance camera for every 11 people in Britain, says CCTV survey," by David Barrett, July 10, 2013. *The Telegraph.* Retrieved from http://www.telegraph.co.uk/technology/10172298/One-surveillance-camera-for-every-11-people-in-Britain-says-CCTV-survey.html.

the organization need improvement the most; and, following the implementation of changes, we will not know whether improvements have been achieved."[71] Relevant to this discussion is the administrative task of evaluating officer performance and evaluating the performance of the agency, especially with respect to using the results of evaluation as an essential ingredient of evidence-based practice.

### Evaluating Officer Performance

There are two types of **performance measures**: hard and soft. A *hard measure* is quantitative and expressed numerically and is rather easy to formulate—the number, rate, percentage, or ratio of something.

Police have consistently used a set of conventional indicators of officer performance that involve the counting of certain desirable law enforcement activities: the number of field reports submitted, number of tickets written, number of referrals made to other agencies, and number of arrests in general or felony arrests in particular.[72] However, the number of arrests and reports only represents the quantitative measures of police performance.

**Policing in Practice Video:**
How is your police performance evaluated?

A *soft measure* is a qualitative or intangible attribute or characteristic that is usually expressed in terms of degree of excellence, desirability, attitude, or perception and is often based on output or outcome: for example, citizen satisfaction with police or citizens' perceived levels of fear.[73] It is more difficult to assess the qualitative measures of policing (order maintenance, community service, and problem solving). Perhaps consequently, law enforcement activities have typically been the most important, prestigious, and rewarded.[74] And besides only representing a portion of the role of the police, quantitative measures are subject to misinterpretation. A crime rate might not indicate that the police department is doing a great job; it may only mean that crime reporting is low, which can occur when the public has no confidence in or mistrusts the police. According to this logic, crime rate measures could be an inverse measure of police performance.

The evaluation of police personnel may be even more challenging in the context of community-oriented policing. For example, how does a supervisor rate an officer who is no longer making arrests because there is not as great a need? How do you quantify interaction with citizens who promote a positive image of the department? (See Chapter 7.)

Performance measures can strongly influence an employee's daily activities. For example, if the number of tickets issued to cyclists for traffic violations is an important part of the department's evaluation instrument, many police officers will issue more citations. Depending on the perceived weight or importance of the evaluation, some officers will ignore other citations and focus only on bicycle violations. "Performance criteria originally selected because of the ease of their measurement may become, in effect, the goals of the police department and the objectives of its individual officers."[75] However, if properly administered, this form of evaluation will advance organizational objectives and accomplish certain career goals. The administrator would have to continually assess the evaluation criteria and ensure that the evaluation process is fair for all police personnel. For example, an officer assigned to the "power shift," from 8 p.m. to 4 a.m., would be less likely to encounter as many bicycle violations as would a day-shift officer.

### Evaluating Agency Performance

**Performance Measures:** Indicators that assess the extent to which police patrol officers achieve the designated outcomes

It is important to note that a substantial part of a department's mission statement often focuses on quality of life, professionalism, respect, and public safety. Qualitative measures of police agency performance could be accomplished through "community leadership meetings and discussions with questionnaires, focus groups from the community where the services were delivered, and community attitude surveys."[76]

Thus, there is no one measure of police performance that accurately describes today's police. In 2006, the Los Angeles Police Department was assessed on the following performance dimensions:

- Crime reduction
- Compliance with federal consent decree
- Deployment strength
- Diversity in hiring and promotion
- Homeland security and disaster preparedness
- Antigang policies
- Fiscal management[77]

Similarly, a multidimensional performance system included critical dimensions that attempted to capture the services provided to the public by the police:

- Reducing crime and criminal victimization
- Holding offenders accountable
- Reducing fear and blight and enhancing personal safety
- Guaranteeing safety in public and semipublic places
- Using financial resources fairly, efficiently, and effectively
- Using force fairly, efficiently, and effectively
- Satisfying customer demands and achieving legitimacy with those policed[78]

**Policing in Practice Video:**
What is the role of citizen comments in police evaluation? What categories are police officers evaluated on?

The value of subjective measures of police performance became apparent during the 1980s, when researchers discovered that public perceptions had behavioral consequences that affected quality of life.[79] For example, fear of crime can produce sickness and cause absenteeism and truancy; suspicion of the police reduces the willingness of people to provide essential information to the police, thereby decreasing the chances that crimes will be solved; fear of victimization can raise distrust among neighbors, undermining the ability of communities to undertake cooperative crime-prevention action; and the fear of crime may contribute to the decline of neighborhoods as people stop maintaining their property, avoid local businesses and places of recreation, and move to safer, more desirable communities.[80]

---

### CASE IN POINT 6.2

**Ferguson Vows Better Policing, Civil Rights Respect on Brown Anniversary**

As the anniversary of the shooting death by police of Michael Brown approached, the town of Ferguson, Missouri, prepared itself. Ferguson has many new actors and a new outlook on the role of the police there. Andre Anderson was filling the role as interim police chief and announced a community policing strategy to the city council:

"I've asked the police department to adopt four things as we start: We want to embrace professionalism, we want to embrace respect, we want to embrace community engagement and we want to make the community safer."

City Manager Ed Beasley stated that the Ferguson community "can expect we're going to be very encouraging, supportive, but also make sure the laws are upheld." He promised to ensure that Ferguson's citizens "have the right to exercise their civil rights the proper way."[81]

# ■ POLICE AND THE MEDIA

No discussion of police operations would be complete without considering the media. The media play a very important role in shaping the public's attitudes and images of the police and the relations between the police and the community. This is especially true after the adoption of community policing, which identified the need for creating a closer relationship with the community by keeping the public informed of the department's actions and strategies.[82]

According to the National Institute of Justice, "episodes where police engage in excessive use of force have been well publicized in the media. Television shows regularly portray excessive use of force. Widespread media attention to these events unfortunately conveys the impression that rates of use of force, or excessive use of force, are much higher than what actually occurs."[83]

> The myth of the crime fighter endures for many reasons. The entertainment media play a major role in popularizing it. Movies and television police shows feature crime-related stories because they offer drama, fast-paced action, and violence. . . . The news media are equally guilty of overemphasizing police crime fighting. . . . A serious crime is a newsworthy event. There is a victim who engages our sympathies, a story, and then an arrest that offers dramatic visuals of a suspect in custody. A typical night's work for a patrol officer, by way of contrast, does not offer much in the way of dramatic news.[84]

**SAGE Journal Article:**
Police-press relations, impression management and the Leveson Inquiry

Unless people have firsthand experience of the system, media images may shape their perceptions of the participants in police encounters, of the issues involved, and of police procedures. Because press, radio, and television select the events, the people, and the issues they cover, and because these are the principal sources of information about what is happening in a community or in the nation as a whole, the media are recognized as very powerful forces.

The media and the police have experienced major changes due to "three separate but intersecting phenomena: the introduction of community policing, the evolving economics of the media industry, and the explosion of communications and information technology."[85] The demands for transparency in police organizations in light of increased public scrutiny and the shift to community policing give added significance to the role of the media in relation to law enforcement.[86] Furthermore, in the past, journalists often developed police stories and printed the results in a newspaper or released the information on local radio or television stations. However, with news breaking on satellite, cable, and the Internet, the media involves an ever-growing number of diverse information outlets. A video of an alleged incident of police brutality can be captured on a cell phone and released on the Internet moments after the activity occurs. And in many cases, large segments of the population can view videos such as these before the police chief is even aware of the incident.

When covering the police in action, the media have a responsibility to the community they serve: to observe with as much objectivity and to report with as much neutrality as possible. To fulfill this responsibility, the media actively seek to discover what is going on and why, and then to inform their readers, viewers, and listeners about their observations. The media may provide background information, and may offer an opportunity for those involved to explain their positions, air their views, and account for their behavior. It is essential that the police are aware of this aspect of the media's role. When appropriate, a department spokesperson should be available to furnish information about the role, obligations, and conduct of the police in the situations being discussed. On the other hand, those involved in disputes with the police are likely to be fully aware of the power of the media to shape public opinion and may view reporters as forces to be manipulated to their own ends. In certain cases, groups deliberately stage events to attract the attention of the press or television cameras

The department's media spokesperson debriefs reporters on a recent, critical incident.

AP Photo/Alex Brandon

and to provoke extreme, inappropriate responses from the police to undermine their reputation and authority. When the police respond to provocation by using excessive force, it can seriously impair police–community relations. In addition, there is the physical harm inflicted on those who are objects of such treatment. Uniformed officers wielding Tasers on crouched or prone civilians are potent images in the minds of many U.S. citizens. It is precisely when the temptation is greatest for the police officer to retaliate in a very personal, violent way that it is essential to respond with the minimum necessary force. Such restraint is a characteristic of a well-trained and disciplined professional police officer.

The relationship between the media and the police has often been antagonistic. Certainly, there are reasons that the police and media are wary of one another. The media may report inappropriate information gleaned from questionable sources within or without the department. And the media can be fickle. What is news one day is not the next day, and editorial opinion often fluctuates. Being evasive with the media only exacerbates images of secrecy and self-protection among police personnel.[87]

To avoid embarrassment to the department, police officials are sometimes reluctant to report certain matters to the general public. This reluctance may conflict with media representatives' responsibilities to keep the public informed and with the department's own commitment to maintain public confidence by being transparent and honest. On many occasions, police resist disclosing information, because doing so threatens investigations, creates a level of fear, or endangers the public.[88] As police organizations have transitioned from a paramilitary structure toward a more open, community-service orientation, they more readily understand that the media can be a valuable resource.

A former commissioner of the London Police Department put it in these terms:

> We had always adhered to the principle "Tell them [the media] only what you must." After consultation with most of the principal editors in London, we reversed this to "Withhold only what you must" and we delegated to station level the authority to disclose matters of fact not subject to judicial privacy or policies within the sphere of the home office.[89]

The police should regard difficult situations as valuable opportunities to demonstrate their ability to keep their cool and to function well under stressful conditions. They should take advantage of such opportunities to display the professional care and skill used to discharge their obligations. The police can keep the public informed about police behavior during such events.

The media can and should be viewed as police allies rather than as critics of policing. The primary goal of the media is to observe life conditions and objectively report these events to the public. The positive influence of the media is often overlooked by the police because of the perceived adversarial nature of their relationship. Media attention is a powerful tool, and continuing personal relationships with media representatives will establish a pattern of repeated coverage. Not all coverage will be completely sympathetic to the police cause, nor should it be, but establishing a solid professional relationship will create a foundation of honesty and mutual respect.[90]

### Media Relations Programs

**Author Video:**
The need for communication between law enforcement officers and the public

It is widely known that the media quickly pick up on any negative behavior on behalf of the police. Corruption, brutality, discrimination, and other forms of misconduct are frequently lead topics on television, radio, print, and Internet news. Prime-time television shows also frequently develop plots based on such negative behavior shortly after the behavior is revealed to the public. "The overwhelming search for news should warn law enforcement that the media will get their story one way or another."[91] Convincing the media to cover routine or positive encounters between the police and other citizens to balance coverage is the task before the police. To accomplish this task, police administrators need to develop and implement media relations programs. For most police administrators, police–media relations are the most important aspect of the police department's community outreach program.[92]

A **media relations policy** is important to every police agency. It must be based on the public's right to know about the workings of government agencies (with certain important exceptions) and the media's obligation to keep the public informed. Although various state laws and departmental policies restrict the release of certain information by the police (e.g., information concerning ongoing or anticipated investigations), police personnel should be willing to explain why such information is withheld. The goal of police departments is to develop a cooperative relationship with the media so that they can appropriately provide information that does not hamper police operations or violate constitutional rights.

Some police agencies appoint a **public information officer (PIO)** to represent the agency in all contacts with the media. This officer typically reports directly to the chief and is responsible for informing and educating the public on matters of public safety. The chief of police also is typically available to address issues of mutual concern, to release information concerning the department, and to provide news releases concerning major crimes and investigations. Funneling all information through these two individuals avoids the confusion that sometimes results from having too many spokespersons. With the explosion of different types of media discussed earlier, PIOs are finding the release of information to the public more challenging.

During a typical shift, a police officer encounters numerous routine, repetitive events that are not newsworthy. However, "the odd call about an alligator in a swimming pool, the vulture that flew into a resident's open living room window, or the deeds of the community's unsung hero are the stories that the media really want."[93] A PIO can distribute accounts of these incidents to build a relationship with the media and to illustrate the department's problem-oriented policing principles.

One context in which the media are especially significant is in their treatment of encounters between the police and protestors. Heavy media coverage can help transform a neighborhood disturbance or protest into a citywide or national phenomenon and, in the process, escalate a local neighborhood issue into a citywide crisis. Decisions by

**■ Media Relations Policy:** Policy based on the public's right to know and the police department's obligation to keep the public informed

**■ Public Information Officer (PIO):** Person who represents the police department in all contacts with any form of media

media executives not to cover or to discontinue coverage of a demonstration severely restrict the extent to which others may become aware of or involved in the event, and raise serious questions about the proper role of the press in society.

In the final analysis, in spite of accusations of bias in coverage and the potential for abusing the public's trust, the presence of the media in the various arenas of community conflict appears to be in the best interests of both the police and the public. Besides functioning as reporters of community events, the fact that media observers are present and that they have the ability to communicate their observations quickly tends to discourage extreme behavior in all parties, in most circumstances. Furthermore, in a democracy, exposure to public scrutiny is a healthy and democratizing experience for powerful forces such as the police.

## Social Media

Many observers see lessons to learn from the Boston Police Department (BPD) and its use of social media after and before the bombing of the Boston Marathon in 2013. As events unfolded rapidly after the incident, the BPD used Twitter to inform the public about the investigation, reassure the public and ask for assistance, and correct erroneous news media accounts. In its Twitter messages, the department confirmed the event, announced road closures and press conferences, expressed sympathy for the victims and their families, posted the number of casualties, and confirmed that no suspect had yet been apprehended. By directly offering official information, the agency established itself as the source of reliable information, as opposed to the news media, where rumors were circulating. That the BPD was successful in its use of social media indicates a level of trust that the department had previously been using social media to build.[94] During the critical hours after the incident, the BPD relied on specially trained staff persons (the bureau chief of public information and her team) to maintain contact personally with department commanders and craft the messages that went out to the public. See Table 6.1 for the types of social media used or planned to be used by police.

As the manhunt for the suspects unfolded, the police asked for the public's cooperation in *not* revealing police activities that could thwart their efforts to apprehend the last suspect, who was eventually found and taken into custody. Afterward, the department was praised for "leading an honest conversation with the public during a time of crisis in a way that no police department has done before."[95]

As illustrated by these events, social media allows police departments to communicate directly with the public, without having to use the news media as an intermediary. Handled properly, it legitimizes them as the source of information. Prior to the bombing,

| Table 6.1 ■ Types of Social Media Used/Planned to Be Used by Police | | |
| --- | --- | --- |
| Social Media Type | Percent of Responding Agencies Currently Using | Percent of Responding Agencies Planning to Begin Using in 2 to 5 Years |
| Agency Website | 100 | — |
| Facebook | 82 | 14 |
| Twitter | 69 | 18 |
| YouTube | 48 | 20 |
| LinkedIn | 34 | 20 |

*Source:* Police Executive Research Forum, *Future Trends in Policing* (Washington, DC: Office of Community Oriented Policing Services, 2014), http://ric-zai-inc.com/Publications/cops-p282-pub.pdf.

*Note:* PERF, with the support of the COPS Office and Target Corporation, disseminated a "Future of Policing" survey in 2012 to more than 500 police agencies; nearly 200 responded.

the BPD had used social media as an avenue for its press releases, which the news media relied on for accurate information.[96]

Agencies can use a social media presence to build a trusting relationship with the community, to gain control over their reputation, to receive questions from the public and to share tips, to coordinate messages and disseminate information quickly, and to enlist the public's help in furthering their investigative efforts. To accomplish all of this, police agencies are in turn learning from public relations experts from the corporate and private sectors, who have elevated communications to an art and a science.

The International Association of Chiefs of Police (IACP) tracks social media metrics on a dedicated website and listed 3,541 agencies in July 2015. It lists the agencies with how many "Likes" they have on Facebook and the number of Twitter followers they have. The site requests that subscribing agencies indicate their other social media platforms—Myspace, YouTube, LinkedIn, Nextdoor, Google+, Pinterest, and Blog.[97]

## 6
## UNDER REVIEW

## CHAPTER SUMMARY

The responsibilities of police have expanded over the last decades. The operations and functions of a police agency are varied and depend largely on factors such as the size of the population they serve and the organizational structure they use to perform their functions. As a result, most police administrators now assess the number and allocation of police personnel on a continuing basis. The duties of police officers range from animal complaint calls and thefts of bicycles to burglary and murder investigations.

The purpose and effects of patrol techniques have been challenged from time to time. Patrol techniques prior to the community-oriented policing era focused on rapid response time to calls for service and the deterrent effect on crime of marked police cars randomly patrolling the community. Key studies identified significant flaws associated with this strategy. Today, police use a variety of strategies.

The evaluation of police performance at the individual and agency levels and media relations are important issues. Performance evaluation criteria should be consistent with the mission and goals of the organization. Evidence-based practice calls for ongoing evaluation. Finally, it is important that police agencies maintain positive relationships with the media and use social media wisely to build community and public respect.

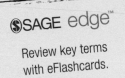

**$SAGE edge™**

Review key terms with eFlashcards.

## KEY TERMS

- Broken windows theory  129
- Zero tolerance  130
- Forensic science  132
- CSI effect  132
- Watchman style  133
- Legalistic style  134
- Service style  134
- Intuitive approach  137

- Comparative approach  137
- Workload analysis  138
- Allocation Model for Patrol (AMP)  138
- Deployment models  139
- Foot patrol  140
- On-view crime  140
- Bicycle patrol  140
- Air patrol  141

- Mounted patrol  141
- 911 policing  141
- Kansas City preventive patrol experiment  141
- Random preventive patrol  142
- Performance measures  144
- Media relations policy  148
- Public information officer (PIO)  148

**$SAGE edge™**

Test your understanding of chapter content. Take the practice quiz.

## DISCUSSION QUESTIONS

1. Discuss the functions of today's police.

2. Describe the investigative function of today's police.

3. Describe Wilson's three styles of policing.

4. Describe the various forms of police patrol.

5. What are the expected outcomes of police patrol?

6. Is random police patrol an effective technique?

7. Compare and contrast the relationship between the strategies of directed patrol, differential response, and saturation patrol and crackdowns.

8. Describe the methods for determining the appropriate number of police personnel and discuss the strengths and weaknesses of each method.

9. Discuss the factors used in the allocation of police personnel.

10. How can we best evaluate police performance?

11. Why are police media relations so important to the police? The public?

## INTERNET EXERCISES

1. Go to the Internet and locate a media policy for a police department. What types and forms of information can be released to the media? Who is in charge of releasing this information?

2. Select one of the police innovations discussed in the chapter (hot spots, directed patrol, third-party policing, etc.). Go to the Internet and find information about this innovation. How is this innovation evaluated? What has been its effectiveness in relation to crime prevention or crime reduction?

## STUDENT STUDY SITE

**$SAGE edge**™  **edge.sagepub.com/coxpolicing3e**

**Sharpen your skills with SAGE edge!**

SAGE edge for Students provides a personalized approach to help you accomplish your coursework goals in an easy-to-use learning environment. You'll find action plans, mobile-friendly eFlashcards, and quizzes as well as videos, web resources, and links to SAGE journal articles to support and expand on the concepts presented in this chapter.

# CONTEMPORARY STRATEGIES IN POLICING

© iStockphoto.com/Jen Grantham

## CHAPTER LEARNING OBJECTIVES:

1. Compare and contrast the underlying tenets of both traditional and community-based styles of policing

2. Describe the strategies associated with problem-oriented policing

3. Evaluate, based on research, the effectiveness of community-based policing and problem-oriented policing

4. Debate the criticisms of community policing

5. Discuss recent innovations in police information, resources, environment, organization, and process

6. Select the form of policing you believe to be the most effective and justify your response with empirical evidence

U.S. police officers are better educated, trained, and equipped than ever before. At the same time, the scope of police duties has expanded in the age of international crime and terrorism. Technology continues to advance, budgets are constrained, and police forces are increasingly diverse. Examples of excessive force, police corruption, and inefficiency still appear frequently in the media, and the police remain unable to prevent most crimes or to apprehend most offenders. Every police agency faces some combination of these challenges and has grappled with ways to improve its effectiveness. In the two decades leading up to the 21st century, policing changed from a closed, incident-driven, reactive bureaucracy to a more open, dynamic, quality-oriented partnership with the community.[1] Such changes are included under the general heading of community policing, which represents the most significant shift in policing in recent history.

Still, as we have seen, corruption, litigation, harassment by some segments of society, inconsistent leadership, and inefficiency are just some of the issues that continue to burden police agencies. Scandals involving theft, use and sale of drugs by officers, police brutality, and other serious violations are still far too common. It appears that many of the ways the police tried to adapt to a rapidly changing society have resulted in or have perpetuated a cycle of isolation and alienation. Specialization, for example, was viewed as one way of providing better service to the public. As a result, agencies developed numerous specialized units (internal affairs, community relations, juvenile, robbery, homicide, drug, sex crimes, and traffic). In many cases, a consequence of such development has been little cross-training, an "it's not my job" attitude, tight-knit and highly secretive units, and too little effective communication between officers in specialized units and patrol officers. When scandals arise in such units, the confidence of both the general public and the noninvolved officers within the police ranks is understandably undermined. In recent times, gangs, drugs, race, ethnicity, immigration, technological innovations, cybercrime, and increasingly violent encounters involving automatic weapons have become focal points. The increased visibility of immigrants and a small number of terrorist incidents within the borders of our country have led to a rebirth of concern about racial and ethnic differences and the reemergence of extreme right-wing groups. Relationships between the police and members of racial and

**Author Video:**
Community Policing

The philosophy of police omnipresence: an effective method for the prevention of crime?

ethnic minority groups continue to be problematic in many cases. All of the new police technology and all of the old police traditions have not been able to solve these distinct but related problems. As a result, a search for innovative approaches continues.

## ■ COMMUNITY POLICING

**Video Link:**
Building trust between police and community

Although it is becoming more widely adopted, there is still some confusion about community policing, what it might be expected to accomplish, and how or why it might be expected to work where other strategies have failed. Some believe **community-oriented policing** (COP) simply retreads shopworn elements of police community-relations programs—that it is little more than a passing fad that will fade away as have many others before it.[2] This may be most true with respect to traditional police agencies that are highly resistant to change; these tend to be characterized by a paramilitary organizational structure and unionization, among other factors.[3]

Community-oriented policing may take a number of different forms. Still, there are elements common to all of the programs, such as police–community reciprocity, areal decentralization of command, reorientation of patrol, and civilianization.[4] A brief discussion of each of these elements helps to clarify community policing.

*Police–community reciprocity* refers to a "genuine feeling" on the part of the police that the public they serve has something to contribute to policing. Further, the police communicate this feeling to the public, learn from public input, and consider themselves accountable to the community they serve. The police and the public become "co-producers" of crime prevention.[5]

*Areal decentralization of command* refers to the establishment of substations, mini-stations, and other attempts to increase interaction between police officers and the public they serve in a particular geographic area.

*Reorientation of patrol* involves moving from car to foot patrol to increase police interaction with other citizens. This may involve permanently assigning certain officers to walking beats or having officers park their cars so they can get out and talk to residents. Positive contacts between officers and other citizens are thought to be one result of foot patrol that can contribute to crime prevention.

Findings from one study in Philadelphia indicated that officers assumed greater responsibility for permanently assigned beats. Whether such effects are long term is a question that must still be addressed, because the officers in this study were observed only for a period of weeks rather than months or years.

*Civilianization* refers to employing civilians in an increasing number of positions within police agencies. For example, an increasing number of civilians work in research and training divisions, in forensics, and as community service officers who handle many non–crime-related tasks. Civilianization has been related to successfully introducing and carrying out programs and policies related to community mobilization and crime prevention.[6] (See also Chapters 4 and 5.)

In reality, then, COP requires adopting both philosophical and operational changes and, to a great extent, turns traditional policing practices upside down. It is, after all, "not easy to transform blue knights into community organizers."[7] Several principles form the basis for this transformation from traditional to community policing.[8] First, COP is a philosophy based on the belief that law-abiding citizens should have input with respect to policing, provided they are willing to participate in and support the effort. Second, community policing is an organizational strategy that requires all police personnel (civilian and sworn) to explore ways to turn the philosophy into practice. Third, police departments that implement community policing must develop community-policing officers (CPOs) to act as links between the police and community residents that have continuous, sustained contact with law-abiding citizens. In addition, community policing implies a contract between the police and other citizens that helps overcome apathy and

**■ Community-Oriented Policing (COP):** A philosophy based on the belief that law-abiding citizens should have input with respect to policing

© iStockphoto.com/swalls

Community-oriented policing focuses on opportunities to create connections between police and the citizens they serve.

curb vigilantism. Further, community policing is proactive, and it helps improve the quality of life for those who are most vulnerable, such as the poor, the elderly, and the homeless. Although community policing uses technology, it relies on human interaction and ingenuity. Finally, community policing must be fully integrated into the department.

Community policing is not a technique to be applied only to specific problems but, rather, a new way of thinking about the police role in the community.[9] Community policing is not the same as public relations, nor is it simply social work renamed. It is not antitechnology, but it uses technology in a different framework. Community policing is not soft on crime, nor is it an independent program within a police department. Community policing is not cosmetic; it requires substantive changes in the relationships between the police and other citizens. Community policing is not a top-down approach; it must involve the entire department. Finally, community policing incorporates traditional policing responses; it is not tradition bound, but requires risk taking and experimentation. According to one observer, "policing becomes less effective and more likely to drive a wedge between law enforcement and the public when conducted outside a comprehensive COP framework."[10]

Community policing is not solely directed at addressing problems that cannot be addressed by traditional policing methods.[11] Suburban and low-crime communities also can use community policing to address the specific needs and problems of their citizens. The community policing philosophy recognizes that patrol officers are the government representatives best positioned to address a number of social problems, and enforcing the law is only one of several strategies the police can employ to cope with such problems.[12] Long-term interaction between police officers and neighborhood residents is thought to help develop relationships based on mutual trust and cooperation. It also encourages the exchange of information between citizens and police officers, including mutual input concerning policing priorities and tactics for specific neighborhoods.[13]

> By challenging people to work as partners in making their communities better and safer places, Community Policing produces a subtle but profound shift in the role and responsibility of the police. No longer are they the experts with all the answers, the "thin blue line" that protects the good people from the bad—"us" versus "them." Community officers are part of the community, generalists who do whatever it takes to help people help themselves.[14]

**Policing in Practice Video:**
What is one example of community policing by your department?

### Implementing COP

Implementing community-oriented policing (COP) requires a number of concrete changes in most police organizations:

- Redefine the department's role in the community.
- Train all officers in COP.
- Evaluate employees differently.
- Assign officers to specific patrol areas.
- Prioritize calls.
- Tailor police work to community needs.

In COP, patrol officers become liaisons, ombudsmen, problem solvers, and mobilizers of community resources. They seek to obtain community or neighborhood cooperation to identify and resolve problems rather than simply handling incidents. They look for patterns of incidents that are indicative of problems that may best be addressed by resources other than, or in cooperation with, the police. In short, they practice problem-oriented policing (POP, introduced in Chapter 2, is discussed in the following section) as a part of the overall COP strategy.

### The LEMAS Survey

The Law Enforcement Management and Administrative Statistics (LEMAS) survey periodically assesses the community policing practices of state and local police departments. Some of the related highlights of the 2013 LEMAS survey are as follows:

- In 2013, about 7 in 10 local police departments, including about 9 in 10 departments that serve a population of 25,000 or more, had a mission statement that included a community-policing component (see Figure 7.1).
- Departments with a community-policing component employed 88% of all local police officers in 2013.
- A majority of the local police departments serving 25,000 or more residents reported that they had one or more problem-solving partnerships or agreements with local organizations in their community in 2013.
- Most departments serving 50,000 or more residents encouraged officer involvement in problem-solving projects.[15]

By the beginning of the 21st century, COP had made some inroads in many departments across the country, in part as a method of fostering trust in communities that are typically skeptical of the police. At the same time, however, the United States was undergoing major changes in diversity with respect to race, ethnicity, and culture. Roughly 1.5 million new immigrants arrive on U.S. shores each year; Hispanics have displaced African Americans as the largest minority group in the nation; and immigrants have moved away from major population centers to establish neighborhoods in more sparsely populated areas of the country.[16] Because police work is affected by all of these changes, it is essential that commensurate changes occur in recruiting and hiring, as well as in familiarization with the values, norms, and customs of an increasingly diverse population. Hispanics tend to have less favorable attitudes toward the police than Whites, and many immigrants don't trust the police enough to contact them for assistance.[17]

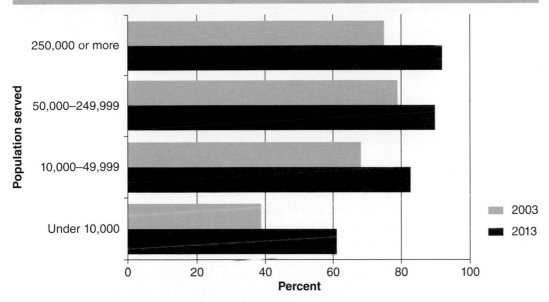

**Figure 7.1** ■ Local Police Departments With a Mission Statement That Included a Community Policing Component, by Size of Population Served, 2003 and 2013

*Source:* Reaves, 2015. Local Police Departments, 2013: Personnel, Policies, and Practices. Bureau of Justice Statistics.

Policing is constantly evolving in many ways to meet changing demands and has now evolved into what might be called the **strategic management era**.[18] The evolution into strategic management was based on the practice of computer-generated crime data and a resulting convergence of police management, technology, strategy, and community involvement. Using technology to process intelligence provided by community resources, changing the roles of police administrators from administrative to operational, and developing strategies to attack identifiable crime hot spots and patterns led not only to the era of strategic management in policing but—some contend—to reductions in crime rates wherever it was implemented.[19]

## ■ PROBLEM-ORIENTED POLICING

The concept of problem-oriented policing (POP) originated in 1979 in the works of Herman Goldstein. Goldstein noted many of the difficulties previously discussed and added that, although many police agencies gave the appearance of being efficient, this appearance failed to translate into benefits for the community. After looking carefully at public expectations of the police, he determined that people want the police to solve problems. Crime statistics were not enough to accurately evaluate this ability or performance. Instead, evaluation needed to focus on the problems encountered and the effectiveness of the police response to such problems.[20]

Problem-oriented police officers, then, need to define the problems they encounter, gather information concerning these problems (frequency, seriousness, duration, location), and develop creative solutions. This model of problem solving is known as the SARA model.[21]

Problem-oriented policing represents a dramatic change from traditional policing, which is incident driven and in which the police typically receive a complaint or call, respond to it, and then clear the incident. Although the specific situation is addressed, the underlying conditions are not—so more calls are likely, requiring further responses to similar incidents. POP regards these incidents as symptoms of underlying conditions that must be addressed to keep the incidents from proliferating.[22] Accordingly, patterns of incidents that are similar

■ **Strategic Management Era:** Based on the practice of computer-generated crime data and a resulting convergence of police management, technology, strategy, and community involvement

SARA stands for a four-step approach.

- *Scanning* means identifying the problem in terms of time, location, and behavior.

- *Analysis* means answering who, what, where, when, how, and why questions.

- *Response* refers to the development of alternative problem-solving approaches and the selection of those most appropriate.

- *Assessment* means evaluating the selected response to determine its effectiveness.

represent problems that must be attended to by the police. Problems—rather than crimes, calls, or incidents—become the basic unit of police work.[23] Line officers become problem identifiers and solvers. Identifying and solving community problems requires input from those who live in the community, as well as from other service providers.

**Web Link:**
How to Fix a Broken
Police Department

Relevant to promoting innovative problem-solving is the willingness of police to engage third parties in furtherance of crime control. Harnessing such capacities is critical to POP given that many public safety problems the police have to address require some level of partnership with external agencies. One reason for this is that many factors that lead to crime have very little to do with the police directly, but instead originate in the functioning of other institutions and the capacity of actors within those settings to assert effective social control. . . . Hence, drawing upon the crime control capacities of external parties as a core aspect of problem analysis and response is essential to the effectiveness of POP in practice.[24]

A closely related strategy was named as an extension of POP—**solution-oriented policing (SOP)**, which focuses on addressing some police–community issues through unique approaches or thinking outside the box. Rather than focusing on apparent causes of such issues, SOP seeks out the best options among potential solutions to problems in a proactive instead of a reactive way. Officers are encouraged to seek such causes and solutions before the resulting problems grow to unmanageable size.[25]

POP and COP share a need for community involvement, and both focus on the conditions that underlie order disruption and crime.[26] POP must continue to be evaluated, but it is surely among the most promising police strategies.[27]

## ■ RESEARCH ON COMMUNITY AND PROBLEM-ORIENTED POLICING

COP and POP have undergone a fair amount of rigorous evaluation over the last several decades, and that evaluation has yielded mixed results.

Some research found that it was difficult to convince police officers to accept the new roles required for community policing, partly due to poor communication from police administrators concerning these new roles.

**Solution-Oriented Policing (SOP):** Focuses on the fact that some police–community issues are best addressed through the development of unique approaches or thinking outside the box

Research revealed the following sorts of challenges:

- Officers who belonged to special units were often distrusted by other officers in more traditional assignments, especially senior officers.

- Other officers felt that they had little or no input into the new program and that community residents were not generally excited about being involved.

- Fear of retaliation from drug dealers had a chilling effect. That fear was based on the assumption that the police would abandon the program and leave them to suffer the consequences.

Still, with proper education and training, community residents did come to report better relationships with the police, even when the program's effects on drugs and crime were difficult to detect. In fact, later research found that community residents tended to have a more positive view of community policing than did the officers involved in COP.[28]

Research from 1992 that used a control group found that citizen complaints about gangs, crime, and disorder in POP neighborhoods decreased over a two-year period, while such complaints remained constant or increased in control neighborhoods.[29] Due to limitations in the research design, the authors stopped short of claiming that POP caused the changes, but the data are certainly suggestive. Overall, these researchers concluded that POP seems to be a good thing in that residents involved in the program seem to be happier about their neighborhoods and the police. "The research suggests that law enforcement agencies that take the time to learn and deal with their constituents' irritants and troubles will be perceived in increasingly positive terms."[30]

One meta-analysis of 12 other studies of community policing found among police officers generally positive effects on job satisfaction, improved relationships with coworkers and citizens, and greater expectations for citizen participation in preventing crimes.[31]

**SAGE Journal Article:** Assessing the Interrelationships Between Perceptions of Impact and Job Satisfaction

A 1998 survey of 82 police departments in Massachusetts communities with fewer than 200,000 inhabitants concluded that deployment strategies such as bike patrol and ministations represented new ways for some departments to perform their policing functions, but that most residents participate only by providing information to departments using these strategies.[32] Residents were more likely to participate in the problem-identification and problem-solving processes associated with community policing when collaborative strategies such as advisory councils and citizen academies were established. These results point to the need for the police to take the initiative for establishing such relationships, particularly in more disadvantaged neighborhoods.

Other research looked at how well officers were being trained in new strategies and the extent to which departments offered the requisite training in the skills and knowledge necessary to make the transition to community policing.[33] One observer concluded that, "without clear guidelines and leadership from the department, efforts to connect the police with the community through the line officer will have no more success than did the old police-community relations programs of the past."[34] Still other research on nine agencies found few accounts of automatic success in the community-policing arena. "In fact . . . most of them failed at both their earlier and recent attempts to implement what they thought were solid police strategies guided by idealized versions of community policing prerogatives that allegedly worked in other departments."[35] Citing cumulative evidence on COP, a 2009 study concluded that many of the strategies employed in COP (storefront offices, neighborhood watch, and community meetings) do not lead to a reduction in serious crime or an increase in police effectiveness.[36]

## ■ CRITICISMS OF COMMUNITY POLICING

There is little doubt that community policing has been a major trend in U.S. policing; in 1999, nearly two-thirds of county and municipal police departments with 100 or more officers had a formally written community-policing plan.[37] Still, some have raised questions about its worth.

### Rhetoric Versus Practice

One common criticism is that many police departments embrace the rhetoric of community policing rather than the philosophy or practice. Indeed, there are police administrators who institute foot patrol programs or establish neighborhood watch programs and claim to have initiated community policing. In some departments, the considerable enthusiasm for community policing has led to its introduction as an organizational objective with little substance in many police departments.[38] This remained the case as we entered the 21st century.[39] These constitute a criticism not of community policing itself, but of those who claim to have implemented it without developing the substance.

### Crime Reduction

There is little empirical evidence to suggest that community policing is effective in reducing serious crime.[40] Indeed, available evidence seems to indicate that, although people involved in community policing efforts feel more secure, crime is not significantly reduced.[41] It may be that people who feel more secure will use the streets and other public places more frequently, thus eventually making it more difficult for criminals to ply their trades. It may also be that people who feel more secure, but are not *in fact* more secure, are more likely to engage in activities that make them available as victims, thus increasing the risk of crime.

**Video Link:**
Mayor to reinforce Community-Oriented Policing after Pittsburgh shootings

### Costs

Implementing COP may decrease the mobility and availability of the officers involved, because the officers are out of their vehicles a good deal of the time and because they are involved in community organization activities and are sometimes unavailable to respond to calls. In fact, in many programs, COP officers no longer perform routine motorized patrol, and other officers must take over this duty so that it can continue. It has also been suggested that the money spent on community policing might be better spent on improving social and economic conditions.[42] In fairness, it must be noted that community policing is seldom touted as a money-saving approach. Although it does cost money to implement any new program, there are various ways of measuring costs and comparing them to benefits. Departmental budgets may have to be increased initially to support COP.[43] However, the strategy may succeed in improving cooperation between the police and other citizens. It is a more elusive matter to measure the savings in crimes prevented or solved as a result of this increased cooperation. Further, some departments have managed costs by rearranging priorities, eliminating services for nonemergency calls, and providing reporting alternatives (telephone, fax, letters) for the public.[44] It appears that the federal government agrees that continued efforts in support of COP are worthwhile. On July 28, 2009, Vice President Joe Biden announced that the Department of Justice Office of COPS (Community Oriented Policing Services) awarded $1 billion in American Recovery and Reinvestment Act funding through its COPS Hiring Recovery Program (CHRP) to state, local, and tribal law enforcement to create or preserve nearly 5,000 law enforcement positions.[45] And, in 2011, the office awarded more than $243 million in grants across the nation.[46]

### Corruption

The permanent assignment of police officers, who have a good deal of independence in operations, enhances the possibility of corruption. This harkens back to corrupt police officers who walked beats, who were not subject to routine supervision, and who frightened neighborhood business persons (legitimate and illegitimate) into paying them for not enforcing the law or for protecting them from other predators. However, the very nature of COP works against such corruption. That is, COP officers work closely with members of the community, often in the setting of a community forum, and are well known on the streets. When these officers truly care about their professional reputations and the relationships they have formed, it is more difficult instead of less so to engage in corruption or abuse.[47]

**Timing**

Some critics argue that the time is simply not right to change from traditional policing strategies to COP. There are always crises to be faced and numerous reasons for not changing strategies. Whether or not the time is right, numerous variations on community policing have emerged across the country.

> If we don't risk changing when the time is right, we will be forced to change when we are not prepared. If we are afraid to change because we are comfortable, we may be holding on just to prove that certainty is better than taking a risk. No one benefits in this scenario. Not the police and certainly not the community.[48]

## ■ THE CURRENT STATUS OF COP AND POP

Over the last three decades, the culture of community policing has permeated the vast majority of police organizations, so much so that tactics and strategies associated with the model have become common knowledge among policing scholars, law enforcement executives, and street-level officers.[52] By now, it appears that "everybody knows" that police organizations need to successfully engage citizens and implement collaborative strategies to solve problems in the community. Although the emphasis has shifted to a number of new policing strategies, there is little doubt that most of these new strategies have incorporated the basic principles of COP and POP. It might, in fact, be argued that the shift toward technological innovations, intelligence gathering, antiterrorist efforts, and information exchange require more cooperation from the public than in the past. As we have noted, the police cannot be everywhere all the time. To be effective in the contemporary world, the police must rely more than ever on the eyes and ears of the public for the information they need to accomplish their tasks. Policing after 9/11 expanded to encompass problem- and community-oriented policing and to include the philosophy of intelligence-led policing. COP and POP have had a role in the development of many other new strategies. Enlisting the help of the Muslim community, for example, is reliant upon those community members accepting the legitimacy of the

### Exhibit 7.3

### CAPS: Chicago Alternative Policing Strategy

Community policing in Chicago is known as CAPS, or the Chicago Alternative Policing Strategy. The program had its origins at the time of rising crime rates in the early 1990s and was in the planning stages for more than a year before it was officially instituted in 1993 in 5 of the city's 25 police districts.[49] During initial phases, the strategy permanently assigned officers to beats and trained them in problem-solving techniques. Citizen committees formed in the various neighborhoods, and police and area residents began to meet on a regular basis. Police and residents worked together to identify and prioritize problems, develop ways of addressing them, and use community resources to accomplish goals. By the spring of 1998, almost 80% of the city's residents were aware of CAPS, over 60% knew about beat meetings in their neighborhoods, and about 15% had attended such meetings. Support for the program has grown among line officers.

To be sure, not all has gone smoothly with CAPS. Within the police department, CAPS challenged the business-as-usual mentality of officers and created initial pessimism among officers who did not care to take on noncrime problems. Developing workable performance measures and incentives has been problematic. It is difficult to quantify the extent to which officers are involved in problem solving and what indications there are of success.[50] A generally positive 10-year evaluation of CAPS noted that "an important point affecting everything that has happened is that CAPS is not simply the Police Department's program, rather it is the city's program. This is not true in most places, and community policing is vulnerable in many cities because of it."[51]

## Community Police in Nepal for Security and Justice

Policing is a vital part of the security institution in Nepal, and efforts have been made to mobilize the police to meet the needs of society. Established in 2004, community police in Nepal have been working to achieve security, justice, and public order. To achieve these goals, community police have coordinated with several social institutions in the community to work on problems such as household violence, children's issues, drugs, and other social ills. In addition, community police focus more on improvement than on punishment.

Apart from security, justice, and public order, community police are involved in humanitarian tasks as well. For example, the community police unit in Chitwan assists in providing shelters for street children and female victims of war and domestic abuse. Community police have also been providing scholarships and stationery to deserving students from poor economic backgrounds in coordination with various educational institutions. Head Constable of Community Policing Gokarna Prasad Dhakal noted, "We give counseling to school and college children for their mistakes rather than taking direct actions on them because in the long run it might have a negative impact on the future of these children. Therefore, if they are caught doing anything wrong, we bring [in] their parents and give counseling together."

There are still a number of obstacles to successful community policing in Nepal, including a lack of resources and budget and the difficulty of establishing coordination and cooperation with the community. On the positive side, Dhakal says, "Since the community is involved, information is delivered very quickly because of which our actions can be prompt."

Dhakal has been involved with community policing as an officer for three years and says, "I am very satisfied with my job. . . . It gives me a feeling of self-contentment to be able to build the society. Now I am directed toward doing something for the society and [helping] the society transform itself as well."

1. Skeptics of Nepal's community policing efforts would argue that law enforcement officers should be fighting crime, not providing counseling to school and college children. What would justify these efforts as the best use of the Security Institution's limited resources?

2. The community police have shifted their focus in many cases from punishment to improvement. Do you believe that these efforts are effective at fighting crime?

3. Is there anything that U.S. law enforcement can learn from Nepal's efforts?

*Source:* Pradhan, P. (2012, February 10). Community police in Nepal for security and justice. *Xinhua News Agency;* Dateline: CHITWAN, Nepal. Record Number: ChkhaeE000047_20120210_GWTFN1_fake. COPYRIGHT 2012 Xinhua News Agency.

police to the degree that they will relay key information. Police build that legitimacy through consistently adhering to fair procedure.[53] In this and other ways, community-oriented policing and homeland security are complementary as strategy and goal.[54]

## ■ INNOVATIONS IN POLICING STRATEGIES

There has been a proliferation of new approaches to preventing and responding to crime. Many innovations departments combine several of these strategies. Evaluation of these approaches continues to inform the growing body of professional knowledge, and so is an important part of this discussion.

Although they are closely related, innovations can be loosely grouped into categories. Some focus on the efficient and strategic use of information of all kinds to craft the best possible approach to dealing with crime problems. These include intelligence-led policing, evidence-based policing, and CompStat. Others use that intelligence to focus resources and officer power where it appears to be needed most. These include hot-spot

### John Crombach, Former Chief of Police, Oxnard Police Department

I received a telephone call from a resident who lived on a cul-de-sac in a nice neighborhood in the north end of town. She was in tears as she described the activity at the house across the street. She told me that she was considering selling her house because they could no longer tolerate the disturbances, loud parties, and traffic in and out of the house during the day and at night. She told me that the police would respond and things would quiet down for a couple of hours, and then the disturbances would start up again. The officers repeat that there isn't much they can do.

After we spoke, I called the captain who was in charge of that area of the city, who confirmed the story. He told me they had done several searches and made several arrests at the house over the past months. He then said, "This house has been a problem for years."

Clearly, the typical police strategies and tactics were not working here. We learned that the owner of the home was living in an assisted living facility and the owner's son was living in the house and renting out the individual rooms and the converted garage to other people. So, when the police made an arrest and removed one occupant, the son quickly found another person to move in—usually a narcotics user or dealer.

After some discussion, the captain and the rest of the leadership for that district decided to step outside the typical strategies and use a more creative and contemporary approach.

The senior lead officer held a meeting with all of the neighbors on the street where the problem house was. The neighbors all agreed to call police for any disturbance they witnessed, and the lead assured the neighbors that the police would deal with the problem.

After enlisting the help of the other neighbors, the senior lead officer for that beat contacted the homeowner at the assisted living facility and made him aware of the events at his house. The homeowner had never authorized his son to occupy the house; however, he was reluctant to tell his son to move. The senior officer contacted the city code compliance officer for that beat as well as the city attorney and inquired about permits for the garage conversion or other city code violations. There were no permits, and the property taxes were current. They learned that Chase Bank held the mortgage on the house. A call to Chase Bank revealed that the son had taken out a reverse mortgage on the property in his father's name. Chase Bank did not know that the father was in assisted living, and a requirement for the reverse mortgage is that the father live in the house. Chase agreed to cooperate with the officers.

With this information, police contacted the son and cited him for the city code violations and informed him that the city attorney was going to declare the residence a public nuisance, due to the number of police events at the house. They kept the father apprised of the investigation, and on his authority all of the "renters" were evicted from the residence. None had rental agreements. The district attorney (DA) prosecuted the son for real estate fraud. The son was convicted; the father sold the house.

At the end of the day, it was the collaboration of the police, code compliance, city attorney, Chase Bank, and the DA's office that cleared out the house and ended the problems in that neighborhood. After years of relying on typical police enforcement strategies and telling the neighbors, "There's not much we can do," a more contemporary problem-solving approach actually solved the problem.

policing, directed patrol, and differential response policing. Still others are based on the idea of thwarting the efforts of individuals who are intent on criminal behavior and making conditions inhospitable for committing crime. These include situational crime prevention, crime prevention through environmental design, and saturation patrol and crackdowns. Others are mostly concerned with collaborating or tight organization to fight crime or respond to emergencies, such as pulling levers policing (discussed later in this chapter), and Incident Command Systems (ICS, introduced in Chapter 3 and discussed further below). Others are more focused on the process of policing and how that can shape behavior and the role of the police. These include broken windows policing and the procedural justice model.

Police administrators would be grateful for some certainty that their strategic efforts will pay off. It requires a great deal of time, effort, and resources on the part of an entire department to move to a new way of doing things. Although researchers have attempted and continue to evaluate policing strategies, there is generally not enough evidence to draw an airtight conclusion either way about their true effectiveness. Research continues, but results are often mixed. Almost all studies measure the correlation of factors, not causal relationships. It is difficult to say that the strategy under evaluation *caused* a reduction (or increase) in crime. Crime rates are influenced by a complex mix of factors, including unemployment, education, drug epidemics, and demographic shifts. However, research design continues to evolve along with policing strategies and may yet yield more useful information.

Research can be categorized according to three common dimensions of crime prevention: the nature of the target, the extent to which the strategy is proactive or reactive, and the specificity or generality of the strategy. So far, proactive, place-based, and specific policing approaches appear much more promising in reducing crime than individual-based, reactive, and general ones.[55]

### Information Innovations
#### Intelligence-Led Policing

SAGE Journal Article: How Intelligence-Led Policing Has Repackaged Common Sense as Transcendental Truth

Intelligence-led policing (ILP) builds on the major developments in law enforcement in the last two decades of the 20th century, including COP and POP. Many describe ILP as a conceptual framework and an information-gathering process that allows police agencies to better understand their crime problems and consider the available resources before deciding on the most effective enforcement tactic or crime-control or -prevention strategy.[56] More specifically, ILP is informant and surveillance based with respect to recidivists and serious crime offenders and provides a central crime intelligence mechanism to facilitate objective decision making. Part of this is the police knowing who is committing the crimes. Much of the crime that is committed in any city is the result of repeat offenders, many of whom have often been recently released from jail or prison. So knowing who these people are and where they are living, and paying extra attention to them, is also part of ILP.

Many of the examples in the literature involve traditional street crimes and gun crimes, but ILP also assisted in the arrests following the London subway and Madrid train bombings.[57] In these cases, intelligence gatherers used surveillance cameras, community informants, and prison officials. ILP tends to focus on threats rather than crimes that have occurred.[58] These cases also indicate that ILP depends on strong community relationships, the belief that crime will continue to be a critical responsibility for the police, and that community support is vital to maintaining an active dialogue between law enforcement and the community.

The implementation of ILP is a challenge for most U.S. law enforcement agencies; the experience and lessons of community policing and CompStat serve as an important foundation. ILP can help law enforcement agencies better prepare for and prevent serious violent crime and acts of terror by taking advantage of the partnerships built through COP. ILP can also benefit from the problem-solving process.[59] ILP is not only consistent with COP but fits well under the COP umbrella. ILP adds a new dimension of community policing based on years of COP experimentation.[60]

#### Evidence-Based Policing

**Evidence-Based Policing:**
Involves using the scientific method to support an informed decision-making process

**Evidence-based policing** involves a scientific method of discovery to support an informed decision-making process.[61] Police administrators use the best available research to create policies and regulations and to conduct training. Police practices are often untested, and in many instances, nobody knows if these practices work.[62] In many cases, even after research has indicated that something does not work, police agencies continue to do it as a result of political pressure, inertia, or lack of awareness.[63] Today, there are a number of policing practices that promise to effectively prevent crime. Police are currently using many of these innovations, but there are some that should be eliminated or modified to better suit the needs of the community. Although there will always be some barriers to research-based policing (as police are asked to do more with less), research will become an even more important part of the decision-making process concerning what works and what does not work in policing.

▶

Policing in Practice
Video:
Crime/Statistical Analyst

### CompStat

The New York Police Department's crime-control model (**CompStat**) is a multifaceted system used to administer police operations. The model is a comprehensive, continuous analysis of results for improvement and achieving prescribed outcomes.[64] CompStat was created to provide police agencies with preliminary crime statistics that would permit tactical planning and deployment of police resources. CompStat is composed of five basic principles: specific objectives, timely and accurate intelligence, effective strategies and tactics, rapid deployment of personnel and resources, and relentless follow-up and assessment.[65] The essence of the CompStat process is to collect, analyze, and map crime data and other essential police performance measures on a regular basis and hold police managers accountable for their performance as measured by these data.[66]

Skeptics have noted that the declines in crime in cities that adopted CompStat were part of a broader trend, as crime rates have been declining nationwide since the mid 1990s.[67] There are some possible conflicts between CompStat and community policing.[68] CompStat gives police command staff most of the responsibility for reducing crime, largely excludes patrol officers from the decision-making process, and focuses on crime reduction.[69] Some also argue that community policing relegates decision making to the street, envisions police and the community as partners in problem solving, and makes officers responsible for a broad spectrum of community problems. "At stake here are two vastly different conceptions of the officer's role in modern society."[70] Others view CompStat as "perhaps the single most important organizational innovation in policing in the latter half of the 20th century."[71] Further, CompStat includes quality-of-life data (an important aspect of COP) in the production of maps and statistics to develop interactive crime prevention and reduction strategies.[72] CompStat has attracted considerable attention from both scholars and practitioners.

Despite its popularity, little empirical research demonstrates the effectiveness of the CompStat strategy. Studies have looked at various aspects of CompStat such as its effectiveness outside New York City; whether it generated a significant increase in "broken windows" arrests; its role in changes in violent, property, and total index crimes; and whether pressures on police managers resulting from CompStat might influence unethical crime reporting.[73] As with many other innovative policing strategies, there is not enough evidence on CompStat to determine its true effectiveness.

### Focused Resources
#### Hot-Spot Policing

Crime **hot spots** involve geographic areas with clusters of criminal offenses occurring within a specific interval of time.[74] Patrol officers have always known the location of consistent problems and responded with more aggressive patrols, surveillance of the area, and other methods. However, until recently, police crime prevention strategies did not focus systematically on hot spots and failed to address the underlying conditions that often give rise to high-activity crime locations.[75] Often, the strategic approach to a hot-spot location involves the police implementing high-visibility patrol, zero-tolerance disorder enforcement, POP, police crackdowns and raids, intensive enforcement of firearms laws through safety frisks during traffic stops, and other strategies.[76] Although there is some question as to what form of hot-spot enforcement has been the most

■ **CompStat:** Stands for computer statistics and is based on collecting and analyzing data from crime maps and other performance measures while holding police administrators accountable for their performance as measured by the data collected; a multifaceted system used to administer police operations based on a comprehensive, continuous analysis of results

■ **Hot Spots:** Geographic areas with clusters of criminal offenses occurring within a specified interval of time

An assistant chief for the Brooklyn South police surveys the CompStat results for his precinct. CompStat is a program designed to disseminate preliminary crime statistics to enable tactical planning.

© New York Daily News Archive/Getty Images.

effective, overall the research has revealed that hot-spot policing can have a meaningful effect on crime without simply displacing crime to nearby areas, which was assumed might happen.[77] Some observers, however, believe that the popularity of this reform may have buffered it from consideration of the potentially disproportionate impact of hot-spot policing on disadvantaged community members and the consequences of this impact for police legitimacy.[78] One study used a randomized experimental design with a panel survey of 371 persons and found that criticisms of hot-spot policing that focus on possible negative effects for residents of the targeted areas may be overstated.[79] It appeared that residents were neither aware of, nor much affected by, a dosage of aggressive order-maintenance policing on their blocks. Still other research suggests that simply increasing police presence does not gain as much community support, nor is it as effective as problem-oriented strategies.[80]

### Directed Patrol

To improve the effectiveness and efficiency of random patrol officers, many departments began to use a form of goal setting. The concept of directed patrol developed in response to the findings from a Kansas City study and was an attempt to alter the outcomes associated with random preventative patrol. **Directed patrol** involves increasing police presence in a specified area. Directed patrol in combination with a general deterrence strategy would saturate a high-crime area, including stops of as many people as possible for all (primarily traffic) offenses. However, directed patrol with a targeted deterrence strategy would focus patrol officers on specific behaviors, individuals, and places.[81] "Under both strategies, perceptions of the probability of punishment for crime generally, and under targeted deterrence, of violent crime in particular, will presumably increase, thereby deterring more individuals from committing crime."[82] Research results are mixed; some directed patrol appears to lead to a decrease in the specific crime the approach focused on, but other evaluation found not statistically significant reductions in crime.[83]

■ **Directed Patrol:** Involves increasing police presence in a specified area

## Differential Response Policing

**Differential response policing** involves rejecting the idea of dispatching each request for assistance or service in the order the call is received. Police have consistently responded to one radio call and returned to the vehicle to answer the next call. Many began to question the effectiveness and efficiency of an immediate response to every type of call received by the dispatcher. Much like triage in a hospital emergency room, differential response programs classify calls by their seriousness: (1) an immediate response by a sworn officer, (2) a delayed response by a sworn officer, or (3) no police response with reports taken over the telephone, by mail, or by having the person come to a police station in person.[84] Some departments support their own web page and allow the public to submit certain types of information online, by fax, or by email directly to the department. For example, the Sacramento Police Department allows residents to make online reports of crimes such as financial identity theft, harassment incidents, hit and run, mail theft, theft from a vehicle, threat incidents, vandalism, and violations of restraining orders.[85] Implementing differential response strategies may increase the time available for patrol, allowing police to focus on crime prevention. Police administrators sometimes use **community service officers (CSOs)** to enhance differential patrol strategies. CSOs are nonsworn employees who perform duties not requiring a police officer (unlock a vehicle, file insurance reports, document minor traffic accidents). CSOs wear different uniforms and patches and drive different vehicles than sworn officers.

## Changing Up the Environment
### Situational Crime Prevention

This innovation provides a means of reducing crime by reducing crime opportunities and increasing the risk to the offenders,[86] which centers on five major strategies:

- Increasing the effort needed to commit the crime
- Increasing the risk associated with the crime
- Reducing the reward derived from the crime
- Reducing the provocation
- Removing excuses for committing the crime[87]

A New York City effort to eliminate graffiti on subway cars serves as an example of **situational crime prevention (SCP)**.[88] Instead of expending resources in an attempt to apprehend the violators in the act of defacing the cars, city authorities decided that any subway car that was painted would not run until completely cleaned. Since graffiti artists derive great pleasure from seeing their artwork travel around New York, the new strategy removed the incentive the offenders had to paint the cars.[89] The officials determined the motivation for the criminal acts, eliminated the rewards, and focused on reducing the opportunity for misconduct and not the individual offenders. Situational crime prevention has been successful in reducing crime rates, though many argue that these types of innovations simply displace criminals into different venues.[90]

A major criticism of SCP strategies is that they simply displace crime from one area to another. If one neighborhood has a robust community watch program, car thieves and vandals are likely to move on to another neighborhood that is poorly monitored. In an analysis of 102 evaluations of situationally focused crime-prevention projects, the authors attempted to determine the extent of crime displacement.[91] Of the 102 studies that examined (or allowed for examination of) displacement, researchers reported displacement in 26% of observations. Because different departments have different ways of monitoring and measuring crime, displacement is easier to detect within a single jurisdiction than from one jurisdiction to another. The same study reported the opposite of displacement—diffusion of benefit—in 27% of observations. Diffusion of benefit occurs when areas near the target neighborhood also see a reduction in crime. Other researchers reported in 2014 that their meta-analysis revealed no significant

**Differential Response Policing:** Involves classifying calls by their seriousness to determine the appropriate police response

**Community Service Officers (CSOs):** Nonsworn employees who perform duties not requiring a sworn police officer

**Situational Crime Prevention (SCP):** Focuses on reducing crime by reducing crime opportunities and increasing risk to the offenders

As noted in the preceding section, intelligence-led policing has proven to be quite effective in the prevention and/or successful investigations of major crime incidents, including acts of terrorism.

© REUTERS/Lucas Jackson

displacement of crime, offering evidence to abut the frequent criticism that place-based policing strategies have only a temporary benefit.[92]

In the 13 studies that allowed for assessment of overall outcomes of the prevention project, when displacement occurred, it tended to be less than the displaced crime, suggesting that the SCP intervention was beneficial.

### Crime Prevention Through Environmental Design

SCP can be tied to an approach referred to as **crime prevention through environmental design (CPTED),** which is based on the following premise: "The proper design and effective use of the built environment can lead to a reduction in the fear of crime and incidence of crime, and to an improvement in quality of life."[93] In other words, schools, banks, businesses, housing, and so on may be constructed in such a way that potential offenders are discouraged from targeting them as a result of the materials employed, the use of open spaces and lighting, the location of the buildings, and a variety of other factors. Although the efficacy of SCP strategies on convenience store safety has received considerable attention, the security of fast-food restaurants has been virtually ignored. A study of 295 convenience stores and 321 fast-food restaurants in Charlotte, North Carolina, attempted to determine whether situational crime control strategies commonly recommended to the convenience store industry were effective at reducing robbery in the fast-food industry. The study also examined whether target-hardening strategies (e.g., removing posters from windows to open the interior of a store to view from the outside, providing better lighting, or obvious use of surveillance cameras to make it less likely that offenders will strike) have similar effects on robbery prevalence rates across the two types of businesses. The results indicate that many target-hardening strategies failed to impact robbery rates for either type of establishment and that those preventive strategies that did work generally appeared to impact one type of establishment or the other, but not both. The authors interpret their findings to mean that effective SCP strategies are situation specific rather than "one size fits all."[94]

### Saturation Patrol and Crackdowns

**Saturation patrol** adds patrol officers and increases police visibility. Crackdowns involve more planning than mere saturation. **Crackdown** refers to an increase in the

■ **Crime Prevention Through Environmental Design (CPTED):**
Based on the premise that proper design and effective use of the built environment can lead to a reduction in the fear of crime and incidence of crime

■ **Saturation Patrol:**
Involves adding patrol officers to a specific area in order to increase police visibility

■ **Crackdowns:**
Increases in the number of police targeted toward a specific type of law violation

number of police targeted toward a specific type of law violation, such as prostitution, drugs, domestic violence, driving under the influence (DUI), and speed and seatbelt violations. These strategies are meant to prevent criminal activities and decrease citizen fears. When a police crackdown is tightly focused, evidence suggests that immediate crime prevention benefits are likely.[95] For example, the Chicago Police Department (CPD) instituted a curfew crackdown and focused police personnel in areas of high gang activity through tactical teams and foot and bicycle patrols in parks and other areas where people congregate.[96] This is a good example of how different strategies can work together. The CPD used intelligence to identify hot spots for saturation patrols.

In most cases, successful third-party policing strategies result in reduced crime for less money, as civil justice mechanisms usually cost less than criminal justice mechanisms.[97] Third-party policing is most often used in drug-prone areas such as parks, malls, and designated street corners. It has also been deployed at locations such as bus stops disposed to robbery, late-night bars, and locations that have spray paint available to minors.[98] In these types of cases, police work with third-party partners to relocate or improve safety at bus stops, reduce hours at late-night bars, and restrict the sale of spray paint to minors.

## Collaboration and Organization
### Pulling Levers Policing

Several police agencies have used an innovation that has its roots in POP. This **pulling levers policing**, or deterrence strategy, focuses attention on a small number of chronic offenders responsible for a large share of the crime problems.[99] More specifically, "the approach consists of selecting a particular crime problem, such as youth homicide; convening an interagency working group of law enforcement, social service, and community-based practitioners; conducting research to identify key offenders, groups, and behavior patterns; [and] framing a response to offenders that uses a varied menu of sanctions (pulling levers)" to halt the criminal behaviors.[100] Continual, direct communication with these offenders is an important segment of the approach. An impact evaluation sponsored by the U.S. Department of Justice suggested that pulling levers policing was associated with a decrease in the monthly number of gun homicides in Stockton, California.[101] The results of a pulling levers reassessment conducted in Indianapolis indicated a significant reduction in homicide following the intervention, while six other similar Midwestern cities did not experience a significant decline in homicide.[102] The study found that gang-related homicides (the target of the pulling levers strategy) declined significantly more than did nongang homicides.

### Incident Command Systems

Incident Command Systems (ICS) involve a "standardized on-scene incident management concept designed specifically to allow responders to adopt an integrated organizational structure equal to the complexity and demands of any single incident or multiple incidents without being hindered by jurisdictional boundaries." (See also Chapter 3.) Such systems are thought to make managing major traffic accidents, terrorist attacks, natural disasters, and hostage situations easier by clarifying the command structure so that personnel from all responding agencies know who is in charge of various functions and the overall incident and whom they are to report to concerning various issues that might arise. ICS have also been used by police at nonemergencies such as large concerts, parades, sporting events, and celebrations. The systems provide a common framework wherein people can work together effectively when assessing the situation, developing and implementing strategies, allocating resources, and reassessing. Many incidents require skills and capacities that are beyond those found in a single organization and therefore require a network of responders from multiple agencies who do not routinely work together. An ICS organizes responses around a central command. At the scene of an accident, the central command may consist of police officers with input from medical and fire personnel.

**Pulling Levers Policing:** An innovation that focuses attention on a small number of chronic offenders responsible for a large share of the crime problems

A commander who tries to single-handedly manage a large-scale operation risks losing sight of the activities related to logistics, media, and other agencies at the scene. Thus, a key principle of the ICS (and the basis for its success when it is properly implemented) is that it divides functions modularly and ensures that no one person is trying to wear all the hats.

In many cases, emergency scenarios and even nonemergency events involve multiple agencies. Examples of multiple jurisdictions include the following:

- Geographic boundaries such as two or more states
- Levels of law enforcement such as local, state, or federal
- Functional responsibilities such as police, fire, or emergency medical personnel[103]

### Policing Processes
#### Broken Windows

Sometimes known as *zero-tolerance policing,* broken windows policing (also discussed in Chapter 6) is based on a theory that suggests that a reduction in minor crimes will lead to a decrease in violent ones.[104] The approach has remained popular over the past quarter of a century, perhaps in large measure because of its alleged success in reducing crime in New York City in the 1990s. The approach suggests that order maintenance within a community (fixing broken windows before they suggest the possibility of burning down the building) can be a major factor in crime control. Further, maintenance of property suggests that residents have a stake in the neighborhood and, by extension, that they will unite to keep the neighborhood safe and in good repair. Thus, broken windows policing seems to make sense, on the surface at least. Some researchers uncovered an unintended consequence of broken windows policing, a sort of "backfiring."[105] They found that such crackdowns can increase the fear of crime among community members and suggested that police needed careful planning to increase the effective benefit of any such intervention.[106]

Unfortunately, however, there is little solid evidence that strict police enforcement with respect to minor violations leads to a reduction in the rate of serious crime.[107] The debate continues over the effectiveness of broken windows policing.

#### Procedural Justice Policing

Police administrators must pay attention to public judgments about how they exercise their authority, because such judgments help to determine the legitimacy of the police and the willingness of individuals to obey the law and to cooperate in efforts to enforce the law. The **procedural justice model** of policing entails four main components of the interaction: citizen participation in the proceedings prior to an authority reaching a decision, neutrality on the part of the authority in decision making, a demonstration of dignity and respect throughout the interaction, and manner that conveys trustworthy motives.[110]

A procedural justice approach thus proposes a significant shift in emphasis for many departments. Procedural justice is:

> grounded in empirical research demonstrating that compliance with the law and willingness to cooperate with enforcement efforts are primarily shaped not by the threat of force or the fear of consequences, but rather by the strength of citizens' beliefs that law enforcement agencies are *legitimate.* And that belief in turn is shaped by the extent to which police behavior displays the attributes of *procedural justice*— practices which generate confidence that policies are formulated and applied fairly so that, regardless of material outcomes, people believe they are treated respectfully and without discrimination. . . . In the procedural justice model, officers are not oriented toward addressing situations primarily with the threat of force. Instead, officers are trained to view every citizen contact as an opportunity to build legitimacy through the tone and quality of the interaction, with force a last resort.[111]

**Audio Link:**
Procedural Justice: Taking the Ego Out of Policing

■ **Procedural Justice Model:**
A model of policing based on empirical research demonstrating that compliance with the law and willingness to cooperate with enforcement efforts are primarily shaped by the strength of citizens' beliefs that law enforcement agencies are legitimate

At a time when an apparent rash of police shootings of unarmed African American men is creating or perpetuating a deep public mistrust of the police—at least among some of the populace—one trouble-ridden city has been making huge strides in turning the tides on that mistrust and on violent crime. Richmond, California, has long been plagued by high rates of violent crime. Even though the rates for violence declined nationally by 20% between 2004 and 2013,[108] in Richmond, they dropped even faster. Homicides in this city of just over 100,000 decreased 40% between 2003 and 2013.[109]

Much of the credit for this turnaround is going to Richmond Police Chief Chris Magnus, who has built strong relationships between the police and the community and implemented improved and effective policies. One of the chief's strategies was geographic policing, which assigns officers to specific beats for extended periods, up to several years. The chief also challenges the department's officers to adopt a more service-oriented attitude and go beyond merely responding to calls. Performance evaluations reflect this change in policy; officers are judged on how well they address the priorities of the town's residents.

In 2006, even though the homicide rate was extremely high, the residents complained to the chief about the number of abandoned vehicles on their streets. Far from putting this issue on the back burner, the chief devoted resources to removing the cars, which helped immeasurably in building trust with the people of Richmond, who saw that the chief was serious about listening to them and responding to their needs. The stronger the community relationships, the more likely the police are to access information useful in preventing or solving crime, especially violent crime. "Just starting a conversation sometimes leads to surprising results," says Magnus.

"Pretty much every department, if you ask them, would say they're doing community policing," says Magnus. "And I think most believe it. But the challenge is: is community policing really policing the community in the way that the community wants to be policed, or is it driven by the police department?"

Many of the national protests against the excessive use of police force ended in violence. In Richmond, the chief stood with the protestors and held a "Black Lives Matter" sign, an act that drew intense criticism. In response, Magnus said, "It seemed to totally represent what we're trying to accomplish, which is respect: this idea that we acknowledge that the relationship between police and the African American community, particularly in many cities, has really been at best strained and at worst incredibly difficult for many, many years."

Magnus stands by his decision and believes that the position that all lives matter is what community policing should be about. Others recognize the chief's insight and effectiveness. The Department of Justice sought out his help by asking for his participation on a panel of experts to review procedures, training, and supervision in St. Louis County, where the police and the community have been engaged in serious conflict over the now iconic shooting death of Michael Brown.

Magnus concedes that the approach is not easy, but that to operate from a position of goodwill in the interest of building trust opens the door to accomplishing goals by working in partnership with the community.

1. Although leadership is critical to instituting reforms, what other factors might be involved in achieving positive results?

2. What strategies have been successful for the Richmond Police Department in lowering crime rates?

3. Do you believe that it is possible for other police departments to duplicate what has happened in Richmond?

*Source:* "Richmond police chief: 'All lives matter. That's really what community policing should be about,'" by Brad Marshland. *Yahoo News* "Richmond reports lowest homicide total in 33 years, credits multipronged efforts," by Robert Rogers. *Contra Costa Times* (January 6, 2014).

The notion of procedural justice is critical to all policing strategies that require public input and support. Nonetheless, implementation of this strategy is far from universal and—in an era where public input to the police is critical—its implementation might pay especially large dividends. A 2013 meta-analysis of procedural justice interventions suggests that they constitute an "important vehicle for promoting citizen satisfaction, confidence, compliance and cooperation with the police, and for enhancing perceptions of procedural justice."[112]

## CHAPTER SUMMARY

Policing continues to evolve as new and different strategies are developed, implemented, and tested in response to allegations of police misconduct and the demands for police services—from the day-to-day necessities of crime control to the increasingly global nature of national security and terrorist activities. Over the last three decades, many police administrators across the country have adopted community-oriented and problem-oriented policing models, tailoring and modifying them according to the needs of their departments and communities. Community-oriented policing represents both a philosophical and a practical shift toward a more collaborative, decentralized, and reciprocal approach to law enforcement. It continues to be tested, and its detractors point to its alleged failures such as poor implementation, ineffectiveness, and cost. There are also significant trends toward innovations that incorporate data gathering, targeting resources, technological advances, and information sharing among police agencies and other government departments. Many feel that strategies that are tailored to more specific problems are also more effective in controlling crime and disorder.

We must still ask how far we have come from the traditional reactive, incident-driven model of policing. Although there is considerable evidence that the traditional model of policing is both ineffective and inefficient, evaluators seek evidence to indicate that the new innovations undertaken produce greater efficiency and effectiveness. These too must be tested for effectiveness.

Research to answer these and other questions is ongoing. As time goes on, evaluators may discover increasingly certain evidence of the effectiveness of specific strategies in determined locations.

To obtain public participation, administrators need to promote citizens' beliefs that law enforcement agencies are legitimate. In return, police agencies stand to gain citizen compliance with the law and cooperation with enforcement efforts.

## KEY TERMS

- Community-oriented policing (COP) 154
- Strategic management era 157
- Solution-oriented policing (SOP) 158
- Evidence-based policing 164
- CompStat 165

- Hot spots 165
- Directed patrol 166
- Differential response policing 167
- Community service officers (CSOs) 167
- Situational crime prevention (SCP) 167

- Crime Prevention Through Environmental Design (CPTED) 168
- Saturation patrol 168
- Crackdowns 168
- Pulling levers policing 169
- Procedural justice model 170

**⑤SAGE edge™**

Review key terms with eFlashcards.

## DISCUSSION QUESTIONS

1. List and discuss some of the problems that characterize traditional policing. Which of the policing strategies discussed in this chapter might successfully address these problems?

2. What is community policing? In your opinion, is it a better approach than traditional policing? Why or why not?

3. What are some of the criticisms of community policing? In your opinion, are these criticisms justified? Why or why not?

4. Discuss problem-oriented policing and its relationship with other policing strategies.

5. What is intelligence-led policing? Is it an improvement over more traditional policing strategies? Why or why not?

6. Discuss the rationale for the development of differential response policing. Given the current economic conditions, does differential response policing make sense?

7. What is the role of researchers in evidence-based policing? Is it reasonable to expect line police officers to willingly accept the recommendations of police researchers? Why or why not?

8. Under what circumstances are Incident Command Systems most likely to prove useful? Can you give an example based on personal knowledge or experience?

9. Describe the policing strategy you feel is most appropriate in light of the contemporary global concerns about terrorism.

**⑤SAGE edge™**

Test your understanding of chapter content. Take the practice quiz.

## INTERNET EXERCISES

1. Use your browser to access articles on hot-spot policing. Summarize the conclusions of the researchers concerning this policing strategy. Does it appear this strategy is worth pursuing further? Why or why not?

2. Locate articles on the Internet dealing with the procedural justice model of policing. Based on your research, is the procedural justice concept new to policing? Is the concept of particular importance in the current policing environment? today?

## STUDENT STUDY SITE

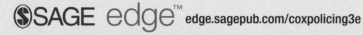 **⑤SAGE edge™** edge.sagepub.com/coxpolicing3e

**Sharpen your skills with SAGE edge!**

SAGE edge for Students provides a personalized approach to help you accomplish your coursework goals in an easy-to-use learning environment. You'll find action plans, mobile-friendly eFlashcards, and quizzes as well as videos, web resources, and links to SAGE journal articles to support and expand on the concepts presented in this chapter.

# HEAR IT FROM THE PROFESSIONALS

▶ edge.sagepub.com/coxpolicing3e

HEAD TO THE STUDY SITE WHERE YOU'LL FIND:

- **Exclusive video interviews** with police professionals discussing their careers, challenges, and advice

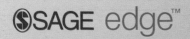

©iStockphoto.com/James Anderson

# POLICE CONDUCT

■■■ PART

III

# CHAPTER 8

# THE POLICE CULTURE AND WORK STRESS

## CHAPTER LEARNING OBJECTIVES:

1. Describe the unique aspects of police subculture

2. Analyze the factors that contribute to police subculture

3. Identify the sources of police stress

4. Discuss the effects and consequences of police stress

5. Assess the influence of police shootings and critical incidents on officers

6. Evaluate the various strategies that both organizations and individual officers can implement to mitigate the negative effects of job-related stress

# ■ WHAT IS CULTURE?

Professional culture exists in many arenas. Culture is the set of assumptions, beliefs, expectations, and philosophy that governs the professional's interactions, performance, and role. A professional arena may have its own unique subculture. Police administrators and the law specify the broad parameters within which officers operate, but the police subculture tells them how to go about their tasks, how hard to work, what kinds of relationships to have with their fellow officers and other categories of people with whom they interact, and how they should feel about police administrators, judges, laws, and the requirements and restrictions they impose. The police subculture also consists of the informal rules and regulations, tactics, and folklore passed from one generation of police officers to another.

The subculture may vary widely from one agency to another. Subculture may be affected by such things as crime rates, leadership values, and long-standing traditions. In a high-crime area that involves perhaps daily violence, a warrior culture may dominate and may help give rise to an "us-versus-them" environment. In a less military-like environment, a command structure may prevail where dialogue between administrators and officers is encouraged and where officers see themselves more as peacekeepers in service to the community. The potency of an agency culture varies among agencies as well. Some departments have deeply ingrained traditions, whereas others may be more dynamic and experimental. Some may welcome or even encourage a questioning attitude, whereas others may demand complete and unquestioning obedience on the part of subordinates. Even though every agency is likely to have officers who approach their work in different ways, personalities that do not fit well into an agency's culture may end up having difficulties adapting to it.

In any case, professional subculture organizes and guides the behavior of its members. Subculture is quite deliberately perpetuated through the police socialization process, which begins in the academy. An organizational culture can have many positive effects and can actually reduce anxiety and uncertainty in relationships and communicate the ideology that defines what the organization is all about.[1] The inherent uncertainty of police work, combined with the need for information control, leads to police teamwork, which in turn generates collective ties and mutual dependency.[2] Police subculture includes "protective, supportive, and shared attitudes, values, understandings and views of the world."[3] These shared values and attitudes are a natural outgrowth of the shared experience of policing.

However, police culture can also demand conformity and exert pressures that take a toll on its members. There are risks that individual officers and entire agencies can become too insulated and separate from the public. The us-versus-them mentality can further isolate the officer from everyone besides other officers. That isolation is both a cause of job stress and a result of it.

Combined, the effects of formal pressures and the pressures that the police subculture generates often lead police officers to experience a great deal of stress in their occupational, social, and family lives—resulting in cynicism, burnout, and a host of physical and emotional ailments. Many officers may not readily recognize the extent to which the police subculture and the pressures of the job affect the way in which they view and act toward others.

## Socialization, Isolation, and the Code

The process of socialization, which creates the "blue fraternity," begins at the police academy. The process continues throughout a police officer's career. If the subculture characterizes the public as hostile, not to be trusted, and potentially violent, this outlook requires secrecy, mutual support, and unity on the part of the police.

The social isolation of the police in turn contributes to a **code of silence** or **blue wall**—a closed police society (also referred to as the "brotherhood" or "blue fraternity"). Where this exists, there may be grave personal or professional consequences for violating it.

■ **Code of Silence (Blue Wall):** Protective, supportive, and shared attitudes, values, understandings, and views of the world associated with the police society

## The Stigma of Being a Cop

In many cases, police officers tend to socialize with other officers (not unlike members of other occupational groups) and come to realize (unlike members of many other occupational groups) that their identities as police officers sometimes make them socially unacceptable, even when off duty. That is, in some circles at least, there is a kind of stigma attached to those who are perceived as being "too close" to police officers; and police officers themselves are sometimes suspicious of the motives of civilians who become too friendly. The dangers associated with policing often prompt officers to distance themselves from the chief source of danger—other citizens.[6] The authority provided to police officers also separates them from other citizens. Thus, police officers are socially isolated from the public and rely on each other for support and protection from a dangerous and hostile work setting. They tend toward a strong sense of loyalty toward other officers.[7]

The more defensive that officers become in their isolation, the more entrenched the us-versus-them attitude becomes. From the outside, the police culture is often viewed negatively, and the code of silence has resulted in police officers *not* being held accountable for misconduct.[4]

Recently, intense public scrutiny has been focused on highly publicized police misconduct cases across the country, including such incidents as the Los Angeles Police Department's Rampart corruption case or the Houston Police Department's shooting of a Mexican immigrant. With each new headline, anxiety and mistrust of police officers and their departments increase. Police executives repeatedly find themselves confronted with the issue of the code of silence. But, how much is fact, and how much is fiction? Reality or perception?[5]

### Erosion of the Public's Trust

Apart from the extent of the code's existence, it is certain that the public believes that it exists. Much of the public believes that officers who are guilty of wrongdoing are protected by the code of silence and are not held accountable for their actions. Regardless of whether a blue wall of silence is a reality, the belief by the public that such a protective environment exists has a negative effect on the relationships between the police and the community. The erosion of public trust in the police inhibits their ability to perform their duties. Police scandals have supporters and critics alike calling for civilian review boards and other external oversight mechanisms.

Recognizing the damage to the public trust, some departments are willing to openly look at their record of complaints. An examination of the internal affairs investigations in the Houston Police Department from 1992 to 2002 found that, in 7 of the 11 years examined, more than 50% of all the complaints investigated were generated internally—by other officers as opposed to external citizen complaints. In one year, almost two-thirds of the complaints were initiated from internal sources. These internal complaints ran the gamut from minor procedural violations to felony criminal activity.[8]

To see whether Houston's Internal Affairs Division data were different from those of other major departments, the city's Planning and Research Division gathered data from 15 departments of the nation's 50 largest cities. Seven of those departments keep track of whether complaints come from internal or external sources. The seven departments are Arlington, Texas; Dallas, Texas; Baltimore, Maryland; Jacksonville, Florida; Columbus, Ohio; Memphis, Tennessee; and El Paso, Texas. These departments had numbers similar to those in Houston.[9] These statistics would tend to indicate that the blue wall or code of silence is not as prevalent as Hollywood would have us believe.

**Author Video:**
The Transformation of the LAPD and the Work that Remans

© Guy Cali/Corbis

This patrol officer is attempting to explain to members of his department's administrative committee on traffic safety why the traffic accident he was involved in was unavoidable.

## Coping

Police officers develop resources to deal with the isolation from the community and even family members, which results from job stress and the police socialization process.[10]

The police are human beings just like everyone else and do make mistakes. In policing, mistakes can have critical consequences. Police must continue to be trained in how to recognize and address the ethical issues they routinely encounter. "Compromising situations frequently occur without warning and with little if any time to think, and as in life-and-death situations, a wrong decision in the ethical arena can have life-changing consequences for the officer."[11]

Ultimately, one way that police officers cope with their organizational environment is by taking a "lay low" or "cover your ass" attitude and adopting a crime-fighter or law-enforcement orientation, which tends to perpetuate the entire dynamic.[12] The establishment of a professional, moral, ethical culture in a police organization can control, prevent, and punish misconduct and corruption. Of course, this type of culture relies in part on the organization's hiring, retention, promotion practices, leadership, and socialization process for new police officers.

## ■ ANALYZING POLICE SUBCULTURE

The **police subculture** is a key concept in the explanation of police behavior and attitudes.[13]

Traditional characterizations of the police culture have focused on describing the shared values, attitudes, and norms created within the occupational and organizational environments of policing.[14]

■ **Police Subculture:** Shared values, attitudes, and norms created within the occupational and organizational environment of policing; a set of informal norms, largely based on tradition and passed on from generation to generation, that greatly influence police behavior and the perception of the public by police. Certain of these subcultural forces have a significant influence on the use of discretion, in both positive and negative ways

One observer identified "six normative orders" within policing—law, bureaucratic control, adventure or machismo, safety, competence, and morality—and concluded these orders serve as boundaries for the subculture that both justify and limit certain actions of police officers.[15]

Some research concerning police culture proposed the existence of different attitudinal subgroups of officers.[16] Some groups of police officers represent many of the negative attitudes of the traditional culture, such as authoritarian, hard line, and aggressive. Others often have attitudes of problem solving and assisting. As police departments

## POLICE STORIES 8.1

### Connie Koski, Professor and Former Police Officer

Police stress is often difficult to truly understand without personal experience. It wasn't until I experienced firsthand the influences of police subculture, expectations from the public, dangerous encounters, and pressures from administrators that I began to fully comprehend how these factors could produce a toxic combination of cynicism and physical and emotional issues.

One particularly serious incident took place on a hot summer evening around the middle of my career. I was a field training officer and senior patrol officer on my shift; I felt confident in my abilities on patrol and took these roles seriously. On the night in question, I was working my fifth 12-hour shift in a row and was feeling the early signs of exhaustion. We received a call of an older Black female harassing a group of older Black men who lived in a senior citizen public housing complex. I recognized the name of the woman causing the problem. She was someone with whom I had a friendly rapport. I told my fellow officers they could remain back at the station to complete shift briefing while I responded to ask her to leave the property. I made the mistake of assuming she would comply, given our friendly relationship, but when I arrived she refused to leave and resisted arrest. As I struggled to place her in handcuffs, the woman grabbed my ink pen from my uniform pocket and began stabbing me in the neck, coming perilously close to my jugular vein. Several of the male callers, also Black, were seated in a gazebo nearby, witnessing the entire struggle. Given that I am White and always worked very hard to treat all people equitably, I made a special effort not to use a significant amount of force to subdue this woman for fear that it would appear either racist or excessive, despite the fact that I was later told by several administrators that I should have done so, given her use of near deadly violence against me. I was finally able to wrestle the woman to the ground without harming her and was able to secure her until backup arrived.

As fellow officers arrived and took custody of the woman, I suddenly and very unexpectedly burst into tears for reasons I could not explain. I was embarrassed in front of my male coworkers and couldn't understand why I was crying. I later discovered that this "adrenaline dump" is what happens to a person's body when he or she experiences sudden violent "fight or flight" situations and has no real release for the adrenaline following the de-escalation of the incident. To compound the situation, the next day I was admonished by administrators for not using deadly force against this woman (as I would have been authorized to do based on the force continuum and her actions toward me), as well as for not having taken backup with me to the call. I was personally proud of my restraint and the ability to bring the incident to a successful resolution without the use of excessive force or inappropriate language in front of other city residents, and was frustrated by the response from my superiors.

I became very cynical and resentful toward my agency's administrators as a result. This attitude became very demotivating for me over the course of the next several months. Rather than seeing this as a sign of stress, many of my superior officers simply saw this as a bad attitude and became very adversarial toward me, rather than helping me understand or seek help, compounding the problem. My behaviors were clearly the result of several years of stress. I was unable to identify it myself, because I had been socialized to believe that I could "handle" it on my own. Most police officers would be untruthful if they told you they never experienced stress at some point during their careers. Some officers ultimately leave the profession as a result of job stress. Others are so heavily indoctrinated into police culture that they resist seeking outside assistance in times of great stress and become almost incapable of recognizing their need for help.

become more heterogeneous, a single department's cohesive police culture may give way to a more multifaceted one.[17] Racial minorities, women, and college-educated personnel bring different outlooks and attributes, based on past experiences, which may affect the way in which police collectively interpret the world around them.[18–19]

At the academy, a new police officer learns the laws and formal rules required before initiating a traffic stop on a motor vehicle. However, beyond these formalities, new officers quickly learn the importance of tone of voice, posture, and initial approach to a hysterical, threatening, or apologetic driver. In many cases, veteran police officers have refined, through years of traffic stops, a ritual or standard approach and accompanying explanation for almost all drivers.

There are different but related forms of organizational culture: artifacts, values, and basic assumptions.[20] The **artifacts** are the most visible parts of the organizational culture and include sounds, architecture, smells, behavior, attire, language, products, and ceremonies. Police culture is in part transmitted and defined by certain artifacts. For example, police recruits quickly learn police jargon, how to address superiors, how to communicate on the radio or computer, a writing style for police reports, and a host of other behaviors unique to policing.

Another police artifact is the patrol officer's uniform, which is a symbol of law and order and allows members of society to readily identify a police officer. Some departments have researched the use of blazers or a more casual form of dress to encourage police–community interactions and de-emphasize the paramilitary associations the uniform can have.

SAGE Journal Article: An Examination of Officers' Occupational Attitudes

The values embedded in the organization are the most important, because they guide the behavior of the organization's members.[21] For example, new police officers often complete months of training on the street with a field training officer or FTO, who has a pivotal role in conveying values such as respect, integrity, honesty, and fairness to a new police officer. The FTO socializes and orients new police officers, and in most cases, the trainee's career and behavioral attributes are impacted by this influence.[22] However, in policing, as in many occupations, some values can set up ethical, moral, and legal conflicts.

Many police officers view themselves as teammates linked together by portable radios, cell phones, and person-to-person messaging, part of a team that is no stronger than its weakest member. As members of the team, they feel a good deal of pressure to live up to the expectations of other team members and to support the practice of secrecy.

Evidence of secrecy is clearly articulated in phrases you might hear among officers, such as "Watch out for your partner first and then the rest of the guys working," "Don't give up another cop," "Don't get involved in anything in another cop's sector," or "If you get caught off base, don't implicate anybody else."[26]

One study reported that in many cases newer police officers were more willing to admit to viewing unethical acts, compared to police officers with more seniority. "One conclusion would be that the [longer the] length of time an officer is exposed to this socialization process, the greater its impact."[27]

What is relevant, recruits are told, is the experience of senior officers who know the ropes or know how to get around things. Recruits are often told by officers with considerable experience to forget what they learned in the academy and in college and to start learning real police work.[28] Among the first lessons learned are that police officers share secrets among themselves; that these secrets, especially when they deal with activities that are questionable in terms of ethics, legality, and departmental policy, are not to be divulged to others; and that administrators often cannot be trusted. Thus, emphasis on the police occupational subculture results in many officers regarding themselves as members of a minority that has to look out for itself.[29]

When officers hold an us-versus-them view of the world, the "us" consists of other police officers; the "them" encompasses almost everybody else. To be sure, members of

■ **Artifacts:** Most visible forms of an organizational culture (sounds, behaviors, language)

other occupational groups also develop their own subcultures and worldviews, but often not to the same extent as the police.[30] According to a classic text, "Set apart from the conventional world, the policeman experiences an exceptionally strong tendency to find his social identity within his occupational milieu."[31]

Rank-and-file police officers sometimes even begin to view their administrators as dangerous outsiders to the patrol subculture and somewhat personally and professionally threatening.[32] This tension between police officers and police administrators is primarily due to the discrepancy between what patrol officers are commanded to do and what they can realistically be expected to accomplish.[33]

Postulates that show the us-versus-them view include the following:

- Don't tell anybody else more than they have to know; it could be bad for you, and it could be bad for them.

- Don't trust a new guy until you have checked him out.

**Organizational Assumptions:** Deeply held beliefs that guide behaviors in an organization

**Ethos:** Fundamental spirit of a culture

- Don't give them (police administrators) too much activity.
- Keep out of the way of any boss from outside your precinct.
- Know your bosses.
- Don't do the bosses' work for them.
- Don't trust bosses to look out for your interests.
- Don't talk too much or too little.
- Protect your ass.[34]

**Web Link:**
Putting Police
Ethics on Trial

## Contributing Factors

Factors inherent in police work contribute to the tendency toward social isolation. Among these factors are danger, authority, and the need to appear efficient.[35]

### Danger

In police work, danger is always a possibility, and it is highly unpredictable, except in certain types of situations. Who knows when the traffic stop at midday will lead to an armed attack on the police officer involved? Who can predict which angry spouse involved in a domestic dispute will batter a police officer (or, for that matter, whether both spouses will)? Who knows when a sniper firing from a rooftop will direct his shots at the windshield of a patrol car? Under what circumstances will a person with a mental disorder turn on an officer attempting to assist? Will drivers approaching an intersection heed the flashing lights and siren of an officer's car? Does the fleeing young burglar have a firearm under his shirt? "The potential to become the victim of a violent encounter, the need for backup from other officers, and the legitimate use of violence to accomplish the police mandate all contribute to a subculture that stresses bravery, which is ultimately related to the perceived and actual dangers of policing."[36]

In fact, because of the unpredictable nature of danger in policing, police officers are trained to be suspicious of most, if not all, citizens they encounter. Police are encouraged to treat them as **symbolic assailants**, to approach them in certain ways, to notify the dispatcher of their whereabouts when making a stop, and to wait for additional officers or backup to arrive before proceeding in potentially dangerous cases.[37] Even though violence occurs in a low percentage of police–civilian interactions, "the highly unpredictable and potentially dangerous person, who cannot be dependably identified in advance, conditions officers to treat each individual with suspicion and caution."[38] Examples of symbolic assailants include two men walking in a quiet residential neighborhood at 3 a.m. or a police officer receiving the description of a person approaching a subway station carrying a "suspicious package." In other words, police officers create in their mind an image of what they perceive to be the behaviors of a threatening person. This image is based on training, past experiences, and sharing of war stories by veteran officers, and it is ever changing depending on the perceived threat to the safety of the officer and the community.

There is a paradox of policing concerning the perception of danger and actual danger.[39] According to some research, it is not the actual danger that results in fear, but the constantly present potential for danger that has the significant impact.[40] The fear of danger by police may be both functional and dysfunctional.[41] The very real hazards of police work require that police be alert to the risks of the job. However, the constant concern over danger can contribute to increased levels of stress and burnout.

During everyday contacts with the public, police officers believe they can minimize the potential danger they will confront, as well as properly display their coercive authority, by always being prepared—or "one up" on the public.[42] One inquiry identified three types: "suspicious persons," "assholes," and "know-nothings."[43] Suspicious persons include those who are most likely about to commit or might have already committed an offense. The assholes include those individuals who disrespect the police and do not

**Symbolic Assailants:** Potentially dangerous citizens to whom police are trained to accord a level of suspicion

Constantly viewing citizens as symbolic assailants and potential threats can lead to burnout and difficulty coping with stress.

© iStockphoto.com/James Anderson

accept the police definition of the situation. These individuals might receive some form of *street justice* or "a physical attack designed to rectify what police take as a personal insult."[44] The know-nothings are the typical citizens who interact with the police when they request service.

### Authority

Academy instructors teach police officers to assess others with whom they are involved in terms of their ability to physically handle such individuals if it becomes necessary and to be aware that in most instances their encounters with other citizens will be perceived as creating trouble for those citizens. Instructors teach officers that they work in an alien environment in which everyone knows who they are, while they lack such information about most of the people with whom they interact.[45]

In addition, of course, as representatives of government, police officers are told they have specific authority to intervene in a wide array of situations. They are equipped with a Taser, a firearm, handcuffs, a portable radio, backup officers, and a uniform to be sure that their image as authority figures is complete and unmistakable. And they are told that, when dealing with a dispute in progress, their definition of the situation must prevail, and they must take charge of the situation. Police are taught that, as a part of their role, they must give orders, exercise control over law enforcement and order maintenance situations, place restraints on certain freedoms, enforce unpopular laws (even ones they do not agree with), conduct searches, make arrests, and perform a number of other duties.[46]

What is not routinely stated to police officers—but what they learn very quickly on the streets—is that other citizens, not infrequently, resent their intervention. And other citizens, when treated suspiciously by the police, may react with hostility, resentment, contempt, and occasionally physical violence. Nor are police officers routinely taught that certain segments of the population hate them or hold them in contempt simply because they wear the badge and uniform. If members of these groups challenge the authority of the police, based on their training, the police will often resort to threats of force or the use of force to impose their authority, which often escalates the level of danger in the encounters. On those relatively rare occasions in which the challenge

Police officers see horrific things, including homicides, rapes, car accidents, and violent assaults, with some of these cases involving children and teenagers. Although some officers may become desensitized over time to certain aspects of the job, it is never easy. And, it is even more difficult to shake the lasting emotional distress that confronting these situations produces. Although we seldom hear about police officers suffering from **post-traumatic stress disorder (PTSD)**, they suffer from it as we now know that military veterans do as well.

Retired Officer Bill Kruger has lived with PTSD ever since killing an escaped convict while on duty. The police usually think they need to "tough it out" when they are having difficulties, that being emotionally challenged is a sign of weakness. Those who do admit a problem risk being stigmatized, being relieved of their badges and guns, and having their peers and superiors assume they are a risk to themselves or others. As with most people who need help, without it, they tend to get worse.

Officer Kruger joined a peer-support group to help cope with his illness. After realizing that his situation would not be kept in confidence, and fearing that staying might jeopardize his career or opportunities for promotion, he decided to leave the group.

Untreated PTSD and other psychological illnesses can lead to drug or alcohol abuse, or even suicide. Officer Kruger acknowledges the effect his PTSD had on his personality. It made him an angry person, and he drank to alleviate his pain. The police community has precious few mental health resources available to officers; agencies retain few trained therapists or psychologists who can properly identify and address PTSD and other conditions. PTSD is sometimes delayed, and retirees may experience an onset of symptoms after they leave the force.

Police administrators need to implement consistent psychological checkups and greater attention to police officer mental health care. Only then will PTSD and other mental health problems be effectively resolved.

1. Should officers with diagnosed cases of severe PTSD be forced to retire from law enforcement? If not, what can law enforcement agencies do with these officers?

2. Do law enforcement agencies have a duty to identify and treat officers with PTSD?

3. Considering the serious nature of PTSD, why would an officer refuse to continue counseling or other treatment services?

4. Should officers be compelled to continue treatment if they do not want counseling or other services?

*Source:* "Toughing it out: Posttraumatic stress in police officers," by Robert T. Muller, 2013. *Psychology Today* (https://www .psychologytoday.com/blog/talking-about-trauma/201302/toughing-it-out-posttraumatic-stress-in-police-officers).

to authority is prolonged or vicious, danger may become the foremost concern of all parties involved, and the capacity to use force, including deadly force in appropriate circumstances, becomes paramount.[47] Under the circumstances, the need for police solidarity and the feelings of isolation and alienation from other citizens become apparent. Police unity bolsters officer self-esteem and confidence, which enables the police to tolerate the isolation from society and the hostility and public disapproval.[48]

## Performance

At the same time, we expect the police to be efficient, and the police themselves are concerned with at least giving the appearance of efficiency, if not the substance, because performance evaluations and promotions often depend on at least the former. Concerns with efficiency and the resulting pressures they produce have increased dramatically with computerization and other technological advances in the police world. Simultaneously, taxpayers have begun to demand greater accountability for the costs involved in policing and the addition of well-educated (and therefore more costly)

■ **Post-traumatic Stress Disorder (PTSD):** Emotional disturbance leading to a numbing of emotions, insomnia, and depression

This officer bears the authoritarian tools of her trade.

© Alex Segre / Alamy

police personnel. The resulting "do more with less" philosophy has led many police executives to emphasize even more the importance of efficient performance. "Citizens expect professional police behavior, respectful treatment, maintenance of human dignity, responsiveness, and a high value on human life. In addition, these increasingly sophisticated taxpayers also insist that the police achieve maximum effectiveness and efficiency in the use of their tax dollars."[49]

In some cases, the police subculture has established standards of acceptable performance for officers and resists raising these standards. Officers whose performance exceeds these standards are often considered *rate-busters* and threats to those adhering to traditional expectations. For example, fueling the patrol car, in some departments, is an operation for which the officer is expected to allot 20 to 30 minutes. Because the operation may actually take less than 5 minutes, administrators concerned about accountability, totaling the amount of time lost in this operation for, say 10 cars, recognize they are losing two to three hours of patrol time if they fail to take action to modify the fueling procedure. At the same time, however, officers concerned about accountability who wish to patrol an additional 15 to 20 minutes and fuel the car in less time make those officers adhering to the 20- to 30-minute standard look bad, and they are under considerable pressure to conform to the established standard. Similar expectations and conflicts exist with respect to the number of drunk drivers who can be processed in a shift, the number of felonies that may be processed, the number of subpoenas that may be served, or the number of prisoners who may be transported. Officers must make choices as to whose expectations

## Exhibit 8.2

### The Police Subculture

The police subculture creates a set of truths, according to which officers are expected to live. Note that there is some basis in fact for each of these subcultural truths and that each makes integration and communication between the police and the citizens they serve more difficult.

- The police are the only real crime fighters.
- No one understands the nature of police work but fellow officers.
- Loyalty to colleagues counts more than anything else.
- It is impossible to win the war on crime without bending the rules.
- Other citizens are unsupportive and make unreasonable demands.
- Patrol work is only for those who are not smart enough to get out of it.[50]

are to be met and sometimes operate in a no-win situation, in which meeting one set of expectations automatically violates the other, leaving the officer under some stress no matter how he or she operates.

### The Police Personality: How Real?

Some have suggested that the impact of police work and the police subculture itself lead to the development of a distinctive **police personality**.[51] The police personality has been conceived as a combination of characteristics and behaviors—a stereotype of the police. Often, these characteristics include a "desire to be in control of the situation, assertions, cynicism, authoritarian attitude, a wish to be aloof from citizens, an increased solidarity with other police officers and a tendency to be physically aggressive."[52] How does such a personality develop? Is it a matter of an individual innately possessing those personality characteristics, or does it develop from the work itself?[53] Some believe policing attracts individuals who possess a certain type of personality, while others propose that the exposure to violence, corruption, and danger creates an elusive personality. On the positive side, one study reported that police applicants differ from the general population in several positive ways: "They are more psychologically healthy than the normative population, as they are generally less depressed and anxious, and more assertive and interested in making and maintaining social contacts."[54]

"There is some evidence for the existence of a police working personality. Most of the evidence points to the influence of socialization and experiences after becoming a police officer as the main source of the unique traits."[55]

Although some of the research on police personalities does appear to distinguish certain traits, no one has been able to "disentangle the effects of a person's socioeconomic background from the demands that police work and its subculture places upon individual officers."[57] The research does not support the existence of a single dominant personality type among police officers. "There is no evidence for such a thing as a typical police personality showing a cluster of traits that is constant across time and space."[58]

## ■ TYPES OF STRESSES IN POLICE WORK

As previously mentioned, the formal police organization and the police subculture both contribute to the stress levels experienced by police. The effects of formal pressure from police organizations and pressures generated by the police subculture often lead police to experience a great deal of stress in their occupational, social, and family lives, resulting at times in cynicism, burnout, and retirement on the job, as well as a host of physical and emotional ailments. Also, those police officers who reported higher levels of stress reported more acts of deviance. Correspondingly, as the stress levels of police officers were reduced through reassignment from high-stress duties, the reported deviance decreased.[59]

Although there does not appear to be a cluster of personality traits that distinguish police officers from other occupational groups, there is no doubt that the nature of police work and the subculture in which it occurs creates difficulties for officers, their families,

■ **Police Personality:** Combination of characteristics and behaviors that are used to stereotype the police

---

### Exhibit 8.3

#### Working Personalities

One system of categorization identifies four working personalities of police: enforcers, idealists, realists, and optimists. Enforcers emphasize the law enforcement function, while idealists focus on individual rights. Realists place little emphasis on social order and individual rights. Optimists view policing as an opportunity to help people.[56]

and their friends. The need to perform under stress is a concern in many professions; policing may not be as stressful as some other occupations such as brain surgery or even teaching. Nevertheless, stress is one of the most common of all occupational hazards for police and can be extremely debilitating, leading to early onset of stress-related illness.[60] Police stress may manifest in a variety of ways.[61]

Of course, the cost associated with a stressful event is a function of how each individual perceives the event.[62] What may be viewed as very threatening to one police officer may be perceived as simply an exciting challenge by another. Those individuals who are capable of venting their feelings and discharging their emotions do not suffer as much from stressful events.[63]

Research on police stress has focused on the sometimes violent nature of the work and the organizational structures found in almost all police agencies.[64]

One top-ranked stressor was concern for fellow police officers being injured or killed.[65] Other research failed to demonstrate a clear association between the dangers of police work and the level of stress that officers experience.[66] A segment of research suggests police officers are "no more stressed than other groups and police work is not especially stressful."[67]

**Author Video:**
How do law enforcement identify and know when officers are under stress? How do law enforcement approach and guide officers to handle stress?

The quasi-military nature associated with some police organizations often breeds alienation among street officers, who are required to use high levels of discretion while being tightly controlled by supervisors and administrative rules.[68] Cops have strict guidelines, and they are dealing with people who are not governed by any rules at all. Additional stressors included public criticism, family demands, career stages, and working the late shift.[69]

To the list of stressors we might add excessive paperwork, red tape, discrimination, lack of participation in decision making, and competition for promotion, among others. One study used saliva and blood samples from police officers to examine their levels of cortisol, which is often referred to as a "stress hormone." The research revealed that police officers "who work the graveyard and swing shifts are more likely to be tired" and have a high rate of injuries, compared to those officers assigned to the day shift.[70]

One study found new and more severe sources of stress for police: increased scrutiny and criticism from the media and the public, and anxiety and loss of morale as a result of layoffs and reduced salary raises.[71] Even positive changes, such as the movement to community-oriented policing, have caused increased levels of stress for many officers. Today, the increasing response to or the threat of terrorism is also a job-related stressor.[72]

The sources of stress can break down into four categories in organizations—task demands, role demands, interpersonal demands, and physical demands.[73]

### Task Demands

Task demands or the lack of them can impose high stress levels on police. Quantitative input overload is a result of too many demands for the time allotted, while qualitative input overload is the result of complexity and limited time.[74] These two types of input overload can lead to **hyperstress**. Quantitative overload occurs when police officers experience stacking of calls or when they receive more calls than they can answer. Emergency calls are prioritized by 911 systems, but minor theft cases, criminal damage to property cases, trespassing violations, and other nonemergency calls are answered in order. An officer on a busy shift might respond to 25 calls for service, with little time for patrol or personal breaks. Obviously, with this number of calls, the quality of the police interaction with the public can suffer. Investigators assigned a large number of cases more readily experience quality overload. Each case must follow case management criteria and may include interviews, interrogations, evidence collection, search warrants, and numerous reports. The number of cases that supervisors assign and the pressure that prosecutors generate to complete an investigation affect the quality of investigation and the extent of overload experienced by individual officers.

**Hyperstress:**
An overload resulting from too many complex demands for the time allotted

Low levels of mental and physical activity cause **hypostress**, which is the result of too little quantitative and qualitative input.[75] Police officers experience high levels of boredom when they work a shift with no calls, when their only activity is random patrol and personal breaks. Answering service call requests—one of the primary roles of a police officer—is often seen by officers as routine, mundane, and boring.

### Role Demands

Role demands develop two types of role stress in the work environment: role conflict and role ambiguity.[76] **Role conflict** is a result of the inconsistent or incompatible expectations. A role conflict can occur when society's expectations of police behavior conflict with certain police principles, beliefs, and behaviors. For example, for many decades, society has condemned the use and sale of illegal drugs. However, the police are limited in their ability to successfully reduce drug sales and trafficking due to many factors outside their sphere of influence, such as search and seizure laws, drug legalization, and limited resources.

> Cops must avoid the harsh glare of the external observation which would reveal (1) that they were frequently in violation of the law, and (2) that they were doing exactly what the public wanted them to do, generating arrests for drugs the only way they can—fabricating evidence, dropsy, lying on the witness stand, entrapment—in a word, by being more criminally sophisticated than the criminals.[77]

Thus, the perceptions of society and the actual behaviors of police performing undercover drug enforcement can generate high levels of stress, especially for police who must become a part of the drug culture, appear in court as a professional police officer, and still maintain relationships with spouses, children, and other family members.

**Role ambiguity** is the confusion a person experiences related to the expectations of others.[78] For example, the police are seen by the public as "alertly ready to respond to citizen demands, as crime-fighters, as an efficient, bureaucratic, highly organized force that keeps society from falling into chaos."[79] However, this is an exaggeration of actual police work. Police work resembles other kinds of work in that it can be boring, tiresome, mentally draining, or technically demanding. It is not always dangerous. And to add to the role confusion, the public has demanded an even higher level of the crime-fighting activities, which are grossly exaggerated in books, movies, electronic games, and television shows.

### Interpersonal Demands

Abrasive personalities, sexual harassment, and the leadership style in the organization are examples of interpersonal demands.[80] Even with general support by the public, police typically encounter individuals with abrasive personalities. Many citizens feel the police are just a little above the evil they fight or believe that the police are against them and misuse their right to use force to uphold the law.[81] The police often perceive the public as extremely harsh critics, leading to increased levels of occupational stress.

In most cases, besides the on-duty demands on police officers, there are also off-duty requirements that affect the stress levels of officers and their families. For example, language similar to the following can be found in most police department policy manuals: "A police officer's character and conduct while off duty must be exemplary, and maintain a position of respect in the community."[82] To an extent, police are never off duty, which adds to high levels of stress in police officers and their families.

Management or leadership styles play an important role in work environment stress levels. There are significant differences in employee stress levels depending on management styles.[83] One study revealed that management styles were one of the primary predictors of stress in employees. This is especially true in police organizations that are characteristically authoritarian but attract college-educated personnel.

**■ Hypostress:** Low levels of mental or physical activity

**■ Role Conflict:** The result of inconsistent or incompatible expectations being communicated to a person

**■ Role Ambiguity:** Confusion a person experiences related to expectations of others

## Physical Demands

Extreme environments, strenuous activities, and hazardous substances create physical demands for people in the workplace. Figure 8.1 illustrates the most common types of serious injuries incurred by police officers. The six types of injuries exhibited in the table account for 89% of all injuries to police officers and investigators. Figure 8.2 indicates the types of calls police officers respond to that led to 76.5% of all injuries described in Figure 8.1. The figures include police officer contact with blood-borne pathogens, which is rarely discussed and includes exposures to relatively minor disease as well as far more serious diseases, such as hepatitis or HIV.

Figure 8.1 ■ Most Common Types of Injuries Incurred by Police Officers

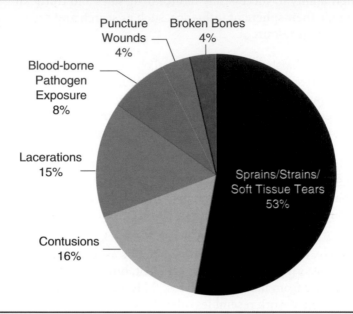

Figure 8.2 ■ Most Common Call Types That Result in Injuries to Police Officers

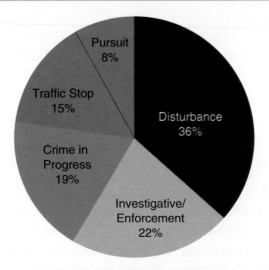

*Source:* Reducing Officer Injuries: FINAL REPORT. The IACP Center For Officer Safety & Wellness, Bureau of Justice Assistance, 2009

Although generally believed to be a very high-stress occupation, more recent research suggests a more moderate environment.[84] This may be due in part to different hiring processes, stress-reduction training classes, and individual characteristics of the officers. However, on a regular basis, police are exposed to situations that other members of society rarely experience.

## ■ EFFECTS AND CONSEQUENCES OF POLICE STRESS

In 2000, the National Institute of Justice (NIJ) concluded that police were experiencing new levels of stress based on a perceived increase in public scrutiny, adverse publicity, and a perceived decline in police camaraderie. Fear of contracting air- and blood-borne diseases (e.g., TB, HIV, and hepatitis), the focus on cultural diversity and political correctness, and the transition to community policing also increased stress levels.[85] Furthermore, these stressors have serious emotional and physical effects on police. The average age of death of a police officer is 67, which is approximately 10 years younger than the average life expectancy for all men in the United States.[86]

---

### Exhibit 8.4

### Categories of Stressors

Stressors experienced by police fall into the following five major categories:

- **Internal stressors:** those originating within the organization, poor supervision, absence of career development opportunities, inadequate reward system, offensive policies, and paperwork

- **External stressors:** absence of career development (not able to transfer to another department), jurisdictional isolation, seemingly ineffective corrections system, courts, distorted press accounts, derogatory remarks, and adverse government actions

- **Performance stressors:** role conflict, adverse work schedules, fear and danger, sense of uselessness, and absence of closure

- **Individual stressors:** feeling overcome by fear and danger, and pressures to conform

- **Effects of critical incidents**[87]

Another typology lists seven police stressors that selectively interact with a police officer's job activities, decision making, and organizational life:

- **Life-threatening stressors:** ever-present potential of injury or death

- **Social isolation stressors:** cynicism, isolation, and alienation from the community; prejudice and discrimination

- **Organizational stressors:** administrative philosophy, changing policies and procedures, morale, job satisfaction, and misdirected performance measures

- **Functional stressors:** role conflict, use of discretion, and legal mandates

- **Personal stressors:** police officer's off-duty life, including family, illness, problems with children, marital stresses, and financial constraints

- **Physiological stressors:** fatigue, medical conditions, and shift-work effects

- **Psychological stressors:** possibly activated by all of the above and the exposure to repulsive situations[88]

### Personal Pitfalls
#### *Desensitization*

Many departments train their officers in handling physical confrontations. Part of this training involves deliberately desensitizing officers out of a natural tendency to avoid either receiving or inflicting physical blows. To be able to maintain control in physically combative situations, officers need to be able to engage and not be hindered by their personal inhibitions. However, the psychological desensitization to trauma can have an ill effect on the officer as an individual and on his or her professional performance. As one officer put it:

> There is a process called occupational socialization that includes the organizationally informal dynamics of becoming blue, for example desensitization and detachment. It is the reason we do not cry over dead bodies or beat child molesters as opposed to reading them their rights. One of the tragedies, yet defense mechanisms this profession "gifts" us with is the ability to separate ourselves from the horrors we see for the sake of getting the paperwork completed.[89]

The consequences of stress and desensitization reported by police include cynicism, suspicion, and emotional detachment from everyday life. In addition, stress leads to reduced efficiency, increased absenteeism, and early retirement, as well as excessive aggressiveness, alcoholism, and other substance abuse. Marital and family problems (extramarital affairs, divorce, domestic violence) and PTSD are additionally related to stress.[90]

#### *Prejudice*

Over the years, the literature on the police has characterized them as more authoritarian and prejudiced than other occupational groups. Authoritarian personalities tend to be conservative, rigid, punitive, and inflexible, and they tend to emphasize authority and rules.[92] **Prejudice** (in this case, unfavorable attitudes toward a group or individual not based on experience or fact) appears to be more common among those with authoritarian traits. Prejudiced individuals tend to develop and adhere to stereotypes based on race, ethnicity, occupational group, and other factors. Police actions based on such stereotypes are discriminatory and clearly inappropriate in a democratic society. Because these stereotypes and prejudices are *attitudes* and are difficult to directly observe, they are also difficult, if not impossible, to eliminate. Discriminatory *actions*, however, are more easily observed, and steps to prevent such actions can and must be taken. The extent to which prejudices and stereotypes translate into discriminatory action remains a question, though there is no doubt that it does sometimes happen.

■ **Prejudice:** Unfavorable attitudes toward a group or individual not based on experience or fact; a feeling about a person or persons based on faulty generalizations

■ **Stress:** Occurs when an event involves a constraint, opportunity, or excessive physical or psychological demand

■ **General Adaptation Syndrome:** Stages of stress experienced by a person after the exposure to stressors

---

### Exhibit 8.5

## Positive Effects of Stress

**Stress** need not always be harmful. In fact, moderate stress appears to be positively related to productivity. Elimination of all stress is neither possible nor desirable. However, the effects of prolonged high levels of stress are clearly associated with dysfunction, producing both debilitating psychological and physical symptoms. In part, the damage caused by stress occurs because of the **general adaptation syndrome**.[91]

In the first stage of this syndrome, the body prepares to fight stress by releasing hormones that lead to an increase in respiration and heartbeat. In the second stage, the body attempts to resist the stressor and repair any damage that has occurred. If the stress continues long enough and cannot be successfully met through flight or fight, then the third stage, exhaustion, occurs. Repeated exposure to stressors that cannot be eliminated or modified by the organism eventually leads to stage three.

These characterizations may be based in part on the previous history of the police. The 1960s was a time of civil unrest and of protests against the police amid accusations of police brutality. Recent changes in policing have had a significant impact on the characterization of the police personality and culture. These changes include more diverse police organizations, more educated police officers, and technical sophistication.[93] In addition, because of the changes in the police role, departments began seeking officers with the personalities and characteristics that were consistent with quality-of-life issues and problem-solving expertise.[94] One of the main reasons for the changes in today's police culture may be the implementation of community-oriented policing, which has dissolved some of the barriers between the police and the community.[95]

Early research found essentially no differences between police officers and those in other occupations with respect to either authoritarianism or prejudice, and studies have found police officers to be intelligent, emotionally stable, and service oriented.[96] In fact, a later study found that years of service as a police officer did not create increased levels of authoritarianism, which runs counter to the "popular belief that years on the job will 'harden' police officers and lead to negative attitudes and traits."[97]

### Cynicism

Cynicism is another feature of the police officer's working personality that is addressed by students of the police. **Cynicism** involves the loss of faith in people, of enthusiasm for police work, and of pride and integrity.[98] Some contend that cynicism peaks in the 7th to 10th year of police service, and the level of cynicism varies with the organizational style of the department and the type of department (urban or rural).[99] "Although most individuals entering police work are idealistic, service-oriented, and outgoing, by about the fifth year in the profession some officers tend to develop attitudes that are cynical, defensive, alienated, authoritarian, and often racist."[100] What causes the changes in a police officer's personality that result in these types of attitudes? Some think it is related to the reality of big-city streets, high crime rates, and anonymity, while others suggest it has to do with length of tenure or socialization.[101]

Within different police subcultures, cynicism is thought to involve different issues, including the public, the police administration, the courts, training and education, dedication to duty, and police solidarity.[102] The study of police cynicism reached its zenith in the 1980s, and it has slowed since, leaving many questions unresolved.[103]

■ **Cynicism:** In this context, involves a loss of faith in people or loss of enthusiasm for police work

### Burnout

Gradually, officers may become disillusioned, bored, frustrated, and later apathetic. Each of the stages entails a variety of stressors. The lack of an appropriate way to relieve stress may lead to **burnout**, which is characterized by emotional exhaustion and cynicism.

■ **Burnout:** Exhaustion and cynicism resulting from repeated exposure to high levels of stress

---

### Exhibit 8.6

### Four Stages That Lead to Police Cynicism

- Stage One—pseudo cynicism: New recruits are idealistic; their desire is to "help people."
- Stage Two—romantic cynicism: Involves the first five years of police work; these officers are the most vulnerable to cynicism.
- Stage Three—aggressive cynicism: Failures and frustrations, resentment, and hostility are obvious and prevalent at the 10th-year mark.
- Stage Four—resigned cynicism: Detachment, passiveness, and acceptance of the flaws of the system characterize seasoned officers.[104]

Individuals unable to cope with stressors reflected in psychological, behavioral, and physical symptoms are said to manifest burnout.[105] Repeated exposure to high levels of stress results in emotional exhaustion, which is often followed by depersonalization of relationships as a coping response. Police who suffer from this level of stress tend to view victims and complainants as case numbers and have little empathy or individual attention for them. An additional contributor to burnout is the fact that police often suppress their emotions. This begins when new recruits observe police academy instructors, field training officers, and veteran officers, and they learn or are told directly to control and hide their emotions, particularly when they are in public view.[106] This control is referred to as displaying a "courtroom face." In general, most believe that police officers exhibit higher rates of burnout compared to other types of occupations.[107]

An advanced stage of burnout involves reduced personal accomplishment, in which the officer loses interest in the job, his or her performance declines, and motivation is lacking. It is important that police administrators understand the implications of burnout, because research has revealed that elevated levels of stress and associated burnout in police officers can decrease job performance.[108]

Officers who experience such stress sometimes turn to alcohol or other drugs, physical aggression, and even suicide in attempting to alleviate it (see below). The literature has theorized that police officers consume more alcohol than the general population.[109] Most believe the consumption of alcohol by police is related to stress or social camaraderie issues. However, one survey of officers revealed drinking levels equivalent to those reported by the general population.[110]

### Stress and Police Families

Some studies have focused on the effects of police work on the police family. A police officer's level of emotional exhaustion was shown to be related to the level of job satisfaction, depersonalization, and marital distress.[111] Furthermore, domestic violence committed by police officers against their intimate partners occurred at the same rate when compared to the general population.[112] However, apart from the fact that most families will

## Exhibit 8.7

## A Day in the Life

An example of the incidents occurring in the first few hours of a police officer's tour of duty will help clarify the stressors to which officers are routinely subjected. Shortly after reporting "in service," the officer receives a call that another officer requires immediate assistance. The officer who responds to the call for help turns on red lights and siren and drives as rapidly as possible to reach a colleague. On the way, he prepares for the possibility of a physical struggle or armed resistance, and the physical changes described are taking place. The officer is tense and excited, but also frightened. The fear experienced may have to do with anticipation about what will happen when he arrives at the scene, but it also has to do with what other drivers, noting the red lights and siren—or failing to note them—will do. Will they yield at intersections? Will they pull off to the right? Will they pull to the left? Will they stop in the middle of the street? Will they slow down or speed up? What will happen if the officer is involved in an accident?

Arriving at the scene, the officer finds the situation under control, a suspect in custody, and the colleague uninjured. As the officer gets back into the patrol car, another call comes from the dispatcher. This call involves an accident with serious injuries. The officer proceeds to the scene (with the same set of concerns about arriving safely). As the first emergency officer to arrive, he finds that several people have been seriously injured and an infant killed. After the accident has been handled, the officer gets into the police vehicle and is told to come to the station to meet with the chief. His concerns on the way are somewhat different but perhaps equally stressful. For the next several hours and, in some cities, for the next several days, weeks, and years, these scenarios are repeated. The ups and downs of police work take their toll, and the officer experiences repeated stress, anxiety, and perhaps burnout.

A study in Khyber Pakhtunkhwa, Pakistan, revealed high levels of anxiety, depression, and stress among police officers. The 2012 study indicated that "female officers, married officers, officers with more years of service, officers with low ranks and officers who work in urban areas have higher levels of depression, anxiety, and stress than male officers, married officers, officers with fewer years of service and officers with high ranks and officers working in rural areas."

The Khyber Pakhtunkhwa Police agree that police officers often face "stress-producing situations." As an example, "terrorists have no qualms about threatening police officers with death . . . and those threats sometimes extend to their families." In some cases, they have seen significant turnover of police officers, and others have lost their commitment to the job. In 2012, there was an attempt to reduce the levels of stress experienced by police. Many have suggested stress counseling, improved safety, and the addition of training related to stress management.

*Source:* "Study finds KP police suffer from psychological pressures," by S. A. Abbas (2012). *Central Asian Online*

not air dirty laundry, domestic violence by police officers was often not detected, due to the officer's strong adherence to a code of secrecy, commitment to camaraderie, and resistance to external intrusion.[113] Similarly, individuals who marry a police officer marry into the police family and are expected to follow the values and norms of the subculture.[114]

There are so many experiences unique to the field of policing that those outside it may find it difficult to understand. Allegiance to the subculture can become almost stronger than the officer's family relationships.[115]

Family-related stress has the potential to adversely affect the job performance of employees. Police officers not experiencing job stress can be adversely affected by problems in the home environment. Several sources of stress commonly cited by police officers' spouses are as follows:

- Shift work and overtime
- Concern over the spouse's cynicism, or need to feel in control in the home
- Inability or unwillingness to express feelings
- Fear that the officer will be hurt or killed in the line of duty
- Police officer's excessively high expectations of his or her children
- Avoidance, teasing, or harassment of the officer's children by other children because the parent is a police officer
- Presence of a weapon in the residence
- Perception the police officer prefers to spend time with other officers rather than with the family
- Perception the officer is paranoid, excessively vigilant, and overprotective
- Problems in helping the officer cope with work-related problems
- Critical incidents or officer's injury or death on the job[116]

The police profession can intrude in various ways into intimate family relationships, disrupting the well-being of marriage and family life. The danger of police work causes fear among family members for the safety of their loved one in uniform. The schedule can entail odd hours and overtime, which complicates family logistics. Spouses may resent the "secret society" nature of the work and the off-limits topics of conversation. Police families can also become the targets of media scrutiny and have to bear that invasion of privacy.[117]

**Policing in Practice Video:**
How do you identify and handle police stress in your department? How do you address relationships with family and friends?

## Police Officer Suicide

Research suggests that personality and situational factors often interact and determine the way the individual experiences and reacts to stress. In some cases, severe stress can lead to suicide.[118]

In a profession where strength, bravery, and resilience are revered, mental health issues and the threats of officer suicide are often "dirty little secrets"—topics very few want to address or acknowledge. Our refusal to speak openly about the issue perpetuates the stigma many officers hold about mental health issues—the stigma that depression, anxiety, and thoughts of suicide are signs of weakness and failure, not cries for help.[119]

### Research on Police Suicide

Despite fairly extensive literature on the subject, many questions persist about the prevalence of police suicide.[120] Although it is very difficult to measure, some estimate that the officer suicide rate is significantly higher than that of the general population. The question of whether the police are at a greater risk for suicide than the average citizen is a potent one. Researchers attempt to answer the question of whether policing contributes to suicide. A 2014 report on the subject analyzed data from the Federal Bureau of Investigation (FBI) and a 2012 National Study of Police Suicides. It claims that police officers died twice as often by suicide than in traffic accidents or as a result of felonious assault.[121] Other researchers conducted a meta-analysis of published suicide rates in law enforcement officers and concluded that they are *less* likely to complete suicide than an age-, race-, and gender-matched population.[122]

Thus, research on this subject has brought in mixed and inconclusive results. It is even uncertain about how to properly measure suicide among police; and there is suspected underreporting, for example, due to the social stigma of suicide.[123] Also, it is difficult to design a proper methodology with a meaningful comparison group.

The police population does not mirror the "general population" in gender, age, employment, or ethnic aspects; therefore, comparing suicide rates of the general public and police may be deceptive.[124] Differences between these two groups include personality traits such as machismo, being over 21 years of age, access to firearms, and working in urban areas.

Besides the stress of police work, other factors contribute to police suicides. Among these are abuse of alcohol and drugs, involvement in deviance and corruption, depression, and (for women) working in a male-dominated organization. Family and economic problems, alienation, and cynicism associated with the police culture; role conflict; and physical and mental health problems are other contributing problems.[125]

Suicide ideation, planning a suicide, and attempts to commit suicide were more likely to occur when individuals were exposed to the suicide of another person.[126] In most cases, police are among the first responders at the scene of a suicide and are required to perform an investigation. Thus, police officers have a much higher exposure to the act of suicide compared to the general population.

In any case, suicide among officers is a problem, given that the majority of officers are psychologically screened prior to hiring and are, by definition, employed and insured populations—which one might think would reduce suicide risk.

The International Association of Chiefs of Police (IACP) recommends the following measures for departments to reduce the risk of suicide among their officers.

- Recruit leaders who care about the mental wellness of their officers and who unequivocally endorse physical and mental wellness parity as critical to a resilient and healthy police force.
- Recruit and hire resilient officers who have demonstrated a commitment to public service and proven stress management skills.

- Establish and institutionalize effective early warning and intervention protocols to identify and treat at-risk officers, for example, by launching awareness campaigns on what to look for and whom to call when officers may be in a mental health crisis or suffering from clinical anxiety or chronic depression.
- Audit existing psychological services and determine whether they are effective in identifying early warning signs of mental wellness issues, including mental illness and suicidal behavior, and in treating at-risk officers.
- Invest in training agency-wide on mental health awareness and stress management.
- Begin mental wellness training at the academy and continue the training throughout officers' careers, with a particular emphasis on first-line supervisors.
- Include family training to reinforce and invest in those critical family connections.
- Establish clear post-event protocols to implement and follow when officers die by suicide.

## ■ POLICE SHOOTINGS AND CRITICAL INCIDENTS

According to preliminary data for 2014, 126 law enforcement officers died in the line of duty in the United States, which is a 24% increase over 2013 (102).[130] Firearms-related incidents were the leading cause of death among officers; there were 50 such deaths in 2014, which represents a 56% increase over 2013 (32). Traffic-related

**Exhibit 8.8**

### Law Enforcement Officer Deaths, 2014

According to the National Law Enforcement Office Memorial Fund, 117 law enforcement officers died in the line of duty in the United States in 2014.[127] Firearms-related incidents were the leading cause of death among officers; there were 48 such deaths in 2014.[128] Auto incidents were the second most frequent cause of death in 2014, killing 32.[129]

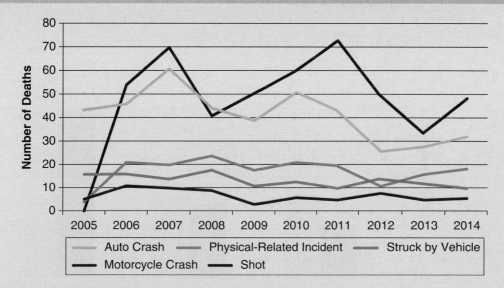

Most Common Causes of Law Enforcement Officer Deaths, 2005–2014

*Source:* National Law Enforcement Officer Memorial Fund, "Causes of Law Enforcement Deaths"

incidents were the second most frequent cause of deaths in 2014, killing 49, which is an 11% increase over 2013 (44).[131] (See Figure 8.3.)

The stress of actually being involved in a shooting, whether as shooter or victim, is very real. In many cases, prior research argued that officers involved in a shooting experienced PTSD. Symptoms associated with this psychological condition include inability to be intimate, sleep disorders, nightmares, feelings of guilt, and reliving the event.[132] However, earlier research from the NIJ found that few police officers involved in shooting incidents suffer long-term negative emotional or physical effects. In fact, "following about one-third of the shootings, officers reported feelings of elation that included joy at being alive, residual excitement after a life-threatening situation, and satisfaction of pride in proving their ability to use deadly force appropriately."[133] Given that officers experience a variety of reactions to traumatic events, the training they receive in preparation for their possible exposure to trauma should also encompass the range of reactions.

Death, extreme physical abuse, and fear of the unknown have significant effects on the physical and mental health of police. For example, after Hurricane Katrina in 2005, approximately 33% of the police officers and firefighters involved with this natural disaster "reported either depressive symptoms or symptoms of posttraumatic stress disorder (PTSD), or both."[134] The top five traumatic events for police officers involve the following:

- Child abuse
- Killing of an innocent person
- Conflict with regulations
- Domestic violence calls
- Hurting a fellow police officer[135]

A more recent study confirmed that the largest stressor for police involved crime and incidents against children. For example, a police officer responding to a trouble call finds that the father has shot his two young children, his wife, and then himself. The public will read only a short abstract about this tragedy in the newspaper, but the image of the young child gripping her doll just before being shot in the head with a shotgun by her father will remain with the officer forever.[136]

**Web Link:**
We Are Not Damaged Goods (Officer PTSD)

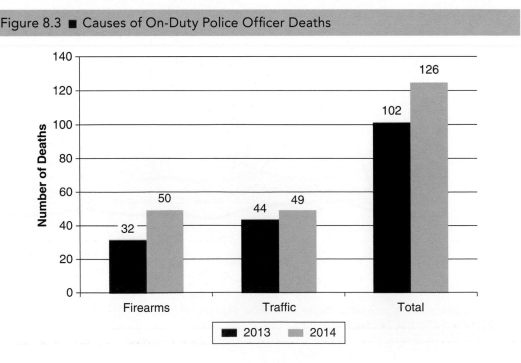

Figure 8.3 ■ Causes of On-Duty Police Officer Deaths

A **critical incident** is a traumatic event that has a stressful impact sufficient enough to overwhelm the otherwise effective coping skills of an individual.[137] Almost every police officer will experience a marked reaction during and after a critical incident. Examples of critical incidents include officer-involved shootings, hostage standoffs, a mass suicide, an infant at the bottom of a pool, a family trapped in a burning vehicle, school shootings, and natural disasters.[138] Additional examples of critical incident hazards include terrorist bombings, exposure to toxic chemicals, and biological or radiation hazards.[139]

The San Jose Police Department considers it important to have a Critical Incident Stress Debriefing Team to address such occurrences.[140] For example, from 1972 to 1987, when the team did not exist, 52 police officers were involved in shootings, and 17 left the department. However, after creation of the team, 122 officers were involved in shootings, and none left the department. Obviously, a number of limitations exist that could have affected the outcomes of this comparison, such as training and individual differences among officers. See Figure 8.4 for a breakdown of the circumstances of fatal shootings of officers.

# ■ COUNTERACTING POLICE STRESS

If stress and its consequences are an inherent part of the work of policing, then handling it appropriately so that it does not become a larger problem—either for the individual officer or for the department—should also be thought of as an inherent part of the job. To the extent that departments have recognized that police work can exact a high toll in personal costs, they have made numerous attempts to identify and lessen the impact of such stress.

There is no exact formula for stress reduction. Individuals differ markedly in the events they define as stressful, in the ways they react to pressure, and in what is effective for them for dealing with stressful events.[141] Higher education and critical reflection by police on their career show great promise for alleviating or mitigating the symptoms of burnout.[142]

It is apparent that stress-reduction training should be provided early in a police officer's career. This can be performed during the initial training period, because police recruits

**Critical Incident:** An event that has a stressful impact sufficient to overwhelm the effective coping skills of a person

---

Figure 8.4 ■ Circumstances of Fatal Shootings of Officers, 2013, 2014

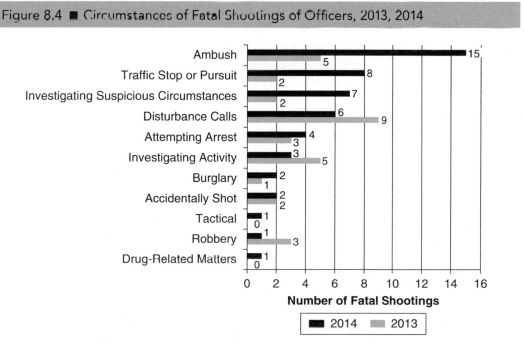

Source: Preliminary 2013 Law Enforcement Officers Deaths

The photo shows the aftermath of the off-duty officer who took his own life, one of the most serious consequence of police burnout.

© ZUMA Press, Inc/Alamy

**Video Link:**
Beyond Ferguson: Warriors to Guardians

are a "captive audience," and because the information may remain with them throughout their entire police career.[143] However, recruit training may not be the most effective time or approach, because most academy attendees are not experienced enough to recognize the stresses of the job. The optimal time to reach a new police officer may be after he or she has worked the street for six to eight months.

Individual police officers often either fail to recognize the signs of stress or fail to seek help when they do recognize the symptoms. This may be due, in part, to the influence of the police subculture, which holds that "real" police officers can handle their own problems and do not need the help of "shrinks," employee assistance programs, clergy, or other outsiders.[144]

To the extent that stress results from discrepancies between the official expectations of police administrators and the unofficial expectations of the police subculture, these discrepancies need to be confronted. Because both official and subcultural expectations will continue to play roles in policing, efforts must be made to reduce existing differences between the two. Revisions to administrative policies that frustrate and create stress for officers can be beneficial.

Officer suicide is perhaps the most significant and urgent reason to address the consequences of job stress. The causes of suicide by police officers are complex and involve a number of factors. Most prevention programs for police involve some type of suicide awareness classes, training to identify "signs" in coworkers, support for employee assistance programs, critical incident stress debriefing, and often some form of mandatory counseling.[145] In the future, police departments may want to open up frank discussions about mental health and alcoholism and encourage officers to get annual voluntary and confidential mental health checks.

It behooves police organizations to directly face the effects of stressful work conditions in the interests of the officer, the department, the officer's family, and the public. These are some of the ways that administrators can help police officers better manage the stresses they encounter:

1. Provide employee assistance programs, including services to officers and families

2. Require orientation programs for the new officer's transition into the police culture

3. Emphasize physical conditioning during pre-academy programs

4. Teach coping mechanisms related to crime, death, and boredom[146]

The Melbourne Police Department in Florida is an example of an agency that has developed a stress-management program to address personal and professional problems and provide support to police officers and their families concerning the effects of critical incident stress. The program specifically involves providing emotional support, identifying conflicts, making referrals, intervention, and debriefing.[147]

The police–public relationships that have continued to evolve are important in the reduction of stress among police officers. If a good deal of the stress experienced by officers results from constant contact with the criminal elements in the community and from constantly working in an environment in which the police are regarded as causing trouble for other citizens, then increasing contacts with law-abiding citizens under positive circumstances should help alleviate some of the stress. To some extent, this gain may be offset by the additional problem-solving responsibilities placed on community-policing officers, but if the administration accepts risks and occasional failures as part of the growing process in community-oriented policing, then this stress can also be reduced.

"Progressive police departments actively implement innovative strategies (e.g., providing peer counselors, encouraging officers and couples to enter confidential counseling, making structural administrative changes, adding diversity programs, changing hiring and training practices, adding critical incident programs, etc.) to help minimize the risk of work stress among police."[148]

**SAGE Journal Article:**
Training Police Leadership to Recognize and Address Operational Stress

## CHAPTER SUMMARY

Most organizations have cultures and subcultures that influence the behavior of employees. Culture involves deeply held beliefs that guide behaviors, among other things. Many subcultures are consistent with the organization's legitimate goals and serve as a positive influence on the operations of these organizations. However, subculture can involve detrimental elements. The police culture can involve extreme loyalty to other police officers, to a problematic degree, overidentification with the role, an intense desire to be accepted by the group, and adherence to a code of silence, which tends to erode the public's trust of the police. Indoctrination into the police culture begins at the academy and continues throughout the officer's career.

As society's concept of the police has changed, so too has police culture. The adoption of and experimentation with community-oriented policing may have altered the occupational and organizational environments of policing, and within these environments, the stresses experienced by police officers.[149] Greater attention to officers' efforts to reduce disorder, solve problems, and build rapport with the public could modify the us-versus-them outlook.[150]

Additional influence of the police culture often involves feelings of isolation from the communities that the officers serve and a mistrust of supervisory ranks. The danger and authority of the work add to these dynamics. Stress and desensitization are other forces that affect police officers, the sources of which are both real and perceived. The isolating us-versus-them attitude can be both a cause and an effect of stress. Policing involves numerous stressors, both individual and organizational in nature.

How officers deal with these various stressors is extremely important. Officers who exhibit responses to stress associated with the negative aspects of the police subculture are much more likely than their counterparts to fall victim to burnout, cynicism, and even criminality. Many police officers cope with stress well by performing daily fitness routines and maintaining their commitment to the legitimate goals of the law enforcement profession.

To counteract the negative influences of the police subculture and the related forms of stress, police administrators and officers alike must be vigilant and recognize their responsibilities to identify and address problem behaviors before they become larger problems.

## KEY TERMS

- Code of silence (blue wall)  177
- Police subculture  179
- Artifacts  181
- Organizational assumption  182
- Ethos  182
- Symbolic assailants  183

- Post-traumatic stress disorder (PTSD)  185
- Police personality  187
- Hyperstress  188
- Hypostress  189
- Role conflict  189
- Role ambiguity  189

- Stress  192
- General adaptation syndrome  192
- Prejudice  192
- Cynicism  193
- Burnout  193
- Critical incident  199

## DISCUSSION QUESTIONS

1. What is the police subculture, and in what ways does it conflict with the official mandates of police work?

2. What are the forms of organizational culture? Give an example of each form.

3. Why is it so difficult for police officers to avoid getting caught up in the subculture? Give specific examples.

4. Is policing a stressful occupation? Why and in what ways?

5. What are some of the major sources of police stress? How might some of these stresses be alleviated? Can they be eliminated?

6. What are the relationships among police stress, alcohol use, suicide, and family disruption?

7. How are police stress and the police subculture interrelated?

8. Discuss the ways in which community policing may help to reduce police stress. Can community policing also increase stress levels among officers? Explain.

## INTERNET EXERCISES

1. Go to the Internet and search for information about *suicide by police*. Is this a recent phenomenon, and how often does it occur? How does involvement in a suicide by police affect the officer, the family, and the police department?

2. Most agree that police officers experience high levels of stress. Using your favorite search engine, go online and search for information on the effects of chronic stress and cardiovascular disease in police officers. How can police officers improve their cardiovascular health? Should police departments require all applicants to complete a cardiac stress test?

## STUDENT STUDY SITE

**$ SAGE edge™** edge.sagepub.com/coxpolicing3e

**Sharpen your skills with SAGE edge!**

SAGE edge for Students provides a personalized approach to help you accomplish your coursework goals in an easy-to-use learning environment. You'll find action plans, mobile-friendly eFlashcards, and quizzes as well as videos, web resources, and links to SAGE journal articles to support and expand on the concepts presented in this chapter.

© AP Photo/Joe Burbank

# CHAPTER

# 9

# LAW, COURT DECISIONS AND THE POLICE

## CHAPTER LEARNING OBJECTIVES:

1. Describe police responsibilities in terms of actions related to the 1st Amendment

2. Discuss the effects the 2nd Amendment has on police

3. Identify the necessary elements for police to conduct search and seizure under the 4th Amendment

4. Describe the implications of the 5th Amendment for police procedure

5. Define due process and its relation to policing and the 14th Amendment

6. Explain the exclusionary rule as it applies to police procedure and evidence collection

7. Identity some of the legal issues associated with police use of force

8. Analyze some of the legal issues associated with the USA PATRIOT Act, homeland security, and terrorism

Discretion, ethics, and accountability influence (or fail to influence) police activity, which is also governed by federal and state constitutions, municipal ordinances, and court decisions. Both the substance and procedures enacted into criminal law (and all other law as well) must be consistent with the U.S. Constitution and with the constitution of the state in which the law is enacted. "American criminal law is mostly statutory, with courts interpreting the meaning of penal codes as necessary."[1] Therefore, laws continue to undergo challenges in the courts, and court decisions have an enormous impact on the meaning of the laws and their impact on police policy and procedure. Understanding the implications of ever-changing case law is another responsibility of the police; administrators must build case law education into ongoing officer training.

**Criminal law** is the body of law established to maintain peace and order, and its basic purpose is to protect society from the injurious acts of individuals. **Civil law** defines and determines the rights of individuals to protect their persons and property. There is considerable overlap between the two basic types of law, and police officers are involved with enforcing not only criminal but also some forms of civil law. In fact, an act causing injury to a person or damage to property may be both a civil wrong, referred to as a *tort*, and a crime.[2]

If laws were written in perfectly clear language, contained no contradictions or ambiguities, and simply involved applying the principles stated in laws to particular situations, and if all officers were thoroughly familiar with all laws, deciding whether a particular law had been violated would be a simple and straightforward task for the officer.[3] Under these circumstances, the need for police discretion would be minimal. Unfortunately, these conditions, taken either singly or in combination, are seldom met. The law in the United States is a huge, complex, sometimes contradictory, and constantly changing collection of prescriptive and proscriptive rules. The fact that professionally trained legal experts make their living arguing over different interpretations of the law gives some indication of the ambiguities and complexities involved in applying the law. Most police officers are not, and for that matter do not need to be, lawyers—but officers need to be familiar with the basics of law to perform their jobs and discharge their responsibilities appropriately. Even the best police training programs provide only limited information on the law; most of the police officer's understanding of the law is achieved indirectly. Through the informal instruction and advice offered by colleagues and supervisors, in-service training programs, cramming for promotional exams, self-initiated reading, day-to-day work experiences, and experiences in the courtroom, however, police officers quickly acquire what might be called a "working knowledge" of the law. This working knowledge constitutes the law as it functions in the day-to-day activities of police officers. It is this work-generated interpretation of the law—which may or may not correspond with the interpretations of lawyers and judicial officials—that guides officers as they carry out their duties.[4]

The law explicitly grants some discretionary powers to police officers and creates a framework within which other discretionary judgments may legitimately be made. It is one measure of the importance of discretion in police work that these are among the first items that become incorporated into the officer's working knowledge of the law. The officer understands, for example, that certain leeway is permitted in determining whether probable cause for a search is present (though legislation and court rulings have increased the confusion surrounding the legal latitude granted the officer in these matters). It is also common knowledge among officers that the overlap that frequently exists among laws gives police officers the opportunity to pick and choose which laws, if any, will be cited once a suspect is apprehended. Thus, the officer can choose to "throw the book" at a suspect by citing violations of several laws or can charge the suspect with a more or less serious offense according to the circumstances. In a variety of ways, then, the law, as interpreted and understood by the police officer, creates the framework within which and sometimes around which the police exercise discretion.[5]

**Policing in Practice Video:**
How does your department handle mandates coming down from state and local governments?

■ **Criminal Law:** Body of law established to maintain peace and order to protect society from the injurious acts of individuals

■ **Civil Law:** Defines and determines the rights of individuals to protect their persons and property

Determining whether a law has been broken is a technical judgment, dependent on the officer's knowledge of the law and capacity to apply the general principles embodied in the law to the particular events that have occurred. However difficult this judgment may be (and it is difficult in many instances), it is a decision that merely sets the stage for a far more consequential one—deciding whether to take official action. If the police officer decides *not* to arrest, the remainder of the legal machinery in the criminal justice network does not normally come into play.[6] The police officer, to be sure, is not alone in making legal decisions. It is the responsibility of the prosecutor (state's attorney, district attorney, attorney general) in a given jurisdiction to advise the police in matters pertaining to law and to help them prepare cases for trial. Cooperation between the prosecutor's office and the police department is essential to both so that the police can follow legal procedures that help the prosecutor obtain convictions.

**Video Link:**
Can US agencies balance security and the Constitution?

This chapter covers some of the general implications of constitutional amendments and legal concepts that govern police behavior, specifically, the relationship of police conduct to the 1st, 2nd, 4th, 5th, 6th, and 14th Amendments and related court decisions. Other amendments also have a bearing on police conduct, but these are the most important to this subject. Both statutory law and court decisions are dynamic. Keeping up with these changes requires ongoing examination of the laws and court decisions that apply in various jurisdictions.

## ■ THE 1ST AMENDMENT

The first 10 amendments to the Constitution are known collectively as the Bill of Rights. The 1st Amendment states that Congress shall make no law prohibiting the free exercise of religion or abridging the rights of free speech and peaceful assembly, and the police are frequently involved in protecting these rights. With respect to the rights of freedom to assemble and free speech, the police, whether or not they agree with protestors' causes or statements, may be called on to protect them from those who disagree with them. For example, police officers may find certain types of protests at military funerals distasteful, but in *Snyder v. Phelps et al.*, the Supreme Court held that the 1st Amendment protects hateful protests at military funerals.

In fact, it is not uncommon for the police to be caught between parties in conflict, both verbal and physical in such situations, nor is it uncommon for members of both parties in the conflict to direct their hostilities toward the police. The Ku Klux Klan marches in cities where its members' views are unwelcome to the majority of residents, and the police attempt to prevent violence between the parties involved. Political protests and demonstration sometimes devolve into violence, with both police and protestors pointing fingers at one another. The most professional of departments train officers to set their own opinions aside to accomplish the job of protecting the lives and property of those subject to the protest as well as the lives of the protestors. They must, of course, protect their own safety at the same time.

Religious activities have also been a focus of police attention, especially following the events of the 9/11 terrorist attacks. For example, when conflict arises between Muslims and those of other religious persuasions, mosques as well as individual members of the faith may be threatened, or Muslims may threaten those who hold other religious beliefs. In such cases, the police may be called on to maintain order or protect lives and property.

In other cases, where protestors fail to follow approved procedures and become destructive or violent, or both, the police are called on to use force to arrest those responsible. At the same time, the police may be involved in undercover operations in which officers infiltrate groups with histories of violence and destruction in order to prevent outbursts during protests through advanced knowledge of events that are likely to occur. Police must ensure, though, that these undercover infiltrations of protests are used to collect only criminal intelligence.

During the civil unrest of the late 1960s, the Chicago Police Department (CPD) was sued civilly due to the actions of members of its Intelligence Unit. The case was adjudicated some 15 years later by virtue of a consent decree between the plaintiffs (Alliance to End Repression and the American Civil Liberties Union [ACLU]) and the CPD. The allegations were that many of the CPD's covert intelligence operations during that time period were not focused on criminal wrongdoing; rather, their intent was to gather information for local and national politicians to use to gain advantages over their opponents. Because of this case and the ensuing consent decree, the official policy of the CPD was that investigations directed at 1st Amendment conduct were prohibited unless express written permission for said conduct was granted and monitored by the superintendent of police. Legal abuses from the past continued to hamper legitimate law enforcement efforts until 2004, when the city of Chicago asked the court to relax the investigative restrictions on their police department, citing changes in case law and judicial philosophy. The court found in favor of the city of Chicago.[7]

In other circumstances, the police may be present at athletic events, holiday parades, and concerts to control pedestrian and vehicular traffic and to deter unruly participants from engaging in activities that would disrupt the enjoyment of those in attendance. For example, consider the case in which the ACLU contended that the Pittsburgh police too frequently issued citations for swearing, making obscene gestures, and other acts deemed disrespectful.[8] The case concerned a man who was arrested for disorderly conduct for flipping his middle finger. In 2006, he made the gesture to another driver, and he made the same gesture when he heard someone yelling at him. The person yelling at him was a police officer. A federal judge ruled that the person should not have been arrested because he was engaging in constitutionally protected expression.[9]

Similarly, the police may become involved in dealing with those whose speech goes beyond the limits of 1st Amendment protections. They may, for instance, arrest an individual whose verbalizations constitute a clear and present danger to others (the classic example being the individual who cries "fire" in a crowded venue when no fire exists, causing panic and perhaps serious injury to some in the crowd). Hate speech, fighting words (words that by their very nature inflict injury or incite violent conduct), and obscenities may also lead to police intervention, though the boundaries that must be crossed for this response to occur are often unclear and call for discretion. The Internet and related technologies have raised additional issues with respect to freedom of speech. The sharing of child pornography via the Internet, for example, has been ruled beyond the protection of the 1st Amendment. Other uses of the Internet to intimidate, harass, or humiliate targets may also be beyond such protection, though the law is not yet well established in this area.

## ■ THE 2ND AMENDMENT

Although the 2nd Amendment does not deal with due process, it is nonetheless important to the police for a variety of reasons. The 2nd Amendment deals with the right to bear arms, which has been the source of considerable litigation. This amendment is of concern to the police not because it spells out appropriate police procedures, as do some of the other amendments discussed in this chapter, but because its interpretation determines to some extent the number of citizens who have access to and permission to carry weapons and the circumstances under which this can legally occur. The right to carry concealed weapons has received a great deal of attention in the last few years, with law enforcement officials supporting both sides of the argument. In addition, attempts by states and municipalities to control licensing, ownership, and carrying of guns have come under scrutiny. Gun control statutes typically impose licensing and registration requirements on gun owners and specify who may and may not legally own a gun (e.g., convicted felons and those with histories of mental illness may be prohibited from gun ownership) and the circumstances under which it may be carried, either openly or concealed. Such statutes further impose requirements on gun dealers by specifying the type of weapons and ammunition they may sell and the waiting period required for delivery of the weapon.[10] At the same time, 49 of the 50 states now allow some form of concealed carry of firearms. The controversy over concealed carry continues, with advocates insisting it helps prevent some violent crimes and opponents arguing it increases injuries and deaths. Police personnel are divided as to the consequences and desirability of concealed carry.

In 2008, in the case of *District of Columbia v. Heller*, the Supreme Court reversed a 70-year position that the 2nd Amendment should apply only to organized militias. The Court ruled that law-abiding individuals have the right to own firearms for self-defense, and relaxed the rules around the storage of those firearms in private homes. This ruling stated that it was unconstitutional for local officials to prohibit the vast majority of Washington, D.C., residents from owning handguns. This represented a watershed moment in the history of government regulation of the conditions of private gun ownership. This federal ruling applied only to the District of Columbia. However, though other cities have continued to ban handgun ownership, *Heller* opened the door for many other challenges to the application of the 2nd Amendment at the state level, without giving useful guidance for how to enact gun control legislation that is consistent with the amendment.

In 2010, the Supreme Court agreed to hear a case that has a definite bearing on these cities. In the case of *McDonald v. Chicago,* the court extended its 2008 decision in support of gun rights in Washington, D.C., to state and local laws.[11] The Supreme Court ruled that the personal right to keep and bear arms applies not only to the federal government, but to state and local governments as well. This is just one of dozens of consequent 2nd Amendment challenges in the courts.[12]

It was suspected that police personnel would more frequently encounter loaded handguns when carrying out regular duties such as entering households or making traffic stops. It remains to be seen whether an extension of the *Heller* decision has resulted or will result in an increased number of incidents involving the police, handguns, and shots fired. However, subsequent to *Heller*, Washington, D.C., enacted specific limitations on assault weapons and large-capacity ammunition magazines, and the District of Columbia has seen a documented decrease in the use of these weapons since the legislation passed.[13]

## ■ THE 4TH AMENDMENT

The 4th Amendment prohibits unreasonable searches and seizures of persons, houses, papers, and effects and requires that probable cause be demonstrated prior to the issuing of warrants. A **search** occurs "when an expectation of privacy that society is prepared to consider reasonable is infringed. A **seizure** of property occurs when

**Author Video:**
Changes in Law Enforcement

■ **Search:** Occurs when an expectation of privacy that society is prepared to consider reasonable is infringed upon

■ **Seizure:** Of property occurs when there is some meaningful interference with an individual's possessory interests in that property

## Concealed Weapons

### Police Say Concealed-Carry Law Would Deter Criminals

Some local police chiefs and other police personnel in the Peoria, Illinois, area indicated that putting fear into the minds of criminals on the streets is one of the best arguments for allowing concealed carry. "If you're not sure if a guy has a gun, you may not try to do some things to him that you might otherwise try to get away with," said Peoria police officer Troy Skaggs, president of the Peoria Police Benevolent Union. "It's the fear of the unknown." Further, the Illinois Sheriffs' Association passed a resolution supporting a concealed-carry law in Illinois, with several conditions in place.

According to Peoria police chief Steven Settingsgaard, who, along with 250 worldwide law enforcement executives, recently spent 10 weeks at the Federal Bureau of Investigation's National Academy, "Everyone I spoke to was in favor of concealed carry."

### Concealed Weapons Bill Meets Objections on Campus

Opposition to a concealed weapons bill comes from the University of Missouri Police Department and two organizations it belongs to—the International Association of Campus Law Enforcement Administrators and the Missouri Association of Campus Law Enforcement.

There is opposition to the bill, because it might expose campus police officers to heightened danger. For instance, if an officer were to respond to a situation in which a Good Samaritan was trying to stop a criminal and both of those parties were armed and had their weapons drawn, how would the officer know who was the aggressor? In such cases, innocent people might be injured or killed. If alcohol played a role in the confrontation, the danger for all concerned would be even greater, and parties and events where alcohol is involved are common on college campuses.

*Source:* "Concealed weapons bill meets objections on campus," by N. Winters and R. Barros, 2009. *Columbia Missourian* (http://www.columbiamissourian.com/stories/2009/04/22/concealed-weapons-bill-met-objections-campus/).

1. Do you believe that laws allowing citizens to carry concealed weapons are effective at deterring crime, as some have argued?

2. What are the possible advantages to concealed carry laws? What are the disadvantages?

3. If possible, would you carry a concealed weapon? Why or why not?

*Source:* "Police say concealed carry law would deter criminals," by R. Ori, 2009. *Journal Star* (http://www.pjstar.com/news/x1730895291/Police-say-concealed-carry-law-would-deter-criminals).

there is some meaningful interference with an individual's possessory interests in that property."[14] With reference to police searches and seizures, in practical terms, the former refers to the fact that a police officer invades the privacy of an individual to seek evidence of a weapon, crime, or contraband, and the latter refers to the confiscation of that weapon, evidence, contraband, or the person suspected of committing the crime in question. In other words, both property and persons may be seized under appropriate circumstances. To comprehend the impact of this amendment, the police must be conversant with the underlying concepts of probable cause and reasonableness. This takes vigilance because the 4th Amendment is probably the most fluid amendment with respect to changes in case law and the requirements that must be met to search persons, properties, and vehicles.

## Probable Cause and Reasonableness

The notion of **probable cause** is derived from the 4th Amendment to the U.S. Constitution, which says, in part, "The right of the people to be secure in their persons, houses, papers, and effects, against unreasonable searches and seizures, shall not be violated, and no warrants shall issue, but on probable cause. . . ." Understanding this concept is important to police officers in the process of stopping and questioning citizens, making arrests, and conducting searches. In regard to effecting an arrest, in *Brinegar v. United States*,[15] the U.S. Supreme Court found that probable cause exists when facts and circumstances within a police officer's knowledge, which are based on reasonably trustworthy information, are sufficient to warrant a person of reasonable caution to believe that an offense has been or is being committed by the person being arrested. It is important to note that the decision recognizes two different ways in which the officer may come into possession of information related to probable cause. First, the officer may observe conduct that leads to the conclusion that an offense is being or has been committed. Second, someone else may observe such conduct and then relay information concerning the conduct to the officer. In the latter case, the officer must reasonably believe that the information provided is from someone who, in the present circumstances, is likely to be reliable.

A further attempt to clarify the standard of probable cause was made by the Court in *Illinois v. Gates*.[16] In this decision, the court noted that the standard for probable cause is a "practical, nontechnical conception" dealing with probabilities based on "factual and practical considerations of everyday life on which reasonable and prudent men, not legal technicians, act." These decisions, of course, raise the issue as to what is reasonable. **Reasonableness** generally refers to what a reasonable person, in similar circumstances, based on similar information, might conclude. For example, arresting someone who happens to be in the general area in which an offense may have been committed, and with no other evidence that the individual in question may be the perpetrator, may well be unreasonable. The individual could be a witness, a nearby resident, a passerby, or even a victim. Arresting that same individual in the area in which an offense was reported and who matched several of the characteristics of the offender (height, gender, race, and clothing) reported by a witness would be reasonable, and this arrest would almost certainly meet the probable cause standard even if the individual arrested turned out not to be the perpetrator. It appears that the courts have determined that reasonableness is not a single standard but may vary from case to case. Taking official action must be balanced against the expectation of privacy guaranteed by the 4th Amendment (*Illinois v. Rodriguez*, 1990).[17] Further, it is important that the officer taking action based on probable cause or reasonable suspicion is able to articulate the facts that justify the action. While simple suspicion is generally insufficient to meet the standard of probable cause, **reasonable suspicion**, based on objective facts and logical conclusions given a specific set of circumstances, may be used as the basis for stopping and frisking suspicious individuals.

The standards for reasonableness are relevant in many aspects of police activity. What constitutes reasonable use of force is a complex equation based on several legal factors. The 1989 unanimous U.S. Supreme Court decision of *Graham v. Connor* established a precedent for the reasonable use of force that persists to today.[18]

> The Fourth Amendment "reasonableness" inquiry is whether the officers' actions are "objectively reasonable" in light of the facts and circumstances confronting them, without regard to their underlying intent or motivation. The "reasonableness" of a particular use of force must be judged from the perspective of a reasonable officer on the scene. . . . The calculus of reasonableness must embody allowance for the fact that police officers are often forced to make split-second judgments—in circumstances that are tense, uncertain, and rapidly evolving—about the amount of force that is necessary in a particular situation.[19]

### Sidebar (left margin)

**Video Link:**
State Court Ruling Makes Searching Cars Easier for Police

■ **Probable Cause:** Exists when facts and circumstances within a police officer's knowledge, which are based on reasonably trustworthy information, are sufficient to warrant a person of reasonable caution to believe that an offense has been or is being committed by the person being arrested

■ **Reasonableness:** Generally refers to what a reasonable person, in similar circumstances, based on similar information, might conclude

■ **Reasonable Suspicion:** When based on objective facts and logical conclusions given a specific set of circumstances, may be used as the basis for stopping and frisking suspicious individuals

Here, a police officer uses forcible entry to execute a search warrant.

The notions of probable cause and reasonable suspicion are important in virtually all aspects of the policing process. To obtain a search warrant, for example, the requesting officer must demonstrate to the issuing judge that it is reasonable to expect to find the items identified at the location specified. Similarly, prior to making a traffic stop, an officer must be able to articulate the reasons for the stop—exceeding the speed limit, equipment problems, weaving back and forth across traffic lanes, and so on. (Exceptions may exist with respect to "safety checks," in which every vehicle is stopped and examined, but these vary considerably by locale.) An important point to keep in mind is that the reasonable suspicion or probable cause must have preceded the stop or arrest and cannot be based on the evidence found *after* the stop or arrest. Failure to act in terms of probable cause typically results in evidence collected during an unreasonable stop or search being excluded at the time of the trial.

Most officers are keenly aware of the importance of a justifiable probable cause as a basis for official action. The temptation can be great, in its absence, to create probable cause so that the fruits of their searches are admissible in court; the ethics of doing so are problematic. However, wrongful searches and seizures cannot be made right in this way, according to the law.

Based on a series of court decisions, there are a number of exceptions to the requirements imposed by the 4th Amendment. The following examples indicate the scope of the amendment as currently interpreted.

### Searches and Seizures With and Without a Warrant

A search **warrant** is an order in writing, issued by a judge, that commands the officer requesting it to search for certain types of property in certain locations and to bring the fruits of that search before the judicial authority in question. An arrest warrant is an order to take a certain person into custody and bring him or her before the judge.[20]

Although a warrant is the preferred means of justifying searches and seizures, the circumstances of police encounters often preclude obtaining a warrant. For example, when a police officer makes a traffic stop and discovers contraband or evidence of a

■ **Warrant:** An order in writing, issued by a judicial authority, authorizing a police officer to take specific actions

crime or when an officer comes on the scene of a crime in progress in which a weapon has been or may be involved, there may be no time to obtain a warrant. Further, if an officer pursues a suspected drug dealer into a building and the suspect runs into a restroom, there is reason to believe the suspect may destroy evidence if immediate action is not taken. For example, in *Kentucky v. King*,[21] the U.S. Supreme Court held that warrantless searches conducted in exigent circumstances do not violate the 4th Amendment so long as the police did not create the exigency by violating or threatening to violate the 4th Amendment. In this case, police officers followed a suspected drug dealer to an apartment complex, smelled marijuana outside an apartment door, knocked loudly, and announced their presence. When the officers began knocking, they heard noises coming from the apartment, which they believed were consistent with the destruction of evidence. The officers announced their intent to enter the apartment, kicked in the door, saw drugs in plain view during a protective sweep of the apartment, and found additional evidence during a subsequent search. The **plain view doctrine** holds that if a police officer sees an incriminating object in plain view during a legitimate stop, he or she may seize the object. There are literally dozens of other exceptions and specifications to stop-and-frisk rules.[22]

As technological advances expand the ability of the police to conduct different kinds of searches, it further challenges the jurisprudence of the 4th Amendment. In the case of *State v. Brossart* (2014), police conducted a warrantless search of a man's home using a drone (or unmanned aerial vehicle UAV). The evidence gained from the UAV search was used to convict Rodney Brossart and his four sons. This is one of the first cases concerned with drones and searches of private individuals. The protections of the 4th Amendment have been debated for the past 200 years, so this issue continues that debate about the needs of the state versus the reasonable expectation of privacy of individual citizens.[23] Part of the issue, when it comes to drones, is whether an aerial view from legally navigable space constitutes a search that should be protected by the 4th Amendment.

Nonetheless, where possible and practical, a warrant is preferred because it requires the officer to demonstrate to an independent third party (magistrate or judge) the probable cause or reasonable suspicion upon which his or her anticipated action is predicated. It also places the burden of proof on the defense, which must demonstrate how the search was unlawful.

## Police Stops

Based on the totality of circumstances that the officer perceives, he or she may stop and briefly detain or —with a warrant—arrest a person if the officer can articulate facts that generate reasonable suspicion that criminal activity has occurred.[24] **Totality of circumstances** is the "whole picture" and requires that an officer have a "particularized and objective basis for suspecting that a particular person" is or has been involved in criminal activity. The totality of circumstances ("the whole picture") includes "various objective observations, information from police reports (if available) and consideration of modes or patterns of operation of certain kinds of lawbreakers" from which the "officer draws inferences and makes deductions" concerning the probability that the party in question is involved in criminal conduct.[25] Again, the officer must be able to provide reasons that justify the stop. After making such a stop, a police officer can briefly detain the person, ask questions, and check identification, because the "law enforcement interests at stake in these circumstances outweigh the individual's interest to be free of a stop and detention that is no more extensive than permissible in the investigation of imminent or ongoing crime."[26] Such stops, often referred to as *Terry* stops, must be discontinued in light of evidence that demonstrates that the officer's initial interpretation of the circumstances was incorrect.[27] The *Terry* case, for which such stops are named, involved an experienced police officer observing Terry engaged in behavior that indicated to the officer that Terry was likely "casing" a store to commit a robbery. On stopping and questioning the suspect, the officer concluded that Terry

**Policing in Practice Video:**
Former Drug Investigator

■ **Plain View Doctrine:** Holds that if a police officer sees an incriminating object in plain view during a legitimate stop, he or she may seize the object

■ **Totality of Circumstances:** Requires that an officer has a particularized and objective basis for suspecting that a particular person is or has been involved in criminal activity

might be armed. A pat-down search led to the discovery of a firearm. The Supreme Court determined that the temporary stop did not violate the 4th Amendment and that such stops are permissible based on reasonable suspicion. Thus, if the officer making a stop reasonably believes that the person stopped may constitute a threat (e.g., may be armed and dangerous), the officer may frisk the suspect. The frisk must be initially limited to a pat down of the suspect's outer clothing and may become more extensive only if the officer detects something that may be a weapon. Absent the discovery of an object that may be a weapon, no further search of the suspect is permissible at this point. If a suspicious object is discovered during the pat down, the officer may reach into the suspect's pockets or clothing for the sole purpose of seizing the weapon. However, any contraband (e.g., illegal drugs) found during the search for a weapon may be confiscated and used as evidence in a criminal trial related to the initial stop.

In *Michigan v. Long*,[28] the Supreme Court extended the range of a search for weapons to include the passenger compartment of the car driven by a suspect if the police have reasonable suspicion (e.g., see a weapon in plain view when approaching the car) that the driver is a dangerous person.[29]

In 2015, the U.S. Supreme Court ruled in *Rodriguez v. U.S.* that prolonging the detention of a person who is subject to a traffic stop for the purpose of waiting for drug-sniffing dogs to arrive and further inspect the vehicle is unconstitutional.[30]

**Web Link:**
Sandra Bland, Samuel DuBose and the rise of 'vehicular stop and frisk'

### Gene L. Scaramella, Former Police Officer, Author, and Educator

My regular partner and I, both younger officers assigned to a busy district in the Chicago Police Department, were assigned to a permanent beat. That particular beat was characterized by a high minority population, a high unemployment rate, and a serious problem with street crime, primarily as a result of the heavy presence of street gangs.

It did not take long to figure out that when we observed young, White males driving by the "hot spots" (where drug dealing occurred) of the district, most of the time they were buying drugs from street gang members. Thus, when we observed this phenomenon, we sat in a covert position and watched. When we witnessed a drug sale, we waited a few moments and then stopped the car driven by the young, White males in question away from where the incident occurred. We then got the occupants out of the car (passengers included, if applicable), searched them and the inside of the car, and, if they had drugs in their possession, placed them under arrest. I recall one particular incident. We were at the station filling out the paperwork and, of course, had to include our probable cause for stopping the car and for searching the driver and the car. I recall asking my partner in a jovial manner why we stopped the car. He replied, "The guy didn't use his turn signal when he turned off of the side street." Regarding the search, I said, "And he gave us permission to search his car! How about that?" Thus, that's how the story was documented with respect to these types of arrests.

Were our actions improper? Sure they were, but we justified our actions by knowing that we had done a good job for the community and the department by removing some drugs from the street. After all, we were in pursuit of a "noble cause," and we weren't going to let silly court rulings stand in our way. The bad guys don't play by the rules, so why should we? Besides, the majority of our arrestees were used later by tactical unit officers to help build a case against the dealers who sold them the drugs. We even received honorable mentions by the department on several occasions.

In retrospect, an "ends justifies the means" approach is not a good idea for obvious reasons. For example, what if one of our cases went to trial rather than being pled out by the prosecutor? We would have had to take the stand and commit perjury. Thankfully, we never had one of those cases go to trial. Faced with similar circumstances today, I would play by the rules for fear of potential consequences and for the sake of professionalism.

© Michael Matthews - Police Images / Alamy.

Justice Ginsburg stated that, "An officer, in other words, may conduct certain unrelated checks during an otherwise lawful traffic stop," but, "he may not do so in a way that prolongs the stop, absent the reasonable suspicion ordinarily demanded to justify detaining an individual." The decision in this case is seemingly opposite a 2005 ruling to which Justice Ginzberg dissented. At that time, the Court held that "a dog sniff conducted during a concededly lawful traffic stop that reveals no information other than the location of a substance that no individual has any right to possess does not violate the 4th Amendment."

Another issue related to police stops has received considerable attention in recent years. The issue in question deals with the rights and obligations of police officers who have probable cause to stop a person they believe may be in the United States illegally, especially in Arizona. The Arizona law before the court, known as SB 1070, authorizes police officers to make warrantless arrests when they have probable cause to believe someone is illegally in the country. Another provision of the law *requires* state and local law enforcement officers, upon reasonable suspicion, to detain anyone stopped or arrested for any reason, no matter how minor, until the immigration status of that person is determined.[31] The governor of Arizona maintained that the law is necessary, because federal authorities have failed to meet their obligation with respect to illegal immigrants. The Obama administration maintained that immigration matters are the domain of the federal government and sued the state in federal court to invalidate the law. In July 2012, the Supreme Court delivered a split decision on the law, sustaining the law's central provision known as the "show me your papers" provision, while leaving the door open to further challenges. The "show me your papers" provision requires state law enforcement officials to determine the immigration status of anyone they stop or arrest if they have reason to suspect that the individual might be in the country illegally. The majority of justices rejected other provisions that would have subjected illegal immigrants to criminal penalties for activities such as seeking work.[32]

### Police Searches Incident to Arrest

Discussing searches incident to arrest requires an understanding of what constitutes an arrest. In general terms, an **arrest** occurs when (1) an individual authorized to take a person into custody detains that person with the intention of making an arrest and (2) when the person being arrested understands that the person making the arrest intends to detain him or her for that purpose. The arrest may be affected with or without a warrant, though the latter is preferable, when possible.

The basic law governing searches related to arrest can be found in *Chimel v. California*.[33] To justify a full search, the suspect must be taken into custody by the officer, and the arresting officer must conduct that search. Further, the search must be conducted at the time of or shortly after the arrest to be legal. In addition, generally speaking, the officer may use the degree of force necessary to protect self and others or to prevent the flight of the suspect or the destruction of evidence. In general, the arresting officer may search the arrestee for weapons or evidence and may extend into any area under the direct or immediate control of the arrestee at the time of the arrest. The search may be extended to companions of the arrestee if the officer reasonably believes that these companions may present a threat or may destroy evidence.[34]

**Author Video:**
4th Amendment

The U.S. Supreme Court decision in *Arizona v. Gant* (2009) addressed the circumstances related to the search of a vehicle related to the arrest of an occupant. Gant was arrested for driving with a suspended license, handcuffed, and locked in a patrol car before police officers searched the passenger compartment of his vehicle and found cocaine and a firearm. The Court held that police may search the passenger compartment of a vehicle incident to a recent occupant's arrest only if it is reasonable to believe the arrestee might access the vehicle at the time of the search or that the vehicle contains evidence of the offense of arrest.[35] In some arrests for traffic violations, there is reasonable basis to believe that the vehicle contains relevant evidence.[36] However, in other cases, such as arrests for possession of controlled substances, the basis of the arrest will supply acceptable rationale for searching the arrestee's passenger compartment and any containers inside. Some might suggest that *Arizona v. Gant* encourages unsafe police practices such as leaving the arrestees unsecured to justify a search incident to arrest. However, according to the Federal Law Enforcement Training Centers (FLETC), Justice Scalia addressed this issue in *Thornton v. United States*.[37] He stated that "if an officer leaves a suspect unrestrained nearby just to manufacture authority to search, one could argue that the search is unreasonable precisely because the dangerous conditions justifying it existed only by the virtue of the officer's failure to follow sensible procedures."

A search must be conducted at the time of or shortly after an arrest.

More recently, in *Florence v. Board of Chosen Freeholders of the County of Burlington* (2012),[38] the Supreme Court further extended the right to search suspects when it held that officials may strip search individuals who have been arrested for any crime before admitting the individuals to jail, even if there is no reason to suspect that the individual is carrying contraband.

## Consent Searches

Another type of search frequently conducted by the police requires

© iStockphoto.com/Robert Ingelhart

If an individual voluntarily waives 4th Amendment rights, police may perform a consent search in a home or, in this case, a vehicle. Lawful consent searches cannot be obtained as a result of coercion or duress.

© iStockphoto.com/EdStock

neither probable cause nor a warrant. A **consent search** occurs when an individual voluntarily waives his or her 4th Amendment rights and allows a police officer to search his or her person, belongings, vehicle, or home. An example of a consent search might involve a traffic stop during which the officer asks the driver of the stopped vehicle if he would mind opening the trunk of the vehicle. Many individuals comply with the request, often because they have nothing to hide from the police or because they are uncertain of the consequences if they refuse the request.

The courts have made it clear that consent searches must be voluntary, that no coercion—either implicit or explicit—may be used, that no deception or misrepresentation may be used, and that the consent be clearly stated (either orally, by gesture, or in writing).[39] The courts have also imposed limits on the scope and object of the search. Finally, in *State v. Lewis* and other cases, it has been held that the consenting party may revoke his or her consent at any time after the search has begun.[40] There are numerous other exceptions and procedures related to the amendment that are beyond the scope of this text.

## ■ THE 5TH AMENDMENT

The 5th Amendment provides that no citizen is to be tried for a capital or "otherwise infamous crime without a presentment or indictment" by a grand jury (exception here is that the grand jury clause does not protect those serving in the armed forces, whether during wartime or peacetime), or may be subject to trial for the same offense twice, or compelled to incriminate himself or herself or be deprived of life, liberty, or property without due process of law. This is a far-reaching amendment, but for our purposes here (due process will be discussed in relation to the 14th Amendment), the right against self-incrimination is of particular importance; it often relates directly to police encounters with suspects. Initially, the **privilege against self-incrimination** seems straightforward. It implies that no person can be compelled to incriminate himself or herself—that the suspect need not answer questions or disclose information that would support his or her own conviction. The courts have ruled that the privilege refers to testimonial communications and does not prevent compelled appearances in lineups or photo lineups, handwriting samples, fingerprints, or blood-alcohol tests, among other

**■ Consent Search:** Occurs when an individual voluntarily waives his or her 4th Amendment rights and allows a police officer to search his or her person, belongings, vehicle, or home

**■ Privilege Against Self-Incrimination:** Implies that no person can be compelled to incriminate himself or herself—the suspect need not answer questions or disclose information that would support his or her own conviction

things.[41] It is interesting to note that, although compulsory appearances in lineups do not constitute constitutional violations for persons in custody, roughly 75% of wrongful convictions found through subsequent DNA analysis involved some form of mistaken eyewitness identification.[42] As a result, several states and some major police agencies are changing their policies concerning photo and in-person lineups.[43]

The impact of the privilege against self-incrimination on police actions is considerable, since it is related to (1) statements, (2) admissions, and (3) confessions given to police officers. The courts have ruled that all three must be given voluntarily and with knowledge on behalf of the suspect that he has the right to remain silent or request the presence of an attorney. Once the police interrogation commences, the 6th Amendment also guarantees the right to counsel. Involuntary confessions are considered to be both unreliable and a violation of due process when resulting from police coercion. This is true even though the statement, admission, or confession itself may actually be reliable. Thus, the Supreme Court held in *Townsend v. Sain* that "any questioning by police officers which in fact produces a confession which is not the product of free intellect renders that confession inadmissible."[44]

A key question for the police concerns the point at which questioning during an investigation becomes an interrogation. In *Escobedo v. Illinois*, the court held that, when "the investigation is no longer a general inquiry into an unsolved crime but has begun to focus on a particular suspect" and "the suspect has been taken into police custody, the police carry out a process of interrogation. . . ."[45] Then, in *Miranda v. Arizona*, the court indicated that when a person is taken into custody or otherwise deprived of his or her freedom by the police and is subjected to questioning, the privilege against self-incrimination is jeopardized.[46] At this point, procedural safeguards must be employed to protect that privilege. This decision resulted in the now-famous warning the police give prior to interrogating suspects: "You have the right to remain silent; anything you say can be used against you in a court of law; you have the right to the presence of an attorney; if you cannot afford an attorney, one will be appointed for you." Suspects are then typically asked whether they understand these rights and whether they wish to continue talking to the police. If a suspect asks for an attorney at this point in the process, or at any other point, the interrogation is to stop until an attorney is present. In *Berghuis v. Thompkins*, the Supreme Court elaborated on *Miranda*, indicating that suspects must explicitly tell police they want to remain silent (rather than simply remain silent) to invoke *Miranda* protections during criminal interrogations.[38] Failure to inform suspects of their rights under *Miranda* likely means that any statement, admission, or confession obtained is inadmissible at the time of trial. Currently, the Obama administration is contemplating legislation to initiate changes in *Miranda* to expand the ability of authorities to question international terrorists.[47]

Not all statements, admissions, or confessions are invalidated by failure to provide the *Miranda* warning. Statements voluntarily made prior to the beginning of any interrogation and not in response to police questioning may be admissible. Similarly, information obtained in the process of routine questioning (e.g., in the booking process) is not generally protected by *Miranda*. Questions spontaneously asked by the police in regard to an emergency or related to public safety, or impulsively asked, are not typically held to be interrogation.[48] Further, it should be noted that *Miranda* applies only to custodial interrogation conducted by the police. Thus, statements, admissions, and confessions made to private citizens are likely to be admissible in court.

Questions often arise concerning whether a suspect knowingly and voluntarily waived his or her rights under *Miranda*. To help ensure that it was indeed voluntary, the police often request a written waiver and may provide the necessary warnings in more than one language. The general rule of thumb for police officers is that it is better to be safe than sorry. Thus, the *Miranda* warning may be given when it is not needed simply to ensure that it has been given should questions arise concerning the privilege against self-incrimination. A recent case indicates the complexities that may be involved in

This suspect has invoked his *Miranda* rights and the police must wait to continue their interrogation until his attorney arrives.

© iStockphoto.com/KatarzynaBialasiewicz

*Miranda* interrogations. In 2003, a police detective tried to question a suspect, who was incarcerated at a Maryland prison as a result of a prior conviction, about his alleged sexual abuse of his son. Shatzer, the suspect, invoked his *Miranda* right to have counsel present during interrogation, and the detective terminated the interview. Shatzer was released back into the general prison population, and the investigation was closed. Another detective reopened the investigation three years later and attempted to interrogate Shatzer, who was still incarcerated. Shatzer waived his *Miranda* rights and made incriminating statements. He was convicted of sexual child abuse. The Supreme Court held that, because Shatzer experienced a break in *Miranda* custody lasting more than two weeks between the first and second attempts at interrogation, his 2006 statements need not be suppressed.[49]

**Author Video:**
Department of Justice: Ferguson Police Department Discriminate Against African Americans

### ■ THE 14TH AMENDMENT

The 14th Amendment is often referred to as the *due process* amendment because it states that no state can deprive any person of life, liberty, or property without due process of law. Currently, the rights guaranteed by the 1st, 4th, and 6th Amendments, along with parts of the 5th and 8th Amendments, have been applied to the states.[50] As it relates to the police specifically, due process requires that evidence of a crime be presented in court and that both testimonial and physical evidence is obtained according to the rules. In addition, the **equal protection clause** of the 14th Amendment applies to the police in that it prevents the federal government and all states from denying the protection of the law to any group of persons by making arbitrary, unreasonable distinctions based on race, religion, gender, and national origin.[51] Thus, this amendment is the basis for a good deal of the civil rights legislation we have seen in the past 50 years. For example, the problems of biased enforcement and racial profiling by the police are clearly prohibited by the equal protection clause.

**■ Equal Protection Clause:** Of the 14th Amendment, applies the equal protection clause to the police in that it prevents both the federal government and all states from denying the protection of the law to any group of persons by making arbitrary, unreasonable distinctions based on race, religion, gender, national origin, and so on

Due process has become a cornerstone of the U.S. legal system, and it is sometimes problematic for the police because of the requirements it establishes for many police activities, including arrest, interrogation, and collection of evidence through searches and seizures, as well as many other activities. Briefly stated, it would be much easier for the police to operate under a crime control model than a due process model. The **crime control model** allows for the arrest of individuals who are known to be factually guilty of committing a crime. The **due process model** requires that evidence of guilt presented in court be obtained according to legal guidelines. The due process model relies on equal treatment of all accused persons and imposes a variety of restraints on the actions of the police. For instance, the police might receive a tip from an anonymous caller who states that a specific individual living in a specific college dorm room is distributing illegal drugs from that location. Using the crime control model, the police break down the door to the room, find the drugs, arrest and charge the offender, and use the drugs as evidence in the ensuing trial. Under the due process model, the police must demonstrate that the tip came from a reliable informant, obtain a proper search warrant, and maintain a proper chain of evidence, or the drugs will be inadmissible as evidence in court and the defendant will be acquitted. In other words, even though the defendant was factually guilty of distributing illegal drugs, he or she is not legally guilty because the procedures established to safeguard the rights of citizens were violated. While the emphasis on technicalities related to due process shifts with political administrations, public opinion, and the judiciary, the underlying right to due process remains. This may be frustrating to the police, who often view due process requirements as obstacles to successful enforcement of the law. Still, most officers would probably agree that if they were the focus of an investigation, they would prefer the due process model.

## ■ THE EXCLUSIONARY RULE

The **exclusionary rule** is a judicially imposed requirement that any evidence obtained by the police using methods that violate an individual's constitutional rights be excluded in a criminal prosecution against that individual. Note that the wrong done by the police must involve constitutional questions for the exclusionary rule to apply. The rule was first expounded in *Weeks v. United States* and applied only to federal law enforcement officers.[52] In *Wolf v. Colorado*, the Supreme Court held that the rule applied to the states as part of the due process clause of the 14th Amendment.[53] Then, in the case of *Mapp v. Ohio*, the court mandated enforcement of the rule by the states.[54]

Interestingly, the exclusionary rule was specifically designed to prevent police misconduct and applies to both police officers and those acting as their agents. Thus, if a police officer without probable cause or a warrant indicates to a private citizen that she might assist the police by searching the purse of a third party, any evidence obtained would be subject to the exclusionary rule. If the same woman searched the same purse on her own initiative, however, the fruits of the search might well be admissible in court proceedings.

The exclusionary rule applies to evidence obtained directly as the result of constitutional violations and also to evidence found indirectly as a result of the violation under what is referred to as the **fruit of the poisonous tree doctrine**. For example, if the police conduct an illegal search and discover stolen property in the home of a suspect and, at the same time, discover evidence that a second suspect was involved in the crime, neither the stolen property nor the name of the second suspect is admissible in court. As you might expect, based on an earlier discussion in this chapter, there are a number of exceptions to the exclusionary rule. Among these are what is known as the good-faith doctrine, the inevitable discovery doctrine, and the independent source doctrine.

The **good-faith doctrine** deals with searches conducted with a warrant, and it states that when a police officer acting in good faith obtains a warrant, conducts a search, and seizes evidence, that evidence will not be excluded from court proceedings even if the warrant is later invalidated.[55] Describing a 2009 decision by the U.S. Supreme Court, a headline in *The New York Times* declared that the court was a "step closer to repeal" of the exclusionary rule.[56] The case in point, *Herring v. United States*, involved a police

**SAGE Journal Article:** The American Exclusionary Rule: Is There a Lesson to Learn from Others?

■ **Crime Control Model:** Allows for the arrest of individuals who are known to be factually guilty of committing a crime

■ **Due Process Model:** Requires that evidence of guilt presented in court be obtained according to legal guidelines

■ **Exclusionary Rule:** A judicially imposed requirement that any evidence obtained by the police using methods that violate an individual's constitutional rights be excluded in a criminal prosecution against that individual

■ **Fruit of the Poisonous Tree Doctrine:** Evidence found indirectly as a result of a constitutional violation

■ **Good-Faith Doctrine:** Involves searches conducted with a warrant and states that when a police officer acting in good faith obtains a warrant, conducts a search, and seizes evidence, that evidence will not be excluded from court proceedings even if the warrant is later invalidated

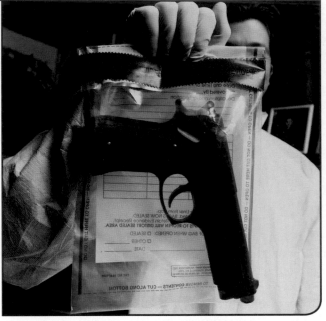

© Digital Vision

investigator who had several run-ins with Mr. Herring. When the police officer saw Herring, he requested a warrant check, and a neighboring county reported there was a warrant for his arrest. Acting on this information, the police officer stopped Herring's vehicle and located methamphetamine in his pocket and a handgun under the seat.[57] Approximately 10 minutes later, the police officer learned that a mistake had occurred and the warrant had been withdrawn five months earlier. The U.S. Supreme Court held that when police mistakes that lead to an unlawful search are the result of isolated negligence attenuated from the search rather than systematic error or reckless disregard of constitutional requirements, the exclusionary rule does not apply.[58]

The **inevitable discovery doctrine** allows the admission of illegally obtained evidence if it would have been discovered lawfully in the "normal course of events" anyway.[59] The normal course of events, for instance, might include routine police procedures or testimonial evidence from a witness. Finally, the **independent source doctrine** (which also uses the biblical reference, "fruit of the poisonous tree doctrine") holds that illegally obtained evidence may be admitted if it was also obtained through an independent source not tainted by police misconduct.

The exclusionary rule indicates the lengths to which the courts have gone in attempting to guarantee constitutional rights by preventing police misconduct. It appears that the courts are not convinced that the police can or will adhere to all procedural requirements without judicial oversight.

### ■ POLICE USE OF FORCE

This discussion of police use of force presents a brief summary of relevant issues versus a comprehensive coverage of all the legal issues related to the use of force. A text on criminal law and procedure would contain a more complete discussion of the issues.

From time to time in the performance of their duties, the police must resort to the use of force to either prevent criminal activity or apprehend criminals. Under common law, police officers could use less-than-lethal force to arrest a felon and, as a last resort, deadly force to arrest a fleeing felon. **Less-than-lethal force** refers to force used by the officer that is not likely to result in serious bodily harm or death, whereas **lethal or deadly force** may result in great bodily harm or death. Examples of less-than-lethal force include launchable and hand-deployable chemical agents, kinetic energy or impact munitions, and electronic control devices (Tasers), among others.[60] In some cases, use of less-than-lethal force has resulted in death or serious injury to suspects. Recently, **Tasers** (electroshock weapons that use electrical current to disrupt voluntary control of muscles) have come under increasing scrutiny in this regard; the ACLU indicated in 2009 that it submitted a petition to the Supreme Court to hear a case on the constitutionality of excessive force related to police use of Tasers.[61]

**■ Inevitable Discovery Doctrine:** Allows the admission of illegally obtained evidence if it would have been discovered lawfully in the normal course of events anyway

**■ Independent Source Doctrine:** Holds that illegally obtained evidence may be admitted if it was also obtained through an independent source not tainted by a failure to follow procedure or police misconduct

**■ Less-Than-Lethal Force:** Force used by an officer that is not likely to result in serious bodily harm or death

**■ Lethal or Deadly Force:** Force that may result in great bodily harm or death

**■ Taser:** Electroshock weapon that uses electrical current to disrupt voluntary control of muscles

© Junglecat

Over time, the maximum penalty for various felonies has been reduced from death to imprisonment. While under common law, police officers would have been permitted to use deadly force against criminals who committed such felonies, the current maximum punishment on conviction would be imprisonment. It made no sense to allow the police to continue to use deadly force in cases where a conviction in court could not result in capital punishment. Thus, police officers today are not empowered to use deadly force against unarmed or otherwise nondangerous offenders.

Generally speaking, police officers are authorized to use reasonable force (recall our earlier discussion of the criteria for reasonableness) to make arrests, to prevent escapes, and to protect themselves and others from harm.[62] The Supreme Court language in *Tennessee v. Garner* best describes the current situation: "A police officer may not seize an unarmed, non-dangerous suspect by shooting him dead," but "where the officer has probable cause to believe that the suspect poses a threat of serious physical harm, either to the officer or to others, it is not constitutionally unreasonable to prevent escape by using deadly force."[63] When determining probable cause in such cases, officers typically consider a series of factors, including the suspects' motivation to harm or escape, their propensity for violence, their current state of mind, their combat experience (in cases where this is known), whether or not they are in possession of a weapon, and the location in which the encounter occurs.[64]

In addition to using force to perform an arrest or prevent an escape, police officers may be confronted with the need to use force to enter a dwelling or a vehicle. Typically, a warrant is required for such entry, but in **exigent circumstances**, the officer may enter without a warrant. Such circumstances may exist when the police are in hot pursuit of a fleeing felon, when there is a danger of imminent destruction of evidence, when a suspect is escaping, or when there is imminent danger to the officer or others. Where the officer has legal authority to enter a dwelling, he should first knock on the door, announce his purpose and identify as a police officer, and demand entry. If the demand to enter is refused or met with silence, the officer may enter after waiting a reasonable (usually quite short) period of time. And in *Wilson v. Arkansas*, the Supreme Court recognized that announcing the presence of a police officer and waiting outside for a response is unreasonable in certain cases.[65] Some instances in which the requirements to knock, announce, and wait may be waived include those in which the safety of the officer or others is at stake, where the procedure may allow the offender to escape, and where knocking and announcing might allow the suspect to destroy evidence.

One additional example of an issue relating to the use of deadly force is that of high-speed police pursuit. In such pursuits, the police vehicle itself may become deadly for

**Policing in Practice Video:**
Within the last few years, has your department changed its policies on use of force? How does implicit bias come into play?

■ **Exigent Circumstances:**
Circumstances that may exist when the police are in hot pursuit of a fleeing felon, when there is a danger of imminent destruction of evidence, when a suspect is escaping, or when there is imminent danger to the officer or others

**Author Video:**
Police use of force

innocent bystanders, those being pursued, or the pursuing police officers. A recent Supreme Court decision shed some light on the current pursuit situation. In *Scott v. Harris*, the Court concluded the following:

> We are loath to lay down a rule requiring the police to allow fleeing suspects to get away whenever they drive so recklessly that they put other people's lives in danger. It is obvious the perverse incentives such a rule would create. . . . A police officer's attempt to terminate a dangerous high-speed car chase that threatens the lives of innocent bystanders does not violate the 4th Amendment, even when it places the fleeing motorist at risk of serious injury or death.[66]

A major concern of police officers everywhere, as well as of police administrators whose forces span out across the city 24 hours a day, is with **liability** for their actions. Under Section 1983 of the U.S. Code—Civil Action for Deprivation of Rights—suits may be brought against both officers and their supervisors, as well as the branch of government they represent in some cases, for failure to train officers properly and for developing unconstitutional policies and practices.[67] These fears seem well founded given that some estimates of the monetary cost of such suits range as high as $780 billion annually—even though most suits are eventually decided in favor of the officer.[68] If the alleged violations by the officer are criminal in nature, prosecutors may take action in addition to the civil action that state and federal courts may take. Thus, the family of an individual killed by a police officer may allege wrongful death and file civil suits in both state and federal courts to collect damages. If a prosecutor has cause to believe that the death resulted from inappropriate behavior on the part of the officer, he or she may file criminal charges as well. The type of defense commonly employed against such actions includes the good-faith doctrine and the reasonable belief that probable cause existed.

> " The decision concerning use of force, particularly deadly force, is one of the most critical a police officer is required to make. Such decisions are typically made in a matter of seconds, but they have consequences that may last a lifetime.

The decision concerning use of force, particularly deadly force, is one of the most critical a police officer is required to make. Such decisions are typically made in a matter of seconds, but they have consequences that may last a lifetime.

## ■ THE USA PATRIOT ACT, HOMELAND SECURITY, AND TERRORISM

Prior to September 11, 2001, very few discussions of police behavior focused on their role in preventing terrorism and apprehending terrorists. Now, terrorism is one of the critical issues of our time for police officers at all levels. According to the Code of Federal Regulations, "**terrorism** consists of the unlawful use of force or threat of force against persons or property to intimidate or coerce a government, a civilian population, or any part thereof in furtherance of political or social objectives."[69] Most terrorists claim to be not criminals, but rather freedom fighters (religion, ideology, special interest). But, almost all terrorist acts violate criminal laws.[70]

Law enforcement officials around the world have reported a significant increase in the range and scope of international terrorist activity in recent years. The public is frequently warned that the danger from terrorists is real and that the nation cannot afford to let down its guard. Further, a visible police presence reminds people of the danger they face every time they travel by air or enter a public building. And, with the continued danger of terrorism comes the continued temptation to dilute constitutional ideals concerning the right to privacy and searches and seizures (note the scanners at airports, coupled with pat-down searches and seizures of bottles of liquid containing more than a few ounces). Similarly, many public buildings, including courthouses and schools, have metal detectors through which employees and visitors alike must pass on entry. Clearly the events of 9/11 have caused Americans to reconsider their approach to national and local security issues.

■ **Liability:** Legal responsibility for costs or damages

■ **Terrorism:** The unlawful use of force or threat of force against persons or property to intimidate or coerce a government, a civilian population, or any part thereof in furtherance of political or social objectives

The passage of the USA PATRIOT Act in October 2001 and the Homeland Security Act in November 2002 raised legal issues that impact the lives of every American. The intent of the USA PATRIOT Act, when it was passed in 2001 as an immediate response to the 9/11 attacks, was to provide federal law enforcement officers with better means to defend against terrorists. Key points included the expansion of surveillance activities, tighter prohibitions on money laundering, and increased information sharing. For example, Section 216 of the act made the Internet subject to surveillance. Section 351 created directives to financial institutions that increased auditing and reporting requirements.[72]

Through the **Homeland Security Act** and the **USA PATRIOT Act**, the U.S. government focuses on several terrorism prevention strategies and tactics.

- Developing public safety programs to protect vulnerable targets and locations
- Enhancing community participation in "terrorist watch" programs
- Improving intelligence by increasing the cooperation among law enforcement agencies worldwide
- Improving training for security forces by developing realistic antiterrorist action scenarios
- Organizing regular exercises for security forces and citizens
- Fostering coordination between security forces and communities on the basis of model local, state, and federal plans for responding to terrorist attacks[73]

The Federal Bureau of Investigation's (FBI) Joint Terrorism Task Force (JTTF) effort, first established in 1980, involves multiple law enforcement agencies working together to increase dialogue, improve relationships, and maximize information sharing.[74] JTTFs have proven successful in thwarting numerous terrorist plots in the United States and in providing an effective venue for local officers to assist in the mission of national security. The FBI benefits from having the JTTF program in that its efforts in counterterrorism are enhanced by cooperation of state and local police officers with street-level experience and knowledge of local jurisdictions. Police departments also benefit from having an officer assigned to a JTTF, because these officers may undergo extensive specialized training and gain experience in managing complex investigations.[75]

The significance of attacks by terrorists throughout the world must not be minimized, but it is also important to consider the possibility of overreaction. The need to monitor people entering the country as well as those already here creates a certain level of tension, as government agencies ask for unprecedented access to personal information.

At the same time, however, the right to privacy requires the protection of personal information. Some argue that parts of the USA PATRIOT Act take away checks on law enforcement and threaten the very rights and freedoms that we are struggling to protect. For example, without a warrant and without probable cause, the FBI now has the power to access private medical records, library records, and student records, and it can prevent anyone from telling those being investigated that it has been done. Another case, however, raised the issue of whether the police have the right to use **global positioning system (GPS)** devices without a warrant to track the movements of suspects.[76] In the case of *United States v. Jones*, the Supreme Court unanimously restricted the ability of the police to use a GPS device to track criminal suspects by ruling that the use of such a device constitutes a search and is governed by 4th Amendment protections. This case is a first test of how privacy rights will be protected in the digital age. Recognizing that questions of privacy and technology represent a legal frontier, the Court stated that the decision should not be construed as a basis for more complex privacy issues. The constitutionality of a variety of police actions under the USA PATRIOT Act is certain to be tested. Police officers, especially, need to know both the scope and the potential hazards of these federal statutes.[77]

■ **Homeland Security Act:** Law passed by the U.S. Congress that focuses on terrorism prevention strategies and tactics

■ **USA PATRIOT Act:** Federal legislation passed in 2002 that represented a major reorganization of national security agencies; it created the Department of Homeland Security, which conducts services previously handled by various other organizations

■ **Global Positioning System (GPS):** A U.S. space-based global navigation satellite system providing positioning, navigation, and timing services to users

# AROUND THE WORLD    9.1

Interpol is the world's largest international police organization. In Tel Aviv, Israel, Interpol holds a three-day, high-profile international conference with senior police officers from 49 countries to discuss cybercrime, counterterrorism, and drug trafficking. Israel's liaison with this organization tells *The Jerusalem Post* about the country's growing cooperation with foreign law enforcement.

Internet-based crime costs countries more money than all drug trafficking combined, and European countries lose a total of 750 billion euros a year due to cybercrime. Targets include global financial institutions, state institutions, and even the Interpol website.

Ronald K. Noble, secretary-general of Interpol, told delegates, "I certainly do not need to convince anyone in this room that crime has become inherently transnational and can touch our citizens from any country in the world where the Internet is in use. . . . What is more, the Internet also facilitates the dissemination of violent, extreme and radical ideologies, enabling radical leaders to reach friendly ears right in our communities and in all corners of the world."

One of Israel's first decisions as a sovereign country was to join Interpol in 1949. Today, Israeli police instantly share information, issue international arrest warrants, and receive such warrants through Interpol's secure Internet network, which connects the Israeli police to 189 Interpol members.

1. Considering the risks to national security, do you believe the government should limit access to the Internet or secretly monitor Internet activity?

2. What steps can law enforcement agencies in the United States take to prevent cybercrime?

3. Because the Internet has international applications, should law enforcement agencies in other countries be able to monitor the Internet activities of U.S. citizens without their knowledge? Why or why not?

*Source:* Lappin, Y. (2012, May 9). Interpol holds high-profile international conference in TA. Police from 49 countries to discuss cyber crime, counter-terrorism, drug trafficking. *The (Israel) Jerusalem Post*, p. 6. Record Number: 13EBF7DB6C19B410.

**Web Link:**
Civil Liberties

It is possible to draw some limited conclusions about the impact of the USA PATRIOT Act and the Homeland Security Act on state and local police. First, the ways in which state and local law enforcement personnel continue to assist in the effort to prevent terrorist attacks are multifaceted and critical. Perhaps contrary to popular belief, police officers encounter known and suspected terrorists in both urban and rural areas. The expanding JTTF concept and enhanced information-sharing techniques have considerably improved the processes of obtaining and analyzing information. With new tools at their disposal, state and local law enforcement authorities will continue to play an important role in preventing future terrorism.[78]

Although it is clear that everyone contends that local police are critical partners with federal officials and are most often the early responders, many of the details about training, coordination, and funding remain unclear. The Department of Homeland Security (DHS) acknowledges that local officers are "the country's eyes and ears on the ground" for antiterrorism efforts, and have formalized some of the structures for technical support, training, and sharing and analyzing information.[79] Two years after the bombing at the Boston Marathon, "1,200 federal officials, explosive ordinance detection teams, canine units, and behavioral detection field officers [were available] to assist the Federal Coordinator in helping the event planners enhance the overall event security."[80] Some of the enhanced measures may be obvious to the public, and some may be behind the scenes. The lessons learned in Boston—according to the DHS—have been adopted at special events across the nation.

Communications between federal and local police have improved, but there is a great deal yet to accomplish. For example, what do the various alert stages (amber, orange,

© iStockphoto.com/EdStock

The USA PATRIOT Act at work—besides routine checks on passengers using basic screening procedures, the act gives law enforcement personnel the authority to conduct additional, more intrusive screening procedures, such as complete searches of the person, use of explosive screening devices, and searches using dogs trained to detect the presence of drugs, explosive materials, and other contraband.

or red) mean to local police in terms of how they should react, what they should look for, and what kinds of information they should provide to the public? What types of intelligence do federal authorities expect from state and local police concerning terrorism?[81] Will constitutional guarantees be further diminished in the attempt to prevent and apprehend terrorists? Among those guarantees that may be in danger, according to some observers, are the very amendments discussed in this chapter. Are compromises involving constitutional rights really necessary to help keep the United States safe from terrorists?

## CHAPTER SUMMARY

It is impossible to comprehensively cover the wide variety of rules and regulations that govern police behavior in the United States. This chapter highlights some of the more important laws and court decisions to indicate the extent of the legal parameters surrounding police activities and the subsequent impact these statutory and judicial decisions have on police policies and procedures. In addition to the issues discussed here, the police are subject to hundreds of state, county, and municipal rules and regulations and to departmental policy.

Police at all levels have a tremendous amount of discretionary authority over their daily practice, such as enforcement of the law, methods used to obtain information, conduct involving interaction with citizens, and the majority of other police actions. The public has the right to protection from any unlawful police practices; related civil and criminal laws exist at both the state and federal levels.

Court decisions and case law add protections at all levels of government. Case law has a major impact on a variety of police actions and administrative policies. Issues such as search and seizure, use of force, interrogation methods, and other related constitutional concerns are often the focus of court decisions issued within a constitutional framework. In addition, case law applicable to the use of deadly force, high-speed vehicle pursuits, negligent training and supervision, negligent retention of personnel, and investigative methodologies that use profiling are examples of areas where the court has an impact on police policy. It is also important to note that when these court-imposed dictates are ignored and violated, individual officers may expose themselves to criminal and civil liability. Their respective agencies can be held civilly liable as well, which may cost agencies millions of dollars.

More recent concerns involve the increasingly global and technological nature of crime. The effects of the USA PATRIOT Act and similar laws have broadened the scope of police power and policies and raised additional constitutional questions concerning police behavior, which may take years to resolve in the courts.

## KEY TERMS

**SAGE** edge™
Review key terms with eFlashcards.

- Criminal law  205
- Civil law  205
- Search  208
- Seizure  208
- Probable cause  210
- Reasonableness  210
- Reasonable suspicion  210
- Warrant  211
- Plain view doctrine  212
- Totality of circumstances  212
- Arrest  214

- Consent search  216
- Privilege against self-incrimination  216
- Equal protection clause  218
- Crime control model  219
- Due process model  219
- Exclusionary rule  219
- Fruit of the poisonous tree doctrine  219
- Good-faith doctrine  219
- Inevitable discovery doctrine  220

- Independent source doctrine  220
- Less-than-lethal force  220
- Lethal or deadly force  220
- Taser  220
- Exigent circumstances  221
- Liability  222
- Terrorism  222
- Homeland Security Act  223
- USA PATRIOT Act  223
- Global positioning system (GPS)  223

## DISCUSSION QUESTIONS

**SAGE** edge™
Test your understanding of chapter content. Take the practice quiz.

1. What are some distinctions between criminal and civil law?

2. Why is it important to understand the role of police discretion when discussing constitutional law and court decisions?

3. What is the proper role of a police officer assigned to work at a protest involving hundreds of people when the officer strenuously disagrees with the protestors?

4. Why might some police officers invent probable cause for a stop they made without such cause?

5. Is it usually preferable for a police officer to make an arrest or conduct a search with or without a warrant? Provide

examples to support your answer.

6. When in doubt, should a police officer administer the *Miranda* warning to a suspect or not? Why or why not?

7. Does the exclusionary rule deal only with the 14th Amendment? If not, what other amendments are involved?

8. What is the purpose of the due process clause? How is the concept of fruit of the poisonous tree related to the due process clause?

9. What is the recognized role of local police officers in the war on terror? What are some resources that are available to the police to help them in their counterterrorism efforts?

## INTERNET EXERCISES

1. Go to the Internet and type in the key words *Muehler et al. v. Mena,* 125 S. Ct. 1495, (U. S. Sup. Ct., No. 03–1423, March 22, 2005).

Review the facts of the case. In your opinion, based on the material discussed in this chapter, were the plaintiff's constitutional rights violated when she was placed in handcuffs during the search of the house she occupied? Why or why not?

2. Type the key words *Groh v. Ramirez*, 540 U. S. 551 (U. S. Sup., No. 02–0811, February 24, 2004), into your search engine.

Review the facts of the case. In your opinion, based on the material discussed in this chapter, were the defendant's 4th Amendment rights violated by the execution of this warrant? Why or why not?

## STUDENT STUDY SITE

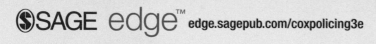
**SAGE edge**™ edge.sagepub.com/coxpolicing3e

**Sharpen your skills with SAGE edge!**

SAGE edge for Students provides a personalized approach to help you accomplish your coursework goals in an easy-to-use learning environment. You'll find action plans, mobile-friendly eFlashcards, and quizzes as well as videos, web resources, and links to SAGE journal articles to support and expand on the concepts presented in this chapter.

## CHAPTER 10

# DISCRETION AND ETHICS IN POLICING

© iStockphoto.com/Ivan Bajic

## CHAPTER LEARNING OBJECTIVES:

1. Define police discretion and the factors that influence it

2. Assess factors that can affect the use of discretion by police

3. Define the term *ethics* and discuss its importance in the field of policing

4. Identify and describe various organizational strategies that can be used to mitigate unethical police conduct

D ue to the multiple roles the police are expected to perform, along with the myriad of external and internal influences that tend to shape police policy and public expectations, the right measure of discretionary authority by the police is essential. Fulfilling the police mission in a competent and responsible manner requires a sustained organizational and individual commitment to underlying ethics, accountability, and professionalism. If the police are to be perceived as professionals, they must exercise discretion wisely and ethically and remain accountable to the public they are sworn to serve.

Professional ethics outline the moral obligation to act in ways that are proper to accomplish professional goals. For police officers, ethical conduct is especially important because of the authority granted to them and because of the difficulty of overseeing the daily behavior of police officers on the street. The public must be able to trust the police to act as if someone were watching, when most of the time, there may be no witnesses.

Figure 10.1 highlights a recent poll that elicited responses regarding community members' confidence in their police officers. As will be discussed in greater detail in Chapter 12, there is often a discrepancy in confidence based on race.

It is appropriate to consider discretion and ethics together, because they are closely interrelated. Discretion is a necessary and desirable part of policing and involves selecting among several possible courses of action. Reducing the number of unethical options is a continuing pursuit of attentive police administrators. Wise exercise of discretion by police officers demands ethical choices. Further, whether the police make wise choices or foolish ones, they are accountable to the public for their actions. Chapter 11 covers the consequences of unethical police behavior and accountability for it.

**Author Video:**
In law enforcement, how important is it for supervisors and others to instill core values?

## ■ POLICE DISCRETION

To perform their role competently and effectively, the police must regularly exercise their discretionary authority, and they must do so ethically and responsibly, if public trust is to be established and maintained. **Police discretion** can be defined simply as "the exercise

---

### Figure 10.1 ■ Community Members' Confidence in Their Police Officers

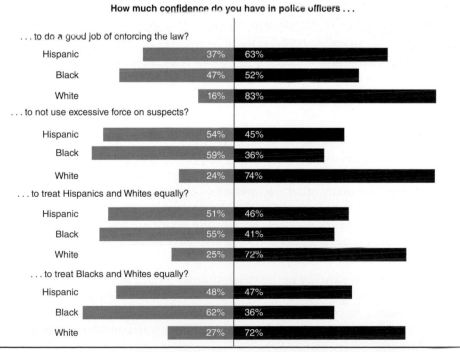

How much confidence do you have in police officers . . .

. . . to do a good job of enforcing the law?

| | JUST SOME / VERY LITTLE | A GREAT DEAL /FAIR AMOUNT |
|---|---|---|
| Hispanic | 37% | 63% |
| Black | 47% | 52% |
| White | 16% | 83% |

. . . to not use excessive force on suspects?

| | | |
|---|---|---|
| Hispanic | 54% | 45% |
| Black | 59% | 36% |
| White | 24% | 74% |

. . . to treat Hispanics and Whites equally?

| | | |
|---|---|---|
| Hispanic | 51% | 46% |
| Black | 55% | 41% |
| White | 25% | 72% |

. . . to treat Blacks and Whites equally?

| | | |
|---|---|---|
| Hispanic | 48% | 47% |
| Black | 62% | 36% |
| White | 27% | 72% |

JUST SOME / VERY LITTLE          A GREAT DEAL /FAIR AMOUNT

**Police Discretion:**
A police officer's exercise of individual choices or judgments concerning possible courses of action

Featured in the photo is a controversial practice referred to as roadblocks or checkpoints to conduct random safety checks on motorists. Many question if these checkpoints are really random in nature.

© iStockphoto.com/belterz

of individual choice or judgment concerning possible courses of action."[1] Discretion amounts to the perceived ability to choose when, how, and in what order to complete assigned work.[2] Efforts to define discretion are important. "If discretion is to be spoken of as a real and variable aspect of policing that is believed to influence police behavior, then it needs to be defined in such a way that it lends it to direct observation and to quantification."[3]

Discretion is a normal, desirable, and unavoidable part of policing that exists at all levels and departments within a police agency and at all levels of policing. It is important that the police are not robotic but have a sense of autonomy, exercise common sense, and interpret the law. There is a great deal of complexity associated with the discretionary decision-making process:

> Whether to enforce the full letter of the law, to simply advise a citizen, or to choose a middle ground, street-level officers must incorporate all of the tools of their trade and select the plan of action most appropriate or reasonable on a case-by-case basis. Though there are many factors to consider regarding officer discretion, personal biases, prejudices, and values are not to be employed in this decision-making process.[4]

Discretion is required, because the code of criminal law—as well as departmental policies—is often expressed in intentionally imprecise terms that make interpretation a necessity. In addition, police resources are limited; the police cannot be everywhere at once. Policing, like many other occupations, consists of a number of specializations, and not all departments have the specialized personnel to investigate all types of crime or provide all types of services. Finally, the police are well aware that the other components of the criminal justice network also have limited capacities (e.g., court time, jail cells).

Although police officers are not in the strictest sense judges or jurors, they must and do perform the functions of both on certain occasions. That is, they must decide the facts in any given encounter, interpret the law with respect to the encounter, and decide how best to bring the encounter to a successful conclusion. They also consider extenuating and mitigating factors.

**SAGE Journal Article:**
Measuring Police Attitudes Toward Discretion

"The extent to which police officers are encouraged to exercise discretion varies from department to department, from shift to shift, and among divisions within the same department, but the exercise of discretion is routine in all police agencies."[5] This is true because of the very nature of policing and because, in most cities, the police simply cannot enforce all the laws all of the time or perform all of the services demanded at the same time.

Thus, both law enforcement and policing are selective processes in which some laws are enforced and some services are provided most of the time, while others are not. The determination of which, and when, services are provided rests to some extent with police administrators, the general public, prosecutors, judges, and other politicians, but police officers do not typically operate under immediate, direct supervision. Therefore, they are relatively free to determine their own actions at any given time.

## Factors That Influence Discretion

Police officer decisions are typically influenced by factors such as the situation, setting, and suspect; departmental policy and culture; the law; victims and public safety; and financial and political expectations. Further, the education, training, and length of service of the officer and the wishes of the complainant have been shown to affect officer decisions.[6]

### The Situation, Setting, and Suspect

Every situation is in some measure unique, and officers must use their personal judgment about the people involved and the context of the situation; a person's age, gender, appearance, mental and emotional state, and economic status are important details that figure into the equation. The officer must calculate these characteristics in light of a host of other things.

However, an officer who decides to render service or enforce the law based solely on the gender, race, or physical appearance of the citizen involved is exercising discretion inappropriately. Agencies can discourage such behavior; proper training can teach why such decisions are unacceptable.

An officer must quickly figure into his or her decision of how to handle a situation by also considering the severity of the offense and the potential for harm, whether there is a clear victim and how vulnerable that person might be, especially to future harm. For example, an officer may decide to follow through on an arrest in a domestic violence situation if a family member is clearly at risk, or if the complaint is not the first one. If an officer has trouble determining who is at fault in the situation, all parties may end up under arrest to ensure the safety of everyone involved.

### Departmental Policy and Culture

For some decisions, there is a range of behaviors that the department may acknowledge and permit. Department practice may allow that a driver who is exceeding the speed limit by three or four miles per hour should not be subject to citation. Leadership may establish a tolerance limit of five miles per hour and instruct officers that those driving over the speed limit, but within the tolerance, need not be cited. Or (as is true in most cases), the decision of whether or not to cite the driver may depend completely on the officer's discretion. Although officers can still cite a driver for driving two or three miles per hour over the speed limit, they know that it is permissible to ignore or warn those who are only marginally speeding.[7]

Officers exercise discretion in performing their duties, as they must do. The agency's leadership and supervision, as well as organizational norms and culture, can lead them to ignore rules and policies; exercise restraint and tolerance and give a person a second chance; choose to refer an individual for treatment or services instead of arrest; resort to

**Author Video:**
How does the blue wall of silence play a role in law enforcement and society?

threats, "street justice," or force; regard tasks not related to enforcement as less than "real" police work; and add another arrest charge to help facilitate an individual's punishment.

Chapter 8 discussed the police subculture and some of its problematic ideas—for example, that people are not to be trusted to follow the law or that people do not like the cops—and officers have to control and demand respect from the public. Depending on the agency, the subculture might reinforce the idea of being lenient with people who have never been in trouble, or it might support the idea that flaws in the criminal justice system justify making decisions about innocence and guilt outside the courtroom. According to the culture of some agencies, preventing crime and enforcing the law depend largely on deterrence, and severe consequences are more likely to achieve deterrence.

### The Law

Of course, officers must know and follow the law. But there is a great deal of gray area in the law, often quite deliberately, and in these situations, discretion plays a critical role. In an effort to curb intimate partner violence, for instance, some states passed laws that require an arrest in many of these instances, thereby removing or significantly limiting police discretion.[8] There are advantages and disadvantages to limiting police discretion. One advantage is greater consistency in terms of how and when police officers enforce a given statute. Among the disadvantages to removing discretion is that the law effectively might have a "new-widening" effect; the police may be constrained to make an arrest when it is not really necessary.

### Political and Economic Pressure

The police are also subject to political pressure to respond to high-profile or hot-button issues, and to ease up or crack down on protestors, drunk drivers, celebrities with drug problems, or undocumented immigrants, to name just a few issues. Officers answer to supervisors, and department leaders have to answer to mayors, commissioners, and lawmakers.

CompStat and other performance measures can and do lead to pressure to meet political and department expectations for citations, which can translate into significant revenue for the jurisdiction.

### The Challenge of Discretion

Author Video: Discretion

Clearly, the exercise of discretion is necessary for effective policing, but it is not neat or easy, and problems arise. The consequences of the police using discretionary authority unethically or otherwise improperly can have devastating outcomes. These consequences include poor morale, civil liability issues, tragic and unnecessary loss of life, and public mistrust of the police.

Maintaining ethical standards within the field of policing is important for reasons that may seem obvious. First and foremost, the police are public servants—agents of the government sworn to uphold the laws of the land. As such, they must be role models, on and off the job. When police officers engage in unethical or illegal behavior, it shakes the trust and confidence of the public they serve. Perhaps even more devastating, when the bond between the public and police is compromised or severed, the ideals of the entire criminal justice network may be called into question. As stated by Federal Bureau of Investigation (FBI) Director Robert Mueller, "Public corruption is the betrayal of the public's sacred trust. It erodes public confidence and undermines the strength of our democracy. Unchecked, it threatens our government and our way of life."[9] More specifically, another high-ranking official from the FBI stated, "The oath taken by the men and women of law enforcement to uphold the law is not an idle one. Corruption cases involving a police officer erode the public trust and thereby complicate and impede the efforts being made by the law enforcement community at all levels."[10]

© iStockphoto.com/ftwitty

Establishing performance standards can have the unintended consequence of promoting biased enforcement because officers under pressure to meet monthly targets for ticketing may turn to inappropriate profiling to find sources for tickets.

## Quotas

**Quotas**—one type of **biased enforcement**—are arbitrary and fixed numbers of citations or stops (or some other measure of activity) that officers are required to meet on a periodic basis. Quotas are unethical and often illegal, because they pressure officers into making decisions to meet the quota requirement rather than what the situation should dictate. Quotas undermine healthy discretion.

Most administrators would deny that there are quotas in their agencies, being fully aware of the controversy about quotas. Rather, they may point to performance standards, which tend to identify acceptable ticket and arrest activity of department members, using measures such as averages and medians. Regardless of the language, officer performance evaluations are often based in part on an officer's number of tickets and arrests. In response, some officers may engage in unethical behaviors such as biased enforcement practices in attempting to meet agency expectations. One former New York Police Department (NYPD) officer turned whistle-blower about the department's quota system, which the department routinely denies. Adhyl Polanco secretly recorded conversations at the Bronx precinct where he worked and later filed suit against the NYPD. The justification for quotas might be that it is a way to ensure productivity from officers, and such numbers are easy to calculate and compare. However, Laurie Robinson, co-chairwoman of President Obama's Task Force on 21st Century Policing, concluded that numbers-based policing sends the wrong message to the public. "If citizens believe that tickets are being issued or arrests are being made for reasons other than the goal of law enforcement, which is about public safety," says Robinson, "then their trust in the legitimacy of the system is really eroded." The problem can be made worse when officers receive pressure from city officials or police administrators to write more citations as a source of revenue. "That, according to the Justice Department, is exactly what happened in Ferguson, Missouri [where] the largely white police there wrote huge numbers of tickets for the city's black residents, collecting millions of dollars in fines every year."[11]

**Audio Link:**
Despite Laws and Lawsuits, Quota-Based Policing Lingers

■ **Biased Enforcement:** Police practice that results from enforcement of the law based on any number of personal and occupational-based biases

■ **Quotas:** Arbitrary and fixed numbers of citations or stops (or some other measure of activity) that officers are required to meet on a periodic basis

## POLICE ☆ STORIES  10.1

### Connie Koski, Professor and Former Police Officer

#### The Relationship Between Police Subculture, Misconduct, and Ethics

When we think of police ethics and police corruption, we often think of personal gain such as the acceptance of gratuities, officers taking bribes or dealing drugs, or stealing items from crime scenes. What happens when officers take advantage of their power to achieve positive policing outcomes? This noble cause corruption is either unethical or illegal behavior, but the motive is pursuit of a benefit to society.

Noble cause corruption represents a form of behavior that is both complex and difficult to study because, at first glance, officers who engage in such behaviors are passionate about protecting the public, a duty they were sworn to uphold.

The pressure is great on today's police officers from administrators, politicians, and the public to "do something about crime," but bolstering the insularity of the police subculture—the "thin blue line"—threatens the delicate bond of trust and legitimacy between the police and those they are sworn to protect.

I worked with a group of five officers who were the pride of my department; they were often used as example of what constitutes "good police work" by many of our top administrators. These officers consistently made the most arrests and were particularly devoted to ridding the city of guns, drugs, and the dealers who distributed them and were particularly skilled at cultivating the information necessary to locate these perpetrators and illegal items. During my time on patrol, however, I often encountered people on the street (both criminals and noncriminals) who informed me that these officers regularly used "drop guns" and "drop bags"—evidence allegedly planted by the officers in question—to make their arrests. Additionally, many of my coworkers admitted to having heard these same accusations, and, although no one would ever admit to having seen the behavior firsthand, many of my fellow officers believed these accusations to be true.

One day, I finally got up the nerve to ask one of the officers directly if he participated in such activities. I could tell by his facial expressions and body language that he was being evasive. He asked, "What difference would it make if I did?" He justified his position by stating that all of the officers in the department knew that this person or that person was a drug dealer who would be caught eventually. Therefore, why might the occasional act of "dropping a bag of dope" on a foot chase ultimately matter in the long run, so long as the dealer was off the streets? I recall being perplexed by this answer and feeling conflicted about this approach to policing. I could certainly agree that getting drugs, guns, and their dealers off the streets was a very positive thing. Ethically, however, I was strongly opposed to the methods and told my fellow officer so. He simply responded that I was naïve and I needed to get some more "TOJ" (time on the job) to understand the value of this approach to fighting crime.

Although there was never enough evidence to substantiate any of the claims against my former coworkers, I often wondered how many residents in my jurisdiction had been affected by such practices. In many ways, I could tell that these behaviors directly and indirectly fed the long-standing mistrust of the police in the minority neighborhoods.

---

**Ethics:** The study of right and wrong, duty, responsibility, and personal character—all of these concepts have an implicit modifier—"moral"—attached to them; ethics is concerned with moral duty, what is morally right and wrong

## ■ ETHICS AND POLICE CONDUCT

Perhaps the most important guide for officers as they make their decisions is ethics. Although there are many different bases for the study of ethics, for the purposes of this text, **ethics** is "the study of right and wrong, duty, responsibility, and personal character. . . . [We] should regard all of these concepts . . . as having an implicit modifier—'moral'—attached to them. Ethics is concerned with moral duty, what is morally right and wrong."[12] Ethical conduct involves "doing the right thing in the right way at the right time for the right reasons."[13] Although ethical issues have always existed in policing, the introduction of community-oriented policing is an example of an organizational transformation that relates to ethical decision making on the part of officers. This focus assists the police in forming a partnership with the community and increasing accountability to the public. "Because of concerns about the types of information being collected by law enforcement and how that information is retained in records, concerns have been expressed that law enforcement may violate citizens' rights in the quest for terrorists."[14] A greater need for more and different types of information has fostered the advancement of intelligence-led policing, which goes a step further than community-oriented policing. (See Chapter 7.)

Ethics has become an increasingly important topic in discussions of police discretion. Many behaviors that were once permitted are no longer tolerated by the public. The behavior of police officers in today's society must be beyond reproach. Police agencies should emphasize ethics in their recruitment, selection, hiring, and promoting practices to ensure the agency employs and rewards individuals of excellent character. "Rewarding ethical behavior is the key to message sending for police executives and middle managers. The logical response to unethical behavior is the appropriate use of general orders, policies, and procedures to discipline officers for unethical behaviors and noncompliance."[15] Former president Theodore Roosevelt stated, "No man can lead a public career really worth leading, no man can act with rugged independence in serious crises, nor strike at great abuses, nor afford to make powerful and unscrupulous foes, if he is himself vulnerable to his private character."[16]

**Web Link:**
Ethics and Integrity

## Ethics in Police Education

It is imperative that the criminal justice curriculum in colleges and universities incorporate and emphasize the study of ethics. The same is true of basic and advanced law enforcement training programs. Ethics should be emphasized continually, and act as a thread that runs through all facets of police hiring, training, and continuing education.

Research on police ethics in education that compares criminal justice students and active police officers indicates a concerning level of tolerance for unethical behavior in both groups, albeit in different areas. Student respondents were nearly twice as likely as their police officer counterparts to respond ethically when dealing with a scenario about an off-duty police officer stopped for driving while intoxicated, theft by a police officer at the scene of a burglary, the use of excessive force by coworkers, witnessing supervisory misconduct, and stopping an off-duty police officer for a serious traffic offense.[17]

**Author Video:**
Ethical Considerations

However, student respondents reported a willingness to perjure themselves to keep themselves or coworkers out of trouble or to ensure the conviction of someone they knew to be guilty. Far fewer police officers and other professionals reported a willingness to perjure themselves for the same reasons.[18]

To help change the cultural aversion to reporting wrongdoings of officers by other officers, criminal justice educators must understand, emphasize, and teach ethics at every opportunity. Also, police officials should require ongoing in-service training in ethical decision making for their officers. Psychological testing and applicant background investigations can focus more on eliminating applicants who have demonstrated unethical behavior. All of these measures may ultimately prove to be ineffective, however, if the police subculture continues to reinforce nonfeasance as an indicator of group loyalty, which is deeply embedded in the tradition.

Officers are called on to recognize the moral dilemma in each situation, decide what to do within ethical boundaries, act with integrity, and follow through consistently. Peer pressure and lax administration are just two of the forces that can thwart good intentions. The 2003 National Business Ethics Survey found that

Undercover policing is a common practice that usually involves a variety of forms of deception. For example, "the police have introduced drugs in prison, undertaken assignments from Latin American drug cartels to launder money, established fencing businesses that paid cash for stolen goods and for 'referrals,' printed counterfeit bills, and committed perjury." These otherwise criminal activities are excused for undercover cops; their "authorized criminality" allows them, for example, to maintain a fictitious identity to gather evidence in building a case against a known offender, for example.

Although undercover operations may sometimes seek merely to observe criminal behavior (surveillance operations) or to prevent crime from occurring (preventative operations), many operations encourage crime commission or consider it a necessity in carrying out a plan (facilitative operations), either through emboldening suspects—short of entrapment—or by weakening potential victims.[22]

1. Should police be authorized to violate the law to carry out activities that are ultimately meant to enforce the law? Be specific.

2. Should undercover policing apply to certain types of crimes and not others? Who should decide which crimes? Explain.

*Suggestions for addressing these questions can be found on the Student Study Site:* **edge.sagepub.com/ coxpolicing3e**

*Source:* "Breaking the law to enforce it: Undercover police participation in crime," by Elizabeth E. Joh, 2009. *Stanford Law Review, 62*(1), 1. Retrieved July 2012 from www.stanfordlawreview.org/print/article/breaking-law-enforce-it-undercover-police-participation-crime.

approximately 40% of those surveyed would not report misconduct if they observed it because of fear of reprisal from management.[19]

Research has demonstrated that ethics education can assist officers in better navigating moral challenges by increasing ethical awareness and moral reasoning—two critical aspects of ethical decision making.[20]

To be effective at changing bad behavior or maintaining good behavior, ethics education must go beyond lectures and must engage officers in challenging dialogue and active tests of reasoning skills.

To maintain high standards, departments must incorporate discussions of ethics into daily operations, stimulating those discussions through a variety of means including video clips, current events, and hypothetical scenarios.[21]

## Evaluating Police Ethics

The vast majority of criminal justice students indicate that they would not turn in a classmate who lied, cheated, or stole.[23] A significant proportion of police officers indicated that, when they became police officers, they would not turn in a fellow police officer who lied, cheated, or stole.[24] Where does the message that it is acceptable to let others do these things without taking action originate? How has doing the right thing become the wrong thing to do?

In 1972, the **Knapp Commission** discovered that the majority of New York City police officers did not aggressively seek out opportunities to engage in unethical conduct, but may have engaged in minor acts of corruption, such as accepting gratuities.[25] The commission referred to these officers as "**grass eaters**." They generally chose not to get involved in unethical conduct; however, they also refused to turn in fellow officers who did—and thus, in effect, condoned unethical acts. This reluctance to report wrongdoing is generally referred to as **nonfeasance** in the professional literature.[26] Do trainers

**Knapp Commission:** Investigative committee formed in 1972 by the city of New York in response to allegations of large-scale corruption among NYPD officers; set the stage for many cities and states in the years that followed

**Grass Eaters:** Term coined by the Knapp Commission to refer to officers who engage in minor acts of corrupt practices (acceptance of gratuities, etc.) and passively accept the wrongdoings of other officers and leaders somehow teach police recruits and tenured officers to condone unethical conduct? Unfortunately, the answer may be yes. And it may be more entrenched than is apparent. (See also Chapter 11.)

Although parents usually teach children not to lie, steal, or cheat, many also teach them not to get involved when others lie, steal, or cheat. "It's not your business—stay out of it!" "Don't get involved!" "You just worry about yourself, not about other people." This and similar advice may indeed lead youth to become grass eaters who simply turn away from lying, cheating, and stealing. They learn very early that "ratting" on another individual is unacceptable behavior in many settings, which is perhaps as detrimental as being directly involved in unethical conduct. Of course, the police subculture often builds on this consideration. Loyalty to the group (other officers) is held out as a virtue, even when it means engaging in seemingly minor unethical conduct (covering, making excuses, telling "white lies") to protect unethical individuals. Yet, police officers are required by the **Code of Conduct** as well as by federal law (Civil Action for Deprivation of Rights, 1871) *not* to condone such behavior. According to the International Association of Chiefs of Police (IACP), a number of factors negatively influence **police ethics**:

- Changing moral standards of contemporary society
- Americans "lacking a moral consensus"
- Increasing number of individuals who reject responsibility for their own actions
- High degree of frustration experienced by today's police officers
- Misinformed or conflicting perceptions of the role of police and conflicting expectations about what is or should be expected from the police
- Law enforcement agencies that fail to clearly draw the legal, ethical, and moral lines in the form of clear policies and procedures, training, supervision, and discipline[27]

In some cases, policy issues reflect the values of administrators who are not adequately committed to ethical conduct.

> After researching thousands of incidents of serious misconduct, the single most damaging category of misconduct in law enforcement is administrators intentionally ignoring obvious ethical problems. There is nothing as negative as a chief, sheriff, director or superintendent knowing his department has ethical problems and intentionally looking the other way, trying to make it to retirement.[28]

In some instances, administrators model unethical conduct on a regular basis, allowing officers to rationalize that their own misconduct is no worse. Placing all the blame for unethical conduct on administrators, however, may encourage individual officers who engage in such conduct to attempt to escape responsibility for their actions.

In a study that examined frontline supervisors' perceptions of police integrity, the supervisors reported reluctance to act on the misconduct of their subordinates because of the perceived unethical practices of high-ranking supervisors in their organization. The researchers posed the following question: "[T]hough supervisors may believe in the need for reform, will they act on those beliefs when they do not believe their own supervisors are legitimately committed to improvement?"[29] Realistically, the answer is probably no.

Certainly, the majority of police officers perform their duties honestly, ethically, and professionally. Still, the officers who engage in inappropriate behavior tarnish the reputation of everyone in policing and place the field in the challenging position of having to constantly convince the public that acts of police malfeasance are not widespread. Far too often, those who do the right thing by telling the truth and exposing corruption and brutality are the victims of attacks from within their ranks.

**Author Video:**
Ethical Theories

**Nonfeasance:**
To the reluctance of generally honest police officers to report misconduct committed by their peers; has been identified as one of the factors perpetuating this issue and is often the result of the influence of the police subculture

**Code of Conduct:**
Formed and adopted by the International Association of Chiefs of Police, which sets forth standards of conduct for police officers on and off duty

**Police Ethics:**
Standards of conduct based on moral and professional principles that influence a variety of actions taken or not taken by police officers on and off duty

Police officers in Wales are held to high professional standards. Officers have been dismissed or resigned for crimes, including "supplying drugs, possessing indecent images of children and drunk-driving." However, many other officers who committed offenses, including "violence, traffic offenses and animal cruelty," were not dismissed. Many argue that every incident or offense must be judged on the merits of the case. This often involves shifting the burden to the officer to prove why he or she should not be dismissed.

The Home Office believes "public confidence in the police is crucial in a system that rests on the principle of policing by consent." Michael Levi, a professor of criminology, argues that the "figures indicate that police officers were less likely to commit crimes than the general population. The general statistics are that one in three males can expect to be convicted of something over their lifetime."

1. Police agencies invest considerable money and resources in identifying, hiring, and training law enforcement officers. Should law enforcement officers be dismissed any time an officer violates the law, regardless of the type of offense? Or should different offenses be treated differently?

2. Considering the importance of public trust, what measure can a police agency take to regain the public trust in the event an officer is disciplined or dismissed for criminal activity?

*Source:* "12 of 32 police in Wales kept jobs after breaking the law, figures show," by Kevin Leonard, 2012. *BBC News.* Retrieved September 2012 from www.bbc.co.uk/news/uk-wales-16508670.

**Racial Profiling:** Occurs when an officer considers race as part of a decision to take, or not to take, law enforcement action; legally, an officer can only consider race as part of a specific, reliable suspect description tied to a particular crime

## Biased Enforcement and Racial Profiling

**Racial profiling** occurs when an officer considers race as part of a decision to take, or not to take, law enforcement action. Legally, an officer can only consider race as part of a specific, reliable suspect description tied to a particular crime. Considering a person's race as a basis for action is unacceptable and grounds for disciplinary action.

The action is still racial profiling, even if the officer does not base his or her decision "solely on race," but considers it as one factor among many. For example, if an officer

Empirical evidence has documented the existence of biased enforcement during routine traffic stops. Black and Hispanic drivers are both ticketed and searched at higher rates than Whites.

© iStockphoto.com/Rich Leg

takes into account a person's race when deciding whom to stop and cite for speeding, it is racial profiling even if the driver is actually violating the law. In this case, the officer has a perfectly legitimate reason to stop and cite, but the fact that he considered race as one of many factors makes the stop illegal. That is very different, however, from a case where a person's race is part of a reliable description tied to a crime—for example, "a male Hispanic wearing a red and blue sweater." In that case, the officer can consider race.

Though it is impossible to know how many, certainly there are police officers who continue to engage in such practices. Indeed, some well-publicized police practices are criticized as overt profiling. New York City's "stop and frisk" program is one such practice. Even if the proportion of officers involved in such practices is small, all officers should be aware that racial profiling is grounds for disciplinary action. Harassment of individuals short of taking official action also is unacceptable. (See Chapter 12.)

**Author Video:**
Racial profiling

> Police are sworn to uphold the "rule of law" in the protection of individual rights, while dutifully enforcing traffic and criminal laws for the protection of the public at large. . . . It is essential that law enforcement administrators take every necessary action to ensure zero tolerance regarding enforcement actions that are discriminatory against any segment of the population.[30]

## ■ LEADERSHIP AND IMPROVING DECISION MAKING

Every police department must establish a clear code of ethical conduct that is based on a set of core values and a mission statement and then go beyond that. Chiefs and supervisors must lead by example, demonstrating that the code applies to everyone in the organization and that everyone is accountable for it.

Because the police department is a public service agency, honesty and accountability to the public are particularly important. It is extremely valuable to recognize and communicate the importance of discretion at all levels in policing. In reality, it is impossible to treat everyone exactly the same. A necessary first step in dealing with discretion is to recognize its existence and importance. Only then can departments address the proper and improper applications of discretion, be more transparent with the public, and improve on effective training.

**Video Link:**
Buffalo Police to mandate ethics training

Although it may not be possible to arrive at a comprehensive set of guidelines for the exercise of police discretion, it is clearly possible to improve on current guidelines. Clarifying guidelines for discretion will assist officers themselves in behaving according to professional standards. It will also assist the community in understanding police actions. The most effective officers grasp the social and historical context in which they operate.

Leaders set the tone for the entire organization; therefore, without a strong commitment to ethical decision making by the chief executive officer and his or her entire command staff, instances of unethical or illegal practices are sure to follow.

> Leaders can and must affect the ethical climate in their organizations. Subordinates learn from observing the behaviors of their superiors and the consequences of those behaviors. If leaders are rewarded for ethical behavior and punished for unethical behavior, their subordinates will learn to emulate the ethical behavior. Nothing any leader can say will have a more powerful effect than what he or she does.[31]

Police agencies must have clear policies and practices. Only then will officers and community members know what is expected. Police leaders must address unethical conduct or other breeches of public trust in the most open, honest, and transparent ways possible. Any reluctance to respond will almost certainly arouse suspicion of wrongdoing

## Figure 10.2 ■ Ethics and Honesty Ranking by Profession

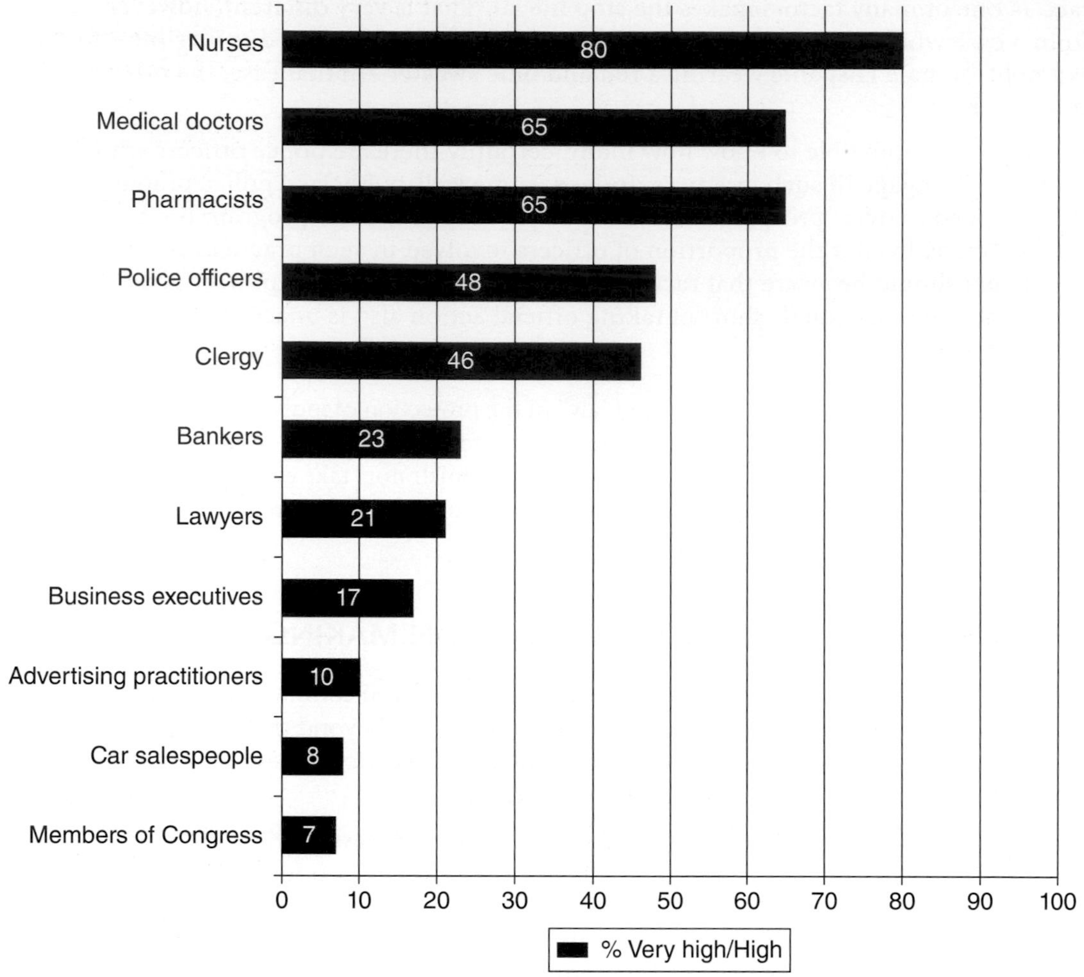

| Profession | % Very high/High |
|---|---|
| Nurses | 80 |
| Medical doctors | 65 |
| Pharmacists | 65 |
| Police officers | 48 |
| Clergy | 46 |
| Bankers | 23 |
| Lawyers | 21 |
| Business executives | 17 |
| Advertising practitioners | 10 |
| Car salespeople | 8 |
| Members of Congress | 7 |

■ % Very high/High

*Source:* http://www.gallup.com/poll/1654/honesty-ethics-professions.aspx

and acts as a barrier to the trust and confidence of the public in the police that are essential if the police are to operate effectively.[32]

> When authority, power, and discretion are granted to public officials . . . rational people presume that they will not use more than they need for their legitimate purposes, because rational people would never grant more authority or discretion to abridge liberty or use force than they believed necessary. The presumption is not of guilt but of official respect for restraint. Citizens expect public officials to justify their use of authority or power when questions arise.[33]

In a 2014 Gallup poll on honesty/ethics in professions, 48% of respondents rated police honesty and ethical standards as high or very high. Figure 10.2 shows how police officers are ranked in comparison to other professions.

One approach that may be more effective in guiding officer discretion involves the use of incentives to promote voluntary compliance with policies. Such incentives include officer participation in policy formulation, establishment of specialized units to deal with specific tasks, positive disciplinary practices aimed at correcting the problem behavior without humiliating the officer involved, and more and better training on discretion in a variety of different situations.[34]

Another departmental approach is to regularly discuss discretion, ethics, and decision making, weaving such discussions into the organizational culture. Rather than waiting for a critical incident to occur, supervisors and managers should engage their officers with scenarios and case studies, taking the opportunity to communicate important agency values, clarify law and policy, and challenge officers to think critically. By making it acceptable to talk about ethics, police agencies can better prepare their officers to face the inevitable difficult choices required of law enforcement officers. However, by discussing common dilemmas before they occur, officers will be better prepared to make the right decisions, rather than to rely solely on individual judgment. In the same way that officers continually train for tactical situations, they should continually train for ethical decisions as well.

Departments must also create systems and foster a culture that rewards ethical behavior. Administrators send key messages by taking allegations of misconduct seriously, protecting confidentiality, and counteracting retaliation for whistle blowing.

It is also important that leaders realize that informal leaders in a police organization also impact police officer attitudes and behaviors. Police leaders must be prepared to immediately confront ethical violations and punish immoral behavior.[35] Law enforcement executives who are committed to ethical behavior can encourage it as follows:

**SAGE Journal Article:**
Whistle-blowing and the Code of Silence in Police Agencies

1. Incorporate the ideals of ethics and integrity into their organization's mission statement

2. Make ethical decision making part of the organization's formal functions

3. Emphasize ethical behavior as part of the agency's organizational philosophy

4. Implement zero-tolerance policies for unethical behavior or decision making[36]

Police administrators can also mandate the study of ethical decision making during training and press training directors to stress this activity at the recruit level. In addition, training directors should revisit their curriculum designs and ensure that trainers are experienced educators who understand and emphasize the importance of ethical considerations and discretionary activities. All policies governing individual and collective police behavior should be consistent with the ideals of justice and morality.

Administrators must build safeguards into department policy that anticipate and address any tendency toward taking shortcuts or other predictable secondary leanings toward the unethical. Leaders must communicate that they support ethical practice.

## Media Relations

As discussed in Chapter 6, the media, both print and broadcast, have the technological ability to transmit news stories throughout the world in a matter of seconds. For a variety of reasons, police–media relations in this country have been problematic. Many police officials—line and staff personnel alike—tend to shun media representatives whenever possible, withholding information on newsworthy events even when disclosing information could not possibly harm anyone or compromise a criminal investigation. In such cases, the media rely instead on questionable sources for information, which frequently results in inaccuracies in the story. Transparency with respect to police operations—for example, when such transparency does not jeopardize ongoing investigations—even if it involves disclosing unethical conduct or poor discretionary choices on the part of the police, may result in more balanced coverage and more focus on the positive contributions of the police.

**Policing in Practice Video:**
What is your department's experience with the use of discretion and media relations? Is there specific training for working with the media?

The conventional wisdom about the most effective way of dealing with the media appears to be changing. Forward-thinking departments are viewing the media as a tool and a partner rather than an adversary from whom they must conceal as much of the truth as possible. Police chiefs are learning from past mistakes and recognizing that clear and

Police departments, like this one in Dallas, use Twitter to inform citizens about crime and traffic enforcement locations, but also to build community relations.

effective communication to the public through the media is a necessity in today's world. They are finding that their integrity and their reputation are key assets in public relations.

Progressive administrators are seeking training in media and public relations. Specialists dedicate themselves to coaching and educating police administrators on interviews, how to respond to reporters in a crisis situation, and defining the conversation and the issues. Trainers advocate for a proactive attitude, stressing the need for the police to "face tough issues head-on and speak-out when news coverage is skewed or inaccurate. . . . Law enforcement has been a victim too long. It's time to stand up and fight back when people make false allegations about [a] department."[37]

Police departments are increasingly using social media as a tool to counter false information, define the version of events as official, and build public relations and community. (See Chapter 6.)

### Intolerance of Malfeasance

Although the next chapter will discuss police misconduct in detail, the discussion of ethics inevitably comes around to how leaders must react to breaches of ethics. Rather than focus on zero-tolerance arrest policies, some police administrators adopted zero-tolerance policies concerning inappropriate conduct by department members. As previously asserted, the vast majority of our nation's police officers perform their duties ethically, professionally, and competently. Those officers who engage in unethical or criminal activities and the departments that allow it damage the reputation of the entire field of policing. Most honest, hardworking officers know who the problem officers are, as do the command staff. The snag here is often the reluctance of officers who believe their own ethics are sound to report the wrongdoings of their colleagues. A National Institute of Justice (NIJ) study designed to promote integrity in the police profession focused on the following issues for agency staff:

- Do they know the rules?
- How much individual and organizational support is there for those rules?
- Are staff familiar with disciplinary actions associated with violations of rules and policies?
- Do staff view disciplinary measures as fair?
- How willing are staff to report misconduct?[38]

As stated in the executive summary of the report, "An agency's culture of integrity, as defined by clearly understood and implemented policies and rules, may be more important in shaping the ethics of police officers than hiring the 'right' people."[39]

The data also indicated that officers quickly learn how various acts of misconduct will be treated by observing their organization's ability to identify unethical conduct and discipline errant officers. "If unwritten policy conflicts with written policy, the resulting confusion undermines an agency's overall integrity-enhancing efforts."[40] The report also offered recommendations for encouraging officers to come forward to report acts of misconduct by their coworkers. They included the following:

1. Making it clear that officers and supervisors who do not report misconduct will be disciplined
2. Terminating any department member caught lying during an internal investigation
3. Issuing rewards, in anonymous fashion, to officers who do report misconduct
4. Allowing for anonymous or confidential reporting
5. Regularly rotating supervisors and officers among shifts, districts or precincts, and other units of assignment (which keeps officers from becoming too comfortable)[41]

## CASE IN POINT 10.1

A Shreveport, Louisiana, police officer was terminated from the department for malfeasance. The termination was based on an incident in 2010. The officer was "assisting in a prisoner transport at the Shreveport City Jail. As the officer reportedly searched the suspect, a police supervisor reported seeing the officer remove an item from the suspect's pocket and hand it to a female standing nearby."

The female was detained, and the investigation revealed the item removed from the prisoner's pocket was a small, plastic bag of suspected marijuana. The officer was arrested for malfeasance in office and obstruction of justice. He was subsequently placed on administrative leave until time of termination.

1. Could there have been a legitimate propose for passing the contents of an arrestee's pockets to a bystander?
2. How should the department inform the staff of the outcome of an investigation into malfeasance? Be specific.
3. What privacy issues might there be for an officer who is under investigation?

*Source:* "Shreveport police officer fired for malfeasance," by KSLA News 12, 2011. Retrieved June 2012 from http://www.ksla.com.

**10**

**UNDER REVIEW**

## CHAPTER SUMMARY

The use of discretion by police is a necessity in the world of policing. The exercise of this broad power is not always underscored by responsible and ethical decision making, and the police subculture has a tremendous influence on the use of discretion.

Discriminatory law enforcement practices erode the public trust, which creates strained police community relations and a dangerous societal divide. One of the most significant such issues is racial profiling, or the targeting of minorities and other certain classes by police for no other reason than race, ethnicity, or perhaps social class. This has weakened the trust between the public and the police, particularly among minority populations.

This was not the only cost as Congress and state legislatures in the nation created laws that require mandatory data collection by police agencies regarding police encounters with citizens pertaining to detention, search and seizure, and arrests or other legal sanctions. The economic cost for the implementation of these new policies came at great expense to individual agencies.

Ethics in policing is extremely important. Unethical conduct by police ranges from violations of department rules and regulations to more serious issues such as unlawful searches and seizures, the use of excessive force, covering up for the malfeasance of fellow officers, and abuse of authority or criminal misconduct.

Police officers must be held to a higher ethical standard than most other citizens because of the oath they take when they enter the field of policing. Honesty, integrity, responsibility, accountability, and professionalism (on and off duty) are the underlying tenets of that oath. When officers breach their fiduciary responsibilities, the consequences can be damaging to the individual officers, their respective agencies, and the communities they serve. A loss of faith or trust by those communities is a serious consequence that is difficult to remedy and helps further degrade public safety.

There are many reasons why unethical practices by some police officers continue, and chief among them are the negative influences of the police subculture, lack of strict accountability on the part of all police officers, ineffective supervisory practices, and weak or ineffective leadership structures.

Discretion, ethics, accountability, and professionalism are dynamically interrelated and must be addressed in a coordinated way.

Ethical practice practice is a requisite for professional status, and if the field of policing is to progress further along the path to professionalization, all parties concerned must commit themselves to achieving this end. Whether the police are able to attain this end depends, in large part, on the responsible and accountable exercise of discretionary authority.

## KEY TERMS

- Police discretion 229
- Biased enforcement 233
- Quotas 233
- Ethics 234

- Knapp Commission 236
- Grass eaters 236
- Code of conduct 236
- Nonfeasance 237

- Police ethics 237
- Racial profiling 238

## DISCUSSION QUESTIONS

1. What are some of the more important ethical issues in policing? Should police recruits be taught ethics?

2. What is police discretion? How extensive is its use?

3. Why is the police subculture important in understanding discretion?

4. What are some possible negative consequences of the exercise of discretion? What are some positive consequences?

5. What factors besides the police subculture affect the exercise of police discretion?

6. Can we eliminate the exercise of police discretion? Should we eliminate it? How might we gain better control over it?

7. Discuss racial profiling as an example of poor discretionary decision making.

8. Discuss the evolution of the police code of ethics or conduct. Why are ethics especially important for the police?

9. List and discuss strategies that may be undertaken to improve the current state of ethical decision making.

## INTERNET EXERCISES

1. Using the key words "international police accountability," locate and discuss information concerning attempts to establish police accountability in at least one foreign country.

2. Use the Internet to locate the code of ethics or code of conduct for a police agency in your area. How does this code compare to the code established by the International Association of Chiefs of Police? In your opinion, is the code enforceable?

3. On the Internet, locate information concerning racial profiling or bias.

## STUDENT STUDY SITE

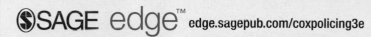 edge.sagepub.com/coxpolicing3e

**Sharpen your skills with SAGE edge!**

SAGE edge for Students provides a personalized approach to help you accomplish your coursework goals in an easy-to-use learning environment. You'll find action plans, mobile-friendly eFlashcards, and quizzes as well as videos, web resources, and links to SAGE journal articles to support and expand on the concepts presented in this chapter.

© iStockphoto.com/Leonardo Patriz

# POLICE MISCONDUCT AND ACCOUNTABILITY

## CHAPTER LEARNING OBJECTIVES:

1. Define the general concept of police corruption and how it is investigated

2. Identify specific examples of police corruption

3. Describe the findings of research on police misconduct and use of force

4. Discuss the impacts of police misconduct, particularly in terms of police–community relations

5. Evaluate some of the alleged causes of police misconduct

6. Describe the relationship between management, administrative issues, and police misconduct

7. Summarize the ways in which police agencies and individuals are held accountable for officer conduct

M isconduct by the police is a reality that agencies and society must address. Problem behavior ranges from minor infractions of rules or policy to egregious criminal acts. Many ethical violations by the police fall under the general heading of conduct unbecoming a police officer. Even though the most troublesome or tragic incidents of misconduct represent a small fraction of the tens of thousands of daily police interactions, police misconduct is a serious matter whenever it occurs. It creates an aura of suspicion, mistrust, and uncertainty. When allegations of corruption arise and are confirmed, or—as seems to occur with increasing frequency—when members of the public document acts of misconduct that seem to go unpunished—it severely inhibits strategies intended to improve policing.

In our present era of policing, law enforcement executives, government officials, community groups, and academicians all advocate policing strategies that include partnerships with the public in the control and suppression of crime, thus providing for an overall improvement in the quality of life. Such strategies require an atmosphere of trust and confidence between the public and those who have been sworn to serve and protect them.

Misconduct may be divided into two broad categories—corruption and physical or emotional abuse. There are many forms of each of these; all are violations of the ethical standards of police officers.

## ■ CORRUPTION

### What Is Corruption?

Corruption occurs when a police officer acts in a manner that places his personal gain ahead of duty, resulting in the violation of police procedures, criminal law, or both.[1] "Corrupt acts contain three elements: 1) They are forbidden by some law, rule, regulation, or ethical standard; 2) they involve the misuse of the officer's position; and 3) they involve some actual or expected material reward or gain."[2]

Police corruption is best viewed not only as the aberrant behavior of individual officers, but as group behavior guided by contradictory sets of norms. It involves a number of specific patterns that can be analyzed according to the acts and actors involved, the norms violated, the extent of peer group support, the degree of organization, and the police department's reaction. Though most likely relatively small, the actual number of police officers involved in corruption nationwide is significant, enough to generate a good deal of negative attention when their acts are exposed. Although most police officers are not directly involved in corrupt activities, large numbers do condone such activities by their failure to speak out or take action against them. These are the officers (referred to as *grass eaters* by the Knapp Commission) who passively accept the presence of corruption as a part of the police world.[3] (See Chapter 10.) **Meat eaters** are those officers, typically far fewer in number, who actively engage in corrupt activities.

### Background of Corruption

Police misconduct is a complicated topic with a long and convoluted history in the United States. The history of the U.S. municipal police is replete with examples and discussions concerning corruption. (See Appendix.) Reform movements have been initiated periodically to reduce or eliminate corruption but have largely failed to achieve their goals. The reform movement of the middle 1800s attempted to remove blatant and undesirable political influence from policing. The civil service reforms of the late 1800s sought the same goal, and though there were some successes, they were bitterly opposed and circumvented.[4] In 1894, the **Lexow Commission**, an investigative group appointed by a coalition of concerned citizens and good government groups, closed its hearings into police corruption and ineffectiveness in New York City.[5] It reported that corruption was systematic and pervasive, a condition that it attributed in large part to malfeasance,

**Video Link:**
Chicago's Gun Violence and Police Misconduct

■ **Meat Eaters:**
Term coined by the Knapp Commission to describe officers who engage widely in corrupt and unlawful practices during the performance of their duties

■ **Lexow Commission:**
Investigative committee formed in 1894 by the city of New York in response to allegations of large-scale corruption amongst NYPD officers; this form of investigation set the stage for many cities and states in the years that followed

misfeasance, and nonfeasance in the higher ranks. The next 15 years saw similar investigations and findings in almost every major U.S. city.

Reforms in the early and middle 1900s emphasized the importance of professionalism as a means of reducing corruption of all types, and reform-oriented chiefs were appointed in many cities across the nation. Yet the problem of corruption resurfaced, sometimes in departments previously marred, other times in departments previously untouched by scandal. "For cops as for anyone else, money works like an acid on integrity. Bribes from bootleggers made the 1920s a golden era for crooked police. Gambling syndicates in the 1950s were protected by a payoff system more elaborate than the Internal Revenue Service."[6] In 1971, Frank Serpico brought to light police corruption in New York City, and the Knapp Commission investigation that followed uncovered widespread corruption among officers of all ranks.

Some departments were built on corrupt foundations, with politicians requiring payments for positions, while others gave police positions away in return for political favors. Allegations of corruption still occur on a regular basis in many large departments, as well as in small- and medium-sized (fewer than 500 sworn personnel) departments.

### Official Investigation Into Corruption

Two highly publicized commissions were formed more recently to investigate police corruption and offer recommendations for change, the first of which was the **Christopher Commission**. Created by former Los Angeles mayor Tom Bradley in 1991 in response to several high-profile media accounts of misconduct by Los Angeles Police Department (LAPD) members, the commission specifically addressed structure and operation, recruitment and training practices, internal disciplinary procedures, and citizen review and oversight issues.[7]

The final report of the Christopher Commission painted a disturbing, but all too familiar, picture of the LAPD for both the public and the police. Key findings of the report included the following:

- A small, but significant, number of police officers systematically engaged in acts involving excessive force.
- Police administrators clearly knew who these problem officers were but took little or no preventive measures to address the problem.
- A new policy needed to be adopted that would hold both individual officers and command staff strictly accountable for future acts of malfeasance.[8]

■ **Christopher Commission:** Investigative body created by former Los Angeles mayor Tom Bradley in 1991 in response to several high-profile media accounts of various acts of misconduct by LAPD members

Whether the LAPD adopted any of these recommendations stemming from the Christopher Commission report is subject to debate. Many remain skeptical that any fundamental changes occurred within the LAPD.

For many of the same reasons cited by Los Angeles public officials and enraged citizen groups, former mayor Rudolph Giuliani of New York City formed a special commission to investigate allegations of corruption within the ranks of the New York Police Department (NYPD). The **Mollen Commission** officially formed in 1994 and was headed by retired New York Supreme Court justice Milton Mollen. The commission was to investigate allegations of misconduct, analyze the effectiveness of anticorruption mechanisms within the department, and offer recommendations for improvement. Key findings and recommendations included the following:

■ **Mollen Commission:** The charge of the committee was to investigate allegations of misconduct, analyze the effectiveness of anticorruption mechanisms within the NYPD, and offer recommendations for improvement

- Much of the corruption was closely tied to the illegal drug market and the use of excessive force.
- Many of the corrupt acts were perpetrated by police officers acting in concert with one another, sometimes with as many as 15 conspiring officers.

- Corruption occurred primarily in crime-ridden precincts, populated predominantly by minority group members.
- The leadership structure of the department demonstrated no sense of commitment to rooting out corrupt practices.
- There existed a strong police subculture that frowned on honest officers reporting the wrongdoings of corrupt coworkers.
- The internal mechanisms responsible for uncovering and investigating misconduct were ineffective and, in many instances, focused on the whistle-blowers rather than the perpetrators.
- There existed a department-wide belief that the identification of corruption would cause the department administrators to retaliate for bringing discredit on the NYPD.
- A recommendation was made to create a permanent, external panel to monitor internal anticorruption measures and conduct investigations.[9]

It appears that the mayor and police administrators have yet to adopt the recommendations of the Mollen Commission and strongly object to oversight from outside the NYPD. This reluctance may be partly responsible for the continued allegations of misconduct that plagues the NYPD. Nearly 15 years after the Mollen Commission findings and recommendations were released, the executive director of the New York Civil Liberties Union stated the following:

> Under his [Commissioner Raymond Kelly] watch the discipline of officers guilty of misconduct has deteriorated dramatically, and many misconduct cases have been closed without any action whatsoever. . . . The police department has sabotaged independent scrutiny of officer practices, creating an atmosphere in which even the most egregious misconduct goes unpunished—unless, of course, a YouTube video puts the lie to the official truth.[10]

Clearly, a brief comparison of the major findings and recommendations of both the Christopher and Mollen Commissions reveals many more similarities than differences: the inability of these two agencies to police themselves, a reluctance to proactively and seriously confront this issue or encourage independent oversight, subcultures that discourage honest police officers from reporting coworker misconduct, and leadership structures that do not actively promote and support anticorruption measures.

Although the reports focused on two of our nation's largest police departments, the critical issues that formed the core of both investigations seem to ring true, albeit in differing magnitude, for all size departments and in all regions of the country. Police agencies at all levels of government are susceptible to police misconduct.

**Policing in Practice Video:**
What do you find are common public misconceptions about police conduct? Is there a public misconception of the level of police misconduct?

## ■ OTHER TYPES OF POLICE MISCONDUCT

Because of their vast legal and discretionary power and authority, and the multiple roles that they perform and assume in a democratic society. The opportunities for all forms of misconduct are, unfortunately, present in the everyday world of policing. The officers who bring discredit on their departments by compromising the police code of conduct causes severe damage to their respective agencies in the areas of public trust, department morale, and overall community relations.

### Nonfeasance, Misfeasance, and Malfeasance

Nonfeasance (Chapter 10) can be contrasted with **misfeasance**, taking inappropriate action or intentionally giving incorrect information, and **malfeasance**, taking hostile or aggressive action against others. In the context of policing, nonfeasance refers to the

■ **Misfeasance:**
Taking inappropriate action or intentionally giving incorrect information

■ **Malfeasance:**
Any intentional act that either is based on illegality or disregards the law enforcement code of ethics or a departmental policy

reluctance of most police officers to report wrongdoings committed by their coworkers. Both misfeasance and malfeasance also occur within the context of police culture. When committing the former, for example, police officers may perjure themselves to cover misconduct; while in committing the latter, they may threaten witnesses or victims to keep them from registering complaints concerning misconduct.

### Drug-Related Corruption

Another form of police misconduct involves drug-related corruption. The large sums of easy money associated with drug selling are a temptation that can prove too hard for many police officers to resist.

> When the wages of sin are incredibly lucrative, as they are in so many instances today, the appeal of corruption is proportionately more alluring. . . . Let me suggest to you that given the potential for misuse of police power, the wonder is that police officers, who witness crime, inhumanity and degradation every day, do not lose their sense of integrity and do not violate their oath of office more frequently.[11]

The 1998 Government Accountability Office (GAO) study provided insight into the systematic, narcotics-related corruption in the field of policing. The study analyzed federal drug investigations and prosecutions of police officers from several state and municipal police departments. The following is a summary of the major conclusions of the GAO report:

- Drug-related police corruption differs from other forms of police misconduct.
- Officers involved in this corrupt practice "were more likely to be actively involved in the commission of a variety of crimes, including stealing drugs and/ or money from drug dealers, selling drugs and lying under oath about illegal searches."

- Power and vigilante justice were found to be additional motives for drug-related corruption.
- A recurring pattern of this form of corruption was that the misconduct involved small groups of officers who consistently conspired and helped one another commit a variety of crimes.
- The culture surrounding drug-related corruption was characterized by the code of silence, blind loyalty to group members, and cynicism about the criminal justice system.
- Younger officers, as well as those lacking experience and at least some higher education, were found to be more susceptible to these corrupt practices.
- A variety of critical management and administrative issues were also associated with this form of corruption, such as lax or incompetent supervision; no real commitment from department leaders to promote integrity; weak or ineffective investigative methods; inadequate training, basic and in-service, particularly in the area of ethical decision making; police brutality; and informal pressures stemming from officers' personal friendships and affiliations with neighborhood figures.[12]

The aftermath of a successful narcotics raid, with the fruits of the crime showing. The seizure of large quantities of illicit drugs and cash has frequently been the downfall of many police officers.

© Photos 12/Alamy Stock Photo

Although the GAO report is somewhat dated, it is nonetheless a seminal piece of research on police corruption. The conclusions appear to be supported by the media and the conclusions of police corruption commissions. (See Appendix.) The issues pertaining to the strength of the police subculture, the support of peers in the commission of acts of misconduct, lax supervisory practices, and ineffective leadership structures seem to be key variables in the continuation of corrupt activities.

## Perjury

To some extent, perjury and other unauthorized deception serve as links between corruption and other forms of misconduct. The line may not always be clear between lying to informants and drug dealers and deceiving one's superiors.

Once perjury and deception gain a foothold, they tend to spread to other officers and to other types of situations until the entire justice system loses credibility. In some cases, perjury becomes accepted as an inherent part of the job in much the same way as corruption.[13]

One researcher interviewed nearly 200 NYPD officers about police misconduct, presenting officers with a variety of hypothetical scenarios.[14] Of the officers interviewed, 77% indicated that perjury "would likely be committed in some of the vignettes presented."[15] The following include other related highlights from the research:

- The three crimes found to be most significant in affecting officers' decisions to perjure themselves were the sale of narcotics, rape, and assault.
- Officers seeking promotion were more likely to perjure themselves.
- Officers with a significant need for overtime pay were highly likely to commit perjury.
- The past performance of officers in this regard was a strong predictor of continued acts of perjury.
- The duty assignments of officers affected their likelihood to commit perjury. Uniformed officers were more than twice as likely as detectives to commit perjury.
- Officers who had been expressly warned by their supervisors on prior occasions not to perjure their testimony or lie on arrest reports were highly unlikely to engage in this form of misconduct again.

### Emotional Abuse and Psychological Harassment

Police officers, like people in other occupational groups, are prone to use stereotypes and divide the world into *us* and *them,* or insiders and outsiders. The police sometimes label those who are perceived as outsiders. This is also referred to as "othering" in psychological terms, which allows people to think of the "others" as less human and less deserving of respect and dignity, thus justifying the abuse or harassment. The use of racial slurs is but one example of this kind of harassment. Other special categories and labels are created for particular types of "deviants," for example, drug dealers, homosexuals, prostitutes, and protestors. The creation of special categories and the ensuing labels are not unique to the police, but as police are public servants who represent the authority of the government, their attitudes can significantly impact the lives of others.

### Corruption of Authority

The **corruption of authority** is the most widespread category of police misconduct and includes "a wide variety of unauthorized material inducements, anything from discounted underwear to free commercial sex."[16]

#### Gratuities

Although the acceptance of gratuities on the part of the police often violates department policy, it does not violate criminal law when the gratuities are offered voluntarily. In many cases, gratuities are viewed as part of the job and are overlooked by police departments unless they become a matter of public concern. In other words, the acceptance of gratuities is often allowed, if not approved.

The difficulty with accepting gratuities is that the officer never knows when the donor may expect or request special services or favors in return. This may never happen, but if it does, it places the officer who has accepted the gratuities in a difficult position. In addition, it becomes difficult to draw a line between such gratuities and other types of corrupt activities in terms of monetary value and violation of ethical standards. To the extent that the public witnesses this kind of special treatment, it acts to further erode confidence and trust in the police.

The issue of police officers and gratuities continues to be debated, but the weight of evidence seems to suggest that they are best avoided when offered by commercial enterprises. Whether or not gratuities pose a major problem when they are offered by a grateful citizen and involve nothing more than a cup of coffee and a cookie remains

**Author Video:**
What are two common types of police misconduct?

■ **Corruption of Authority:** The most widespread category of police misconduct; includes a wide variety of unauthorized material inducements or gratuities

### All Africa News: *Ghanaian Chronicle*: Crack the Whip on Erring Police Officers

A total of 947 policemen and women have been dismissed from the Ghana Police Service for various acts of misconduct within three years, according to the vice president of Ghana, who is also the chairman of the National Police Council. He continued by stating that, "although we have bad nuts in every establishment, I want to commend the police administration for cracking the whip" on offenders and indicated the dismissals should "go a long way to deter other officers from indulging in acts against the code of conduct of the Police Service."

The vice president warned that the government would deal ruthlessly with the culprits who want to derail the house-cleaning by the police service and cautioned the police against using the media to settle their personal and organizational grievances, since that might expose divisions within the police service, which criminals might be able to use to their advantage.

The inspector general of police cautioned personnel against indulging in activities that could tarnish the image of the service, adding, "As personnel of the Police Service, you must demonstrate a high level of professionalism, in words and in deeds, by exhibiting impartiality and fairness to all parties . . ."

1. The chairman described the 947 officers as "bad nuts." Do you believe the officers represent isolated cases of "bad nuts," or do you believe there is something deeply flawed within the police service itself? Explain your position.

2. Do you think the steps the Ghana Police Service took constitute a true deterrent to future misconduct by officers?

*Source:* "AAGM: Crack the whip on erring police officers." *Ghanaian Chronicle* (Ghana), February 28, 2012.

---

controversial. Clearly, if an officer ignores an existing departmental policy prohibiting acceptance of any form of gratuity, it establishes a bad precedent.

### Kickbacks

**Kickbacks** refer to the practice of obtaining goods, services, or money for business referrals by police officers.[17] Those involved in offering these *quid pro quo* schemes could include lawyers, doctors, towing contractors, auto body shop operators, and others who reward police officers who refer customers to them. Some of the forms of misconduct in this category are not illegal; in fact, it is easy to cross the line between violations of department rules and regulations and illegal activities. The difficulties inherent in such activities are obvious, but in some police departments, they too are condoned, unless a public issue arises as a result.

### Shakedowns

**Shakedowns** occur when officers take money or other valuables and personal services from offenders they have caught during the commission of a crime.[18] Drug dealers, prostitutes, and motorists seem to be favorite targets, though incidents like these may occur when any arrestee is willing to buy his or her way out of an arrest.

### Bribery

This type of malfeasance can assume many different forms. Sometimes referred to as *the fix*, it involves police officers taking no enforcement action when they are normally

**■ Kickbacks:** Type of police corruption that refers to the practice of obtaining goods, services, or money for business referrals by police officers

**■ Shakedowns:** Type of corruption that involves officers taking money or other valuables and personal services from offenders they have caught during the commission of a crime

required to do so, usually in exchange for money.[19] Common examples include officers who accept a payment to let a motorist go without a ticket, deliberately misdirect an investigation, or perjure their court testimony to ensure a favorable outcome for the defendant.[20]

### Opportunistic Theft

This form of misconduct pertains to police officers who steal money or other valuables when, for example, they are guarding a crime scene—as in the case of a burglary—or steal other such goods from unconscious, inebriated, or dead people.[21] Similar activity also may occur when money and other property are stolen from arrestees either prior to or during the booking process.

### Protection of Illegal Activities

**Protection of illegal activities** is one of the most egregious forms of misconduct, and it involves police officers taking money or other valuables in exchange for their protection of criminal activities.[22] The most common forms of criminal activity protected by police are narcotics trafficking, gambling, prostitution, the fencing or sale of stolen property, and chop shop or auto theft operations. Unfortunately, allegations of this type of behavior occur all too frequently. To protect the illegal behaviors, a good deal of organization is often required. It does little good for one officer to look the other way when gambling occurs, if his or her replacement (for days off and vacations) or officers on other shifts fail to protect the parties involved.

### Excessive Use of Force

Nothing seems to grip the attention of the public more than the accounts of police officers engaging in **excessive use of force** to affect an arrest, coerce information from, or simply bully people over whom they have power. What constitutes excessive force is

**■ Protection of Illegal Activities:** The most egregious of all forms of misconduct; involves police officers taking money or other valuables in exchange for their protection of criminal activities

**■ Excessive Use of Force:** Also referred to as police brutality, this form of malfeasance pertains to situations in which officers overextend their legal authority by using excessive force to arrest or coerce information from individuals with whom they interact during the course of their duties

## John Crombach, Former Chief of Police, Oxnard Police Department

On May 4, 2012, Keith Herrera, a former Chicago Police Department officer assigned to the Special Operations Section, was sentenced to two months in prison. Herrera pleaded guilty to charges including civil rights violations and tax evasion. He was the last of 11 officers charged with stealing money from suspected drug dealers, making illegal traffic stops, and conducting illegal searches. The Special Operations Section targeted drug dealers, gang members, and other career criminals; the arrest scandal resulted in the disbanding of Special Operations in 2007. According to Herrera, rather than being sanctioned for his behavior, he received "commendations" and an "honorable mention" from his supervisors.

Officer Herrera, who initially faced up to 13 years in prison, had his sentence reduced by working undercover with federal authorities, including wearing a wire to secretly record incriminating conversations with other members of the Special Operations Section. Herrera spoke publicly about the scandal for the first time with CBS News correspondent Katie Couric in May 2008. Officer Herrera described a culture where "getting the bad guy off the street" by any means necessary was common practice among members of the Special Operations Section. They falsified reports, planted evidence, and lied in court—behaviors that do not come naturally to police officers, Herrera argued. Rather, officers are "taught" how to falsify reports; other, more-experienced officers coach younger ones in completing reports. One officer who worked closely with Herrera was Officer Jerome Finnigan, whom officials charged with being the scandal's ringleader. Herrera described Finnigan as his boyhood hero—as "superman." It was only when Finnigan solicited Herrera's help in a plot to murder another member of Special Operations Section, that Herrera approached the Federal Bureau of Investigation (FBI) for help. With Herrera's cooperation, Finnigan ultimately pleaded guilty to conspiracy to commit murder, for which he was sentenced to 12 years in prison.

An idealistic young man when he began his law enforcement career, Officer Herrera read to the court during his sentencing from a handwritten note, saying, "Words cannot describe how ashamed I am of my actions." Officer Herrera's case illuminates failures at every level of the police department, including failures at the highest levels of leadership. It also points to the importance of oversight, appropriate training, and good role models. Police officers, like the rest of us, want to fit in. Unfortunately, when it came to Officer Herrera, fitting in meant violating his professional ethics and succumbing to pressures to cover up the misconduct of others. His choices have forever tarnished the image of the Chicago Police Department and changed his professional life forever.

*Sources:* "Ex-Chicago cop gets 2 months for participating in Special Ops misconduct scandal." *Chicago Tribune*, May 5, 2012. "Corrupt cop reflects on career gone bad: 2-month sentence closes last chapter in sordid Special Ops case," by Cynthia Dizikes. *Chicago Tribune*, May 5, 2012.

almost always a matter of judgment. The police usually defend their actions as using the force necessary to, for example, defuse a threat or to subdue someone who is resisting arrest. The police are authorized to use the force necessary to gain compliance. There is a continuum of force, beginning with a verbal request, then a demand, then chemical sprays, then physical force (ranging from grabbing, punching, and kicking to the use of batons or Tasers), then lethal force. The public usually has limited knowledge of actual police procedure and may not have all the facts or may not be in a position to understand a judgment call by the police.

Problems arise when the police explanation is unconvincing, even taking the police perspective into consideration.

Infamous cases such as the Rodney King incident in Los Angeles and the Abner Louima case in New York City are indelibly etched into the minds of many Americans. More

Officers are shown using physical force to subdue an arrestee. Some would characterized the officers' action as excessive and others claimed it is justified.

REUTERS/Keith Bedford

recently, the tragic deaths involving the police of Oscar Grant (Oakland, California), Michael Brown (Ferguson, Missouri), and Eric Garner (New York City, New York) are a few of the most publicized. These and other incidents have ignited a movement to rectify race relations and the police. Some advocates point out that these events are not new, that the African American community has suffered such losses on a continuing basis. Partially to illustrate the ongoing and pervasive nature of violence against the Black community, one website (Gawker.com) has posted a list of all of the unarmed Black men and women that have been killed by the police from 1999 to 2014.

## ■ RESEARCH ON POLICE MISCONDUCT AND USE OF FORCE

Measuring the extent of police corruption is a difficult, if not impossible, task. The following are just several factors to consider.

**Author Video:**
Number of police officers engaging in police misconduct

- How do researchers quantify corruption?
- There is currently no official source of data on corruption, such as those provided by the Uniform Crime Reports and National Crime Victimization Survey for most other crimes.
- If it cannot be measured, how can researchers determine if anticorruption strategies are working?
- Actual crimes that indicate corruption, such as bribery, are not labeled as such.
- Data on misconduct are difficult to obtain. Without public statistics, researchers generally must rely on police administrators, who are often reluctant to share such information.[23]

Given this difficulty, it is also a challenge to assess the extent to which anticorruption programs have been successful.

In one study, researchers examined the responses of 3,235 police officers from 30 different agencies in multiple states to several different hypothetical scenarios involving various forms of misconduct. They developed a number of questions and recommendations related to the issue of integrity:

- Do all officers in the agency know the rules? If not, they must be taught.
- How strongly do officers support the rules? If they do not, they should be told why they should be supportive.
- Do officers know the disciplinary actions associated with breaking the rules? It is imperative that this be well known and publicized.
- Do the officers believe the disciplinary actions associated with rule violations are fair? If they do not, the chief must either modify the discipline or correct the officers' perceptions.
- How willing are officers to report misconduct of their colleagues? If they are unwilling, the chief must establish a policy that encourages the reporting of misconduct, such as rules that call for the termination of any officer who has knowledge of misconduct and does not report it, guarantees of anonymity to officers who come forward and report misconduct, and so forth.[24]

Survey data from a random sample of police officers employed in the Philadelphia Police Department helped explore the role of organizational justice in police misconduct.

> Officers who view their agency as fair and just in managerial practices are less likely to adhere to the code of silence or believe that police corruption in pursuit of a noble cause is justified. Furthermore, perceptions of organizational justice are associated with lower levels of engagement in several forms of police misconduct (fewer citizen complaints, fewer Internal Affairs Division investigations initiated, and fewer disciplinary charges). The results suggest that organizational justice is a promising framework to understand police misconduct and may help guide police administrators in the implementation of effective management strategies to reduce the incidence of the behavior.[25]

To close the loop, the Lynchburg Police Department in Virginia administrators constantly encourage and reward ethical practice by their officers. This too is part of their routine, and is a key ingredient in their recipe for individual and organizational success.[26]

Only a small percentage of police–public interactions involve the use of force, with an even smaller percentage resulting in conduct that would be classified as excessive.

In 2011, 6% of drivers pulled over in traffic stops experienced some type of force used against them, from shouting and cursing, to verbal threats of force or other action, to physical force, including hitting, handcuffing, and pointing a gun, and only 33.3% of these thought that the use of force was excessive.[27] Of that 6%, only 1% report that physical force was used.

Some data on use of force collected in 2008 by the Bureau of Justice Statistics show the following:

- Of the 39,914 residents surveyed across the United States, 776 individuals experienced the use or threat of force by police.
- Individuals aged between 16 and 29 accounted for approximately 58% of the instances in which force was used or threatened by police.
- Males were more likely than females to have force used or threatened against them during their most recent contact with police.
- Blacks were more likely than Whites or Hispanics to experience use or threat of force.
- Of persons who had force used or threatened against them by police, an estimated 74% felt those actions were excessive.
- Of those individuals who had force used or threatened against them, about half were pushed or grabbed by police.

- Individuals police suspected of wrongdoing accounted for 16.6% of the force incidents, and persons whose contact occurred during a criminal investigation accounted for 21.6% of force incidents.
- An estimated 10.4% of persons who experienced the use or threat of force reported that police found illegal items, such as drugs or a weapon.
- About 19% of persons who experienced the use or threat of force by the police reported being injured during the incident.
- Among persons experiencing police use or threat of force, an estimated 22% reported that they argued with, cursed at, insulted, or verbally threatened the police.
- About 12% of those involved in a force incident reported disobeying or interfering with the police.
- Among individuals who had force used or threatened against them, an estimated 40% were arrested during the incident.
- An estimated 84% of individuals who experienced force or the threat of force felt that the police acted improperly. Of those who experienced the use or threat of force and felt the police acted improperly, 14% filed a complaint against the police.
- An estimated 9 out of 10 residents who had contact with police felt the police acted properly.[28]

See Table 11.1 for some types of force used or threatened by police.

The evidence cited is consistent with a 2005 National Institute of Justice (NIJ)–sponsored research project regarding citizen contacts with the police.[29] Of the 43.5 million persons who reported having face-to-face contact with police, approximately 2.3% reported experiencing force or threat of force by police at least once during that time period. In addition, of those respondents who reported experiencing force or threat of force,

- 55% claimed that police actually used force (i.e., pushing, pointing a gun, and use of chemical sprays);
- 28% reported force being threatened by police, but no force was used;
- 10% reported police officers shouting or cursing at them but not applying force; and
- approximately 17% admitted to provoking the officers by threatening them or resisting arrest.[30]

The NIJ reports also identified areas in need of further research such as administrative policies, hiring practices, disciplinary procedures, use of technology, and the various influences of situational characteristics on the use of force.

### Table 11.1 ■ Types of Force Used or Threatened by Police, 2008

| Type of Force Police Used or Threatened | Force Was Used or Threatened |
| --- | --- |
| Pushed or grabbed | 53.5% |
| Kicked or hit | 12.6 |
| Sprayed chemical/pepper spray | 4.9! |
| Electroshock weapon (stun gun) | 4.1! |
| Pointed gun | 25.6 |
| Threatened force | 76.6 |
| Shouted at resident | 75.5 |
| Cursed at resident | 39.1 |

Research on the use of Tasers by the police has led to some interesting findings. One study, based on 24,000 use-of-force records, found that most use-of-force encounters result from defensive efforts by suspects trying to resist physical control.[31] Another finding was that Tasers (also known as conductive energy devices or CEDs), when used too frequently or over too long a time period, may result in serious harm. These authors recommend that officers be trained to use Tasers only with active resisters. They also note that their data were based largely on officer accounts, which might be biased; there were differences between some officers' versions and victims' accounts.

# ■ THE IMPACTS OF MISCONDUCT

One of the most significant impacts of misconduct is to increase the amount of suspicion and distrust of the justice system among all parties, which damages the very foundation of democracy.

> When officers use unlawful means to gain a desired end, they damage the system they represent. Beyond the damage to the justice system, however, officers who engage in illegal behavior denigrate not only the uniform of the guardian but also the individual within. The eventual result to society is a loss of confidence in those charged with the protection of others, leading to a fraying of the tapestry of the culture that binds communities together.[32]

**Video Link:**
Police Accounts Appear to Differ With Laquan McDonald Shooting Video

Other important consequences of police misconduct are exacerbating racial tension, exposing departments to costly civil lawsuits, and degrading the morale of the workforce—making the job of policing that much harder.

Unfortunately, media accounts of police misconduct are not hard to find. Even more alarming for police executives is that criminal conduct perpetrated by police officers represents only a small percentage of the activities routinely classified as police misconduct.

Police misconduct and race continues to be an issue of paramount importance. A Gallup news poll taken in 2011 examined the amount of confidence different racial and ethnic groups expressed with respect to police honesty and ethical standards. A majority of Whites rated the police as honest and ethical and reported having considerable confidence in them; a minority of Blacks agreed with that assessment. (See Figure 11.1.)

## Race and Police Harassment

Members of minority groups, particularly in high-crime areas, report that **psychological or emotional abuse** is a routine part of their encounters with the police. And, in fact, the best available evidence supports this contention.

There is widespread perception that citizen encounters with the police frequently and unnecessarily turn violent in minority communities in cities of all sizes across the country. The perception creates hostility and resentment on behalf of some citizens who view themselves as particularly likely to be victims of harassment and brutality and on behalf of the police who view themselves also as likely to be harassed, challenged, and criticized.

Disillusioned with what they see as a lack of accountability by police—a failure of justice—wary and mistrustful citizens have taken to monitoring the police themselves and sharing that information freely. Certainly, the proliferation of cell phone cameras has introduced a new and widespread means for public monitoring. The Cato Institute has established a website that maintains a daily list of incidents.[33]

■ **Psychological or Emotional Abuse:** Type of wrongdoing normally associated with the use of racial slurs and other negative descriptions of certain classes of citizens (e.g., gays, drug addicts, homeless persons, and protestors, to name the most common)

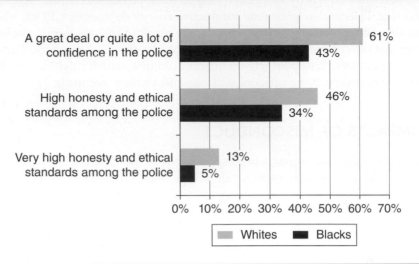

Figure 11.1 ■ Gallup Survey of Confidence in the Police

The American Civil Liberties Union (ACLU) has launched a phone app that allows citizens to record footage of the police and upload it directly onto an ACLU server for storage and sharing.[34] And three youngsters from Georgia have developed a website and invited others to publicly share their accounts of interactions they have had with the police. Related to public wariness is, of course, the issue of race, which continues to dog police departments, officers, and interactions of all kinds. The question of racial fairness in law enforcement reflects the fact that our society is still very troubled when it comes to what racism means and the persistent and vast differences in the ways that different groups of people are treated and experience life in the United States.

In spite of misgivings on both sides, the vast majority of police encounters with other citizens occur without physical brutality on the part of either party.

In several studies, foremost among the complaints of minority group members about the police were the use of improper forms of address (use of terms such as *boy*, or use of a first name when a surname is appropriate) and stopping and questioning people for no apparent reason other than their race or ethnicity.[35] (See Chapters 10 and 12 for more on profiling.)

Research indicates that harassment and psychological brutality continue to occur in police encounters with certain segments of the population. Repeated public opinion polls show that minority groups look less favorably on the police than Whites. For example, a *CBS News/New York Times* poll taken in July 2008 asked respondents whether they felt they had ever been stopped by the police just because of race or ethnicity. Just 7% of Whites responded yes to the question compared to 43% of Blacks and 30% of Hispanics.[36]

During recent federal testimony, police accountability expert Samuel Walker asserted that disrespectful and offensive language by the police is "extremely important because of its pervasiveness, its impact on police-community relations, and its special impact on communities of color."[37] Verbal disrespect was a significant impediment to police–community relations in the 1960s and is still pervasive today.[38]

Citing citizen complaint data, Walker outlined four key adverse consequences resulting from this form of police behavior:

1. Personal psychological injury to the member of the community involved

2. A pervasive distrust of the police among those people most often the target of such language, particularly communities of color

3. Provocation of hostility toward the officer, leading to an escalation of the encounter into more aggressive behavior on the part of both parties, sometimes tragically resulting in the unnecessary use of force by the officer, including even the use of deadly force

4. An undermining of standards of professionalism in the police department as officers learn by experience that they will not be disciplined for such conduct[39]

Walker concluded his testimony by proposing the President's Task Force on 21st Century Policing implement a respectful policing initiative (RPI) and outlined the action items that would include.

Additional seminal research examined the perceptions of four types of police misconduct—verbal abuse, excessive force, unwarranted traffic stops, and corruption by White, Black, and Hispanic respondents and the factors that shape these perceptions. The researchers' findings explain why and how perceptions and trust of the police are heavily influenced by race. Their primary conclusion is that "[d]ominant groups should perceive the police as an institution allied with their interests, whereas minorities should be inclined to view the police as contributing to their subordination. This . . . does increase the odds that [minorities] will believe police misconduct is a serious problem, whereas whites tend to discount or minimize it and perhaps view criticisms as a threat to a revered institution."[40]

Other research acknowledges that racial and ethnic minorities are often disproportionately on the receiving end of aggressive behaviors on the part of the police. However, they conclude further that such aggression is part of "ordinary social-psychological processes triggered by the characteristics of neighborhoods."[41]

### Research on Profiling

Researchers have long been occupied with measuring profiling to prove that it does indeed exist and to understand its forms and true prevalence. Observers describe racial profiling as most prevalent in the context of street-level crime, counterterrorism, and immigration law enforcement.[42]

Policing practices in New Jersey and Maryland in 1998 put a spotlight on racial profiling and evoked a huge public outcry, when members of the New Jersey and Maryland State Police were formally accused of stopping Black motorists on state highways for no reason other than race.[43] Empirical evidence gained from data collection efforts regarding traffic stops, detention and investigation, and arrests of Black drivers on New Jersey and Maryland highways paints an alarming picture. In New Jersey, researchers measured rates to ascertain whether state troopers stopped, ticketed, or arrested Black motorists at rates significantly higher than other racial and ethnic groups.[44]

The results of the data collection efforts in New Jersey were disturbing. The analysis of the approximately 42,000 cars involved in the study led to the following conclusions:

- There was little or no difference concerning the frequency and type of traffic violations committed by Black and White motorists.
- Approximately 73% of the motorists stopped and arrested were Black, but only about 13% of the vehicles involved in stops had a Black driver or passenger.
- Blacks drove or occupied only about 13% of the vehicles in question, but accounted for 35% of the total number of stops.

Results from a similar study in Maryland yielded remarkably similar results. In this case, 6,000 vehicles were included in the data collection, and, as in the New Jersey study, the purpose was to discover whether Maryland state troopers were stopping, issuing citations, searching, or arresting predominantly minority-group motorists. The following quotation summarized the Maryland results:

> Blacks and whites drove no differently; the percentage of blacks and whites violating the traffic code were virtually undistinguishable. More importantly . . . analysis found that although 17.5% of the population violating the traffic code on the road . . . studied was black, more than 72% of those stopped and searched were black. In more than 80% of the cases, the person stopped and searched was a member of some racial minority.[45]

Since these studies were completed, many other police agencies have come under scrutiny for similarly biased enforcement practices, prompting legislatures from all levels of government to sponsor and adopt laws to eradicate this form of police malfeasance. Complaints came not only from the African-American community, but from other racial and ethnic groups as well. The complaints from the minority citizens were so numerous that the ACLU posted an online complaint form and questionnaire to compile statistical data that would bolster a plea to government agencies for support in eliminating these biased practices. Currently, each state and the federal government have adopted laws requiring the collection and reporting of data pertaining to traffic stops (e.g., ticket issues, driver or occupant searches).

## ■ CAUSES OF MISCONDUCT—BAD APPLES OR BAD BARRELS?

Many police administrators seem to readily offer the "bad apple" explanation that corruption is the result of the weaknesses of individual officers. Most forms of corruption require some degree of organizational support, at least in the sense that others within the organization turn their heads and refuse to confront the corrupt officer. This failure to take action against corrupt officers, even on the part of other officers who clearly dislike such activities, may be due to a complex set of factors, including the police subculture.

There is a code of silence among police officers with respect to a variety of types of deviant behavior.[46] Such deviance has been called an "open secret" within the fraternity, but its existence is denied to those outside the group.[47] For Bernie Cawley, a New York police officer, it was "nothing to lie to grand juries, to steal drugs, weapons, and money, and to protect other cops doing the same thing."[48] His fellow officer, Michael Dowd, testified, "Cops don't want to turn in other cops. Cops don't want to be a rat."[49] Many observers agree that the code of silence and lack of physical evidence hampers many investigations. In the absence of reliable and cooperative witnesses, corruption cases are nearly impossible to prosecute successfully. In such cases, the witnesses are often other police officers.[50]

In some departments, officers who are "straight" are regarded as stupid for failing to benefit from corrupt activities. When an officer does decide to take action against corrupt colleagues, the fraternity may react violently and is very likely to ostracize the one who violated the code or broke faith.

Why does police misconduct persist? The answer seems to lie with individuals, with agencies, and—at least in part—in the relationship between the police and the larger society.

### Individual

Of course there are individuals who are unsuitable for police work due to flaws in their character. Some of these individuals still make it through the recruiting and hiring process. The absence of appropriate controls such as adequate background checks, performance evaluations, or continuous training can result in subsequent behavior

SAGE Journal Article: Police Corruption and Psychological Testing: A Strategy for Preemployment Screening

problems. Agencies need to have policies and practices in place that prevent the bad apples from having undue influence.

In part, police corruption may be related to economic conditions, but that relationship is complex. When police and other wages are low, the temptation to accept dirty money may be great. Not to excuse the behavior, some observers find it exceedingly understandable.

### Agency

It is impossible to explain the extent of police misconduct and corruption with the bad apple theory, however. One could argue that police misconduct is behavior that can only be learned on the job. A corrupt environment can teach improper behavior to otherwise law-abiding and upstanding officers.

The police subculture, especially the code of silence among police officers, results in collective feelings and attitudes of cynicism, isolation from the community, and a sense of blind loyalty to colleagues.

Psychologist Philip Zimbardo is responsible for the famous 1971 Stanford experiment on how normal individuals easily become corrupted by power and authority. Zimbardo argues that the line between good and evil is permeable, not solid, and the context (in this case, the negative side of the police culture) can corrupt individuals. Other famous psychological experiments have demonstrated the human capacity for inflicting pain on others out of obedience to authority, out of a sense that the victim is the "other," and out of a belief that the responsibility for wrongdoing is shared among the group.[51] For these and many other reasons, police departments must actively counteract the tendency toward corruption.

The cycle of corruption persists also because honest police officers, due to fear of retaliation from coworkers and supervisors, often hesitate to report the illegal and unethical acts of coworkers. Until this aspect of the police subculture can be significantly diminished, and honest police officers develop the courage to do the right thing, police misconduct is likely to continue.

**SAGE Journal Article:**
Organizational Justice and Police Misconduct

# Exhibit 11.1

## Justifications for Misconduct

To help illuminate the psychology that underlies police misconduct, it is useful to analyze and categorize the cognitive rationalizations that can contribute to unethical behavior. Developing a culture of ethics can mitigate misconduct, even before it actually occurs.

Decades of empirical research have supported the idea that whenever a person's behaviors are inconsistent with his or her attitudes or beliefs, the individual will experience an uncomfortable state of psychological tension—a phenomenon referred to as cognitive dissonance.[48] People modify contradictory beliefs or behaviors in ways intended to reduce or eliminate discomfort. Officers can reduce psychological tension by changing how they think about their actions and the consequences of those actions, or by adjusting their activities, attitudes, or beliefs in ways that are consistent with their values and self-image. In general, attitudes are less resistant to change than behaviors are.

Officers can cognitively restructure unethical behaviors in ways that make them seem personally and socially acceptable, thereby allowing immoral behavior while preserving a self-image as an ethical person.

Most officers do not jump headfirst into large-scale misconduct—instead, they change incrementally.

The strength and ease with which officers can rationalize unethical behavior also depends, at least in part, on how they view their conduct, the people harmed by their actions, and the consequences that flow from their actions. An officer's initial slide down the slippery slope of misconduct can begin with nothing more than simple policy violations that, if left unchecked, generate a mild feeling of psychological tension or discomfort. However, by learning to rationalize wrongdoing in ways that make it psychologically and morally acceptable, officers are able to relieve any feelings of distress or discomfort, effectively disengaging their moral compasses.

Officers can employ cognitive rationalizations prospectively (before the corrupt act) to forestall guilt and resistance, or retrospectively (after the misconduct) to erase any regrets. In either case, the more frequently an officer rationalizes deviant behavior, the easier each subsequent instance of misconduct becomes. This is because the more frequently an officer rationalizes, the easier it becomes to activate similar thought patterns in the future. With time and repeated experience, rationalizations can eventually become part of the habitual, automatic, effortless ways that officers think about themselves, their duties, and the consequences of their actions, eventually allowing increasingly egregious acts of misconduct with little, if any, of the guilt or shame commonly associated with wrongdoing.

Table 11.2 lists common rationalizations that officers might use to neutralize or excuse unethical conduct.

### Table 11.2 ■ Rationalizing Misconduct

| Strategy | Description |
| --- | --- |
| Denial of Victim | Alleging that because there is no legitimate victim, there is no misconduct |
| Victim of Circumstance | Behaving improperly because the officer had no other choice, because of either peer pressure or unethical supervision |
| Denial of Injury | Because nobody was hurt by the officer's action, stating that no misconduct actually occurred |
| Advantageous Comparisons | Minimizing or excusing one's own wrongdoing by comparing it to the more egregious behavior of others |
| Higher Cause | Breaking the rules because of some higher calling—that is, removing a known felon from the streets |
| Blame the Victim | Believing that the victim invited any suffering or misconduct by breaking the law in the first place |
| Dehumanization | Using euphemistic language to dehumanize people, thereby making them easier to victimize |
| Diffusion of Responsibility | Relying on the diffusion of responsibility among the involved parties to excuse misconduct |

*Source:* Adapted from "Understanding the psychology of police misconduct," by Brian D. Fitch. *The Police Chief 78* (January 2011), 24–27. Retrieved from http://www.nxtbook.com/nxtbooks/naylor/CPIM0111/#/24.

## Society

It is commonly said that police are a reflection of the society or community they serve, and this is true with respect to police corruption. Simply put, a large percentage of corrupt practices by police could be stopped quickly if the society were organized to eliminate them. For example, if other citizens stopped offering bribes, free services, and other gratuities, and started reporting all police attempts to benefit in unauthorized fashion from their positions—as was recommended by the Knapp Commission in 1972—it would be very difficult for some forms of police corruption to persist as they do.

To some extent, it appears that we want our police to be corrupt, or at least corruptible. It gives critics something to talk and write about, it provides a general sense that the police are not morally superior to others, and it perhaps gives many a feeling of power over those who in some way are more powerful. Does society want the police to be totally honest and trustworthy? Or is it preferable to believe that they would overlook at least minor violations as a result of the favors they get? Most of the police do in fact adhere to high ethical standards, and they are, after all, basically citizens like everyone else. It is easy to cast stones at the police, because the average citizen has no idea what the police go through, and because too many of the police succumb to the pull of corruption. It is fairly convincing to the average citizen that corruption is inherent in the police role and that there is little that could change it.

## Noble Cause Corruption

As the phrase implies, **noble cause corruption** pertains to various situations in which officers circumvent the law to serve what they perceive to be the greater good. The following dilemma describes this behavior: "If you have a perpetrator in custody, and he has information that could save the life of an innocent victim, is it right to use extreme methods to get the information?"[53] Although such questions always generate debate, the answer is actually quite clear—police officers are sworn to uphold the law and should never, under any circumstances, willfully violate the rights of anyone in their custody. Those who disagree with this assertion point to the high stakes creating the need to temper the requirements of the law; this is a classic ends-justifies-the-means situation.[54]

The debate about noble cause corruption might apply to more commonplace activities encountered by police officers. Imagine plainclothes officers approaching an individual on the street to conduct a field interview. The person in question abruptly turns a corner and, while temporarily out of view of the officers, drops a quantity of illegal narcotics to the ground. The police then find the contraband and arrest

> **Noble Cause Corruption:** Form of misconduct pertaining to various situations in which officers circumvent the law in order to serve what they perceive to be the greater good (e.g., manufacturing probable cause, perjury to gain a conviction in court)

**Detective Harry Callahan.**
You don't assign him to murder cases.
You just turn him loose.
**Clint Eastwood Dirty Harry**

© Photos 12 / Alamy Stock Photo

> Noble cause corruption is often glorified in films that portray cops who are willing to break the rules to get the job done. A classic example is Dirty Harry.

the subject. What should the officers do? If they tell the truth, the case will most likely be dismissed in court. If they elect to fabricate their report and possibly perjure themselves in court, they have removed a dope dealer from the street. The problem with adhering to the noble cause corruption philosophy is that two wrongs never make a right. If left unchecked, the collective behavior of officers may eventually even assume a vigilante-like mentality.[55]

## ■ MISCONDUCT: MANAGEMENT AND ADMINISTRATIVE ISSUES

**Author Video:**
Preventing abuse
of authority

The reluctance by chief executive officers to take appropriate disciplinary action against officers engaged in unethical behavior serves only to strengthen the police subculture and the influence it exerts on so many officers. Moreover, these types of attitudes by chiefs send a very disturbing but clear message to subordinates: that more often than not—at least with respect to this research population—the penalty for malfeasance will not be commensurate with the seriousness of the offense. In any event, this view of corruption by chiefs of police is an issue that begs more attention, through both research and professional development activities.[56]

Although one type of corruption does not necessarily lead to another, where one finds more serious types of corruption, one is also likely to find most of the less serious types. Consider, for example, a department that condones internal payoffs. If a supervisor attained her position by paying someone for it, her authority to deal with less serious forms of corruption among those supervised is compromised. In the long run, such a department is likely to be characterized by all other forms of corruption. In addition, services to the public are likely to be less efficient and effective than they might otherwise be, because promotions are not usually based on merit, and less competent or incompetent people may become supervisors.

> Discipline may be especially weak since any action might lead to unpleasant publicity. If a large portion of a police department is implicated in such corrupt relations, no one can enforce the law against the police themselves. Officers outside the network of payoffs have to turn their backs on what goes on around them and deny publicly that any such activity exists. . . . Moreover, what is the effect on a young patrolman who learns that his colleagues and commanders are often more interested in profiting from the law than enforcing it?[57]

> Daniel Sullivan, former head of the [New York City] department's Internal Affairs division, testified that the message from the top brass to his investigators was simple: "We shouldn't be so aggressive because the department doesn't want bad press." . . . Honest officers testified that their efforts to report and investigate corruption ran into resistance and retaliation.[58]

Many police agencies fail to discipline officers who are guilty of misconduct. This failure to act sends a clear message to line officers: We are not committed to ethical conduct. The resulting consequences may be disastrous.[59]

The various commissions that investigated the misconduct in question found one common denominator in problem agencies—the leadership demonstrated no real sense of commitment to detecting and investigating corruption from within. Many police chiefs will point to the bad apples as the problem, but corruption can result from faulty leadership structures and administrative policies that avoid rather than promote strict accountability for all misconduct.[60]

The organizational culture of many police agencies actually fosters corruption. Research has indicated that ". . . incentive structures within police agencies increase the problem of corruption."[61] Arrest quotas and arrest rates of officers are often used as criteria for more sought-after assignments, such as gang crime and vice, and are even used for promotion; these are not good management practices.

## Whistle-blowing

The Mollen Commission report pointed to the existence of a department-wide belief that the identification of corruption would cause department administrators to retaliate for bringing adverse public attention to the agency. Whistle-blowing is particularly difficult among the police, due to the code of silence and the extreme emphasis on loyalty among the police. Whistle-blowers have often been the targets of retaliation.[62] Unfortunately, the history of the treatment of whistle-blowers is full accounts of threats made and carried out.

In response to data such as those in the Mollen Commission report, some chiefs emphasize the harm done to community relations when misconduct becomes public. They believe that covering up, ignoring, or simply having wrongdoers resign rather than face the disciplinary ramifications commensurate with their misdeeds is for the greater good. However, critics of this view believe that

> [m]anagement accountability is perhaps the most important, effective and most difficult proactive tool for preventing and detecting police corruption. This is not a program or a device, but rather a thorough rethinking of the meaning of supervision and management responsibility. The driving assumption underlying accountability is that commanders are responsible for all police activity that takes place on their command. At its simplest, a policy of accountability means that commanders may not plead ignorance and surprise when corruption is discovered in their areas.[63]

## Addressing Misconduct

No matter how one analyzes the situation, any administrative action short of holding all members of the organization strictly accountable for their misdeeds serves only to perpetuate the problem and send a disturbing message down the organizational ladder—a message that tacitly approves of corrupt practices.

Eliminating or reducing misconduct warrants a well-constructed and well-delivered message that it will not be tolerated. After New York City implemented a new police strategy in 1994, crime was dramatically decreasing, and the number of citizen complaints against police was dramatically increasing. However, two police precincts in the South Bronx managed to reduce the number of citizen complaints to below the 1993 level.[64] The decrease appeared to be related to two key variables: (1) a new department-wide policy called CPR (courtesy, professionalism, and respect) and (2) the dedication to improving community relations by the precincts' commanding officers. The latter was accomplished through commanding officers taking a keen interest in "repeat offender" officers, or those receiving multiple citizen complaints. It did not take long for officers to figure out that their commanders were keeping tabs on them. The most likely explanation for the decline in citizen complaints in these two precincts was the "efforts made by precinct commanders to promote respectful policing and change a police culture that tolerated citizen complaints."[65]

Other management techniques for detecting misconduct include the use of field associates, "turning" officers who have been caught engaging in misconduct, and the rotation of assignments. **Field associates** are officers who are specially trained and sometimes recruited to obtain information on misconduct while performing normal police functions. This information is relayed to management without other officers knowing who the informants are (ideally, at least). If the program is discovered, however, it can create an atmosphere of suspicion among officers. Turning involves offering leniency or immunity to officers who have been caught engaging in misconduct and who agree to provide information on other problem officers.

Rotating personnel across shifts and geographic assignments is a technique used to disrupt possible misconduct by making it difficult for officers and other citizens to establish permanent ties.

**Field Associates:** Specially trained officers used to obtain intelligence regarding corrupt police practices

Leaders must weigh this strategy with some caution. Although rotation may have a positive effect on misconduct, it may also disrupt the flow of information between officers and other citizens, negatively impact community relations, and make community-oriented policing more difficult.

Leaders cannot realistically expect the best outcomes by relying on strictly punitive measures for their officers' misconduct. Punishment alone is no more effective with disciplining police officers than it is with controlling the behavior of public citizens.

Another strategy that may reduce misconduct is selective recruitment. Recruiting police personnel of high moral character and providing training in ethics early in their careers appear to be steps in the right direction.[66] If the department and subculture also foster an anticorruption attitude, promote on the basis of merit, and pay relatively well, the allure of corruption may decrease. Internal affairs units and external review boards have also been used to help curb corruption by identifying and charging those involved.

## ■ ACCOUNTABILITY

In a democratic society, public servants are accountable to the community through the political process; to some degree, the public expresses its desires through elections. Presidents, governors, county and municipal administrators, and legislative bodies are responsible for overseeing the performance of public servants, including the police. These overseers must balance the public's wishes with legal considerations.[67]

**Video Link:**
Rebuilding accountability and trust after police shooting

Because the powers granted the police are considerable, citizens are understandably vigilant in monitoring police actions and are aware of their right to demand that the police account for their behavior. Requirements that the police issue periodic reports concerning their activities are one indicator of such vigilance, as is the increasing demand for transparency in policing.

Over the years, the police have attempted to demonstrate accountability by becoming more professional, using internal affairs units, improving citizen complaint procedures, increasing the transparency of their process and decisions, and using **early intervention programs**. These focus on identifying officers whose behavior is problematic, intervening to correct the problem behavior, and following up with those who have received intervention.[68] Although all of these agency attempts to ensure accountability are worthwhile, police officers themselves have an obligation to demand peer-to-peer accountability when they believe professional transgressions have occurred.[69] This is a difficult but desirable goal.

In the traditional police world, innovation is seldom rewarded. A typical response to attempts to control, prevent, or correct discretionary behavior is the use of negative sanctions, which tends to lead to temporary rather than permanent change, inappropriate emotional behavior, inflexibility, degradation of desirable behavior, and fear or distrust of administrators. Further, stigma can have negative effects on self-esteem and status; punishment and humiliation can lead to anger and hostility.[70] Depending on how a department holds its officers accountable for their behavior, there may be positive as well as negative consequences for the individual officers and for the agency.

■ **Early Intervention Programs:**
Administrative practice of identifying officers whose behavior is problematic, intervening to correct the problem behavior, and monitoring intervention of those who have received it

### Accountability and Community Policing

Some police administrators view community-oriented policing as a positive step toward accountability. The emphasis on community policing may be uneven across the nation, but there is reason to believe that many departments have incorporated its core elements. Genuine partnerships between the police and the public and the increased visibility of police operations help to bridge the gap between the police and the public. Implementing ride-along programs, citizen police academies, and neighborhood watch groups improves relationships and enables the public to learn about actual police operations, which is the second part of the equation. Just as officers need to be culturally competent and understand segments of society with fluency and sensitivity, society as a whole needs to grow in its understanding of what the police experience and why they conduct themselves as they do. Mutually, the two sides can work together to bridge the gap between them.

## Citizen Oversight Groups

The public has attempted to hold the police accountable through litigation, public protest, and citizen oversight groups. Many of these attempts have focused on holding the police legally and ethically responsible for their actions by drawing attention to the problem and establishing limits on discretionary conduct; some efforts involve increased reporting on police performance. Success in these attempts has been limited by the failure to adopt uniform standards of accountability, by failure to maintain those standards that are established, and by lack of supervisory oversight. Still, some observers believe that police will continue to embrace and expand accountability.

> We expect to see more police agencies conducting their own routine public surveys, as many do now, holding themselves accountable not only for reducing reported crime, but also for reducing fear and the perception that crime is a problem in particular neighborhoods or for especially vulnerable residents.[71]

When such accountability exists, the public can judge for itself how successful the police are in exercising discretion wisely and in conducting themselves ethically.

Some police agencies rely on **citizen or civilian panels or boards** as a method of external review. Civilian review boards consist of a group of citizens (other than police officers) who investigate complaints against the police and recommend consequences. Some argue that citizens who do not serve as police officers cannot understand the issues involved in policing and therefore should not be allowed to judge officers. Others argue that it is precisely *because* these citizens are not police officers that they can judge the impact of officer actions from a different perspective and render more independent judgments.

**Audio Link:**
Police are Learning To Accept Civilian Oversight, but Distrust Lingers

■ **Citizen or Civilian Panels or Boards:** Groups of citizens (other than police officers) who investigate complaints against the police and recommend punishment in cases where it appears to be justified by the facts

The Indianapolis Metropolitan Civilian Police Merit Board met to hear testimony and consider the dismissal of an officer accused of using excessive force. Civilian review boards such as this one have been established to investigate complaints against the police and to provide the impartiality of those outside the force.

© AP Photo/Michelle Pemberton.

## Internal Affairs

**Internal affairs** officers are designated to receive complaints, whether from other citizens or other officers. They conduct investigations to determine whether the facts in a case point to officer misconduct and report to their supervisors to decide whether to take action against the officers. As might be expected, internal affairs officers are often not popular with their fellow officers, and internal investigations is a career path in and of itself in some larger departments. In smaller departments, internal investigations are often conducted by the highest-ranking officers. This, of course, begs the question, "Who watches the watchers?" There is evidence that corruption exists even among internal affairs divisions and personnel. For example, there are allegations that Chicago's Independent Police Review Authority (IPRA) deliberately drags cases out, resulting in a dismissal of charges in some serious cases. Some of these cases have lingered for years, jeopardizing the firings of police officers that the superintendent had deemed unfit to serve.[72] According to the head of IPRA, the investigations are often complex and need to be thorough. IPRA was formed in 2007 by city ordinance and investigates about 2,800 complaints of police misconduct each year. The office faced a daunting task beginning several years ago when it was created to replace the Office of Professional Standards (OPS). IPRA inherited OPS's caseload and was charged with restoring the public's trust that allegations against police officers would be taken seriously.[73] Recognizing the importance of building trust and providing professional internal review of police actions, in September 2009, the International Association of Chiefs of Police (IACP) and the Office of Community Oriented Policing Services (COPS) released *Building Trust Between the Police and the Citizens They Serve.* This guide examines all aspects of internal affairs operations and recommends strategies to improve and sustain community trust building.[74]

**Internal affairs units** typically perform the following functions:

- Receive and investigate complaints concerning police misconduct
- Investigate other possible indicators of police misconduct (deadly force incidents, unethical conduct)
- Prosecute officers who appear to be responsible for serious misconduct
- Collect intelligence on misconduct and share it with police administrators
- Keep complainants and victims of police misconduct informed of departmental actions related to their cases

## Police Discipline

Police officers who engage in misconduct or violate department policy are subject to different types of discipline, depending on the severity of their misconduct. Similar to other citizens, police officers may be prosecuted criminally for acts committed either on or off duty. For example, a police officer who is arrested for drunk driving while off duty is prosecuted for his or her crime in the same way as other citizens would be. The police make the arrest, the arresting officer completes an incident report, and evidence is presented to the office of the district attorney, who determines what charges, if any, the officer will face. An officer convicted of a criminal offense may face a fine, a term on probation, or time in jail or prison. The arrestee also has the option of allowing a jury to decide his or her guilt. The same is true with criminal offenses committed while on duty. An officer who uses unreasonable force may be prosecuted for a variety of criminal charges, including assault under color of authority.

Unlike many other professionals, law enforcement officers may also be charged with violating their department's policy. An officer who is convicted on a charge of drunk driving faces not only punishment assigned by the court, but also administrative discipline for violating department policy. The officer may be required to attend training,

**Web Link:**
Metropolitan Police Department, Internal Affairs Bureau

**Internal Affairs Units:** Units within police agencies that receive and investigate complaints concerning police misconduct, investigate possible indicators of police misconduct, prosecute officers who appear to be responsible for serious misconduct, and collect intelligence on misconduct and share it with police administrators

to accept a suspension without pay, or to face termination. The type of administrative discipline an officer receives depends on the severity of the offense, any prior discipline the officer has received, and other mitigating or aggravating factors, such as the officer's willingness to accept responsibility and truthfulness.

Many large law enforcement agencies have special units devoted to the investigation of alleged criminal violations and administrative policy violations. Officers who are charged with violating a criminal statute are entitled to the same legal protections as other citizens. The officer may not be compelled to speak to investigators or testify in court, all evidence used in trial must be legally obtained, and the officer may cross-examine witnesses.

Officers also have certain administrative rights; however, an officer's criminal rights may conflict with administrative rights. For example, an officer charged with a crime cannot be compelled to speak with investigators; on the other hand, most police departments have administrative policies that require officers to answer all questions asked during an administrative inquiry. As a result, police agencies separate the criminal and administrative investigations. When an officer is charged with violating both a criminal statute and administrative policy, investigators complete the criminal portion first. It is only after the criminal investigation has concluded that the administrative investigation begins. An officer who is suspected of committing a criminal violation as well as a policy violation faces convictions for both, for one or the other, or for neither.

An officer convicted of a criminal offense may, like other citizens convicted of a crime, appeal his or her conviction. Similarly, an officer who is convicted of an administrative policy violation may contest the finding or discipline.

1. Studies have shown that police officers have a much more narrow definition of serious misconduct than private citizens. How do you account for the difference?

2. What role does the "code of silence" play in identifying and addressing issues of misconduct?

3. Many professions practice a "code of silence." Are there ways in which the "code of silence" is beneficial to law enforcement? Should departments attempt to eliminate it altogether?

## AROUND THE WORLD 11.2

Researchers have studied many of these same issues in another international context, focusing on 1,055 police officers from Bosnia and the Czech Republic.[75] The results with respect to officers' opinions about the seriousness of police malfeasance, associated disciplinary actions, and willingness to report misconduct were remarkably similar to those reported for officers in the United States. They concluded that the most significant finding was that the disciplinary culture of the two countries affected the views of individual officers more than any other variable. Specifically, officers from both countries had the following similarities:

1. They shared an understanding of what constitutes serious issues of misconduct.

2. The majority of respondents from both countries observed the infamous code of silence, unless the misconduct at issue fell on the serious end of the misconduct continuum.

3. Officers from the Czech Republic were more willing to expect disciplinary action for rule violations, and officers from Bosnia felt that discipline was controlled by an informal set of rules and norms—and most felt they would not receive any discipline at all, unless the misconduct was viewed as severe.[76]

### Cameras

Many police departments have adopted policies that require video cameras that are capable of recording sight and sound to be mounted inside police vehicles, and increasing numbers of departments are using body-worn cameras.

This technology could potentially help ensure the safety of both officers and citizens. In addition, cameras provide a more or less permanent record of events captured during police encounters, should any of the parties involved allege misconduct. All tapes are collected and maintained for review, if the need arises. Because the videotape is in a sense a form of supervision, many officers claim that this makes them better officers, more professional and more than ever willing to abide by department policy. (See Chapter 13.)

## CHAPTER SUMMARY

The issue of misconduct is a problem that has always plagued the field of policing. Regardless of how infrequently misconduct occurs or by how few or many officers, it does damage to individuals, agencies, and communities. Misconduct foments public mistrust of its supposed protectors, exposes departments to costly litigation, and degrades the morale of individual officers and entire agencies.

As a result of high-profile police-involved shootings, police–community relations are extremely challenging at the present time. Racial and political tensions are running high. Police officers and departments are under intense public scrutiny as society struggles with the issue of how to police the police.

All misconduct is a breach of the public trust in one way or another. There are many forms of misconduct, including corruption, which involves personal material or financial gain and an abuse of power, such as with bribery. Depending on a person's level of involvement with corrupt activities, misconduct can be nonfeasance, misfeasance, or malfeasance. Officers succumb to the temptations of drugs and drug money, opportunistically bending and breaking the rules to make the job easier or less risky, or—in its worst form—committing actual crimes, sometimes violent crimes. Getting in even deeper, officers may lie to cover up misdeeds, even in court and under oath. Individuals often construct elaborate rationalizations to counteract the psychological unethical behavior.

Corruption is always a risk that follows power. Despite periodic efforts and formal investigations to expose and eliminate it, corruption persists and is an issue that every police agency must grapple with. Corruption in particular can be contagious within an agency; peer pressure is one of the more significant forces that influences the behavior—good and bad—of the police at every level.

There is ample evidence that the "bad apple" theory is not as potent an explanation for misconduct as the "bad barrel" theory. Police culture—and agency leadership—create the atmosphere and set the tone for the conduct of its members. Many feel that misconduct is largely learned within the agency, not borne there by unsuitable candidates.

There have been many recommendations made by police researchers, police executives, and governmental agencies to mitigate the frequency of the many forms of police. The International Association of Chiefs of Police and the U.S. Department of Justice have also offered many sound recommendations. Leadership lies at the foundation of the solutions to this issue. Supervisory personnel must lead by example, and the examples need to start at the very top. To do otherwise makes department leaders part of the problem rather than the solution. One theme that consistently emerges is that police misconduct tends to flourish in the absence of genuine commitment from leadership to put an end to corrupt policing practices.

# APPENDIX

## Table A.1 ■ Examples of Police Misconduct in the United States

| Author(s) | Title | Year | Summary of Misconduct |
|---|---|---|---|
| Strunsky, S., Associated Press | "Two More Officers Charged in Newark Police Corruption Case" | 2004 | At least four indictments occurred of officers charging the sale of narcotics and shaking down drug dealers for money and drugs. |
| Associated Press | "Fourth Defendant Sentenced in Memphis Police Corruption Case" | 2006 | Sting operation. Cases involved taking money to protect drug dealers, burglary, and transporting prostitutes to remote casinos. |
| Associated Press | "Topeka Police Corruption Story" | 2006 | Case involved two officers accused of stealing thousands of dollars intended for undercover drug buys. |
| Associated Press | "Chicago Police Dept. Not Doing Enough to Stop Corruption" | 2006 | Chicago officials were accused of a "practice of indifference to corruption . . . making officers who engage in misconduct feel protected." |
| Tram, M., Associated Press | "More Arrests as Chicago Police Corruption Investigation Widens; 3 Officers Charged" | 2006 | Officers accused of shaking down drug dealers, home invasion, and armed violence. Earlier in the same year, four other officers from the same gang crimes unit were charged with robbery, kidnapping, and making false arrests. |
| Melia, M., Associated Press Worldstream | "Police in Puerto Rico Rocked by Scandals" | 2007 | Ten officers were accused of planting drugs on people and making false arrests. This indictment came amid several police scandals with more than 50 federal indictments of police officers the previous year. The protection of drug dealers was the most common offense regarding those cases. |
| Anonymous, *Police Department Disciplinary Bulletin* | "Big Police Scandal in Small Town" | 2009 | The Massachusetts Department of Public Health suspended the license of Hamilton's police-run ambulance service after an investigation revealed that a majority of the town's officers—including the chief—participated in a scheme to falsify emergency medical technician training and certification records. The successful scheme enabled them to continue to run the ambulance service—and receive thousands of dollars in bonus pay as officer-EMTs—despite the apparent failure to keep up with mandatory continuing education and refresher training designed to protect the public. |
| Gorenstein, N., *Inquirer* | "Closing Arguments Offer Competing Views of Testimony in Camden Police Corruption Case" | 2010 | Jurors at the trial of two former Camden police officers heard analyses of testimony describing 13 incidents in 2008 and 2009 in which the officers allegedly broke the law by stealing cash, planting evidence, and lying in reports and to state grand juries, while making drug arrests. |
| Koppel, N., *The Wall Street Journal* | "San Fran Confidential: Cases Dropped Due to Alleged Police Corruption" | 2011 | Prosecutors in the Bay Area have been forced to dismiss over 800 criminal cases there in the past year because of allegations of police corruption, including selling drug evidence, conducting unlawful searches, and conspiring to get men drunk and then arrest them on drunk-driving charges. |
| Emery, T., *The New York Times* | "Baltimore Police Scandal Spotlights Leader's Fight to Root Out Corruption" | 2012 | A scheme to divert cars damaged in traffic accidents to a body shop in return for payoffs resulted in one of the widest police corruption scandals in Baltimore history. Ten officers have been sentenced to prison; a total of 14 officers pleaded guilty to federal extortion charges. At least 14 suspended officers still face departmental discipline and possible state charges. |

**Table A.2** ■ Historical Attempts at Investigating Police Corruption in the United States

| Name of Commission | Year of Report | Conclusions | Recommendations |
|---|---|---|---|
| Lexow Commission (Cox & McCamey, 2008; defense of the Lexow measures, 1895) | 1894 | Corruption was pervasive and systematic in the NYPD, largely due to malfeasance, misfeasance, and nonfeasance in the higher ranks. Political corruption from the infamous Tammany Hall played a significant role as well. | Appointment of honest and capable police magistrates; appointment of honest, efficient, and responsible police administrators; passage of the "Police Magistrates Bill." |
| Wickersham Commission (American Law and Legal Information Law Library, 2009) | 1932 | The report was titled "Lawlessness in Law Enforcement." Findings included widespread nationwide use of brutality by police, bribery, entrapment, evidence tampering, intimidation and coercion of witnesses, unlawful wiretapping, and collusion with organized criminal gangs. | Widespread reforms not just in policing but in the entire criminal justice system. Need for more professional police departments, higher qualifications for the job of a police officer, and insulation of the police from political influences. |
| Knapp Commission (Knapp Commission Report on Police Corruption, 1973) | 1972 | Started as a result of police whistle-blowers. Widespread corruption in the NYPD; identification of two types of corrupt officers, grass eaters and meat eaters; and citizens' willingness to bribe police for preferential treatment that perpetuates corruption. | Increased supervisor accountability for actions of subordinates, creation of internal affairs units in all units of the department, improved screening and increased qualifications for all ranks, and undercover informants to be assigned to all units in the agency. |
| Christopher Commission (Human Rights Watch, 1998) | 1991 | Corrupt LAPD police culture that tolerated various acts of misconduct, a relatively small group (44) of officers responsible for a significant portion of malfeasance (group received no discipline) committed during the "CRASH" years (gang suppression efforts begun in 1977), planting evidence, brutality, and perjury. | Improved selection and training criteria, implementation of community-oriented policing strategies, and more supervisor accountability for the actions of subordinates. |
| Mollen Commission (Treaster, 1994) | 1994 | Significant amount of corruption tied to the drug markets, weak leadership structure with no commitment to uncovering corrupt practices, strong police subculture encouraging officers not to rat on one another, weak internal affairs unit, and many acts of corruption committed by officers acting together in small groups. | Change in leadership structure, more department-wide emphasis on anticorruption measures, better-trained internal affairs unit, and an external panel to oversee misconduct investigations. |

## KEY TERMS

**$SAGE edge™**
Review key terms with eFlashcards.

- Meat eaters 247
- Lexow Commission 247
- Christopher Commission 248
- Mollen Commission 248
- Misfeasance 249
- Malfeasance 249
- Corruption of authority 252

- Kickbacks 253
- Shakedowns 253
- Protection of illegal activities 253
- Excessive use of force 253
- Psychological or emotional abuse 259

- Noble cause corruption 265
- Field associates 267
- Early intervention programs 268
- Citizen or civilian panels or boards 269
- Internal affairs units 270

## DISCUSSION QUESTIONS

1. Why is police accountability important, and how can it best be promoted?

2. What are some of the obstacles to police accountability?

3. What constitutes police misconduct? Can you cite examples of police misconduct from your own experiences?

4. Why is corruption of authority (accepting gratuities such as free coffee, food, etc.) critical in understanding police corruption in general?

5. Does society desire or demand police who are incorruptible? Why or why not?

6. What are the relationships between internal corruption in police agencies and other forms of corruption?

7. Do circumstances involving the philosophy of "the end justifies the means" or "noble cause corruption" mitigate the serious nature of misconduct by police? Why or why not?

8. Why would a police officer perjure him- or herself? What is the impact of such perjury on the criminal justice network and other citizens in general?

9. Is psychological brutality an important form of police misconduct? Why and in what ways?

10. What recommendations have been offered to mitigate the frequency and depth of police corruption?

11. Do you think police misconduct is as serious a problem now as it was a decade or so ago? Support your answer.

12. Why is domestic abuse by police officers problematic? How might the problem be alleviated?

$SAGE edge™
Test your understanding of chapter content. Take the practice quiz.

## INTERNET EXERCISES

1. Using the web, locate examples of three "real life" scandals pertaining to at least three different forms of corruption identified in the chapter.

2. Using the web, locate what recent strategies are being used by law enforcement and other government personnel in their fight against the drug cartels of Mexico.

3. Research the term or phrase *narcoterrorism*, and define it in detail. Document at least two examples of this form of terrorism.

## STUDENT STUDY SITE

 $SAGE edge™ edge.sagepub.com/coxpolicing3e

**Sharpen your skills with SAGE edge!**

SAGE edge for Students provides a personalized approach to help you accomplish your coursework goals in an easy-to-use learning environment. You'll find action plans, mobile-friendly eFlashcards, and quizzes as well as videos, web resources, and links to SAGE journal articles to support and expand on the concepts presented in this chapter.

# REVIEW » PRACTICE » IMPROVE

▶ edge.sagepub.com/coxpolicing3e

HEAD TO THE STUDY SITE WHERE YOU'LL FIND:

- **eFlashcards** to strengthen your understanding of key terms.

- **Practice quizzes** to test your comprehension of key concepts.

- **Videos and multimedia** content to enhance your exploration of key topics

**$SAGE** edge™

©iStockphoto.com/Bastiaan Slabber

# CONTEMPORARY ISSUES IN POLICING

PART IV

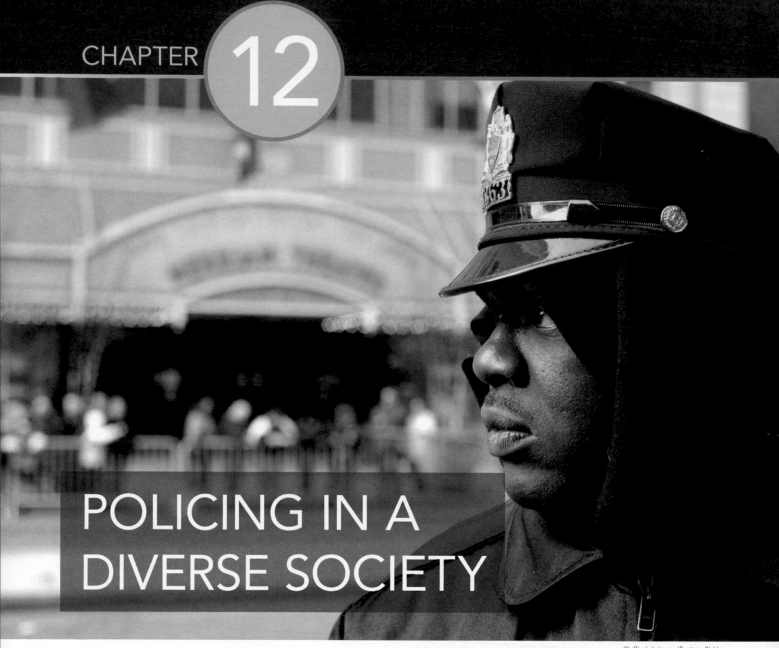

# CHAPTER 12

# POLICING IN A DIVERSE SOCIETY

© iStockphoto.com/Bastiaan Slabber

## CHAPTER LEARNING OBJECTIVES:

1. Identify the characteristics of a democratic and multiethnic society that impact police–multicultural relations

2. Describe the historical origins of the current problems associated with multicultural relations and the police

3. Discuss the various strategies that can be implemented by both the police and the public to improve the perception of police

4. Identify various strategies that may be implemented to mitigate acts of discrimination and improve

police officers' understanding of racial and ethnic diversity in the communities they serve

5. Explain the historical and current roles and challenges that women have in policing

6. Discuss the evolution of the treatment experienced by minority group members in policing and whether or not you believe the current treatment of these groups is fair and impartial

I n a democratic society, community relations are the cornerstone of good policing. Without public support, the police are uninformed about most crimes, are likely to receive inadequate resources, are not able to collect information needed to solve cases and apprehend offenders, and are challenged in recruiting quality employees. The police are, or should be, protectors of civil liberties and civil rights, as well as of life and property. If the police are to serve the community effectively and in a manner acceptable to citizens, they must demonstrate their effectiveness in these areas and establish a fruitful working relationship with the public.

## ■ POLICING IN A MULTICULTURAL AND MULTIETHNIC SOCIETY

The term **police–community relations** can be misleading. There is not a single, large, homogeneous group that is the public, but many diverse publics, groups that are identifiable by geography, race, gender, age, social class, respect for law and order, and degree of law-abiding behavior.[1] These different publics have unique interests and concerns that distinguish them from one another in many ways. The police, as public servants, must serve everyone. However, because the expectations of members of these different publics are often dissimilar, providing effective service is often difficult.

**Author Video:** Policing in a multicultural setting

These different, sometimes conflicting, expectations point out that good police–community relations are not easy to achieve. In a large, industrialized multiethnic society based on values such as democratic decision making, individual freedom, and tolerance for diversity, to some extent, conflict between the police and other citizens is inevitable and perhaps even healthy, within limits. However, conflict with specific subgroups that becomes chronic or habitual is a serious problem.

Even though successful community relations depend on reciprocity, the public cannot be forced to see and understand things from the police perspective. Therefore, the burden of trying to improve police–community relations often rests with the police.

### Changing Demographics

Developing positive working relationships in a rapidly changing, multicultural society is difficult. The U.S. population is becoming increasingly diverse (see Figure 12.1). Changes in the demographic proportions of minority groups result from differences in birth and death rates as well as immigration. Hawaii, New Mexico, California, Texas, and Washington, DC, have high levels of immigration and have more than 50% racial and ethnic minority populations.[2]

According to the U.S. Census Bureau, in 2010, slightly more than one-third of the population reported their race and ethnicity as something other than non-Hispanic White.[3]

The minority population (in terms of race and ethnicity) increased from 86.9 million to 111.9 million between 2000 and 2010, representing a 29% increase.[4] Asians and Hispanics continued to be the two fastest-growing minorities. In 2010, California had the largest minority population in the nation with 22.3 million, followed by Texas (13.7 million), New York (8.1 million), Florida (7.9 million), and Illinois (4.7 million).[5] Time will tell if these trends continue. According to the U.S. Census Bureau, the percentage of non-Hispanic Whites was 62% in 2014.[6]

What was recognized decades ago certainly remains the case today.

> Our communities are changing quickly—often too quickly for law enforcement to keep up. Failing to understand many of these changes, and still trying to conduct business as usual, we find that the tools and rules that worked before don't work now. For many seasoned officers, their main concern is to make it through each shift and go home in one piece. This only serves to reinforce a force-oriented culture that brings officers closer to each other and further from the community they serve.[7]

**■ Police–Community Relations:** Consists of both human and public relations

The Asian population grew from about 4% in 2000 to about 5.3% in 2014.[8] More than half of the 10-year growth in the total U.S. population was due to the increase in the Hispanic population. There were 57.7 million U.S. Hispanics projected for 2015 compared to 49.7 million in 2000. If present trends continue, estimates are that non-Hispanic Whites will account for no more than 50% of the population by 2044.[9]

At the same time, the national population is aging, and the elderly constitute an increasing proportion of our population. A new type of generation gap is arising with most people over age 60 being non-Hispanic Whites.

In addition, gays and lesbians, the homeless, the mentally ill, religious minorities, political extremists, and refugees from the Middle East, Central and South America, and island countries all constitute significant minorities.

Many of these diverse groups bring different languages, religious observances, dress, and lifestyles, and different views of the police. Some immigrants who come from countries where the police are integrated with the military and police actions are not regulated by strong constitutional and human rights guarantees have very negative images of the police,[10] while others have more positive images.[11]

All create challenges for the police in providing adequate services while dealing with problems related to language and cultural understanding. Further complicating matters is the fear that terrorists from abroad may hide among the numerous immigrants, while terrorists from within continue to present very real threats as well. All in all, the police at all levels face ever-changing issues related to the nation's demographics.

**Policing in Practice Video:**
What does your department do to foster community relations in consideration that Oxnard is a multicultural city?

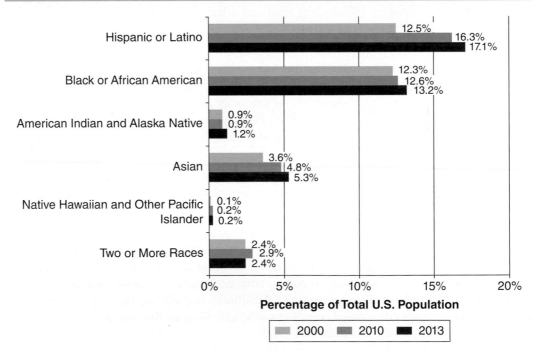

Figure 12.1 ■ Racial and Ethnic Minority Population, 2000, 2010, 2013

*Source:* Adapted from "Overview of race and Hispanic origin: 2010," by K. Humes, N. Jones, and R. Rameriz, March 2011. U.S. Census Bureau (http://www.census.gov/prod/cen2010/briefs/c2010br-02.pdf).

*Note:* To comprehend the composition of each of the categories and to view a number of cautionary statements related to the use of the data presented in Table 12.1, see the U.S. Census Bureau website. Data presented here represent a general summary of census information.

Department personnel should represent the racial, ethnic, and gender makeup of the citizens they serve. Some police departments actively outreach to recruit women and minority residents.

## Immigration

Immigrants and refugees have typically tended to remain in physical and cultural isolation, which can leave them vulnerable to crime victimization both from members of their own ethnic group and from the larger community. Interactions between immigrants and the police often involve social misunderstanding, causing further alienation. Police agencies characterized by ethnic diversity serve the public better—especially with community and problem-solving approaches—by providing sworn officers who can deliver effective services within their own ethnic communities and to the community as a whole.

Community-oriented strategies are particularly challenging in the face of anti-immigration legislation, which is designed to stem the flow of illegal immigrants or to facilitate their removal. Community cooperation is required for effective policing and is enhanced when residents believe that laws are enforced fairly. Cynicism and distrust of the police undermine the public's willingness to cooperate. Some suggest that recent trends toward strict local enforcement of immigration laws might undercut police efforts by creating fear and cynicism in immigrant neighborhoods.[12] The constitutionality of these laws is being tested in the courts.

To complicate matters further, many immigrants entering the United States come from countries where the police are corrupt, brutal, unreliable, and insensitive. For members of these groups who have been subject to both prejudice and discrimination in their home countries, learning to trust the police and accept them as public servants rather than as a group of armed and dangerous thugs is not easy and takes time.

## Mentally Ill

Another population that has increasingly involved the police and that the police do not fully understand is individuals who are mentally ill or mentally disturbed. Mental health systems around the country continue to be affected by budgetary concerns, and police officers are often forced to step in to provide emergency services to those with mental illness. In doing so, the police encounter a variety of problems. For example,

**Video Link:**
Supreme Court Upholds
Controversial Part of
Immigration Law

some facilities may only accept patients who agree to treatment, and persons who are mentally ill often refuse help. Further, dealing with those who have mental illness is frustrating, because the police often find they have few options, yet the public expects the police to "do something." In some instances, the police transport persons with mental illness to receiving centers (perhaps over and over again). If the receiving center refuses to accept the individual who is mentally ill, jail may be the only alternative, and most officers would agree that is not a long-term solution.[13] In response to this need, many departments have specially trained crisis intervention personnel; some departments have an entire team or teams dedicated to a more skilled and knowledgeable response to this vulnerable population.

In major U.S. cities, such as New York, Chicago, and Los Angeles, jails have become de facto mental institutions, because there are so many people with mental illness on the streets.[14] Their acting-out behavior often lands them behind bars, where the options for treatment are few and the conditions of confinement are far from therapeutic. In fact, jail or prison conditions often make mental conditions worse.

## ■ THE PROBLEM AND PROMISE OF DIVERSITY

Many other subgroups in our complex society have characteristics that can make it hard for the police to understand and respond effectively. There are differences of age, culture, religion, geography, sexual orientation, and gender status. It would be an enormous task for anyone to completely understand the customs and norms of every subgroup of U.S. society. Partly for this reason, the police must rely on community partnerships and a positive public image to become more effective in communities that are more opaque to them.

The millions of day-to-day encounters involving the police and the public that take place are the foundation of human relations, good or bad. These encounters do not occur in a vacuum. Most people have preconceived notions and deep misconceptions about members of different racial, religious, age, or ethnic groups. The public also has preconceived notions about police officers. Such **stereotypes** may be based on prior experience, rumor, and media images. These notions may be partially accurate or entirely inaccurate. Either way, stereotypes influence the nature of the interaction. This is most problematic when the assumptions are completely erroneous.

The misunderstanding and prejudice between the police and social subgroups lead to avoidable strife and spiraling polarization. The consequences of this disconnect are many and significant. Police morale suffers under the weight of public outrage and scorn; the public mistrusts the police to do their job in a professional and just manner. A reluctance to call for help makes it more difficult for the police to gather information from reliable community sources, which, in turn, creates barriers to preventing or solving crime and protecting victims, especially in the roughest neighborhoods.

In a diverse society, these problems are perhaps inevitable to some extent, as we divide the world into *us* and *them* groups, interact with and tend to support members of the *us* group, and distrust members of the *them* group. In addition, as the global nature of crime and policing continues to expand, the importance of understanding and operating in multicultural and multiethnic settings becomes increasingly significant.

## ■ POLICE–COMMUNITY CONFLICT

Conflict between the police and other citizens continues to widen the gap that separates the police from other citizens. Police are often referred to as if they are not part of society, but, of course, they are citizens too—legally, historically, and traditionally.

In many respects, the police are viewed as adversaries not only by those involved in criminal activities, but also by basically law-abiding citizens who occasionally violate

**Video Link:**
Mental Health: Crisis in North Carolina, pt. 2

**Policing in Practice Video:**
Community Relations Specialist

**Stereotypes:**
Preconceived notions based on prior encounters, word of mouth/rumor/gossip, and information provided by the media

speed limits, or drive when they have had one too many drinks, or fail to go through proper channels to obtain a permit.

Residents of the ghetto or barrio may perceive the presence of the patrol car as police harassment, while the police may believe they are acting in the best interests of these minority groups by providing as many personnel as possible in those areas where citizens are most likely to commit or be victims of crime. Police may regard the slang, dress, and behavior of Black and Latino youth as a challenge to their personal and professional authority.

Imagine an encounter between a uniformed police officer and another citizen. The officer is easily identifiable because of the uniform, badge, nightstick, handcuffs, and gun; and all of these help identify his or her role in the encounter. The officer's trappings indicate power and authority and that the officer's definition of the situation will be the prevailing one—that is, that the officer is in control or will gain control.

The other side of the equation is that the other party will defer to the officer's authority, treat the officer with some degree of respect, and comply with directions. To do otherwise is to challenge the officer's authority and risk provoking the officer to more drastic actions. Some officers are extremely sensitive to such challenges and to losing face and so may feel compelled to respond quickly and forcefully to maintain control. This kind of spiraling encounter is even more likely when negative or erroneous stereotypical assumptions are at play. When the police or the other parties are primed for a negative confrontation, reason suggests that it is more likely to occur than not occur.

Although most encounters with police are civil and are characterized by some degree of mutual concern, understanding, and respect,[15] there is no denying that some are likely to be more problematic than others, depending on a number of factors. These include the impressions brought to the encounter, the setting in which the encounter occurs (private or public, familiar or unfamiliar), the number and types of participants involved, the degree of control exercised by the participants, and what actually happens during the encounter. For example, the mere sight of a police officer puts some people on guard.

They drive more slowly and more carefully; if they are involved in illegal activities, they may try to appear innocent, and they may treat other persons more civilly. For their part, police officers are trained to be suspicious of everyone, especially when past experience or present knowledge leads them to believe an offense may be involved.

In every situation, police officers have to make sense out of all sorts of information, sometimes with split-second timing. When they have the wrong idea about the meaning of behavior or language or signals from a person whose culture they do not understand, it is that much more difficult to analyze and react appropriately, and conflicts often arise.

### Police–Minority Encounters

Because of history, stereotypes, and cultural illiteracy, police encounters with minority individuals are emotionally charged beyond the position of authority the police already hold. One of the most controversial areas of police–community relations is encompassed by these encounters, particularly those with Blacks and Hispanics, but also with other racial and ethnic minorities, and more recently with Middle Easterners.

Negative impressions also often exist when the police are called into a domestic violence situation in which they regard the offender with suspicion, and the offender believes that police intervention into his home and into an essentially private matter is improper. This may be doubly true when there are also cultural prohibitions against involving outsiders in intimate family matters, making the officer's intervention even more problematic. This may be especially pronounced in domestic situations that involve individuals from Latin American countries or from the Middle East, for example.

Sadly, our country has a long history of conflict between the police and minority communities. Certainly, for the African American community, slavery, segregation, and discriminatory laws have shaped the troubled relationship with both the police and Blacks. Segregation and sexual orientation laws in the United States were long enforced by the police, who treated Blacks, Native Americans, gays and lesbians, and others as second-class citizens (in terms of existing laws, they were). Morally and ethically objectionable as these laws were, police officers were legally obligated to obey them. Officers who agreed with the laws may have done so with pleasure. When the laws changed as a result of civil rights activism, some police were slow to adapt, and community members were slow to believe the police could change, even if the law had.

### Exhibit 12.1

## Prejudice and Discrimination

There is a difference between *prejudice* (a feeling about a person or persons based on faulty generalizations) and *discrimination* (which involves behavior that, in its negative form, excludes all members of a certain group from some rights, opportunities, or privileges).[17] We all have prejudices that may or may not result in discrimination. Prejudice undoubtedly exists among police officers (as it does among all other occupational groups), and though race relations have advanced (changes in civil rights legislation, hiring practices of police agencies, the election of a African American president, the appointment of Black and Hispanic Supreme Court justices, and the appointment of numerous minorities to cabinet-level and other important governmental positions), there is still a long way to go.

There are few ways to measure the existence of prejudice except to ask police officers and other citizens about their feelings.[18] Further, whatever these feelings may be, they are not themselves illegal. However, when these feelings carry over into behavior (discrimination), serious problems may result, and community relations suffer.

Prejudice and discrimination are not limited to the police, and therefore, the police alone cannot ensure good community relations.

Just in the last six decades, patterns of heightened tensions between minority communities and the police have flared and subsided. To touch on the subject, during the 1960s, five years of riots involved Blacks and the police.

In the 1990s, the highly publicized Rodney King beating by Los Angeles police officers ignited serious clashes and waves of violent protest, especially in major urban areas. More recently, a number of police shootings of young, unarmed Black men has focused attention on what appears to many both inside and outside the African American community to be a tragic and troubling pattern of police behavior. These and countless similar incidents are some of the reasons that members of minority groups that are based on race, ethnicity, or sexual orientation are hostile or wary of the police.

Although minority group members often regard the numbers of police in their neighborhoods as excessive and as a form of harassment, the police argue that minority neighborhoods typically have high crime rates and therefore require police presence. In fact, some have argued that race is totally irrelevant to the police in most high-crime neighborhoods because nearly all of the residents are minorities.[16]

Some may argue that police presence contributes to high crime rates (the more police, the more crimes they discover); however, it is equally true that the number of victims and offenders found in such neighborhoods compels the police to respond. Regardless, there is no justification for the use of discriminatory tactics in minority neighborhoods.

## Peer Pressure

Many police officers who might not otherwise be involved in discriminatory practices fall victim to **occupational discrimination**. That is, even though an individual officer may not believe in acting in a discriminatory fashion, his colleagues may exhibit such behavior. To be included as a part of the subculture described earlier, the officer may emulate the behavior of his peers, thus harassing or abusing minority group members—not because he believes it is right, but because he wishes to be perceived as a member of the "in-group."

## Forms of Discrimination

The most common form of discrimination is **psychological harassment** such as the use of racial slurs and other attempts to embarrass or humiliate people. Failure to use proper forms of address (e.g., use of first name rather than *Mr.* or *Ms.* and last name) has been and remains a major complaint of minority group members.[19]

Verbal abuse by police officers continues to be one of the most common complaints about the police expressed by citizens. Racial or ethnic slurs not only demean citizens but also deny them equal treatment. They, too, may respond by harassing and verbally abusing the police for assumed or perceived injustices. In general, in an atmosphere of mistrust, situations that might be defused with cooler heads often escalate and end up requiring the use of force.

Failure to respond rapidly to calls in ghetto or barrio areas has also been an issue. And unreasonable use of stop-and-question and stop-and-frisk tactics alarms minority group members. Further, the relatively infrequent but totally unacceptable use of excessive force on the part of the police in dealing with members of minorities (or, for that matter, the dominant group) is of major concern.[20] Such incidents become legend in minority neighborhoods and further damage the already negative image of the police. (See Chapter 11.)

## Profiling

Minority group members believe that the police single them out for harassment and abuse.

> Minorities are arrested, stopped and questioned and shot and killed by the police out of all proportion to their representation in the population. . . . The police play a far more visible role in minority group neighborhoods compared with white neighborhoods. . . . An African-American or Hispanic American is much more likely than a white American to see or have personal contact with a police officer.[21]

■ **Occupational Discrimination:** Discrimination that results, in part at least, from being a member of a particular work group

■ **Psychological Harassment:** Harassment based on the use of racial slurs and other attempts to embarrass or humiliate members of the minority group

Exhibit 12.2

## Arrest Rates by Race, by Crime

Police use arrests as a strategy for resolving a variety of problems (many of which are noncriminal in nature) in the ghettos. In some instances, the probability of a Black man being arrested during his lifetime approaches 90%.[26] The distribution of arrests for 2013 can be seen in Figure 12.2a. According to the census, African Americans made up 13.2% of the total U.S. population in 2014.[27] The graph clearly indicates that Blacks were disproportionately arrested for most types of crimes in 2013.[28] (See Figures 12.2b and 12.2c.)

Figure 12.2a ■ Arrests by Race, 2013

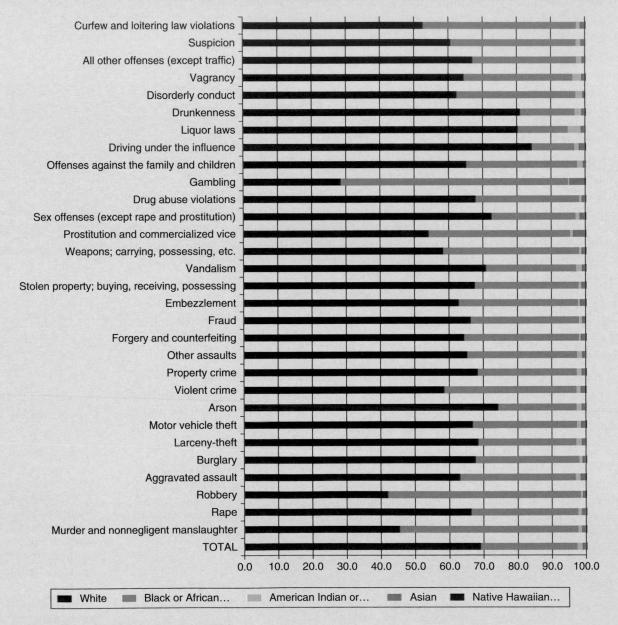

¹ Because of rounding, the percentages may not add to 100.0.

² Violent crimes are offenses of murder and nonnegligent manslaughter, forcible rape, robbery, and aggravated assault. Property crimes are offenses of burglary, larceny-theft, motor vehicle theft, and arson.

*Source:* Federal Bureau of Investigation (2013), *Crime in the United States* (Table 43).

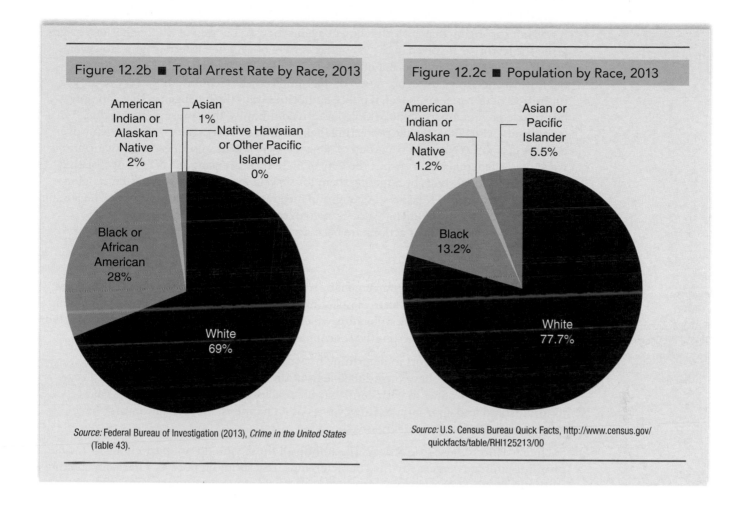

**Figure 12.2b ■ Total Arrest Rate by Race, 2013**

- American Indian or Alaskan Native 2%
- Asian 1%
- Native Hawaiian or Other Pacific Islander 0%
- Black or African American 28%
- White 69%

*Source:* Federal Bureau of Investigation (2013), *Crime in the United States* (Table 43).

**Figure 12.2c ■ Population by Race, 2013**

- American Indian or Alaskan Native 1.2%
- Asian or Pacific Islander 5.5%
- Black 13.2%
- White 77.7%

*Source:* U.S. Census Bureau Quick Facts, http://www.census.gov/quickfacts/table/RHI125213/00

Human relations problems involving the police and minority group members persist.

> One national study found that more than half of all black men report they have been victims of racial profiling by law enforcement. Overall, roughly 4 in 10 blacks and 3 in 10 Hispanics believe they have been unfairly stopped by the police simply because of their race or ethnicity.[22]

And, in 2012, the issue of targeting minorities remained a major concern for at least some citizens of New York City who claim that "stop and frisk" policies continue to target minorities.[23]

Elected officials in New York City have challenged the New York Police Department's (NYPD) policies related to "stop and frisk," which allow the police to target racial and ethnic minorities.[24] "The policy is either accidentally, incidentally, or purposely racist, however you slice it," according to Councilman Jumaane Williams.[25] Former mayor Michael Bloomberg and NYPD commissioner Ray Kelly argue that the program prevents crime and saves lives. The issue here is whether NYPD officers apply the policies ethically (as well as legally).

### Profiling the Muslim Community

Following the events of 9/11, federal agents swept through Arab, Muslim, and South Asian neighborhoods throughout the country, apprehending men on the street, as well as from their homes, workplaces, and mosques.[29] "It soon became clear that most, if not all, of the several thousand detainees picked up by federal agents in the immediate aftermath of 9/11 were guilty of little more than being Arab, Muslim, or South Asian and were in the wrong place at the wrong time. . . . Of the thousands of men who were detained and questioned, not one has been publicly charged with terrorism."[30]

It was not surprising that law enforcement agents focused on men of Middle Eastern origin, given the terrorists involved in the 9/11 attacks were of Middle Eastern origin. However, lengthy incarceration of innocent individuals, coupled with verbal and physical abuse, did little to encourage the cooperation of the Middle Eastern community in preventing future acts of terrorism.[31] In fact, if police authorities want the intelligence that can only be provided by members of the Middle Eastern community, they must first treat that community with respect while protecting their civil rights and dignity. A controversy over this in the NYPD centered on a group of New Jersey residents, mosques, and organizations who "filed a federal lawsuit against the City of New York, accusing the NYPD of violating their constitutional rights by targeting them for surveillance on the basis of their religion—outside of mosques, in Muslim student group meetings, and at religious schools. The lawsuit could help define how far investigators can go in the name of national security."[32] The NYPD responded that their actions are necessary to safeguard against future terrorism.

### Legislation on Profiling

**SAGE Journal Article:**
Racial Profiling and
Postmodern Society

The controversy over biased enforcement by some police officers has reached a critical point. As one attempt to control this form of police misconduct, most states have passed legislation referred to as **mandatory data collection**, which requires police to record detailed information on the race or ethnicity of persons they encounter and to attend sensitivity training.

As mentioned, in the effort to determine how much racial profiling exists, various communities or states have introduced legislation mandating that officers record race and ethnicity. The concern with confronting racial profiling where it exists is easy to understand and appropriate. However, as often happens, the legislation may have numerous unintended consequences.

Such legislation may cause officers (including all those who do not participate in racial profiling) to focus on exactly the characteristics they should ignore as a basis for making stops or arrests. Such reporting clearly causes officers to focus on racial and ethnic characteristics precisely because they have to record them. Officers must learn to note racial and ethnic data once the stop has occurred, not as a reason for the stop.

Officers may feel pressure to come up with the right numbers by the end of their shift. Emphasis on the numbers can lead to intentional misreporting. If officers feel the numbers are more important than the quality of their interactions with the public, they may develop their own quota systems. On the one hand, this may lead to false reporting or motivate officers to not make stops or arrests that they would normally make because they fear being reprimanded for stopping too many persons of a particular race or ethnicity. On the other hand, data collection and analysis can be an excellent defense against allegations of biased enforcement when the analysis shows no evidence of such enforcement styles.

Solving such dilemmas is difficult precisely because discrimination in law enforcement can occur in a variety of contexts, ranging from traffic stops, to airport screenings, to field interrogations, to complaints of providing shabby services.

### Driving or Walking While Black

■ **Mandatory
Data Collection:**
Primarily in response to
the racial profiling issues
associated with the late
1990s and early 2000s,
the federal government
and each individual
state mandated that law
enforcement agencies
maintain data regarding
various demographic
issues during police
stops of vehicles

Police officers frequently respond to calls from the public concerning "suspicious persons." In some cases, the only thing "suspicious" about the person is his or her race. In a far too common scenario, Whites observing young Blacks in predominantly White neighborhoods may regard them as suspicious persons. They call the police and then watch to see what happens.

No matter how obvious the racial bias of the caller, the police still have to decide what to do. If the officer does not respond, he or she may be criticized for failing to do his or her duty, especially if a problem does occur. And common sense suggests to the officer that something should be done. Taking no action goes against the training the officer has received. If the officer does respond, the manner in which this occurs makes all the difference. The officer's assumptions about what constitutes "suspicious" conduct, as well as the law, influence the manner of the response.

If the officer takes a low-key approach and has some competence and skill in questioning members of the public, the situation may resolve without incident. Further, when the police respond, members of the public are less compelled to take matters into their own hands.

If the stop or questioning becomes harassing in nature, this tends to inflame the situation and feeds the individual's and the public's belief that the police routinely act with racial bias. If an officer tells the young Black man to "move along" or to "go back to your own neighborhood" or threatens to take (unjustified) official action, this tends to be seen as biased enforcement.

Public perception that the police engage in profiling is not limited to minority communities. The Gallup organization conducted numerous national polls to gauge these issues, and the results are summarized below.

- When racial profiling was defined as "police officers stop motorists of certain racial or ethnic groups because the officers believe that these groups are more likely than others to commit certain types of crimes," 59% of the adults surveyed believed this practice to be widespread, regardless of the respondent's race or ethnicity. In addition, 81% of the respondents disapproved of this practice.

- More than 4 out of 10 African American respondents believed they had been stopped by the police because of their race at some time. Moreover, of those, 6 out of 10 said they had been stopped three or more times. The responses varied significantly by age and gender within the African American community: ". . . it is black men, and especially young black men, aged 18 [to] 34, who are most likely to report having been stopped because of their race."[33]

- When respondents were asked to give their opinions of both their local and their state police, among Whites there was barely a difference, with 85% giving favorable opinions of their local police and 87% giving favorable opinions of their state police. Researchers stated that Blacks had a less favorable opinion of both, with 58% having a favorable opinion of their local police, and 64% of state troopers. Once again, age was a significant factor. More than 50% of young Black men, aged 18 to 34, had unfavorable opinions of both groups of police. Unfavorable opinions of the police dropped to 36% among the respondents in the age group of 35- to 49-year-olds.[34]

- When respondents were asked during interactions with their local and state police if they felt they were treated unfairly, race, age, and gender seemed to account for the most pronounced differences. For Whites, the number of those who reported being treated unfairly was small—7% for local police, and 4% for state police. Black respondents reported quite differently—27% for local police, and 17% for state police. When age was factored in, 53% of Black men, aged 18 to 34, reported being treated unfairly by local police, and 29% reported being treated unfairly by state police.[35]

- A comprehensive plan involving policy reform, officer training, and voluntary data collection may help in this regard.[36] Ultimately, however, the issue of racism must be dealt with by the larger society if biased enforcement and racial profiling are to be alleviated.

- The practice of profiling by race, ethnicity, religion, or national origin runs counter to what is arguably the core principle of U.S. democracy: that humans are created equal, and are entitled to be treated equally by the government, irrespective of immutable characteristics like skin color, faith, and ethnic or national origin.[37] (See Chapter 11.)

### Research on Police Discrimination

Research indicates that African Americans and Hispanics are significantly more dissatisfied with the police than Whites.[38] Neighborhood crime conditions, direct experiences with police, and mass media representations of police have all been found to impact residents' attitudes toward police.[39] Hispanics and African Americans hold more critical views

of police based on their disproportionate adverse experiences with police, exposure to negative media depictions of police, and residence in high-crime neighborhoods where policing practices may be contentious. However, a 2011 analysis involving an anonymous mailed survey of over 16,000 residents of a large western city (focusing on individual and community-level relationships between race or ethnicity and willingness to cooperate with the police in a community anticrime initiative) found that, contrary to previous research, African Americans who responded to the survey reported a greater willingness to work with the police than did White respondents.[40] The results, in part, rely on the specific survey questions about a willingness to work with the police. There were other limitations to the study as well. Still, both the nature of prior experiences with police and perceptions of the police based on encounters detailed by others appear to be important in determining a person's willingness to work with the police.[41] Citizens' perceived procedural justice during personal contacts with the police is related to their evaluations of the ability of police to keep their communities safe from serious violence.[42]

**Legal cynicism** (is a cultural orientation in which the law and the agents of its enforcement are viewed as illegitimate, unresponsive, and ill equipped to ensure public safety) and often exists in high-crime neighborhoods.[43] In neighborhoods characterized by high levels of legal cynicism, crimes are much less likely to lead to an arrest than in neighborhoods where citizens view the police more favorably.

One survey of youths enrolled in public high school found race to be one of the most powerful variables in explaining public attitudes toward the police. The researchers found that in this specific sample, "both African Americans and Latinos who had been stopped and disrespected by the police were less willing to assist them and less likely to believe that the police care about their neighborhoods."[44] They suggested that adverse contact between police officers and such youths might have an additive effect on juveniles' reactions to the

■ **Legal Cynicism:**
A cultural orientation in which the law and the agents of its enforcement are viewed as illegitimate, unresponsive, and ill equipped to ensure public safety

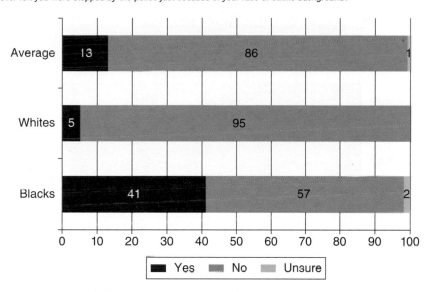
police. The authors concluded that youth are more inclined to cooperate with the police if they have been treated fairly and with respect. It is important to measure the impact of accumulated negative experiences in order to better understand police–minority relations.[45]

Responses from a Gallup poll taken in 2011, concerning the honesty and ethical standards and amount of confidence expressed with respect to the police by different racial and ethnic groups, address this issue and are shown in Figure 12.4.

A study of Taser use found a moderate relationship between race and ethnicity and such use.[46] Hispanic suspects were twice as likely as Whites to have Tasers used against them. Hispanic ethnicity, although not the primary determinant of Taser use, did increase the likelihood that a suspect would be subdued with a Taser. Similarly, another study examined police officer decision making during automobile stops to determine whether Black and Hispanic drivers were searched as frequently as nonminorities, and the researchers found that Blacks are overrepresented among searches overall and among searches involving greater officer discretion to search.[47] However, after introducing other explanatory variables, researchers concluded that factors other than minority status may provide explanations for the searches. Specifically, minorities are differentially involved in searches, because police frequently engage minorities under circumstances consistent with searches, suggesting that it is the social context of the stop—rather than the race or ethnicity of the driver—that primarily influences searches. A study of some 36,000 traffic stops found that perceived culpability is the primary reason that searches are performed for the entire sample of traffic stops as well as those for Black and White subsamples.[48] Of course, what constitutes culpability is subjective and could be influenced by stereotype.

A 2003 study suggested that race and ethnicity may be more important in citizens' assessments of police officer demeanor than in performance assessment and that the media had little effect on assessments of either performance or demeanor.[49] The study concluded that the police can improve public opinion by increasing informal contacts with citizens and can increase approval of their job performance by "participating in community meetings, increasing officers' visibility in neighborhoods, and talking

*Respondents' Ratings of the Honesty and Ethical Standards of the Police by Race:*

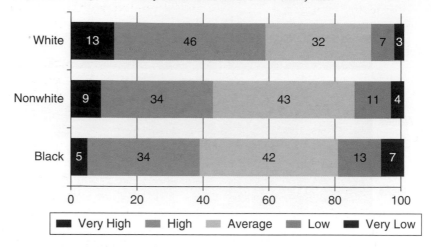

*Reported Public Confidence in Police by Race:*

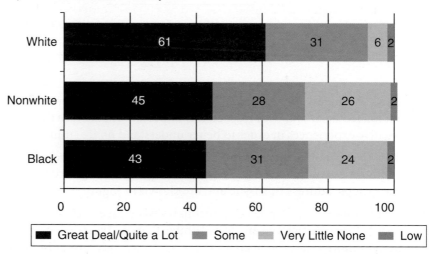

*Source:* Adapted from Sourcebook of Criminal Justice Statistics Online. Retrieved May 29, 2012, from http://www.bing.com/search?q=sourc ebook+of+criminal+justice+statistics&form=MSNH14&qs=AS&sk=AS1&pq=sourcebook&sp=2&sc=8-10&x=121&y=20.

with citizens," at least in what they refer to as disorderly neighborhoods.[50] However, more recent research found that attitudes about the prevalence of racial profiling are susceptible to the manner in which the media construct incidents of police misconduct.[51]

Negative stereotypes are often inaccurate or based on fear, or worse, and their persistence makes sharing a definition of the situation or mutual understanding difficult, if not impossible. Young Arab Americans became a focus of police attention following the events of 9/11. As might be expected, encounters between the police and Arab Americans have increased since then. One study examined how the terrorist attacks affected relationships between the police and residents in Arab American neighborhoods.[52] Among the difficulties noted were mutual distrust between Arab American communities and law enforcement, lack of cultural awareness among law enforcement officers, language barriers, and residents' concerns about immigration status. Residents of some Arab American communities indicated that they feared law enforcement agencies, "especially federal ones, more than acts of hate or violence, despite an increase in hate crimes. They specifically cited immigration enforcement, surveillance, and racial profiling"[53] as the source of fear, which is concerning, because more than 80% of hate crimes involve serious behaviors, including violent crimes such as rape or other sexual assault, robbery, or assault.[54] Even though minorities may be fearful of crime, they are often hesitant to report even serious crimes to the police, making it difficult, if not impossible, for the police to solve such crimes.

There are an estimated 5 to 7 million Muslims in the United States representing a number of different nationalities and ethnicities.[55] These U.S. Muslims likely represent the best source of information regarding those who have been dangerously radicalized within their communities, and it is critical to gather such information for counterterrorism efforts. It would be much easier to gather such information if police officers had accurate perceptions and understandings of the Muslim population. A relatively small study of the knowledge and stereotypes held by police commanders concerning Muslims found that a majority did not hold negative stereotypes of Muslims; this was especially true with respect to police personnel who had participated in a residential program with Muslims. Still, some officers were not eager to learn from or about Muslims. And a study based on interviews with Muslim Americans found support for the notion that perceived procedural justice of police activities is important in establishing cooperation with the police.[56] The researchers found room for improvement among police commanders in understanding both Muslims and Islam.

## CASE IN POINT 12.1

### Use "Terrorist" Label Carefully

An article in *USA Today* describes an analysis by Professor Tung Yin who found that race and religion impact views of terrorism to the extent that similar crimes tend to be viewed differently in the United States when the perpetrators are Muslim or of Arab descent. Ideas about what constitutes terrorism and who is likely to commit it may have an effect on both the police and the courts.

Stereotyping all Muslims as terrorists is clearly unfair, and those investigating alleged terrorism cases run the risk of failing to consider non-Muslims as suspects. Or, in an attempt not to stereotype Muslims as terrorists, authorities may ignore warnings that might otherwise point to Muslims as suspects. "Those who defend American Muslims are tempted at times to obscure the religious and terrorist angles when Muslims do perpetrate violence; this to protect Muslims from reprisals . . ."

"If the religious dimension helps identify a suspect, and if the t-word helps law enforcement and the public understand the nature of an act of mass violence, its use is justified. If the label fits, apply it. But fairly, please."

1. Using labels like "terrorist" is a slippery slope. Under what circumstances should law enforcement use the label, and under what circumstances should the label not be used?

2. Members of the Arab and Muslim communities are especially sensitive to labels like "terrorist." How can law enforcement investigate and prevent terrorist acts, some of which are perpetrated by persons of Arab and Muslim descent, without unfairly labeling law-abiding members of the Arab and Muslim communities?

3. In what ways can the Arab and Muslim communities assist law enforcement in identifying, preventing, and investigating terrorist acts?

*Source:* "Use 'terrorist' label carefully," by T. Krattenmaker, June 11, 2012. *USA Today,* p. 7A.

## ■ PUBLIC IMAGE OF THE POLICE

Although community relations programs are doomed to fail if the day-to-day human relations practices of participants are poor, publicizing the positive practices and programs of police departments can certainly affect the impression of the police in the minds of other citizens.

Department outreach, such as police literature, public-speaking engagements, websites, and department-sponsored programs, are all parts of police **public relations** efforts, as are policy and procedure and media relationships. The uniform of the officer, the symbol on the squad car, and the response of the dispatcher or receptionist at police headquarters all create an impression of the police and also fall within the public relations domain.

*Policy* consists of decisions, statements, and plans made by management in an attempt to influence public opinion. Ill-conceived policies, policies formulated but not acted on, or policies formulated but not explained or understood can hardly be expected to result in sound practice. The second component, *practice,* is the process of putting the policies into action.[57] In most police agencies, policies are formulated by the chief in consultation with staff and city manager, mayor, and councilpersons, while putting the policies into operation is typically a task of rank-and-file officers.

As in most areas of police operations, good communication is essential, perhaps in particular in the area of public relations. Policies developed without communication and input from those they will affect or those who will eventually be responsible for putting them into action are often of little value. Many police administrators fail at implementing effective community relations programs. Some administrators recognize the importance of policy making and work hard at developing policies with appropriate input. Some recognize the importance of human relations and emphasize to every officer the importance of encounters with other citizens. Far fewer appear to recognize that policy making and practice are intimately intertwined and that policy makers and those who implement the policies must be in constant communication to allow for feedback and evaluation on a routine basis.

■ **Public Relations:** From the police perspective, they include all of the activities in which police engage while attempting to develop or maintain a favorable public image

Seattle police officer Debra Pelich, right, wears a video camera on her eyeglasses as she talks with Alex Legesse before a small community gathering in Seattle.

© AP Photo/Elaine Thompson

© AP Photo/Hector Mata

In preparation for immigration demonstrations, the Los Angeles Police Department mobilized public information officers. PIOs are responsible for establishing relationships with media outlets as well as performing outreach to community stakeholders.

Such feedback and evaluation should focus in an ongoing way on measuring and evaluating public opinion concerning the police, and on developing and implementing policies to maintain favorable public opinion or to improve it. Public relations is a continuous process, as conditions and opinions change. Public relations programs will maintain or lead to a favorable image only if they accurately reflect practices that are acceptable to the public.

## ■ POLICE IN THE COMMUNITY

The police sometimes feel separate from and in conflict with other citizens, but they are still members of the community in which they serve. Both groups are controlled by the same government, both pay taxes to support the police and other public service agencies, the children of both groups attend the same schools, and both share in the fate of the community. By and large, the police are recruited from, hired by, and sworn to serve this same community. Further, the functions of the police are essential to the community.

Emphasizing this common community membership is a key to improving relations.

A department that reflects the racial and ethnic composition of that community sends a message of willingness to participate as partners in the community. It shows a mentality of appreciation for the many benefits of having a diverse populace and representative workforce. These benefits include additional skills among the workforce, such as language, a familiarity with the locals, and more avenues for investigation, to name a few.

Active efforts to recruit qualified minorities into policing are essential in this regard, as are promotions based strictly on merit. A multiethnic police department will not be problem free, but it has a definite advantage in developing good community relations. In some California departments, White officers are already in the minority.

Innovative, regular training in human and public relations skills is an important requirement for police officers, as is training in cultural diversity. Cultural diversity or awareness programs are designed to familiarize police officers with people and customs that are different from those they are used to. Assigning an officer to police a ghetto

**Web Link:**
Do diverse police forces treat their communities more fairly than almost-all-white ones like Ferguson's?

or barrio without such an introduction virtually guarantees that he or she will have problems. Programs should be designed to provide officers with some structure and preparation, to anticipate the types of crises that might arise in the community, and to help alert officers to the potential possibilities that might occur.

The types of multicultural issues discussed in this chapter are not unique to the United States or U.S. policing, but occur in all societies where diverse populations exist.

### Cultural Diversity and Awareness Training

Training in cultural diversity typically focuses on improving communication skills, recognizing signs of prejudice and bias, understanding the perspectives of people of different backgrounds, and appreciating the benefits of diversity.[58] Before being assigned to a beat, officers should receive orientation on the various groups residing in the area. Further, as police agencies become more culturally diverse, internal problems may

## AROUND THE WORLD 12.1

### Introducing a Human Approach in Policing

A newspaper editorial in *The New Nation* (Dhaka, Bangladesh) points out that the responsibility of ensuring justice and security of the citizens in every country is vested with the police. In Bangladesh, while the government has taken some initiative to modernize police services, a colonial legacy remains in some areas of police activities. There are both internal and external pressures on the police to develop a more human approach to justice and security.

The article goes on to state that the more democratic a country, the more the police are respectful in dealing with citizens. In any country, the police face the challenge of building good relations with the citizens they serve. In Bangladesh, the police are ready to help citizens, and citizens definitely want more services from police. The author asks, "Then what is the problem?" and concludes that the problem is communication. Many people have a traditional fear of the police.

In recent years, some organizations and alliances have been working for good governance in policing by bringing the police and the public closer to ensure justice and security. In April 2004, six established nongovernmental organizations (NGOs) and academic centers joined together to form an alliance called Altus.

Altus works across continents to minimize the gap between the police and the public by forming a multicultural perspective to improve public safety and maintain justice. Altus helps public officials identify or develop empirically tested models of respectful policing, quality legal services for the poor, and other good practices.

Police Station Visitors Week (PSVW) is a global event organized by Altus to assess the quality of services delivered in the participating police departments, to identify some of the best practices in use by police, to strengthen the accountability of police to the local citizens whom they serve, and to promote human rights standards.

Bangladesh police cooperate in this event in an attempt to build closer ties between people and police. The five core categories of the police assessment are "community orientation, physical conditions, and equal treatment of the Public without bias based on age, gender, ethnicity, nationality, minority status, age or sexual orientation, transparency and accountability, and detention conditions."

1. What role does a "more human approach to justice" play in U.S. law enforcement?

2. How important is "communication" between U.S. law enforcement and its citizenry? Explain.

3. What steps can a police agency take to improve communication and cooperation with law enforcement?

*Source:* Adapted from an editorial. "Introducing human approach in policing," October 22, 2010. *The New Nation* (Dhaka, Bangladesh). Retrieved June 11, 2012, from http://infoweb.newsbank.com.ezproxy.wiu.edu/iw-search/we/InfoWeb?p_product=AWNB&p_theme=aggregated5&p_action=doc&p_docid=133055BC32A558E8&p_docnum=3&p_queryname=10.

develop, so training should address hate crimes, racial profiling, derogatory language, racial and ethnic slurs, and ethnic jokes in the context of the police organization.[59] The development of action plans that serve diverse communities and training sessions that include active participation and establishment of a meaningful context are equally important components of diversity training.[60]

Training programs require police administrators to recognize that multicultural relations require effort on behalf of every individual officer and the police management team. The former determine the nature of human relations in daily encounters; the latter, in consultation with these officers and the various publics in the jurisdiction, determine and evaluate the policies to be implemented and their effectiveness in practice.

## Police Responsiveness

Two key terms related to police success in multicultural relations are *responsiveness* and *accountability*. **Responsiveness** refers to the provision of appropriate police services promptly and competently and referrals to appropriate services outside of police jurisdiction. This requires that police administrators recognize and convey to the public that it may be impossible or inappropriate for the police to respond to all citizen requests for service.

Departments must use available resources according to established priorities and strategies, in partnership with the community. They must communicate those strategies clearly and assure the public that they take requests seriously.

Tulsa, Oklahoma, serves as an example of such efforts. Tulsa has seen a dramatic increase in the number of people whose primary language is Spanish and who may have limited proficiency in English. To overcome language barriers and cultural misunderstandings, the Tulsa Police Department (TPD) developed a strategic plan to improve services to these individuals.[61] The plan included information gathering, education, police–Hispanic liaisons, media relations, helplines with Spanish speakers, and a Spanish interpreters' ride-along program. The TPD has seen "substantial gains in law enforcement's positive influence within the Hispanic community and has enjoyed a healthy start to improving the trust and cooperation of those citizens."[62]

**Accountability** is the second key to police efforts to establish and maintain positive relationships with all segments of the community. As employees of the community they serve, police officers are accountable to their employers for their actions. Accountability may be accomplished in a variety of ways, ranging from periodic reports to the public on police activities, to annual reports, to developing and using an internal affairs unit, to cooperation in developing a civilian review board, to hearing complaints concerning the police, to establishing informative websites, to developing and implementing outreach programs for diverse segments of the community. (See Chapter 10.)

## The Community Role in Multicultural Relations

Aware or unaware, the community plays an important role in policing. Fully accepting this role allows the public more equality in working with the police. The police may be required to take the lead in developing community-relations efforts, but the public is an important part of the team necessary for the success of such efforts. If the community does not engage in open dialog and building positive relationships, police-initiated programs cannot be as effective as possible. To demonstrate good faith, community residents and civic action groups can develop programs to support police efforts and recognize police performance, such as informing the police during investigations and serving as witnesses in court.

Citizen oversight of the police was an established fact of life in U.S. law enforcement by the end of the 20th century. It existed in many large cities and steadily spread to smaller communities. The spread of oversight marked a momentous change since the tumultuous 1960s. Most important, citizen involvement in the complaint process was increasingly recognized as an important means for achieving police accountability.[63] (See Chapter 10.)

**Responsiveness:** Refers to the provision of appropriate police services promptly and competently, with appropriate referrals in cases not within agency jurisdiction

**Accountability:** Refers to the fact that the police are public employees and are therefore accountable to the public for their actions

### Citizen Complaints

Good community relations require that citizens feel free to discuss with appropriate authorities their complaints about police officer behavior. Systematic efforts to determine what those served by the police think of the services they receive should be an integral part of police management. Such efforts may be conducted by department personnel, by university personnel, or by private consultants and should attempt to establish a baseline of public opinion and then compare those opinions with related data that the department collects on a regular basis. A part of this process should include the developing and publicizing of policies related to citizen complaints. Citizens should know whom to contact and what to expect when they make such contact. Further, complainants should be kept advised of the efforts made to investigate their complaints and the final disposition of the complaint.

**Video Link:**
Police, upset citizens mediate differences

According to the 2003 Law Enforcement Management and Administrative Statistics (LEMAS) report, state and local law enforcement agencies with 100 or more sworn officers received more than 26,000 citizen complaints about officer use of force for the year 2002.[64] This figure breaks down to rates of 33 complaints per agency or 6.6 complaints per 100 full-time sworn personnel. About 8% of use-of-force complaints were sustained, meaning there was sufficient evidence to justify disciplinary action against the officer(s) involved.[65] The misuse of force is among the more serious complaints filed against police officers and represents a small minority of all citizen complaints, most of which are never brought to the attention of the authorities.

One relevant study examined citizen complaints filed against police officers in Florida, Illinois, Missouri, Pennsylvania, and Washington. Approximately 50% of all the complaints focused on the verbal conduct and overall demeanor of the officers. An additional quarter of the total complaints involved a wide variety of nonviolent, illegal conduct committed by officers on and off duty. The remaining quarter of complaints dealt with excessive force issues, once again by officers on and off duty.[66]

In an attempt to better understand police contacts with other citizens by investigating perceptions and behaviors during encounters that result in physical resistance and force, researchers used interviews with citizens who resisted or were accused of resisting lawful police commands and the officers who used force to control them. The research results indicated that officers and other citizens might focus on different issues when interacting. Police officers frequently used force to maintain their authority and in response to perceived threats. Individuals with whom the police interacted often admitted partial culpability and claimed they failed to acquiesce due to perceived procedural injustices.[67]

Many citizens who feel they have been abused or harassed by the police do not know how to file a complaint or fear retaliation from the officer involved or his or her colleagues if they do complain. Public relations messages indicating the desire of police administrators to know about such complaints, coupled with prompt, fair action when such complaints are received, can only help to improve community relations. Recognizing this fact, the Denver Police Department developed a **community–police mediation program** to address the challenges of resolving complaints in a timely manner and in a way that attempts to satisfy officers and community members. This process of determining the validity of allegations of misconduct has the potential to strengthen (or weaken) police–community relations.

**Community–Police Mediation Program:**
A voluntary process in which community members and officers sit down in a neutral and confidential setting facilitated by a professional mediator to discuss their differences

Mediation is a voluntary process in which community members and officers sit down in a neutral and confidential setting facilitated by a professional mediator to discuss their differences. This alternative to the traditional complaint-handling process provides an opportunity for each party to be heard and to consider the other's perspective about an incident. The intent is to promote mutual understanding so that similar situations can be prevented.[68]

Although efforts to improve the citizen complaint process are worthwhile, most citizens who have complaints about the police may never voice them directly to the police.[69] Some citizens who strongly support the police file complaints in the hope of helping the police improve.

### A Representative Workforce

Over the past 40 years, police departments have attempted to recruit more women and minorities into policing to more accurately reflect the community's demographics. Hiring minority officers legitimizes the department and helps the police to overcome obstacles to effective partnerships.

In discussing women and minorities in policing, it is important to acknowledge the impact of "tokenism." "Tokens" (members who comprise less than 15% of a group's total) may experience a variety of hardships in the workplace, ranging from feelings of heightened visibility, to isolation, to limited opportunities for advancement. Although most of the policing literature on tokens defines the concept in terms of gender, researchers examined tokenism as a function of gender, ethnicity, and race, paying particular attention to Latino officers.[70] Research revealed that, for the most part, token police officers do experience the effects of tokenism. All minorities experienced some level of tokenism; however, Black males and Black females experienced greater levels of tokenism than Latino officers.

## ■ WOMEN IN POLICING

As indicated earlier, when women enter a male-dominated workplace, they are often viewed as "tokens," at least initially. They are subjected to enhanced scrutiny and polarization from men, stereotyped, and passed over for promotions,[71] resulting in added stress on the job.

### Background

When police departments began hiring women in the 1800s, they sometimes hired widows of deceased officers as a kind of death benefit. Women were hired to guard other women or to protect the "moral safety" of young women. The first women in policing, thus, were charged with duties more akin to social work than law enforcement or order maintenance and were paid less than men.

During World War I, the task of policewomen was to keep prostitutes away from military camps and to assist in the return of runaway women and girls.[72] The "women's bureau" was a separate division; policewomen did not wear uniforms, nor were they armed. They typically received less pay than their male counterparts, though they were considerably better educated.[73]

During the Great Depression, most jobs were saved for men; during World War II, many women went to work for the police as dispatchers or clerical workers or to assist men. The 1950s and 1960s saw increasing numbers of women going into the field of policing and working toward more responsibility.

Not until the 1960s did opportunities for policewomen begin to improve. The President's Commission on Law Enforcement and the Administration of Justice (1967) found that policewomen could be an invaluable asset to modern law enforcement and recommended that their role be broadened to include patrol and investigative duties as well as administrative responsibilities. It was during this time that women were first given regular patrol duties. In 1972, Congress amended Title VII of the 1964 Civil Rights Act to prohibit discrimination by both private and public employers based on the sex of the applicant. At the same time, the FBI and the Secret Service appointed their first

**Author Video:**
Women and minorities in policing

female field agents. A number of cities (St. Louis, Washington, DC, and New York City) placed uniformed female officers in patrol positions and conducted studies to evaluate their performance. Throughout the remainder of the 20th century, women made some gains, albeit often hard won, in being hired in greater numbers and being promoted to positions of authority.[74]

Nationwide in 2013, as shown in Figure 12.5, 24.4% of full-time law enforcement officers were females, and 67.9% of full-time civilian law enforcement employees were females. Cities with populations of over 1 million inhabitants employed the highest percentage (17%) of female officers, while cities with populations of 10 to 25,000 employed the lowest percentage (7.9%) of full-time female officers. Cities with populations of 100,000 to 249,999 inhabitants had the highest percentage (74%) of female civilian law enforcement employees.[75]

A well-rounded and diversified police department should include an adequate share of women officers and administrators, as well as civilians. A 2010 study demonstrated that "female candidates are more likely to be college educated and less likely to receive citizen complaints, misconduct charges, or claims of excessive force than male officers. With rapidly evolving gender roles, women bring unique skills and competencies to enhance departments' service delivery strategies. By focusing efforts on attracting female candidates, agencies are likely to identify a valuable untapped resource."[76]

### Women of Color

In 2006, researchers concluded that several factors contributed to a significant proportion of Black women in municipal policing. First, Black women often see policing as an attractive option compared to the narrow ranges of occupations that are often open to them. Black women have been leaders in their communities, and serving as a police officer enables a Black woman to "wield power in the African American community and to work to alter an organization often viewed as oppressive."[77]

Figure 12.5 ■ Full-Time Law Enforcement Employees, Women, 2013

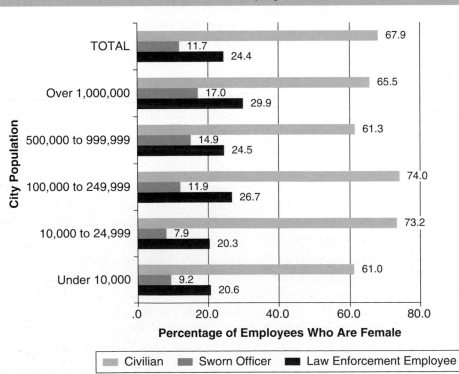

*Source:* Federal Bureau of Investigation (2013), *Crime in the United States* (Table 74).

Some use the term **double marginality** in discussing the stresses experienced by Black police officers, referring to the fact that Black officers were not fully accepted by their White coworkers and were also distrusted by other Blacks. The same term may be applied to women in police work who are not fully accepted as equals by their male coworkers and who often find other women (especially male officers' wives) somewhat suspect of their motives for entering police work. Based on these considerations, we might expect that policewomen would have relatively high turnover rates, and this appears to be the case in at least some departments.[78] Such turnover may be due to discrimination on behalf of male officers, lack of equal promotional opportunities, and the constant pressure to prove themselves.[79]

As might be expected, African American policewomen are even more likely to be viewed as outsiders within their own departments. There is evidence that they are often isolated from both White women and Black men on the force.[80]

### Challenges for Women Police Officers

Even though significant changes have occurred over the past decades with respect to integration of occupations by gender, some occupational groups have been slow to accept such changes. This is perhaps particularly true in occupations such as policing, which are imbued with traditional conceptions of masculinity as a required trait. The presence of women in what has typically been referred to as the police *fraternity* may undermine the sense of masculine identity that accompanies that subculture.

Studies of supervisors' attitudes toward policewomen are scarce, and those that do exist are conflicting. A Washington, DC, study, for example, indicated predominantly negative attitudes toward women officers on the part of supervisors, while studies in St. Louis and New York showed supervisors to be more positive.[81] One chief put it in these terms: "I could see all kinds of problems . . . jealous wives, injuries. . . . It was a headache I didn't want."[82]

With changes brought on by movements for equal rights for women, by hiring better educated officers, and as a result of competent performance of women in the police role, these sex role stereotypes continue to change. One study, for example, found that there has been a small shift toward more favorable attitudes concerning female officers, but

**Audio Link:**
What Changes as Women Rise through Law Enforcement's Ranks

**■ Double Marginality:** Refers to the fact that Black officers were not fully accepted by their White coworkers and were also distrusted by other Blacks

It wasn't that long ago when it was commonplace to see no women working in the patrol division of most police agencies. Today, the situation has changed somewhat with women joining the ranks of law enforcement agencies.

© iStockphoto.com/inhauscreative

about 20% of male officers still did not want to work with female officers on patrol.[83] "Perhaps the problem is that some hard-liners persist in the argument that such changes [more female officers] represent a feminization of policing; that real policing was, and still is, the so-called masculine image of crime-fighting."[84]

The negative attitudes of policemen toward policewomen are most often based on personal belief, not actual experience: "No research has shown that strength is related to an individual's ability to manage successfully a dangerous situation. . . . There are no reports in the literature of bad outcomes because a policewoman did not have enough strength or aggression."[85] In spite of the defenses of policewomen, many male police officers continue to be highly critical of them.

Others have noted that agility, a cool head, and good communication skills may be more important than strength in dangerous situations.[86] Some suggest that the presence of a policewoman may actually help to defuse a potentially violent situation.[87]

Some studies found that, while citizens generally believed policemen were preferable in violent situations, they also generally approved of policewomen.[88]

> Police work requires thinking and courage. It can be a physical job, yes, but it's first and foremost a mental exercise. As big and strong as I am, I've been tossed around like a rag doll—and any idiot with a gun and a will to do so can easily shoot me dead. We survive and get the job done by using our heads. I would sooner work with a female cop with brains and guts than any male cop who's stupid or timid, regardless of the size of his biceps.[89]

In spite of these concerns, in some communities, policewomen have been accepted by male coworkers and the public alike. Further, there is evidence that minorities and better-educated officers are more likely to accept women, and their numbers are increasing. Because women account for about 51% of the population, and because the evidence is clear that they are capable of performing a wide variety of police functions, they should be viewed as a valuable asset in the struggle to make police departments more representative of the communities they serve and, ultimately, in the effort to reintegrate police and community. The presence of female officers diversifies views on policy and practice in policing and demonstrates that women can successfully perform policing tasks.[90]

## ■ MINORITY POLICE OFFICERS

Some of the most problematic encounters involving the police occur between White police officers and minority citizens. In a sense, the police are a reflection of the society and its dysfunctions. Encounters between the police and Blacks, Hispanics, Native Americans, Asians, and Middle Easterners indicate that significant hostility remains in the larger social context as a result of racist attitudes, historical distrust, and past discrimination. (See Figure 12.6.)

Because the police are a reflection of society, it is not surprising that they sometimes have poor working relationships with minority group members. As previously mentioned, the national debate about policing and race has reignited in the wake of the shootings of unarmed Black men. The Ferguson Police Department in Missouri has 50 White officers and three Black officers. The town of Ferguson is 67% Black. Diversifying the police department is viewed as a potential solution to the lack of trust between communities of color and the police. The U.S. Department of Justice considers increased police diversity to be one of a series of reforms that include new training practices, new hiring practices, and a shift in departmental culture.

Some researchers are delving into the question of precisely what effect greater diversity may have on policing practices and police effectiveness. A 2015 study is measuring

## POLICE ⬡ STORIES  12.2

## Connie Koski, Professor and Former Police Officer

Women in federal, state, and local law enforcement agencies have, in many ways, overcome numerous obstacles in employment and promotion. Additionally, the research on women in policing has generally transitioned from assessing whether they "can they do the job" to "how they do the job differently" (and, occasionally, more effectively than their male counterparts). Women in law enforcement have come a long way. Yet, scholarly research shows that women in law enforcement still have a long way to go.

One of my graduate school professors told a kind of story that is rarely heard anymore. She became the first woman officer in her precinct in a large metropolitan police department in the Southwest in the late 1970s. Since she was the only woman, they had no locker room for her, so they assigned her to the janitor's closet within the precinct. She would come to work to find her uniform tied in knots or covered in fecal matter, or was locked in the closet while preparing for her shift while her male counterparts stood outside mocking her.

I began my career in the early 1990s and, prior to employment, I had been a police Explorer with an agency that not only readily accepted me and the other women in my group, but was extremely supportive of my decision to pursue a career in law enforcement. I knew there would still be some difficulties, but assumed these would be few. Shortly after I and another woman were hired, we attended a retirement party for a male officer who had served the department for 30 years. Many of our department's senior officers, administrators, and recent retirees were there, and one of them approached me and my coworker and began to fervently explain why women did not belong in law enforcement. This enraged my coworker, and she began to argue her case as to why he was incorrect. A very tall man with large hands, he held up his right hand and said to her, "Put your hand on my hand." Perplexed, my female coworker, a woman of approximately 5'7" who was in excellent physical shape, placed her hand on his hand, as requested. To our surprise, her hand was amazingly smaller than this man's hand. He smiled wryly and simply stated, "That, ladies, is why women should not be police officers!" With a wink, he smugly walked away and left us fuming while all of the male officers who had gathered around laughed and toasted this fellow with their drinks.

In fact, I had a male training officer who had been trained by an officer with similar attitudes and who outwardly exhibited his disapproval of women as police officers. He told me to sit in the passenger seat of the patrol car and keep my mouth shut because I had nothing of value to say. As time went on, my female coworker and I worked extremely hard to prove ourselves to our male coworkers in the face of much resistance. We eventually gained the respect of the vast majority of them. By the time we became field training officers (FTOs) ourselves, many of the incoming male officers looked up to us and our knowledge and experience. We watched as our agency began promoting many of the women within the ranks, and eventually one of our female coworkers even became chief of police.

Success stories such as these exist all across the country today. Although barriers to employment for women in law enforcement are far fewer than just a decade ago, there are still many obstacles to acceptance. As recently as 2014, in fact, I was having a conversation with a young male officer who worked for a university police department in the South. When I asked if his department had any female officers on the force, he rolled his eyes and smugly stated, "No, thank god. Female officers are basically useless!"

As a retired female officer and now college professor, I make it a point to enhance both my male and my female students' understanding of just how far women in law enforcement have come. I also make sure to highlight the unique attributes women bring to the job. Whenever possible, I also seek out opportunities for them to explore female officers' perspectives and personal experiences through the use of speakers, ride-alongs, and case studies. I would argue that college professors, dedicated academy instructors, top administrators, and effective FTOs could be the greatest agents of social change with regard to the future of women in law enforcement.

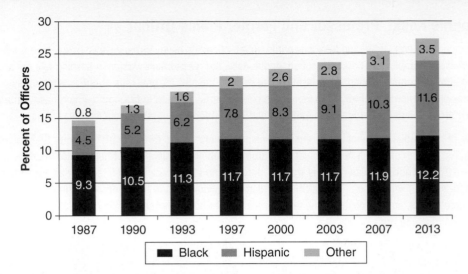

**Figure 12.6 ■ Minority Representation Among Full-Time Sworn Personnel in Local Police Departments, 1987–2013**

About 130,000 minority local police were employed in 2013. The total represented an increase of about 78,000 (150%) since 1987. Minority representation among local police officers increased from 14.6% in 1987 to 22.6% in 2000 to 27.3% in 2013.

*Source:* B. Reaves, NCJ 248677 (Washington, DC: Bureau of Justice Statistics, May 2015).

police effectiveness from the perspective of both the department and the community. For the police, effectiveness is measured by the clearance rate of crimes, which is how often crimes are solved. For the community, the measure of effectiveness is the level of community complaints.

### African American Police Officers

*Background*

During slavery, it was, of course, unthinkable that a Black man could have authority over any White man. Indeed, White police officers, especially (but not exclusively) in the southern states where the majority of African Americans lived, enforced racist laws. Early "slave patrols" protected the economic order of the South and ensured that no rebellions were able to form and that runaway slaves were apprehended and returned to their owners.[91] Even after the Civil War and Emancipation, violence against Blacks persisted or grew worse, and vigilantism took hold, most infamously in the form of the Ku Klux Klan. The legal order has changed over time, but it has its roots in slavery, segregation, and discrimination, all of which the police were responsible for upholding.

Some would argue that the full potential of police professionalism first envisioned during the Reform Era did not even begin to include Blacks or other minorities until the civil rights era of the 1960s, which led to a more progressive political climate and the election of African American mayors in some cities.[92] (See Chapter 2.)

> It was that movement, led primarily by black Americans, and that political empowerment that finally began to produce the putative benefits of professional policing: a fairer distribution of police services, less use of deadly force, greater respect for individual rights, and equal opportunity for minorities within the Nation's police departments. Without that movement, the promise of professional policing would have remained hollow.[93]

### Why Become Police?

Research noted some time ago that police work is attractive to Blacks for the same reasons it is attractive to Whites—reasonable salary, job security, and reasonable pension.[94] This idea was supported in 2008:

> Despite the passage of time, many . . . conclusions remain valid: a dislike of police in general is still present in many minority communities; despite social differences between black and white police officers, the job is seen as a basis for cooperation that overrides race; overt appeals from suspects for racial solidarity fall on deaf ears; and African Americans are more likely to become police officers because of the benefits in a civil service job rather than wanting to be a police officer *per se*.[95]

### Department Benefits

Police departments have a good deal to gain by hiring African Americans in terms of **protective coloration.** Black police officers can often gather information that would be extremely difficult for White officers to gather; having Black police officers on the force may make charges of racial brutality against the police less likely; and federal funding is partly dependent on equal employment opportunity and affirmative-action programs. Nonetheless, the general premise behind the effort to increase the number of Black police officers involves improving police–community relations while decreasing biased police behavior.[96]

It is also obvious that White police officers, whether undercover or not, will arouse suspicion in predominantly Black groups. And with respect to police brutality toward minority groups, it is apparent that when Black police officers resort to the use of force in dealing with Black citizens, the issue of interracial brutality is avoided (though the issue of police brutality remains).

The best reason for hiring and promoting qualified Black applicants is the fact that a tremendous amount of talent is wasted if they are excluded from police work. Because there is no evidence that White officers perform the policing function better than Black officers, it is ethically and morally appropriate to hire applicants who are Black. Further, integrated police departments are more representative, and Black officers may serve as much-needed role models in the community. In addition, Black leadership may account for movement toward more progressive and effective strategies overall.

### Challenges for African American Police Officers

Black police officers confront a number of problems in addition to those confronted by their White counterparts. Although many Black officers are assigned to police the ghettos in hopes of alleviating racial tensions, not all Black citizens prefer Black officers to White. Black officers sometimes have more trouble dealing with Black citizens than do White officers.[97] As mentioned previously, Black police officers suffer from double marginality resulting from the fact that they are sometimes distrusted by their White counterparts and are often viewed as traitors by other members of the African American community.[98] Black officers may be perceived as more Black than blue (i.e., police oriented) by White officers and more blue than Black by others in the Black community. When researchers examined whether racial variation in public evaluations of police behavior is moderated by the race of the officer, they found that officer race may be an important factor in shaping citizen perceptions of police stops, particularly among Black citizens.[99] This finding provides some evidence that increasing the number of minority officers may be one viable option for improving citizen–officer relations.

Black police officers, like their White colleagues, must arrest unwilling suspects, intervene in domestic squabbles, and keep order on the streets. They represent the interests of order, property, and the status quo in some neighborhoods where large numbers of unemployed minority youth, among others, do not share a commitment to the same values.[100]

■ **Protective Coloration:** Refers to the facts that Black police officers can often gather information that would be extremely difficult for White officers to gather; that having Black police officers on the force may make charges of racial brutality against the police less likely; and that federal funding is partly dependent on equal employment opportunities and affirmative-action programs

A 2006 study found that a police officer's race has a direct influence on arrest outcomes and that differences exist between White and Black officers concerning the decision to arrest. They found that "white officers were more likely to arrest suspects than black officers, but black suspects were more likely to be arrested when the decision maker was a black officer."[101] Encounters between Black officers and White citizens do not always proceed smoothly either. Black officers report being subjected to racial slurs, mistrust, and avoidance. Some Whites are also concerned about whether Black officers will respond first as members of their race or as police officers when dealing with interracial situations. In some parts of the country, Blacks in positions of authority are uncommon, and Whites are apprehensive about recognizing the authority of an African American man or woman.

Black police officers have typically reported that their relationships with White officers, at least while on duty, are satisfactory. They appear to be confident that White officers will back them up in emergency situations, and they indicate that they would do the same for White officers. However, "despite an outward emphasis on the unity of blue over any division between black and white, black and white police officers remain two distinct shades of blue, with distinct attitudes toward each other and the community they serve."[102] In some instances, Black officers have formed their own associations in police departments, with agendas different from, and sometimes in sharp contrast to, those of White officers.

## Hispanic Police Officers

There is little information about Hispanic police officers, in part because their numbers have been very small until recently. In the last few years, the number of Hispanic officers—especially in large departments—has greatly increased. The LAPD has over 50% Hispanic officers.[103]

Police contacts with Hispanics are already frequent and are likely to increase dramatically as this community increases in size. Without a Spanish-speaking workforce, these contacts are likely to be somewhat problematic because of language and culture differences. In addition to whatever immediate reason the police have for initiating contact with Hispanics, they may also be dealing with illegal immigrants, who can be deported if detected and reported to Immigration and Customs Enforcement (ICE). Fears about this scenario run high in immigrant communities.

In one study, just under half (46%) of Hispanics expressed confidence that police officers would *not* use excessive force on suspects, and 45% were confident the police would treat Hispanics fairly.[104]

### Challenges for Hispanic Police Officers

There are some community-specific barriers to diversifying the workforce and creating a more representative police agency. Education is one such barrier. A study by the Pew Hispanic Center discovered that only 16% of Latino high school graduates earn four-year college degrees by age 29, compared with 37% of non-Hispanic Whites and 21% of African Americans.[107] Others concluded that college education is still disproportionately inaccessible to both Blacks and Hispanics, raising the possibility that a college-degree requirement for entry-level officers may be discriminatory in its effect.[108]

The language barrier, physical size requirements,[109] the general belief that Hispanics are not highly sought after by police departments, and the belief that other occupations or professions were more highly prized by Hispanics probably account for the relatively small number of Hispanic officers in the past.

## Asian Police Officers

Although the highest concentrations of Asian Americans are in Hawaii and California, Asian immigrants and refugees have developed large and growing populations

**Exhibit 12.2**

## Clarifying Terminology

The term *Hispanic* or *Latino* often implies that all members of these minorities are the same regardless of country of origin or ethnic background. This, of course, is not the case, and it is often helpful to the police to be aware of the differences in both language and customs.[105]

According to the U.S. Census Bureau, "Hispanic or Latino" refers to a person of Cuban, Mexican, Puerto Rican, South or Central American, or other Spanish culture or origin regardless of race.[106]

throughout the country.[110] Still, either a very small fraction or none of the police officers in most departments are Asian American. One of the reasons may be that Asian parents—many of whom endured the upheaval of immigration—have high educational ambitions for their children and do not value police work.[111] Many Asian families consider police work to be too dangerous an occupation for their sons and daughters.[112] Furthermore, Asian experiences with corrupt police officers in their country have resulted in many mature Asians expecting that U.S. police officers are also corrupt, unhelpful to citizens, and untrustworthy.[113] Another study concluded that the majority of Chinese immigrants rated police positively in overall performance and specific areas of effectiveness, integrity, and demeanor.[114]

As the Asian American population increases, along with crime rates in some Asian American communities, and as Asian Americans become more organized in pursuit of equality, the need for Asian American police officers increases as well. Although there is little information about Asian American police officers, one study of Chinese American officers in 1987 indicated that Chinese American police officers share many of the same problems as other minority officers.[115]

It appeared to researchers that Chinese American officers tend to distance themselves from other Chinese Americans in some ways, much as some officers who represent other minority groups tend to distance themselves from their racial or ethnic groups. It appears, also as with others, that they prefer to be viewed first and foremost as police officers, at least while on duty.

The Asian American force has grown significantly in New York City, from 200 officers in 1990 to over 2,100 in 2015, which represents 6% of the force's total, still below the city's 15% Asian American population. About half of these officers are Chinese American. Given their numbers, Asian American officers are assigned to all New York precincts, not just Asian neighborhoods.[116]

Other Asian minorities also require the attention of the police. Refugees from Vietnam, Cambodia, and Laos have formed enclaves in many urban areas, establishing their communities as their numbers increase. Numerous officers have reported difficulties communicating with and understanding the culture of such refugees. Korean and Japanese neighborhoods also exist in cities around the United States, and residents of these areas may also present difficulties in terms of providing (or requesting) police services. Further, once thought to be crime-free areas, Asian neighborhoods are no longer viewed as such. Many have entrenched gang problems that are difficult for police to address if the community members mistrust them.

### LGBTQ Police Officers

Less is known about other minorities in policing, although the body of research is growing. What we know about lesbian, gay, bisexual, transgender, and questioning (LGBTQ) people in policing suggests that successful integration of this population

© Richard Levine/Alamy

NYPD officers from the Gay Officers Action League (GOAL) march in the annual Gay Pride Parade on Fifth Avenue in New York.

into law enforcement is yet to be achieved. As a result, most LGBTQ police officers do not openly admit their sexual orientation for fear that fellow officers will view them negatively.[117] Those officers who openly admit their sexuality frequently find themselves ostracized and the target of jokes.[118] Whether a bias against LGBTQ officers emerges on the job due to unfavorable contact with this population or whether discrimination is based on preemployment conceptions is unknown.

In the past, being an LGBTQ police officer was grounds for dismissal, but this type of employment discrimination is no longer officially condoned. Still, harassment of LGBTQs became such a widespread issue that some police departments were compelled to enact a zero-tolerance policy toward homophobic actions.[119] In fact, LGBTQs have filed lawsuits against police departments claiming denial of employment based on their same-sex preference (see, for example, *Childers v. Dallas Police Department*[120]). In recent years, some metropolitan police departments, such as those in Los Angeles, New York, and Seattle, have actively recruited officers from the LGBTQ community.[121] In what may well be an unusual circumstance, one smaller department in South Carolina was embroiled in a political and controversial dismissal of an openly lesbian chief of the department in the town of Latta (population 1,400). Crystal Moore came to be highly regarded as chief, but was fired by the mayor, who claimed her sexual orientation was not a factor in the dismissal. The city council was attempting to have Moore reinstated.[122]

Some urban police departments have gone so far as to create LGBTQ liaison units, staffed by openly LGBTQ officers, to provide police response to the community.[123] Others, such as the Indianapolis Metropolitan Police Department, have participated in gay pride parades.[124]

**SAGE Journal Article:**
Shared Perceptions Among Lesbian and Gay Police Officers

One study in 2003 explored how police officers manage a homosexual orientation in a "potentially hostile environment."[125] The findings suggest that these officers support a more humane approach to policing and see themselves as particularly qualified to work within marginal communities. Despite the structural barriers of homophobia and sexism that tempered these officers' full acceptance and access to the police subculture, LGBTQ officers struggled to balance job demands with their sexual orientation, their gender, their race/ethnicity, and other dimensions of their identities.

### Recruiting and Retaining Minorities as Police Officers

Inside and outside of police departments, equal treatment—regardless of race, ethnicity, religion, or gender—is the foundation for a truly democratic society. The recruitment and promotion of qualified minority group members is essential. Understanding and communicating with men and women and different racial and ethnic groups that are characterized by different cultural values, attitudes, and beliefs are essential for any public servant in a multicultural, multiethnic society. In addition, minority group members who become police officers may serve as living proof that it is possible to "get up and get out" for minority youngsters who need such role models.

However, simply diversifying the workforce is not a complete solution to racism within or from the police department. And diversification can be handled badly, which can be counterproductive, especially if a department recruits and hires candidates for reasons other than their ability and competency. Whether qualified or not, minority group members are in the spotlight in many police organizations. Their behavior is critically scrutinized at every turn, making them feel as if they are on trial, increasing the stress under which they operate, which, in turn, may make it more difficult for them to perform well.

The solution to this dilemma is obvious but difficult to achieve. In simple terms, race, ethnicity, and gender should not be considerations when hiring or promoting police personnel. There is no evidence to support the belief that any of these factors directly determines success or lack of success in policing.

Eliminating gender and racial factors in the hiring and promotional process means developing tests that are not inherently biased in terms of such factors.

## CHAPTER SUMMARY

Policing in a multicultural and multiethnic society is fraught with problems. Successful policing requires both knowledge and understanding of various cultures, races, ethnic groups, sexual orientation, age, mental stability, and gender. Police–community relations are all critical to effective policing. Avoiding such practices as biased enforcement and racial profiling and promoting proper handling of citizen complaints is also necessary if the public is to believe in the legitimacy of the police.

Prejudice and stereotyping are influences across all of society, not just among the police. The police cannot solve the problem of diversity by themselves. They can and do develop and implement community programs and training oriented toward improving relationships with a wide variety of groups, but public cooperation is needed if these programs are to prove successful. Police responsiveness and accountability are prerequisites to obtaining such support.

Judging by the numbers, minority officers have made progress in achieving representation commensurate with their proportion of the general population. Although they have the same legal rights and responsibilities as other police officers, they may still face discrimination in regard to duty assignments and promotions, for example. Numerous agencies have attempted to eliminate discrimination in hiring and promoting practices. However, this has proven to be a difficult and complex task, as there are educational and cultural barriers that hinder minority recruitment efforts.

As a result of these factors, court decisions, and civil rights legislation, the police entry-level and promotional requirements have changed in some departments. Some fear that police agencies are lowering their standards; others maintain that unbiased recruiting without sacrificing standards is possible.

Simply inserting women and minorities into the existing culture of a department is not the answer to addressing public mistrust, officer morale, and litigation against the police. Departments that voluntarily diversify their personnel perhaps have a more progressive and inclusive culture all around, so that the stereotype has no place or relevance, either within the department or in encounters with the public.

## KEY TERMS

- Police–community relations 279
- Stereotypes 282
- Occupational discrimination 285
- Psychological harassment 285
- Mandatory data collection 288
- Legal cynicism 290
- Public relations 294
- Responsiveness 297
- Accountability 297
- Community–Police Mediation Program 298
- Double marginality 301
- Protective coloration 305

## DISCUSSION QUESTIONS

1. Discuss the historical origins of some of the current problems in police relations with various racial or ethnic minority groups.

2. What characteristics of a multiethnic, industrial, democratic society make police–community relations particularly problematic?

3. As reflected in public opinion surveys, what is the general perception of the police? What are some of the important factors in determining these perceptions?

4. List and discuss some specific steps the police can take to help improve relations with diverse communities. List and discuss the same thing from the public perspective.

5. What is the impact of biased law enforcement on police–community relations?

6. Why and how have women been excluded from police work over the years?

7. Based on the research relating to the performance of policewomen on patrol, are you convinced that policewomen are as capable as policemen? Why or why not?

8. Why and how have member of racial and ethnic minority groups been excluded from police work?

9. What are the basic advantages to police departments in hiring members of racial or ethnic minorities?

10. What stresses do minority officers experience in addition to those experienced by White police officers?

11. What steps can police departments take to address occupational discrimination and to improve understanding among police officers of different racial or ethnic groups?

## INTERNET EXERCISES

1. Based on your own experience, estimate the percentages of individuals living in your home city or county who belong to various racial groups. Use the website for the U.S. Census Bureau (www.census.gov) to find official data for the same area. Compare your estimates to Census data. Did you find any surprises? If so, what were they?

2. Locate two articles that deal with police–minority relations in other countries. What countries did you select? Describe the nature of police–minority relations in each of the countries you researched. How do such relations compare with police–minority relations in the United States?

## STUDENT STUDY SITE

**⑤SAGE edge™** edge.sagepub.com/coxpolicing3e

**Sharpen your skills with SAGE edge!**

SAGE edge for Students provides a personalized approach to help you accomplish your coursework goals in an easy-to-use learning environment. You'll find action plans, mobile-friendly eFlashcards, and quizzes as well as videos, web resources, and links to SAGE journal articles to support and expand on the concepts presented in this chapter.

# HEAR IT FROM THE PROFESSIONALS

► edge.sagepub.com/coxpolicing3e

HEAD TO THE STUDY SITE WHERE YOU'LL FIND:

- **Exclusive video interviews** with police professionals discussing their careers, challenges, and advice

$SAGE edge™

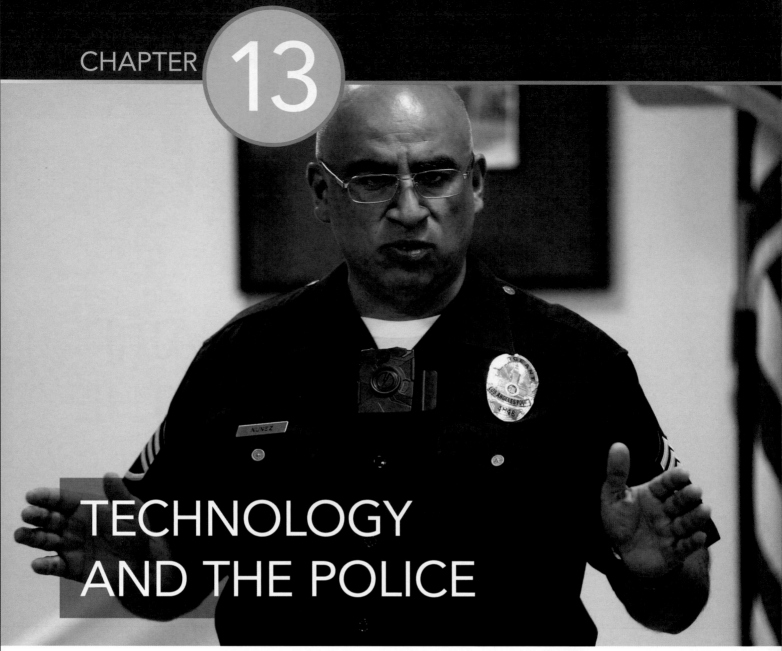

# CHAPTER 13

# TECHNOLOGY AND THE POLICE

© POOL New

## CHAPTER LEARNING OBJECTIVES:

1. Evaluate the cost and benefits of technology in policing

2. Summarize the variety of ways that computers have affected policing

3. Identify and describe the issues surrounding the increased use of video cameras by police and the private security industry

4. Describe the many constitutional issues now confronting judicial and legislative bodies presented by the growth of surveillance technologies

5. Explain how crime mapping is used in crime analysis and crime prevention

6. Describe the four main biological identifiers and how they are used in investigations

7. List the main tools officers use for speed detection

8. Discuss the effects of technology on police armor and weaponry, both lethal and nonlethal, and identify any legal issues associated with the use of these various technologies

"Technology, in a very real sense, is transforming policing in fundamental respects. New and emerging technologies are playing an increasingly crucial role in the daily work of frontline police officers, equipping them with enforcement and investigative tools that have the potential to make them better informed and more effective."[1] The first technological advances that changed policing in the United States were the telephone, the two-way radio, and the automobile (see Figure 13.1).[2] There are two basic currents in new police technologies: information technology and "hard" technology.

© Signatures Collection

The "eye in the sky" image is an example of the sophisticated technologies available to law enforcement and private security personnel.

## ■ THE COSTS AND BENEFITS OF TECHNOLOGY

Technology has continued to change rapidly. The Internet has become an invaluable communication and information resource. Wireless computer and cell phone applications appear unlimited, digital technology in televisions and cameras advance at a rapid pace, global positioning systems (GPS) are now standard equipment in many vehicles and on most smartphones, surveillance and targeting are now possible through the use of unmanned aircraft, and all of these are linked together not only on a national level, but internationally. These dramatic changes have affected the police perhaps as much as any other institution, and often in very positive ways. However, as is the case with technological changes at the societal level, not all the changes in policing have been positive. Proper deployment of technological devices in policing, whether in the public or private sector, requires officer training, judicious discretionary behavior, and a thorough understanding of the legal and ethical issues involved.

All technology users have to be concerned about its misuse as well. Internet users risk hackers obtaining their personal information and using it for illegitimate purposes. The police must be able to understand and investigate a variety of Internet crimes, which include child pornography, conspiracies to commit financial crimes, or identity theft. Cell phones and computers may be used to facilitate terrorism, and GPS can be used to locate the exact positions of police cars with the purpose of evasion.

Increasingly, citizens are worried about the misuse of technological devices to track their every movement and invade their privacy. For example, the ability to hear and "see" through walls may be used to conduct surveillance on us in our most private moments without our knowledge or consent. In fact, almost every innovation seems to create new ways to invade individual privacy; thus, there is an ongoing tension over how much leeway the police should have in using technology and how much privacy the citizen should retain. The procedural safeguard of privacy is the requirement of a search warrant. For example, thermal imaging detects changes in heat and is especially useful for helping to identify indoor marijuana grows. The powerful lights used to grow marijuana indoors produce a significant amount of detectable heat, and that information can support probable cause for a search warrant. However, attempting to balance the needs of investigation with privacy rights of individuals, the U.S. Supreme Court ruled in *Kyllo v. United States* that the police are required to obtain a search warrant even before examining a private dwelling using the imaging technology.[3]

**Author Video:**
Technology and policing

**Author Video:**
How does law enforcement use social media and new means of technology?

## Figure 13.1 ■ Historic Technological Advances of the 19th and 20th Centuries

| | |
|---|---|
| 1850s | Systematic photography for criminal identification was first used in San Francisco. |
| 1877 | Police use of the telegraph began in Albany, New York. |
| 1878 | The telephone was used in police precinct houses in Washington, DC. |
| 1901 | Scotland Yard adopted a fingerprint classification system. |
| 1923 | The first police crime laboratory in the United States was established by the Los Angeles Police Department, and the Teletype machine was inaugurated by the Pennsylvania State Police. |
| 1928 | Detroit police began using the one-way radio. |
| 1934 | Boston police began using the two-way radio. |
| 1930 | The prototype of the present-day polygraph was developed. |
| 1948 | Radar was introduced to traffic law enforcement. |
| 1955 | The New Orleans Police Department was one of the first departments in the country to install an electronic data processing machine. |
| 1960s | The first computer-assisted dispatching system was installed in the St. Louis Police Department. |
| 1966 | The National Law Enforcement Telecommunications System, a message-switching facility linking all state police computers except Hawaii, was established. |
| 1967 | The Federal Bureau of Investigation (FBI) inaugurated the National Crime Information Center (NCIC), the first national law enforcement computing center. NCIC is a computerized national filing system on wanted persons and stolen vehicles, weapons, and other items of value. |
| 1968 | The number 911 for emergencies was first used. |
| Late 1960s | Attempts to develop riot control technologies and use-of-force alternatives were initiated. Wooden, rubber, and plastic bullets; tranquilizer guns; electrified batons; strobe lights that caused giddiness, fainting, and nausea; and stun guns were tested. One of the few successful technologies to emerge was the Taser, which shoots tiny darts into victims, delivering a 50,000-volt shock. |
| 1970s | The large-scale computerization of U.S. police departments began. Major computer-based applications included computer-aided dispatch (CAD), management information systems, centralized call collection using three-digit phone numbers (911), and centralized integrated dispatching of police, fire, and medical services. |
| 1972 | The development of lightweight, flexible, and comfortable protective body armor for the police (Kevlar) took place. |
| Mid-1970s | The study of night vision gear for police officers led to widespread use of the devices. |
| 1975 | The first fingerprint reader was installed at the FBI. |
| 1979 | The Royal Canadian Mounted Police implemented the first actual automated fingerprint identification system (AFIS). |
| 1982 | Pepper spray was first developed (oleoresin capsicum or OC spray). |
| 1990s | More than 90% of U.S. police departments serving a population of 50,000 or more were using computers for applications such as criminal investigations, budgeting, dispatch, manpower allocation, and mapping and analysis of crime patterns. |
| 1996 | The National Academy of Sciences announced that there was no longer any reason to question the reliability of DNA evidence. |
| 1999 | Taser (already in use) develops a new technology that uses a patented neuromuscular technology. |
| 2000s | Crime labs begin using "Touch DNA," or testing surfaces for invisible traces that a suspect may have left. This next generation of DNA testing requires only a small number of cells (15–30). |
| 2010 | Scientists begin to work on "bacterial fingerprints" (specifically identifiable bacterial traces left behind by an individual), which have the potential to be a powerful forensic tool. |
| 2013 | San Diego Police Department uses facial recognition software to collect information on arrestees. |
| 2014 | First pioneered in the United Kingdom in the 1990s, license plate reader systems are used by 70% of local police agencies in the United States. |
| 2015 | North Dakota legalizes the use of unmanned drones to deploy "less lethal" weapons, such as OC spray and Tasers. |

*Sources:* Adapted from *The Evolution and Development of Police Technology,* by Seaskate, Inc., 1998, National Institute of Justice; "Touch DNA: From the crime scene to the crime laboratory," by J. Minor, April 12, 2013. *Forensic Magazine*; "Law enforcement investigation tools expand beyond DNA to bacteria," by D. Weiss, January 22, 2015. *Public Safety*; "Facial recognition software moves from overseas wars to local police," by T. Williams, August 12, 2015. *The New York Times*; "70 percent of U.S. police departments use license plate readers," by J. Hsu, July 8, 2014. *IEEE Spectrum*; "North Dakota legalizes armed police drones," by L. Wagner, August 27, 2015. *NPR*.

Technological advances have an allure for all of us. Careful evaluation of the benefits relative to the costs is essential. Technology has the potential to divert critical resources away from more traditional crime prevention and police strategies that may do more to protect public safety than the newest device.[4]

Although data can be a useful tool, the overreliance on data can be a shortcoming. Data can supply important information about crime trends and patterns, including when, where, and how crimes occur in a particular area. This helps police agencies to direct valuable resources strategically and with maximum effectiveness. However, many serious crimes are still solved using information gained from community members, who in many cases are better informed about the events in the neighborhood than police officers. It is vital that police departments continue to develop and maintain community partnerships.

There is little argument that technological advances have improved the effectiveness, the efficiency, and even the productivity of police. However, "technology should not move officers away from the interpersonal contact with the community that is vital to developing collaborative partnerships and solving neighborhood problems."[5] In other words, it is important that technologies such as mobile data terminals, video cameras, and automated nameplate recognition systems do not prevent police officers from interacting and communicating with the community.

Not all the effects of increased technology in police agencies are positive. In 2011, for example, "Highly computerized cities reported larger shares of employees in technical positions, spent more per capita, and reported fewer officers per capita than cities with lower computerization levels."[6]

Each new technology comes at a cost, and police departments have limited budgets. Moreover, the newer a technology, the more expensive it generally is to purchase and to maintain. Highly advanced or cutting-edge technologies often contain "bugs," defects that have yet to be corrected by the manufacturer. As a general rule, the more advanced, complex, or sophisticated a technology, the more that can go wrong. The cost of a malfunction, depending on the type of technology, can be serious. For example, when an officer's MDC (see below) fails because of poor cellular coverage, the officer may lose his or her ability to communicate with other officers in the field, or to receive certain calls for service. In addition, with time, other technologies designed to thwart the latest police tool become available; there is a market for those as well—for example, methods to defeat polygraph tests or urine tests, "bug" detection devices, and radar alarms, to name a few.[7]

**Web Link:**
New Cellphone Surveillance Safeguards Imposed on Federal Law Enforcement

## CASE IN POINT 13.1

A Chicago police officer investigating a robbery of an iPhone recently made use of the "Find My iPhone" application to make an arrest. Police stopped the suspect and typed in the victim's Apple ID and password, and "instantly her stolen phone was pinpointed on the map."

Police have received training and used similar apps to "track down other brands, such as Droids and BlackBerrys." In another case, police used the "Find My iPhone" application to locate a phone in a residence, which resulted in the arrest of the perpetrator and the recovery of the phone.

1. How can law enforcement make better use of emerging technologies like "Find My iPhone?"
2. Should police agencies be allowed to use emerging technologies like "Find My iPhone" to apprehend criminals without waiting for the victim or owner's consent?

*Source:* From "Chicago case shows how to use iPhone app to find a thief," by Frank Main, May 2012. *Chicago Sun-Times.*

Additionally, the greater the amount of information available to police officers, the greater the potential gravity of its misuse or abuse. Police officers often have access to personal information about citizens not available to the general public. The information about where people live and the types of vehicles they drive is useful to law enforcement, but can be misused. As the type and amount of information becomes more readily available to the police through advances in technology, agencies will need to take increasing steps to ensure that information is properly controlled.

Technological and scientific advances make it possible to collect and preserve a wide variety of types of evidence, but the probative value of such evidence varies from case to case. In an attempt to establish some degree of balance between scientific evidence collected through the use of new technologies and presented by expert witnesses in court and the knowledge and understanding of such evidence on behalf of judges and jurors, a set of rules has been established. The *Daubert* Standard, as articulated in Rule 702 of the Federal Rules of Evidence, is particularly instructive:

> If scientific, technical, or other specialized knowledge will assist the trier of fact to understand the evidence or to determine a fact in issue, a witness qualified as an expert by knowledge, skill, or experience, training, or education, may testify thereto in the form of an opinion or otherwise, if: (1) the testimony is based on sufficient facts or data, (2) the testimony is the product of reliable principles and methods, and (3) the witness has applied the principles and methods reliably to the facts of the case.[8]

The subsections of Rule 702 make it clear that the police must be trained in the collection and preservation of scientific evidence and that they must use appropriate and reliable technology in such collection and preservation. Only then can expert testimony in support of the evidence be admitted and considered by judges and jurors.[9] Other federal rules of evidence and other court decisions apply as well,[10] but the *Daubert* example should suffice as a caution against the belief that police technology guarantees success in court.

## ■ COMPUTERS

Over four decades have passed since LEAA (Law Enforcement Assistance Administration) first began its effort to bring technology to the fight against crime. Computers, and especially wireless computers, have become an integral part of the tools of law enforcement.

Officers use computers to access a number of databases, to fill out paperwork, and to record witness statements while they are still at the scene. They can also use wireless technology to upload digital photos they have taken of crime scenes and to check license plate numbers or suspect IDs against a database of stolen cars or outstanding warrants. They can retrieve a suspect's criminal record and photograph on the screen in front of them, without having to relay information through a dispatcher. In 2007, about 9 in 10 local police officers worked for a department that used in-field computers, compared to 3 in 10 officers in 1990.[11] By 2013, over 90% of departments that serve communities of at least 25,000 residents had in-field computerized access to driving and vehicle records and outstanding warrants.[12]

**Mobile digital communicators or mobile digital computers (MDCs)** in patrol vehicles have been one of the most important technological tools for patrol officers since the introduction of radio communications. In fact, "radio communications for law enforcement may soon be a thing of the past."[13] In some police departments, MDCs communicate with the city's main computer system using a **computer-aided dispatch (CAD)** system, which operates on a cellular radio frequency.[14] In addition to receiving radio assignments using voice communication, officers are able to view assignments on the MDC screen and have car-to-car communication capability. Officers can also receive certain radio assignments by MDC, thereby keeping voice communications to

**■ Mobile Digital Communicator (MDC):** Digital dispatch and data communications system for field officers; also called a **mobile digital computer**

**■ Computer-Aided Dispatch (CAD):** A system in which dispatch is accomplished through the use of computers

a minimum and security levels high. Coordinating with GPS technology, dispatchers can see where the patrol cars are on a digital map. Data communications via MDC have several distinct advantages over voice communications:

- Supervisors are able to review pending assignments, check the status of all patrol units, and communicate directly with any unit by using the MDC. This permits supervisors to spot potential problems and take a proactive approach to managing their resources and workload.

- Transmissions are secure, eliminating concerns about unauthorized scanning and interception of sensitive transmissions.

- MDCs increase available airtime, freeing existing voice frequencies for both officers and dispatchers when engaging in priority transmissions.

- Officers no longer have to "stand by" while other officers and dispatchers are engaged with priority transmissions. Officers have the ability to recall up-to-the-minute pertinent data, premise history, and information on radio assignments.

- Queries of wanted persons, stolen vehicles, or National Crime Information Center (NCIC) status can be done directly by an officer in an MDC-equipped vehicle. Officers can query as many vehicles and personnel as required, whenever or wherever needed.

- Information is accessed and received faster and more efficiently. Unlike our present voice communications, all MDC-equipped vehicles can make NCIC queries simultaneously.

The use of MDCs allows for the collection of time use statistics, which enable better time management of officers and, thus, greater efficiency. In addition, dispatch-related transactions such as dispatch receipt, status updating, busy updating, and on-view and traffic-stop updating, as well as access to the status of other units, other complaints, location information (hazards/alerts, history, contacts, etc.), optional map display, and unit history, are all possible.[15] Police also use handheld scanners to scan documents or photos and later view these types of images on a computer. For example, fraudulent checks, driver's licenses, and other documents can be scanned and transferred to a computer via a USB cable or Micro SD (secure digital memory) card.[16]

The integration of CAD, records, mobile, and **automatic vehicle location (AVL)**— including mapping—and many other features and functional tools is another step forward using combined technologies. Each vehicle reports its position to a computer in dispatch and displays that position on a map. GPS involves a combination of hardware and software that uses satellite technology to provide the latitude and longitude of specific locations.[17] This aids dispatchers when they receive a high-priority call by permitting them to look at the map and determine which officer is closest to the call location. At the same time, patrol officers also see a real-time AVL map in their vehicles and can decide who is closest to the location in question.[18] The technology is particularly useful for remote, often-rural areas that lack specific addresses, including large forest preserve areas. GPS has also been used by police on vehicles of persons under investigation for committing a crime. However, the U.S. Supreme Court ruled in *United States v. Jones* (2012)[19] that police agencies seeking to use a GPS tracking device on a vehicle of a person under investigation must first obtain a search warrant, which refers back to the issue of individual privacy versus the needs of law enforcement.[20]

An additional component associated with the AVL is the **geographic information system (GIS)**. A GIS is software that captures, analyzes, and stores spatial data. These programs make it easy to visualize and interpret geographic information and examine the effects of crime, traffic safety, home foreclosures, and urban planning to mention a few.[22] Although GISs are in use in approximately 63% of large police departments, researchers still know little about the location of police officers when they are not responding to calls for service.[23]

■ **Automatic Vehicle Location (AVL):** A means for automatically determining the geographic location of a vehicle and transmitting the information to a requester, most often through the use of GPS

■ **Geographic Information System (GIS):** Computer software that captures, analyzes, stores, and presents spatial data and makes it easy to visualize and interpret geographic information

In Chicago, beginning in 2005, police officers gained access to some 5 million mug shots and other computerized crime information without having to return to the station.[24] Wireless portable data terminals gave police officers on the street instant access to **Illinois Citizen and Law Enforcement Analysis and Reporting (I-CLEAR)**, a computerized data warehouse designed to allow them to search for suspects based on nicknames, tattoos, country of origin, vehicle make and model, and other characteristics. Files are said to contain everything from information on gang membership and a history of previous police calls at an address to crime reports, arrest warrants and citations, and vital homeland security information, including watch lists and terrorism alerts.[25] Police officers are able to show mug shots to crime victims while they remain at a crime scene and while events are still fresh in the victim's mind. The longer the time between a crime and the identification of a possible suspect, the greater the chance for error. Officers have the advantage of entering case reports into the system from their vehicles, eliminating the bulk of the previously required paperwork. "I-CLEAR represents an unprecedented partnership between the Illinois State Police (ISP) and the Chicago Police Department, one that promises to position Illinois well in the regional data-sharing arena."[26]

**Psychophysiological detection of deception (PDD)**, previously referred to as a polygraph or lie detector, is another evolving technology. The PDD is a device that registers involuntary physical processes such as pulse rate and perspiration and is often used in an attempt to detect whether or not a suspect is telling the truth. The theory is that lying causes stress, and the instrument is designed to detect the physiological evidence of stress in the body. The early lie detectors were instruments with needles that scribbled lines on a single strip of scrolling paper. These analog machines have been replaced by digital computerized equipment. The scrolling paper has been replaced with sophisticated algorithms and computer monitors. Such computerized PDD systems allow a trained examiner to do voice and audio recordings, to read a subject's pulse, and to gauge voice responses and other physiological markers. Algorithms allow comparisons of the data collected from a suspect with information known to be truthful and deceptive. In theory, at least, the computerization of the polygraph makes it extremely difficult for a suspect to deceive the instrument.[27]

**Illinois Citizen and Law Enforcement Analysis and Reporting (I-CLEAR):** A computerized data warehouse designed to allow police officers to search for suspects based on nicknames, tattoos, country of origin, vehicle make and model, and other characteristics in partnership with the Illinois State Police and residents of Chicago

**Psychophysiological Detection of Deception (PDD):** A device that registers involuntary physical processes that is often used in an attempt to detect whether or not a suspect is telling the truth

The Pentagon issued handheld PDDs to U.S. soldiers in Afghanistan to screen local police officers, interpreters, and allied forces for access to U.S. military bases.[28] Such handheld devices are available in other settings as well. For example, portable devices using voice tension technology to measure varying degrees of vibration in the voice are available. Changes in vibrations are alleged to be caused by the person being tested going from a state of calm to a state of nervousness. These devices may even be connected to cell phones and used to measure changes in vibrations at a distance.[29] It is still questionable whether these devices yield reliable results.

It can take time and experimentation for the limits of a technology to become apparent to the field. The PDD serves as a good example of that process.

The reliability of PDD results has been the source of a long-standing controversy. Proponents assert that the most advanced PDD can be calibrated to the individual and that questioning is structured to be individualized and precise. Critics question their reliability, pointing out that some people actually believe their falsehood is the truth or they can control their physical responses and fool the machine.

The **Employee Polygraph Protection Act of 1988 (EPPA)** recognized and attempted to safeguard against the abuse of information collected by the technology of the time.[30] The act prohibits employers from requiring applicants to take a polygraph test; with certain exceptions, employers are prohibited from using PDD results in the hiring or promoting of employees or as a basis for discipline or discharge.[31]

Also, given the potential for error, many courts do not consider PDD results as evidence admissible in court. See Chapter 4 for a discussion of polygraph use in the hiring of police officers.

Functional magnetic resonance imaging (fMRI) is being tried as a method of detecting deception. The fMRI reveals areas of the brain or other anatomy that are experiencing momentary changes in blood flow or electrical activity.[32]

> Neurophysiologists know that certain areas of the brain activate when recalling memories, while others are stimulated when we're being creative, e.g. lying. The idea is that a lie requires some creative thought, while answering a question truthfully relies only on memory. Similarly, a suspect can be shown pictures of a crime scene and their brain activity analyzed to see if the image is registering as something never seen before (because they had not been present at the scene of the crime).[33]

## ■ VIDEO CAMERAS

Police use of cameras has proliferated dramatically over the past two decades. As digital technology has become increasingly available, the use of cameras to record and store evidence has become invaluable to the police. Cameras are now attached to everything from patrol cars to uniform lapels to Tasers, and they are increasingly deployed by both public and private police to assist in the surveillance of property, traffic patterns, crowds, airports, other transportation hubs, and more. The police also used thermal imaging and infrared cameras during searches both by land and by air. For example, indoor marijuana growing operations can be located by thermal imaging, but the U.S. Supreme Court ruled in *Kyllo v. United States* (see page 313) that police are required to obtain a search warrant before examining a private dwelling with this technology.[34]

The use of **CCTV** (closed-circuit television) in England has been widely publicized, as has the use of **red light cameras** (which record stoplight violations at intersections) and police in-car cameras. In the United States, systems also exist today that can photograph suspects who are vandalizing property and notify the police that the vandalism is in progress.[35] **Graffiti cameras** (talking surveillance cameras) warn intruders to leave the area and that their photograph has been obtained. An additional video camera advancement involves the use of an eight-pound, remote-controlled submarine that can

**Policing in Practice Video:**
Director of IT and Electronic Security

■ **Employee Polygraph Protection Act of 1988 (EPPA):** Prohibits employers from requiring applicants to take a polygraph test or from using PDD results in the hiring or promoting of employees or as a basis for discipline or discharge

■ **CCTV:** Closed-circuit television

■ **Red Light Cameras:** Record stoplight violations at intersections

■ **Graffiti Cameras:** Talking surveillance cameras

send video footage to police.[36] The submarine has been used to search underwater for missing persons and explosives.

### Vehicle Cameras

Police vehicles are increasingly being fitted with video cameras (with sound-recording capability) that can record activity inside or outside the car. Such cameras record information that can later be used to determine whether officers followed departmental policy, whether officers or those they encountered were harassed, whether anyone violated the law, the identities of those involved in an encounter, facts about the location of a stop, and the make and license number of a vehicle stopped by the police. Evidentiary information recorded can later be used in court to prove or disprove witness statements or can be evaluated as evidence in itself.

Advocates of the cameras say they provide officers with additional evidence to convict traffic offenders, especially in DUI (driving under the influence) cases. The cameras are also touted as a way of protecting officers against false complaints of brutality and racial profiling. Motorists benefit from the camera, because officers are less likely to misbehave during traffic stops if they know they are being taped. As one officer put it, "With the video camera, it makes you a better officer because you know you're being videotaped. . . . I would never want to work without a camera. If I had to, I'd feel it was a disadvantage."[37] Today the video display can "show not only what's being seen by the in-car video cameras of that one officer's squad, but also get tactically significant video from another officer's car—or another video feed like traffic cameras or security cameras connect to the system—to get eyes on the target before even arriving at a scene."[38] Based on numerous similar accounts, police agencies throughout the country have adopted these cameras for the benefit of both the public and their officers. The advantages in terms of improved community relations and increased professionalism appear thus far to outweigh the disadvantages. (See Figure 13.2.)

In 2005, the International Association of Chiefs of Police (IACP) conducted research to evaluate the impact of in-car camera systems on state police and highway patrol agencies.

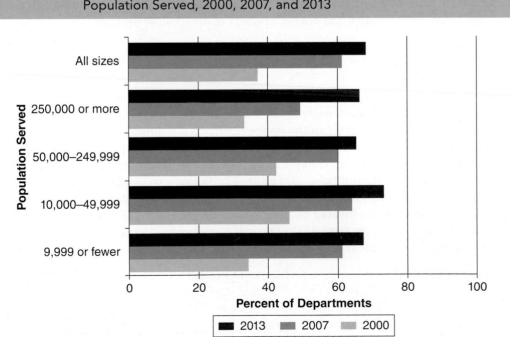

**Figure 13.2** ■ Use of In-Car Video Cameras by Local Police Departments, by Size of Population Served, 2000, 2007, and 2013

*Source:* Local police departments, 2013: Equipment and technology, by B. A. Reaves, 2015. Bureau of Justice Statistics.

Study results, based on surveys, focus groups, and on-site interviews, indicated that the cameras were of considerable value in the following ways:

- Enhanced officer safety
- Improved agency accountability
- Reduced agency liability
- Simplified incident review
- Enhanced new recruit and in-service training (post-incident use of videos)
- Improved community and media perceptions
- Strengthened police leadership
- Advanced prosecution/case resolution
- Enhanced officer performance and professionalism
- Increased homeland security
- Upgraded technology policies and procedures[39]

The authors of the report also found that agencies sometimes failed to view the entire camera system continuum by neglecting components such as storing, filing, and retrieving video evidence. Some agencies also failed to gather sufficient information on officer attitudes, long-term equipment maintenance costs, and other policy areas.[40]

### Body-Worn Cameras

Following the 2014 police shooting of Michael Brown, an unarmed Black man, in Ferguson, Missouri, a grand jury acquitted the officer involved. The African American community erupted in protest, to which the police responded with force and military-style equipment; more violence ensued. In the wake of these events, the discussion of body-worn cameras for the police expanded. President Obama asked for $263 million to support community policing efforts to help rebuild trust in the police, $75 million of which was designated for body-worn cameras, also known as "cop cams" or "body cams."[41] Previously, a New York judge included these cameras in her judicial order after ruling that the city's "stop and frisk" program was unconstitutional.[42]

**Policing in Practice Video:**
What are the advantages and disadvantages of body cameras?

These recording devices may seem like the answer to the problem of the police acting with impunity. They are like the public's eyes on the cops. In 2013, approximately one-third of departments were already using body cameras.[43] Many officers welcome them and feel they offer protection against unjustified accusations. Some communities are already reporting a reduction in complaints of excessive use of force.[44]

However, there are still many important questions about the use of body cameras on police officers. To begin with, the cameras still offer only one point of view. Different people can look at the same video and interpret it in two completely different ways.[45] So, a video from the police officer's point of view does not necessarily provide the best-possible perspective. The cameras are only one of many tools, and there is a danger in relying too heavily on them. The question of who controls the on-off switch is of critical importance. If officers can turn their cameras off themselves, the question of discretion is still at the forefront. If officers cannot turn the cameras off, there is the problem of whether the department can protect the privacy rights of witnesses, bystanders, confidential informants, victims, and officers themselves. In these times of increasing government surveillance, there is the question of whether the police use of body-worn cameras constitutes an unjust expansion of that surveillance. In addition, there are the questions of the storage and security of the footage. Video files must be carefully protected to maintain their integrity as evidence and to ensure they won't be tampered with or improperly leaked to the public.[46] Without proper training and procedures in the use of body cameras, this tool has the potential to increase instead of reduce the public's mistrust of the police. Of course, agencies will also have to address the issue of

**Video Link:**
Can technology and training strengthen community policing after Ferguson?

the costs to buy, maintain, and use the equipment. There is as yet very little research to support any claims of effectiveness, so most of these questions remain to be answered, possibly in the courts.

### Mobile Phone Cameras

In addition to cameras installed by the police department, the majority of citizens are walking around with cameras in their pockets. Since the pivotal moment of the Rodney King beating by Los Angeles police officers in 1991, witnesses have taken videos of police interactions in a more or less happenstance way. In most of these cases, the police were unaware of the filming; their behavior was documented without their knowledge, which tends to alarm the public and lead to the conclusion that police act badly on their own when they think no one is watching.

Because citizens are increasingly aware of problematic police interaction, they may be more likely to pull their phones out of their pockets and document what they see. The police as well are likely to be increasingly aware of the possibility of being filmed at any time. Some observers are taking this a step farther into the prevention of unwanted police behavior, not only the "proof" of it.

The American Civil Liberties Union (ACLU) of California has developed an application for mobile phones that allows citizens to record police actions. The recorded video goes directly to an ACLU server that stores the footage even if the phone is destroyed. Additionally, a user can alert other nearby users about the incident. The ACLU is making a "Know Your Rights" guide available as part of the launch of this tool, which over 40,000 people downloaded in the first week.[47]

Similar applications were already in use in New York City to record stop-and-frisk incidents and in Ferguson, Missouri. Compelled by events in Missouri, three Georgia teenagers developed a phone app called "Five-O" that allows users to record and rate their interactions with police officers and then share the reports they create with others. The user can immediately alert a predefined list of recipients of the incident as it is happening, and the app pinpoints the user's location through GPS.[48] Though inspired by incidents of excessive force and serious police misconduct, these tools have the potential to record positive interactions with the police as well.

This is an example of the public taking a proactive approach to holding the police accountable for their actions. However, citizen documents may be problematic in many of the same ways that cameras worn by police officers or installed in patrol cars are—for example, the issue of protecting the privacy of bystanders or victims and ensuring the integrity of the footage.

**Policing in Practice Video:**
What is one example of how technology helped to solve a call?

## ■ SURVEILLANCE TECHNOLOGY

Wiretapping originated before the invention of the modern telephone, when telegraph wires were literally tapped to intercept communications. Statutes prohibiting the use of wiretaps in this regard were enacted in the 1860s, and, from the 1890s until the present day, it has been illegal in the United States for unauthorized persons to listen in on or record private phone conversations.

However, in 1928, the U.S. Supreme Court approved the practice of wiretapping by the police and other government officials, and it was not until the 1960s that the requirement that police personnel obtain a court order to listen in on private conversations (under most circumstances) came into existence. Specifically, in 1968, Congress passed the Omnibus Crime Control and Safe Streets Act, which established strict procedures for conducting interception of wire, oral, and electronic communications.[49]

With the development and expansion of the Internet, new concerns arose. Because Internet communications are not actually verbal conversation, they were not protected by the same laws that protected traditional phone use. This became and remains a concern, because government officials as well as others can view information transmitted over the Internet using sophisticated technology. In 1986, the U.S. government enacted the **Electronic Communications Privacy Act (ECPA)** wiretapping regulation, which protects email, pagers, and cell phone calls.[50] Technology changes extremely rapidly and mostly in the private sector; politics and legislation are constantly trying to catch up and respond to the new situations created by an evolving technosphere.

The events of September 11, 2001, changed many things, including laws having to do with electronic eavesdropping. In October 2001, former president Bush signed legislation expanding the ability to tap telephones and track Internet usage in the hunt for terrorists. The bill, known as the USA PATRIOT Act (see Chapter 9), updated and clarified the ECPA and gave federal authorities much wider latitude in monitoring Internet usage and expanded the way such data are shared among different agencies. Under the **Foreign Intelligence Surveillance Act (FISA)**, for example, the purpose of electronic surveillance must be to obtain intelligence in the United States on foreign powers (such as enemy agents or spies) or individuals connected to international terrorist groups. The government must show the FISA court probable cause that the target of the surveillance is a foreign power or agent of a foreign power to obtain authorization to eavesdrop. However, if the attorney general determines that an emergency exists, he or she may authorize the emergency employment of electronic surveillance before obtaining the necessary authorization from the FISA court. Having taken such emergency measures, the attorney general must notify a judge of the court not more than 72 hours after the authorization of such surveillance.

Since the 1980s, **National Security Letters (NSLs)**, which are written demands from the Federal Bureau of Investigation (FBI) that compel Internet service providers, credit companies, financial institutions, and others to hand over confidential records about their customers (such as subscriber information, phone numbers, email addresses, websites visited, and more), have been used to collect extensive information concerning electronic communications. The USA PATRIOT Act expanded the kinds of records that could be obtained with an NSL. These letters do not require court approval. The FBI need merely assert that the information requested in the NSL is relevant to an investigation, and recipients are prohibited from disclosing that they have received the NSL.[51]

In 2010, President Obama signed a one-year extension of some sections of the USA PATRIOT Act (which had previously been extended by the Bush administration) without approving any new limits on the provisions allowing the government, with permission from the FISA court, "to obtain roving wiretaps over multiple communication devices, seize suspects' records without their knowledge, and conduct surveillance of a so-called 'lone wolf,' or someone deemed suspicious but without any known ties to an organized terrorist group."[52]

In keeping with the changes occurring following 9/11, the FBI developed "a sophisticated, point-and-click surveillance system that performs instant wiretaps on almost any communications device."[53] The **Digital Collection System Network (DCSNet)** "connects FBI wiretapping rooms to switches controlled by traditional land-line operators, internet-telephone providers and cellular companies."[54]

DCSNet consists of software that collects, sifts, and stores phone numbers, phone calls, and text messages.

> The system directly connects FBI wiretapping outposts around the country to a far-reaching private communications network. . . . The surveillance system[s] let FBI agents play back recordings even as they are being captured (like TiVo), create master wiretap files, send digital recordings to translators, track the rough location of targets

Technology changes extremely rapidly and mostly in the private sector; politics and legislation are constantly trying to catch up and respond to the new situations created by an evolving technosphere.

■ **Electronic Communications Privacy Act (ECPA):** Wiretapping regulation that protects email, pagers, and cell phone calls

■ **Foreign Intelligence Surveillance Act (FISA):** Specifies that the purpose of electronic surveillance must be to obtain intelligence in the United States on foreign powers (such as enemy agents or spies) or individuals connected to international terrorist groups

■ **National Security Letters (NSLs):** Written demands from the FBI that compel Internet service providers, credit companies, financial institutions, and others to hand over confidential records about their customers (such as subscriber information, phone numbers, email addresses, and websites visited)

■ **Digital Collection System Network (DCSNet):** Connects FBI wiretapping rooms to switches controlled by traditional landline operators, Internet-telephone providers, and cellular companies in real time using cell-tower information, and even stream intercepts outward to mobile surveillance vans.[55]

As might be expected, the expansion of government powers authorized in post-9/11 legislation has caused considerable concern. Can any of us be certain that conversations we regard as private are not being monitored? Should we give up some degree of privacy in the interests of homeland security? How far should invasion of privacy go? Should we accept not only having our communications monitored but permitting full-body scans at airports? These and other questions related to technological advances and the potential for abuse by police and other government (and perhaps some private) officials are complex and not easily answered.

In combination, computers and cameras have proven useful to the police. For example, in Murrysville, Pennsylvania, police vehicles are equipped with laptops that receive live video feeds from school buildings in the district and are able to access electronic floor plans and building diagrams. According to Chief Tom Seefield, "We're trying to be proactive and be prepared for anything that lies ahead for us. If we have an incident in the school district, such as a gunman or somebody in there trying to kidnap a child, we would be able to go on the laptops, and the cameras in each school giving us the ability to get a live video feed. . . . That gives us eyes from outside the building to help us better prepare and plan

**Policing in Practice Video:**
What technology in your department do you find important? Why?

---

## Exhibit 13.1

## A Policy Framework for the Deployment of Police Technology

In response to the proliferation of new and unregulated technologies, and in recognition of their surveillance power, potential dangers, and encroachment into the private lives of citizens, the International Association of Chiefs of Police (IACP) developed a policy framework for the deployment of police technology.

The IACP emphasizes the need for comprehensive policy that covers technology objectives, deployment, privacy protections, records management, data quality, systems security, data retention and purging, access and use of stored data, information sharing, accountability, training, and sanctions for noncompliance. Its specific recommendations include the following:

1. Determine the intended use and the benefits to law enforcement goals and public safety requirements

2. Engage the community in the planning process and assure the public and the media of the agency's intentions to protect privacy

3. Inform the public of all use

4. Operate equipment only with trained and certified personnel; approve all use by a supervisor

5. Fully document all use and audit all documentation

6. Do not equip a remote apparatus with weapons

7. With specific and arguable exceptions, secure a search warrant prior to conducting surveillance or searches

8. Do not retain images[56]

In addition, the IACP describes the need for appropriate policies. "Policies function to reinforce training and to establish an operational baseline to guide officers and other personnel in proper procedures regarding its use. Moreover, policies help to ensure uniformity in practice across the agency and to enforce accountability. Policies should reflect the mission and values of the agency and be tightly aligned with applicable local, state, and federal laws, regulations, and judicial rulings."[57]

prior to entering the building."[58] In police departments in Denver, Colorado; Washington, DC; Ann Arbor, Michigan; and Louisville, Kentucky; among others, mobile cameras read license plates of parked and moving vehicles and compare them to vehicle databases.[59] The system, known as a **license plate recognition (LPR) system**, helps the police fight motor vehicle theft and identify unregistered cars, and it may be of use in AMBER Alert searches as well. LPRs are one version of **automatic number plate recognition (ANPR)**, which uses optical character recognition to read the license plates on vehicles. The system takes pictures of a vehicle license plate and processes the numbers and letters using the optical recognition software against a known database.[60] While some are concerned about potential misuse as revenue generators and as devices to track vehicle movements for questionable purposes, the technology appears to be gaining acceptance across the country.[61] Although LPR technology has increased in use, research results have not found a significant crime deterrent effect, either general or offense specific.[62] (See Figure 13.3.)

**Internet protocol (IP) cameras** are basically CCTV cameras that use the Internet to transmit image data and control signals over an Ethernet link. These cameras are commonly used by the police for surveillance and are typically deployed in a network with a digital video recorder (DVR) or a network video recorder (NVR) to form a video surveillance system.[63] Output from multiple cameras can be monitored from remote locations and images stored securely for future use. Police applications include traffic monitoring through the use of cameras placed at appropriate intervals along roadways, in subways, or in tunnels. IP camera networks can also be used to monitor employees in cases involving theft, involving compliance with regulatory requirements, and where employees are suspected of conspiring to commit crimes or acts of terrorism. Further, the cameras can be used to provide views of remote sites that are not easily accessible or are extremely dangerous, such as suspected terrorist training camps.[64] Thus, IP applications cover the gamut of police activities, ranging from local traffic control through Department of Homeland Security (DHS) surveillance of suspects and sensitive locations. As is the case with all surveillance technology, opportunities for abuse using IP technology certainly exist.

■ **License Plate Recognition (LPR) System:** Reads license plates of parked and moving vehicles and compares them to vehicle databases

■ **Automatic Number Plate Recognition (ANPR):** Technology that uses optical character recognition to read the license plates on vehicles

■ **Internet Protocol (IP) Cameras:** CCTV cameras that use the Internet to transmit image data and control signals over an Ethernet link

© Signatures Collection

This police car is fitted with two forward-facing automatic number plate recognition (ANPR) units mounted on the trunk, which can be used to take pictures of license plates and check them against police databases.

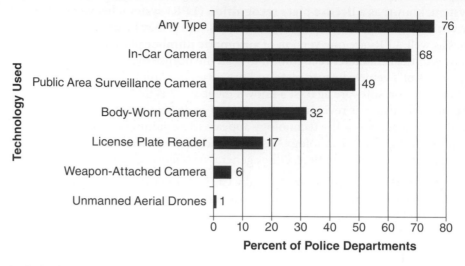

**Technology Used**

| | Percent |
|---|---|
| Any Type | 76 |
| In-Car Camera | 68 |
| Public Area Surveillance Camera | 49 |
| Body-Worn Camera | 32 |
| License Plate Reader | 17 |
| Weapon-Attached Camera | 6 |
| Unmanned Aerial Drones | 1 |

**Percent of Police Departments**

*Source: Local police departments, 2013: Equipment and technology,* by B. A. Reaves, 2015. Bureau of Justice Statistics.

## Drones and Robots

Technology that has potential benefits for the police continues to expand. More than 50 institutions, including dozens of universities and law enforcement agencies, have received a certificate of authorization (COA) from the Federal Aviation Administration (FAA) to operate remotely piloted aircraft known as **drones**. In the United States, the FAA has "the responsibility to ensure that the privacy of individuals is protected and that the public is fully informed about who is using drones in public airspace and why," according to the same legislators.[65] It appears that dozens of companies are currently developing over 100 different drone systems, ranging from miniature models to those

■ **Drones:** Aircraft without a human pilot on board controlled either by computers or remotely by an operator on the ground or in another vehicle

Sgt. Jim Linn retrieves the Alameda County Sheriff's Office drone while demonstrating a search and rescue operation on Friday, Aug. 14, 2015, in Dublin, Calif. As law enforcement joins the ranks of hobbyists sending drones into California skies, civil liberties advocates are raising the specter of unchecked police surveillance and state lawmakers are drafting limits.

AP Photo/Noah Berger

with wingspans comparable to airliners.[66] Those approved include not only agencies such as the Department of Homeland Security but also smaller ones such as police departments in North Little Rock, Arkansas, and Ogden, Utah, as well the University of North Dakota and Nicholls State University in Louisiana.[67] However, the FAA will not release the number of agencies it has issued COAs.[68]

Robots are emerging quickly as another seemingly futuristic trend in many arenas, including policing. Potentially ranging from R2-D2 to RoboCop, robot developers may have the goal of reducing crime in mind. However, the for-profit companies involved in technology innovation are not necessarily thinking about the Constitution. One such company, Knightscope, is developing an autonomous bot that roams around and collects data through thermal imaging and facial and license recognition sensors, among other things.[69] Proponents claim that robots will expand the capacity of the police to monitor a burgeoning population, which would otherwise outpace the traditional police. It doesn't seem that they have yet addressed the vulnerability of such equipment on the streets of the United States' tough cities. The extreme scenario for robot technology would be fully autonomous weapons, which are allegedly being developed for the military.

As is the case with most new police technology, drones and robots are controversial and raise many issues related to safety and privacy rights and whether the use of such technology for surveillance is consistent with the U.S. Constitution and U.S. values. This may be especially true in the case of these new technologies, because "even the smallest drones can carry a host of surveillance equipment, from video cameras and thermal imaging to GPS tracking and cellphone eavesdropping tools. They can also be equipped with advanced forms of radar detection, license plate cameras, and facial recognition."[70]

■ **Crime Mapping:**
The process of using a GIS to conduct spatial analysis of crime problems and other police issues

## ■ CRIME MAPPING

**Crime mapping** has long been associated with crime analysis and is a process that uses a GIS to conduct spatial analyses of crime problems and other police issues. **Crime analysis** is the systematic study of crime and disorder problems to assist police in apprehending criminals, reducing and preventing crime and disorder, and evaluating methods.[71]

■ **Crime Analysis:**
The systematic study of crime and disorder problems, including sociodemographic, spatial, and temporal factors

## AROUND THE WORLD 13.1

"Western Australian police are using number-plate recognition technology to spot motorists with drug convictions and then subject them to roadside saliva testing and vehicle searches." The technology is able to scan a vehicle plate and reveal convictions against the owner of the vehicle, outstanding warrants, and whether the owner has a valid driver's license and valid vehicle license. Police determined that the prior convictions of the motorists met the standard of a reasonable suspicion required to conduct a search.

1. Western Australian police report that the technology is assisting them in "intelligence-led" operations. Prior to the use of number-plate recognition technology, police stopped drivers "in a random manner." However, one police minister is "not convinced that the police had the legal right to search private vehicles solely based on the basis that the driver had a drug conviction." The U.S. Constitution provides a reasonable expectation of privacy. Do you believe that number-plate recognition technology constitutes a "reasonable" search? Explain.

2. Do you believe that prior drug offenses provide sufficient reasonable suspicion to search a motorist's vehicle? Why or why not?

*Source:* From "Police use of technology to target drug users," by Ronan O'Connell, July 2011. *The Western Australian*. Retrieved June 2012 from http://au.news.yahoo.com.

Some of the earliest crime mapping involved sticking different-colored pins into a wall map to indicate the location of reported crimes. The problem with wall maps is they are difficult to keep updated and accurate and can only display limited data.[72] Another form of crime mapping involves computer maps. The third type of crime mapping, briefly discussed earlier in this chapter, involves a GIS and is different from the pin and computer maps. The GIS "allows an analyst to view data behind the geographic features, combine various features, manipulate the data and maps, and perform statistical functions."[73]

For example, at the Jacksonville County Sheriff's Office in Florida, the Crime Analysis Unit cleans, classifies, and merges data from multiple tables in the Record Management System.[74] This information is geocoded and delivered to a base map containing a variety of geographic layers. The analysts at Jackson County employ geospatial and temporal techniques to identify emerging crime patterns and at the same time analyze long-term crime problems. The county uses criminal incidents, field interviews, arrests, and other data in its analysis.[75]

Additional analysis often involves the creation of **density analysis maps**, which are commonly referred to as "hot spots."[76] Density analysis can reveal areas of elevated crime activity and can also be used to perform geographic profiling. The National Institute of Justice (NIJ) discovered that the statistical program CrimeStat and a desktop GIS will permit police to accomplish the following tasks:

- Identify and analyze hot spots within larger areas
- Plot crime incidents on a map
- Track offender behavior over time
- Estimate a serial offender's residence[77]

The interest in crime mapping and analysis has not been confined to police agencies. WikiCrimes is a unique new use of Internet technology to promote collaborative relationships between citizens and law enforcement by providing a "common interaction space for the general public where they can note criminal activity and track the locations where such crimes occur." Although the effectiveness of WikiCrimes has not yet been evaluated, both law enforcement and the academic community might use WikiCrimes as a means for partnership.[78]

**Video Link:**
New crime mapping system in Greensboro

■ **Density Analysis Maps:** Maps used to reveal areas with elevated crime activity, known as hot spots

## CASE (IN) POINT    13.2

Americans are increasingly tracking crime trends as police departments install Internet-based crime mapping services. The services obtain live feeds from police agencies and immediately post them to their Internet site.

Many crime-mapping sites were developed in 2007 with the addition of Google Maps. "An Internet-enabled mapping service that provides satellite images for most urban areas, Google maps gave crime mapping a cost-effective foundation. The crime mapping services were then able to focus exclusively on software that recognized addresses and build systems capable of pulling data from police records."

1. Although crime-mapping tools can provide a host of useful information, what might the privacy issues be surrounding the use of crime-mapping data?

2. If you were the victim of a crime, how would you feel about sharing that information on a public forum?

*Source:* From "New programs put crime stats on the map," by B. White, 2009. *The Wall Street Journal*, p. D1.

## Legislature Could Try Again on Eavesdropping

Although some Illinois legislators made serious attempts to change the state's strict eavesdropping statute, many criticized bills that would have allowed both the police and other citizens to audio record one another. There were at least three serious attempts to change the state's strict eavesdropping statute during the legislative session in 2012.

The Senate considered the third attempt—House Bill 1263—as it went into legislative overtime. Some lawmakers criticized the bill, which would have allowed both police officers and citizens, in public and when interacting with one another, to record each other.

"Our state constitution has specific language in it that speaks to eavesdropping, and we're throwing out our constitution on June 1. . . . We ought not to do this," said Sen. Kwame Raoul (D-Chicago).

HB1263 was intended to require the person recording to inform everyone else involved that the recording was under way. Raoul said in his conversation with the bill's chief sponsor, Sen. Michael Noland (D-Elgin), the only notification a police officer would need is his uniform and his badge.

The Senate never voted on the measure. After 15 minutes of debate on the bill, Noland withdrew it.

"Obviously, there is a great deal of misinformation on this bill, and it's going to take a little more education of my colleagues here," Noland said.

Rep. Elaine Nekritz (D-Northbrook) said she is very reluctant to support Noland's version of the legislation. "I think you're opening the door to police being able to engage in a conversation, get people to say things on the record—when that person may or may not be involved in anything—without having to go out for a warrant or read their *Miranda* rights," Nekritz said. "I am very leery of that."

During a North Atlantic Treaty Organization (NATO) summit held in Chicago in May 2012, the police did not enforce a state law that would have made it a felony to record someone without that person's permission. Thus, protestors and demonstrators using smartphones and video cameras could record the police without their knowledge. Enforcement would have been extremely difficult under the circumstances, and the constitutionality of the Illinois law was subsequently challenged in court. Still, some argue that, whether or not it is enforced, as long as the law prohibiting audio recording without permission remains on the books, it is problematic.

Chicago's police superintendent said that the "Illinois eavesdropping law is a 'foreign concept' to him. He said the police can benefit from having events recorded so there are no false accusations of misconduct later."[79]

In 2014, the Illinois Supreme Court held that the state eavesdropping law "criminalized innocent conduct" and violated free-speech rights by prohibiting recording conversations with police or another citizen without that person's permission.[80] However, late in the year, the state house and senate reinstated the prohibition by wide voting margins. The new bill makes it a felony to "surreptitiously record a private conversation" if at least one person had a reasonable expectation of privacy. The law is vague about what constitutes a public encounter and therefore what constitutes an expectation of privacy. Ironically, it appears that the legislature acted to prevent the public from recording the police and not the other way around.[81]

1. Do you believe that police officers and private citizens should be allowed to record each other in public places, such as coffee shops, restaurants, and parks? Why or why not?

2. Do you believe that an officer's uniform and badge is enough notification to surreptitiously record conversations with private citizens? Why or why not?

3. With the proliferation of cell phone cameras and recording devices, is there any reason to continue debating privacy issues? Should people simply behave as if every conversation is being recorded and useable as evidence in the event of a crime?

*Sources:* "Legislature could try again on eavesdropping in fall," by D. Thomas, June 4, 2012. *The State Journal-Register.* "Chicago police can be recorded at NATO summit," by J. Keyser, April 29, 2012. *Journal Star* (Peoria), p. B7; "Illinois Gen. assembly revives recording ban," December 5, 2014. IllinoisPolicy.org.

## ■ BIOLOGICAL IDENTIFIERS

### Fingerprints

Because they identify unique individuals, fingerprints have been used for many years to identify victims, suspects, and perpetrators. They are also used to access secure facilities and equipment and to check for criminal records. The police have routinely kept fingerprints of criminals on file for years, but because they had to be checked by hand for a match, and because the files were often maintained locally and not shared with other agencies, they were seldom used to their full potential. Currently, however, prints are stored as electronic pictures on computers and are accessible to police around the world. Computers can now rapidly scan millions of files and can locate possible matches. If a suspect's fingerprints are on file somewhere in the world, it is likely that a specific police agency can locate them and identify the suspect.[82]

One development in fingerprint technology is the increasingly widespread use of **fingerprint scanners**. A fingerprint scanner system has two basic jobs—it needs to get an image of the finger, and it needs to determine whether the pattern of ridges and valleys in this image matches the pattern of ridges and valleys in prescanned images.

Once the scanner processor ascertains that a clear image has been captured, it compares the print to stored data. This is done using algorithms to compare specific features of the fingerprint, known as minutiae. To get a match, the scanner system has to find a sufficient number of minutiae patterns that the two prints have in common.[83] There are numerous uses of fingerprint scanners in both private and public policing. There are clear-cut advantages over ink and paper prints, those most obvious being the speed with which analysis can be accomplished.

### Facial Recognition

New surveillance and identification techniques that can be used to identify and eavesdrop on unwitting community members are emerging quickly and being implemented before society can determine the legitimate use of those tools. There are always reasons to adopt more powerful law enforcement tools, but these must be weighed against the constitutional rights to privacy of regular citizens, which the new

---

**Policing in Practice Video:**
What technology should students interested in policing careers learn or be educated on?

■ **Fingerprint Scanner:** Takes an image of the finger and determines whether the pattern of ridges and valleys in the image matches the pattern of ridges and valleys in prescanned images

---

The use of fingerprint scanners has greatly accelerated the speed with which law enforcement can complete comparison analysis.

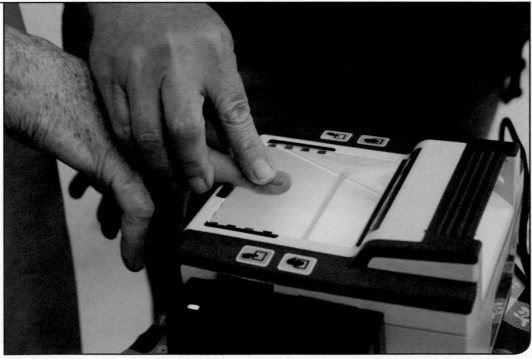

© Signatures Collection

tools increasingly undermine. Proponents of new technologies often claim that they help the police respond immediately to crimes in progress or to intercept criminals before they can carry out their plans. On the other hand, we have seen the erosion of constitutional privacy rights and ever more intrusive means of gathering information. The police are becoming capable of identifying a person stopped for a traffic violation with only a photo, amassing huge databases and accessing existing ones such as driver's license photos, storing information of law-abiding citizens. This may be a case of it being easier to ask for forgiveness than permission.

In 2013, the Chula Vista Police Department, near San Diego, began piloting the use of facial recognition technology. The Tactical Identification System matches photos that officers take in the field to those stored in databases of 350,000 arrestees and 1.5 million booking photos. With facial recognition, the police can compare a photo of an individual almost instantly to the faces in the database and identify the person in question, no ID required. Without a photo, they can view driving records, criminal records, and immigration status. The police can also identify someone who is injured and unresponsive.

The program—in use by the San Diego Police and Sheriff's Departments—was rolled out quietly, without any public hearing or notice. This came at a time when the debate on the sharing of massive amounts of data on the public is widespread and ongoing.[84] The information storage is a key factor; the San Diego Police Department claims that the data are safeguarded, but it appears to be up to individual officers to delete photos from their handheld devices.[85]

The technology was originally developed for use in the wars in Iraq and Afghanistan; thus, this is another example of military technology being adapted for domestic use in law enforcement.

## DNA

DNA evidence can be used to identify a perpetrator—even decades after the commission of a crime.[87] **DNA (deoxyribonucleic acid)** is one of two types of molecules that encode genetic information. While only about one-tenth of a percent of DNA (about 3 million bases) differs from one person to the next, scientists can use these variable regions to

**DNA (Deoxyribonucleic Acid):** One of two types of molecules that encode genetic information

---

**Exhibit 13.2**

### Facial Recognition Software

Facial recognition is one of several types of biometric information on the cutting edge of identity technology. The FBI has developed a comprehensive program called Next Generation Identification, which comprises the following developing technologies:

- Advanced Fingerprint Identification Technology increases accuracy, processing speed, and system availability.

- The Repository for Individuals of Special Concern (RISC) allows officers to rapidly identify wanted persons, suspected terrorists, and registered sex offenders.

- The Interstate Photo System is a database of 23 million photos that provide leads but not positive identification.

- The Universal Latent File and National Palm Print System (NPPS) contain millions of palm prints that are searchable on a nationwide basis.

- The Rap Back Service notifies law enforcement agencies of criminal activity by parolees and probationers.

- Iris Recognition is a new tool to accurately identify individuals that is becoming more accurate and more widespread.[86]

## Sheriff's Department Surveillance Program Angers Residents

The sheriff's department in Los Angeles had detected a string of necklace snatchings in Compton and were looking for a solution. Over nine days in early 2012, the Los Angeles County Sheriff's Department flew a small plane in a continuous loop over the city of Compton, filming it in real time. The plane was equipped with a dozen wide-angle industrial imaging cameras that recorded low-resolution footage of every area in the city (the equivalent of 800 video cameras) and sent them to Compton Sheriff's Station. At the station, deputies observed the local crime, as well as the everyday activities of the city's residents. The flights were part of an aerial surveillance campaign aimed at fighting crime in the cities and unincorporated county areas under the sheriff's jurisdiction. The desert community of Lancaster, approximately 80 miles north of Compton, was also part of the same pilot observation program.

The sheriff's department publicized the aerial surveillance program at a council meeting in Lancaster. However, anticipating resistance to the idea, the sheriff did not inform the residents of Compton. Two years later, they found out about it from the Center for Investigative Reporting. The revelation angered many Compton residents. In response, Compton mayor Aja Brown proposed a "citizen privacy protection policy" to require sheriff's officials to make public notification next time they deploy monitoring equipment.

The surveillance program not only angered residents and civil libertarians, but at least one technologist expressed doubts about whether the video was intrusive enough to actually impact crime. The images may be comprehensive, but they are not detailed enough to use for positive identification. The program came at a time of increasing debate over the advantages and dangers of high-tech surveillance techniques, which can be used to eavesdrop on unwitting community members.

Sheriff's department officials attempted to defend the program by pointing out that Compton residents had already been under surveillance since 2007 with ground-based video monitoring. A spokesperson for the sheriff's department stated that the department had decided against fully deploying the program because "it didn't enhance the law enforcement capacity of the department." Lancaster officials decided to hire a private contractor to continue to supply them with aerial views for a cost of $90,000 a month.

1. Do you think the sheriff's department deployed the program appropriately? Why or why not?

2. How much notification should the public receive about police surveillance?

3. What restrictions should the police have to observe with regard to aerial surveillance?

*Source:* Adapted from "Sheriff's secret air surveillance of Compton sparks outrage," by A. Jennings, R. Winton, and J. Rainey, April 23, 2014. *Los Angeles Times.* "Hollywood-style surveillance technology inches closer to reality," by G. W. Schulz and A. Pike, April 11, 2014. *The Daily Reveal.*

generate a DNA profile of an individual, using samples from blood, bone, hair, and other body tissues and products. In criminal cases, this generally involves obtaining samples from crime scene evidence and a suspect, extracting the DNA, and analyzing it for the presence of a set of specific DNA regions or markers.[88]

The analysis technologies used in forensic DNA investigations are beyond the scope of this text; it is safe to say, however, that proper collection and preservation of DNA evidence by crime scene technicians or investigators can both help convict the guilty and exonerate the innocent. According to the Innocence Project, for example, some 200 male prisoners who have served a combined total of 2,496 years have been exonerated by DNA evidence.[89] Although it may be impossible to determine the number of suspects convicted as a result of DNA analysis, the number is certainly significant, and even more advanced technology appears to be on the horizon. It is predicted that DNA chip technology (in which thousands of short DNA sequences are embedded in a tiny chip) will enable faster, less expensive analyses using many more probes and raising the odds against coincidental matches.[90]

Still other developments that may aid police officers in apprehending offenders hold promise for the future. For example, fingerprints can be smudged or impossible to obtain on some surfaces, and blood, tissue, semen, or saliva may not always be present in sufficient quantities for analytic purposes, but each of us leaves a unique trail of bugs (in this case, hand germs or bacteria) behind as we conduct our daily activities. Some have predicted that bacterial trail will become a valuable new tool for forensic scientists.[91] These bacteria are abundant, can be lifted from small areas, and remain essentially unchanged after two weeks at room temperature. According to some researchers, it may be easier to recover bacterial DNA than human DNA from touched surfaces, although they caution that additional studies are needed to confirm initial results.[92]

Among the objections to DNA databases, for example, are the allegations that DNA typing is not a mature enough technology to avoid false matches, that extracting DNA samples invades bodily integrity, that forensic genotyping reveals intensely personal information, that offender databases and data banks might be used for purposes other than criminal justice, that DNA data banking invades the privacy of innocent relatives, and that using samples from offender data banks for genetics research violates the Nuremberg Code.[93] Other databases are subject to criticism on variations of these objections—for example, that databases on sex offenders sometimes contain inaccurate information and that they punish innocent relatives by identifying them with the listed offenders.

**Audio Link:**
After SCOTUS DNA Ruling, What Changes for Police?

## Exhibit 13.3

## Police Databases

There are dozens of databases, other than the Integrated Automated Fingerprint Identification System (IAFIS) and DNA data banks, that contain information useful to or provided by police agencies, and many of these are also accessible to the public:

*Bureau of Alcohol, Tobacco, Firearms and Explosives (ATF)*—with the advent of the Internet, seizes the opportunity to employ Internet subscribers in its continuing effort to combat violent crime by advertising wanted persons

*Drug Enforcement Administration (DEA) Fugitives*—contains information about DEA fugitives who are being tracked and are listed by field division, and information concerning major international fugitives and captured fugitives is also available

*Federal Bureau of Investigation (FBI) Crime Alerts/FBI Most Wanted List*—provides information about the FBI's efforts to locate fugitives and missing persons

*FBI Most Wanted Terrorists*—includes information concerning alleged terrorists who have been indicted by federal grand juries in various jurisdictions in the United States for the crimes reflected on their wanted posters

*FBI National DNA Index System*—contains data or records (e.g., the genotypes), and data banks store the original samples taken from offenders

*Immigration and Customs Enforcement (ICE) Most Wanted Fugitives*—provides information on ICE's top fugitives

*Interpol Most Wanted*—the official site of the International Criminal Police Organization (Interpol) provides rapid access to official, controlled information (National wanted websites, http://www.interpol.int/Crime-areas/Fugitive-investigations/National-wanted-websites).

### Bacterial Forensics

The next frontier for investigations may be the analysis of bacterial traces that can identify specific individuals for forensic purposes. Scientists now believe they can analyze the bacterial exchange between humans and their environment. According to researchers, individuals leave highly detectable microbes behind when they touch things, through their footprints, and on their cell phones.[94] The microbial "fingerprint" appears to be quite stable as well, remaining identifiable up to a year after its collection.[95] As this technology develops, it may in many cases replace the need for DNA analysis, for example in sexual assault cases.[96]

## ■ SPEED DETECTION DEVICES OR SYSTEMS

**■ Radio Detection and Ranging (RADAR) Systems:**
Use remote sensors that emit electromagnetic radio waves to determine vehicle speeds

Police have used a variety of detection systems to monitor vehicle speeds and issue traffic citations for violators. Use of patrol car speedometers was one of the first techniques and may still be used occasionally when more technologically sophisticated systems are unavailable or inoperable. Since the late 1940s, police have used **radio detection and ranging (RADAR) systems**, which use remote sensors that emit electromagnetic radio waves to determine vehicle speeds. These systems may be either moving (e.g., mounted in patrol cars, aircraft) or stationary to measure the speed of oncoming or receding traffic. They often track one or two targets at a time. Detection ranges vary, but may be up to a mile or more.[97]

**■ Photo Radar:**
Automatically detects a speeding violation and photographs or video records the driver, the vehicle, and the license plate, and records vehicle speed and typically the date, time, and location

**Photo radar** automatically detects a speeding violation and photographs or video records the driver, the vehicle, and the license plate and records vehicle speed and the date, time, and location.[98] In addition, photo radar often connects to a computer or printer to retrieve stored data, including the number and type of prior violations. In many cases, violators do not even know they have been detected and recorded until they receive a ticket and a photograph of the driver and license plate in the mail. Even though the registered owner of the vehicle may not be the driver in the photograph, he or she still receives the ticket.

**■ Laser Radars:**
LADARs (LAser Detection And Ranging) or LIDARs (LIght Detection And Ranging) use laser light to determine speed

**Laser radars** (referred to as LADARs [LAser Detection And Ranging] or LIDARs [LIght Detection And Ranging]) were introduced in the early 1990s and use laser light instead of the radio waves that are the basis of conventional radar to determine speed

Police use handheld RADAR systems to detect the speed of oncoming or receding traffic.

© Courtesy of the U.S. Air Force, http://www.kirkland.af.mil/

(the term *laser radar* is technically inappropriate).[99] As is the case with other speed detection systems, a number of rules apply to the use of lasers to detect speed. These include the following:

1. Adequate training and experience on the part of the operator

2. Certification of the device as acceptable in the jurisdiction in question

3. Verification or calibration of the detection device prior to the beginning of the operator's shift and again at the end of the shift (to ensure the unit is operating properly)

4. Proper inspection and maintenance by the manufacturer

5. Testimony of the operator indicating that the speed reading was properly obtained and was within the limits of the equipment

6. Proper identification of the targeted vehicle

7. Testimony that the detection device was properly operated and positioned at the time of the reading[100]

A **Visual Average Speed Computer and Recorder (VASCAR)** is a semiautomated technique for determining the speed of a moving vehicle is used by the police to apprehend speeders in jurisdictions where RADAR or LIDAR are illegal or to prevent detection by drivers using radar detectors. A VASCAR unit couples a stopwatch with a simple computer. The operator calculates a vehicle's speed by recording the time it takes the vehicle to pass between two fixed objects that are a known distance apart.[101]

The **Electronic Non-Radar Detection Device (ENRADD)** speed detection system uses infrared beams to measure a car's speed as it passes through a three-foot-long section of road. Sensors detect when a vehicle enters and leaves the section. A display unit indicates the resulting number for the officer.[102] Police officers must start and stop the timing device. Motorists who challenge their citations sometimes allege operator error. When using ENRADD, the vehicle triggers the switches starting and stopping the clock. The officer has no hands-on role but simply reads the display, removing this particular challenge to citations.[103]

The key to the use of speed detection devices or systems is officer training. When properly deployed, such systems accurately detect not only speed, but also the make and model and license number of the vehicle. In some cases, they also provide identification of the driver.

## ■ ARMOR AND WEAPONS

### Body Armor

Humans have been wearing various forms of **body armor** for thousands of years, so the concept is an old one. In the 1960s, engineers developed a unique form of soft body armor constructed from advanced woven fibers that could be sewn into vests and other soft clothing.[104] As a result, more than 3,000 police officers' lives have been saved by body armor since the mid-1970s.[105] However, it is important to note that bulletproof body armor does not exist. Today, body armor can provide protection against various types of handgun ammunition, and the armor is usually categorized and rated for different threat levels. For example, additional protection is normally employed for SWAT team operations, hostage rescues, and special operation assignments in which police officers are exposed to greater threats that require additional protection than regular-duty body armor.[106] In some of these high-risk incidents, even the perpetrators wear body armor to protect themselves from police weapons.

Most agree that body armor affords police officers protection from a variety of assaults and accidents. A police officer *not* wearing body armor is 14 times more likely to suffer a fatal injury compared to an officer wearing body armor.[107] However, though the number

**Visual Average Speed Computer and Recorder (VASCAR):** A semiautomated technique for determining the speed of a moving vehicle by recording the moment that a vehicle passes two fixed objects that are a known distance apart and the time the target vehicle takes to travel between them

**Electronic Non-Radar Detection Device (ENRADD):** A speed detection system using infrared beams to measure a car's speed as it passes through a three-foot-long section of road using sensors placed on each side of the road to detect when a vehicle enters and exits the section

**Body Armor:** A defense covering worn by police officers that is usually constructed of woven fibers that are sewn into a vest or soft clothing

appears to be increasing, many officers fulfill their duties without the protection of body armor. A 2002 survey by DuPont indicated that 45% of U.S. police departments failed to mandate vest wearing by policy. By 2007, however, 67% of local police officers were employed by a department that required them to wear protective body armor at all times while in the field.[108] By 2013, approximately 71% of police departments required officers to wear body armor.[109] (See Figure 13.4.)

Future body armor research will most likely benefit from experiments being conducted for the U.S. Army. The army hopes to develop an advanced infantry uniform that integrates nanotechnology, exoskeletons, and liquid body armor by 2020.[110] This may exist only in concept, but the basic components include the following:

- *Helmet*—houses a GPS receiver, radio, and wide and local area network connections
- *Warrior psychological status monitoring system*—layers closest to the body that contain sensors that monitor heart rate, blood pressure, and hydration
- *Liquid body armor*—consists of a magnetorheological fluid that remains in a liquid state until a magnetic field is applied, at which time it transforms from a soft to a rigid state in thousandths of a second
- *Exoskeleton*—lightweight composite devices that attach to the legs and augment the strength of the person wearing the uniform

**Video Link:**
Anderson Police Trade Batons for Nunchucks as Nonlethal Weapon of Choice

### Police Weapons

Society has provided the police with the authority and obligation to enforce the law, sustain order, and ensure the safety of citizens. To fulfill these obligations, police officers need credible means of countering threats.[111] Thus, according to the research, several factors pertain to the weapons police officers use in society—including human considerations, judicial and societal requirements, and tactical and technical issues.

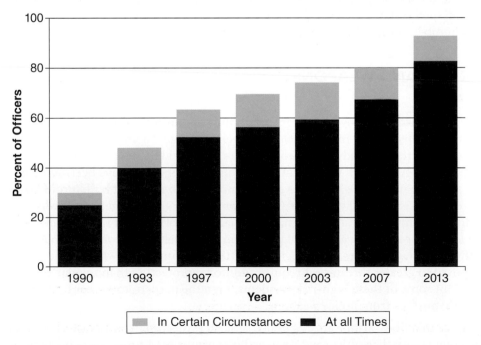

Figure 13.4 ■ Local Police Officers Employed by a Department With Body Armor Wear Requirements for Patrol Officers, 1990–2013

*Source: Local police departments, 2013: Equipment and technology, by B. A. Reaves, 2015. Bureau of Justice Statistics.*

© AP Photo/Grand Rapids Press, Chris Clark

Body armor is an important aspect of a police officer's uniform, though no body armor is completely bulletproof.

In most cases, police employ a use-of-force options chart to assist officers in determining the amount of force to use in a specific situation. The chart dictates the appropriate options based on the subject's conduct. For example, if a person is assaultive, the officer has the option of using a personal weapon, control holds, or OC spray. In effect, more severe circumstances require more force, and less force is required in less serious circumstances. Less-lethal force is most often appropriate under the following conditions:

- Lethal force is not appropriate.
- Lethal force is justified, but lesser force may subdue the person or resolve the situation.
- Lethal force is justified but could cause collateral effects, such as injury to innocent bystanders.[112]

The following are several examples of technology that police officers can use in less-than-lethal-force situations:

- **Conducted energy device**—involves devices, such as Tasers, stun guns, or stun belts, that induce involuntary muscle contractions that temporarily incapacitate the person. These electrical devices produce an immediate effect. In 2011, over 15,000 police and military agencies used conducted energy devices such as Tasers, compared to 47% in 2003.[113]
- **Directed energy devices**—technology that uses radiated energy to achieve similar effects to blunt force, but with a lower probability of injury (Tasers). In many cases, this device stimulates nerve endings, which causes intolerable discomfort to the person but no lasting or long-term effects.
- **Chemicals**—involves chemicals such as OC spray, tear gas, and stink bombs.
- **Distraction**—temporarily incapacitates individuals while causing little harm—includes the laser-based dazzler, bright lights, and noise.

■ **Conducted Energy Devices:** Devices such as a Taser that can induce involuntary muscle contractions that can temporarily incapacitate people

■ **Directed Energy Devices:** Use radiated energy to achieve the same effect as blunt force with a lower probability of injury

- **Vehicle-stopping technology**—includes devices that disrupt and stall a vehicle's electrical system and tire-deflator devices that immobilize vehicles.
- **Barriers**—nets, foams, and physical barriers.
- **Blunt force**—projectiles such as the rubber bullets used in crowd control.[114]

Although Tasers are generally considered devices that deliver less-than-lethal force, there have been many incidents in which a person died following being exposed to a Taser by the police. Officers generally resort to a Taser if an individual is noncompliant or resisting arrest. Still, there may be complicating circumstances, such as the individual's health status, his or her intoxication level, and the specific "dose" from the device. Certainly, given the potential for unnecessary harm, ongoing and improved training on Taser use could help decrease the number of unintentional killings from this less-than-lethal weapon.[115] (See Figure 13.5.)

**Physical restraints** involve a variety of products that are employed to physically restrain or impede the movement of an individual. They are almost always used in conjunction with less-than-lethal devices. A net gun can discharge a large net and incapacitate people.[116] The net can snare an individual in a web of indestructible nylon and immobilizes the person without physical contact. Another form of physical restraint is a surface chemical substance that makes a surface extremely slippery or extremely sticky.

Finally, research is continuing into the use of calmative agents as a less-than-lethal option for police officers. **Calmative agents** involve pharmaceuticals or sedative drugs that produce a calming or tranquil state.[117]

Excellent examples of new technologies being tested include a handheld detector of concealed weapons that should be available in a few years and the use of acoustic (sonic or ultrasonic) weapons to confuse or incapacitate offenders. The federal government has

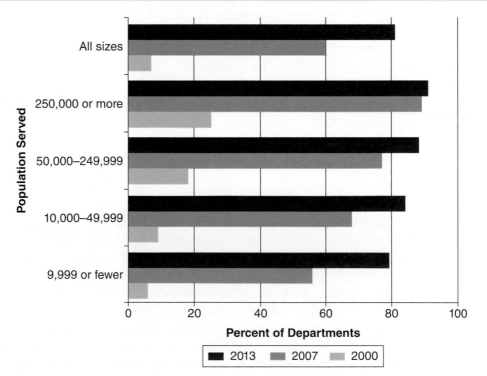

Figure 13.5 ■ Local Police departments authorizing the use of conducted energy weapons, by size of population served, 2000, 2007, and 2013

*Source: Local police departments, 2013: Equipment and technology*, by B. A. Reaves, 2015. Bureau of Justice Statistics.

**Physical Restraints:** A variety of products employed to physically restrain or impede the movement of a person

**Calmative Agents:** Pharmaceutical or sedative drugs that produce a calming or tranquil state

invested in a weapons detector that emits a sonic pulse; when a knife or gun is present, the pulse is reflected back, triggering an alarm and a light. At least some researchers are convinced that findings clearly demonstrate that acoustic technology is a low-cost alternative to conventional imaging methods for concealed weapons detection.[118] This technology has applications for municipal police as well as DHS officials in settings such as airports, trains, and bus terminals, to mention just a few.

Other sonic or ultrasonic research has focused on the use of weapons that can distract, harass, injure, or even kill a target using sound. At enough decibels, sound can rupture the eardrums and cause extreme pain. Such weapons have been used on some ships to prevent pirates from gaining control, indicating potential international applications of the technology.[119]

Police patrol cars throughout the United States are among the most technologically sophisticated and well-equipped vehicles on the road today. Configured with laptop computers or mobile digital terminals/computers, in-car cameras, automated license plate readers, multiband radios, RADAR/LIDAR devices, automated vehicle location, emergency lights, sirens, and much more, the cockpit of the typical police car might appear to the uninitiated to be nearly as complicated as that of a jet airplane and every bit as crowded.[120]

## CHAPTER SUMMARY

There is perhaps no single issue that has affected the field of policing more than technological advancements. Not that long ago, officers used in-car radios to communicate with their dispatchers and facsimile machines to transmit the fingerprint cards of arrestees to the state bureaus of identification to check for possible outstanding warrants or to learn the criminal histories of their suspects. Now, many departments devote significant resources to equip their officers with highly sophisticated technologies that are used as a matter of routine. The benefits and capacities of technological innovation generally outweigh their financial costs, the possibility of malfunction or misuse, and the department's potential vulnerability due to its dependence on a fallible tool.

Some examples of police technology are compact, mobile radios that connect instantly with dispatchers; in-car video cameras to record officers' interactions with citizens; laptop computers to compose officers' written reports, conduct driver's license checks, and receive criminal histories on suspects instantaneously; a computer screen that can scan a suspect's hand to determine a suspect's true identity by comparing the prints in question with millions of records maintained by the FBI and state bureaus of identification; cameras in public areas that can record the actions of citizens caught by the camera lenses; new and improved forensic capabilities such as DNA testing; and dozens of other capabilities used in the fight against crime.

These improvements in technology, however, come with potentially serious legal issues—particularly with respect to privacy rights of individuals. Constitutional issues such as invasion of privacy and lack of probable cause have been the subject of much debate among the legal community with respect to these new technologies. The courts have yet to rule extensively on these matters. Many cases will have to work their way through the legal system.

Finally, sophisticated computer technology has given law enforcement the ability to map crime and gather all of the pertinent details associated with individual acts of crime. Systems like CompStat and I-CLEAR are good examples of these types of police databases. Such programs are of great assistance in the fight against crime, particularly with respect to the prevention of crime. But they too have drawbacks and limitations.

There is no doubt that technology will continue to play an important role in policing. Police departments across the nation and of all sizes must carefully evaluate the tendency toward increased invasion of privacy. The innovations required for the implementation of intelligence-led policing, predictive policing, and other new strategies will likely continue the rapid development of new police technologies. As this occurs, police administrators and the courts will be challenged to stay current with the necessary limits on the use of technology to ensure that police authority is not abused.

## KEY TERMS

- Mobile Digital Communicator (MDC)  316
- Computer-Aided Dispatch (CAD)  316
- Automatic Vehicle Location (AVL)  317
- Geographic Information System (GIS)  317
- Illinois Citizen and Law Enforcement Analysis and Reporting (I-CLEAR)  318
- Psychophysiological Detection of Deception (PDD)  318
- Employee Polygraph Protection Act of 1988 (EPPA)  319
- CCTV  319
- Red light cameras  319
- Graffiti cameras  319

- Electronic Communications Privacy Act (ECPA)  323
- Foreign Intelligence Surveillance Act (FISA)  323
- National Security Letters (NSL)  323
- Digital Collection System Network (DCSNet)  323
- License Plate Recognition System (LPR)  325
- Automatic Number Plate Recognition (ANPR)  325
- Internet protocol (IP) cameras  325
- Drones  326
- Crime mapping  327
- Crime analysis  327
- Density analysis maps  328

- Fingerprint scanner  330
- DNA (deoxyribonucleic acid)  331
- Radio Detection and Ranging (RADAR) systems  334
- Photo radar  334
- Laser radars  334
- Visual Average Speed Computer and Recorder (VASCAR)  335
- Electronic Non-Radar Detection Device (ENRADD)  335
- Body armor  335
- Conducted energy devices  337
- Directed energy devices  337
- Physical restraints  338
- Calmative agents  338

## DISCUSSION QUESTIONS

1. Technological changes in policing may have both positive and negative consequences. Discuss some of the potentially positive consequences. What are some of the ethical considerations involved in the proper use of police technology?

2. What are some of the technological applications of mobile data terminals, GPS, and CAD systems in private and public policing? Are there any major disadvantages to these applications?

3. How do video cameras in police cars (and other mobile video cameras as well) help ensure accountability? What is the role of such cameras in protecting officers and other citizens during police encounters? What are the disadvantages to having mobile cameras record such encounters?

4. Why have crime mapping and associated crime analysis become so popular in policing today? Is the evidence concerning the results of crime mapping and analysis convincing to you? Why or why not?

5. If you were to note one major advantage of DNA analysis for the police, what would it be? What is the major advantage for suspects? What is the major disadvantage for suspects?

6. In your opinion, has the variety of speed detection devices employed by the police reduced the number of drivers who violate speed laws? Why or why not?

7. What have been the major improvements in the area of police body armor and weaponry during the past decade? Is there any downside to the use of either?

## INTERNET EXERCISES

1. View two articles that discuss future trends in policing technology. What are the most recent developments? What are the companies that are producing these technologies?

2. Using JUSTNET.org, choose one of the items on the "Tech Topics" menu and compare that information to two other news articles on the same topic.

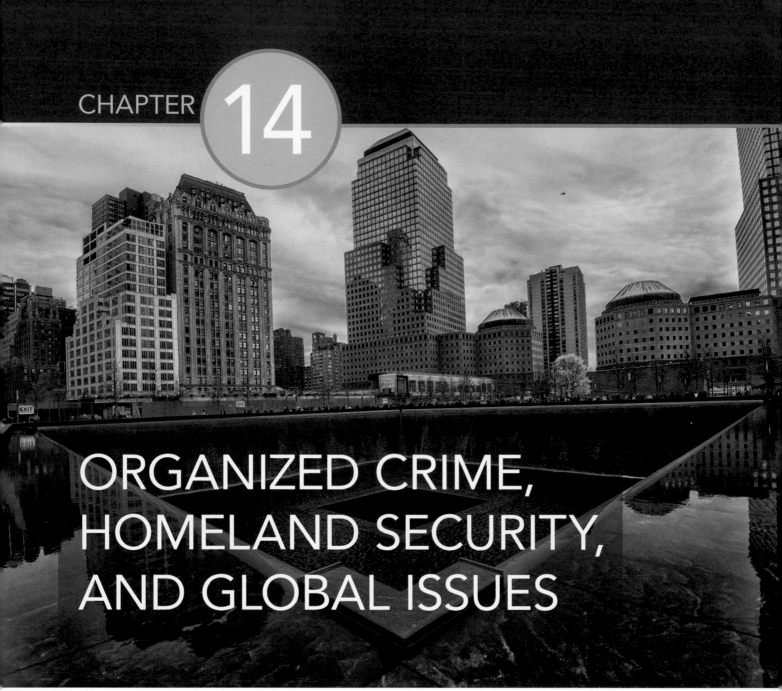

CHAPTER

# 14

© Signature Collection

# ORGANIZED CRIME, HOMELAND SECURITY, AND GLOBAL ISSUES

## CHAPTER LEARNING OBJECTIVES:

1. Identify the various factors that have vastly expanded transnational crime

2. Discuss the economic, social, and political costs associated with white-collar crime

3. Describe local and global conditions that give rise to acts of terrorism

4. Identify recommendations for improved law enforcement and citizen responses to terrorism and transnational organized crime

In this age of international organized crime, terrorism, and homeland security priorities, the police community at all levels can no longer afford to ignore criminal activities once faced only by members of federal law enforcement or by the police in other countries. Continuous progress in technology, the increased mobility of persons from one country to another, significant changes in the socioeconomic conditions of the global marketplace, weak governments in unstable nations, and modified legal agreements and shifting political relationships between the United States and other countries have combined to dramatically change the way the police community operates. These interrelated and overlapping global issues significantly impact the roles and responsibilities of police in the United States.

Transnational crime, organized crime, white-collar crime, and terrorism are extremely complex; each of these topics is the subject of entire textbooks. This chapter provides context to the environment of terrorism, the need for homeland security, and the requirement that police agencies at all levels become involved in responding to global issues.

## ■ TRANSNATIONAL CRIME

Transnational crime (actually often transcontinental crime) encompasses terrorism and organized crime. (See Appendix.) The former tends to be ideological in nature, and the latter is mostly driven by financial gain. In its broadest sense, **transnational crime** is defined as "crime that takes place across national borders [and] has had profound consequences for the ordering of the world system."[1] Criminal organizations whose operations were once confined primarily to their countries of origin now operate in multiple countries throughout the world.

Political, economic, and social upheavals throughout the world, such as the **North American Free Trade Agreement (NAFTA)**, the breakdown of the former Soviet Union, **Perestroika**, and the transition to a unified monetary system in most of Europe have created opportunities for crime with an increased geographic scope. Transnational crime is especially problematic in states where the rule of law is weak and the government is unstable. Crime of this nature and scale generates vast sums of money and undermines the legitimacy of authority and economic growth.

The Millennium Declaration adopted by the Heads of State meeting at the United Nations in September 2000 reaffirmed the principles underlying U.S. efforts. The declaration states that "men and women have the right to live their lives and raise their children in dignity, free from hunger and from the fear of violence, oppression or injustice."

### Transnational Organized Crime

The Federal Bureau of Investigation (FBI) defines **organized crime** as follows:

> Any group having some manner of a formalized structure and whose primary objective is to obtain money through illegal activities. Such groups maintain their position through the use of actual or threatened violence, corrupt public officials, graft, or extortion, and generally have a significant impact on the people in their locales, region, or the country as a whole.[3]

Transnational organized crime (TOC) organizations are driven more by financial gain and power acquisition than by political or religious ideology. They tend to be hierarchical in structure, are governed by informal and formal rules, have a distinct division of labor, and are exclusive of membership. Their methods of dominating the illicit activity in a geographical area include bribery and violence.[5] The United Nations Office on Drugs and Crime (UNODC) defines TOC broadly as "any serious transnational offense undertaken by three or more people with the aim of material gain." The office suggests that the trend among transnational crime organizations is toward a more decentralized, "cell" structure, patterned after terrorist groups. This more diffuse

**■ Transnational Crime:** "Crime that takes place across national borders . . . [that] is poorly understood but has had profound consequences for the ordering of the world system"[2]

**■ North American Free Trade Agreement (NAFTA):** Agreement for free trade between the United States, Canada, and Mexico that became effective in 1994

**■ Perestroika:** Formal policy implemented by Russian authorities following the collapse of the former Soviet Union, whose goal was to introduce a more democratic form of government and a free-market economy for Russian citizens

**■ Organized Crime:** Any group having some manner of a formalized structure and whose primary objective is to obtain money through illegal activities; such groups maintain their position through the use of actual or threatened violence, corrupt public officials, graft, or extortion, and they generally have a significant impact on the people in their locales, their region, or the country as a whole[4]

The intricate body tattooing depicted is a telltale membership sign of Japan's most notorious transnational crime organization, Boryokudan, a.k.a. Yakuza.

**Video Link:**
Global Perspectives: William Brownfield

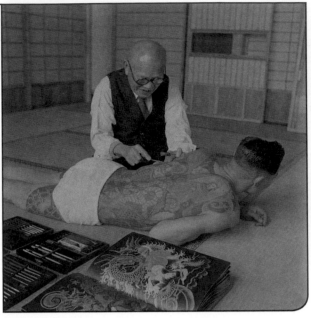

© Horace Bristol/CORBIS

organization means that the enterprise remains focused on the market for illicit activity, and the criminal activity can continue even if personnel are arrested or incarcerated.[6]

### Types of TOC

The most important categories of transnational organized crimes are human trafficking,[7] migrant smuggling, cybercrimes, environmental resources crimes (e.g., pollution, hazardous waste dumping, poaching), marine piracy, and trafficking in counterfeit goods, firearms, and heroin and cocaine.

The UNODC describes the TOC world as a network of "flows" or trafficking routes between suppliers and consumers that span international boundaries and continents. Figure 14.1 shows the main commodities and routes.

---

Figure 14.1 ■ Transnational Organized Crime Flows

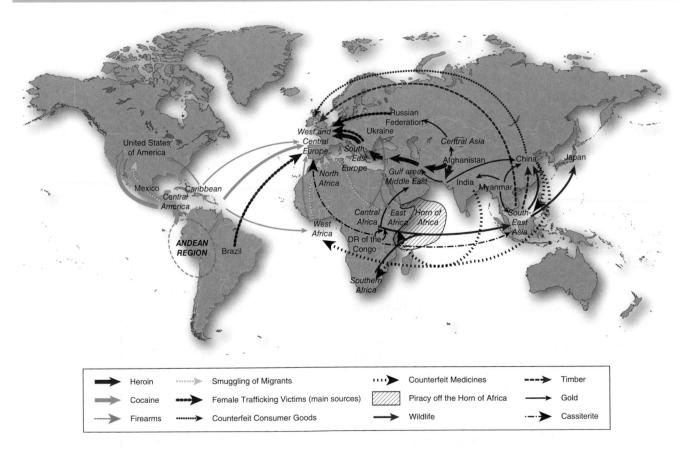

*Source:* United Nations. (2010). *The globalization of crime: A transnational organized crime threat assessment.* United Nations Office on Drugs and Crime.

---

The FBI indicates that Russian mobsters, groups from African countries like Nigeria, Chinese tongs, Japanese **Boryokudan**, other Asian crime rings, and criminals based in Eastern European nations like Hungary and Romania all have a presence in the United States or have targeted Americans from afar using the Internet and other technologies.[8]

**Boryokudan:** Also known as the Yakuza, the criminal organization initially formed in Japan that has since developed into a transnational organized crime group

## CASE IN POINT 14.1[9]

### Cybercrime and the Department of Justice

In April 2015, Assistant Attorney General Leslie Caldwell gave an address to a roundtable of cybercrime experts. Caldwell oversees the Computer Crime and Intellectual Property Section (CCIPS), whose attorneys are specialists in the "Computer Fraud and Abuse Act; electronic surveillance laws related to monitoring or gathering information from computers; and the constitutional framework for the collection and use of electronic evidence."[10]

In her remarks, Caldwell praised the efforts of the CCIPS and its "takedowns of botnets made up of hundreds of thousands of computers, to massive online identity theft operations, to other crimes facilitated by complex technologies." She then cautioned the group about the growing threat and challenges of cybercrime. She cited studies that estimate the United States leads the world with 76% of data breaches and that cybercrime costs $400 billion annually. She went on to say that organized criminals are "experts in exploiting technology to conceal their activities, causing crimes of unprecedented scale and sophistication—often invading the privacy and jeopardizing the security of information belonging to millions of individual victims."

Still, she claimed that cybercrime is stoppable and suggested that the key is in changing the game on criminals who see hacking as a "low-risk, high-reward proposition." Clearly, the federal government will want to work closely with the private sector in combating data breaches and other cybercrime.

1. How should responsible agencies measure the effectiveness of their anti-hacking efforts?

2. Consider and discuss the possible harms that cybercrime can cause.

3. Should the federal government be concerned about too much participation by the private sector in fighting cybercrime? Why or why not?

*Source:* U.S. Department of Justice. (2015, April 29). "Justice news: Assistant Attorney General Leslie R. Caldwell delivers remarks at the criminal division's cybersecurity industry roundtable"

## YOU ??? DECIDE    14.1

For decades, prosecution of organized crime was based on regular state and federal statutes. Since bosses and kingpins typically employed lower-level members to carry out the crimes, the management usually avoided prosecution. The Racketeer Influenced and Corrupt Organizations Act, or **RICO Act**, solved that problem. Prosecutors are now able to arrest and convict high-level members based on the actions of those who worked for them.

Although the initial intent was to combat organized crime, RICO has been used on any criminal undertaking that fits within the language of the statute. Under the state and federal RICO laws, police agencies and prosecutors can keep confiscated property and cash linked to a variety of crimes committed for financial gain and use that money later for gang prevention, substance abuse treatment, and fighting crime.

Defense attorneys feel that state laws allowing seizure of cash and property from defendants suspected of committing a variety of crimes for financial gain encourage police to lay claim to everything they can, and then later try to link the seized assets to criminal activity that falls under RICO.

1. Do you feel this system of "keeping the spoils" will cause police to bend rules or cross the line in search and seizure laws in order to obtain money or cars?

2. Besides gang prevention and substance abuse treatment, what else do you feel would be appropriate to use RICO funds for?

*Suggestions for addressing these questions can be found on the Student Study Site:* **edge.sagepub.com/coxpolicing3e**

**Web Link:**
Justice Department Sets Sights on Wall Street Executives

■ **RICO Act:** Federal legislation enacted in 1970 that allows prosecutors to go after the organization rather than individuals; defines racketeering in a broad manner and makes it a crime to belong to an organization involved in a pattern of racketeering

■ **White-Collar Crime:** "Illegal or unethical acts that violate the fiduciary responsibility of public trust by an individual or organization, usually during the course of legitimate occupational activity, by persons of high or respectable social status for personal or organizational gain"[12]

■ **Money Laundering:** Attempts to disguise the original source of monies, normally through illegal means, and infuse said monies into the legitimate marketplace

## ■ WHITE-COLLAR CRIME

The term *white-collar crime* was coined in 1939, when the field of criminology was asserting that high-level financial crime was as important as street crime, if not more so. **White-collar crime** has evolved into a multibillion-dollar-per-year criminal enterprise. Much of white-collar crime is transnational in scope.

> White-collar crimes are illegal or unethical acts that violate fiduciary responsibility of public trust by an individual or organization, usually during the course of legitimate occupational activity, by persons of high or respectable social status for personal or organizational gain.[11]

White-collar crime is a problem both domestically and internationally and may involve individuals as well as crime organizations. The most common white-collar offenses include antitrust violations, computer and Internet fraud, credit card fraud, phone and telemarketing fraud, bankruptcy fraud, health care fraud, environmental law violations, insurance fraud, mail fraud, government fraud, tax evasion, financial fraud, securities fraud, insider trading, bribery, kickbacks, counterfeiting, public corruption, **money laundering**, embezzlement, economic espionage and trade secret theft.

### Costs of White-Collar Crime

White-collar crime is often considered to be "victimless." Of course, this is far from the truth. According to the FBI, white-collar crime is estimated to cost the United States more than $300 billion annually. Even more staggering are the estimates pertaining to the global economic costs of white-collar crime. The World Federation of United Nations Associations estimated the global costs of white-collar crime in 2008 to be in excess of $10 trillion.[13] The social costs include a weakening of respect for the law, the loss of faith in various institutions, and erosion of the reputations of governments.

## ■ TERRORISM

No discussion of contemporary policing would be complete without consideration of terrorism—a phenomenon that has plagued numerous societies throughout the world for many years. Only in the last two decades or so have the effects of terrorist acts been felt in the United States. (See Appendix, Table A.1.)

**Audio Link:**
White Collar Crimes Drives Up London Property Prices

For most Americans, the events of September 11, 2001 (9/11), define terrorism in this country. On that infamous date, al-Qaeda terrorists hijacked four passenger jets and intentionally crashed two of them into the Twin Towers of the World Trade Center in New York City. Everyone on board was killed, as were many of those working in the buildings. Both towers collapsed, destroying nearby buildings and damaging others. The hijackers crashed a third airliner into the Pentagon, just outside Washington, DC. The fourth plane crashed into a field in rural Pennsylvania after some of its passengers and flight crew attempted to retake control of the plane, which the hijackers had redirected toward Washington, DC. There were no survivors from any of the flights. All told, 2,976 victims and 19 hijackers died in the attacks. The vast majority of casualties were civilians, including nationals from over 90 countries.

**Video Link:**
San Bernardino, California, shooting

Before 9/11, there was the bombing of the federal building in Oklahoma City in 1995 and the first attack on the World Trade Center in 1993. Other incidents of foreign terrorism affected the United States in earlier years as well.

Before 9/11, the FBI's definition was as follows: "Terrorism is the unlawful use of force or threat of violence against persons or property to intimidate or coerce a government, the civilian population, or any segment thereof, in furtherance of political or social objectives."[14] Through the years, however, researchers and law enforcement officials have changed their definitions of terrorism to be more current.

> Terrorism is a premeditated and unlawful act in which groups or agents of some principal engage in a threatened or actual use of force or violence against human or property targets. These groups or agents engage in this behavior intending the

purposeful intimidation of governments or people to affect policy or behavior with an underlying political objective.[15]

### Foreign and Domestic Terrorists

**Web Link:**
Paris Attacks and Other Assaults Seen as Evidence of a Shift by ISIS

Some acts of terrorism in the United States are transnational in origin and nature, while others are the "homegrown" or domestic variety. That is, some terrorists form their ideological hatred in cultures and societies outside the United States, and they organize their plots largely outside U.S. borders. Clearly, 9/11 was one such incident. Homegrown terrorists may have equally strong ideology but are products of U.S. society. They plan and carry out their attacks on U.S. soil and often are reacting to aspects of their own society. The Oklahoma City bombing by Timothy McVeigh and Terry Nichols and countless acts of terror by the Ku Klux Klan are examples of these. Other examples include a loose network of individuals who live in the United States called **"sovereign citizens,"** who believe they can reject the authority of the federal government and are thus exempt from paying taxes or following other federal laws. They believe that the government operates illegally and that they have a justified license to kill.[16]

Both of these—foreign enemies that are unfathomable or a neighbor who is determined to turn on his or her fellow citizens—are of intense concern to law enforcement agencies, the purpose of which is to protect and serve.

### Types of Terrorism

**Sovereign Citizens:**
A loose network of individuals living in the United States who profess to believe that federal, state, and local governments operate illegally

Terrorism takes many forms, all of which are serious and some of which are not so obvious. (See Appendix, Table A.1.) In addition to bombings, which tragically have become commonplace around the world, emergency service personnel must be able to respond to biological, chemical, and technological (or cyberterrorism) attacks. For example, just after 9/11, mail to news outlets and Senate offices were contaminated with the deadly anthrax virus. The attack killed 5 people and injured 17 others.[17] There is increased potential for "tampering with data and software in the virtual system [that] could have major repercussions in the physical world, involving such things as disruption of air traffic control systems and tampering with automated pharmaceutical

The 9/11 terrorist attacks greatly increased state and local law enforcement's involvement in preventing terrorism. Local agencies increasingly make use of new technologies and strategies such as this New York Police Department harbor launch unit used in counterterrorism patrols.

© Signatures Collection

### Nuclear Trafficking Incidents

Many criminal organizations have become international security threats. For example, the breakup of the former Soviet Union in 1991 left the infrastructure of the region quite vulnerable to exploitation. One of the key elements of that infrastructure was the military and its stockpile of weapons, including an array of nuclear materials; since 1991, many of those nuclear materials have been stolen.

The International Atomic Energy Agency's (IAEA) Office of Nuclear Security (ONS) and its Database on Illicit Trafficking (of nuclear and radioactive materials) had 116 member states in 2012.

The ONS established the database—actually, a data-collection system—as far back as 1995 to address this issue of international concern. With respect to international terrorism, a new era began after September 11, 2001. In this post-9/11 "framework," countries have augmented their detection equipment; thus, reporting of trafficking incidents involving nuclear materials has also increased. Still, the ONS only reports confirmed incidents. As of 2012, there were 2,200 reported incidents. All nuclear material is radioactive and exists in most countries in the world. Security conditions are variable; however, higher-risk materials are generally better protected. Material is often transported by truck, and sometimes these are lost or stolen by thieves who want the vehicle and are ignorant of its contents. Only a small fraction of theft of nuclear material is intended for sale to terrorists. The security network for the protection of these materials is fairly robust; traffickers have a difficult time finding buyers and are frequently apprehended.

or food production."[18] These are realities that law enforcement and counterterrorist specialists must anticipate and investigate and, of course, prevent.

It is part of the strategy and purpose of terrorists to go undetected and to take their targets by complete surprise, making the task of thwarting attacks extremely complex; further, "motivations, financing, methods of attack and choice of target are constantly changing. Terrorist acts often defy national borders; one act of terrorism can involve activities and actors from numerous countries."

As stated by one FBI agent, "Undoubtedly, terrorism is here to stay and it is the greatest threat to national security. Increased mobility, improved communication, and the potential use of weapons of mass destruction, such as biological threats, will be major challenges for investigators."[19]

**SAGE Journal Article:**
The analytical study of terrorism: Taking Stock

### Intersecting Crime Flows

The FBI estimates the worldwide monetary costs of organized crime to be in the area of $1 trillion. The trade in illicit goods, especially heroin and cocaine, generates billions of dollars. The lucrative profits of TOC sometimes end up funding insurgent groups or tempting them to forego their ideology for the pursuit of personal wealth. Migrant workers sometimes end up indentured to work in the trade of selling counterfeit goods. Unstable governments are vulnerable to a cycle of undermining control by organized criminals, and in some cases, the criminal organizations have become more powerful than the government of the state.

The illegal trade in nuclear materials, large-scale arms smuggling, and international narcotics trafficking was identified as a way of financing other transnational crimes like terrorism and illegal alien smuggling, "exacting an even higher human cost in large numbers of source and destination countries."[20] Also, the massive profits generated by transnational crime groups, estimated at billions of dollars, much of which is laundered through the world economic markets, place the security of these marketplaces at serious risk. Finally, due to the huge profits generated by these crimes, the resultant public corruption places all governments and legal systems at great risk as well. Many of these same issues are central themes related to global changes in organized crime and terrorism.[21]

## ■ LOCAL RESPONSE TO TERRORISM AND TRANSNATIONAL ORGANIZED CRIME

The international community has obviously recognized the continually changing nature and levels of transnational organized crime and terrorism. Disrupting and thwarting these activities is an international priority, especially where such threats are the most potent. U.S. authorities must coordinate their activities on the global stage; another level of coordination is required within national borders and among U.S. agencies.

For the most part, the burden of counterterrorism has fallen squarely on the shoulders of federal law enforcement agencies. However, it has become clear that policing at all levels must assume some responsibility for and commitment to containing both domestic and international terrorism and other transnational criminal activity. This updated priority has created a number of concerns for criminal justice administrators, ranging from budgetary deficiencies and training issues to investigative techniques and expanded police powers that may be subject to constitutional abuse in the name of national defense.

Prior to 9/11, many in the police community predicted that acts of terrorism would proliferate if authorities did not begin to focus on the "front end" of the terrorist problem from a "proactive and preventive organizational dynamics perspective."[22] The problem with the traditional U.S. response to terrorism was

**Video Link:**
Assessing Terror Threat for Transportation

> that the terrorists [were] always one attack ahead of the law enforcement and security professionals, and as a result of this advantage, [were] frequently successful. This advantage can be neutralized by reinforcing the government's counter-terrorist information collection and by integrating threat analysis and threat based security countermeasures tailored to interdiction operations.[23]

Local law enforcement officers have at times played a significant role in the identification, investigation, and apprehension of terror suspects, especially when those attacks occurred on U.S. soil. They are often the first to have contact with a terror suspect before, during, or after an attack. Unlike federal law enforcement agents, who have little routine contact with the public, officers from municipal, county, and state agencies contact thousands of persons each day. Some such contacts involve simple traffic stops or suspicious person calls, which can result in the identification and arrest of potential terror suspects. In other cases, investigators may uncover evidence of a terrorist plot during the service of search or arrest warrants. Similarly, subjects who are planning or who have committed acts of terror may be arrested on other, unrelated charges. The chances that local law enforcement officers will stumble upon evidence of a terror plot, encounter a terror suspect, or knowingly or unwittingly arrest someone guilty of a terrorist act are probably greater than commonly assumed.

Many police agencies now mandate some form of terrorism training that focuses on recognition and reporting. The recognition training components detail the intelligence gathering and sharing processes, collaboration among law enforcement agencies, types of terrorism, weapons of mass destruction, and safety precautions. One particular focus of the training is the recognition of suspicious activity that may not, by itself, amount to terrorism, but may be part of a larger plot. For example, if an officer stops a motorist and discovers a map of Universal Studios, radical literature, and several pounds of gunpowder, the officer is trained to take additional steps to identify the motorist, document the items, report his findings, and, if possible, arrest the motorist for a lesser crime. By recognizing the precursors of terrorist acts, the officer may identify a potential (and as yet unknown) terror suspect and prevent a terror attack.

### Antiterrorism and Organized Crime Legislation

Shortly after 9/11, and in response to the warnings from the police community, former president George W. Bush and the U.S. Congress passed two key pieces of legislation that have changed the way the United States deals with terrorism. Some federal regulations are designed to protect the U.S public while they travel. There are still other federal protections of water and food supplies, as well as power sources (gas, oil, and electric). Although the most visible changes in security have occurred in the country's airports, most of the increased protection is now under direct law enforcement control.

### Department of Homeland Security

When the Department of Homeland Security (DHS) was initially formed in 2001, its mission was

> to develop and coordinate the implementation of a comprehensive national strategy to secure the United States from terrorist threats or attacks . . . and . . . coordinate the executive branch's efforts to detect, prepare for, prevent, protect against, respond to, and recover from terrorist attacks within the United States.[24]

According to a 2001 report by the U.S. General Accounting Office (GAO), these executive-level mandates are to be accomplished by implementing a risk-management approach to reduce the risk and mitigate the consequences of future terrorist attacks:

- Conducting threat assessments "to evaluate the likelihood of terrorist activity against a given asset or location . . . [which] helps to establish and prioritize security program requirements, planning, and resource allocation"
- Conducting vulnerability assessments to identify and respond to "weaknesses in physical structures, personnel protection systems, processes, or other areas that may be exploited by terrorists"
- Performing criticality assessments "designed to systematically identify and evaluate important assets and infrastructure in terms of various factors, such as the mission and significance of a target"[25]

**Policing in Practice Video:**
How do local police departments work with federal agencies?

The DHS has broadened its scope over the past several years. Current legislation now includes specifically defined roles for the intelligence community and the U.S. military; promotes and funds public–private partnerships, including "citizen ready" initiatives; provides recommendations and funding for improved critical infrastructure protection, including "the transportation and communications and information technology industries"; and includes "preparation for and responding to incidents involving weapons of mass destruction and natural disasters."[26] The DHS has adopted a multiagency approach and related complexities regarding the national strategy in the fight against terrorism.[27]

### The USA PATRIOT Act and Information Sharing

Congress also passed the USA PATRIOT Act (see Chapter 9), which was designed to combat terrorism more effectively and proactively. USA PATRIOT is an acronym for the Uniting and Strengthening America by Providing Appropriate Tools Required to Intercept and Obstruct Terrorism.

One of the more significant components of the legislation involved police agencies and pertained directly to the relaxing of restrictions on sharing valuable intelligence among law enforcement organizations at all levels of government. There is perhaps no greater obstacle to effective criminal investigation than the lack of intelligence. This phenomenon sometimes occurs because of bureaucratic disclosure restrictions, which may be intended to maintain the integrity of an investigation, but more often than not have to do with petty jealousies or the fear of being upstaged by a different agency. Speaking to this very issue in a speech to the U.S. Conference of Mayors, FBI Director Robert Mueller III said, in part, that

> no one agency or entity at any level, whether it is federal, state or local, has the length or the breadth of talent and expertise. We must work together. Law enforcement, quite simply, is only as good as its relationships. . . . I have asked the special agents in

charge in cities where we do not already have a joint terrorism task force to get one up and running quickly. . . . They do break down stereotypes and communications barriers, more effectively coordinate leads, and help get the resources in the right places. In short, they are an excellent tool for melding us together in ways that make information sharing a non-issue.[28]

This "siloing" is not unique to law enforcement, and when it occurs, it can be an obstacle to achieving agency goals. Research shows that collaboration among law enforcement agencies *does* exist, but there is still a great deal of room for improvement.[29]

This antiterrorism law was designed to dramatically expand federal law enforcement and intelligence-gathering authority. Specifically, this new law expands federal police powers in the following ways:

- Authorizing roving wiretaps or the need for just one court order to tap multiple phone numbers, including cell phones, fax machines, and pagers

- Allowing for the detention of non-U.S. citizens suspected of terrorist activity for up to seven days without formal charges

- Giving law enforcement officials greater subpoena power for email records of suspected terrorists

- Relaxing of restrictions on information sharing between U.S. law enforcement and intelligence-gathering agencies

- Expanding current money laundering statutes by requiring more record keeping and account holder information

- Lengthening the statute of limitations for prosecuting acts of terrorism described as being "egregious"[30]

### Racketeer Influenced and Corrupt Organizations (RICO) Act

Although laws addressing the various crimes perpetrated by individual members of transnational criminal organizations are numerous, none of them reaches the depth and breadth of the RICO Act. Enacted into law as part of the Organized Crime Control Act of 1970, this far-reaching conspiracy statute addresses the criminal organization itself, in effect making it unlawful to belong to an organization that is involved in a pattern of racketeering. New crimes are added to those lists on a consistent basis as the nature and type of transnational crimes evolve.

The goal of prosecutors who use this statute is to demonstrate a pattern of crimes (racketeering) through an organization or enterprise. The statute defines an enterprise as "any individual, partnership, corporation, association or other legal entity, and any union or group of individuals associated in fact, although not a legal entity."[31] Thus, prosecutors no longer have the burden of proving separate conspiracies, because RICO— for all intents and purposes—makes it a crime in and of itself to belong to an enterprise involved in a pattern of racketeering, even if said crimes that constitute the pattern of racketeering are committed by other persons in the enterprise. This prosecutorial tool, which was designed to attack the leadership structures of these criminal organizations, has been quite effective. Prior to RICO, the leaders of such enterprises were insulated because the individual crimes were committed by lower-ranking members, albeit via the direction of higher-ranking members.[32] To fulfill the pattern requirement of RICO, prosecutors must prove the commission of at least two of the crimes the statute names within a 10-year time span.

RICO, however, also has its critics. The major criticism of the statute by attorneys familiar with this law is that it is unconstitutionally vague, especially the definitions of racketeering.[33] Nonetheless, the use of RICO against criminal organizations and other entities has proven to be quite effective. The issues surrounding this law are extremely complex and are consistently being modified through case law.

**Video Link:**
Will Leaked Secrets Damage Efforts by U.S. Intelligence?

## Race, Ethnicity, and the Police Response to Transnational Crime

Another area of great public concern regarding the new police response to terrorism is the issue of racial profiling or biased enforcement, discussed at length in Chapter 10. There is some controversy on whether the risk of terrorism justifies racial profiling. Expanded police powers must be tempered by the responsible exercise of discretionary authority. A close monitoring of the actions of the law enforcement community is called for.

A relatively recent issue related to the potential abuse of power by law enforcement officials is 2010 legislation in the state of Arizona that authorizes state and local police officers—acting under the legal doctrine of reasonable suspicion—to detain and question persons suspected of being illegal immigrants. Many politicians and citizen groups claim the law is unconstitutional, and others feel the law is necessary due to the failure of federal officials to secure the state's borders. Litigation at the state and federal levels is challenging this law. As indicated in Chapter 9, the Supreme Court delivered a split decision, sustaining its central provision known as the "show me your papers" provision (but leaving the door open to further challenges). The majority of justices rejected other provisions that would have subjected illegal immigrants to criminal penalties for activities such as seeking work.[34]

**Video Link:**
U.S. Secretary of Homeland Security Discusses Immigration

In 2015, the African American community suffered yet another and all-too-familiar blow when Dylann Roof (age 21) shot and killed nine members of a Charleston, South Carolina, church in an act of self-professed White supremacy. Part of the fallout of this tragic event was a question of whether domestic antiterrorism efforts needed to adjust and change strategy. Another of the questions this event raises is whether the acts of disturbed lone individuals who have adopted an extremist ideology constitute a rising terror threat. Other similarly concerning events include a 2011 killing spree in Norway by Anders Breivik, the 2012 shootings in Wisconsin at a Sikh temple, the infamous Boston marathon bombing of 2013, and a 2015 coffee-shop siege in Sydney, Australia. In the case of the Charleston shooting, observers are suggesting the need for a law enforcement response that goes well beyond gun control and banning of the Confederate flag, which many regard as a symbol of racial hatred.

## First-Responder Preparedness

Even with the creation of the DHS, with the expansion of powers given to the police, and with the public's heightened awareness, the threat of terrorism is an ongoing reality, both internationally and domestically. Prudence calls for preparedness for similar acts in the future.

As **first responders** in emergency situations, the law enforcement community can do a number of things to accomplish the objectives of preparedness. Although the federal government must assume the lead role in this endeavor, the nation's response to terrorism must be a concerted, multilevel effort on behalf of the police and other agencies. A variety of strategies and plans have been implemented and performed at the state and local levels. For example, states and municipalities must continue to cooperate with the various joint **task forces** sponsored by federal law enforcement organizations such as the FBI, Immigration and Customs Enforcement (ICE), the Drug Enforcement Administration (DEA), and the U.S. State Department. Using this strategy, local police officers are assigned to these and other federal agencies and are officially sworn to enforce federal laws. The advantages are numerous, especially with regard to intelligence sharing, and the benefits in terms of preparedness are significant.[35]

Some observers are concerned with the possible impacts of terrorism on police performance. Their basic concern is that increased terrorist threats will reduce resources that are devoted to ordinary policing functions. However, others suggest that heightened surveillance due to terrorist threats could have unintended crime prevention benefits at the community level.[36]

**First Responder:** In the context of law enforcement or emergency response preparedness, these are the individuals to provide the first line of defense (police officers, firefighters, emergency medical personnel, public utility personnel, etc.)

**Task Force:** Law enforcement strategy based on the promotion and use of interagency cooperation; these units are normally headed by a federal law enforcement agency with local police officers being detailed or assigned to work on the various task forces

Local law enforcement officers can use their authorities of arrest and seizure against individuals. Local police agencies are positioned to be the "eyes and ears" of federal authorities. They can be a conduit for the most current information on the street and are more likely to have relationships with the community members who may have useful antiterrorist or anti–organized crime information.

For police administrators, the implications are clear. Merely having a plan to respond to transnational crime activities is not sufficient to protect the public from the devastating effects of transnational crime in all its forms. A comprehensive approach is necessary to adequately protect the public. Enhanced and comprehensive training from a variety of sources; disseminating detailed plans to personnel; familiarizing officers with the available equipment; and comprehensive practicing of existing plans are all necessary to maintain the level of readiness required to protect the public.[37]

Smaller communities with limited budgets also must encourage their police departments, fire departments, social service agencies, health care professionals, and volunteer organizations to work together to increase their level of preparedness in response to the varied threats that acts of terrorism pose. Agencies will develop at an earlier stage of investigations better intelligence concerning terrorist activities if officers learn effective intelligence-gathering tactics such as how to identify new indicators and warnings, how crime and terrorism tactics evolve, how to place events

## POLICE ⬟ STORIES 14.1

### John Crombach, Former Chief of Police, Oxnard Police Department

The events of 9/11 had a significant impact on local policing. Even though we were pretty sure Islamic terrorists were not going to attack our community, our elected officials gave us the task of evaluating critical infrastructure and developing strategies for its security. Much of our focus shifted from local neighborhood problems to the threat of terrorism.

The special agent in charge of the local FBI office called to inform us that the Federal Bureau of Investigation would no longer be assisting us on "local" crime issues such as bank robbery and narcotics trafficking. Their focus was strictly terrorism. We trained our officers on Islamic fundamentalists and their tactics and how to identify signs of their presence in the community. After a couple of years of this, the police chiefs and the sheriff decided to blend this attention on homeland security with an "all crimes" approach. We still had local street gangs who were becoming more organized and violent. They were communicating across the border into Mexico for narcotics smuggling and hiding wanted criminal suspects. We believed that these criminal organizations were our own "local terrorists" who were victimizing our communities at a far greater rate than al-Qaeda.

Although we satisfied the requirements of the federal government for homeland security funding, we also were able to reengage the FBI, the federal marshal, and the Drug Enforcement Administration to form a task force to deal with the gangs who were responsible for homicides, narcotics trafficking, extortion, and other violent street crimes. After a two-year operation into this organized gang, we were able to arrest and prosecute over 80 of its members, along with several high-ranking gang members, two of whom were in Mexico. This successfully reduced the gang activity and the violent crime it perpetrated within the entire county.

It took the collaboration of the sheriff, the local police departments, and the federal agencies to make this model work. We complied with the federal requirements to evaluate and assess critical infrastructure and developed plans for intelligence gathering and for responding to incidents involving mass casualties or evacuations. In many ways, this evolution was good for our county, which borders Los Angeles County. The communication, cooperation, and collaboration were greater than ever in my history with the organization. We continued to simultaneously attack local crime, organized crime issues, and homeland security.

A Seattle Police officer looks over a Metro passenger bus, heavily damaged during a mock terrorist "dirty bomb" explosion, as part of a terrorism response exercise.

© Reuters Photograph

and actions in context, how to analyze components of a threat, and how to combine all of these tools to develop sound threat assessments.[38]

One example of the importance of intelligence gathering and cooperation can be seen in the New York City suburban counties of Rockland, Orange, and Sullivan where state, county, and local law enforcement officers and firefighters are committed to an interagency cooperative effort to fight terrorism.[39] Federal, state, county, and local agencies work together through New York State Division of Homeland Security and Emergency Services to field proactive counterterrorism action teams and intelligence officers to deter and prevent terrorist activities in their area. One result has been the creation of the Counter Terrorism Action Teams (CTATs). The first CTAT operation focused on the commuting public. State, county, and local police officers, deputies, and troopers spread out to train stations and bus stations within the zone, conducting security checks, giving out informational flyers, and riding the trains and buses. Officers engaged the commuting public in discussion, identifying what suspicious activity to look for and how to report it. The CTATs also deployed to shopping malls and schools. The public reacted positively to the teams, and the law enforcement agencies in the zone felt they were getting a great return in both security and public relations for the resources they devoted to it. All involved took proactive steps instead of reacting to terrorism.

Another obvious component of the local response to terrorism should be to provide state and local emergency service personnel with meaningful continuing education and training activities. The content of such training, in addition to focusing on terrorism, should stress the topics of ethics, professionalism, and the judicious exercise of discretionary authority. These efforts should assist in mitigating potential abuses that may arise during the efforts of the police to combat terrorism successfully.

### The Role of the Public

Public awareness is also an essential element in defending against terrorism. A good example of this heightened public awareness in the years following 9/11 occurred in New York City. On May 1, 2010, in the crowded Times Square area, a car bomb was discovered when a T-shirt vendor saw something suspicious (smoke coming from an unoccupied SUV on 45th Street near 7th Avenue) and alerted police. The would-be car bomber left an SUV loaded with propane and gas cans, fireworks, timing devices, and more than 100 pounds of fertilizer on the street, though luckily the fertilizer the offender chose was not the type that explodes. Police evacuated the crowds from the vicinity of the vehicle, and the bomb squad disabled the device. Within two days, police investigators working for all levels of government identified, located, and arrested the offender. In addition to professional police work, investigators were aided by video recordings from surveillance cameras in the nearby area and, ultimately, by the actions of an alert citizen who reported the suspicious vehicle to police.[40]

To better position itself to adapt to this changing threat environment, the FBI is undergoing a transformation in the way it collects and uses intelligence. The FBI continues to enhance its relationships with intelligence and law enforcement partners at all levels of government and abroad. In the words of FBI Director Mueller, "working side by side is not only our best option, it is our only option."[41]

## CHAPTER SUMMARY

Continuous advances in technology, the increased mobility of persons from one country to another, significant changes in the socioeconomic conditions of the global marketplace, and modified legal agreements and changing political relationships between the United States and other countries have combined to dramatically change the way in which the police community operates.

These and other related factors, have given rise to a global crime phenomenon known as transnational crime. Included in this broad category of crime are complex forms of organized crime, white-collar crime, and terrorism.

In all of its forms, the repercussions caused by transnational crime are devastating on a number of fronts. In addition to the human tragedies that have occurred throughout the world, costs to the global financial markets have been significant—estimated to be at least several trillion dollars annually. Moreover, the social and political costs associated with transnational crime are significant as well. These costs are felt in the form of an overall loss of faith or trust in governments by their citizens and the strained political relationships among leaders of many countries due to violations of national and international sovereignty.

The post-9/11 local police response to these crime threats has changed significantly from being reactive to being proactive in nature. There will always be more to do, but significant gains have taken place. For example, proactive police practices such as participation with federal law enforcement task forces, improved intra- and interagency cooperation in sharing pertinent information, and engaging in continuous planning and training for first-responder preparedness have become major goals of local law enforcement agencies. The issue of preparedness must also include input from emergency medical services personnel and academicians, via their curriculum offerings on international issues, and a continued focus on public awareness campaigns.

Recent legislation such as the USA PATRIOT Act and other effective laws such as RICO must continue to be applied toward these global crime organizations, and agreements between countries on effective international laws and treaties must continue as well.

The final, and perhaps most significant, point to be made from the discussion in this chapter is that if the United States, as a nation, is to respond to terrorism effectively, its efforts must be just, lawful, and responsible, and perhaps most important of all, the nation must be guided by the spirit of interagency and interdisciplinary cooperation and public awareness.

## KEY TERMS

- Transnational crime  343
- North American Free Trade Agreement (NAFTA)  343
- Perestroika  343
- Organized crime  343
- Boryokudan  345
- RICO Act  346
- White-collar crime  346
- Money laundering  346
- Sovereign citizens  348
- Task force  353
- First responder  353

## DISCUSSION QUESTIONS

1. What major global issues have affected local police operations in the United States?

2. What particular international incidents have led to the vast expansion of transnational crime?

3. What did the United Nations survey of other countries reveal about the different forms of transnational crime?

4. Based on the characteristics of the various transnational groups listed throughout the chapter, what common attributes do they share?

5. Are any of the categories of white-collar crime listed in the chapter transnational in nature? If yes, identify those categories.

6. What are some of the many economic, social, and political costs associated with white-collar crime?

7. Do you agree with Nader's notion of postponed violence? Why or why not?

8. What global conditions gave rise to the frequency of acts of terrorism?

9. What are the major functions of the Department of Homeland Security?

10. Do the fundamental constructs of the USA PATRIOT Act and the RICO statute overlap? How so?

11. What are some of the various roles of local law enforcement with respect to terrorism?

12. What recommendations can you make for improved law enforcement and citizen responses to terrorism?

## INTERNET EXERCISES

1. Identify at least three international organizations that are involved in the fight against transnational crime.

2. Identify other key legislation that was part of the Organized Crime Control Act of 1970 (in addition to RICO) and that is effective against members of transnational criminal organizations.

3. Find out what you can about sovereign citizens and other homegrown extremist groups.

4. Research the most recent incidents of terrorism and which groups are claiming responsibility for them.

## APPENDIX

The specific categories of crimes fitting such a definition are numerous, and most of the following crimes can be transnational in nature.[43]

- *Crimes against the consumer:* consumer fraud, telemarketing fraud, false advertising, price fixing, price gouging, and knockoff rip-offs

- *Manufacture and sale of unsafe products:* motor vehicles, tools, foods, pharmaceutical products, and medical devices

- *Environmental crime:* water pollution, air pollution, environmental racism (relegation of toxic dump sites to low-income communities), toxic terrorism (the unlawful disposal of toxic waste both inside and outside of our borders), and violations of the provisions of the Occupational Safety and Health Act (OSHA)

- *Institutional corruption:* corruption of the mass media, and religious frauds (e.g., phony faith healers, embezzlement of funds by church leaders, and the televangelist scandals of the 1980s)

- *Securities, investment, insurance, and banking frauds:* insider trading, manipulation of the stock and bond industries, pension fund fraud, insurance fraud in its many forms, the fraud-induced collapse of the savings and loan industry during the 1980s, and the more recent collapse of some of the largest banks in the United States and the subsequent government buyout

- *Crimes by the government:* eugenics and the use of human beings as guinea pigs, violations of sovereignty, and the abuse of power by governmental agencies

- *Corruption of public officials:* political corruption in all three branches of government, and at all levels; unlawful acts such as bribery, unlawful campaign contributions, ghost payrolling, influence pedaling, and many forms of police misconduct

- *Medical crime:* fraudulent equipment sales, home care fraud, hospital frauds, Medicare and Medicaid fraud, and nursing home abuses

- *Computer crime:* embezzlement and other financial theft, hacking, the intentional infusion of viruses into computer networks, espionage, unlawful gambling, and distribution of adult and child pornography

Terrorist attacks are usually well-planned and -coordinated efforts, often involving a number of steps.

**Target Selection**

As the goal of terrorism is political or ideological change, targets are usually selected because they have some kind of significance or symbolism to the terrorist objective or they could catastrophically disrupt business as usual, such as critical infrastructure or resources.

A terrorist attack in symbolic places such as the White House or JFK Airport would cause mass hysteria and draw significant media attention. When regular citizens suspect suspicious activity, their first instinct is not usually to call the FBI; rather, it is to contact their local police department.

For example, Jeffrey Labelle was arrested by the Montreal Police after a tip from family members. Family members became concerned and notified law enforcement about Labelle's radical views. Police officers searched Labelle's home, where they found a map, which depicted the coordinates of four different police stations. Although Labelle made no direct threat, he was arrested as a "preventive measure" and charged with one count of the terrorism hoax section of Canada's criminal code.[44]

## Planning

The planning stage includes selecting the type of weapon to be used and the person who will carry out the attack, as well as surveillance and rehearsals. The target determines the type of weapon. In many cases, it is local law enforcement officers who uncover the terror plot after responding to a call of suspicious activity.

For example, in Las Vegas, Nevada, local police officers were summoned to an extended-stay hotel room after a 57-year-old man complained of difficulty breathing. The following day, a relative of the man went to the hotel to claim his possessions and found a plastic bag containing ricin. The relative took the poison to the manager's officer, who notified the police. The police later searched the room, where they found firearms and an "anarchist-type textbook" with the entry for ricin clearly marked.[45]

## Funding

It is also necessary for terrorists to fund their activities, which may involve committing other crimes such as fraud or theft. Because local law enforcement officers are called to investigate local thefts, they stand the greatest chance of identifying and arresting terror suspects at this stage.

For example, Kevin James was arrested for a string of armed robberies of gas stations. According to authorities, he did it to obtain money for terrorist attacks against "US military operations, 'infidels,' and Israeli and Jewish facilities in the Los Angeles."[46] James ultimately received a 16-year sentence for his crimes.

## Deployment

During this active stage, the "weapon" is on route to the target. If deployment of the weapon is interrupted, there is a good chance that local law enforcement will somehow be involved. This might involve an officer stopping the driver of the deployment vehicle for a simple traffic violation and noticing something suspicious.

For example, a local law enforcement officer foiled a terrorist attack when a customs agent arrested an al-Qaeda agent with a trunk full of explosives. The agent says it was her "gut instinct" that led her to investigate Ahmed Ressam, who was attempting to enter the United States on a ferry from Canada. Agents later discovered that his plan had been to blow up Los Angeles International Airport.[47]

## Attack

During an active attack, local law enforcement is likely to be the first on scene, as is typical, or the police are already present as force protection at a large event.

For example, this is precisely what happened at Fort Hood when a local police officer confronted a gunman who had already massacred 13 people, the worst such incident at an army base in U.S. history. The officer ended the massacre by shooting the suspect four times after a chance encounter.[48] The officer was also injured during the encounter.

## Escape

Any terrorist that survives the attack must next flee the scene.

For example, despite months of planning his attack on the Oklahoma City federal building, Timothy McVeigh was captured by a state trooper for an expired registration as he fled the scene. The officer, who believed the vehicle might be stolen, asked for the registration, which McVeigh did not have. When McVeigh reached into his rear pocket, supposedly for his driver's license, the officer discovered a .45 caliber pistol in a suicide holster, along with a knife and an additional magazine and arrested McVeigh. It wasn't until two days later that the officer received a call from the FBI expressing interest in McVeigh as a possible suspect in the bombing.[49]

## Exploitation

After an attack, terrorists use it to bring attention to their cause and claim it as a victory.

For example, serial bomber Eric Robert Rudolph remained one of the most hunted men in U.S. history. Rudolph's luck, however, ran out the day he bombed the New Woman All Women Health Clinic and a premed student observed Rudolph fleeing the scene. Witnesses provided law enforcement officials with Rudolph's license plate number, but for the next five years, Rudolph eluded authorities.

However, early on May 31, 2004, a rookie police officer encountered Rudolph foraging for food in a Dumpster. Rudolph gave the officer a fake name, but the second officer recognized Rudolph from school. Rudolph's fingerprints confirmed the officers' suspicions. Rudolph pled guilty and told authorities where he had stashed more than 250 pounds of dynamite.[50]

## Table A.1 ■ Terrorist Attacks in the United States and Against Americans

**1920**

**September 16, New York City:** TNT bomb planted in unattended horse-drawn wagon exploded on Wall Street killing 35 people and injuring hundreds more.

**1975**

**January 24, New York City:** Bomb set off in historic Fraunces Tavern killed 4 and injured more than 50 people.

**1993**

**February 26, New York City:** Bomb exploded in basement garage of World Trade Center, killing 6 and injuring at least 1,040 others.

**1995**

**April 19, Oklahoma City:** Car bomb exploded outside federal office building, collapsing wall and floors. 168 people were killed.

**2001**

**September 11, New York City, Arlington, VA, and Shanksville, PA:** Hijackers crashed 2 commercial jets into Twin Towers of World Trade Center; 2 more hijacked jets were crashed into the Pentagon and a field in rural Pennsylvania. Total dead and missing numbered 2,992.

**2009**

**June 1, Little Rock, AR:** Abdulhakim Muhammad, a Muslim convert from Memphis, Tennessee, was charged with shooting two soldiers outside a military recruiting center. One was killed and the other wounded.

**December 25:** A Nigerian man on a flight from Amsterdam to Detroit attempted to ignite an explosive device hidden in his underwear. The explosive device failed to detonate.

**2010**

**May 1, New York City:** A car bomb was discovered in Times Square after smoke was seen coming from a vehicle. The bomb was ignited, but failed to detonate and was disarmed before it could cause any harm.

**May 10, Jacksonville, FL:** A pipe bomb exploded while approximately 60 Muslims were praying in a mosque. The attack caused no injuries.

**October 29:** Two packages were found on separate cargo planes. Each package contained a bomb consisting of 300–400 grams (11–14 ounces) of plastic explosives and a detonating mechanism.

**2011**

**January 17, Spokane, WA:** A pipe bomb was discovered along the route of the Martin Luther King Jr. memorial march. The bomb was defused without any injuries.

**2012**

**September 11, Benghazi, Libya:** Armed militants fire upon the U.S. consulate, killing U.S. ambassador to Libya Christopher Stevens and three other embassy officials. U.S. Secretary of State Hillary Clinton said the United States believed that al-Qaeda orchestrated the attack.

**2013**

**April 15, Boston, MA:** Multiple bombs exploded near the finish line of the Boston Marathon. Three people were killed, and more than 260 people were injured. The suspects were brothers Tamerlan Tsarnaev, age 26, whom authorities killed, and Dzhokhar A. Tsarnaev, age 19, who eventually went to trial and was condemned to death in May 2015.

**2014**

**August 19:** Members of the Islamic State in Iraq and Syria (ISIS) beheaded U.S. journalist James Foley, 40, in apparent retaliation for U.S. airstrikes against the group. Foley, who worked for *GlobalPost*, went missing in Syria in November 2012.

**September 2:** An ISIS militant decapitated another U.S. journalist, Steven Sotloff, 31, who worked for *Time* and other news outlets. He was abducted in 2013 in Syria.

**2015**

**June 17, Charleston, SC:** Gunman killed nine people and injured one at a prayer meeting in Emanuel African Methodist Episcopal Church.

**December 3, San Bernardino, CA:** Two attackers reportedly inspired by ISIS killed 14 and injured 21 at a county employee holiday party; both attackers were killed hours later in a shootout with police in which 2 police officers were injured.

*Source:* Adapted from "Terrorist attacks in the U.S. or against Americans" (www.infoplease.com/ipa/A0001454.html#ixzz1xyTe1MjgThe). Johnston, Robert. "Terrorist attacks and related incidents in the United States." (http://www.johnstonsarchive.net/terrorism/wrjp255a.html)

# CHAPTER 15

# PRIVATE POLICE

## CHAPTER LEARNING OBJECTIVES:

1. Describe the history and background of private police

2. List the size of the current private security force

3. Summarize the various roles and employment information of private and contract security personnel

4. Discuss the authority, requirements, and accountability of private security personnel

5. Explain the differences between private and public police, as well as the risks and benefits of a privatized police force

6. Identify possible strategies that could be implemented to mitigate the current discord between police and private security personnel

# ■ HISTORY AND BACKGROUND

Private or contract policing came to the United States along with the early settlers. The need to protect property and people led to the use of fortifications in some cases and the hiring of night watchmen. The slow development of public policing at all levels, along with increasing crime rates, eventually led to the emergence of private security forces. In important ways, private security interests have expanded into areas that were once the responsibility of public agencies alone.[1]

Some of the security companies that have names familiar to most people today were established in the 1800s. In the middle 1800s, Allan Pinkerton founded the Pinkerton National Detective Agency. The agency conducted investigations and provided security for railroads, railroad yards, and other industrial concerns.[2] The Pinkertons worked for the federal government collecting intelligence during President Abraham Lincoln's term, and the agency is credited with foiling a plot to assassinate President Lincoln.

At about the same time, Henry Wells and William Fargo established Wells Fargo and Company, which provided detective services and armed security personnel to guard freight shipments. A few years later, Washington Brink established Brink's Inc., which provided services similar to those of Wells Fargo but eventually expanded into armored-car and carrier services. During the same era, Edwin Holmes became the first to offer burglar alarm service, and American District Telegraph (ADT) also began installing and servicing alarm systems.[3]

William Burns, who headed the Bureau of Investigation, Secret Service (the forerunner of the Federal Bureau of Investigation), founded a detective agency under his own name in the early 1900s. The William J. Burns International Detective Agency was to become the second largest contract guard and investigative service in the United States (second only to the Pinkerton agency) until the end of the 20th century. During this period, the first fire control and detection system was developed as well under the title of Baker Industries.

Throughout the 20th century, industrial business relied almost exclusively on private agencies to protect their property. Few businesses hired their own security staffs. However, with the United States' entry into World War II, industrial firms started developing their own security systems. Today there are both.

Soon after the end of the Korean War (1953), managers who handled security operations during both World War II and the Korean War formed the American Society for Industrial Security (ASIS). ASIS was the first professional security association in the United States and has its roots in military operations. Today, it has grown into a global representative for security interests. ASIS was founded in 1955, which signifies the beginning of modern security for most security professionals.[4]

In the 1960s and 1970s, loss prevention had become a major focus for private security firms, and repositories of security information were developed and shared through various alliances, bureaus, or security institutes.

© Alexander Gardner

This photo shows Allan Pinkerton of the National Detective Agency to the left of President Abraham Lincoln. Private police from the early days of the private security industry engaged in many duties now associated with public policing.

In 1993, the National Industrial Security Program established the first federal standards for modern private security operations. These standards were designed to protect the war industry and its secrets. The program oversees private industry's need for access to classified information.[5]

### The Rise of the Modern Private Security Industry

For a variety of reasons, the use of private and contract police services increased greatly between 1980 and 2000 and has remained slightly more level since then.[6] Reflecting changing societal conditions, such as increased demands on the public police, these services grew in importance in many sectors—commercial, industrial, residential, and government. As fraud, arson, and employee theft, among other crimes committed against hotels, hospitals, warehouses, and retail establishments, became increasingly sophisticated, security consulting and private investigations firms arose to fill security needs.

**Audio Link:**
With Robberies Up, Oakland Residents Turn to Private Cops

A number of other factors have influenced the growth of private police. More affluent Americans—such as those who live in gated communities—wanted to feel safer and more insulated from criminal elements, and they could pay for premium services. Areas that had upward trends in street crime and violent crime, cutbacks in police services, or both were good markets for private security companies. More widespread use of sophisticated technology and related storage and transmission of highly sensitive data expanded a relatively new set of markets.[7]

During the economic downturn that started in 2008, the number of public police began to decline in many cities around the country.[8] Local budget cuts resulted in layoffs, furloughs, and unfilled positions. The recession altered local law enforcement in the United States by forcing some agencies to close precincts, merge with other agencies in similar straits, or even shut down. Society is used to thinking of the police as a basic and untouchable service, but many departments are struggling to provide the most basic services.[9]

Among the changes the public may observe are longer response times and reduced police presence in some areas.[10] In response to police cutbacks, in many areas in the United States, those living in townhouses, apartments, and condominiums have jointly hired private protection agents. This is not a new development, but one that has a history dating back to the early '90s.

In some low-income housing projects here [Los Angeles], the U. S. Department of Housing and Urban Development pays for security guards to protect residents from gang warfare. New York City uses private guards to police schools. Miami hires rent-a-cops to patrol its Metrorail system. . . . In Kansas City, MO, police want to contract private companies to pick up 22 jobs done by the department. Already they've replaced civilian officers at school crossings and may soon be hired to respond to security alarm calls.[11]

# ■ THE CURRENT PRIVATE SECURITY FORCE

## Numbers

It is difficult to accurately count the numbers of private police. Private agencies aren't completely transparent, employees who have only some security functions are likely to be undercounted, and it is quite impossible to know how many public police engage in private duty.

However, in 2009, private security companies in the United States numbered over 10,000, with estimated annual revenues exceeding $15 billion.[12] According to the Bureau of Labor Statistics (BLS), the number of people employed in the private security industry far exceeds the number of public police officers. In 2014, there were over 1 million security guards, compared to approximately 640,000 police officers.[13] Some estimate that there will be about 1.3 million people employed in private security by 2018.[14] Due to the sheer numbers, some suggest that the average person is much more likely to interact with private police than public police on a daily basis.

The states with the highest employment level in this occupation are California, New York, Texas, Florida, and Illinois.[15] (See Figure 15.1.)

Figure 15.1 ■ Employment of Security Guards, by State, May 2014

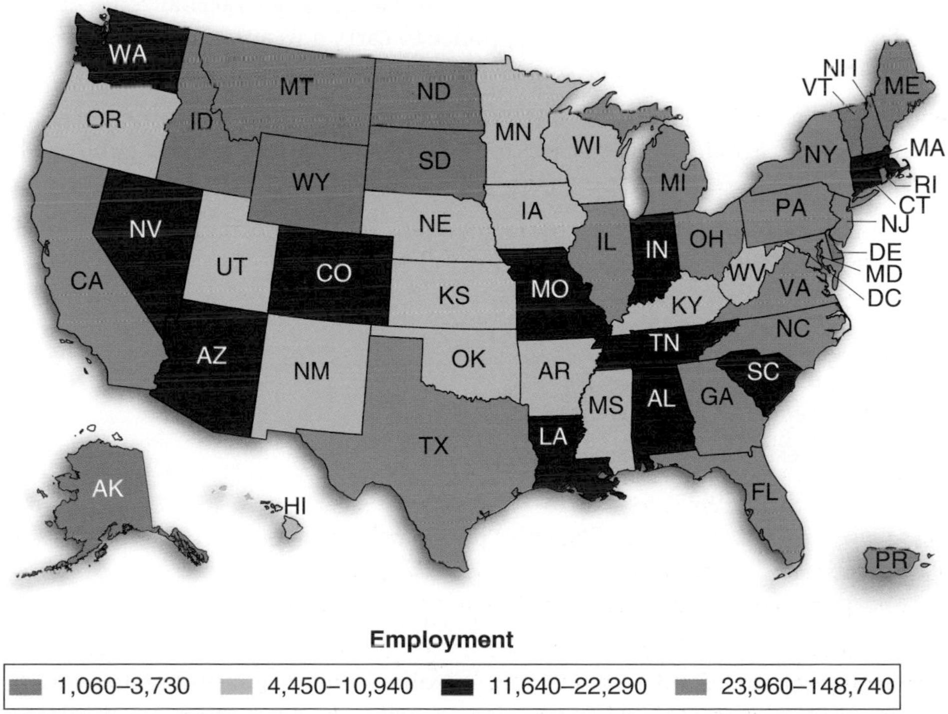

**Employment**

| 1,060–3,730 | 4,450–10,940 | 11,640–22,290 | 23,960–148,740 |

*Source:* Bureau of Labor Statistics, 2014b.

**Web Link:**
Private police carry guns
and make arrests, and
their ranks are swelling

The federal government hires thousands of contract security officers who patrol federal buildings and provide security at military bases. And in cities across the United States, private security officers protect courthouses and other public facilities.[16] As the threat of terrorism within the United States has grown, so has the need to use all forms of security to prevent and apprehend terrorists.

## ■ PRIVATE AND CONTRACT SECURITY PERSONNEL

### Who Are They?

Many individuals choose to take a direct path into the ranks of private security services; others fall back on jobs in the private sector if they fail to meet the requirements for public service. Still others—investigators in particular—enter the field after serving in law enforcement, the military, government auditing and investigation, or federal intelligence as a second career. Some agents and officers retire at 55 or even earlier and seek out lucrative private sector employment; private offers may attract others before their retirement.

Most computer forensic investigators learn their trade while working for a law enforcement agency, either as a sworn officer or as a civilian computer forensic analyst. In fact, some argue that since 9/11 the private security industry has been draining the New York Police Department (NYPD) of "serious, smart and experienced officers the city needs the most in a crisis."[17]

Much of the activity of private security forces that work internationally for counterterrorism involves former military and police personnel who provide "everything from diplomatic, convoy, embassy weapon storage and energy infrastructural security to gathering intelligence, conducting interrogations, patrolling borders on land, fighting pirates on sea and transporting goods and personnel by air."[18]

### What Roles Do They Fill?

There are different categories of private security personnel who act in a wide range of different roles. **Contract security personnel** (security guards or officers hired by security firms and then contracted to another firm) are sometimes referred to as "third-party" police. **In-house security personnel** typically are employed by and conduct security activities for a specific organization. These are also referred to as internalized security officers. They are more likely than contract police to carry a weapon, to execute a stop and frisk, and to use force to arrest a suspect.[19] **Hybrid systems** combine elements of both.

In addition, public police officers sometimes perform security work for private concern during their off-duty hours. In such cases, private security personnel and public police officers are one and the same.

■ **Contract Security
Personnel:** Security
guards or security officers
hired by organizations
from outside agencies
to secure and protect
assets and personnel

Private security personnel—whether performed by contract, internal, or moonlighting public police—can be generally categorized as follows:

- Security managers
- Security guards
- Personal security (bodyguards)
- Private investigators and detectives
- Security consultants
- Security equipment and service sales personnel
- Locksmiths
- Computer and intellectual property security personnel

■ **In-House Security
Personnel:** Typically
employees who conduct
security activities within
an organization

■ **Hybrid Systems:**
Consist of in-house
management personnel
with contract officers

There are numerous other roles for security personnel such as hospital security, airport and airline security, campus security, banking security, loss prevention, alarm response, and technology experts. For example, armored car guards protect money and valuables during transit, and they protect individuals responsible for making commercial bank deposits from theft or injury. **Gaming surveillance officers** act as security agents for casino managers and patrons. They observe casino operations for irregular activities, such as cheating or theft; monitor compliance to rules, regulations, and laws; and sometimes walk the casino floor.[20]

All of these roles can be fulfilled more effectively if there is coordination and cooperation with public police.

Public and private police frequently perform similar services, such as patrol and protection of threatened individuals, though the former are community or society oriented, while the latter tend to be client oriented. Security officers monitor security video in real time, control door and entrance access, and use motion detection tied to radio dispatch to mitigate theft risks.[21] Private police engage in conducting searches and seizures; detaining, questioning, and arresting individual citizens; and engaging in surveillance and investigation. Of course, some roles entail more coercive activities than others, but the private police are allowed to use reasonable force to conduct a citizen's arrest.[22]

© Jupiterimage

Private security officers are found in virtually all large office complexes and buildings. Owners of these structures mitigate potential civil liability in case of someone being assaulted or otherwise injured on the premises by having security officers on scene. In addition, these security officers control access to the buildings in question and will detain anyone who may have committed a criminal offense on their property. The offenders are then turned over to public police agencies.

The range of the private police is extremely wide and varied, and it is outside the scope of this text to provide an exhaustive list or complete details of all of the roles that private security personnel fill. The following profiles provide some examples.

## Security Officers

Just some of the fields **security officers** (or security guards) work in are industry, retail, hospitals, airlines, hotels, universities, and banks. Security guards often work with undercover store detectives to prevent theft by customers or employees and help apprehend shoplifting suspects. Some patrol parking lots to deter car thefts and robberies. Others work in office buildings, banks, and hospitals, maintaining order and protecting customers, staff, and property. Still others work at air, sea, and rail terminals and other transportation facilities, protecting people, freight, property, and equipment. Security guards also work in public buildings such as museums, factories, laboratories, government buildings, data processing centers, and military bases, where they protect information, products, computer codes, and defense secrets and check the credentials of people and vehicles entering and leaving the premises. Working at universities, parks, and sports stadiums, security personnel perform crowd control, supervise parking and seating, and direct traffic.[23]

Security officers may detain or arrest criminal violators, answer service calls concerning criminal activity or problems, and issue traffic violation warnings. In many instances, private security personnel investigate thefts, fraud, drugs, and violence in the workplace. In addition to providing security, they may monitor safety issues and collect critical data and information specific to clients' needs.[24]

Security guards patrol and inspect property to protect against fire, theft, vandalism, terrorism, and other illegal activity. They use radio and telephone communications for

■ **Gaming Surveillance Officers:** Hired to act as security agents for casino managers and patrons

■ **Security Officers:** Privately hired to patrol and inspect property to protect against fire, theft, vandalism, terrorism, and illegal activity

assistance from police, fire, or emergency medical services, as needed. Security guards must usually document their observations and activities. In addition, they may interview witnesses or victims, prepare case reports, and testify in court.[25] Their specific tasks depend on whether they work in a static security position or on a mobile patrol. Guards assigned to static security positions stay at one location for a specified length of time; they become closely acquainted with the property and people associated with their station and often monitor alarms and CCTV (closed-circuit television) cameras. Guards assigned to mobile patrol drive or walk from one location to another and conduct security checks within an assigned geographical zone.

### Employment

Security guards and gaming surveillance officers held over 1 million jobs in 2012.[26] More than half of all jobs for security guards were in investigation and security services, including guard and armored car services. Most other security officers were employed directly by educational services, hospitals, restaurants and bars, hotels, department stores, manufacturing firms, lessors of real estate (residential and nonresidential buildings), and governments. Gaming surveillance officers work primarily in gambling industries, casino hotels, and local government.[27] (See Table 15.1.)

## Private Detectives and Investigators

Most **private detectives and investigators** have some college education, even though there are no formal education requirements for most private detective and investigator jobs. A majority of states require private detectives to be licensed. Although related experience is usually required, some people enter the occupation directly after graduation from college, generally with an associate's or bachelor's degree in criminal justice or police science.

Private detectives and investigators held about 30,000 jobs in 2012.[28] They work in a wide variety of environments, depending on the case that they are working on. Some spend more time in their offices conducting computer searches and making phone calls. Others spend more time in the field, conducting interviews or surveillance. Investigators generally work alone, but they may work with others for specific tasks. Some of the work involves confrontation, so the job can be stressful and dangerous. Some situations—such as certain bodyguard assignments for corporate or celebrity clients—call for the investigator to be armed. In most cases, however, a weapon is not necessary, because private detectives and investigators are mostly concerned with information gathering and not law enforcement or criminal apprehension.[29]

**■ Private Detectives and Investigators:** Detectives (investigators) who are not members of the police but are hired by individual clients or companies and are often licensed by the state

| Table 15.1 ■ Security Guards and Gaming Surveillance Officers* | |
|---|---|
| 2012 median pay | $24,020 per year $11.55 per hour |
| Entry-level education | High school diploma or equivalent |
| Work experience in a related occupation | None |
| On-the-job training | Short-term on-the-job training |
| Number of jobs, 2012 | 1,083,600 |
| Job outlook, 2012–22 | 12% (average) |
| Employment change, 2012–22 | 130,200 |

*Source:* Bureau of Labor Statistics. (2015, July). *Occupational outlook handbook: Security guards and gaming surveillance officers.*

*BLS combines these two types of jobs into one category. Gaming surveillance officers are less than 1% of the total.

Some private investigators are self-employed, while others work in private detective agencies, in various jobs in private commercial enterprises, state and local government, legal services firms, employment services companies, insurance agencies, law firms, credit mediation establishments, and banks and other depository institutions.[30] (See Table 15.2.)

| Table 15.2 ■ Private Detective/Investigator Information | |
| --- | --- |
| 2012 median pay | $45,740 per year $21.99 per hour |
| Entry-level education | High school diploma or equivalent |
| Work experience in a related occupation | Less than 5 years |
| On-the-job training | Moderate on-the-job training |
| Number of jobs, 2012 | 30,000 |
| Job outlook, 2012–22 | 11% (average) |
| Employment change, 2012–22 | 3,300 |

Source: Bureau of Labor Statistics. (2015, July). *Occupational outlook handbook: Private detectives and investigators.*

### Executive Protection Agents

Every year in the United States, hundreds of individuals fall victim to workplace crimes such as violence and stalking. Experienced **executive protection agents** use strategies based on U.S. Secret Service methods to ensure the safety of at-risk individuals such as corporate executives, attorneys, wealthy families, sports celebrities, movie stars, national news and talk show personalities, political figures, presidential candidates, and civil rights leaders.[31]

## ■ AUTHORITY, REQUIREMENTS, AND ACCOUNTABILITY

Most private security personnel do not have police powers equivalent to those of public officers, but in some circumstances, private security personnel are granted such powers in specific areas on specific premises by statute. Contract personnel (typically uniformed), for example, tend to do policing more often than in-house personnel, but there are circumstances and contexts in which in-house personnel conduct policing activities very similar to those of public police and contract personnel.[32]

### Hiring Requirements

There typically are no specific education requirements for security guards, but employers usually prefer to fill armed-guard positions with people who have at least a high school diploma. Gaming surveillance officers often need some education beyond high school.

The amount and quality of training that guards receive varies widely. It is more rigorous for armed guards, for instance, because their employers are legally responsible for any use of force; armed guards receive formal training in areas such as weapons retention and laws covering the use of force. In many states, ongoing training is a legal requirement for retention of licensure.[33]

A 2012 study found that private police are "chronically undertrained" and nearly a third nationwide face almost no regulation.[34] Guards who are employed at establishments that place a heavy emphasis on security usually receive more extensive formal training. For example, guards at nuclear power plants undergo several months of training before going on duty—and even then, they perform their tasks under close supervision for a significant

SAGE Journal Article: Walking the line on police privatization: efficiency, accountability and court decisions

■ **Executive Protection Agents:** Private security personnel hired to protect executives, attorneys, wealthy families, sports celebrities, movie stars, and political figures, among others

period of time. They are taught to use firearms, administer first aid, operate alarm systems and electronic security equipment, and spot and respond to security problems.

In 1990, only 25 states licensed or regulated the security industry. A study completed in 2005 found that 43 states had such requirements.[35] As of 2010, all but nine states had some form of licensing and training requirements—administered through some form of licensing board—for companies, individual personnel, or both.[36] Even so, the requirements vary widely from state to state.

In most states, to be licensed as a security guard, an individual must be at least 18 years old, pass a background check and drug test, and complete classroom training in such subjects as property rights, emergency procedures, and detention of suspected criminals. However, the average training provided to security personnel is a small fraction of the typical training for police officers.[37]

Guards who carry weapons must be licensed by the appropriate government authority, and some receive further certification as special police officers, allowing them to make limited types of arrests while on duty. As an example, according to the Washington, DC, Police Department, any private security employee who is armed must be licensed as a "special police" officer with arrest powers.[38] Washington, DC, at one time, had over 4,000 special police officers.

## CASE IN POINT 15.1

### Manassas, Virginia

Michael Youlen stopped a local driver and cited him for driving with a suspended license. Youlen wears a badge and carries a gun. He is not a member of the local public police, but the chief and sole officer of the private police force that he created himself.

Virginia state law contains a provision that allows the courts to grant authority to private citizens to become Special Conservators of the Peace (SCOPs). An SCOP can carry a gun, wear a badge, and arrest people. The number of these state-authorized citizen police is 750, which represents a 100% increase in roughly 10 years. The state legislature has recently increased the training requirements from 40 to 130 hours. Apparently, this is fewer hours than what the state's nail salon workers need. The SCOP designation is not unique to Virginia; other states have similar systems.

The concept is a precursor of the modern police officer, having its roots in the legal allowance for business proprietors to protect their property. There is no authority to monitor or hold accountable the state's SCOPs.

Youlen contracts his services to housing complexes, and his business is growing. A former upstate New York police officer, he claims that his work complements that of the public police, and that he can handle minor matters such as loitering, noise complaints, and minor drug offenses that are beyond the capacity and resources of the Manassas Police Department. Youlen's clients claim that he has cleaned up petty crime and helps residents feel secure. Youlen turns over more serious matters to the police and is available to testify in court, if necessary.

There have been more serious problems associated with some SCOPs. For example, an SCOP in Newport News named Bukowski got into an argument with a woman over a parking space. He and a partner drew and pointed their guns at the woman, who was in the car with a friend and two children. Bukowski was charged and convicted of abduction. The state also revoked his SCOP registration.[41]

1. Should a state keep or abandon the concept of authorizing citizens to be SCOPs?

2. What requirements should a person have to meet to become an SCOP?

3. Who should have the responsibility for overseeing the activities of a state's SCOPs?

Most states license private detectives and investigators. However, some states have few requirements, and others have stringent regulations. In most states, detectives and investigators who carry handguns must meet additional requirements, and some states require an additional license to work as a bodyguard. There are no licenses specifically for computer forensic investigators; some states require them to be licensed private investigators, which allows them to do follow-up and related investigative work.[39]

Even though the accountability of the public police has come under serious scrutiny, there are still far more legal and formal systems of oversight and accountability in place for them compared to those for private security agents. As mentioned, private agents are accountable to their employees rather than their communities. Some believe private police tend to focus on the priorities of their employers and not the priority of public safety and individual rights.[40]

**Web Link:**
Private Protective
Services Board

# ■ PRIVATE VERSUS PUBLIC POLICE

The differences between private and public police are anything but clear and easily defined. This text will define some of the similarities and differences between the two groups, both of which are hugely varying in themselves. Perhaps the most important difference is that the police are charged with serving and protecting the public, and the purpose of private security is to protect private property. Further, because private police are charged with protecting private assets, they are mostly concerned about prevention of loss more than successfully prosecuting wrongdoers.

POLICE ✪ STORIES 15.1

## Brian Fitch, Author and Retired, LA County Sheriff's Department Lieutenant
### Private Citizens and Searches

I remember well the first time I encountered a security officer at the local high school who had found drugs on a student. I worked as a patrol officer, mostly in the evenings and early morning hours, for the first few years of my career, so I had no contact with school security. However, not long after being assigned to day shift, I received a call about school security personnel detaining a student with drugs. When I arrived, the school security officer, commonly referred to as the school "narc," presented me with a bag of marijuana. "How did you find this?" I asked. The officer told me how he had received information from a student that another student was holding marijuana. When the officer saw the suspicious student, he simply detained the student, reached into the student's pockets, and recovered the marijuana. Somewhat dumbfounded, I replied, "You can't do that! I mean, you can't just detain a student and search him based on suspicion." Without hesitation, the officer replied, "Sure I can. I do it all the time." I went on to explain how the 4th Amendment prohibits unreasonable searches. The security officer simply repeated his earlier statement, "Look, I do it all the time, and I have never had a problem."

I turned to the vice principal, who was listening to the conversation, and said, "I need to call the district attorney's office for a legal opinion." A few minutes later, I spoke with a deputy district attorney who informed me that, indeed, the security officer was correct. In fact, he had every legal right to detain and search a student based on mere suspicion. The deputy district attorney went on to explain that as a peace officer, I was expected to know the law, especially law related to search and seizure. If I seized evidence illegally, the evidence could not be used at trial. However, the security officer was not a peace officer. He was a private citizen. And as such, he is not expected to understand and follow the laws pertaining to search and seizure. Somewhat surprised, I took the student and evidence into custody. And, even more surprisingly, the student was charged with possession of marijuana on school grounds.

### The Benefits of Private Police

Private security represents a significant extension of protection services, diffusing them well beyond what the public police could possibly accomplish. Privatization of certain police functions may help solve some of the problems that hinder law enforcement agencies' efforts to achieve their goals. "Some cities are pushing for armed private security personnel to patrol the streets, perform arrests and transport civilians."[42] Some could argue that private security personnel can help fill the gap caused by reduced funding of public police, freeing valuable police resources to concentrate on violent crimes and respond rapidly to serious crimes.

In some cases, especially in the post-9/11 world, many regard private security as an essential component of homeland security, especially in the area of critical national infrastructure. After the Boston Marathon bombing in 2013, commercial enterprise provided photographs and video surveillance tapes that aided the public police.[43] To those holding that view, the private security force increases equity. If the better-off can better protect themselves, the police can better tend to the needs of poorer and more vulnerable segments of the community. Of course, as discussed in Chapter 12, the kind of attention paid by the police is a key to whether the effect on the community is positive or negative.

Finally, many contractors may have specialized skills or resources that the average U.S. police department could not afford or mobilize for a specific task.

### The Risks of Privatizing the Police

Private agents are constitutionally characterized as citizens unless they are officially deputized. As such, they can do things that the public police cannot do. Perhaps most importantly, there is no 4th Amendment protection against unreasonable search and seizure. Private security agents are not required to issue *Miranda* warnings. And evidence obtained by private agents is not subject to the normal rules for excluding it in court.

As with the public police, there are concerns about abuses of power, violations of civil liberties or privacy, and inadequate training among private security personnel—very long-standing tensions between public and private policing organizations. Public police officers perhaps understandably complain that private ones are untrained, unprofessional, unregulated, and unaccountable "wannabes" who at times hinder their work.

Some argue that private police promote equality by extending the security force and freeing up public resources to handle major crimes more effectively. Others maintain that the profit motive inherent in private industry distorts any tendency toward the public good. The logic of the argument is if the wealthy can just buy more protection, the less fortunate and more vulnerable will have less access to safety. This amounts to a "disinvestment in public safety and the increased investment in private safety [which] raises issues of class, equality, and the increasing gap between the rich and the poor."[44]

The lack of training, especially firearms training, can easily contribute to the frequency of the misuse of force or mistakes that have tragic consequences. Further, any improper actions of the private police can damage the reputation of public police officers. Police unions may have legitimate grounds to complain about the spread of private security, as their purpose is to protect the jobs and the interests of their constituents. Additionally, contract and internal private police are not positioned to balance the interests of different groups in society. Whether the public police do an adequate job of this is a question for debate, but that is certainly their mandate.

## ■ COORDINATING PUBLIC POLICE AND PRIVATE SECURITY

The work of a national advisory committee reviewed the private security industry for the purposes of establishing new standards for personnel, regulation, and interagency cooperation. The Task Force on Private Security published its report in 1976 indicating that public and private security efforts should be complementary. Indeed, public and

## Santa Cruz to Beef Up Downtown Patrol—Private Security Guards to Help Monitor Area

Downtown visitors in Santa Cruz, California, will see more uniformed officers patrolling Pacific Avenue, but the new faces will not be police. A pilot program that puts private security guards downtown during the morning and early afternoon has been launched with the intent to provide increased police presence in the business district plagued by vagrants and crime. Security guards who have been trained in municipal ordinances and equipped with police radios will share the daily patrols, augmenting public policing in the area.

Santa Cruz police are looking for creative ways to provide additional public safety resources downtown. The private security officers will not carry guns and will have no police powers. They can detain people and notify police dispatchers of problems that require the attention of a sworn officer.

The head of the Downtown Association said business owners support the proactive police initiative. "The more of a presence of enforcement downtown, the more security people have," he said.

The Santa Cruz city manager said the security guards will help "change the culture so that bad behavior is not acceptable."

The president of First Alarm Security & Patrol Inc. said his company often provides support services to area law enforcement and this latest assignment is an exciting opportunity for his staff.

1. What do you think about the city of Santa Cruz spending tax dollars on security guards who are not armed and have no police powers? Would the money used to hire three security guards be better spent by hiring a smaller number of police officers?

2. Members of the public who see a security guard are likely to believe the new guard is more highly trained than he or she actually is. Do you believe the presence of the guards will lower crime? Will this present problems for the police department and the public?

3. What are the upsides to using less-expensive and less trained security officers? What are the downsides?

*Source:* Squires, J., & Brown, J. M. (2010, September 4). Santa Cruz to beef up downtown patrol—Private security guards to help monitor area. *San Jose Mercury News* (CA), 4B. Record Number: 1442395. Copyright (c) 2010 *San Jose Mercury News*.

private officers frequently interact cooperatively. However, the relationship between the two groups is often uneasy for several reasons, including the following:

- Lack of mutual respect
- Lack of communication
- Lack of enforcement knowledge of private security personnel
- Perceived competition
- Lack of standards for private security personnel
- Perceived corruption of public officers
- Jurisdictional conflicts
- Confusion of identity
- Mutual image and communication problems
- Provision of services in overlapping areas
- Moonlighting policies for public police
- Differences in legal powers
- False alarm rates[45]

In spite of all these potential problems, cooperation between the two types of police may be improving in some areas. Law enforcement and private security must work collaboratively, because neither possesses the necessary resources to completely prevent crime, and in particular terrorism. Continued improvement in the relationship between public police and private security personnel may depend on the following:

- Upgrading private security, including statewide statutes requiring background checks, training, ethical codes, and licensing
- Increased knowledge of the value of private security functions on the part of the police
- Increased interaction on joint projects
- The possible transfer of some public police functions to the private sector[46]

Some progress has already occurred and is exemplified by various partnerships across the country that pursue mutual goals in their communities. For example, the NYPD has an antiterrorism program called NYPD Shield. In the commissioner's own words, "After September, 11, the Police Department's relationship with New York's private security professionals took on a vast new significance for the city. Collaboration and communication are essential to modern policing. The world of private security is a critical partner in the law enforcement network and NYPD Shield is an important mechanism for broadening this partnership."[47]

An ASIS program called "Operation Cooperation" represented a major national initiative to encourage partnerships between public police and private security professionals. Partnerships offer a number of benefits to both sides:

- Creative problem solving
- Increased training opportunities
- Data and intelligence gathering and sharing
- "Force multiplier" opportunities
- Access to the community through private sector communications technology
- Reduced recovery time following disasters[48]

**Properly defined and managed partnerships with private security firms might well make the efforts of police officers more effective and rewarding.**

Alliances share information, sometimes by subscription or membership, and by circulating "hot" lists and newsletters electronically. Some of the more prominent of these are the National Insurance Crime Bureau, the Jewelers Security Alliance, and the International Association of Arson Investigators.[49]

In the interest of enhancing the counterterrorism effectiveness of private security, the Department of Justice now allows private security employers in all 50 states to access FBI criminal background information.[50]

Properly defined and managed partnerships with private security firms might well make the efforts of police officers more effective and rewarding.[51]

### Moving Forward

It is likely that the private sector will continue to increase its presence in crime prevention activities. Alliances between the two sectors may be gaining prominence on the strength of the idea that they can cooperate and coproduce security, thus enhancing safety for all Americans. Forward-thinking public agencies will try to make the most of the opportunities that partnership presents.

Still, there are areas of concern and conflict that slow the growth of understanding and cooperation. Some companies do not report criminal offenses to the police to protect the company image. The company may cite lax charging policies, court proceedings that might be damaging to the organization, and a general feeling that the courts are not

© Alfonso Vicente / Alamy Stock Photo

The complex public safety issues of the time require cooperation and coordination of planning between police, fire, and private security personnel. As mentioned throughout the chapter, this has been one of the top priorities of the public safety sector since the 9/11 terrorist attacks.

sympathetic to business losses.[52] Private security personnel are often not granted access to information on criminal cases, even as a follow-up to cases they initially investigated. As a group, they tend to suffer from a poor professional image as indicated by the use of terms such as *rent-a-cops* and *wannabes*.

Continued problem solving—possibly through other joint task forces—is thus sure to be a focus in the field. The problems with private policing are not necessarily inherent but are issues that can be resolved. Perhaps most important will be the sharing of information. Improved regulation is also likely to be a key area.

In 2004, the National Policy Summit project (sponsored by the Department of Justice) partnered with the International Association of Chiefs of Police, ASIS, the National Association of Security Companies, and the International Security Management Association. The group produced five recommendations:

1. Leaders in law enforcement and private security should make a formal commitment to cooperate.

2. The federal government should fund research and training on relevant legislation, private security, and law enforcement cooperation.

3. The federal government should create an advisory council composed of law enforcement and private security professionals to oversee implementation issues related to partnerships.

4. Leaders among federal local law enforcement departments and private security agencies, along with relevant membership organizations, should promote a cooperative agenda.

5. There should be local partnerships set to address the following:

   - Joint response to critical incidents
   - Coordinated infrastructure protection
   - Improved communications and data interoperability
   - Better information and intelligence sharing
   - Coordinated responses to workplace security issues[53]

**Video Link:**
Lawmaker Calling for Private Police Departments to Increase Transparency

## U.K. Police Invite Private Security Firms to Bid for Probing Crimes

The issues related to private security are not unique to the United States but are global in nature. Countries such as Australia—where the government regulates the security industry—and South Korea are also experiencing major growth in the private security industry and are focused on improving relationships between the public security and the private security.

According to *Asian News International*, two of England's largest police forces have invited bids from private security companies to investigate some crimes and patrol neighborhoods. The private security firms could be involved in supporting victims and managing high-risk individuals, but would not be empowered to arrest suspects.

This news led critics—who were reacting to suggestions from the British home secretary that private forces could help protect "front-line policing" by delegating some work to the private sector—to warn that privatizing police services would make forces less accountable to the public. With much less of a free-market ideology than the United States, Britain has a long history of maintaining a strict separation between the public police, with authority conferred by the state, and private security companies, which have no commensurate public mandate. Until the "New Labour" era of Tony Blair and Gordon Brown, the British Home Office refused to regulate the private industry out of concern that regulation would signal recognition and approval of the private forces.[54]

Over seven years, the contract has a potential value of up to 3.5 billion pounds, making it the largest contract to date for a private company to provide police services.

According to a West Midlands police officer, "The areas of service listed in this notice are deliberately broad to allow the force to explore the skills, expertise and solutions a partnership could bring."

Critics complained that "bringing the private sector into policing is a dangerous experiment with local safety and taxpayers' money" and urged "police authorities not to fall into the trap of thinking the private sector is the answer" to budget cuts.

1. As a private citizen, how do you feel about private security officers patrolling your neighborhood instead of sworn police officers?

2. Are there jobs that private security officers may be better suited for than sworn law enforcement officers?

3. Because private security officers receive considerably less training than sworn law enforcement officers, they are often held to a different standard. Do you believe that different standards for different people working for the same police agency can present problems for the public? Explain.

## CHAPTER SUMMARY

The private police have proliferated during the past several decades. This growth intensified after 9/11, and private police now far outnumber public police officers. The reasons for this growth in the private security industry include the inability of the public police to respond to all of the requests for security-related services due to manpower shortages; the needs of office buildings, large retail stores, museums, sports arenas, and the like to provide for the safety of the public; and a need of the private sector for specialized services such as executive security, computer security, insurance fraud protection, security of gated communities, and protection against financial crimes such as embezzlement and internal thefts.

Through the years, public police and private security personnel have not always worked well together. Probably the most significant reasons for this strained relationship center on discrete, but related, issues. Many police officers view security personnel as "police wannabes" who lack the capabilities and wherewithal to properly perform law enforcement functions. State-imposed training and education requirements for private security personnel are often less in comparison to their public counterparts. The public tends to perceive uniformed security guards as being less than competent. In response to these and other issues, ASIS, the largest professional organization in the world representing the private security industry, attempts to increase training and education requirements and standards. ASIS also attempts to promote better working relationships between the police and security personnel.

The private security industry is expected to continue to grow in the foreseeable future and to continue the movement toward professionalization to increase its effectiveness and to improve the competence and accountability of security officers. It is important that public police and private security personnel coordinate their efforts and work together to combat both crime and catastrophic events.

## KEY TERMS

- Contract security personnel  366
- In-house security personnel  366
- Hybrid systems  366
- Gaming surveillance officers  367
- Security officers  367
- Private detectives and investigators  368
- Executive protection agents  369

**SAGE edge™**
Review key terms with eFlashcards.

## DISCUSSION QUESTIONS

1. Discuss the extent of the growth of private security in the United States and some of the reasons for this growth.

2. What is the importance of licensing requirements for private detectives and investigators? What are some possible consequences of failure to license?

3. What is the impact of the events of 9/11 on the private security industry in the United States?

4. Relationships between private security personnel and public police are not always pleasant. Discuss some of the reasons for this state of affairs.

5. What, in your opinion, does the future hold with respect to cooperation and coordination between private and public police?

**SAGE edge™**
Test your understanding of chapter content. Take the practice quiz.

## INTERNET EXERCISES

1. Search for information on the requirements for becoming a private detective or investigator in your state. Do these requirements seem reasonable to you? Why or why not?

2. Locate and discuss articles dealing with police and private security partnerships. Do such partnerships appear to be mutually beneficial to the partners? Why or why not?

## STUDENT STUDY SITE

 **SAGE edge™** edge.sagepub.com/coxpolicing3e

**Sharpen your skills with SAGE edge!**

SAGE edge for Students provides a personalized approach to help you accomplish your coursework goals in an easy-to-use learning environment. You'll find action plans, mobile-friendly eFlashcards, and quizzes as well as videos, web resources, and links to SAGE journal articles to support and expand on the concepts presented in this chapter.

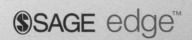

# LOOKING AHEAD

■■■■■ PART V

Chapter 16: The Future of Policing in the United States

AP Photo/Wilfredo Lee

# CHAPTER 16

# THE FUTURE OF POLICING IN THE UNITED STATES

## CHAPTER LEARNING OBJECTIVES:

1. Discuss the changing context of policing in the United States

2. Identify some of the ongoing and strategic changes of police departments

3. Describe the likely roles to be played by police agencies with respect to terrorism in the future

P redicting the future is impossible, but envisioning the way to it is not only possible, but necessary. The following discussion of the future of policing in the United States is based on an analysis of current trends, projected demographic changes, and the best thinking in the field. In this world of increasing complexity due to terrorism and Internet crime, the police find themselves challenged to improve upon their traditional role and accept new responsibilities at the same time.

As this text has shown, police strategies do not exist in a vacuum. Legislation, political attitudes, and local resources are just some of the influences on policing strategies. To keep pace with social developments, changes in attitudes and resources are a critical ingredients in effective policing.

## ■ THE CHANGING CONTEXT

Future police organizations may or may not resemble today's police. For example, "the twenty-first century has put policing into a whole new milieu—one in which the causes of crime and disorder often lie outside the immediate community, demanding new and innovative approaches from police."[1] Street crimes of the past often involved perpetrators and victims from the same local area. Thus, prevention included some form of surveillance, analyzing activity in the immediate area, and taking action to head off problems (problem-oriented policing). However, in many areas, various types of reported street crime have declined, and we have seen the rise of terrorism and Internet crimes. In many instances, "offenders are thousands of miles away while planning and even committing these crimes. Hackers and crackers halfway around the globe can shut down a community's Internet dependent monetary and energy system."[2] The U.S. Attorneys Office recognized identity theft as the United States' fastest-growing crime in 2012.[3]

Even earlier, some observers predicted the following changes in police strategies:

- Deployment of community policing, including more authority for remote supervisors and human service and communications training for officers
- Proactive planning and intelligence to include planned and unplanned events, including critical incident and hot-spot management and centralized rapid-response teams organized for instant deployment
- Greater dependence on private police, auxiliary police, and community volunteers; major corporation private police beginning to have more public police powers
- Police executives with greater education and professionalism and moving between major police departments[4]

**Author Video:**
What directions do you envision policing in America going in the future?

### Demographics

The police must always understand the context in which they operate. A number of demographic, economic, and workforce changes will affect the future of policing. The U.S. population is expected to increase to somewhere between 399 million and 458 million by 2050 depending on the level of international migration.[7] Also by 2050, 83.7 million people will be age 65 and over, almost double the 2012 estimate of 43 million.[8] This means that about 20% of the population will be senior citizens. In 2010, this population segment was 13.8% of the total, and in 1970, it was 9.8%.

In the future, elderly persons will present a significant challenge to health care, police, and local government organizations. Some implications of this trend for the police include increased calls for service for real and perceived victimizations, different types of crime, and a new potential class of perpetrators—senior citizens.[9]

In addition, the United States is expected to experience a rapid growth in racial and ethnic diversity. The bulk of international migration into the United States is expected to be Hispanic and Asian. Depending on specific levels of migration, the Hispanic segment of the population will continue to grow to about 30% of the total in 2050.[10] In the 21st century,

Members of the New York City Bomb Squad display their bomb disposal robot (L) and their response vehicle and equipment at a demonstration of security technologies at Police headquarters in New York City.

REUTERS/Reuters Photographe

**CASE IN POINT** 16.1

## Computer Hacking

Law enforcement officials at all levels are in the position of having to play "catch up" with technologically sophisticated criminals, whose very motive is to stay a step ahead.

In July 2015, the U.S. government revealed a data breach of staggering proportions at its Office of Personnel Management (OPM). Highly personal information obtained by conducting background checks for security clearances included State Department posts, Social Security numbers, addresses, medical histories, criminal background information, drug use profiles, and romantic histories. The fear was that hackers could use the information for the purposes of blackmail or any number of nefarious purposes.

Far exceeding original estimates, the hackers accessed data on 22.1 million current, former, and prospective government employees and contractors, and their friends and family members, which is approximately 7% of the nation's population.[5]

The incident was considered one of the most damaging to date, given the number of people affected and the sensitivity of the information the hackers obtained. Katherine Archuleta headed the organization and expressed an intention to remain in place as the agency's leader, despite calls for her resignation. The White House National Security Council stopped short of an official accusation, but investigators told the news service that a team with links to China's ministry of state security was a suspect in the hacking incident. The data were not encrypted, and parts of the agency's computer system were likely outdated. Hackers appeared to have used malicious software to carry out the "cyber intrusion," considered by some to be an "aggressive act of espionage."[6] It was not yet known how the information would be put to use. Some of the individuals whose personal data was stolen received information from the government about containing and responding to the incident, such as a promise of three years of credit monitoring; others have received scant information.

1. Discuss how this incident could exemplify the need for effective public/private law enforcement partnerships.

2. How can federal and local law enforcement most effectively respond to the hacking of personal information?

issues related to race and ethnicity will be even more prevalent in the administration of justice. During the "tough-on-crime" era, the criminal justice system shifted from a rehabilitative model to one of increased incarceration due in part to increasingly harsh sentencing laws and retributive politics. Minority communities, the poor, and the legally underrepresented are those most impacted—disproportionately so—by a more punitive criminal justice environment. There are many signs that suggest a move toward a more measured, "smart-on-crime" approach to corrections.

Just when police are challenged to face these changes, they are also facing diminishing resources and a crisis of confidence and trust among the public. Students of organizational process and change point out that trial and error is sometimes the only way to move forward and that a failure to try to change or a fear of failure can stifle innovation. And yet, the police cannot be all things to all people, and the police can be most effective only if they have widespread community support. From the start, the municipal police emerged as a result of citizen needs. Those needs, however, change at a sometimes staggering pace, depending on such factors as economics, demographics, and social policies. To continue to meet the changing demands of citizens, police agencies at all levels must first have a realistic view of these needs and then invite citizen input as to how best to achieve them.

## Economics

The recession that began in December 2007 affected the economic status of community- and problem-oriented policing programs. Researchers found that many local departments eliminated antidrug programs, purchases of squad cars, gang-prevention programs, and after-hour presentations to citizen groups concerning home security and other issues.[11] Shrinking budgets have helped fuel the discussion on the "need for change in delivery of police services from a mid-20th century model to a more forward looking 21st century model":

> Police service delivery can be categorized into three tiers. The first tier, emergency response is not going to change. Tier two is non-emergency response; where officers respond to calls after the fact, primarily to collect the information and statements necessary to produce reports. These calls, while an important service, do not require rapid response—the business has already been vandalized, the bike already stolen. Tier three deals with quality of life issues, such as crime prevention efforts or traffic management duties. They help make our communities better places to live, but they are proactive and ongoing activities. The second and third tiers have always competed for staffing and financial resources, but as local budgets constrict, the competition becomes fiercer.[12]

Although there is debate over the relationship between crime and the economy, many believe the recession will result in a rise in crime. Of the 233 police departments surveyed by the Police Executive Research Forum, 44% reported a rise in certain types of crime that many attributed to the United States' worst economic and financial crisis in decades.[13]

## Research and Planning

A key to understanding where the police are today and what direction they need to go is adequate, accurate, and meaningful information. There are enormous gaps in what is known about the efficacy of policing. The National Police Research Platform cautioned that current police managers are hampered by a shortage of evidence concerning their organizations and their workforce.[14]

> Just some of the topics that researchers might address to inform the professional field are (1) the quality of supervision and leadership, (2) the perceived fairness of department policies and procedures, (3) employee acceptance of racial, ethnic, and gender diversity, (4) levels of employee stress, and (5) factors that affect employee morale and productivity.

**Policing in Practice Video:**
What directions do you envision policing in America going in the future?

It is incumbent upon every law enforcement agency to determine how to respond to these differing public priorities, how to account for different types of officer responses, and the styles of policing that are best suited to particular communities. There are other questions about terrorism and crime management, level of satisfaction with supervisors, amount of perceived stress among officers, civil and criminal liability of police personnel, and dozens of other areas that can best be informed through research and addressed through appropriate planning. And trend data are generally more useful than "snapshot" or cross-sectional data.

Past years have shown a number of dramatic changes in policing. A few of these changes include the following:

- Budget cuts resulting in the layoff of police officers and the reduction of type and level of services offered to the community
- Increased demand for accountability of police officers
- Improved interagency cooperation and communication between federal, state, and local law enforcement agencies, and with private security organizations
- Use of various types of information technology
- Additional surveillance authority provided to the police pertaining to terrorism and other crimes
- Increased paramilitary training for police officers

Research and planning in these areas will become increasingly important and useful to police administrators who must justify new programs and demonstrate the value of existing efforts.

## ■ ONGOING AND STRATEGIC CHANGE

**Web Link:**
COPS Office: President's Task Force

In December 2014, President Barack Obama established the Task Force on 21st Century Policing. The crisis of confidence between the public and the police has come to be known as the police/citizen divide. The job of the task force was to identify best practices and recommend strategies for reducing crime and building public trust. The task force produced the final report summarizing its months of inquiry.

The main topic areas of the task force inquiry were organized around six "pillars":

1. Building trust and legitimacy
2. Policy and oversight
3. Technology and social media
4. Community policing and crime reduction
5. Officer training and education
6. Officer safety and wellness

These categories are useful in a considered discussion of interrelated topics pertaining to the future of policing. This chapter includes community-oriented policing as one of several operational approaches, and includes training and education in a broader discussion of police personnel issues. Police departments will need to continually strategize on operations, personnel issues, and community relations to be their most effective. Most of these subjects are covered in more detail in their respective chapters and sections throughout the book but are mentioned here in the context of looking forward as this new century unfolds.

### Trust and Legitimacy

Building trust and legitimacy has perhaps never been more important to policing in the United States than it is today. Research shows that "people are more likely to obey the law when they believe that those who are enforcing it have authority that is perceived as legitimate."[15] The findings of the task force support adopting a guardian versus a warrior mindset. A procedural justice approach shows the most promise of achieving that end. Some of the keys to procedural justice are fairness in the application of the law, unbiased decision making, and giving the public fair voice and representation. "Fair and impartial policing is built on understanding and acknowledging human biases."[16] An active cultural shift that emphasizes the use of intellect, language, powers of persuasion, empathy, and humanity is called for, as these can often achieve a more positive outcome than exercising force.

SAGE Journal Article: Defining the Meaning of a "Fair" Procedure

Another key to trust among the public for the legitimacy of the police is establishing and maintaining a culture of transparency and accountability. Law enforcement agencies need to proactively engage the public, measure and analyze the level of trust the communities have in them, and create as diverse a workforce as possible. "Every interaction a police officer has with a community member should be seen as an opportunity to make a positive difference."[17]

These values have enormous potential to contribute to racial reconciliation. To that end, officers need to operate under fair conditions themselves to be capable of treating the public similarly.

## Policy and Oversight

The task force concluded that policy and oversight must represent the values of the community. Especially where crime is the highest, collaboration between law enforcement and community members is essential. Policies must be clear and complete, particularly with regard to the use of force, mass demonstrations, gender identification, and racial profiling. The public must understand the performance measures that their officers are expected to meet. The public must also have faith in investigations and prosecutions of officer misconduct. Aggregated data should be available to the public. Policy should be dynamic and periodically evaluated. The task force also recommended strategies for small police agencies such as interagency collaboration, sharing services, and regional training.[18]

Video Link: The importance of police oversight

## Technology and Social Media

No discussion of the future of policing would be complete without a brief look at the impact of advancing technology on the field. As discussed in Chapter 13, recent technological innovations in policing are poised on the threshold of challenging and controversial possibilities.

Technology and social media are undeniable forces that change rapidly and present a constant challenge for police departments. Departments have to balance the need to keep pace with rapid changes and the need to have a coherent and well-thought-out plan for the use of technology. The task force concerned itself with the large questions of protecting civil and human rights, agency and jurisdictional implementation needs, and standards for research and development.

Video Link: Midwest City police using social media to help catch criminals

The advancements in technology vary widely among police agencies—some of which have implemented wireless access to law enforcement databases, mug shot files, agency communications, scheduling and management tools, and voice recognition to simplify data processing along with speed report writing.[19]

New technology is a double-edged sword—it creates new forms of crime at the same time it assists the police in fighting crime. Police chiefs around the world are facing a number of pressures, which include

> a political expectation that crime will keep falling; a political imperative to cut budgets to meet falling public revenues; and the all-too-familiar political commitment to keep cops on the street and visible. In these circumstances, too many chiefs have decided to cut their scientific and technological support services. . . . This is a short term fix that will lead to big problems down the road.[20]

The application of technology, which is not a solution by itself, must be tempered with careful evaluation of its effectiveness in furthering the values and the mission of the department.

## Policing Strategies

### Patrol

Specialization may continue to characterize police in the 21st century; however, patrol officers will remain the backbone of policing at the local level due to their sheer numbers, their visibility, and the frequency of contact with the public. Police patrol will continue to be necessary for random and planned acts of violence, domestic disputes, vehicular accidents, lost children, and countless other situations.[21] However, patrol will experience further changes in methods, equipment, communications, and the caliber of police officers. For example, with more sophisticated surveillance equipment and techniques, including robots, future patrols may rely less on the physical location of the patrol officer.[22]

### Community-Oriented Policing

Community-oriented policing stresses the coproduction of public safety, engaging the department and the residence of neighborhoods in the interest of durable solutions and meaningful results. The task force made a special point of naming the protection of dignity, especially for children and youth at risk for crime and violence. It called for the police to have an expanded role in youth development as opposed to youth discipline.

There is little doubt that the wave of the future in policing will include expanded involvement of civilians in police work as employees in police agencies; as members of advisory, planning, and direct support groups; as critics and reviewers of police activities; and as sources of information to fight terrorism. The message is clear: The police cannot control crime or maintain order by themselves. The involvement of citizens other than police officers in crime prevention, apprehension of offenders, and order maintenance is absolutely essential. A partnership is required, but the partnership must be legitimate. In the past, police partnerships with other citizens meant citizens

A woman police officer practices high speed driving skills in a patrol car simulator with a real steering wheel and seat.

© Marmaduke St. John / Alamy Stock Photo

were minimally involved in police activities while the police served as the experts, citizen input was sought in certain areas but denied in others, and policy making remained the exclusive right of the police.

The future will continue to involve increased police efforts to improve citizen cooperation in high-crime areas. In many cases, additional patrols and specialized units were assigned to areas identified as high-crime-density locations or hot spots. However, economic factors could mean that many police departments will no longer have these options available to reduce crime and violence.[23] The reality is that most of the people living in such areas are not criminals but victims. They continue to be victims, because gangs and other less well-organized but equally predatory criminals control the streets. Police will continue to provide patrol to these areas and to maintain a semblance of order, but those strategies are far less effective without cooperation from the community.

### Predictive Policing

**Predictive policing** is an emerging strategy that could "effectively deploy resources in front of crime in order to do more with less and change outcomes."[24] As police face new budget restraints and limitations, the question to ask with more urgency is, "why just count crimes when you can anticipate, prevent and respond more effectively?"[25] Predictive policing takes crime mapping to a new level. It involves software that uses complex algorithms that process vast crime data sets and produce statistical predictions of where and when crime is likely to occur.[26]

The concept of predictive policing builds on and melds parts of community-oriented policing, intelligence-led policing, and hot-spot policing.[27]

> At the simplest level, this might mean using crime analysis to determine the likely patterns of drive-by shootings, then deploying the police officers to the areas and at the times these are most likely to occur in order to preempt the crime. At a more complex level, it might mean watching the trends in the spot copper price, and implementing strategies (such as legislation and scrap business monitoring) to reduce the marketability of stolen copper in advance of an anticipated spike in thefts.[28]

Predictive policing includes both strategic and tactical applications and employs forecasting techniques similar to those used by businesses to anticipate market conditions and industry trends over time.[29] Predictive policing models in the future will likely include the following:

- Statistical analysis to forecast CompStat-like performance
- Advanced models to determine the risk of offending or victimization of particular individuals or groups
- Advanced analytical tools, including social network analysis tools and intelligent decision support systems related to relationships between suspects, victims, and others
- Geospatial tools to analyze trends in demographics, land use, income, and other sources to predict allocation of police resources
- Integrated sensor and information systems to protect critical public spaces
- Crime prediction models using a variety of input variables
- Forensic tools to detect and interdict criminal activity[30]

In 2011, the National Institute of Corrections funded Chicago, Illinois, and Shreveport, Louisiana, to pilot predictive policing programs. The Chicago Police Department focused on pattern-matching software that is currently used for medical diagnosis and was adapted for crime analysis. The final evaluation of that project is due in 2016. In Shreveport, researchers used an experimental design with control groups to evaluate

**■ Predictive Policing:** A model that involves using data and analysis to predict future police problems and implement strategies to resolve problems

a version of broken windows policing and see if there was a reduction in such crimes as shootings, robbery, burglary, auto break-ins, and auto thefts.[31] The 2014 final report of the Shreveport pilot concluded that the program did not result in any statistically significant reduction in property crime.[32]

However, there may have been some benefits in terms of overtime costs, community partnerships, assistance to readers in making decisions, and more targeted use of resources.

Proponents of predictive policing make claims of its great potential. "Predictive policing [strategies] have become so powerful that these complex computerized algorithms can now help reveal localized future crime patterns before they even emerge."[33] Critics of predictive policing cautioned against the potential for perpetuating racial profiling and over-policing in already targeted communities. As with other strategic policing tools, it is essential to use it prudently. Data collection must be thorough and consistent. Departments must exercise care in designating a neighborhood as a "high-crime area," as the designation can lower the threshold for reasonable suspicion and give the police enhanced powers to conduct searches. The courts must be involved in determining the boundaries of civil protections, which may lead to establishing best practices and uniform standards.[34]

### Evolving Police Personnel

#### Training and Education

Training and education of officers is critical to achieving all of these goals. Today's officers are faced with a wide range of challenges including terrorism, immigration, a changing legal landscape, diverse cultural values, evolving technology, and a crisis in mental health. Police departments will be challenged to ensure that training and education are high quality and effective. The federal government can play a part in promoting consistent standards. One idea is to create a national postgraduate institute for senior executives.

Police personnel will have increasing opportunities to participate in training offered by a variety of training institutes. All training is, or should be, interrelated. The special skills learned at training institutes need to be updated on a continuing basis and can be shared

---

## YOU ??? DECIDE — 16.1

The Los Angeles Police Department has implemented a program titled Predictive Policing, which involves "predicting where crimes will happen" and "putting officers on the scene before crimes occur." The LAPD is now using computers to analyze the times, dates, and places of recently reported crimes.

The "crime prediction boxes" or hot spots used in predictive policing are generated by mathematical calculations that are similar to those used to "predict earthquakes and aftershocks." The LAPD believes predictive policing and increased police patrol will reduce opportunities for criminals. Early results of predictive policing reveal that "burglaries are down 33% and violent crime is also down 21%."

According to LAPD Chief Charlie Beck, "I am not going to get more money, I'm not going to get more cops. But, I have to be better at using what I have and that is what Predictive Policing is about."

1. Are there privacy implications and 4th Amendment issues related to the implementation of predictive policing? Explain.

2. Is predictive policing different from community-oriented policing, problem-oriented policing, and other innovations that are currently in place in many police departments? Explain.

*Suggestions for addressing these questions can be found on the Student Study Site:* **edge.sagepub.com/ coxpolicing3e**

*Source:* "LAPD computer program prevents crime by predicting it," by Bob Orr, 2012. *CBS Evening News.*

with others through in-service training by those who have attended the institutes, which is both cost-effective for departments and rewarding for trainees.

Departments must evaluate training to ensure that it is high quality and effective. Meaningful evaluation includes a pretest of attendees' knowledge of the material to be presented and a posttest following the training. A failure to evaluate training may lead to a waste of training resources.

The traditional military model for police training, which served well in the past, has come under question. "The sophistication of today's culturally diverse, quick paced, ever-changing, technically advanced and globally influenced society" demands a set of skills and competencies that are substantially different and more complex compared to the past.[35]

### Police Leadership

As we have seen, the quality of leadership in police organizations varies tremendously. Some agencies carefully select entry-level personnel, carefully evaluate their potential for promotion, promote based on merit, and prepare those who are to be promoted by sending them to appropriate training or educational programs. Other police organizations do none of these. There is little rigorous research concerning police leadership—"most of which is limited to case studies of how chiefs matter or try to matter in shaping the policies, practices and performance of their departments."[36]

**Audio Link:**
NYPD's Union Rift Confronted by a Wider Shift in Leadership Style

## Connie Koski, Professor and Former Police Officer

It has been said that law enforcement agencies are some of the slowest organizations to adopt change. During my career, I was able to observe this firsthand in many different areas, but the contribution of higher education to the efficient policing of my community was one area in particular that really stood out. As noted throughout this text, there is still much debate over the benefits higher education can bring to the law enforcement profession.

My agency, for instance, required nothing more than a high school diploma or GED for employment, and many of my coworkers (including top administrators) had just that. In the early 1990s, I was the first of the next generation of officers entering the department with bachelor's degrees. I was labeled a "snot-nosed college brat" and "book-smart and street-dumb" by many of my fellow officers and administrators. Most of the members of my department believed that it was in-service training that taught you the tactics and strategies necessary to do the job. In fact, during a debate over the value of community-oriented policing, one coworker who had a high school diploma concluded his argument that a college education is not important by noting that he made the same amount as I did, so what difference did all of the expense of a college degree matter anyway? I found it difficult to convince many of my coworkers that higher education, regardless of major, had many mind-opening benefits and instilled the ability to seek innovative solutions to the root causes of community problems, beyond the traditional police role of enforcing the law and arresting offenders.

It is only in hindsight that I am able to see how gradual changes in perspective toward the value of higher education have benefited my agency. Citizens of my jurisdiction and city administrators eventually raised the educational requirement for our chief of police to a four-year degree, and gave extra consideration to those on the promotional list who possessed such degrees. Additionally, although higher education is still not a mandate for employment, the overwhelming majority of line officers and administrators now have at least an associate's degree. The result has been an agency that has increased its levels of professionalism, accountability, use of innovative technologies and evidence-based enforcement strategies, and improved trust and respect from both community residents and neighboring agencies. Trends similar to this in law enforcement agencies across the country have the potential to positively impact the efficiency and effectiveness of the police to prepare for and adapt to the rapid changes and needs facing our communities in the 21st century.

However, a department with a strong sense of mission and clearly defined values and culture has an easier time identifying and selecting the leaders that have the right skills and experience to steer the organization in the desired direction.

### Private and Contract Security Personnel

As discussed in Chapter 15, there is likely to be a considerable increase in private and contract security personnel in the future. Policing in rural areas is becoming an increasingly expensive proposition as standards for police officers improve, as some criminals try to exploit small-city and small-town areas with fewer police, and as the technology of policing becomes more sophisticated and more costly.

This trend indicates both a desire and a need for improved communication and cooperation between the police, private security, and business communities. However, territorial conflicts between police agencies and private security firms that are responsible for the needs of corporations and wealthy communities remain a concern and a challenge to overcome.[37]

### Civilianization

The decrease in sworn personnel in some police departments and a lack of qualified applicants in others has resulted in the "hiring of more civilians to assist sworn personnel with non-enforcement tasks."[38] Civilians are involved in neighborhood watch groups, school and mall monitors, crime prevention patrol, writing reports, and photographing and collecting evidence. Employing civilians helps to break down barriers between the police and other citizens, often frees police officers to concentrate more of their time on matters for which they have been specifically trained, and fosters a sense of ownership among the public for both order maintenance and law enforcement.

### Accreditation

To an extent, the incorporation of high standards of performance and conduct can improve the image of the police.

A growing number of state and local police agencies have demonstrated their desire to be considered among the best in the profession by undergoing the painstaking, lengthy process of accreditation by the Commission on Accreditation for Law Enforcement Agencies. Departments originally accredited have now been through the reaccreditation process.

Many other agencies are doing self-evaluations to determine whether to pursue accreditation. Even for those who decide not to apply for accreditation, there is, for the first time, a set of standards that allow police personnel to examine the extent to which they are operating according to the recognized standards of the profession. Some states have formed associations that help individual agencies prepare for accreditation, and this has fostered improved communications among agencies. In addition, accreditation now requires the use of community surveys on a regular basis, thereby enhancing the police–community partnership and the use of research techniques by police personnel.

### Officer Wellness and Safety

Officer wellness and safety is another aspect of public safety. Officers need proper support to maintain their own mental and physical health and the health of their families.

## ■ TERRORISM AND FUTURE POLICING

As discussed in Chapter 14, police officers assume an important role in the attempts to prevent terrorism. There are a number of links between traditional crime and terrorism. In fact, many terrorist groups commit crimes, including fraud, money laundering, drug trafficking, and identity theft, to provide the revenues needed to commit terrorist attacks.[39] Police officers have the capability to "identify potential terrorists" who live and

**Web Link:**
The Commission on Accreditation for Law Enforcement Agencies, Inc.

"operate in their jurisdictions" and who are involved in these crimes, "help to protect vulnerable targets," and "coordinate the first response to terror attacks."[40]

The partnership elements of community-oriented policing are the most useful in preventing terrorism.[41] "Just as street-level knowledge is important to breaking up narcotics activities in a neighborhood, community partnerships and trusting relationships will inspire the confidence of citizens to pass along information that can help to uncover terrorist individuals or cells."[42] The relationship between crime and terrorist acts should assist the police agencies that have embraced community-oriented policing in the transition to the prevention and investigation of terrorist threats.[43] For example, in New York City, the police department tip line received a number of calls about a person's anti-American rhetoric. An investigation revealed the plans for an attack at the Herald Square subway station in 2004, near the time of the Republican National Convention.[44]

Traumatic events such as terrorist attacks can be a serious setback and cause organizations to fall back on more traditional methods of doing business and in some cases eliminate community policing.[45] There has been some concern that the close association with the military and the terrorist-oriented mission of the police will accelerate the militarization and isolation of the police rather than bring them closer to the community partnerships that served as the source of legitimacy for community policing.[46] More specifically, since 9/11, some have called for police to take a more active stance in counterterrorism activities, which emphasize intelligence gathering, covert investigations, information sharing, and immigrant enforcement.[47] Many police agencies have yet to shift their core goals and priorities to reflect homeland security policing.

> There has been some concern that the close association with the military and the terrorist-oriented mission of the police will accelerate the militarization and isolation of the police rather than bring them closer to the community partnerships that served as the source of legitimacy for community policing.

### Intelligence-Led Policing and Terrorism

Intelligence-led policing (ILP) "in the simplest terms is a model of policing in which criminal intelligence serves as a guide to operations, instead of the reverse."[48] ILP supports decision makers through data collection and intelligence analysis and is vital for the prevention, response to, and mitigation of terrorist attacks, crime incidents, and natural disasters.[49] Some agencies—larger ones especially—dedicate officers to

It is predicted that the concept of gated communities will proliferate, and residents will look to private security personnel for their community's protective services.

© iStockphoto.com/Rich Legg.

## AROUND THE WORLD  16.1

Metropolitan commissioner Bernard Hogan-Howe believes "modern policing is multidimensional, encompassing a diversity of tasks beyond just preventing and detecting crime." He proposes that police adopt a "more well-rounded depiction of the police function in society than those formulations that pivot around just one aspect (crime-fighting, zero-tolerance policing, intelligence-led policing, etc)."

In the past, metropolitan police in London were specialized. According to the commissioner, "Police focused on one task, dealing with only one section of the public, may view the whole world through that lens and struggled when called upon to police other situations."

In the future, rather than doing "more with less," metropolitan police officers may begin doing "less with more" and intervene less often, but with more impact. In other words, police officers with a broad range of skills will address more problems and not be required to refer problems to specialists.

1. Do you believe the police should focus on preventing and detecting crime or adopt a more "well-rounded depiction"?

2. How do you feel about law enforcement doing "less with more"? For example, the police will only respond when required, the police will be less visible in the lives of ordinary citizens. However, when the police are called out, they will have more resources to solve crimes and address problems. Explain your position.

*Source:* "'Total policing' requires doing less, not more," by Martin Innes, 2012. *The Guardian.*

counterterrorism, employ intelligence experts, hire officers fluent in many foreign languages, and monitor news sources and intelligence data.[50]

**SAGE Journal Article:**
Intelligence-Led Policing as a Framework for Responding to Terrorism

As with other innovations, a healthy skepticism is advisable pending more evaluation. Every approach may reveal its flaws over time. One potential flaw of ILP is assuming wrongly that, "if the police simply collect as much information as they can, they will at some point identify suspicious activity"[51] that will lead them to terrorist activity. Behaviors and events labeled as suspicious leave open the opportunity for individuals to exercise prejudices and preconceptions. Plus, there is always the challenge of weeding out the useless information from the useful. Also as with other innovations, it is vital to employ the concept faithfully and not merely use the terms or trifle with implementation.

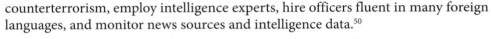

## CHAPTER SUMMARY

It is risky to forecast the future of policing in the United States. However, a number of issues will more than likely impact the future of police agencies. These issues include the continued advance in technology; the future roles or duties of police related to global issues, such as transnational crime; adequate and effective continuing education and training; increased responsibilities for the private security industry; effective leadership capabilities; and an increased need for a holistic response to crime and disaster incidents to reconcile the rift between the police and the public, based on cooperative efforts and partnership.

In light of these important issues, police officials are well advised to concentrate on breaking down barriers between the police and the private security sectors; formulating response plans for acts of terrorism and other disasters, natural or otherwise; continuing to improve relations with the public; and practicing those plans and continuing to evaluate and modify them as new information comes to light.

- Predictive policing  387

## DISCUSSION QUESTIONS

1. What is the role of community policing in the future of U.S. policing?

2. Discuss the current relationship between the private security industry and public policing. Is that relationship likely to change in the next few years? If so, in what ways? Explain.

3. What qualifications should we look for in tomorrow's police leaders?

4. Will the emphases on police education and training remain the same in the years to come? If not, what changes do you anticipate?

5. Discuss some technological changes that are likely to have a major impact on policing in the future.

6. Discuss the role of the municipal police in dealing with terrorism. What recommendations can you make as to how this role could best be fulfilled?

## INTERNET EXERCISES

1. Find information about intelligence-led policing and predictive policing. What is the level of effectiveness of these innovations? How can we evaluate intelligence-led policing and predictive policing? Explain.

2. Search for information on new technologies to detect and prevent terrorism. Will the development of new technologies in the future alter the nature of terrorism? Explain.

## STUDENT STUDY SITE

 **⑤SAGE edge™** edge.sagepub.com/coxpolicing3e

**Sharpen your skills with SAGE edge!**

SAGE edge for Students provides a personalized approach to help you accomplish your coursework goals in an easy-to-use learning environment. You'll find action plans, mobile-friendly eFlashcards, and quizzes as well as videos, web resources, and links to SAGE journal articles to support and expand on the concepts presented in this chapter.

# HEAR IT FROM THE PROFESSIONALS

▶ edge.sagepub.com/coxpolicing3e

HEAD TO THE STUDY SITE WHERE YOU'LL FIND:

- **Exclusive video interviews** with police professionals discussing their careers, challenges, and advice

**Academy of Criminal Justice Sciences (ACJS):** One of the largest professional organizations in the world dedicated to the advancement of knowledge in the criminal justice profession

**Accountability:** Refers to the fact that the police are public employees and are therefore accountable to the public for their actions

**Accreditation:** Development of standards containing a clear statement of professional objectives

**Affirmative Action:** Programs that are intended to prevent discrimination in present hiring and promotion practices and to actively promote proportional representation and equitable opportunity

**Air Patrol:** Police patrolling from fixed-wing aircraft and helicopter

**Allocation Model for Patrol (AMP):** A model involving several variables for estimating the number of required police personnel

**Arrest:** Occurs when an individual authorized to take a person into custody detains that person with the intention of making an arrest and when the person being arrested understands that the intention of the person making the arrest is detaining him or her for that purpose

**Artifacts:** Most visible forms of an organizational culture (sounds, behaviors, language)

**Assessment Center:** A formal process that involves a series of exercises (simulation and role playing) designed to test how well a candidate would perform in a job

**Automatic Number Plate Recognition (ANPR):** Technology that uses optical character recognition to read the license plates on vehicles

**Automatic Vehicle Location (AVL):** A means for automatically determining the geographic location of a vehicle and transmitting the information to a requester, most often through the use of GPS

**Biased Enforcement:** Police practice that results from enforcement of the law based on any number of personal and occupational-based biases

**Bicycle Patrol:** Police patrolling while riding bicycles; this is a popular form of patrol because of the low cost and possible coverage compared to foot patrol

**Body Armor:** A defense covering worn by police officers that is usually constructed of woven fibers that are sewn into a vest or soft clothing

**Bona Fide Occupational Qualification (BFOQ):** An exception to the prohibition against basing hiring decisions on religion, race, sex, age, or national origin, if such basis is shown to be a requirement necessary to the specific functions of the job

**Boryokudan:** Also known as the Yakuza, the criminal organization initially formed in Japan that has since developed into a transnational organized crime group

**Broken Windows Theory:** A theory stating that neighborhood social disorder causes a decline of the overall condition of the neighborhood, which leads to criminal activity

**Burnout:** Exhaustion and cynicism resulting from repeated exposure to high levels of stress

**Calmative Agents:** Pharmaceutical or sedative drugs that produce a calming or tranquil state

**CCTV:** Closed-circuit television

**Chain of Custody:** The chronological documentation that shows the seizure, custody, control, transfer, analysis, and disposition of physical or electronic evidence

**Christopher Commission:** Investigative body created by former Los Angeles mayor Tom Bradley in 1991 in response to several high-profile media accounts of various acts of misconduct by LAPD members

**Citizen or Civilian Panels or Boards:** Groups of citizens (other than police officers) who investigate complaints against the police and recommend punishment in cases where it appears to be justified by the facts

**Civil Law:** Defines and determines the rights of individuals to protect their persons and property

**Code of Conduct:** Revised as of 2005, this code was formed and adopted by the International Association of Chiefs of Police, which sets forth standards of conduct for police officers on and off duty

**Code of Ethics:** A set of principles that guide decision making and behavior for police officers, both on and off duty; the code defines the standards for professionalism, which is key to the integrity of police officers and their credibility with the public

**Code of Silence (Blue Wall):** Protective, supportive, and shared attitudes, values, understandings, and views of the world associated with the police society

**Collective Bargaining:** Negotiations between an employer and groups of employees to determine conditions of employment

**Commission on Accreditation for Law Enforcement Agencies (CALEA):** Established in 1979 (operational in 1983), the commission conducts evaluations based on specific standards for law enforcement agencies and accredits agencies meeting the criteria

**Community-Oriented Policing (COP):** A philosophy based on the belief that law-abiding citizens should have input with respect to policing

**Community-Police Mediation Program:** A voluntary process in which community members and officers sit down in a neutral and confidential setting facilitated by a professional mediator to discuss their differences

**Community Policing:** A model of policing based on establishing partnerships among police and other citizens in an attempt to improve quality of life through crime prevention, information sharing, and mutual understanding

**Community Relations Programs:** Programs sponsored by police agencies that attempt to improve police–community relations

**Community Service Officers (CSOs):** Nonsworn employees who perform duties not requiring a sworn police officer

**Comparative Approach:** Involves comparing the number of police officers between cities of similar characteristics or the ratio of police officers to population

**CompStat:** Stands for computer statistics and is based on collecting and analyzing data from crime maps and other performance measures while holding police administrators accountable for their performance as measured by the data collected; a multifaceted system used to administer police operations based on a comprehensive, continuous analysis of results

**Computer-Aided Dispatch (CAD):** A system in which dispatch is accomplished through the use of computers

**Conducted Energy Devices:** Devices such as a Taser that can induce involuntary muscle contractions that can temporarily incapacitate people

**Consent Decree:** Agreement related to an employer achieving a balance in terms of race, ethnicity, and gender in the workforce

**Consent Search:** Occurs when an individual voluntarily waives his or her 4th Amendment rights and allows a police officer to search his or her person, belongings, vehicle, or home

**Contract Security Personnel:** Security guards or security officers hired by organizations from outside agencies to secure and protect assets and personnel

**Corruption of Authority:** The most widespread category of police misconduct; includes a wide variety of unauthorized material inducements or gratuities, ranging from discounted clothing and meals to free alcoholic beverages and commercial sex

**Crackdowns:** Increases in the number of police targeted toward a specific type of law violation

**Crime Analysis:** The systematic study of crime and disorder problems, including sociodemographic, spatial, and temporal factors

**Crime Control Model:** Allows for the arrest of individuals who are known to be factually guilty of committing a crime

**Crime Mapping:** The process of using a GIS to conduct spatial analysis of crime problems and other police issues

**Crime Prevention Through Environmental Design (CPTED):** Based on the premise that proper design and effective use of the built environment can lead to a reduction in the fear of crime and incidence of crime

**Criminal Law:** Body of law established to maintain peace and order to protect society from the injurious acts of individuals

**Critical Incident:** An event that has a stressful impact sufficient to overwhelm the effective coping skills of a person

**CSI Effect:** Refers to the perception of scientific testing by television viewers

**Cynicism:** In this context, involves a loss of faith in people or loss of enthusiasm for police work

**Department of Homeland Security (DHS):** Federal agency responsible for a unified national effort to secure the country and preserve freedom

**Deployment Models:** The assignment of police personnel to districts, zones, and areas

**Differential Response Policing:** Involves classifying calls by their seriousness to determine the appropriate police response

**Digital Collection System Network (DCSNet):** Connects FBI wiretapping rooms to switches controlled by traditional landline operators, Internet-telephone providers, and cellular companies

**Directed Energy Devices:** Use radiated energy to achieve the same effect as blunt force with a lower probability of injury

**Directed Patrol:** Involves increasing police presence in a specified area

**Discrimination:** Treating people differently because of their race, gender, religion, or national origin; involves behavior that, in its negative form, excludes all members of a certain group from some rights, opportunities, or privileges

**Disparate Impact:** Involves an employment policy or practice that, although seemingly neutral, adversely impacts a person or group

**DNA (Deoxyribonucleic Acid):** One of two types of molecules that encode genetic information

**Double Marginality:** Refers to the fact that Black officers were not fully accepted by their White coworkers and were also distrusted by other Blacks

**Drones:** Aircraft without a human pilot on board controlled either by computers or remotely by an operator on the ground or in another vehicle

**Drug Abuse Resistance Education (DARE):** Educational programs presented by police officers in cooperation with school authorities in an attempt to prevent abuse of drugs by youth

**Due Process Model:** Requires that evidence of guilt presented in court be obtained according to legal guidelines

**Early Intervention Programs:** Administrative practice of identifying officers whose behavior is problematic, intervening to correct the problem behavior, and monitoring intervention of those who have received it

**Education:** The provision of familiarity with the theoretical concepts and principles underlying the training

**Electronic Communications Privacy Act (ECPA):** Wiretapping regulation that protects email, pagers, and cell phone calls

**Electronic Non-Radar Detection Device (ENRADD):** A speed detection system using infrared beams to measure a car's speed as it passes through a three-foot-long section of road using sensors placed on each side of the road to detect when a vehicle enters and exits the section

**Employee Polygraph Protection Act of 1998 (EPPA):** Prohibits employers from requiring applicants to take a polygraph test or from using PDD results in the hiring or promoting of employees or as a basis for discipline or discharge

**Equal Protection Clause:** Of the 14th Amendment, applies to the police in that it prevents both the federal government and all states from denying the protection of the law to any group of persons by making arbitrary, unreasonable distinctions based on race, religion, gender, national origin, and so on

**Ethics:** The study of right and wrong, duty, responsibility, and personal character—all of these concepts have an implicit modifier—"moral"—attached to them; ethics is concerned with moral duty, what is morally right and wrong

**Ethos:** Fundamental spirit of a culture

**Evidence-Based Policing:** Involves using the scientific method to support an informed decision-making process

**Excessive Use of Force:** Also referred to as police brutality, this form of malfeasance pertains to situations in which officers overextend their legal authority by using excessive force to arrest or coerce information from individuals with whom they interact during the course of their duties

**Exclusionary Rule:** A judicially imposed requirement that any evidence obtained by the police using methods that violate an individual's constitutional rights be excluded in a criminal prosecution against that individual

**Executive Protection Agents:** Private security personnel hired to protect executives, attorneys, wealthy families, sports celebrities, movie stars, and political figures, among others

**Exigent Circumstances:** Circumstances that may exist when the police are in hot pursuit of a fleeing felon, when there is a danger of imminent destruction of evidence, when a suspect is escaping, or when there is imminent danger to the officer or others

**Field Associates:** Specially trained officers used to obtain intelligence regarding corrupt police practices

**Field Training:** Occurs immediately following successful recruit training; during field training, new officers are paired with specially trained veterans and are evaluated on how they perform on the street, normally in the patrol division; field training programs normally last anywhere from six weeks to six months

**Field Training Officers (FTOs):** Officers who have been selected and trained to direct, evaluate, and correct the performance of recruits immediately after their basic academy training

**Fingerprint Scanner:** Takes an image of the finger and determines whether the pattern of ridges and valleys in the image matches the pattern of ridges and valleys in prescanned images

**First Responder:** In the context of law enforcement or emergency response preparedness, these are the individuals to provide the first line of defense (police officers, firefighters, emergency medical personnel, public utility personnel, etc.)

**Foot Patrol:** The original form of police patrol; often employed today at parades, concerts, and sporting events

**Foreign Intelligence Surveillance Act (FISA):** Specifies that the purpose of electronic surveillance must be to obtain intelligence in the United States on foreign powers (such as enemy agents or spies) or individuals connected to international terrorist groups

**Forensic Science:** Any branch of science used in the resolution of legal disputes

**Fruit of the Poisonous Tree Doctrine:** Evidence found indirectly as a result of a constitutional violation

**Functional Organization Design:** Creation of positions and departments in an organization based on specialized activities

**Galvanic Skin Response:** Changes in electrical resistance in the skin over time

**Gaming Surveillance Officers:** Hired to act as security agents for casino managers and patrons

**General Adaptation Syndrome:** Stages of stress experienced by a person after the exposure to stressors

**Geographic Information System (GIS):** Computer software that captures, analyzes, stores, and presents spatial data and makes it easy to visualize and interpret geographic information

**Global Positioning System (GPS):** A U.S. space-based global navigation satellite system providing positioning, navigation, and timing services to users

**Good-Faith Doctrine:** Involves searches conducted with a warrant and states that when a police officer acting in good faith obtains a warrant, conducts a search, and seizes evidence, that evidence will not be excluded from court proceedings even if the warrant is later invalidated

**Graffiti Cameras:** Talking surveillance cameras

**Grass Eaters:** Term coined by the Knapp Commission to refer to officers who engage in minor acts of corrupt practices (acceptance of gratuities, etc.) and passively accept the wrongdoings of other officers

**Hierarchies:** Organizational structures that take the shape of a pyramid, with many employees at the bottom and a few management personnel at the top

**Homeland Security Act:** Law passed by the U.S. Congress that focuses on terrorism prevention strategies and tactics

**Hot Spots:** Geographic areas with clusters of criminal offenses occurring within a specified interval of time

**Hybrid Systems:** Consist of in-house management personnel with contract officers

**Hyperstress:** An overload resulting from too many complex demands for the time allotted

**Hypostress:** Low levels of mental or physical activity

**Illinois Citizen and Law Enforcement Analysis and Reporting (I-CLEAR):** A computerized data warehouse designed to allow police officers to search for suspects based on nicknames, tattoos, country of origin, vehicle make and model, and other characteristics in partnership with the Illinois State Police and residents of Chicago

**Immutable Characteristics:** Characteristics determined at birth or characteristics individuals should not be asked to change

**Incident Command System (ICS):** Coordinates police personnel, allocates resources, and allows emergency responders to adopt and integrate organization structure; attempts to achieve effective coordination of police personnel while ensuring appropriate allocation of resources and providing emergency responders an integrated organizational structure unhindered by jurisdictional boundaries

**Independent Source Doctrine:** Holds that illegally obtained evidence may be admitted if it was also obtained through an independent source not tainted by a failure to follow procedure or police misconduct

**Inevitable Discovery Doctrine:** Allows the admission of illegally obtained evidence if it would have been discovered lawfully in the normal course of events anyway

**In-House Security Personnel:** Typically employees who conduct security activities within an organization

**In-service Training:** Also known as **continuing professional education**, the intent is to keep professionals up to date with continuous changes that affect their practice

**Institutional Discrimination:** Unfair testing procedures, hiring practices, job assignments, and educational requirements

**Integrity Test:** Test used to assess a candidate's honesty and propensity for counterproductive behavior on the job, such as drug use or theft

**Intelligence-Led or Intelligence-Based Policing:** A policing model that originated in Britain and focuses on risk assessment and risk management. Involves identifying risks or patterns associated with groups, individuals, and locations to predict when and where crime is likely to occur; builds on community policing and problem-oriented policing and includes an information gathering process that allows police agencies to better understand their crime problems and take a measure of resources available to be able to decide on enforcement and prevention strategies

**Internal Affairs Units:** Units within police agencies that receive and investigate complaints concerning police misconduct, investigate possible indicators of police misconduct, prosecute officers who appear to be responsible for serious misconduct, and collect intelligence on misconduct and share it with police administrators

**Internet Protocol (IP) Cameras:** CCTV cameras that use the Internet to transmit image data and control signals over an Ethernet link

**Intuitive Approach:** Little more than an educated guess concerning the appropriate number of police personnel

**Job Action:** Occurs when negotiations fail to lead to an agreement and can include blue flu, work slowdowns, and work speedups

**Kansas City Preventive Patrol Experiment:** One of the most comprehensive assessments of police patrol

**Kickbacks:** Type of police corruption that refers to the practice of obtaining goods, services, or money for business referrals by police officers (e.g., attorneys, doctors, tow truck operators, auto body shops, and board-up service companies)

**Knapp Commission:** Investigative committee formed in 1972 by the city of New York in response to allegations of large-scale corruption among NYPD officers. This form of investigation set the stage for many cities and states in the years that followed

**Laser Radars:** LADARs (LAser Detection And Ranging) or LIDARs (LIght Detection And Ranging) use laser light to determine speed

**Law Enforcement Assistance Administration (LEAA):** During the 1960s and 1970s, provided a billion dollars each year to improve and strengthen criminal justice agencies

**Law Enforcement Officer:** A specially designated citizen who focuses on enforcing laws through detection and apprehension

**Legal Cynicism:** A cultural orientation in which the law and the agents of its enforcement are viewed as illegitimate, unresponsive, and ill equipped to ensure public safety

**Legalistic Style:** Focus is on law enforcement and arrests

**Less-Than-Lethal Force:** Force used by an officer that is not likely to result in serious bodily harm or death

**Lethal or Deadly Force:** Force that may result in great bodily harm or death

**Lexow Commission:** Investigative committee formed in 1894 by the city of New York in response to allegations of large-scale corruption amongst NYPD officers; this form of investigation set the stage for many cities and states in the years that followed

**Liability:** Legal responsibility for costs or damages

**License Plate Recognition (LPR) System:** Reads license plates of parked and moving vehicles and compares them to vehicle databases

**Line Personnel:** Perform actual police work and include patrol officers and investigators

**Malfeasance:** Any intentional act that either is based on illegality or disregards the law enforcement code of ethics or a departmental policy

**Mandatory Continuing Education (MCE):** Career-long training standards for police professionals to maintain and improve their professional competence

**Mandatory Data Collection:** Primarily in response to the racial profiling issues associated with the late 1990s and early 2000s, the federal government and each individual state mandated that law enforcement agencies maintain data regarding various demographic issues during police stops of vehicles (i.e., race of the driver and occupants of the vehicle stopped, reason or probable cause for the stop, whether or not any occupants or the vehicle was searched, justification for the search, length of detention, and whether or not any tickets were issued or arrests made)

**Matrix Structure:** Involves multiple support systems and authority relationships often found in a drug task force

**Meat Eaters:** Term coined by the Knapp Commission to describe officers who engage widely in corrupt and unlawful practices during the performance of their duties

**Media Relations Policy:** Policy based on the public's right to know and the police department's obligation to keep the public informed

**Misfeasance:** Taking inappropriate action or intentionally giving incorrect information

**Mobile Digital Communicator (MDC):** Digital dispatch and data communications system for field officers; also called a **mobile digital computer**

**Mollen Commission:** Created by former New York City mayor Rudolph Giuliani in 1994 and headed by retired New York Supreme Court justice Milton Mollen, the charge of the committee was to investigate allegations of misconduct, analyze the effectiveness of anticorruption mechanisms within the department, and offer recommendations for improvement

**Money Laundering:** Attempts to disguise the original source of monies, normally through illegal means, and infuse said monies into the legitimate marketplace

**Mounted Patrol:** Police patrolling on horseback

**Multiple-Hurdle Procedure:** A battery of tests or hurdles that must be completed before a recruit can become a police officer; the failure to pass any of the sequential hurdles disqualifies the candidate

**National Advisory Commission on Civil Disorders (1967):** Another major effort to better understand styles of policing, police–community relations, and police selection and training

**National Advisory Commission on Criminal Justice Standards and Goals (1973):** Another attempt to better understand styles of policing, police–community relations, and police selection and training

**National Security Letters (NSLs):** Written demands from the FBI that compel Internet service providers, credit companies, financial institutions, and others to hand over confidential records about their customers (such as subscriber information, phone numbers, email addresses, and websites visited)

**Night Watch System:** Early policing system that required able-bodied males to donate their time to help protect cities

**911 Policing:** Allocation of police resources in a case-by-case fashion

**Noble Cause Corruption:** Form of misconduct pertaining to various situations in which officers circumvent the law in order to serve what they perceive to be the greater good (e.g., manufacturing probable cause, perjury to gain a conviction in court)

**Nonfeasance:** In the context of policing, this form of misconduct refers to the reluctance of generally honest police officers to report misconduct committed by their peers; this reluctance on the part of honest officers has been identified as one of the factors perpetuating this issue and is often the result of the influence of the police subculture

**North American Free Trade Agreement (NAFTA):** Agreement for free trade between the United States, Canada, and Mexico that became effective in 1994

**Occupational Discrimination:** Discrimination that results, in part at least, from being a member of a particular work group

**Office of the Police Corps and Law Enforcement Education:** Created by the U.S. Department of Justice in 1999, the goal of this program was to weave a college education with state-of-the-art police training to produce highly qualified personnel who would be able to confront the demands and intricacies of 21st-century policing; unfortunately, funding for the program has been eliminated, and the Police Corps is no longer awarding scholarships or providing training

**On-View Crimes:** Crimes that the police officer actually observes while on patrol

**Organization:** A rational, efficient form of grouping people

**Organizational Assumptions:** Deeply held beliefs that guide behaviors in an organization

**Organized Crime:** Any group having some manner of a formalized structure and whose primary objective is to obtain money through illegal activities; such groups maintain their position through the use of actual or threatened violence, corrupt public officials, graft, or extortion, and they generally have a significant impact on the people in their locales, their region, or the country as a whole[4]

**Patrick Colquhoun:** Superintending magistrate of the Thames River Police, a forerunner of the Metropolitan Police and author of works on metropolitan policing

**Peace officer Accredited TRaining OnLine (PATROL):** Innovative and inexpensive way to provide a myriad of in-service training opportunities to officers on a statewide basis; this asynchronous, online training initiative was formed by a partnership between the Minnesota Chiefs of Police Association, the Minnesota Sheriffs' Association, and the League of Minnesota Cities Insurance Trust

**Pendleton Act:** Required that government jobs be awarded on the basis of merit rather than on the basis of friendship or political favor

**Perestroika:** Formal policy implemented by Russian authorities following the collapse of the former Soviet Union, whose goal was to introduce a more democratic form of government and a free-market economy for Russian citizens

**Performance Measures:** Indicators that assess the extent to which police patrol officers achieve the designated outcomes

**Photo Radar:** Automatically detects a speeding violation and photographs or video records the driver, the vehicle, and the license plate, and records vehicle speed and typically the date, time, and location

**Physical Restraints:** A variety of products employed to physically restrain or impede the movement of a person

**Place Design:** Geographical establishment of primary units in an organization, including assignment of personnel to beats, zones, districts, and areas

**Plain View Doctrine:** Holds that if a police officer sees an incriminating object in plain view during a legitimate stop, he or she may seize the object

**Police:** Derived from the Greek words *polis* and *politeuein*, which refer to being a citizen who participates in the affairs of a city or state

**Police Association for College Education (PACE):** Formerly known as the American Police Foundation, PACE is a professional organization dedicated to the professionalization of law enforcement through higher education

**Police–Community Relations:** Consists of both human and public relations

**Police Discretion:** A police officer's exercise of individual choices or judgments concerning possible courses of action

**Police Ethics:** Standards of conduct based on moral and professional principles that influence a variety of actions taken or not taken by police officers on and off duty

**Police Officer:** A specially designated citizen whose functions include order maintenance, provision of services, and law enforcement

**Police Paramilitary Unit:** A highly specialized police unit such as a special response team

**Police Personality:** Combination of characteristics and behaviors that are used to stereotype the police

**Police Subculture:** Shared values, attitudes, and norms created within the occupational and organizational environment of policing; a set of informal norms, largely based on tradition and passed on from generation to generation, that greatly influence police behavior and the perception of the public by police. Certain of these subcultural forces have a significant influence on the use of discretion, in both positive and negative ways

**Police Training Officer (PTO) Program:** Recently developed field training program that many researchers and police executives claim is effective at helping new officers entering the field develop problem-solving skills rarely seen at the early stages of their career; the PTO program involves two primary training areas: substantive topics and core competencies

**Polygraph:** A device that registers involuntary physical processes that is often used in an attempt to detect whether or not a suspect is telling the truth

**Post-traumatic Stress Disorder (PTSD):** Emotional disturbance leading to a numbing of emotions, insomnia, and depression

**Predictive Policing:** A model that involves using data and analysis to predict future police problems and implement strategies to resolve problems

**Prejudice:** Unfavorable attitudes toward a group or individual not based on experience or fact; a feeling about a person or persons based on faulty generalizations

**President's Commission on Law Enforcement and Administration of Justice (1967):** Represented a major effort to better understand styles of policing, police–community relations, and police selection and training

**Private Detectives and Investigators:** Detectives (investigators) who are not members of the police but are hired by individual clients or companies and are often licensed by the state

**Privilege Against Self-Incrimination:** Implies that no person can be compelled to incriminate himself or herself—the suspect need not answer questions or disclose information that would support his or her own conviction

**Probable Cause:** Exists when facts and circumstances within a police officer's knowledge, which are based on reasonably trustworthy information, are sufficient to warrant a person of reasonable caution to believe that an offense has been or is being committed by the person being arrested

**Probationary Period:** The period starting on the first day of recruit training, during which the performance of new officers is evaluated; this period ranges from six months to two years, depending on the agency; during probation, officers are "employees at will" and do not enjoy any of the employment protections (such as grievance procedures) granted to officers who have successfully completed their probationary periods

**Problem-Oriented Policing:** Encourages officers to take a holistic approach, working with other citizens and other agency representatives to find long-term solutions to a variety of recurrent problems

**Procedural Justice Model:** A model of policing based on empirical research demonstrating that compliance with the law and willingness to cooperate with enforcement efforts are primarily shaped by the strength of citizens' beliefs that law enforcement agencies are legitimate

**Profession:** Occupation often requiring some form of accreditation, certification, or licensing and usually including a code of ethics

**Professionalism:** An end state that is largely based on ethical practice and other related characteristics such as good personal character, personal and organizational accountability, a commitment to higher education and continuous training, and intolerance for misconduct

**Protection of Illegal Activities:** The most egregious of all forms of misconduct; involves police officers taking money or other valuables in exchange for their protection of criminal activities

**Protective Coloration:** Refers to the fact that Black police officers can often gather information that would be extremely difficult for White officers to gather; that having Black police officers on the force may make charges of racial brutality against the police less likely; and that federal funding is partly dependent on equal employment opportunities and affirmative action programs

**Psychological or Emotional Abuse:** Type of wrongdoing normally associated with the use of racial slurs and other negative descriptions of certain classes of citizens (e.g., gays, drug addicts, homeless persons, and protestors, to name the most common)

**Psychological Harassment:** Harassment based on the use of racial slurs and other attempts to embarrass or humiliate members of the minority group

**Psychophysiological Detection of Deception (PDD):** A device that registers involuntary physical processes that is often used in an attempt to detect whether or not a suspect is telling the truth

**Public Information Officer (PIO):** Person who represents the police department in all contacts with any form of media

**Public Relations:** From the police perspective, they include all of the activities in which police engage while attempting to develop or maintain a favorable public image

**Pulling Levers Policing:** An innovation that focuses attention on a small number of chronic offenders responsible for a large share of the crime problems

**Qualified Individual With a Disability:** Interpreted to mean the job applicant must be able to perform the essential elements of the job with or without reasonable accommodation

**Quotas:** Arbitrary and fixed numbers of citations or stops (or some other measure of activity) that officers are required to meet on a periodic basis

**Racial Profiling:** Occurs when an officer considers race as part of a decision to take, or not to take, law enforcement action; legally, an officer can only consider race as part of a specific, reliable suspect description tied to a particular crime

**Radio Detection and Ranging (RADAR) Systems:** Use remote sensors that emit electromagnetic radio waves to determine vehicle speeds

**Random Preventive Patrol:** Method of performing police work that permits officers to control their area

**Rank Structure:** Chain of command that identifies who communicates with whom and identifies lines of authority

**Reasonable Accommodation:** Refers to new construction or modification of existing facilities and work schedules, as long as the modification does not cause the agency undue hardship, such as significant expense or difficulty

**Reasonable Suspicion:** When based on objective facts and logical conclusions given a specific set of circumstances, may be used as the basis for stopping and frisking suspicious individuals

**Reasonableness:** Generally refers to what a reasonable person, in similar circumstances, based on similar information, might conclude

**Recruit Training:** Also known as basic training, refers to the initial training successful police applicants are exposed to; training covers criminal law, traffic code enforcement, arrest techniques, firearm training, self-defense tactics, vehicle searches, and a host of similar topics; successful recruit training culminates in certification as a sworn police or peace officer

**Red Light Cameras:** Record stoplight violations at intersections

**Reform Era (Reform Movement):** Involved radical reorganization of police agencies, including strong centralized administrative bureaucracy, hiring and promotion based on merit, highly specialized units, and application of science to crime through improved record keeping, fingerprinting, serology, and criminal investigation

**Responsiveness:** Refers to the provision of appropriate police services promptly and competently, with appropriate referrals in cases not within agency jurisdiction

**RICO Act:** Federal legislation enacted in 1970 that allows prosecutors to go after the organization rather than individuals; defines racketeering in a broad manner and makes it a crime to belong to an organization involved in a pattern of racketeering

**Role Ambiguity:** Confusion a person experiences related to expectations of others

**Role Conflict:** The result of inconsistent or incompatible expectations being communicated to a person

**Saturation Patrol:** Involves adding patrol officers to a specific area in order to increase police visibility

**Search:** Occurs when an expectation of privacy that society is prepared to consider reasonable is infringed upon

**Security Officers:** Privately hired to patrol and inspect property to protect against fire, theft, vandalism, terrorism, and illegal activity

**Seizure:** Of property occurs when there is some meaningful interference with an individual's possessory interests in that property

**Service Style:** Searches for alternatives to arrest and the uses of formal sanctions

**Shakedowns:** Type of corruption that involves officers taking money or other valuables and personal services from offenders they have caught during the commission of a crime; drug dealers, pimps, and motorists are among the favored targets for this practice

**Sheriff:** Typically, an elected official responsible for county law enforcement and, in many instances, the county jail

**Simulation or Work Sample Test:** Measures job skills of an applicant using samples of behavior under realistic job-like conditions

**Sir Robert Peel:** The founder of modern territorial policing (London Metropolitan Police) in 1829 in London

**Situational Crime Prevention (SCP):** Focuses on reducing crime by reducing crime opportunities and increasing risk to the offenders

**Solution-Oriented Policing (SOP):** Focuses on the fact that some police–community issues are best addressed through the development of unique approaches or thinking outside the box

**Sovereign Citizens:** A loose network of individuals living in the United States who profess to believe that federal, state, and local governments operate illegally

**Span of Control:** Ratio of supervisors to subordinates

**Status Test:** Related to an applicant's citizenship, possession of or ability to obtain a driver's license, residency requirement, and age and education level

**Stereotypes:** Preconceived notions based on prior encounters, word of mouth/rumor/gossip, and information provided by the media

**Strategic Management Era:** Based on the practice of computer-generated crime data and a resulting convergence of police management, technology, strategy, and community involvement

**Stress:** Occurs when an event involves a constraint, opportunity, or excessive physical or psychological demand

**Symbolic Assailants:** Potentially dangerous citizens to whom police are trained to accord a level of suspicion

**Taser:** Electroshock weapon that uses electrical current to disrupt voluntary control of muscles

**Task Force:** Law enforcement strategy based on the promotion and use of interagency cooperation; these units are normally headed by a federal law enforcement agency with local police officers being detailed or assigned to work on the various task forces

**Terrorism:** The unlawful use of force or threat of force against persons or property to intimidate or coerce a government, a civilian population, or any part thereof in furtherance of political or social objectives; "[t]he premeditated and unlawful act in which groups or agents of some principal engage in a threatened or actual use of force or violence against human or property targets. These groups or agents engage in this behavior intending the purposeful intimidation of governments or people to affect policy or behavior with an underlying political objective"[71]

**Terrorism-Oriented Policing:** Adds new duties to those already assumed by the police in an attempt to detect and prevent terrorist acts

**Time Design:** An organizational design that involves assignment of personnel based on watches, tours, or shifts

**Totality of Circumstances:** Requires that an officer has a particularized and objective basis for suspecting that a particular person is or has been involved in criminal activity; may be based on a variety of objective observations, information from police reports, and consideration of modes or patterns of operation of certain kinds of offenders from which a police officer may draw inferences and make deductions concerning the probability that the party in question is involved in criminal conduct

**Training:** The provision of basic skills necessary to perform essential job functions

**Transnational Crime:** "Crime that takes place across national borders . . . [that] is poorly understood but has had profound consequences for the ordering of the world system"[2]

**Unity of Command:** Each member of the organization has an immediate supervisor

**USA PATRIOT Act:** Federal legislation passed in 2002 that represented a major reorganization of national security agencies; it created the Department of Homeland Security, which conducts services previously handled by various other organizations

**Use of Force Training Simulator (UFTS):** Technology that employs computer-generated images (CGI) and speech technology that enable variability in characters and scenarios as well as character and scenario responses to user commands and conversation

**Visual Average Speed Computer and Recorder (VASCAR):** A semiautomated technique for determining the speed of a moving vehicle by recording the moment that a vehicle passes two fixed objects that are a known distance apart and the time the target vehicle takes to travel between them

**Warrant:** An order in writing, issued by a judicial authority, authorizing a police officer to take specific actions

**Watchman Style:** Focuses on an order maintenance style of policing

**White-Collar Crime:** "Illegal or unethical acts that violate the fiduciary responsibility of public trust by an individual or organization, usually during the course of legitimate occupational activity, by persons of high or respectable social status for personal or organizational gain"[12]

**Workload Analysis:** Consists of an elaborate information system with defined levels of police performance for computing the number of appropriate police personnel

**Zero Tolerance:** An aggressive policing strategy in which all violators are ticketed or arrested and which disregards extenuating circumstances

## ■ PREFACE

1. U.S. Department of Justice, Civil Rights Division, *Investigation of the Ferguson Police Department* (March 4, 2015), available from http://www.justice.gov/sites/default/files/opa/press-releases/attachments/2015/03/04/ferguson_police_department_report.pdf

2. J. Halpern, "The Cop: Darren Wilson Was Not Indicted for Shooting Michael Brown. Many People Question Whether Justice Was Done," *The New Yorker* (August 10, 2015).

## ■ CHAPTER 1

1. G. Gately, "Why Is Violent Crime Surging In Many Cities?" *The Crime Report* (July 13, 2015): http://www.thecrimereport.org/news/inside-criminal-justice/2015-07-why-is-violent-crime-surging-in-many-cities; M. Kaste, "Nationwide Crime Spike Has Law Enforcement Retooling Its Approach," *National Public Radio* (July 1, 2015): http://www.npr.org/2015/07/01/418555852/nationwide-crime-spike-has-law-enforcement-retooling-their-approach

2. H. Haddon, "Killings of New York Police Officers Spark Backlash to Protests," *The Wall Street Journal* (December 21, 2014): http://www.wsj.com/articles/after-police-shootings-protesters-vow-to-continue-1419192944

3. M. Rubinkam, "Bryon Dickson, PA State Trooper Killed in Ambush, to Be Laid to Rest," *Huffington Post* (September 18, 2014): http://www.huffingtonpost.com/2014/09/18/bryon-dickson-funeral_n_5841726.html

4. Gately, "Why Is Violent Crime Surging in Many Cities?"

5. M. Kaste, "Nationwide Crime Spike Has Law Enforcement Retooling Its Approach," *National Public Radio* (July 1, 2015): http://www.npr.org/2015/07/01/418555852/nationwide-crime-spike-has-law-enforcement-retooling-their-approach

6. H. Toch and J. D. Grant, *Police as Problem Solvers* (New York, NY: Plenum, 1991).

7. International Association of Chiefs of Police, *Discover Policing* (2012): http://discoverpolicing.org.

8. J. P. Crank, C. Kadleck, and C. Koski, "The USA: The Next Big Thing," *Police Practice & Research* 11, no. 5 (2010): 405–422.

9. B. K. Melekian, "Policing in the New Economy: A Report on the Emerging Trends From the Office of Community Oriented Policing Services," *The Police Chief* 79 (2012): 16–19.

10. B. A. Reaves, "Census of State and Local Law Enforcement Agencies, 2008," NCJ 233982 (Bureau of Justice Statistics, 2011): http://www.bjs.gov/content/pub/pdf/fleo08.pdf

11. Federal Bureau of Investigation, "Full Time Law Enforcement Employees, Table 74," *Crime in the United States, 2011* (2011a): https://www.fbi.gov/about-us/cjis/ucr/crime-in-the-u.s/2011/crime-in-the-u.s.-2011/tables/table_74_full-time_law_enforcement_employees_by_population_group_percent_male_and_female_2011.xls

12. Federal Bureau of Investigation, "Full Time State Law Enforcement Employees, by State, Table 76," *Crime in the United States, 2011* (2011b): https://www.fbi.gov/about-us/cjis/ucr/crime-in-the-u.s/2011/crime-in-the-u.s.-2011/tables/table_76_full-time_state_law_enforcement_employees_by_state_2011.xls

13. R. Roberg, K. Novak, and G. Cordner, *Police & Society*, 3rd ed. (Los Angeles, CA: Roxbury, 2005).

14. Reaves, "Census of State and Local Law Enforcement Agencies, 2008."

15. Crank et al., "The USA: The Next Big Thing."

16. B. Krisberg and S. Marchionna, *Fact Sheet: Police, Prisons, and Public Safety in California* (Berkeley, CA: Earl Warren Institute on Law and Social Policy, April 2013).

17. Community Oriented Policing Services, U.S. Department of Justice, "The Impact of the Economic Downturn on American Police Agencies" (n.d.): http://www.cops.usdoj.gov/Default.asp?Item=2602

18. Melekian, "Policing in the New Economy."

19. M. Gamiz Jr., "Private Security Industry Grows as Pay Rate Stays Flat," *The Morning Call* (March 2, 2010): http://www.mcall.com/business/local/outlook/all-security-030908%2C0%2C2413617.story; K. O. Morgan and S. Morgan, *Crime: State Rankings 2011* (Washington, DC: CQ Press, 2011).

20. International Association of Chiefs of Police, *Discover Policing* (2012): http://discoverpolicing.org.

21. Division of Public Safety, *Crime Prevention, Safety Programs and Presentations* (2012): www.dps.illinois.edu/universitypolice/index.html.

22. Indiana Sheriff's Association, *What Is a Sheriff?* (2012): http://www.indianasheriffs.org.

23. Illinois Department of Natural Resources, *Conservation Police Officer Career Opportunities* (2012): http://dnr.state.il.us.

24. Bureau of Justice Statistics, *Tribal Law Enforcement* (2008c): www.bjs.ojp.usdoj.gov.

25. Bureau of Justice Statistics, *Tribal Law Enforcement*, 1.

## ■ CHAPTER 2

1. M. Lee, *A History of the Police in England* (Montclair, NJ: Patterson Smith, 1971), 27.

2. W. Miller, "The Good, the Bad & the Ugly: Policing America," *History Today* 50, no. 8 (August 2000), 29–35.

3. D. R. Johnson, *American Law Enforcement: A History* (St. Louis, MO: Forum Press, 1981), 7.

4. Miller, "The Good, the Bad, & the Ugly."

5. S. Walker, *The Police in America* (Boston, MA: McGraw-Hill, 1999).

6. H. D. Barlow, *Criminal Justice in America* (Upper Saddle River, NJ: Prentice Hall, 2000), 166; R. Lane, "Urban Police and Crime," in M. Tonry & N. Morris (Eds.), *Modern Policing* (Chicago, IL: University of Chicago Press, 1992), 6–7.

7. Barlow, *Criminal Justice in America*, 165–166; B. L. Berg, *Law Enforcement: An Introduction to Police in Society* (Boston, MA: Allyn and Bacon, 1992), 31.

8. Miller, "The Good, the Bad, & the Ugly."

9. B. Sweatman and A. Cross, "The Police in the United States," *C. J. International* 5, no. 1 (1989): 11–18.

10. "FBI Celebrates 100 Years," *Police Chief* (July 2008), available from http://www.policechiefmagazine.org/magazine/index.cfm?fuseaction=display.

11. D. Wells, "The Boston Police Department," *Police Chief* 73, no. 5 (May 2006), available from http://www.policechiefmagazine.org/magazine/index.cfm?fuseaction=display_arch&article_id=900&issue_id=52006.

12. Anonymous, "In Our Century," *The American City & County* 125, no. 11 (November 2010): 70.

13. G. L. Kelling and M. H. Moore, *The Evolving Strategy of Policing: Perspectives on Policing* (Washington, DC: Government Printing Office, November 1998), 3.

14. J. A. Conser and G. D. Russell, *Law Enforcement in the United States* (Gaithersburg, MD: Aspen, 2000), 167; R. Roberg and J. Kuykendall, *Police in Society* (Belmont, CA: Wadsworth, 1993), 59.

15. Conser and Russell, *Law Enforcement in the United States*, 168; Kelling and Moore, *The Evolving Strategy of Policing*, 4.

16. J. F. Richardson, *Urban Police in the United States* (Port Washington, NY: Kennikat Press, 1974), 33–34.

17. Richardson, *Urban Police in the United States*, 47.

18. Conser and Russell, *Law Enforcement in the United States*, 168; Lane, "Urban Police and Crime," 12.

19. D. E. Barlow and M. H. Barlow, *Policing in a Multicultural Society: An American Story* (Prospect Heights, IL: Waveland Press, 2000).

20. D. R. Johnson, *American Law Enforcement: A History* (St. Louis, MO: Forum Press, 1981), 1.

21. Barlow, *Criminal Justice in America*, 167; Roberg and Kuykendall, *Police in Society*, 61–66.

22. Walker, *The Police in America*.

23. L. K. Gaines, V. E. Kappeler, and J. B. Vaughn, *Policing in America*, 3rd ed. (Cincinnati, OH: Anderson, 1999).

24. Richardson, *Urban Police in the United States*, 57.

25. R. H. Langworthy and L. F. Travis III, *Policing in America: A Balance of Forces* (Englewood Cliffs, NJ: Prentice Hall, 1999).

26. Richardson, *Urban Police in the United States*, 70.

27. A. R. Hunt, "Murder Wave Still Swamps a Resurgent New Orleans," *Harrisburg Daily Register* (April 3, 2012), A4.

28. J. Blumgart, "New Orleans Cops Ignore Federal Oversight," *Al Jazeera* (April 13, 2014), available from http://america.aljazeera.com/articles/2014/4/13/doj-and-nopd.html

29. Hunt, "Murder Wave Still Swamps a Resurgent New Orleans," A4.

30. S. Paulson, "Chicago Is the Most Corrupt City in the U.S.," *Chicago Examiner* (February 15, 2012), available from http://www.examiner.com/article/chicago-is-the-most-corrupt-city-the-united-states

31. Barlow, p. 167; D. Jackson, "Sordid Ties Tarnishing City Police," *Chicago Tribune* (October 22, 2000), A1.

32. H. Goldstein, *Policing a Free Society* (Cambridge, MA: Ballinger), 151–152.

33. Langworthy and Travis, *Policing in America*.

34. Walker, *The Police in America*.

35. Barlow and Barlow, *Policing in a Multicultural Society*.

36. R. G. Dunham and G. P. Alpert, *Critical Issues in Policing: Contemporary Readings*, 3rd ed., (Prospect Heights, IL: Waveland Press, 1997).

37. Barlow and Barlow, *Policing in a Multicultural Society*.

38. Dunham and Alpert, *Critical Issues in Policing*; D. Green, "Changes in Policing," *Law & Order* (January 2003), available from http://policechiefmagazine.org/magazine/.

39. Bouza, A. V. (1990). *The police mystique*. New York, NY: Plenum, pp. 270–271.

40. G. P. Alpert and R. G. Dunham, *Policing Urban America*, 3rd ed., (Prospect Heights, IL: Waveland Press, 1997).

41. J. Petersilia, "Influence of Research on Policing," in R. G. Dunham and G. P. Alpert (Eds.), *Critical Issues in Policing: Contemporary Readings* (Prospect Heights, IL: Waveland Press, 1993), 220.

42. Conser and Russell, *Law Enforcement in the United States*, 197.

43. J. P. Crank, C. Kadleck, and C. Koski, "The USA: The Next Big Thing," *Police Practice & Research* 11, no. 5 (2010), 410.

44. Green, "Changes in Policing."

45. Green, "Changes in Policing."

46. Kelling and Moore, *The Evolving Strategy of Policing*, 10.

47. Barlow and Barlow, *Policing in a Multicultural Society*, 43.

48. M. D. Lyman, *The Police: An Introduction* (Upper Saddle River, NJ: Prentice Hall, 1999).

49. H. Goldstein, "Improving Policing: A Problem-Oriented Approach," *Crime and Delinquency* 25 (1979), 236–258.

50. L. W. Sherman, *The Quality of Police Education* (San Francisco, CA: Jossey-Bass, 1978), 4.

51. M. Corsianos, "Responding to Officers' Gendered Experiences Through Community Policing and Improving Police Accountability to Citizens," *Contemporary Justice Review* 14, no. 1 (2011), 11.

52. J. Lee, "Policing After 9/11: Community Policing in an Age of Homeland Security," *Police Quarterly* 13, no. 4 (2010), 347–366.

53. D. P. Rosenbaum, L. M. Graziano, C. D. Stephens, and A. M. Schuck, "Understanding Community Policing and Legitimacy-Seeking Behavior in Virtual Reality: A National Study of Municipal Police websites," *Police Quarterly* 14, no. 1 (2011), 25–47.

54. Crank, Kadleck, and Koski, "The USA," 419

55. W. M. Oliver, "The Era of Homeland Security: September 11, 2001 to . . . ," *Journal of California Law Enforcement* 40, no. 3 (2006), 19–30.

56. Oliver, "The Era of Homeland Security."

57. B. Brown, "Community Policing in Diverse Society," *Law Enforcement Executive Forum* 4, no. 5 (2004), 49–56.

58. J. Gottstein, *Intelligence-Based Policing* (September 2008), available from http://www.hendonpub.com/resources/articlearchive/details.aspx?ID=207059

59. R. Roberg, K. Novak, and G. Cordner, *Police & Society*, 3rd ed. (Los Angeles, CA: Roxbury, 2005), 566.

60. G. Newman and R. Clarke, *Policing Terrorism: An Executive's Guide* (Offices of Community Oriented Police Service, U.S. Department of Justice, July 2008), 10.

61. Newman and Clarke, *Policing Terrorism*, 6.

62. Newman and Clarke, *Policing Terrorism*, 6.

63. Newman and Clarke, *Policing Terrorism*, 16.

64. Newman and Clarke, *Policing Terrorism*, 10.

65. G. Kelling and W. Bratton, "Policing Terrorism," *Civic Bulletin* 43 (New York: Manhattan Institute for Policy Research, September 2006), in G. Newman and R. Clarke, *Policing Terrorism: An Executive's Guide* (Offices of Community Oriented Police Service, U.S. Department of Justice, July 2008), 10.

66. Newman and Clarke, *Policing Terrorism*, 16.

67. Roberg, Novak, and Cordner, *Police & Society*, 8.

68. R. J. Meadows, "Legal Issues in Policing," in R. Muraskin and A. R. Roberts (Eds.), *Visions for Change: Crime and Justice in the Twenty-First Century* (Upper Saddle River, NJ: Prentice Hall, 1998), 145.

69. D. J. Walsh and V. Conway, "Police Governance and Accountability: Overview of Current Issues," *Crime, Law & Social Change* 55, no. 2/3 (2011), 61, 62.

70. D. Weisburd and A. Braga, *Police innovation: Contrasting Perspectives* (New York, NY: Cambridge University Press, 2006).

71. A. A. Braga and D. Weisburd, *Police Innovation and Crime Prevention: Lessons Learned From Police Research Over the Past 20 Years* (Paper presented at the National Institute of Justice Policing Research Workshop: Planning for the Future, Washington, D.C., May 2007).

## ■ CHAPTER 3

1. E. R. Maguire, *Organizational Structure in American Police Agencies* (Albany, NY: State University Press, 2003).

2. Maguire, *Organizational Structure in American Police Agencies*, 3.

3. U.S. Department of Labor, *What Is an Incident Command System?* (Washington, DC: Occupational Safety and Health Administration, 2012), available from http://www.osha.gov/SLTC/etools/ics/what_is_ics.html

4. M. Jones, "A Complexity Science View of Modern Police Administration," *Public Administration Quarterly* 32, no. 3 (2008), 433–458.

5. G. Kerilikowske, "The End of Community Policing: Remembering the Lessons Learned," *FBI Law Enforcement Bulletin* 73, no. 4 (2004), 6–9.

6. W. Engelson, "Leadership Challenges in the Information Age," *Police Chief* 66 (1999), 64–66.

7. R. L. LaGrange, *Policing American Society*, 2nd ed. (Chicago, IL: Nelson-Hall, 1998), 318.

8. J. F. Hodgson and C. Orban, *Public Policing in the 21st Century: Issues and Dilemmas in the United States and Canada* (Monsey, NY: Criminal Justice Press, 2005).

9. R. R. Roberg and G. Cordner, *Police and Society*, 4th ed. (New York, NY: Oxford University Press, 2009), 100.

10. S. L. Muzzatti, "The Police, the Public, the Post-Liberal Politics of Fear: Paramilitary Policing Post–9/11," in J. F. Hodgson and C. Orban (Eds.), *Public Policing in the 21st Century: Issues and Dilemmas in the U.S. and Canada* (Monsey, NY: Criminal Justice Press, 2005), 107–125.

11. S. Mastrofski, "Community Policing: A Skeptical View," in D. Weisburg and A. A. Braga (Eds.), *Police Innovation Contrasting Perspectives* (New York, NY: Cambridge University Press, 2006), 64.

12. Jones, "A Complexity Science View of Modern Police Administration," 4.

13. S. M. Cox and J. D. Fitzgerald, *Police in Community Relations: Critical Issues*, 3rd ed. (Madison, WI: Brown & Benchmark, 1996); J. H. Skolnick and D. H. Bayley, *The New Blue Line: Police Innovation in Six American Cities* (New York, NY: Free Press, 1986); M. K. Sparrow, M. H. Moore, and D. M. Kennedy, *Beyond 911: A New Era for Policing* (New York, NY: Basic Books, 1990); H. Toch and J. D. Grant, *Police as Problem Solvers* (New York, NY: Plenum, 1991).

14. D. J. Stevens, *An Introduction to American Policing* (Sudbury, MA: Jones and Bartlett, 2008), 140.

15. G. L. Kelling, T. Pate, D. Dieckman, and C. E. Brown, *The Kansas City Preventive Patrol Experiment: A Summary Report* (Washington, DC: Police Foundation, 1974); K. Lavery, "Changing Patrol Operations. Why? One Word: Survival," *Officer.com* (August 25, 2008), available from http://www.officer.com; Skolnick and Bayley, *The New Blue Line;* Toch and Grant, *Police as Problem Solvers.*

16. P. W. Greenwood, J. Chaiken, and J. R. Petersilia, *The Criminal Investigation Process* (Lexington, MA: D.C. Heath, 1977).

17. C. A. Kostelac, *Civilianization in Law Enforcement Organizations* (Paper presented at the annual meeting of the American Society of Criminology, Los Angeles, CA, 2006), available from http://www.allacademic.com/meta/p126524_index.html; author research.

18. National Institute of Justice, *Fighting Crime With COPS and Citizens* (2000), available from http://www.ojp/usdoj.gov/nij/publications/cops/impact.html

19. C. Wexler, "Subject to Debate: De-civilianization of Policing: A Big Step Backwards," *Newsletter of the Police Executive Research Forum* 23 (2009), 1–5.

20. C. Stenberg and S. L. Austin, *Managing Local Government Services: A Practical Guide* (Atlanta, GA: ICMA Press, 2007).

21. Stenberg and Austin, *Managing Local Government Services,* 334.

22. D. Hellriegel and J. W. Slocum, *Organizational Behavior,* 13th ed. (Cincinnati, OH: South-Western Cengage Learning, 2011).

23. Y. C. Turner, "Decentralizing the Specialized Unit Functions in Small Police Agencies," *Police Chief* 77 (2000), 50.

24. New York Police Department, *Precincts* (2012), available from http://home2.nyc.gov/html/nypd/html/home/precincts.shtml

25. W. Tucker, J. Jordan, and R. Deliums, *Police Reform White Paper* (Oakland, CA: Oakland Police Department, 2007)

26. L. K. Gaines, M. D. Southerland, and J. E. Angell, *Police Administration* (New York, NY: McGraw-Hill, 1991), 106

27. S. P. Robbins, *Organizational Behavior,* 11th ed. (Upper Saddle River, NJ: Prentice Hall, 2005)

28. Maguire, *Organizational Structure in American Police Agencies.*

29. R. Balko, "The Militarization of America's Police Forces," *Cato's Letter* 11, no. 4. (2003), 1–5.

30. Balko, "The Militarization of America's Police Forces."

31. Balko, "The Militarization of America's Police Forces."

32. American Civil Liberties Union (ACLU), *War Comes Home: The Excessive Militarization of American Policing* (2014), available from https://www.aclu.org/sites/default/files/field_document/jus14-warcomeshome-report-web-rel1_1.pdf

33. M. Apuzzo, "War Gear Flows to Police Departments," *The New York Times* (June 8, 2014).

34. ACLU, *War Comes Home.*

35. R. N. Holden, *Modern Police Management,* 2nd ed. (Englewood Cliffs, NJ: Prentice Hall, 2000).

36. A. D. Sapp, "Police Unionism as a Developmental Process," in A. S. Blumberg and E. Niederhoffer (Eds.), *The Ambivalent Force: Perspectives on the Police,* 3rd ed. (New York, NY: Holt, Rinehart & Winston, 1985), 412–419.

37. Bureau of Labor Statistics, *Economic News Release* (Washington, DC: United States Department of Labor, 2012), available from http://www.bls.gov/news.release/union2.nr0.htm

38. J. Sherk, "Mandatory Public-Safety Collective Bargaining Could Be Made Less Onerous," *The Heritage Foundation* (2008), available from http://www.policyarchive.org/bitstream/handle/10207/13660/wm_1923.pdf.sequence.

39. T. Caplow, *Managing an Organization* (New York, NY: Holt, Rinehart & Winston, 1983).

40. K. Johnson, "Police Agencies Find It Hard to Require Degrees: Education Standards Tricky for Short-Handed Departments," *USA Today* (September 18, 2006), A3.

41. Bureau of Justice Assistance, *Police Chiefs Desk Reference* (Washington, DC: Office of Justice Programs, 2004), 157.

42. Bureau of Justice Assistance, *Police Chiefs Desk Reference.*

43. CALEA, *Law Enforcement Program: The Standards* (2012), available from http://www.calea.org

44. J. Chriss, *From Generalist to Specialist Back to Generalist: The Shifting Roles of Police Over Time* (Paper presented at the annual meeting of the American Society of Criminology, Atlanta, GA, 2007), available from http://www.allacademic.com/meta/p174160_index.html

45. Chriss, *From Generalist to Specialist Back to Generalist.*

## ■ CHAPTER 4

1. D. Orrick, "Recruiting During the Economic Downturn," *Police Chief Magazine* 79. (2012), 1–6, available from http://policechiefmagazine.org

2. K. Johnson, "Police Agencies Buried in Resumes," *USA Today* (2009), available from http://www.usatoday.com/news/nation/2009-03-11-copjobs_N.htm

3. B. Wright, M. Dai, and K. Greenbeck, "Correlates of Police Academy Success," *Policing: An International Journal of Police Strategies & Management* 34 (2011), 626.

4. F. L. McCafferty, "The Challenge of Selecting Tomorrow's Police Officers From Generations X and Y," *Journal of the American Academy of Psychiatry and the Law* 31 (2003), 79.

5. D. Sanders and A. Stefaniak, "To Protect and Serve: What Generation Y Brings to Law Enforcement and How Police Agencies Can Benefit," *Police Perspectives* (University of Utah, Center for Public Policy & Administration, 2008), available from www.cppa.utah.edu/publications/work force.PP_To_Protect_and_Serve.pdf

6. J. P. Henchey, "Ready or Not, Here They Come: The Millennial Generation Enters the Workforce," *The Police Chief* 72, no. 9 (September 2005).

7. Sanders and Stefaniak, "To Protect and Serve," 5.

8. McCafferty, "The Challenge of Selecting Tomorrow's Police Officers From Generations X and Y."

9. C. Raines, *Managing Millennials, Generations at Work* (2002), available from http://generationsatwork.com/articles/millenials.htm

10. J. R. Lundborn, "Managing the Generation Yers—Simply Put," *Police and Security News* (2002), available from http://www.policeandsecuritynews.com/julyaug02/genyers.htm

11. J. Beck and M. Wade, *Got Game: How the Gamer Generation Is Reshaping Business Forever* (Boston, MA: Harvard Business School Press, 2004); Sanders and Stefaniak, "To Protect and Serve."

12. B. Harrison, "Gamers, Millennials and Generation Next: Implications for Policing," *Police Chief Magazine* 74 (2007), 5, available from http://policechiefmagazine.org/magazine/index.cfm?fuseaction=display_arch&article_id=1312&issue_id=12007.

13. Henchey, "Ready or Not, Here They Come."

14. A. Schapiro, "How Community Policing Has Changed What Police Departments Are Looking for in Recruits," *Community Policing Dispatch* 1 (2008), 1, available from http://www.cops.usdoj.gov/html/dispatch/october2008/nugget.htm

15. Henchey, "Ready or Not, Here They Come"; L. Eldridge, "The 'Me' Generation and the Future of Law Enforcement," *All Law Enforcement Is Local* (September 13, 2012), available from http://www.policeone.com/police-jobs-and-careers/articles/5980033-The-me-generation-and-the-future-of-law-enforcement/

16. Ibid.

17. D. Bell, *Race, Racism and American Law,* 6th ed. (New York, NY: Aspen, 2004).

18. Ibid.

19. Equal Employment Opportunity Commission (EEOC), *Employers and Other Entities Covered by EEO Laws* (2009), available from http://www.eeoc.gov/aboutee/overview_coverage.html.

20. Bell, *Race, Racism and American Law.*

21. U.S. Department of Commerce, *NOAA Civil Rights Office* (2010), available from http://www.eeo.noaa.gov/glossary.htm

22. EEOC, *Employers and Other Entities Covered by EEO Laws.*

23. F. Pincus, *Reverse Discrimination: Dismantling the Myth* (Boulder, CO: Lynne Rienner, 2003).

24. Ibid.

25. A. Thernstrom, "The Supreme Court Says No to Quotas," *The Wall Street Journal* (July 1, 2009), A13.

26. R. A. Epstein, "Ricci v. DeStefano," *Forbes.com,* available from http://www.forbes.com/2009/06/29/ricci-destefano-new-haven-supreme-court affirmative-action-opinion-column

27. J. A. Burns, "Supreme Court Creates New Risk for Employers Who Use Tests or other Screening Devices," *Employment Law Watch* (2009), available from http://www.employmentlawwatch.com/tags/ricci-v-destefano/

28. S. M. Cox and J. D. Fitzgerald, *Police in Community Relations: Critical Issues,* 3rd ed. (Dubuque, IA: Brown & Benchmark, 1996).

29. G. Billikopf, *Validating the Selection Process* (University of California, 2006), available from http://www.cnr.berkeley.edu/ucce50/ag-labor/71abor/03.htm

30. EEOC, *Employers and Other Entities Covered by EEO Laws.*

31. Ibid.

32. District of Columbia Fire and Emergency Medical Services Department, "Pregnancy Policy," *Bulletin* 29 (2008), available from http://fems.dc.gov/fems/lib/fems/pdf/bull._29_pregnancy_ policy_.pdf

33. EEOC, *Employers and Other Entities Covered by EEO Laws.*

34. R. A. Rhodes, "Legal Discrimination in Four Letters: BFOQ," *Connecticut Employment Law Letter* (2002), available from http://www.halloran-sage.com

35. F. Landy and E. Salas, *Employment Discrimination Litigation: Behavioral, Quantitative, and Legal Perspectives* (Hoboken, NJ: John Wiley, 2005), 266–267.

36. EEOC, *Americans with Disabilities Act: Questions and Answers* (2002), available from http://www.ada.gov/q%26aeng02.htm

37. U.S. Department of Justice (DOJ), *ADA Settlement and Consent Agreement* (Settlement agreement between the United States of America and Illinois State Police, 2011), available from www.ada.gov/settlement.htm

38. T. D. Colbridge, "The Americans with Disabilities Act: A Practical Guide for Police Departments," *FBI Law Enforcement Bulletin* 70 (2011), 23–32.

39. Colbridge, "The Americans with Disabilities Act," 26.

40. DOJ, *Questions and Answers: The Americans with Disabilities Act and Hiring Police Officers*, available from http://www.ada.gov/copsq7a/.htm

41. J. Ashcroft, D. Daniels, and S. V. Hart, *Hiring and Keeping Police Officers* (U.S. Department of Justice, 2004), 9, available from http://www.ncjrs.gov/

42. H. Brandon and B. Lippman, "Using the Web to Improve Recruitment," *Police Chief* 67 (2000), 37–41.

43. National Center for Women and Policing (NCWP), *Recruiting and Retaining Women: A Self-Assessment Guide for Law Enforcement* (2001), 22–27, available from http://www.ncjrs.org/pdffiles1/bja/185235.pdf

44. NCWP, *Recruiting and Retaining Women*, 21–27.

45. D. Milgram, "Recruiting Women to Policing: Practical Strategies That Work," *Police Chief Magazine* 53 (2002), 23–29, available from http://www.iwitts.org

46. NCWP, *Recruiting and Retaining Women*; L. M. Tuomey and R. Jolly, "Step Up to Law Enforcement, A Successful Strategy for Recruiting Women Into the Law Enforcement Profession," *The Police Chief* (June 2009), available from http://www.policechiefmagazine.org/magazine/index.cfm?fuseaction=display_arch&article_id=1820&issue_id=62009#8

47. C. E. Rabe-Hemp, "Survival in an 'All Boys Club': Policewomen and Their Fight for Acceptance," *Policing* 31, no. 2 (2008b), 251.

48. C. A. Archbold, K. D. Hassell, and A. J. Stichman, "Comparing Promotion Aspirations Among Female and Male Police Officers," *International Journal of Police Science & Management* 12, no. 2 (2010), 287–303.

49. J. Mroz, "Female Police Chiefs, a Novelty No More," *The New York Times* (April 6, 2008), available from http://www.nytimes.com/2008/04/06/nyregion/nyregionspecial2/06Rpolice.html

50. M. Dulaney, "Black Police in America" (1996), in R. G. Dunham and G. P. Alpert (Eds.), *Critical Issues in Policing* (Long Grove, IL: Waveland Press, 2010).

51. J. Kuykendall and D. Burns, "The Black Police Officer: An Historical Perspective," *Journal of Contemporary Criminal Justice* 1 (1980), 103–113.

52. S. Leinen, *Black Police, White Society* (New York, NY: University Press, 1984).

53. R. Margolis, *Who Will Wear the Badge? A Study of Minority Recruitment Efforts in Protective Services* (Washington, DC: Government Printing Office, 1971).

54. P. S. Sullivan, "Minority Officers: Current Issues," in R. Dunham and G. Alpert (Eds.), *Critical Issues in Policing: Contemporary Readings* (Prospect Heights, IL: Waveland, 1989); L. Williams, "Police Officers Tell of Strains of Living as a 'Black in Blue,'" *The New York Times* (February 14, 1988), 26.

55. J. M. Kennedy, "Latino FBI Agents Bias Victims: Judge," *Journal Star* (October 1, 1988), A2.

56. R. M. Shusta, D. R. Levine, P. R. Harris, and H. Z. Wong, *Multicultural Law Enforcement: Strategies for Peacekeeping in a Diverse Society* (Englewood Cliffs, NJ: Prentice-Hall, 1995).

57. J. McKeever and A. Kranda, "Recruitment and Retention of Qualified Police Personnel: A Best Practices Guide," *Big Ideas for Smaller Departments* 1, no. 3 (Summer 2000), 14.

58. Ibid.

59. D. A. Decicco, "Police Officer Candidate Assessment and Selection," *FBI Law Enforcement Bulletin* 69 (2000), 1–6.

60. C. Smith and A. D. Angie, *Developing a Multiple Hurdle Approach to Hiring* (PowerPoint presentation, HR Research & Assessment Division, U.S. Secret Service IPAC Conference, Washington, D.C., July 2011), available from http://annex.ipacweb.org/library/conf/11/smith.pdf

61. Federal Bureau of Investigation, *FBI Police Officer Physical Requirements* (2009), available from http://www.fbijobs.gov/1261.asp

62. Los Angeles Police Department, *Qualifications* (2012), available from http://www.joinlapd.com/qualifications.html

63. EEOC, *Employers and Other Entities Covered by EEO Laws.*

64. L. K. Gaines and V. E. Kappeler, *Policing in America,* 6th ed. (Cincinnati, OH: Anderson Publishing, 2008), 110.

65. Philadelphia Police Department (PPD), *Veteran's Preference* (2012b), available from http://www.ppdonline.org/career/career_vets.php

66. PPD, *Preference Points* (2012a), available from http://phillypolice.com/careers/preference-points

67. Memphis Police Department, *Requirements* (2012), available from http://mpdacademy.com/requirements.php

68. Decicco, "Police Officer Candidate Assessment and Selection."

69. G. Cordner and A. Cordner, "Obstacles to Recruitment, Selection, and Retention of Women Police Officers," *Police Quarterly* 14 (2011), 221.

70. Cordner and Cordner, "Obstacles to Recruitment, Selection, and Retention of Women Police Officers," 222.

71. K. A. Lonsway, "Failing Grades: Physical Agility Tests in Police Selection," *Women Police* 38 (2004), 7–11.

72. Ibid.

73. F. Landy and J. M. Conte, *Work in the 21st Century: An Introduction to Industrial and Organizational Psychology*, 3rd ed. (Hoboken, NJ: Wiley-Blackwell, 2009), 151.

74. Med-Tox Health Services, *Law Enforcement Physical Agility Testing* (2009), available from http://www.med-tox.com/policetest.html

75. K. A. Lonsway, "Failing Grades: Physical Agility Tests in Police Selection," *Women Police* 38 (2004), 7–11.

76. New York State Police Recruitment Center, *Height and Weight Standards* (2012), available from http://www.nytrooper.com/height_weight.cfm

77. R. N. Holden and L. L. Gammeltoft, "*Toonen v. Brown County*: The Legality of Police Vision Standards," *American Journal of Police* 10 (1991), 59–66.

78. G. W. Good, S. C. Maisel, and S. D. Kriska, "Setting an Uncorrected Visual Acuity Standard for Police Officer Applicants," *Journal of Applied Psychology* 83 (1998), 817–824.

79. Med-Tox Health Services, *Law Enforcement Physical Agility Testing*, 1.

80. Pittsburgh Personnel and Civil Service Commission, *Police officer Examination and Selection* (2012), available from http://www.city.pittsburgh.pa.us/personnel/html/exam_and_selection.html

81. International Public Management Association for Human Resources (IPMA), *Entry-Level Police Tests* (Alexandria, VA: Author, 2009), available from http://www.ipma-hr.org

82. C. A. Winters, "Socio-economic Status, Test Bias, and the Selection of Police," *Police Journal* 65 (1992), 125–135.

83. C. R. Bartol and A. Bartol, *Introduction to Forensic Psychology: Research and Application* (Thousand Oaks, CA: Sage, 2008), 49.

84. M. Tawney, "Integrity Testing: The Selection Tool of the Future," *Law and Order* 56 (2008), 34–39.

85. M. L. Dantzker, "Psychological Preemployment Screening for Police Candidates: Seeking Consistency If Not Standardization," *Professional Psychology: Research and Practice* 42, no. 3 (2011), 276–283, available from http://www.apa.org/pubs/journals/features/pro-42-3-276.pdf; "Pre-employment Psychological Evaluation Services Guidelines," ratified by the IACP Police Psychological Services Section (Los Angeles, CA, 2004), available from http://www.policepsych.com/screening.pdf

86. R. D. Meier, R. E. Farmer, and D. Maxwell, "Psychological Screening of Police Candidates: Current Perspectives," *Journal of Police Science and Administration* 15 (1987), 210–215.

87. Dantzker, "Psychological Preemployment Screening for Police Candidates."

88. Bartol and Bartol, *Introduction to Forensic Psychology*.

89. R. E. Cochrane, R. P. Teft, and L. Vandecreek, "Psychological Testing and the Selection of Police Officers," *Criminal Justice and Behavior* 30 (2003), 511–537.

90. Ibid.

91. Y. S. Ben-Porath, J. M. Fico, N. S. Hibler, R. Inwald, J. Kruml, and M. R. Roberts, "Assessing the Psychological Suitability of Candidates for Law Enforcement Positions," *Police Chief* 78 (2011), 64–70.

92. A. W. Benner, "Psychological Screening of Police Applicants," pp. 72–86 in R. G. Dunham and G. P. Alpert (Eds.), *Critical Issues in Policing: Contemporary Readings* (Prospect Heights, IL: Waveland, 1989), 83.

93. Ben-Porath et al., "Assessing the Psychological Suitability of Candidates for Law Enforcement Positions."

94. Bartol and Bartol, *Introduction to Forensic Psychology*, 49.

95. G. P. Alpert and R. G. Dunham, *Policing Urban America*, 3rd ed. (Prospect Heights, IL: Waveland, 1997).

96. Find Law, *Pre-employment Background Check Laws* (2012), available from http://employment.findlaw.com/hiring-process/preemployment-background-check-laws.html

97. Decicco, "Police Officer Candidate Assessment and Selection."

98. Privacy Rights Clearinghouse, *Employment Background Checks: A Jobseeker's Guide* (2011), available from http://www.privacyrights.org/fs/fs16-bck.htm

99. N. Baxley, "Recruiting Police Officers in the New Millennium," *Law and Order* 48 (2000), 371.

100. Santa Rosa Police Department, *Illegal Drug Use Guidelines* (2009), from

http://cisanta-rosa.ca.us/doclib/Documents/Drug-Standard.pdf

101. K. R. Humphrey, K. P. Decker, L. Goldberg, H. G. Pope, J. Gutman, and G. Green, "Anabolic Steroid Use and Abuse by Police Officers: Policy and Prevention," *Police Chief* 75 (2008), 1–10, available from http://policechiefmagazine.org

102. Ibid.

103. DOJ, *Questions and Answers*.

104. Decicco, "Police Officer Candidate Assessment and Selection."

105. N. J. Gordon, "Today's Instrument for Truth Testing," *Police Chief* 75 (2008), 1–9, available from http://www.policechiefmagazine.org

106. Ibid.

107. P. R. Wolpe, K. R. Foster, and D. D. Langleben, "Emerging Neurotechnologies for Lie-Detection: Promises and Perils," *American Journal of Bioethics* 5, no. 2 (2005), 39–49.

108. S. M. Cox and J. D. Fitzgerald, *Police in Community Relations: Critical Issues*, 3rd ed. (Dubuque, IA: Brown & Benchmark, 1996).

109. S. Falkenberg, L. K. Gaines, and T. C. Cox, "The Oral Interview Board: What Does It Measure?" *Journal of Police Science and Administration* 17 (1990), 32–39.

110. J. Holloway, "Oh, Those Oral Board Blues," *Women Police* 34, no. 3 (2000), 14.

111. Henchey, "Ready or Not, Here They Come."

112. K. Love and S. DeArmond, "The Validity of Assessment Center Ratings and 16PF Personality Trait Scores in Police Sergeant Promotions: A Case of Incremental Validity," *Public Personnel Management* 36, no. 1 (2007), 21.

113. T. L. Cosner and W. C. Baumgart, "An Effective Assessment Center Program: Essential Components," *FBI Law Enforcement Bulletin* 69 (2000), 1–5.

114. Executive Office for Administration and Finance, *Regional Assessment Center Initiative* (2009), available from http://www.mass.gov

115. L. R. O'Leary, "Assessment Centers," pp. 28–30 in W. G. Bailey (Ed.), *The Encyclopedia of Police Science* (New York, NY: Garland, 1989), 28.

116. M. McLaurin, "How to Run an Assessment Center," *Police Magazine* (2005), available from http://www.policemag.com

117. Ohio Association of Chiefs of Police, *Assessment Center Exercise Menu* (2001), available from www.oacp.org/advise/exercise.pdf

118. McLaurin, "How to Run an Assessment Center, 3.

119. Ibid.

120. C. Hale, "Assessment Centers," *Law and Order* 53 (2005), 22–24.

121. T. Kroecker, "Developing Future Leaders: Making the Link to the Promotional Process," *Police Chief* 67 (2000), 64–69.

122. Ibid.

123. B. Frankel, "Police Chiefs Worry About Job Security," *USA Today* (November 19, 1992), 10A.

## ■ CHAPTER 5

1. P. J. McDermott and D. Hulse, "Interpersonal Skills Training in Police Academy Curriculum," *FBI Law Enforcement Bulletin* 81, no. 2 (2012), 16–20.

2. A. Baro and D. Burlingame, "Law Enforcement and Higher Education: Is There an Impasse?" *Journal of Criminal Justice Education* 10 (Spring 1999), 57–73.

3. T. J. Jurkanin, "Police Education and Training: An Intelligence-Led Future," *The Police Chief* 78, no. 11 (2011), 20–23.

4. Jurkanin, "Police Education and Training," 20.

5. M. Bostrom, "The Influence of Higher Education on Police Officer Work Habits," *The Police Chief* 72, no. 10 (October 2005), 18, 20–25.

6. O. Polk and D. Armstrong, "Higher Education and Law Enforcement Career Paths: Is the Road to Success Paved by a Degree?" *Journal of Criminal Justice Education* 12 (2001), 77–99.

7. J. Broderick, *Police in a Time of Change* (Prospect Heights, IL: Waveland, 1987).

8. P. Carlan and F. Byxbe, "The Promise of Humanistic Policing: Is Higher Education Living Up to Societal Expectation?" *American Journal of Criminal Justice* 24 (2000), 235–245.

9. Office of Justice Programs, *Department of Justice Names New Police Corps Director* (Washington, DC: U.S. Department of Justice, 2004), available from http://www.ojp.usdoj.gov/archives/pressreleases/2004/OPC04089.htm

10. Oregon State Police, *Police Corps* (2007), available from http://www.oregon.gov/OSP/CJS/police_corps.shtml

11. C. Swanson, L. Territo, and R. Taylor, *Police Administration: Structures, Processes, and Behavior*, 4th ed. (Upper Saddle River, NJ: Prentice-Hall, 1998), 211–212).

12. D. Carter and A. Sapp, "College Education and Policing: Coming of Age," *FBI Law Enforcement Bulletin* 61 (January 1992), 8–14; National Advisory Commission on Criminal Justice Standards and Goals, *Report on the Police* (Washington, DC: Government Printing Office, 1973).

13. J. Travis, *Education in Law Enforcement: Beyond the College Degree* (February 10, 1995), available from www.nij/gov/about/speeches/past-directors/police.htm

14. D. Stevens, "College Educated Police Officers: Do They Provide Better Police Service?" *Law and Order* 47 (1999), 37–40.

15. C. Patterson, "Adding Value? A Review of the International Literature on the Role of Higher Education in Police Training and Education," *Police Practice and Research* 12, no. 4 (2011), 286–297.

16. D. Liming and M. Wolf, "Job Outlook by Education, 2006–16," *Occupational Outlook Quarterly* 52, no. 3 (Fall 2008).

17. L. Mayo, "Support for College Degree Requirements: The Big Picture," *Police Chief* 73, no. 8 (2006), available from http:www.policechiefmagazine.org/magazine/index.cfm?fuseaction=display_arch&article_id=959&issue_id=82006

18. Patterson, "Adding Value?"
19. A. Sapp, D. Carter, and D. Stephens, "Police Chiefs: CJ Curricula Inconsistent With Contemporary Police Needs," *ACJS Today* 7 (1989), 1, 5.
20. M. J. Hickman and B. A. Reaves, *Local Police Departments 2003* (Washington, DC: Bureau of Justice Statistics, 2006), in J. Rydberg and W. Terrill, "The Effect of Higher Education on Police Behavior," *Police Quarterly* 13 (2010), 92–120.
21. Carter and Sapp, "College Education and Policing," 11.
22. *Davis v. City of Dallas,* 777 F.2d 205 (5th Cir. 1985, certiorari denied to Supreme Court May 19, 1986).
23. Minnesota Board of Peace Officer Standards and Training, *How to Become a Police Officer in Minnesota* (2012), available from http://dps.mn.gov
24. Directory of Accredited Criminal Justice Schools, http://www.criminaljusticeprograms.com/
25. P. Carlan, "The Criminal Justice Degree and Policing: Conceptual Development or Occupational Primer?" *Policing: An International Journal of Police Strategies and Management* 20, no. 4 (2007), 608–619.
26. Academy of Criminal Justice Sciences, *ACJS Certification Standards* (2012), available from http://www.acjs.org/pubs/167_667_3517.cfm
27. Ibid.
28. Bostrom, "The Influence of Higher Education on Police Officer Work Habits," 24.
29. Bostrom, The Influence of Higher Education on Police Officer Work Habits," 49.
30. L. W. Sherman and M. Blumberg, "Higher Education and Police Use of Force," *Journal of Criminal Justice* 9 (1981), 317–331.
31. E. Daniels, "The Effect of a College Degree on Police Absenteeism," *Police Chief* 49 (September 1982), 70–71.
32. G. Griffin, *A Study of Relationships Between Level of College Education and Police Patrolman's Performance* (Saratoga, NY: Twenty One, 1980).
33. M. Meagher, *Perceptions of the Police Patrol Function: Does Officer Education Make a Difference?* (Paper presented at ACJS meeting, San Antonio, TX, March 1983).
34. E. A. Paoline, W. Terrill, and M. T. Rossler, "Higher Education, College Degree Major, and Police Occupational Attitudes," *Journal of Criminal Justice Education* 26, no. 1 (2015), 49–73.
35. E. M. Baeher, J. E. Furcon, and E. Froemel, *Psychological Assessment of Patrolman Qualifications in Relation to Field Performance* (Washington, DC: Government Printing Office, 1968).
36. A. Smith, B. Locke, and W. Walker, "Authoritarianism in Police College Students and Non-police College Students," *Journal of Criminal Law, Criminology, and Police Science* 59 (1968), 440–443.
37. B. Cohen and J. Chaiken, *Police Background Characteristics: Summary Report* (Washington, DC: Government Printing Office, 1972).
38. B. Cox and R. Moore Jr., "Toward the Twenty-First Century: Law Enforcement Training Now and Then," *Journal of Contemporary Criminal Justice* 8 (1992), 235–256.
39. S. Cunningham, "The Florida Research," *Police Chief* 73, no. 8 (August 2006), 20–22.
40. C. W. Telep, "The Impact of Higher Education on Police Officer Attitudes Towards Abuse of Authority," *Journal of Criminal Justice Education* 22, no. 3 (2011), 392–419.
41. M. Landahl, "WANT TO GET AHEAD? Stop Stalling and Go Get Your Degree," *Sheriff* 1, no. 1 (2009), 26–29; R. Roberg and S. Bonn, "Higher Education and Policing: Where Are We Now?" *Policing: An International Journal of Police Strategies and Management* 27, no. 4 (2004), 469–486.
42. J. Manis, C. A. Archbold, K. D. and Hassell, "Exploring the Impact of Police Officer Education Level on Allegations of Police Misconduct," *International Journal of Police Science & Management* 10, no. 4 (2008), 509–523.
43. Telep, "The Impact of Higher Education on Police Officer Attitudes Towards Abuse of Authority."
44. V. Kappeler, A. Sapp, and D. Carter, "Police Officer Higher Education, Citizen Complaints and Departmental Rule Violations," *American Journal of the Police* 11 (1992), 37–54.
45. J. Rydberg and W. Terrill, "The Effect of Higher Education on Police Behavior," *Police Quarterly* 13 (2010), 92–120.
46. Ibid.
47. Carter and Sapp, "College Education and Policing."
48. Ibid.
49. Sapp et al., "Police Chiefs."
50. Sapp et al., "Police Chiefs," 5.
51. J. Krimmel and P. Lindenmuth, "Police Chief Performance and Leadership Styles," *Police Quarterly* 4, no. 4 (2001), 469–483.
52. Krimmel and Lindenmuth, "Police Chief Performance and Leadership Styles," 481.
53. S. L. Feemster and J. V. Collins, "Beyond Survival Toward Officer Wellness (BeSTOW): Targeting Law Enforcement Training," *The Police Chief* 77, no. 11 (2010), 33–43.
54. Ibid.
55. R. Means, R. (2008). Evaluation and recognition systems," *Law & Order* 56, no. 7 (2008), 17–20.
56. G. L. Pritchett, "Interpersonal Communication: Improving Law Enforcement's Image," *FBI Law Enforcement Bulletin* 62 (1993), 22–26; A. J. Reiss Jr., *The Police and the Public* (New Haven, CT: Yale University Press, 1971).
57. W. Overton and J. Black, "Language as a Weapon," *Police Chief* 65 (1994), 46; Pritchett, "Interpersonal Communication."
58. M. Schwartz and S. Yonkers, "Officer Satisfaction With police In-service Training: An Exploratory Evaluation," *American Journal of Police* 10 (1991), 49–63.
59. D. H. Bracey, *Future Trends in Police Training* (Paper presented at the Third Annual Sino-American Criminal Justice Institute, Taipei, Taiwan, August 1990a).
60. J. Magers and L. Klein, "Police Basic Training: A Comparative Study of States' Standards in the United States," *Illinois Law Enforcement Executive Forum* 2, no. 2 (2002), 108.
61. M. L. Birzer, "Police Training in the 21st Century," *FBI Law Enforcement Bulletin* 68 (1999), 17.
62. Feemster and Collins, "Beyond Survival Toward Officer Wellness (BeSTOW)."
63. Birzer, "Police Training in the 21st Century."
64. Bureau of Justice Statistics, *State and Local Law Enforcement Training Academies, 2006* (NCJ 222987) (Washington, DC: Author, 2009), available from http://bjs.ojp.usdoj.gov/content/pub/pdf/slleta06.pdf
65. A. T. Chappell, "Police Academy Training: Comparing Across Curricula," *Policing: An International Journal of Police Strategies & Management* 31, no. 1 (2008), 36–56, available from http://ww2.odu.edu/~achappel/curricula.pdf
66. Commission on Peace Officer Standards and Training, *Field Training Program* (2012), available from http://post.ca.gov/field-training.aspx
67. E. Nowicki, "New Dogs, New Tricks," *Police* 14 (1990b), 34.
68. S. Pitts, R. Glensor, and K. Peak, "Police Training Officer (PTO) Program: A Contemporary Approach to Postacademy Recruit Training," *The Police Chief* 74, no. 8 (2007), 34–40.
69. Virginia Community Policing Institute, *The Police Training Officer Program* (2012), available from www.vcpionline.org
70. H. G. Rainey, *Understanding & Managing Public Organizations*, 3rd ed. (San Francisco, CA: Jossey-Bass, 2003).
71. R. V. del Carmen and J. T. Walker, *Briefs of Leading Cases in Law Enforcement*, 4th ed. (Cincinnati, OH: Anderson, 2000).
72. Ibid.
73. Calvin College, "The History of Licensure," in J. McCarthy, *Licensure: The Good, the Bad and the Unknown* (Doctoral thesis, Sarah Lawrence College, Bronxville, NY, 2005), Microform 1455063, available from http://www.calvin.edu; S. Schmerler, "Licensure: Two Sides of the Coin on the 'Head' Side," *Perspectives in Genetic Counseling* 19, no. 4 (1997/1998), 1–13, in J. McCarthy, *Licensure: The Good, the Bad and the Unknown* (Doctoral thesis, Sarah Lawrence College, Bronxville, NY, 2005), Microform 1455063.
74. National Law Enforcement and Corrections Technology Center, *Imaging, Speech Technology Boost Simulation Training* (Washington, DC: U.S. Department of Justice, 2008).
75. Ibid.
76. PATROL Minnesota, "Police Accredited Training Online," *League of Minnesota Cities Insurance Trust* (2009), available

from http://www.nexportsolutions.com/patrolminnesota/index.html

77. R. M. Schwartz, J. Rogers, and P. M. Plaisted, "Partnering for Progress: Maine Law Enforcement Online Training Initiative," *The Police Chief*, 76, no. 11 (2009), 3.

78. J. Bumgarner, "Evaluating Law Enforcement Training," *Police Chief* 68 (2001), 32–36; H. Marsh and E. Grosskopf, "The Key Factors in Law Enforcement Training: Requirements, Assessments and Methods," *Police Chief* 58 (1991), 64–66.

79. M. J. Hickman, *State and Local Law Enforcement Training Academies, 2002* (U.S. Department of Justice, Bureau of Justice Statistics, 2005), available from bjs.ojp. usdoj.gov/content/pub/ascii/slleta02.txt

80. Ibid.

81. Ibid.

82. T. Golden and P. Seehafer, "Delivering Training Material in a Practical Way," *FBI Law Enforcement Bulletin* (February 2009), 21–24.

83. M. Massoni, "Field Training Programs: Understanding Adult Learning Styles," *FBI Law Enforcement Bulletin* (February 2009), 1–5.

84. Massoni, "Field Training Programs," 2–3.

85. Massoni, "Field Training Programs," 3–4.

86. Massoni, "Field Training Programs," 5.

87. Golden and Seehafer, "Delivering Training Material in a Practical Way."

88. E. Nowicki, "Eight Qualities of Highly Effective Trainers," *Law & Order* 54, no. 7 (2006), 32–34.

89. K. Johnson, "Police Training Halts as Agencies Face Budget Cuts," *USA Today* (2010), available from http://www.usatoday.com/news/nation/2010-10-04-cop-training

90. H. Hedden, "International Law Enforcement Educators and Trainers Association," in D. Griffith, "Coping With Budget Cuts," *Police Magazine* (2011), available from http://www.policemag.com.

91. Mobile Team Training Unit IV (2012), available from http://www.mobileteamtrainingiv.org

92. L. Phillips, "Is Mandatory Continuing Professional Education Working?" *Mobius* 7 (1987), 57–63.

93. S. Frye, "Mandatory Continuing Education for Professional Re-licensure: A Comparative Analysis of Its Impact in Law and Medicine," *Journal of Continuing Higher Education* 38 (1990), 16–25.

94. K. Rockhill, "Mandatory Continuing Education for Professionals: Trends and Issues," *Adult Education* 33 (1983), 106–116.

95. G. Maple, "Continuing Education for the Health Sciences," *Australian Journal of Adult Education* 27 (1987), 22–27.

96. California Commission on Peace Officer Standards and Training, *Command College Program* (2012), available from http://www.post.ca.gov/Training/Command_College.

97. Ibid.

98. Bumgarner, "Evaluating Law Enforcement Training."

99. L. Phillips, "Is Mandatory Continuing Professional Education Working?" *Mobius* 7 (1987), 57–63.

100. Ibid.

# ■ CHAPTER 6

1. Forensic Science: A Fundamental Perspective," *The Police Chief* 74, no. 11 (2007), available from http://policechiefmagazine.org

2. Michigan Commission on Law Enforcement Standards, *Statewide Job Analysis of the Patrol Officer Position* (2006), available from http://www.michigan.gov/documents/mcoles/Detroit_Police_Department_185900_7.pdf.

3. Honolulu Police Department, *Powers, Duties and Functions* (2012), available from http://www.honolulu.gov/csd/budget/23hpd.pdf

4. T. Jurkanin, L. Hoover, J. Dowling, and J. Ahmad, *Enduring, Surviving, and Thriving as a Law Enforcement Executive* (Springfield, IL: Charles C. Thomas, 2001).

5. A. Golub, B. D. Johnson, A. Taylor, and J. Eterno, "Quality of Life Policing: Do Offenders Get the Message?" *Policing: An International Journal of Police Strategy and Management* 26 (2003), 690–707, in J. Good, *Are We Fixing Broken Windows?* (Paper presented at the annual meeting of the American Sociological Association, Montreal, Quebec, Canada, 2006).

6. D. Brook, "The Cracks in 'Broken Windows,'" *The Boston Globe* (February 19, 2006), available from http://www.boston.com

7. D. Thacher, "Order Maintenance Reconsidered: Moving Beyond Strong Causal Reasoning," *Journal of Criminal Law and Criminology* 381, no. 94 (2004).

8. Ibid.

9. W. H. Sousa, "Paying Attention to Minor Offenses: Order Maintenance Policing in Practice," *Police Practice and Research* 11, no. 1 (2010), 45–59.

10. A. E. Taslitz, *Reconstructing the Fourth Amendment* (New York, NY: NYU Press, 2006), 271.

11. H. Lamb, L. E. Weinberger, and W. J. DeCuir, "The Police and Mental Health," *Psychiatric Service* 53 (2002), 1266–1271.

12. M. Palmiotto, *Criminal Investigation* (Lanham, MD: University Press of America, 2004).

13. College of Policing, Investigation Process (2013), available from https://www.app.college.police.uk/app-content/investigations/investigation-process/

14. D. H. Bayley, *What Works in Policing* (New York, NY: Oxford University Press, 1998), 71.

15. J. N. Gilbert, *Criminal Investigation*, 5th ed. (Upper Saddle River, NJ: Prentice-Hall, 2001); J. N. Gilbert, *Criminal Investigation*, 8th ed. (Upper Saddle River, NJ: Prentice-Hall, 2009); P. Greenwood, *The Rand Criminal Investigation Study: Its Findings and Impacts to Date* (Santa Monica, CA: RAND, 1979).

16. P. W. Greenwood and J. Petersilia, *The Criminal Investigation Process: Volume I. Summary and Policy Recommendations* (Santa Monica, CA: RAND, 1975).

17. FBI, *What We Investigate* (2012), available from http://www.fbi.gov/hq.htm

18. B. Caddy and P. Cobb, "Forensic Science," in P. C. White (Ed.), *Crime Scene to Court: The Essentials of Forensic Science* (Philadelphia, PA: Royal Society of Chemistry, 2004).

19. West Virginia State Police Forensic Laboratory, *Laboratory Field Manual* (2015), available from http://www.wvsp.gov/about/Documents/CrimeLab/LabManual062015.pdf

20. Associated Press, "CSI Effect Floods Connecticut Labs With Crime Evidence," *CBS Connecticut* (2011), available from http://Connecticut.cbslocal.com.

21. D. E. Shelton, "The 'CSI Effect': Does It Really Exist?" *National Institute of Justice Journal* (2008), available from http://www.ojp.usdoj.gov.nij.journals/259/csi-efect.htm

22. J. Roman, S. Reid, J. Reid, A. Chalfin, W. Adams, and C. Knight, "Cost-Effectiveness Analysis of the Use of DNA In the Investigation of High-Volume Crimes," *The Urban Institute* (2009), from http://www.urban.org

23. J. Wilson, *Varieties of Police Behavior: The Management of Law and Order in Eight Communities* (Cambridge, MA: Harvard University Press, 1968).

24. Wilson, *Varieties of Police Behavior*, 140–171.

25. Wilson, *Varieties of Police Behavior*, 172–199.

26. Wilson, *Varieties of Police Behavior*.

27. J. Broderick, *Police in a Time of Change* (Morristown, NJ: Gene Learning Press, 1977).

28. Broderick, *Police in a Time of Change*; J. S. Dempsey and L. S. Forst, *An Introduction to Policing*, 5th ed. (Florence, KY: Delmar Cengage Learning, 2009).

29. J. R. Greene, *The Encyclopedia of Police Science*, 3rd ed. (Boca Raton, FL: CRC Press, 2006).

30. L. W. Brooks, "Police Discretionary Behavior: A Study of Style," in R. G. Dunham and G. P. Alpert (Eds.), *Critical Issues in Policing*, 3rd ed. (Prospect Heights, IL: Waveland Press, 1997); R. Roberg, K. Novak, and G. Cordner, *Police and Society*, 3rd ed. (Los Angeles, CA: Roxbury Publishing, 2005), as discussed in J. R. Greene, *The Encyclopedia of Police Science*, 3rd ed. (Boca Raton, FL: CRC Publishing, 2006).

31. G. P. Alpert and R. G. Dunham, *Policing Urban America*, 3rd ed. (Prospect Heights, IL: Waveland, 1997).

32. M. Moore, D. Thacher, A. Dodge, and T. Moore, *Recognizing Value in Policing* (Washington, DC: Police Executive Forum, 2002).

33. G. Anderson, *A Patrol Staffing Study of the Aurora, Elgin, and Joliet, Illinois Police Departments Utilizing the Allocation Model for Police Patrol* (Unpublished master's thesis, Western Illinois University, Macomb, IL, 2008).

34. "Officer, Suspect Injured in Confrontation In Morrisville" (*ABC Action News*, February 14, 2015), available from http://6abc.com/news/officer-suspect-injured-in-confrontation-in-morrisville/517463/

35. R. Roberg, J. Kuykendall, and K. Novak, *Police Management*, 3rd ed. (New York, NY: Oxford University Press, 2002).

36. D. H. Bayley, *Police for the Future* (New York, NY: Oxford University Press, 1994).

37. Ibid.

38. Roberg et al., *Police Management*. (3rd ed.).

39. Ibid.

40. G. Cordner and R. Sheehan, *Police Administration*, 4th ed. (Cincinnati, OH: Anderson, 1999), 442.

41. N. Famega, N. Frank, and L. Mazerolle, "Managing Police Patrol Time: The Role of Supervisor Directives," *Justice Quarterly* 22 (2005), 540–560.

42. Justex Systems Inc., *Allocation Model for Patrol* (2008), from http://www.justex.com

43. J. Douglass, "Tactical Deployment: The Next Great Paradigm Shift in Law Enforcement," *Geography & Public Safety* 1 (2009), 6–8.

44. J. Douglass, "Tactical Deployment: The Next Great Paradigm Shift in Law Enforcement," *Geography & Public Safety* 1 (2009), 6.

45. Douglass, "Tactical Deployment."

46. D. Harris, "Patrol Deployment Alternatives for the San Jose Police Department," *Corona Solutions* (2010), available from http://www.sanjoseca.gov

47. Harris, "Patrol Deployment Alternatives for the San Jose Police Department."

48. B. Reaves, *Local Police Departments, 2007* (Law Enforcement Management and Administrative Statistics [LEMAS], 2007a), available from http://bjs.ojp.usdoj.gov/index.cfm?ty=pbdetail&iid=1750

49. T. F. Adams, *Police Field Operations*, 7th ed. (Upper Saddle River, NJ: Prentice-Hall, 2007), 164.

50. D. Levinson, *Encyclopedia of Crime and Punishment,* Vols. I–IV (Thousand Oaks, CA: Sage, 2002).

51. W. Pelfrey, "Precipitating Factors of Paradigmatic Shift in Policing," in G. Alpert and A. Piquero (Eds.), *Community Policing* (Prospect Heights, IL: Waveland, 1998).

52. M. Moore, "Problem-Solving and Community Policing," in G. Alpert and A. Piquero (Eds.), *Community Policing*, 2nd ed. (Prospect Heights, IL: Waveland, 1992).

53. J. Q. Wilson and G. L. Kelling, "Broken Windows," pp. 154–167 in V. E. Kappeler (Ed.), *The Police and Society,* 2nd ed. (Prospect Heights, IL: Waveland, 1999), 154.

54. K. Craven, "Foot Patrols: Crime Analysis and Community Engagement to Further the Commitment to Community Policing," *Community Policing Dispatch* 2 (2009), available from http://cops.usdoj.gov

55. J. Young, "Community policing in Savannah, Georgia," pp. 305–323 in G. Alpert and A. Piquero (Eds.), *Community Policing*, 2nd ed. (Prospect Heights, IL: Waveland, 2000), 315.

56. City of Portland, *Community Foot Patrols* (2012), available from http://www.portlandonline.com

57. Metro Nashville Police Department, *Bicycle Patrol* (2000), available from http://www.nashville.net/~police/citizen/bicycle_patrol.htm

58. Seattle Police Department, *Bike Patrols* (2011), available from http://www.seattle.gov

59. C. Menton, "Bicycle Patrols: An Underutilized Resource," *Policing* 31 (2008), 93.

60. Denver Police Department, *Air Support Unit* (2000), available from http://www.denvergov.org/content/template2922.asp

61. Chicago Police Department, *Mounted Patrol Unit* (1998), available from http://www.ci.chi.il.us/communitypolicing/DistrictHome/Special Functions/Mounted.html

62. R. B. Parks, S. D. Mastrofski, C. Dejong, and M. K. Gray, "How Officers Spend Their Time With the Community," *Justice Quarterly* 16 (1999), 484–518.

63. G. Kelling, T. Pate, D. Dieckman, and C. Brown, *The Kansas City Preventive Patrol Experiment: A Summary Report* (Washington, DC: Police Foundation, 1974), in A. B. Thistlewaite and J. D. Wooldredge, *Forty Studies That Changed Criminal Justice* (Upper Saddle River, NJ: Pearson, 2010).

64. D. H. Bayley, *What Works in Policing* (New York, NY: Oxford University Press, 1998), 27.

65. Police Foundation, *The Kansas City Preventive Patrol Experiment* (2009), available from http://www.policefoundation.org/docs/kansas.html

66. J. P. Crank, *Understanding Police Culture* (Cincinnati, OH: Anderson, 1998).

67. R. Engel, *How Police Supervisory Styles Influence Patrol Officer Behavior* (Rockville, MD: National Institute of Justice, 2003).

68. J. R. Greene and C. B. Klockars, "What Police Do," pp. 273–284 in C. B. Klockars & S. D. Mastrofski (Eds.), *Thinking About Police: Contemporary Readings*, 2nd ed. (New York, NY: McGraw-Hill, 1991).

69. J. S. Dempsey, *Policing*, 2nd ed. (St. Paul, MN: West, 1999).

70. Longmont, CO, Police Department, *Staffing Study: Updated 2006*. (2006), available from http://www.ci.longmont.co.us

71. G. Cordner and K. E. Scarborough, *Police Administration*, 6th ed. (Cincinnati, OH: Anderson, 2007), 345.

72. R. L. LaGrange, *Policing American Society*, 2nd ed. (Chicago: Nelson-Hall, 1998), 365.

73. J. M. Shane, *What Every Chief Executive Should Know: Using Data to Measure Police Performance* (Flushing, NY: Looseleaf Law, 2007).

74. Roberg et al., *Police Management*, 166.

75. G. Cordner and K. E. Scarborough, *Police Administration*, 6th ed. (Cincinnati, OH: Anderson, 2007), 350.

76. E. A. Thibault, L. M. Lynch, and R. B. McBride, *Proactive Police Management,* 5th ed. (Upper Saddle River, NJ: Prentice-Hall, 2001), 57

77. P. McGreevy, "Panel Gives Bratton Vote of Confidence," *Los Angeles Times* (2006), available from http://www.latimes.com/news/local/la-me-chief20dec20,1,7062859.story, in Shane, *What Every Chief Executive Should Know.*

78. Shane, *What Every Chief Executive Should Know;* M. Moore, D. Thacher, A. Dodge, and T. Moore, *Recognizing Value in Policing* (Washington, DC: Police Executive Forum, 2002).

79. D. H. Bayley, *Police for the Future* (New York, NY: Oxford University Press), 98.

80. Bayley, *Police for the Future;* J. Q. Wilson and G. L. Kelling, "Broken Windows," pp. 154–167 in V. E. Kappeler (Ed.), *The Police and Society,* 2nd ed. (Prospect Heights, IL: Waveland, 1999).

81. J. Meckles, "Ferguson Prepares for Anniversary of Death," *KSDK* (July 28, 2015), available from http://www.ksdk.com/story/news/local/ferguson/2015/07/29/ferguson-prepares-for-weekend-of-august-9th/30816571/

82. B. F. Kingshott, "Effective Police Management of the Media," *Criminal Justice Studies: A Critical Journal of Crime, Law and Society* 24, no. 3 (2011), 241–253.

83. National Institute of Justice, *Statistics on the Use of Force* (Washington, DC: U.S. Department of Justice, Office of Justice Programs, 2009), available from http://www.ojp.usdoj.gov/nij/topics/law-enforcement/use-of-force/statistics.htm

84. S. Walker, *The Police in America*, 3rd ed. (Boston, MA: McGraw-Hill, 2008), 4–6.

85. S. Braunstein, "Adapting to Change in Law Enforcement Public Information," *Police Chief Magazine* 74 (2007), 42.

86. Ibid.

87. S. M. Cox and J. M. Fitzgerald, *Police in Community Relations: Critical Issues,* 3rd ed. (Dubuque, IA: W. C. Brown, 1996), 67.

88. Greene, *The Encyclopedia of Police Science.*

89. R. Mark, *Policing a Perplexed Society* (London, UK: Allen & Unwin, 1977), 50–51.

90. E. Scaramella and A. Newman, "Community Education and the Media: A Partnership for Effective Crime Control," *Crime and Justice International* 15 (1999), 9–10, 12.

91. D. Staszak, "Media Trends and the Public Information Officer," *FBI Law Enforcement Bulletin* 70 (2001), 11.

92. Greene, *The Encyclopedia of Police Science.*

93. E. M. Morley and M. Jacobson, "Building a Successful Public Information Program," *Police Chief Magazine* 74 (2007), 1, 3.

94. E. F. Davis III, A. A. Alves, and D. A. Sklansky, *Social Media and Police Leadership: Lessons From Boston. New Perspectives in Policing Bulletin* (NCJ 244760) (Washington, DC: U.S. Department of Justice, National Institute of Justice, 2014), available from https://www.ncjrs.gov/pdffiles1/nij/244760.pdf

95. K. Bindley, "Boston Police Twitter: How Cop Team Tweets Led City From Terror to Joy," *Huffington Post* (April 26, 2013), available from http://www.huffingtonpost.com/2013/04/26/boston-policetwitter-marathon_n_3157472.html

96. Ibid.

97. IACP Center for Social Media, "Directory," available from http://www.iacpsocialmedia.org/Directory.aspx

# ■ CHAPTER 7

1. D. J. Stevens, *Case Studies in Community Policing* (Upper Saddle River, NJ: Prentice-Hall, 2001).

2. Stevens, *Case Studies in Community Policing*, 7–8; W. L. Tafoya, "The Current and Future State of Community Policing," pp. 304–314 in R. W. Glensor, M. E. Correia, and K. J. Peak (Eds.), *Policing Communities: Understanding Crime and Solving Problems* (Los Angeles, CA: Roxbury, 2000); R. C. Trojanowicz, "Community Policing Is Not Police-Community Relations," *FBI Law Enforcement Bulletin* 59 (1990), 6–11.

3. J. Crank, C. Kadleck, and C. Koski, "The USA: The Next Big Thing," *Police Practice & Research* 11, no. 5), (October 2010), 405–422; J. H. Skolnick and D. H. Bayley, *The New Blue Line: Police Innovation in Six American Cities* (New York, NY: Free Press, 1986); Stevens, *Case Studies in Community Policing*, 11; Tafoya, "The Current and Future State of Community Policing."

4. Skolnick and Bayley, *The New Blue Line*, 212–220.

5. Skolnick and Bayley, *The New Blue Line*, 212–213.

6. Skolnick and Bayley, *The New Blue Line*.

7. Skolnick and Bayley, *The New Blue Line*, 211.

8. R. C. Trojanowicz, V. E. Kappeler, L. K. Gaines, and B. Bucqueroux, *Community Policing: A Contemporary Perspective*, 2nd ed. (Cincinnati, OH: Anderson, 1998).

9. Ibid.

10. C. Reed, "The Community Policing Umbrella," *FBI Law Enforcement Bulletin* 77, no. 11 (2008), 22–25.

11. L. R. Carey, "Community Policing for the Suburban Department," *Police Chief* 61 (1994), 24–26.

12. A. P. Cardarelli, J. McDevitt, and K. Baum, "The Rhetoric and Reality of Community Policing in Small and Medium-Sized Cities and Towns," *Policing* 21 (1998), 397–415.

13. P. M. Walters, "Community-Oriented Policing: A Blend of Strategies," *FBI Law Enforcement Bulletin* 62 (1993), 20–23.

14. According to R. C. Trojanowicz and B. Bucqueroux, "Preventing Individual and Systemic Corruption," *Footprints* 4 (1992), 1–3.

15. B. A. Reaves, *Local Police Departments, 2013: Personnel, Policies, and Practices* (NCJ 248677) (Bureau of Justice Statistics, 2015), 8–9, available from http://www.bjs.gov/content/pub/pdf/lpd13ppp.pdf

16. B. Brown, "Community Policing in a Diverse Society," *Law Enforcement Executive Forum* 4, no. 5 (2004), 49–56.

17. Brown, "Community Policing in a Diverse Society," 50–51; Y. Lai and J. Zhao, "The Impact of Race/Ethnicity, Neighborhood Context, and Police/Citizen Interaction on Residents' Attitudes Toward the Police," *Journal of Criminal Justice* 38, no. 4 (2010), 685–692; C. Rennison, "An Investigation of Reporting Violence to the Police: A Focus on Hispanic Victims," *Journal of Criminal Justice* 38, no. 4 (2010), 390–399.

18. J. R. Kobolt and K. A. Tucker, "The Fourth Era of American Policing: Strategic Management," *Law Enforcement Executive Forum* 4, no. 5 (2004), 61–69.

19. Kobolt and Tucker, "The Fourth Era of American Policing," 68.

20. H. Goldstein, "Improving Policing: A Problem Oriented Approach," *Crime and Delinquency* 25 (1979) 236–258.

21. J. E. Eck and W. Spelman, *Problem-Solving: Problem-Oriented Policing in Newport News* (Washington, DC: National Institute of Justice, 1988); H. Goldstein, *Problem-Oriented Policing* (New York, NY: McGraw-Hill, 1990); Stevens, *Case Studies in Community Policing*.

22. D. E. Barlow and M. H. Barlow, *Policing in Multicultural Society: An American Story* (Prospect Heights, IL: Waveland, 2000), 44.

23. H. Toch and J. D. Grant, *Police as Problem Solvers* (Newark, NY: Plenum, 1991), 18.

24. A. Cherney, "Harnessing the Crime Control Capacities of Third Parties," *Policing* 31, no. 4 (2008), 631.

25. R. Garner, "Solution-Oriented Policing: Application in Practice," *Law Enforcement Executive Forum* 4, no. 5 (2004), 43–47.

26. W. M. Oliver and E. Bartgis, "Community Policing: A Conceptual Framework," *Policing, 21,* 490–509; Stevens, *Case Studies in Community Policing*, 14–15.

27. R. Boba, *Crime Analysis With Crime Mapping* (Thousand Oaks, CA: Sage, 2009).

28. J. Liederbach, E. J. Fritsch, D. L. Carter, and A. Bannister, "Exploring the Limits of Collaboration in Community Policing: A Direct Comparison of Police and Citizen Views," *Policing* 31, no. 2 (2008), 271–291.

29. P. Jesilow, J. Meyer, D. Parsons, and W. Tegler, "Evaluating Problem-Oriented Policing: A Quasi-experiment," *Policing* 21 (1998), 449–464.

30. Jesilow et al., 460.

31. A. J. Lurigo and D. P. Rosenbaum, "The Impact of Community Policing on Police Personnel: A Review of the Literature," pp. 147–163 in D. P. Rosenbaum (Ed.), *The Challenge of Community Policing: Testing the Promises* (Thousand Oaks, CA: Sage, 1994).

32. A. P. Cardarelli, J. McDevitt, and K. Baum, "The Rhetoric and Reality of Community Policing in Small and Medium-Sized Cities and Towns," *Policing* 21 (1998), 397–415.

33. M. G. Breci, "The Transition to Community Policing: The Department's Role in Upgrading Officers' Skills," *Policing* 20 (1997), 766–776.

34. Breci, "The Transition to Community Policing," 774.

35. Stevens, *Case Studies in Community Policing*, 1–2.

36. Bobam, *Crime Analysis With Crime Mapping*, 2009.

37. Bureau of Justice Statistics, *State and Local Law Enforcement Statistics* (1999), available from http://www.nrc.uscg.mil/insum2005/facilityfire1.html

38. C. Offer, "COP Fads and Emperors Without Clothes," *Law Enforcement News* 19 (1993), 8.

39. Stevens, *Case Studies in Community Policing*, 2001; M. J. Palmiotto, *Police Misconduct: A Reader for the 21st Century* (Upper Saddle River, NJ: Prentice-Hall, 2000); M. Morabito, "Understanding Community Policing as an Innovation: Patterns of Adoption," *Crime & Delinquency* 56, no. 4 (October 2010), 564–587.

40. Stevens, *Case Studies in Community Policing*, 2001.

41. Boba, *Crime Analysis With Crime Mapping*; Crank et al., "The USA: The Next Big Thing."

42. A. L. Pisani, "Dissecting Community Policing—Part 1," *Law Enforcement News* 18 (1992), 13.

43. Palmiotto, *Police Misconduct*, 211; S. Sadd and R. M. Grinc, "Implementation Challenges in Community Policing," pp. 97–116 in R. W. Glensor, M. E. Correia, & J. K. Peak (Eds.), *Policing Communities: Understanding Crime and Solving Problems* (Los Angeles, CA: Roxbury, 2000), 116.

44. B. Burgreen and N. McPherson, "Neighborhood Policing Without a Budget Increase," *The Police Chief* 59 (1992), 31–33.

45. COPS Office, *CHRP Announcement Toolkit* (July 28, 2008), available from http://www.cops.usdoj.gov/Default.asp?Item=2208

46. COPS Office, *COPS Hiring Program (CHP)* (2012), available from http://www.cops.usdoj.gov/Default.asp?Item=2628

47. R. C. Trojanowicz and B. Bucqueroux, "Preventing Individual and Systemic Corruption," *Footprints* 4 (1992), 1–3.

48. B. Burgreen and N. McPherson, *Neighborhood Policing Without a Budget Increase* (1992), 31.

49. S. M. Hartnett and W. G. Skogan, "Community Policing: Chicago's Experience" (NCJ 177464), *National Institute of Justice Journal* (April 1999), 2–11.

50. Hartnett and Skogan, "Community Policing," 10.

51. W. G. Skogan, L. Steiner, C. Bonitoz, J. Bennis, S. Borchers, J. DuBois, R. Gondocs, S. Hartnett, S. Y. Kim, and S. Rosebaum, *CAPS at ten community policing in Chicago: An evaluation of Chicago's alternative policing strategy.* (Springfield, IL: State of Illinois, January 2004), available from https://portal.chicagopolice.org/i/cpd/clearpath/Caps10.pdf

52. J. Liederbach, E. J. Fritsch, D. L. Carter, and A. Bannister, "Exploring the Limits of Collaboration in Community Policing: A Direct Comparison of Police and Citizen Views," *Policing* 31, no. 2 (2008), 271–291.

53. T. R. Tyler, S. Schulhofer, and A. Z. Huq, "Legitimacy and Deterrence Effects in Counterterrorism Policing: A Study of Muslim Americans," *Law & Society Review* 44 (2010), 365–402. doi: 10.1111/j.1540-5893.2010.00405.x

54. J. V. Lee, "Policing After 9/11: Community Policing in an Age of Homeland Security," *Police Quarterly* 13, no. 4 (2010), 347–366.

55. C. Lum, C. Koper, and C. Telep, "The Evidence-Based Policing Matrix," *Journal of Experimental Criminology* 7, no. 1 (2011), 3–26.

56. J. H. Ratcliffe and R. Guidetti, "State Police Investigative Structure and the Adoption of Intelligence-Led Policing," *Policing* 31 (2008), 109–119.

57. E. F. McGarrell, J. D. Freilich, and S. Chermak, "Intelligence-Led Policing as a Framework for Responding to Terrorism," *Journal of Contemporary Justice* 23 (2007), 142–158.

58. D. L. Carter and J. G. Carter, "Intelligence-Led Policing: Conceptual and Functional Considerations for Public Policy," *Criminal Justice Policy Review* 20, no. 3 (2009), 310–325.

59. C. Reed, "The Community Policing Umbrella," *FBI Law Enforcement Bulletin* 77, no. 11 (2008), 22–25.

60. Ibid.

61. D. J. Stevens, *An Introduction to American Policing* (Sudbury, MA: Jones and Bartlett, 2008).

62. L. Sherman, *Evidence-Based Policing: Ideas in American Policing* (Washington, DC: Police Foundation, 1998), available from http://www.policefoundation.org/pdf/sherman.pdf

63. C. J. Jensen, "Consuming and Applying Research Evidence-Based Policing," *The Police Chief* 73 (2006), 2–5.

64. P. P. McDonald, *Managing Police Operations* (Belmont, CA: Wadsworth/Thomson, 2002), 7.

65. McDonald, *Managing Police Operations*, 8.

66. Boba, *Crime Analysis With Crime Mapping*; Philadelphia Police Department, *CompStat Process* (2009), available from http://www.ppdonline.org/hq_compstat.php

67. J. L. Truman and L. Langton, *Criminal Victimization, 2013* (NCJ 247648) (Washington, DC: Bureau of Justice Statistics, 2014), available from http://www.bjs.gov/content/pub/pdf/cv13.pdf

68. H. Williams, "Foreword," in L. Willis, S. Mastrofski, and D. Weisburd, *CompStat in Practice: An In-Depth Analysis of Three Cities* (Washington, DC: Police Foundation, 2003), available from http://www.policefoundation.org/pdf/compstatinpractice.pdf

69. Ibid.

70. Ibid.

71. E. Silverman, "Compstat's Innovation," in D. L. Weisburd and A. Braga (Eds.), *Police Innovation: Contrasting Perspectives* (Cambridge, UK: Cambridge University Press, 2006), 267.

72. Boba, *Crime Analysis With Crime Mapping*.

73. J. Hyunseok, L. T. Hoover, and J. Hee-Jong, "An Evaluation of CompStat's Effect on Crime: The Fort Worth Experience," *Police Quarterly* 13, no. 4 (2010), 387–412; J. A. Eterno and E. B. Silverman, "The NYPD's CompStat: Compare Statistics or Compose Statistics?" *International Journal of Police Science & Management* 12, no. 3 (2010), 426–449. doi:10.1350/ijps.2010.12.3.195.

74. Institute for Pure and Applied Mathematics, *Crime Hot Spots: Behavioral, Computational and Mathematical Models* (2007), available from http://www.ipam.ucla.edu/programs/chs2007/

75. A. A. Braga, *Crime Prevention Research Review No. 2: Police Enforcement Strategies to Prevent Crime in Hot Spot Areas* (Washington, DC: U.S. Department of Justice, Office of Community Oriented Policing Services, 2008a).

76. Ibid.

77. D. Weisburd and A. Braga, "Hot Spots Policing as a Model for Police Innovation," pp. 225–244 in D. Weisburd and A. Braga (Eds.), *Police Innovation: Contrasting Perspectives* (New York, NY: Cambridge University Press, 2006).

78. T. Rinehart Kochel, "Constructing Hot Spots Policing: Unexamined Consequences for Disadvantaged Populations and for Police Legitimacy," *Criminal Justice Policy Review* 22, no. 3 (2011), 350–374.

79. D. Weisburd, J. Hinkle, C. Famega, and J. Ready, "The Possible 'Backfire' Effects of Hot Spots Policing: An Experimental Assessment of Impacts on Legitimacy, Fear and Collective Efficacy," *Journal of Experimental Criminology* 7, no. 4 (2011), 297–320.

80. A. A. Braga, A. V. Papachristos, A. V., and D. M. Hureau, "The Effect of Hot Spots Policing on Crime: An Updated Systematic Review and Meta-Analysis," *Justice Quarterly* 31, no. 4 (2014), 633–663.

81. J. Wilson, T. F. Hiromoto, G. Tita, and J. Riley, *Homicide in San Diego: A Case Study Analysis* (WR-142-OJP) (Santa Monica, CA: Rand, 2004).

82. Wilson et al., *Homicide in San Diego*, 12.

83. E. McGarrell, S. Chermak, and A. Weiss, *Reducing Firearms Violence Through Directed Police Patrol: Final Report on the Evaluation of the Indianapolis Police Department's Directed Patrol Project* (Washington, DC: U.S. Department of Justice, 2002).

84. S. Walker, *The Police in America*, 3rd ed. (Boston, MA: McGraw-Hill, 2008).

85. Sacramento Police Department, *File Online Reports Now* (2009), available from http://www.sacpd.org/reports/fileonline/filenow

86. J. R. Greene, *The Encyclopedia of Police Science*, 3rd ed. (Boca Raton, FL: CRC Press, 2006).

87. D. B. Cornish and R. V. Clarke, "Opportunities, Precipitators and Criminal Decisions: A Reply to Wortley's Critique of Situational Crime Prevention," *Crime Prevention Studies* 16 (2003), 41–96.

88. N. Vance and B. Trani, "Situational Prevention and the Reduction of White Collar Crime," *Journal of Leadership Accountability and Ethics* (Fall 2008), 9–13.

89. Ibid.

90. T. J. Holt, K. R. Blevins, and J. B. Kuhns, "Examining the Displacement Practices of Johns With On-line Data," *Journal of Criminal Justice* 36 (2008), 522–528.

91. R. T. Guerette and K. J. Bowers, "Assessing the Extent of Crime Displacement and Diffusion of Benefits: A Review of Situational Crime Prevention Evaluations," *Criminology* 47, no. 4 (2009), 1331–1368.

92. C. W. Telep, D. Weisburd, C. E. Gill, Z. Vitter, and D. Teichman, "Displacement of Crime and Diffusion of Crime Control Benefits in Large-Scale Geographic Areas: A Systematic Review," Journal of Experimental Criminology 10, no. 4 (2014), 515–548. DOI: 10.1007/s11292-014-9208-5.

93. National Institute of Crime Prevention, *Crime Prevention Through Environmental Design* (2009), available from http://www.cptedtraining.net.

94. M. Exum, J. B. Kuhns, B. Koch, and C. Johnson, "An Examination of Situational Crime Prevention Strategies Across Convenience Stores and Fast-Food Restaurants," *Criminal Justice Policy Review* 21, no. 3 (2010), 269–295.

95. W. Skogan and K. Frydl, *Fairness and Effectiveness in Policing: The Evidence* (Washington, DC: The National Academies Press, 2004).

96. C. Sadovi, "Chicago Police Plan Curfew Crackdown," *Chicago Breaking News* (April 2, 2009), available from http://www.chicagobreakingnews.com/2009/04/curfew-chicago-police-crackdown-students-killed.html

97. T. L. Meares, "Third-Party Policing: A Critical View," in D. Weisburd and A. Braga (Eds.), *Police Innovation: Contrasting Perspectives* (New York, NY: Cambridge University Press, 2006).

98. M. Mitchell and J. Casey, *Police Leadership and Management* (Annandale, AU: Federation Press, 2007).

99. A. A. Braga, "Pulling Levers: Focused Deterrence Strategies and the Prevention of Gun Homicide," *Journal of Criminal Justice* 36 (2008b), 332.

100. A. A. Braga and D. L. Weisburd, *Police Innovation and Crime Prevention: Lessons Learned From Police Research Over the Past 20 Years* (Paper presented at the National Institute of Justice Policing Research Workshop: Planning for the Future. Washington, DC, November 28–29, 2006), available from http://ncjrs.gov/pdf files1/nij/grants/218585.pdf

101. Braga, "Pulling Levers."

102. N. Corsaro and E. F. McGarrell, "Testing a Promising Homicide Reduction Strategy: Re-assessing the Impact of the Indianapolis 'Pulling Levers' Intervention," *Journal of Experimental Criminology* 5, no. 1 (2009), 63–82. doi:10.1007/s11292-008-9065-1.

103. National Response Team, *National Response Center: Analysis Report* (June 2005), available from http://nrt.org/production/NRT/NRTWeb.nsf/AllAttachmentsByTitle/A-429NRCAnalysisReport/$File%20NRC%20Analysis%20Report.pdf?OpenElement.

104. W. Sousa and G. Kelling, "Of 'Broken Windows,' Criminology, and Criminal Justice," pp. 77–97 in D. L. Weisburd and A. Braga (Eds.), *Police Innovation: Contrasting Perspectives* (Cambridge, UK:

Cambridge University Press, 2006); J. Wilson and G. Kelling, "Broken Windows: The Police and Neighborhood Safety," *Atlantic Monthly* 24, no. 9 (1982), 29–38.

105. D. Weisburd, J. Hinkle, C. Famega, and J. Ready, "The Possible 'Backfire' Effects of Hot Spots Policing: An Experimental Assessment of Impacts on Legitimacy, Fear and Collective Efficacy," *Journal of Experimental Criminology*, 7, no. 4 (2011), 297–320.

106. D. Weisburd, C. W. Telep J. C. Hinkle, and J. E. Eck, "The Effects of Problem-Oriented Policing on Crime and Disorder" (*Campbell Systematic Reviews* 2008), 14. DOI: 10.4073/csr.2008.

107. P. Chauhan, M. Cerdá, S. F. Messner, M. Tracy, K. Tardiff, and S. Galea, "Race/Ethnic-Specific Homicide Rates in New York City: Evaluating the Impact of Broken Windows Policing and Crack Cocaine Markets," *Homicide Studies* 15, no. 3 (2011), 268–290. doi:10.1177/1088767911416917; B. E. Harcourt and D. E. Thacher, "Is Broken Windows Policing Broken?" *Legal Affairs* (October 17, 2005), available from http://www.legalaffairs.org/webexclusive/debateclub_brokenwindows1005.msp; W. Skogan, *Impact of Policing on Social Disorder: Summary of Findings* (Washington, DC: U.S. Department of Justice, Office of Justice Programs, 1992).

108. FBI, "Crime in the United States, 2013" (Table 1), available http://www.fbi.gov/about-us/cjis/ucr/crime-in-the-u.s/2013/crime-in-the-u.s.-2013/tables/1tabledatadecoverviewpdf/table_1_crime_in_the_united_states_by_volume_and_rate_per_100000_inhabitants_1994-2013.xls

109. R. Rogers, "Richmond Reports Lowest Homicide Total in 33 Years, Credits Multipronged Efforts," *Contra Costa Times* (January 6, 2014).

110. L. Mazerolle, S. Bennett, J. Davis, E. Sargeant, and M. Manning, "Procedural Justice and Police Legitimacy: A Systematic Review of the Research," *Journal of Experimental Criminology* 9 (2013), 245–274.

111. S. Schulhofer, T. Tyler, and A. Huq, "American Policing at a Crossroads: Unsustainable Policies and the Procedural Justice Alternative," *Journal of Criminal Law & Criminology* 101, no. 2 (2011), 335–374.

112. Mazerolle et al., "Procedural Justice and Police Legitimacy, 245–246.

# ■ CHAPTER 8

1. J. E. Champoux, *Organizational Behavior*, 3rd ed. (Cincinnati, OH: Thomson South-Western, 2006).

2. P. K. Manning, *Police Work: The Social Organization of Policing* (Cambridge, MA: MIT Press, 1977).

3. Manning, *Police Work*, 227.

4. A. Frye, "Blue Wall of Silence Perceived in Police Force," *Daily Bulletin* (February 12, 2006), available from http://www.dailybulletin.com.

5. C. E. Ferrell, "Code of Silence: Fact or Fiction?" *The Police Chief* 70 (2003), 9–11.

6. W. Terrill, E. A. Paoline, and P. K. Manning, "Police Culture and Coercion," *Criminology* 41, no. 4 (2003), 1003–1035.

7. Ibid.

8. Ferrell, "Code of Silence: Fact or Fiction."

9. Ibid.

10. J. A. Inciardi, *Criminal Justice*, 3rd ed. (San Diego, CA: Harcourt Brace Jovanovich, 1990).

11. Inciardi, *Criminal Justice*, 2.

12. E. A. Paoline, S. Myers, and R. Worden, "Police Culture, Individualism, and Community Policing: Evidence From Two Police Departments," *Justice Quarterly* 17 (2000), 575–605.

13. W. Westley, *Violence and the Police* (Cambridge, MA: MIT Press, 1970).

14. E. A. Paoline, "Shedding Light on Police Culture: An Examination of Officers' Occupational Attitudes," *Police Quarterly*, 7, no. 2 (2004), 205–236.

15. S. Herbert, "The Police Subculture Reconsidered," *Criminology* 36 (1998), in N. Conti, *Weak Links and Warrior Hearts: A Framework for Judging Self and Others in Police Training* (Working Paper No. 24, International Police Executive Symposium, 2010), available from http://www.ipes.info

16. Paoline, "Shedding Light on Police Culture."

17. E. A. Paoline, "Taking Stock: Toward a Richer Understanding of Police Culture," *Journal of Criminal Justice* 31 (2003), 199–214.

18. Paoline et al., "Police Culture, Individualism, and Community Policing."

19. Conti, *Weak Links and Warrior Hearts*.

20. Champoux, *Organizational Behavior*, 70–91.

21. Ibid.

22. G. Ryan, *Field Training Officer Styles Within an Urban Police Organization* (Paper presented at the American Society of Criminology Annual Meeting. Philadelphia, PA, 2009), available from http://www.obscohost.com

23. Champoux, *Organizational Behavior*, 70–91.

24. D. E. Nelson and J. C. Quick, *Organizational Behavior: Foundations, Reality and Challenges,* 5th ed. (Florence, KY: Cengage Learning, 2006).

25. L. K. Gaines, V. E. Kappeler, and J. B. Vaughn, *Policing in America*, 6th ed. (Cincinnati, OH: Anderson, 2008), 327–330.

26. E. Reuss-Ianni, *Two Cultures of Policing* (New Brunswick, NJ: Transaction Books, 1983), 14–16.

27. R. Martin, "Police Corruption: An Analytical Look Into Police Ethics," *FBI Law Enforcement Bulletin* 80 (2011), 11–17.

28. D. H. Bayley and E. Bittner, "Learning the Skills of Policing," *Law and Contemporary Problems* 47 (1989), 35–59.

29. S. M. Cox and J. D. Fitzgerald, *Police in Community Relations: Critical Issues*, 3rd ed. (Dubuque, IA: W. C. Brown, 1996); J. H. Skolnick and J. J. Fyfe, *Above the Law: Police and the Excessive Use of Force* (New York, NY: Free Press, 1993).

30. J. Skolnick, *Justice Without Trial* (New York, NY: Wiley, 1966).

31. Skolnick, *Justice Without Trial*, 52.

32. V. E. Kappeler, R. Sluder, and G. Alpert, *Forces of Deviance: Understanding the Dark Side of Policing* (Prospect Heights, IL: Waveland, 1998), in R. R. Bennett and E. L. Schmitt, "The Effect of Work Environment on Levels of Police Cynicism: A Comparative Study," *Police Quarterly* 5, no. 4 (2002), 493–522.

33. Bennett and Schmitt, "The Effect of Work Environment on Levels of Police Cynicism: A Comparative Study."

34. Reuss-Ianni, *Two Cultures of Policing*, 14–16.

35. J. Skolnick, *Justice Without Trial* (New York, NY: Wiley, 1966).

36. Gaines et al., *Policing in America*, 327.

37. T. Barker, R. D. Hunter, and J. P. Rush, *Police Systems & Practices: An Introduction* (Englewood Cliffs, NJ: Prentice Hall, 1994); Skolnick, *Justice Without Trial*.

38. L. B. Johnson, M. Todd, and G. Subramanian, "Violence in Police Families: Work-Family Spillover," *Journal of Family Violence* 20, no. 1 (2005), 3–9.

39. F. Cullen, F., Link, B., Travis, L. T., & Lemming, T. (1983). Paradox in policing: A note on perceptions of danger. *Journal of Police Science and Administration, 11,* (1983), 457–462, in J. P. Crank, *Understanding Police Culture*, 2nd ed. (Cincinnati, OH: Anderson Publishing Company, 2004).

40. Crank, *Understanding Police Culture*, 158.

41. Cullen et al., "Paradox in Policing."

42. J. Rubinstein, *City Police* (New York, NY: Farrar, Straus and Giroux, 1973); R. E. Sykes and E. E. Brent, "The Regulation of Interaction by Police: A Systems View of Taking Charge," *Criminology* 18 (1980), 182–197, in E. A. Paoline, "Taking Stock: Toward a Richer Understanding of Police Culture," *Journal of Criminal Justice* 31 (2003), 199–214.

43. J. Van Maanen, "The Asshole," pp. 221–238 in J. VanMaanen and P. K. Manning (Eds.), *Policing: A View From the Street* (Santa Monica, CA: Goodyear, 1978).

44. Van Maanen, "The Asshole," 310.

45. Rubenstein, *City Police*.

46. G. P. Alpert and R. G. Dunham, *Policing Urban America,* 3rd ed. (Prospect Heights, IL: Waveland, 1997).

47. L. R. Carey, "Community Policing for the Suburban Department," *Police Chief* 61 (1994), 24–26.

48. Alpert and Dunham, *Policing Urban America*.

49. Carey, "Community Policing for the Suburban Department," 24.

50. M. K. Sparrow, M. H. Moore, and D. M. Kennedy, *Beyond 911: A New Era for Policing* (New York, NY: Basic Books, 1992), 51.

51. B. L. Berg, *Policing in Modern Society* (Burlington, MA: Butterworth-Heinemann, 1999).

52. Berg, *Policing in Modern Society*, 297.

53. A. Twersky-Glasner, "Police Personality: What Is It and Why Are They Like That?" *Journal of Police and Criminal Psychology* 20, no. 1 (2005), 56–65.

54. B. Carpenter and S. Raza, "Personality Characteristics of Police Applicants: Comparisons Across Subgroups and Other Populations," *Journal of Police Science and Administration* 15 (1987), 10–17.

55. Alpert and Dunham, *Policing Urban America,* 112.

56. J. J. Broderick, *Police in a Time of Change,* 2nd ed. (Prospect Heights, IL: Waveland, 1987), in K. J. Peak, *Policing America: Challenges, and Best Practices* (6th ed. (Upper Saddle River, NJ: Pearson Prentice-Hall, 2009), 22–115.

57. W. C. Terry, "Police Stress: The Empirical Evidence," *Police Science and Administration* 9 (1989), 61–75.

58. A. D. Yarmey, *Understanding Police and Police Work: Psychosocial Issues* (New York, NY: New York University Press, 1990), 42.

59. M. Arter, "Stress and Deviance in Policing," *Deviant Behavior* 29, no. 1 (2008), 43–69.

60. T. F. Adams, *Police Field Operations,* 7th ed. (Upper Saddle River, NJ: Prentice-Hall, 2007).

61. S. Torres, D. L. Maggard, and C. To, "Preparing Families for the Hazards of Police Work," *The Police Chief* 70, no. 10 (October 2003), 108–114, available from http://www.policechiefmagazine.org/magazine/index.cfm?fuseaction=display_arch&article_id=120&issue_id=102003

62. J. A. Waters and W. Ussery, "Police Stress: History, Contributing Factors, Symptoms, and Interventions," *Policing* 30, no. 2 (2007), 169–178.

63. Ibid.

64. J. Zhao, N. He, and N. Lovrich, "Predicting Five Dimensions of Police Officer Stress: Looking More Deeply Into Organizational Settings for Sources of Police Stress," *Police Quarterly* 5, no. 1 (2002), 43–62.

65. L. Garcia, D. K. Nesbary, and J. Gu, "Perceptual Variations of Stressors Among Police Officers During an Era of Decreasing Crime," *Journal of Criminal Justice* 20, no. 1 (2004), 33–50.

66. Zhao et al., "Predicting Five Dimensions of Police Officer Stress."

67. J. M. Shane, "Organizational Stressors and Police Performance," *Journal of Criminal Justice* 38 (2010), 807–818, available from http://www.ebscohost.com

68. R. T. Golembiewski and B. S. Kim, "Burnout in Police Work: Stressors, Strain, and the Phase Model," *Police Studies* 14 (1991), 74–80.

69. Garcia et al., "Perceptual Variations of Stressors Among Police Officers During an Era of Decreasing Crime."

70. D. Nadvornick, "Night Shift Police Prone to Health Problems," *Washington State University News Center* (2011), available from http://wsunews.wsu.edu.

71. National Institute of Justice, "On-the-Job Stress in Policing" (NCJ 180079), *National Institute of Justice Journal* 19, no. 24 (2000), available from http://www.ncjrs.gov/pdffiles1/jr000242d.pdf

72. F. G. Dowling, G. Moynihan, B. Genet, and J. Lewis, "A Peer-Based Assistance Program for Officers With the New York City

Police Department: Report of the Effects of September 11, 2001," *American Journal of Psychiatry* 163 (2006), 151–153, in R. Gershon, B. Barocas, A. Canton, X. Li, and D. Vlahov, "Mental, Physical, and Behavioral Outcomes Associated With Perceived Work Stress in Police Officers," *Criminal Justice and Behavior* 36, no. 3 (2009), 275–289.

73. D. E. Nelson and J. C. Quick, *Organizational Behavior: Foundations, Reality and Challenges,* 5th ed. (Florence, KY: Cengage Learning, 2006), 217–221.

74. P. M. Whisenand, *Supervising Police Personnel,* 4th ed. (Upper Saddle River, NJ: Prentice-Hall, 2001), 206.

75. Ibid.

76. Nelson and Quick, *Organizational Behavior.*

77. Crank, *Understanding Police Culture,* 298.

78. Nelson and Quick, *Organizational Behavior.*

79. Manning, *Police Work: The Social Organization of Policing* (Cambridge, MA: MIT Press, 1977), 100.

80. Nelson and Quick, *Organizational Behavior.*

81. Alpert and Dunham, *Policing Urban America.*

82. University of Oklahoma Police, *Mission Statement* (2008), available from http://www.ou.edu/oupd/mission.htm

83. S. L. Lind and F. L. Otte, "Management Styles, Mediating Variables, and Stress Among HRD Professionals," *Human Resource Development Quarterly* 5, no. 4 (2006), 301–316.

84. R. Roberg, J. Crank, and J. Kuykendall, *Police and Society* (Los Angeles, CA: Roxbury, 2000), 466.

85. National Institute of Justice, "On-the-Job Stress in Policing," 19.

86. J. M. Violanti, "Police Suicide: A National Comparison With Fire-fighter and Military Personnel," *Policing* 33 (2010), 270–279, available from http://proquest.umi.com

87. K. J. Peak, *Policing America,* 6th ed. (Upper Saddle River, NJ: Prentice-Hall, 2009), 377–381.

88. D. L. Carter and L. A. Radelet, *The Police and the Community,* 6th ed. (Upper Saddle River, NJ: Prentice-Hall, 1999).

89. S. Silverii, "Beware the 'Gift' of Socialization," *Law Enforcement Today* (January 7, 2013), available from http://www.lawenforcementtoday.com/2013/01/07/beware-the-gift-of-socialization/

90. NIJ, "On-the-Job Stress in Policing."

91. H. Selye, *Stress Without Distress* (Philadelphia, PA: Lippincott, 1974).

92. T. W. Adorno, E. Frenkel-Brunswik, D. Levinson, and N. Sanford, *The Authoritarian Personality* (New York, NY: Harper, 1950).

93. L. Siegel, *Introduction to Criminal Justice,* 12th ed. (Florence, KY: Wadsworth-Cengage Learning, 2009), 280.

94. Carter and Radelet, *The Police and the Community,* 186.

95. M. L. Dantzker, *Understanding Today's Police* (Monsey, NY: Criminal Justice Press, 2005), 279.

96. W. C. Terry, "Police Stress: The Empirical Evidence," *Police Science and Administration* 9 (1989), 61–75.

97. L. Laguna, A. Linn, K. Ward, and R. Rupslaukyte, "An Examination of Authoritarian Personality Traits Among Police Officers: The Role of Experience," *Journal of Police Criminal Psychology* 25 (2009), 99–104.

98. A. Niederhoffer, *Behind the Shield: The Police in Urban Society* (Garden City, NY: Doubleday, 1967), 96.

99. R. M. Regoli and E. D. Poole, "Specifying Police Cynicism," *Journal of Police Science and Administration* 6 (1978), 98–104.

100. L. Gould, "A Longitudinal Approach to the Study of the Police Personality: Race/Gender Differences," *Journal of Police and Criminal Psychology* 15, no. 2 (2000), 41–51.

101. W. Graves, "Police Cynicism: Causes and Cures," *FBI Law Enforcement Bulletin* 65. (1996), 16–20; R. R. Dorsey and D. J. Giacopassi, D. J. (1987). Demographics and work-related correlates of police officer cynicism," pp. 173–188 in D. B. Kennedy and R. J. Homant (Eds.), *Police and Law Enforcement* (New York, NY: Ames Press, 1987); M. J. Hickman, N. L. Piquero, and A. R. Piquero, "The Validity of Neiderhoffer's Cynicism Scale," *Journal of Criminal Justice* 32, no. 1 (2004), 1–13.

102. A. V. Bouza, *The Police Mystique: An Insider's Look at Cops, Crime, and the Criminal Justice System* (New York, NY: Plenum, 1990).

103. A. L. Johnson, *Organizational Cynicism and Occupational Stress in Police Officers* (Unpublished dissertation abstract, Central Michigan University, Mt. Pleasant, MI, 2007), available from http://www.proquest.com

104. Niederhofer, *Behind the Shield,* 95.

105. L. B. Johnson, M. Todd, and G. Subramanian, "Violence in Police Families: Work-Family Spillover," *Journal of Family Violence* 20, no. 1 (2005), 3–9.

106. Johnson et al., "Violence in Police Families."

107. L. M. Schaible and V. Gecas, "The Impact of Emotional Labor and Value Dissonance on Burnout Among Police Officers," *Police Quarterly* 13 (2010), 316–326, available from http://www.ebscohost.com

108. A. M. Goodman, "A Model for Police Officer Burnout," *Journal of Business and Psychology* 5, no. 1 (1990), 85–89, in W. P. McCarty, J. Zhao, and B. Garland, "Occupational Stress and Burnout Between Male and Female Police Officers: Are There Any Gender Differences?" *Policing* 30, no. 4 (2007), 672–679.

109. V. Lindsay, W. B. Taylor, and K. Shelley, "Alcohol and the Police: An Empirical Examination of a Widely-Held Assumption," *Policing* 31, no. 4 (2008), 596–605.

110. Ibid.

111. J. R. Picanol, *Coping Styles That Have a Negative Influence on Police Marriages* (Unpublished doctoral dissertation, Carlos Albizu University, Miami, FL, 2009), available from http://proquest.umi.com

112. S. Prabhu and N. Turner, "Rising to the Challenge: Preventing Police Officer Domestic Violence," *Police Chief* 67, no. 11 (2000), 43–55.

113. R. Klein, "The Extent of Domestic Violence Within Law Enforcement: An Empirical Study," in L. B. Johnson, M. Todd, and G. Subramanian, "Violence in Police Families: Work-Family Spillover," *Journal of Family Violence* 20, no. 1 (2005), 3–9.

114. Johnson, Todd, and Subramanian, "Violence in Police Families."

115. R. Martin, "Police Corruption: An Analytical Look Into Police Ethics," *FBI Law Enforcement Bulletin* 80 (2011), 11–17.

116. R. Borum and C. Philpot, "Therapy With Law Enforcement Couples: Clinical Management of the High-Risk Lifestyle," *American Journal of Family Therapy* 21 (1993), 122–135.

117. A. S. Blumberg and E. Niederhoffer, "The Police Family," in A. S. Blumberg and E. Neiderhoffer (Eds.), *The Ambivalent Force: Perspectives on the Police*, 3rd ed. (New York, NY: Holt, Rinehart & Winston, 1985).

118. Honig as discussed in J. Ritter, "Suicide Rates Jolt Police Culture," *USA Today* (February 9, 2007), 3A.

119. International Association of Chiefs of Police (IACP), *IACP National Symposium on Law Enforcement Officer Suicide and Mental Health: Breaking the Silence on Law Enforcement Suicides* (Washington, DC: Office of Community Oriented Policing Services, 2014), available from http://www.theiacp.org/Portals/0/documents/pdfs/Suicide_Project/Officer_Suicide_Report.pdf

120. A. M. B. Hem and O. Eckberg, "Suicide in Police—A Critical Review," *Suicide and Life-Threatening Behavior* 31, no. 2 (2001), 224–233; R. Loo, "A Meta-Analysis of Police Suicide Rates: Findings and Issues," *Suicide and Life-Threatening Behavior* 33, no. 3 (2003), 313–325; and J. M. Violanti, "Police Suicide Research: Conflict and Consensus," *International Journal of Emergency Mental Health* 10, no. 4 (2008), 299–307.

121. IACP, *IACP National Symposium on Law Enforcement Officer Suicide and Mental Health.*

122. D. W. Clark, E. K. White, and J. M. Violanti, "Law Enforcement Suicides: Current Knowledge and Future Directions," *The Police Chief* (April 2015), available from http://www.policechiefmagazine.org/magazine/index.cfm?fuseaction=display_arch&article_id=2669&issue_id=52012

123. J. M. Violanti, "Suicide or Undetermined? A National Assessment of Police Suicide Death Classification," *International Journal of Emergency Mental Health* 12, no. 2 (2010), 89–94.

124. Gaines et al., Policing in America, 345–346.

125. Gaines et al., Policing in America, 346.

126. A. E. Crosby and J. J. Sacks, "Exposure to Suicide: Incidence and Association With Suicidal Ideation and Behavior: United States, 1994," *Suicide and Threatening Behavior* 32 (2002), 321–328, in J. M. Violanti, D. Fekedulegn, and M. E. Charles, *American Journal of Criminal Justice* 34, no. 1 (2009), 41–57.

127. National Law Enforcement Officer Memorial Fund, "Causes of Law Enforcement Deaths,"

available from http://www.nleomf.org/facts/officer-fatalities-data/causes.html

128. Ibid.

129. Ibid.

130. Preliminary 2014 Law Enforcement Officers Fatality Report, available from http://www.nleomf.org/assets/pdfs/reports/Preliminary-2014-Officer-Fatalities-Report.pdf

131. Ibid.

132. NIJ, *Causes of Officer Stress and Fatigue* (2012), available from http://www.nij.gov

133. NIJ, "Police Response to Officer-Involved Shootings," *National Institute of Justice Journal* 53 (NCJ 21226, 2006), available from http://www.ojp.usdoj.gov

134. B. P. Bernard, R. J. Driscoll, M. Kitt, S. W. Tak, and C. A. West, "Health Hazards Evaluation of Police Officers and Firefighters After Hurricane Katrina," *Morbidity and Mortality Weekly Report* 55 (2006), 456–458, available from http://go.galegroup.com

135. D. J. Stevens, "Police Officer Stress," *Law and Order* 47 (1999), 77–81.

136. O. Johnson, *Blue Wall of Silence: Perceptions of the Influence of Training on Law Enforcement Suicide* (Dissertation Abstract, University of Phoenix, Phoenix, AZ, 2010), available from http://dissertation.com

137. P. Kulbarsh, "Critical Incident Stress," *Officer.com* (2007), available from http://www.officer.com

138. Ibid.

139. D. Paton, "Critical Incident Stress Risk in Police Officers: Managing Resilience and Vulnerability," *Traumatology* 12 (2006), 198–210.

140. A. Benner, "The Challenge for Police Psychology in the Twenty First Century: Moving Beyond Efficient to Effective" (1994), in M. Chapin, S. J. Brannen, M. I. Singer, and M. Walker, "Training Police Leadership to Recognize and Address Operational Stress," *Police Quarterly* 11 (2008), 338–351.

141. K. Ellison, *Stress and the Police Officer* (Springfield, IL: Charles C. Thomas, 2004), in U.S. Department of Justice, *Stress and Stress Management* (2005), available from http://lbilibrary.fbiacademy.edu

142. G. Scaramella, E. Shannon, and M. Giannoni, "Rekindling Police Burnout: Implications for the Motivation and Retention of Personnel," *Professional Issues in Criminal Justice* 1, no. 1 (2005), 1–15.

143. NIJ, "On-the-Job Stress in Policing" (NCJ 180079), *National Institute of Justice Journal* 19, no. 24 (2000), available from http://www.ncjrs.gov/pdffiles1/jr000242d.pdf

144. A. V. Bouza, *The Police Mystique: An Insider's Look at Cops, Crime, and the Criminal Justice System* (New York, NY: Plenum, 1990).

145. O'Hara, *Police Suicides in New Jersey.*

146. S. Torres and D. L. Maggard, "Preparing Families for the Hazards of Police Work," *Police Chief* 70, no. 10 (2003), 1–7.

147. Melbourne Police Department, *Stress Management* (2012), available from http://www.melbourneflorida.org/police/stress_management.htm

148. Gershon et al., "Mental, Physical, and Behavioral Outcomes Associated With Perceived Work Stress in Police Officers."

149. Paoline et al., "Police Culture, Individualism, and Community Policing," 581.

150. Ibid.

## ■ CHAPTER 9

1. N. M. Garland, Criminal Law for the Criminal Justice *Professional, 2nd ed. (Boston, MA: McGraw Hill, 2009).*

2. S. M. Cox and W. P. McCamey, *Introduction to Criminal Justice: Exploring the Network* (Thousand Oaks, CA: Sage, 2008).

3. Ibid.

4. Ibid.

5. J. A. Conser and G. D. Russell, *Law Enforcement in the United States* (Gaithersburg, MD: Aspen Press, 2000); S. M. Cox, *Police: Practices, Perspectives, Problems* (Needham Heights, MA: Allyn & Bacon, 1996); Cox and McCamey, Introduction to Criminal Justice.

6. Cox and McCamey, *Introduction to Criminal Justice.*

7. *Alliance to End Repression et al., v City of Chicago*, 356 F. 3d 767 (7th Cir. 2004).

8. "Pittsburgh Police Trial on First Amendment Delayed" (*Philadelphia Inquirer*, 2009), available from http://www.philly.com/inquirer/loca/nj/20090909

9. Ibid.

10. Garland, *Criminal Law for the Criminal Justice Professional.*

11. "Court Looks at Reach of Second Amendment," Associated Press (March 2, 2010), available from http://www.msnbc.msn.com/id/35671214

12. Law Center to Prevent Gun Violence, *The Second Amendment Battleground: Victories in the Courts and Why They Matter* (2012), available from http://smartgunlaws.org/the-second-amendment-battleground-victories-in-the-courts/#footnote_20_19642

13. "About the Project: The Hidden Life of Guns" (*The Washington Post*, January 22, 2011), available from http://www.washingtonpost.com/wp-dyn/content/article/2011/01/22/AR2011012204243.html

14. *United States v. Jacobsen*, 466 U.S. 109,113 (1984).

15. *Brinegar v. United States*, 338 U.S. 160 (1949).

16. *Illinois v. Gates*, 462 U.S. 213 (1983).

17. *Illinois v. Rodriguez*, 497 U.S. 177 (1990).

18. M. Clark, "Understanding *Graham v. Connor*," *Police: The Law Enforcement Magazine* (October 27, 2014), available from http://www.policemag.com/channel/patrol/articles/2014/10/understanding-graham-v-connor.aspx.

19. *Graham v. Connor*, 490 U.S. 386 (1989). P. 396-397, available from http://caselaw.findlaw.com/us-supreme-court/490/386.html.

20. J. N. Ferdico, *Criminal Procedure for the Criminal Justice Professional* (Belmont, CA: Wadsworth/Thomson, 2002), 160.

21. *Kentucky v. King*, 563 U.S. 131 S.Ct. 1849, 1856, 179 L.Ed.2d 865 (2011).

22. Discussion of these particulars is beyond the scope of this text but may be found in any text on criminal procedure or through a search of cases related to stop and frisk on the Internet.

23. T. Bryan, *State v. Brossart*: Adapting the Fourth Amendment for a Future With Drones," 63 Cath. U. L. Rev. 465 (2014), available from http://scholarship.law.edu/lawreview/vol63/iss2/9.

24. Ferdico, *Criminal Procedure for the Criminal Justice Professional*.

25. *United States v. Cortez*, 449 U.S. 411, 417, 101 S. Ct. 690, 695, 66 L. Ed. 2d 690 (1981).

26. *United States v. Hensley*, 469 U.S. 221, No. 83-1330 (1985).

27. *State v. Garland*, 482 A.2d 139, 144 (Me. 1984); *Terry v. Ohio*, 392 U.S. 1, 88 S. Ct. 1868, 20 L. Ed. 2d 889 (1968).

28. *Michigan v. Long*, 463 U.S. 1032 (1983).

29. *Michigan v. Long*, 463 U.S. 1032, 103 S. Ct. 3469, 77 L. Ed. 2d 1201 (1983).

30. A. Liptak, "Justices Rule That Police Can't Extend Traffic Stops" (*The New York Times*, April 21, 2015, available from http://www.nytimes.com/2015/04/22/us/supreme-court-limits-drug-sniffing-dog-use-in-traffic-stops.html?_r=1; *Rodriguez v. United States*, 575 U.S. (2015).

31. N. Totenberg, "Controversial Arizona Law Reaches Supreme Court" (NPR, 2012), available from http://www.npr.org/2012/04/25/151281643/controversial-arizona-law-reaches-supreme-court.

32. A. Liptak and J. H. Cushman, "Blocking Parts of Arizona Law, Justices Allow Its Centerpiece," *The New York Times* (June 25, 2012), available from http://www.nytimes.com/2012/06/26/us/supreme-court-rejects-part-of-arizona-immigration-law.html?pagewanted_all&_r=0

33. *Chimel v. California*, 395 U. S.752, 762–63 (1969).

34. *United States v. Simmons*, 567 F.2d 314, 320 (1977).

35. *Arizona v. Gant*, 556 U.S. 332, No. 07–542 (2009).

36. Federal Law Enforcement Training Center (FLETC), "*Arizona v. Gant*" (2009), available from http://www.fletc.gov/training/programs/legal-division/the-informer/Arizona-vs-gant.pdf/view

37. *Thornton v. United States*, 541 U.S. 615, 124 S. Ct. 2127, 158 L. Ed.2d 905 (2004).

38. *Florence v. Board of Chosen Freeholders of the County of Burlington*, 621 F.3d 296 (2012).

39. *Schneckloth v. Bustamonte*, 412 U.S. 218, 228 (1973); *United States v. Gonzalez-Basulto*, 898 F.2d 1011, 1012–13 5th Cir. (1990).

40. *State v. Lewis*, 611 A.2d.69 (Me. 1992).

41. Ferdico, *Criminal Procedure for the Criminal Justice Professional*, 18.

42. K. Johnson, "States Revamp Photo Lineups Used by Police," *USA Today* (September 17, 2009), 3A.

43. Ibid.

44. *Townsend v. Sain*, 372 U.S. 293, 307–08 (1963).

45. *Escobedo v. Illinois*, 378 U.S. 478, 4 Ohio Misc. 197, 84 S. Ct. 1758, 12 L. Ed. 2d 977 (1964).

46. *Miranda v. Arizona*, 384 U.S. 457–58, 86 S.Ct. 1602, 16 L.Ed.2d 694 (1966).

47. *Berghuis v. Thompkins*, 560 U. S. 130 S. Ct. 2250 (2010); C. Zash, "Miranda Rights Rule Changes, Must Say Want to Be Silent," *Digtriad.com* (June 2, 2010), available June 3, 2010, from http://www.digtriad.com/news/local_state/article.aspx?storyid=143135.

48. S. Ferrechio, "Holder Wants Changes in *Miranda* Rule," *Washington Examiner* (May 10, 2010), available from http://www.washingtonexaminer.com/politics/Holder-wants-changes-in-Miranda-rule-93240504.html#ixzz0ppGpHshJ

49. Ferdico, *Criminal Procedure for the Criminal Justice Professional*, 483.

50. *Maryland v. Shatzer*, No. 08–680, 405 Md. 585, 954 A. 2d 1118 (2010).

51. Ferdico, *Criminal Procedure for the Criminal Justice Professional*, 9; Garland, *Criminal Law for the Criminal Justice Professional*, 17–18; S. T. Reid, *Criminal Law: The Essentials* (New York, NY: Oxford University Press, 2009), 12–14.

52. Reid, *Criminal Law*.

53. *Weeks v. United States*, 232 U.S. 383, 34 S. Ct. 341, 58 L. Ed. 652 (1914).

54. *Wolf v. Colorado*, 338 U.S. 25, 69 S.Ct. 1359, L.Ed. 1782 (1949).

55. *Mapp v. Ohio*, 367 U.S. 643, 655 (1961).

56. *United States v. Leon*, 468 U.S. 897, 104 S. Ct. 3405, 82 L. Ed. 2d 677 (1984).

57. D. Savage, "Who's Policing the Fourth Amendment?" *ABA Journal* (April 1, 2009), available from http://www.abajournal.com

58. Ibid.

59. *Herring v. United States*, 555 U.S.,135, 129 S. Ct. 695, 172 L. Ed. 2d 496 (2009).

60. *Murray v. United States*, 487 U.S. 533, 539, 540 [101 L.Ed.2nd 472, 482] (1988).

61. D. Dowe, "Everything You Need to Know About Less-Than-Lethal Options: Part 1," *Tactical Response* 7, no. 3 (2009), 38–43.

62. J. Senter, "ACLU Taking Taser Use to Supreme Court," *Santa Rosa Press Gazette* (February 7, 2009), available from http://www.srpressgazette.com/news/court-6101-supreme-aclu.html

63. Ferdico, *Criminal Procedure for the Criminal Justice Professional*, 130–131; D. T. Skelton, *Contemporary Criminal Law* (Boston, MA: Butterworth-Heinemann, 1998), 349.

64. *Tennessee v. Garner*, 471 U.S. 1, 11–12 (1985).

65. R. Means and G. Seidel, "Maintaining Proportionality and Managing Force Escalations," *Law & Order* 57, no. 2 (2009), 31–33.

66. *Scott v. Harris*, 127 S. Ct. 1769, U. S. Sup. Ct., No. 05–1631 (2007).

67. 42 U.S.C. § 1983.

68. V. E. Kappeler, *Critical Issues in Police Civil Liability*, 3rd ed. (Prospect Heights, IL: Waveland, 2001).

69. Federal Bureau of Investigation, *Terrorism 2002–2005* (2006), available from http://www.fbi.gov/publications/terror/terror ism2002_2005.htm

70. R. J. Fischer, E. Halibozek, and G. Green, *Introduction to Security*, 8th ed. (Burlington, MA: Elsevier, 2008).

71. G. Martin, *Understanding Terrorism*, 2nd ed. (Thousand Oaks, CA: Sage, 2006), 48.

72. ACLU, *ACLU Memo to Interested Persons Regarding the Conference Report on the USA PATRIOT Improvement and Reauthorization Act of 2005* (2005), available from http://www.aclu.org/cpredirect/22384

73. J. Devanney and D. Devanney, "Homeland Security and Patriot Acts," *Law and Order* 51 (August 8, 2003), 10–12.

74. B. Barker and S. Fowler, "The FBI Joint Terrorism Task Force Officer," *FBI Law Enforcement Bulletin* 77, no. 11 (2008), 12–17.

75. Ibid.

76. *United States v. Jones*, 565 U. S. (2012).

77. ACLU, *ACLU Memo to Interested Persons Regarding the Conference Report on the USA PATRIOT Improvement and Reauthorization Act of 2005*.

78. W. McCormack, "State and Local Law Enforcement: Contributions to Terrorism Prevention," *FBI Law Enforcement Bulletin* 78, no. 3 (2009), 1–8.

79. DHS, "Law Enforcement Partnerships," available from http://www.dhs.gov/topic/law-enforcement-partnerships

80. DHS, "Boston Marathon Two Years Later . . . A Coordinated Effort for Security" (April 20, 2015), available from http://www.dhs.gov/blog/2015/04/20/boston-marathon-two-years-later%E2%80%A6a-coordinated-effort-security

81. D. C. Sheehan, G. S. Everly, and A. M. Langlieb, "How Agencies Help Law Enforcement Officers Cope With Major Critical Incidents," *FBI Bulletin* 73, no. 9 (September 2004), 1–12.

## ■ CHAPTER 10

1. S. Cox and W. McCamey, *Introduction to Criminal Justice: Exploring the Network*, 5th ed. (Durham, SC: Carolina Academic Press, 2008).

2. E. Nickels, "A Note on the Status of Discretion in Police Research," *Journal of Criminal Justice* 35, no. 5 (September/October 2007), 570.

3. Nickels, "A Note on the Status of Discretion in Police Research," 577.

4. T. J. Martinelli, "Updating Ethics Training-Policing Privacy Series: Noble Cause Corruption and Police Discretion," *The Police Chief* 77 (2011), 60–62.

5. A. J. Reiss, "Police Organization in the Twentieth Century," pp. 50–98 in M. Tonry and N. Morris (Eds.), *Modern Policing* (Chicago, IL: University of Chicago Press, 1992), 74.

6. L. W. Brooks, "Police Discretionary Behavior: A Study of Style," pp. 140–164 in R. G. Dunham and G. P. Alpert (Eds.), *Critical Issues in*

*Policing: Contemporary Readings*, 2nd ed. (Prospect Heights, IL: Waveland, 1993).

7. R. H. Langworthy and L. F. Travis, *Policing in America: A Balance of Forces* (New York, NY: Macmillan, 1994), 294–295.

8. R. Iyengar, "The Protection Battered Spouses Don't Need" (*The New York Times*, August 7, 2007), available from http://www.nytimes.com/2007/08/07/opinion/07iyengar.html?_r=0; C. R. Rowe, "Where Is the Middle Ground Between Mandatory and Discretionary Domestic Violence Legislation?" (*re/search*, 2012), available from https://ssrcdepaul.wordpress.com/2012/02/14/dv-mandatory-arrest/.

9. R. Mueller III, *Federal Bureau of Investigation, Major Executive Speeches* (Speech presented at City Club of San Diego, San Diego, CA, May 11, 2006), available from http://fbi.gov/pressrel/speeches/mueller051106.htm.

10. U.S. Department of Justice, *Former Cedartown Police Officer Pleads Guilty to Stealing Money From Hispanic Motorists During Traffic Stops* (2007), available from www.justice.gov/usao/gan/press/2007/03-12-07b.pdf.

11. J. Rose, "Despite Laws and Lawsuits, Quota-Based Policing Lingers" (*NPR*, April 4, 2015), available from http://www.npr.org/2015/04/04/395061810/despite-laws-and-lawsuits-quota-based-policing-lingers

12. D. Close and N. Meier, *Morality in Criminal Justice: An Introduction to Ethics* (Belmont, CA: Wadsworth, 1995), 3.

13. E. Delattre, *Character and Cops*, 5th ed. (Washington, DC: AEI Press, 2002), 6

14. Community Oriented Policing Services, *Intelligence-Led Policing: The Integration of Community Policing and Law Enforcement Intelligence* (2008), available from www.cops.usdoj.gov.

15. Martinelli, "Updating Ethics Training–Policing Privacy Series," 62.

16. N. Stephens, "Law Enforcement Ethics Do Not Begin When You Pin on the Badge," *FBI Law Enforcement Bulletin* 75, no. 11 (November 2006), 22–23.

17. G. Scaramella, "Attitudes of Undergraduate Criminal Justice Majors Toward Ethical Issues in Criminal Justice," *Illinois Law Enforcement Executive Forum* 1 (February 2001), 9–25; G. Scaramella, R. Rodriguez, and J. Allen, "A Longitudinal Analysis of Four Inquiries of Ethical Attitudes of Criminal Justice Higher Education Students and Police Officers," *Contemporary Issues in Criminology and the Social Sciences* 4, no. 2 (2009), 1–20; J. Allen, B, Mhlanga, and E. Khan, "Education, Training and Ethical Dilemmas: Responses of Criminal Justice Practitioners Regarding Professional and Ethical Issues," *Professional Issues in Criminal Justice* 1, no. 1 (2006), 3–28; R. Turano, *A Comparative Study of Undergraduate Criminal Justice College Students and DuPage County Police Officers Involving Ethical Attitudes* (Unpublished master's thesis, Western Illinois University. Macomb, IL, 2001).

18. Scaramella, "Attitudes of Undergraduate Criminal Justice Majors Toward Ethical Issues in Criminal Justice"; Scaramella et al., "A Longitudinal Analysis of Four Inquiries of Ethical Attitudes of Criminal Justice Higher Education Students and Police Officers"; Allen et al., "Education, Training and Ethical Dilemmas: Responses of Criminal Justice Practitioners Regarding Professional and Ethical Issues"; Turano, *A Comparative Study of Undergraduate Criminal Justice College Students and DuPage County Police Officers Involving Ethical Attitudes.*

19. Ethics Resource Center, *2003 National Business Ethics Survey* (NBES) (May 21, 2003), available from http://www.ethics.org/resource/2003-national-business-ethics-survey-nbes.

20. B. D. Fitch, "Rethinking Ethics in Law Enforcement," *FBI Law Enforcement Bulletin* 80 (2011), 18–23.

21. For a more complete discussion on facilitation, see P. Renner, *The Art of Teaching Adults: How to Become an Exceptional Instructor and Facilitator* (Vancouver, Canada: Training Associates, 2005).

22. E. E. Joh, *Stanford Law Review* 62, no. 1 (2009), available from www.stanfordlawreview.org/print/article/breaking-law-enforce-it-undercover-police-participation-crime.

23. S. Cox, Personal interview with Cox (Macomb, IL, May 20, 2002), in *Police: Practices, Perspectives, Problems* (Boston, MA: Allyn & Bacon, 1996).

24. Scaramella et al., "A Longitudinal Analysis of Four Inquiries of Ethical Attitudes of Criminal Justice Higher Education Students and Police Officers," *Contemporary Issues in Criminology and the Social Sciences* 4, no. 2 (2009), 1–20.

25. Knapp Commission, *Report on Police Corruption* (New York, NY: George Braziller, 1972).

26. E. Delattre, *Character and Cops*, 5th ed. (Washington, DC: AEI Press, 2002).

27. International Association of Chiefs of Police, *Police Ethics: Problems and Solutions Part I* (2012), available from http://www.theiacp.org.

28. N. Trautman, "Administrator Misconduct," *Law and Order* 50 (2002), 118–126.

29. J. Schafer and T. Martinelli, "First-Line Supervisor's Perceptions of Police Integrity: The Measurement of Police Integrity Revisited," *Policing,* 31, no. 2 (2008), 306–323.

30. T. J. Jurkanin, Editorial, *Illinois Law Enforcement Executive Forum* (July 2001), i.

31. A. M. Jacocks and M. D. Bowman, "Developing and Sustaining a Culture of Integrity," *The Police Chief* 73 (2006), 16–22.

32. Delattre, *Character and Cops.*

33. Ibid.

34. L. W. Brooks, "Police Discretionary Behavior: A Study of Style," pp. 140–164 in R. G. Dunham and G. P. Alpert (Eds.), *Critical Issues in Policing: Contemporary Readings*, 2nd ed. (Prospect Heights, IL: Waveland, 1993).

35. B. D. Fitch, "Rethinking Ethics in Law Enforcement," *FBI Law Enforcement Bulletin* 80 (2011), 18–23.

36. B. Zuidema and H. Duff Jr., "Organizational Ethics Through Effective Leadership," *FBI Law Enforcement Bulletin* 78, no. 3 (March 2009), 8–11.

37. Police Media Relations, "Police Media Pro Speaks at Police Chiefs Conference," available from http://policemediarelations.com/police-media-pro-speaks-at-police-chiefs-conference/

38. C. B. Klockars, S. K. Ivkovich, Harver, and M. R. Haberfeld, "The Measurement of Police Integrity" (National Institute of Justice *Research in Brief*, May 2000), available from https://www.ncjrs.gov/pdffiles1/nij/181465.pdf.

39. National Institute of Justice (NIJ), *Enhancing Police Integrity* (Washington, DC: U.S. Department of Justice, Office of Justice Programs, December 2005), 1.

40. NIJ, *Enhancing Police Integrity*, 1.

41. NIC, 2005.

# ■ CHAPTER 11

1. G. W. Lynch, "Police Corruption From the United States Perspective," *Police Studies* 12 (1989), 165–170.

2. T. Barker and D. L. Carter, *Police Deviance* (Cincinnati, OH: Pilgrimage, 1986), 3–4.

3. Knapp Commission, *The Knapp Commission Report on Police Corruption* (New York, NY: George Braziller, 1973).

4. D. R. Johnson, *American Law Enforcement: A History* (St. Louis, MO: Forum Press, 1981); J. F. Richardson, *Urban Police in the United States* (Port Washington, NY: Kennikat Press, 1974); R. Trojanowicz, "Preventing Individual and Systemic Corruption," *Footprints* 4 (1992), 1–3.

5. D. H. Bracey, "Proactive Measures Against Police Corruption: Yesterday's Solutions, Today's Problems," *Police Studies* 12 (1989), 175–179.

6. R. Lacayo, "Cops and Robbers," *Time* (October 11, 1993), 43–44.

7. Human Rights Watch, *Shielded From Justice: Police Brutality and Accountability in the United States* (Los Angeles, CA: The Christopher Commission Report, 1998), available from http://www.hrw.org/reports98/police/usp073.htm.

8. Christopher Commission, *Report of the Independent Commission on the Los Angeles Police Department* (Los Angeles, CA: Author, 1991); Human Rights Watch, *Shielded From Justice.*

9. M. Tran, "Corruption Riddles New York Police: Inquiry Says Drug Dealing Rogue Cops Acted Like Gangs," *The Gazette* (Montreal, July 8, 1994), A9; J. Treaster, "Mollen Panel Says Buck Stops With Top Officers," *The New York Times* (Sec. 1, July 10, 1994), 21.

10. D. Lieberman, "A Closer Eye on the Police [Letter to the Editor]," *The New York Times* (August 17, 2008), available from http://www.nytimes.com.

11. Lynch, "Police Corruption From the United States Perspective."

12. U.S. General Accounting Office, *Drug-Related Police Corruption* (Washington, DC: Government Printing Office, 1998), 3–5.

13. P. Chevigny, *Police Power: Police Abuses in New York City* (New York, NY: Vintage Press, 1969); E. Cray, *The Enemy in the Streets: Police Malpractice in America* (Garden City, NY: Anchor Books, 1972); P. K. Manning, "Police Lying," *Urban Life* 3 (1974), 283–306; J. H. Skolnick, *Justice Without Trial* (New York, NY: Wiley, 1966); R. R. Roberg and J. Kuykendall, *Police in Society* (Belmont, CA: Wadsworth, 1993).

14. M. Foley, *Police Perjury: A Factorial Analysis,* National Institute of Justice (NCJ 181241) (Doctoral dissertation, City University of New York, Queens, 2000).

15. Foley, *Police Perjury*, 132.

16. S. Rosoff, H. Pontell, and R. Tillman, *Profit Without Honor: White Collar Crime and the Looting of America*, 4th ed. (Upper Saddle River, NJ: Prentice-Hall, 2007), 448.

17. Rosoff et al., *Profit Without Honor*.

18. Ibid.

19. Ibid.

20. W. Hyatt, "Parameters of Police Misconduct," pp. 75–99 in M. Palmiotto (Ed.), *Police Misconduct* (Upper Saddle River, NJ: Prentice-Hall, 2001).

21. Rosoff et al., *Profit Without Honor*.

22. Ibid.

23. S. Ivkovic, "To Serve and Collect: Measuring Police Corruption," *Journal of Criminal Law and Criminology* 93, no. 2/3 (2003), 593.

24. C. Klockars, S. Ivkovich, and M. Haberfeld, *Enhancing Police Integrity* (National Institute of Justice, Research for Practice, December 2005), available from http://www.ojp.usdoj.gov//nij.

25. S. E. Wolfe and A. R. Piquero, "Organizational Justice and Police Misconduct," *Criminal Justice and Behavior* 38, no. 4 (2011), 332–353.

26. B. Zuidema and H. Duff Jr., "Organizational Ethics Through Effective Leadership," *FBI Law Enforcement Bulletin* (March 2009), 8–11.

27. L. Langton and M. Durose, *Police Behavior During Traffic and Street Stops, 2011* (NCJ 242937) (Bureau of Justice Statistics, September 2013), available from http://www.bjs.gov/content/pub/pdf/pbtss11.pdf

28. C. Eith and M. R. Durose, *Contacts Between Police and the Public, 2008* (NCJ 234599) (Bureau of Justice Statistics, 2011), available from http://www.bjs.gov/content/pub/pdf/cpp08.pdf.

29. M. Durose, E. Smith, and P. Langan, *Contacts Between the Police and the Public, 2005* (NCJ 215243) (National Institute of Justice, April 2007), available from http://www.ojp.usdoj.gov//nij.

30. Ibid.

31. G. P. Alpert and R. G. Dunham, "Policy and Training Recommendations Related to Police Use of CEDs: Overview of Findings From a Comprehensive National Study," *Police Quarterly* 13, no. 3 (2010), 235–259.

32. B. Harrison, "Noble Cause Corruption and the Police Ethic," *FBI Law Enforcement Bulletin* 68 (August 1999), 1–7.

33. Cato Institute, "The National Police Misconduct Reporting Project," available from http://www.policemisconduct.net/

34. American Civil Liberties Union (ACLU), "Mobile Justice," available from https://www.aclu.org/video/mobile-justice

35. National Advisory Commission on Civil Disorders, *Report* (Washington, DC: Government Printing Office, 1968); A. J. Lurigio, R. G. Greenleaf, and L. L. Flexon, "The Effects of Race on Relationships With the Police: A Survey of African American and Latino Youths in Chicago," *Western Criminology Review* 10, no. 1 (2009), 29–42.

36. *CBS News/New York Times* poll (July 7–14, 2008), available from http://www.pollingreport.com/institut.htm

37. S. E. Walker, *A Respectful Policing Initiative: Statement to the President's Task Force on 21st Century Policing* (2015), available from http://www.cops.usdoj.gov/pdf/taskforce/submissions/Walker-Samuel-Testimony.pdf

38. A. Reiss, "Police Brutality . . . Answers to Key Questions," pp. 10–19 in M. Lipsky (Ed.), *Police Encounters* (Chicago, IL: Aldine, 1968).

39. Walker, *A Respectful Policing Initiative*, 2–3.

40. R. Weitzer and S. A. Tuch, "Race and Perceptions of Police Misconduct," *Social Problems* 51, no. 3 (2004), 305–325.

41. M. D. Holmes and B. W. Smith, "Intergroup Dynamics of Extra-Legal Police Aggression: An Integrated Theory of Race and Place," *Aggression and Violent Behavior* 17, no. 4 (2012), 344–353.

42. The Leadership Conference. 2011. *Restoring a National Consensus: The Need to End Racial Profiling in America,* http://www.civilrights.org/publications/reports/racial-profiling2011/racial_profiling2011.pdf.

43. H. Barovick, "DWB: Driving While Black," *Time,* 151, no. 23 (June 15, 1998), available from http://www.pathfinder.com/time/magazine/1998/dom/980615/nation_driving_while.html.

44. W. Harris, "Recruiting Women: Are We Doing Enough?" *Police* 23, 18–23.

45. Ibid.

46. E. R. Stoddard, "The Informal Code of Police Deviance: A Group Approach to 'Blue-Coat Crime,'" *Journal of Criminal Law, Criminology and Police Science* 59 (June 1968), 201–213.

47. A. V. Bouza, *The Police Mystique: An Insider's Look at Cops, Crime, and the Criminal Justice System* (New York, NY: Plenum, 1990); B. Frankel, "'You'll Be in the Fold' by Breaking Law," *USA Today* (1993a), 1A; S. K. Klockars, W. E. Ivkovich, W. E. Harver, and M. R. Haberfeld, *The Measurement of Police Integrity* (Research in Brief, National Institute of Justice) (Washington, DC: Government Printing Office, May 2000); D. Weisburd and R. Greenspan, *Police Attitudes Toward Abuse of Authority: Findings From a National Study* (Research in Brief, National Institute of Justice) (Washington, DC: Government Printing Office, May 2000).

48. Frankel, "'You'll Be in the Fold' by Breaking Law," 1a.

49. Frankel, "'You'll Be in the Fold' by Breaking Law," 3a.

50. K. Johnson, "Milwaukee Beating Case Busts Officers' 'Code of Silence,'" *USA Today* (December 17, 2007), available from http://www.usatoday.com/news/nation/2007–12–17-Copside_N.htm.

51. E. Wargo, "Bad Apples or Bad Barrels? Zimbardo on the 'Lucifer Effect,'" *Observer* 19, no. 8 (August, 2006).

52. For a discussion of research on cognitive dissonance, see J. Cooper, R. Mirabile, and S. J. Scher, "Actions and Attitudes: The Theory of Cognitive Dissonance," pp. 63–80 in *Persuasion: Psychological Insights and Perspectives*, ed. Timothy C. Brock and Melanie C. Green (Thousand Oaks, CA: Sage Publications, 2005), 63–80.

53. C. Seron, J. Pereira, and J. Kovath, "Judging Police Misconduct: 'Street-Level' Versus Professional Policing," *Law & Society Review* 38, no. 4 (2004), 665–710.

54. E. Delattre, *Character and Cops*, 4th ed. (Washington, DC: AEI Press, 2002), 85.

55. M. A. Caldero and J. P. Crank, *Police Ethics: The Corruption of Noble Cause*, 3rd ed. (New York, NY: Routledge, 2015).

56. Delattre, *Character and Cops*.

57. H. Lee and M. S. Vaughn, "Organizational Factors That Contribute to Police Deadly Force Liability," *Journal of Criminal Justice* 38, no. 2 (2010), 193–206.

58. J. F. Richardson, *Urban Police in the United States* (Port Washington, NY: Kennikat Press, 1974), 154.

59. B. Frankel, "For NYC Cops, License for Crime," *USA Today* (October 7, 1993b), 3A.

60. S. Walker, C. Spohn, and M. DeLone, *The Color of Justice: Race, Ethnicity, and Crime in America*, 4th ed. (Belmont, CA: Wadsworth/Thompson Learning, 2006).

61. Delattre, *Character and Cops*; Klockars et al., *Enhancing Police Integrity*.

62. G. Marche, "Integrity, Culture, and Scale: An Empirical Test of the Big Bad Police Agency," *Crime, Law and Social Change* 51, no. 5 (June 2009), 463.

63. R. A. Johnson, Roberta Ann, "Whistleblowing and the Police," *Rutgers University Journal of Law and Urban Policy* (2005), available from http://www.bmartin.cc/dissent/documents/Johnson.pdf

64. D. H. Bracey, "Proactive Measures Against Police Corruption: Yesterday's Solutions, Today's Problems," *Police Studies* 12 (1989), 175–179.

65. R. Davis, P. Mateu-Gelabert, and J. Miller, "Can Effective Policing Also Be Respectful? Two Examples in the South Bronx," *Police Quarterly* 8 (2005), 229–247.

66. Davis et al., "Can Effective Policing Also Be Respectful?" 229.

67. O. E. Cooksey, "Corruption: A Continuing Challenge for Law Enforcement," *FBI Law Enforcement Bulletin* 60 (September 1991), 5–9; G. W. Lynch, "Police Corruption From the United States Perspective," *Police Studies* 12 (1989), 165–170; E. Meese and P. J. Ortmeier, *Leadership, Ethics, and*

*Policing: Challenges for the 21st Century* (Upper Saddle River, NJ: Prentice-Hall, 2003).

68. S. E. Walker and C. A. Archbold, *The New World of Police Accountability*, 2nd ed. (Thousand Oaks, CA: Sage Publications, 2014).

69. K. Lersch, T. Bazley, and T. Mieczkowski, "Early Intervention Programs: An Effective Police Accountability Tool, or Punishment of the Productive?" *Policing* 29, no. 1 (2006), 58–77.

70. J. Bills, K. Ching-Chung, R. Heringer, and D. Mankin, "Peer-to-Peer Accountability," *FBI Law Enforcement Bulletin* 78, no. 8 (2009), 12–20.

71. Klockars et al., *Enhancing Police Integrity*.

72. C. Stone and J. Travis, "Toward a New Professionalism in Policing," *New Perspectives in Policing* (National Institute of Justice, 2011), available from http://www.ncjrs.gov/pdffiles1/nij/232359.pdf.

73. A. Sweeney and J. Gorner, "Police Misconduct Cases Drag on for Years: Investigative Agency's Delays Can Lead to Dismissal of Charges," *Chicago Tribune* (June 17, 2012), available from http://www.chicagotribune.com/news/local/ct-met-cop-investigations-delayed-20120617,0,7334405.

74. Ibid.

75. U.S. Department of Justice, *Building Trust Between the Police and the Citizens They Serve: An Internal Affairs Promising Practices Guide for Local Law Enforcement*, available from http://www.theiacp.org/portals/0/pdfs/BuildingTrust.pdf.

76. S. Ivkovic and T. Shelley, "The Contours of Police Integrity Across Eastern Europe: The Case of Bosnia and Herzegovina and the Czech Republic," *International Criminal Justice Review* 18, no. 1 (2008), 59.

## ■ CHAPTER 12

1. S. M. Cox and W. P. McCamey, *Introduction to Criminal Justice: Exploring the Network* (Durham, NC: Carolina Academic Press, 2008), 12–13.

2. U.S. Census Bureau, "QuickFacts Beta: United States," available from http://www.census.gov/quickfacts/.

3. K. Humes, N. Jones, and R. Ramire, *Overview of Race and Hispanic Origin: 2010* (U.S. Census Bureau, March 2011), available from http://www.census.gov/prod/cen2010/briefs/c2010br-02.pdf.

4. Ibid.

5. Ibid.

6. U.S. Census Bureau, "State & County QuickFacts," available from http://quickfacts.census.gov/qfd/states/00000.html.

7. S. M. Hennessy, "Achieving Cultural Competence," *Police Chief* 60 (August 1993), 46–54.

8. Humes et al., *Overview of Race and Hispanic Origin*.

9. S. L. Colby and J. M. Ortman, "Projections and Composition of the U.S. Population: 2014–2060" (P25-1143, March 2015), available from http://www.census.gov/content/dam/Census/library/publications/2015/demo/p25-1143.pdf.

10. G. Barak, J. M. Flavin, and P. S. Leighton, *Class, Race, Gender and Crime* (Los Angeles, CA: Roxbury, 2001), 257–259; E. L. Scott, "Cultural Awareness Training," *Police Chief* 60 (1993), 26–28.

11. Y. Wu, I. Y. Sun, and B. W. Smith, "Race, Immigration, and Policing: Chinese Immigrants' Satisfaction With Police," *JQ: Justice Quarterly* 28, no. 5 (2011), 745–774.

12. D. S. Kirk, A. V. Papachristos, J. Fagan, and T. R. Tyler, "The Paradox of Law Enforcement in Immigrant Communities: Does Tough Immigration Enforcement Undermine Public Safety?" *Annals of the American Academy of Political & Social Science* 641, no. 1 (2012), 79–98.

13. A. Thomas, "Police Find Dealing With Mentally Ill a Tough Task," *Times-Georgian* (January 11, 2011), available from http://www.times-georgian.com/view/full_story/10969560/article-Police-find-dealing-with-mentally-ill-a-tough-task?instance=TG_home_story_offset.

14. T. Williams, "A Psychologist as Warden? Jail and Mental Illness Intersect in Chicago" (*The New York Times*, July 30, 2015), available from http://www.nytimes.com/2015/07/31/us/a-psychologist-as-warden-jail-and-mental-illness-intersect-in-chicago.html?hpw&rref=us&action=click&pgtype=Homepage&module=well-region&region=bottom-well&WT.nav=bottom-well&_r=1.

15. A. J. Reiss, "Police Brutality—Answers to Key Questions," *Trans-action* 5 (July/August 1968), 15–16.

16. H. MacDonald, "The Myth of Racial Profiling," *City Journal* 11 (2001), 14–27.

17. R. T. Schaefer, *Racial and Ethnic Groups*, 8th ed. (Upper Saddle River, NJ: Prentice-Hall, 2000).

18. A. Bouza, *Police Unbound: Corruption, Abuse, and Heroism by the Boys in Blue* (Amherst, NY: Prometheus Books, 2001); K. Thornton, R. L. McKinnie, and M. Stetz, "Treatment of Minorities Harsher, Officers Admit," *Union-Tribune* (August 29, 1999), available from http://www-psy.ucsd.edu/~eebbesen/psych16298/162PolicePrejdice.html.

19. R. K. Brunson and J. Miller, "Young Black Men and Urban Policing in the United States," *British Journal of Criminology* 46 (2006), 613–640; Cox, S. M. (1984). Race/ethnic relations and the police: Current and future issues. *American Journal of the Police, 3*, 169–183; A. Hacker, *Two Nations: Black and White, Separate, Hostile, Unequal* (New York, NY: Ballantine Books, 1992); National Advisory Commission on Civil Disorders (Kerner Commission), *Report* (Washington, DC: Government Printing Office, 1968); K. Thornton, R. L. McKinnie, and M. Stetz, "Treatment of Minorities Harsher, Officers Admit," *Union-Tribune* (August 29, 1999), available from http://www-psy.ucsd.edu/~eebbesen/psych16298/162PolicePrejdice.html; S. Walker, C. Spohn, and M. DeLone, *The Color of Justice: Race, Ethnicity, and Crime in America* (Belmont, CA: Wadsworth, 1995); R. Weitzer and S. A. Tuch, *Rethinking Minority Attitudes Toward the Police—Final Technical Report* (NCJ 207145) (Washington, DC: U.S. Department of Justice, June 2004), available from http://www.ncjrs.gov/pdffiles1/nij/grants/207145.pdf.

20. B. F. Chavis and J. D. Williams, "Beyond the Rodney King Story: NAACP Report on Police Conduct and Community Relations," *NAACP News* 93 (1993), 42; "Police Continue to Use Excessive Force Against Hispanics [Editorial]," *La Prensa San Diego* (May 4, 2007), available from www.laprensa-sandiego.org/archieve/2007/may04-07/police.htm; A. J. Reiss, *The Police and the Public* (New Haven, CT: Yale University Press, 1970); S. Walker, C. Spohn, and M. DeLone, M. (1995). *The color of justice: Race, Ethnicity, and Crime in America* (Belmont, CA: Wadsworth, 1995).

21. Walker et al., *The Color of Justice*, 85, 89.

22. E. Kane, "In 2001 America, Whites Can't Believe Blacks Treated Unfairly," *Milwaukee Journal Sentinel* (July 15, 2001), B3.

23. M. Eversley, "Officials Target 'Stop and Frisk' as Racist," *USA Today* (June 8, 2012), 3A.

24. Ibid.

25. Ibid.

26. D. E. Barlow and M. H. Barlow, *Police in a Multicultural Society: An American Story* (Prospect Heights, IL: Waveland, 2000), 94.

27. U.S. Census Bureau, "State & County QuickFacts."

28. Federal Bureau of Investigation (FBI), *Crime in the United States, 2010* (2011), available from http://www.fbi.gov/about-us/cjis/ucr/crime-in-the-u.s/2010/crime-in-the-u.s.-2010/.

29. ACLU (American Civil Liberties Union), *Sanctioned Bias: Racial Profiling Since 9/11* (New York, NY: Author, 2004), available from http://www.aclu.org/FilesPDFs/racial%20profiling%20report.pdf.

30. ACLU, *Sanctioned Bias*, 5.

31. B. Brown, "Community Policing in a Diverse Society," *Law Enforcement Executive Forum* 4, no. 5 (2004), 49–56.

32. K. Loria, "New Jersey Muslims Sue NYPD to End Surveillance," *The Christian Science Monitor* (June 7, 2012), available from http://www.csmonitor.com/USA/Justice/2012/0607/New-Jersey-Muslims-sue-NYPD-to-end-surveillance.

33. F. Newport, "Racial Profiling Is Seen as Widespread, Particularly Among Young Black Men," *Gallup News Service* (December 9, 1999), available from http://www.gallup.com/poll/3421/racial-profiling-seen-widespread-particularly-among-young-black-men.aspx.

34. Ibid.

35. Ibid.

36. G. Carrick, "Professional Police Traffic Stops: Strategies to Address Racial Profiling," *FBI Law Enforcement Bulletin* 69 (2000), 8–10.

37. ACLU, *Sanctioned Bias*, 18.

38. R. Weitzer and S. A. Tuch, *Rethinking Minority Attitudes Toward the Police—Final Technical Report* (NCJ 207145) (Washington,

DC: U.S. Department of Justice, June 2004), available from http://www.ncjrs.gov/pdffiles1/nij/grants/207145.pdf.

39. L. Graziano, A. Schuck, and C. Martin, "Police Misconduct, Media Coverage, and Public Perceptions of Racial Profiling: An Experiment," *JQ: Justice Quarterly* 27, no. 1 (2010), 52–76.

40. M. M. Wehrman and J. De Angelis, "Citizen Willingness to Participate in Police-Community Partnerships: Exploring the Influence of Race and Neighborhood Context," *Police Quarterly* 14, no. 1 (2011), 48–69.

41. Ibid.

42. J. Gau, "A Longitudinal Analysis of Citizens' Attitudes About Police," *Policing* 33, no. 2 (2010), 236–252.

43. D. S. Kirk and M. Matsuda, "Legal Cynicism, Collective Efficacy, and the Ecology of Arrest," *Criminology* 49, no. 2 (2011), 443–472.

44. A. Lurigio, R. Greenleaf, and J. Flexon, "The Effects of Race on Relationships With the Police: A Survey of African American and Latino Youths in Chicago," *Western Criminology Review* 10, no. 1 (2009), 29–41. 38

45. R. K. Brunson and J. Miller, "Young Black Men and Urban Policing in the United States," *British Journal of Criminology* 46 (2006), 613–640.

46. J. Gau, C. Mosher, and T. Pratt, "An Inquiry Into the Impact of Suspect Race on Police Use of Tasers," *Police Quarterly* 13, no. 1 (2010), 27–48.

47. S. W. Fallik and K. J. Novak, "The Decision to Search: Is Race or Ethnicity Important?" *Journal of Contemporary Criminal Justice* 28, no. 2 (2012), 146–165.

48. G. E. Higgins, G. F. Vito, and E. L. Grossi, "The Impact of Race on the Police Decision to Search During a Traffic Stop: A Focal Concerns Theory Perspective," *Journal of Contemporary Criminal Justice* 28, no. 2 (2012), 166–183.

49. C. Maxson, K. Hennigan, and D. C. Sloane, *Factors That Influence Public Opinion of the Police* (NIJ 197925, June 2003), available from http://www.ncjrs.gov/txtfiles1/nij/197925.txt.

50. Ibid.

51. L. Graziano, A. Schuck, and C. Martin, "Police Misconduct, Media Coverage, and Public Perceptions of Racial Profiling: An Experiment," *JQ: Justice Quarterly* 27, no. 1 (2010), 52–76.

52. N. J. Henderson, C. W. Ortiz, N. F. Sugie, and J. Miller, *Policing in Arab-American Communities After September 11* (NCJ 221706) (Washington, DC: U.S. Department of Justice, July 2008), available from http://www.ncjrs.gov/app/publications/abstract.aspx?ID= 243589.

53. Henderson et al., *Policing in Arab-American Communities After September 11*, 2.

54. C. W. Harlow, *Hate Crimes Reported by Victims and Police* (NCJ 209911) (Washington, DC: Bureau of Justice Statistics, November 2005), available from http://bjs.ojp.usdoj.gov/index.cfm?ty=pbdetail&iid=949.

55. D. Keeling and T. Hughes, "Police Officer Attitudes Toward Muslims and Islam: 'Worlds Apart'?" *American Journal of Criminal Justice* 36, no. 4 (2011), 307–318.

56. T. R. Tyler, S. Schulhofer, and A. Z. Huq, "Legitimacy and Deterrence Effects in Counterterrorism Policing: A Study of Muslim Americans," *Law & Society Review* 44, no. 2 (2010), 365–402.

57. S. M. Cox and J. D. Fitzgerald, *Police in Community Relations: Critical Issues*, 3rd ed. (New York, NY: McGraw-Hill, 1996); L. W. Nolte, *Fundamentals of Public Relations: Professional Guidelines, Concepts, and Integrations* (New York, NY: Pergamon, 1979).

58. D. E. Barlow and M. H. Barlow, *Police in a Multicultural Society: An American Story* (Prospect Heights, IL: Waveland, 2000); T. Bickham and A. Rossett, "Diversity Training: Are We Doing the Right Thing?" *Police Chief* 60 (1993), 43–47; California Commission on Peace Officer Standards and Training, *Cultural Diversity Program* (2009), available from http://www.post.ca.gov/training/diversity.asp; Cox and Fitzgerald, *Police in Community Relations: Critical Issues*; T. Grove, "Implicit Bias and Law Enforcement," *The Police Chief* 78 (October 2011), 44–56; S. M. Hennessy, "Achieving Cultural Competence," *Police Chief* 60 (August 1993), 46–54; E. L. Scott, "Cultural Awareness Training," *Police Chief* 60 (1993), 26–28.

59. Barlow and Barlow, *Police in a Multicultural Society*; California Commission on Peace Officer Standards and Training, *Cultural Diversity Program*; Scott, "Cultural Awareness Training."

60. S. M. Hennessy, C. Hendricks, and J. Hendricks, "Cultural Awareness and Communication Training: What Works and What Doesn't," *Police Chief* 68 (2001), 15–19.

61. M. Sherwood "Developing a Multifaceted Approach to Hispanic Outreach," *The Police Chief* 78 (March 2011), 54–55.

62. Sherwood, "Developing a Multifaceted Approach to Hispanic Outreach," 55.

63. S. Walker, *Police Accountability: The Role of Citizen Oversight* (Belmont, CA: Wadsworth, 2001), 44.

64. M. J. Hickman, *Citizen Complaints About Police Use of Force* (Washington, DC: U.S. Department of Justice, June 2006), available from http://www.ojp.usdoj.gov/bjs/pub/pdf/ccpuf.pdf.

65. Ibid.

66. R. Johnson, "Citizen Complaints: What the Police Should Know," *FBI Law Enforcement Bulletin* 67 (December 1998), 1–5.

67. J. Rojek, G. P. Alpert, and H. P. Smith, "Examining Officer and Citizen Accounts of Police Use-of-Force Incidents," *Crime & Delinquency* 58, no. 2 (March 2012), 301–327.

68. A. Clemmons and R. Rosenthal, "Mediating Citizen Complaints: The Denver Program," *Police Chief* LXXV, no. 8 (2008), available from http://www.ncjrs.gov.

69. R. J. Homant, "Citizen Attitudes and Complaints," pp. 54–63 in W. G. Bailey (Ed.), *The Encyclopedia of Police Science* (New York, NY: Garland Press, 1989); Walker, *Police Accountability*, 20–21, 53–80; S. Walker, C. Spohn, and M. DeLone, *The Color of Justice: Race, Ethnicity, and Crime in America* (Belmont, CA: Wadsworth, 1995), 106–107.

70. M. S. Stroshine and S. G. Brandl, "Race, Gender, and Tokenism in Policing: An Empirical Elaboration," *Police Quarterly* 14, no. 4 (2011), 344–365.

71. R. Kanter, *Men and Women of the Corporation* (New York, NY: Basic Books, 1977); S. E. Martin, "Female Officers on the Move? A Status Report on Women in Policing," pp. 312–329 in R. G. Dunham and G. P. Alpert (Eds.), *Critical Issues in Policing: Contemporary Issues* (Prospect Heights, IL: Waveland, 1993).

72. D. J. Bell, "Policewomen—Myths and Reality," *Journal of Police Science and Administration* 10 (1982), 112–120; C. H. House, "The Changing Role of Women in Law Enforcement," *The Police Chief* 60 (1993), 139–144.

73. P. Horne, *Women in Law Enforcement* (Springfield, IL: Charles Thomas, 1980).

74. B. R. Price, "A History of Women in Policing" (National Center for Women in Policing, 1996), available from http://womenandpolicing.com/history/historytext.htm.

75. FBI, *Crime in the United States* (2013), available from https://www.fbi.gov/about-us/cjis/ucr/crime-in-the-u.s/2013/crime-in-the-u.s.-2013.

76. D. Orrick, "Recruiting During the Economic Turndown," *The Police Chief* 79, no. 1. (January 2012), 22–24, available from http://www.policechiefmagazine.org/magazine/index.cfm?fuseaction=display&article_id=2577&issue_id=.

77. S. E. Martin and N. C. Jurik, *Doing Justice, Doing Gender: Women in Legal and Criminal Justice Occupations*, 2nd ed. (Thousand Oaks, CA: Sage, 2006), 58.

78. L. Fry, "A Preliminary Examination of the Factors Related to Turnover of Women in Law Enforcement," *Journal of Police Science and Administration* 11 (1983), 149–155; W. Harris, "Recruiting Women: Are We Doing Enough?" *Police* 23 (1999), 18–23.

79. S. E. Martin, "Female Officers on the Move? A Status Report on Women in Policing," pp. 312–329 in R. G. Dunham and G. P. Alpert (Eds.), *Critical Issues in Policing: Contemporary Issues* (Prospect Heights, IL: Waveland, 1993).

80. W. P. McCarty, J. Zhao, and B. E. Garland, "Occupational Stress and Burnout Between Male and Female Police Officers: Are There Any Gender Differences?" *Policing* 30, no. 4 (2007), 672; M. Pogrebin, M. Dodge, and H. Chatman, "Reflections of African-American Women on Their Careers in Urban Policing. Their Experiences of Racial and Sexual Discrimination," *International Journal of the Sociology of Law* 28 (2000), 311–326.

81. J. Balkin, "Why Policemen Don't Like Policewomen," *Journal of Police Science and Administration* 16 (1988), 29–37.

82. Harris, "Recruiting Women," 18.
83. M. C. Grown and R. D. Carlson, "Do Male Policemen Accept Women on Patrol Yet? Androgyny, Public Complaints, and Dad," *Journal of Police and Criminal Psychology* 9 (1993), 10–14.
84. M. E. Gold, "The Progress of Women in Policing," *Law & Order* 48 (2000), 159–161.
85. Balkin, "Why Policemen Don't Like Policewomen," 34.
86. M. T. Charles, "Women in Policing—The Physical Aspect," *Journal of Police Science and Administration* 10 (1982), 194–205; J. McDowell, "Are Women Better Cops?" (*Time,* February 17, 1992), 70–72; Rogers (1987), as cited in Balkin, "Why Policemen Don't Like Policewomen."
87. Gold, "The Progress of Women in Policing"; R. J. Homant and D. B. Kennedy, "Police Perceptions of Spouse Abuse—A Comparison of Male and Female Officers," *Journal of Criminal Justice* 13 (1985), 29–47; Martin, "Female Officers on the Move?"; L. J. Sherman, "Evaluation of Policewomen on Patrol in a Suburban Police Department," *Journal of Police Science and Administration* 3 (1975), 434–438.
88. D. J. Bell, "Policewomen—Myths and Reality," *Journal of Police Science and Administration* 10 (1982), 112–120; M. G. Breci, "Female Officers on Patrol: Public Perceptions in the 1990s," *Journal of Crime & Justice* 20 (1997), 153–166.
89. B. Cohen, "Are Female Cops a Safety Risk? One Cop's Answer," *Women Police* 34 (2000), 3.
90. E. Linn and B. R. Price, "The Evolving Role of Women in American Policing," pp. 69–80 in A. S. Blumberg and E. Niederhoffer (Eds.), *The Ambivalent Force: Perspectives on the Police*, 3rd ed. (New York, NY: Holt, Rinehart and Winston, 1985).
91. V. E. Kappeler, "A Brief History of Slavery and the Origins of American Policing" (Eastern Kentucky University, 2014), available from http://plsonline.eku edu/insidelook/brief-history-slavery-and-origins-american-policing.
92. H. Williams and P. V. Murphy, *The Evolving Strategy of the Police: A Minority View* (National Institute of Justice, 1990), available from https://www.ncjrs.gov/pdffiles1/nij/121019.pdf
93. Williams and Murphy, *The Evolving Strategy of the Police*, 2.
94. N. Alex, *Black in Blue* (New York, NY: Appleton-Century-Crofts, 1969).
95. P. C. Moskos, "Two Shades of Blue: Black and White in the Blue Brotherhood," *Law Enforcement Executive Forum* 5 (2008), 57–86; Alex, *Black in Blue.*
96. R. A. Brown and J. Frank, "Race and Officer Decision Making: Examining Differences in Arrest Outcomes Between Black and White Officers," *Justice Quarterly* 23 (2006), 96–127.
97. C. Jackson and I. Wallach, "Perceptions of the Police in a Black Community," pp. 382–403 in J. R. Snibbe and H. M. Snibbe (Eds.), *The Urban Police in Transition*

(Springfield, IL: Charles C. Thomas, 1973); Alex, *Black in Blue*; N. Alex, *New York Cops Talk Back* (New York, NY: Wiley, 1976).
98. Alex, *Black in Blue.*
99. J. C. Cochran and P. Y. Warren, "Racial, Ethnic, and Gender Differences in Perceptions of the Police: The Salience of Officer Race Within the Context of Racial Profiling," *Journal of Contemporary Criminal Justice* 28, no. 2 (2012), 206–227.
100. J. B. Jacobs and J. Cohen, "The Impact of Racial Integration on the Police," *Journal of Police Science and Administration* 6 (1978), 179–183.
101. Brown and Frank, "Race and Officer Decision Making."
102. P. C. Moskos, "Two Shades of Blue: Black and White in the Blue Brotherhood," *Law Enforcement Executive Forum* 5 (2008), 57–86.
103. R. Uranga, "More Latino Officers Than Whites in LAPD Now," *Los Angeles Daily News* (February 20, 2008), available from http://www.dailynews.com/20080220/more-latino-officers-than-whites-in-lapd-now.
104. "Hispanics and the Criminal Justice System," *State News Service* (April 7, 2009), available from http://www.lexisnexis.com.
105. S. M. DiPietro and R. J. Bursik, "Studies of the New Immigration: The Dangers of Pan-ethnic Classifications," *Annals of The American Academy of Political & Social Science* 641, no. 1 (2012), 247–267.
106. Humes et al., *Overview of Race and Hispanic Origin: 2010.*
107. M. Navarro, "For Hispanics, Extra Barriers Can Complicate College More," *The New York Times*, Section A (February 10, 2009), 14.
108. D. L. Carter and A. D. Sapp, *Police Education and Minority Recruitment: The Impact of a College Requirement* (Washington, DC: Police Executive Research Forum, 1991).
109. D. W. Chen, "In New York City, a Toll Is Newly Felt as Asians Rise in the Police Ranks" (*The New York Times*, January 3, 2015), available from http://www.nytimes.com/2015/01/04/nyregion/in-new-york-city-a-toll-is-newly-felt-as-asians-rise-in-the-police-ranks.html?ref=topics&_r=0
110. A. N. Ancheta, *Race, Rights and the Asian American Experience,* 2nd ed. (Chapel Hill, NC: Rutgers University Press, 2006).
111. J. Berger, "Influx of Asians in New Jersey Is Not Reflected in Police Ranks," *The New York Times* (May 1, 2006, available from http://www.nytimes.com.
112. Voice of America, "US Police Departments Face Challenges Recruiting Asian-Americans" (March 7, 2012), available from http://www.voanews.com/content/us-police-departments-face-challenges-recruiting-asian-americans-141905613/180743.html.
113. D. D. Daye, *A Law Enforcement Sourcebook of Asian Crime and Cultures: Tactics and Mind Sets* (Boca Raton, FL: CRC Press, 1997).
114. C. C. Doris and S. J. H. Linda, "Chinese Immigrants' Attitudes Toward the Police in San Francisco," *Policing* 33, no. 4 (2010), 621–643.

115. T. Lin, *Chinese-American Police Officers in New York City* (Unpublished master's thesis, Western Illinois University, Macomb, IL, 1987).
116. Chen, "In New York City, a Toll Is Newly Felt as Asians Rise in the Police Ranks."
117. A. Belkin and J. McNichol, "Pink and Blue: Outcomes Associated With the Integration of Open Gay and Lesbian Personnel in the San Diego Police Department," *Police Quarterly* 3, no. 1 (2002), 63–95; A. C. Wooditch and J. M. Ruiz, "Out of the Closet and Into the Blue: An Inquiry Into Biases in Policing," *Police Forum* 18, no. 2 (2009), available from http://www.sulross.edu/policeforum/docs/archives/Volume_18_ Number_2.pdf.
118. E. Fletcher, "Roseville Police Settle Anti-gay Discrimination Suit," *McClatchy—Tribune Business News* (May 11, 2011), available from http://search.proquest.com.ezproxy.wiu.edu/docview/865912888?account id=14982; N. Jurik, S. Miller, and K. Forest, "Diversity in Blue: Lesbian and Gay Police Officers in a Masculine Occupation," *Men and Masculinities* 5, no. 4 (2003), 355–385.
119. Belkin and McNichol, "Pink and Blue."
120. *Childers v. Dallas Police Department*, 671 F. 2d 1380
121. Ibid.
122. Police Women in Law Enforcement, "Residents of Small S.C. Town Rally Behind Fired Lesbian Police Chief" (April 29, 2014), available from http://www.policemag.com/channel/women-in-law-enforcement/news/2014/04/29/residents-of-small-south-carolina-town-rally-behind-fired-lesbian-police-chief.aspx.
123. Gay and Lesbian Liaison Unit, *About the Gay and Lesbian Liaison Unit* (Washington, DC: Author, 2009), available from http://www.gllu.org/resources/index.htm#pubs.
124. H. MacWilliams, "IMPD to Walk in Gay Pride Parade for First Time," *McClatchy—Tribune Business News* (June 9, 2011), available from http://search.proquest.com.ezproxy.wiu.edu/docview/871 120925?accountId=114982.
125. S. L. Miller, K. B. Forest, and N. C. Jurik, "Diversity in Blue: Lesbian and Gay Police Officers in a Masculine Occupation," *Men and Masculinities* 5, no. 4 (2003), 355–385.

## ■ CHAPTER 13

1. D. J. Roberts, "Technology Is Playing an Expanding Role in Policing," *The Police Chief* 78 (January 2011), 72–73, available from http://www.nxtbook.com/nxtbooks/naylor/CPIM0111/#/72.
2. J. Byrne and G. Marx, "Technological Innovations in Crime Prevention and Policing: A Review of the Research on Implementation and Impact," *Journal of Police Studies* 3, no. 20 (2011), 17–40, available from https://www.ncjrs.gov/pdffiles1/nij/238011.pdf.
3. *Kyllo v. United States*, 533 U.S. 27 (2001).
4. Byrne and Marx, "Technological Innovations in Crime Prevention and Policing."

5. S. Dye, "Policing in Local Law Enforcement: A Commitment to Getting Out-of-the-Car," *The Police Chief* 76, no. 10 (October 2009), available from http://www.policechiefmagazine.org/magazine/index.cfm?fuseaction=display&article_id=1908&issue_id=102009.

6. S. Nunn, "Police Information Technology: Assessing the Effects of Computerization on Urban Police Functions," *Public Administration Review* 61, no. 2 (2001), 221–234.

7. G. Marx, "A Tack in the Shoe and Taking Off the Shoe: Neutralization and Counter-neutralization Dynamics," *Surveillance and Society* (2009), available from http://web.mit.edu/gtmarx/www/shoe.pdf.

8. Benchmark Institute, "Expert Witness," *Federal Rules of Evidence* (2012), available from http://www.benchmarkinstitute.org/t_by_t/expert/index.htm.

9. *Daubert v. Merrell Dow Pharmaceuticals, Inc.*, 43 F. 3d 1311—Court of Appeals, 9th Circuit (1995).

10. For example, *Frye v. United States* 293F, 1013 [1923]).

11. B. Reaves, *Local Police Departments, 2007* (NCJ 231174) (U.S. Department of Justice, 2010), available from http://bjs.ojp.usdoj.gov/index.cfm?ty=pbdetail&iid=1750.

12. B. A. Reaves, *Local Police Departments, 2013: Equipment and Technology* (Bureau of Justice Statistics, 2015), available from http://www.bjs.gov/content/pub/pdf/lpd13et.pdf.

13. K. Buczynski, "New Computer System for Local police," *SSPTV.com* (2012), available from http://ssptv.com/new/new-computer-system-for-local-police/.

14. Dispatch Magazine Online, *Mobile Data for Public Safety* (2012), available from http://www.911dispatch.com/info/mobiledata.html.

15. P. Paterra, "Pa. Police to Watch Schools With Help of Laptops: The Video Feeds Are to Be Used Only in Emergencies," *PoliceOne* (2010), available from http://www.policeone.com/police-technology/mobile-computers/articles/1995855-Pa-police-to-watch-schools-with-help-of-laptops/.

16. J. Rivera, "Magically Scan Documents and Photos on Patrol," *PoliceOne* (May 22, 2012), available from http://www.policeone.com/police-products/investigation/Investigative-Software/articles/5587149-Magically-scan-documents-and-photos-on-patrol/.

17. R. Boba, *Crime Analysis With Crime Mapping* (Thousand Oaks, CA: Sage, 2009).

18. Paterra, "Pa. Police to Watch Schools With Help of Laptops."

19. *United States v. Jones*, 132 S. Ct. 945, 565 U.S. ___ (2012).

20. D. Wyllie, "Product Review: Silvercloud GPS Tracker From LandAirSea," *PoliceOne.com News* (2012), available from http://www.policeone.com.

21. L. Greenemeier, "What Is the Big Secret Surrounding Stingray Surveillance?" *Scientific American* (June 25, 2015), available from http://www.scientificamerican.com/article/what-is-the-big-secret-surrounding-stingray-surveillance/?page=2; ACLU, "Stingray Tracking Devices," available from https://www.aclu.org/issues/privacy-technology/surveillance-technologies/stingray-tracking-devices.

22. National Institute of Justice, *MAPS: Automobiles and Traffic Safety* (Washington, DC: U.S. Department of Justice, 2009a), available from http://www.ojp.usdoj.gov/nij/maps/traffic-safety-projects.htm.

23. Ibid.

24. F. Spielman, "Computers Bringing Police Files to Cop Cars in Chicago: 'Squad Cars of the Future,'" *The Associated Press* (October 27, 2004), available from http://www.policegrantshelp.com/news/93093-Computers-Bringing-Police-Files-to-Cop-Cars-in.

25. Ibid.

26. J. DuBois, W. Skogan, S. Hartnett, N. Bump, and D. Morris, *CLEAR and I-CLEAR: A Report on New Information Technology in Chicago and Illinois* (Evanston, IL: Illinois Criminal Justice Authority, August 2007), available from www.idaillinois.org/cdm/compoundobject/collection/ed/id/84264/rec/17.

27. A. Chansanchai, *No Lie: Polygraph Exams Go Portable. Shrinking Technology Means Professional Examiners Can Easily Come to You* (April 16, 2008), available from http://www.msnbc.msn.com/id/24114951/ns/technology_and_science-tech_and_gadgets/.

28. B. Deedman, *New Anti-Terror Weapon: Hand-Held Lie Detector* (April 9, 2008), available from http://www.msnbc.msn.com/id/23926278/.

29. Brickhouse Security, *Portable Voice Lie Detector* (2010), available from http://www.brickhousesecurity.com/portable-lie-detector.html.

30. U.S. Department of Labor, "Fact Sheet #36: Employee Polygraph Protection Act of 1988" (2008), available http://www.dol.gov/whd/regs/compliance/whdfs36.htm.

31. Ibid.

32. T. Dees, "Will We Ever Have a True Lie Detector?" *PoliceOne.com News* (2012), available from http://www.policeone.com.

33. Dees, "Will We Ever Have a True Lie Detector?" 1.

34. L. Wilson and W. Spencer, "The Impact of *Kyllo*: Don't Discard Those Thermal Imaging Devices," *The Police Chief* 68, no. 6 (2001), 10–12.

35. Schultz, P. D. (2008). The future is here: Technology in police departments. *The Police Chief, 75*(6), 19–27.

36. D. Wyllie, "IACP 2010: New Real-Time Video Capabilities From Motorola," *PoliceOne* (October 28, 2010), available from http://www.policeone.com/police-products/radios/surveillance/articles/2853876-IACP-2010-New-real-time-video-capabilities-from-Motorola/.

37. B. Keoun, "Video Cameras in Squad Cars Gain Popularity Among Police [Electronic version]," *Chicago Tribune,* Sec. 2 (May 22, 2000), 2.

38. Wyllie, "IACP 2010," p. 1.

39. International Association of Chiefs of Police (IACP), *In-Car Camera Report* (Alexandria, VA: IACP Research Center Directorate, 2005), available from http://www.theiacp.org/PublicationsGuides/Projects/InCarCameraTechnicalAssistance/2005IACPIncarCameraReport/tabid/340/Default.aspx.

40. IACP, *In-Car Camera Report*; see also Maghan, J., O'Reilly, G. W., & Chong Ho Shon, "Technology, Policing, and Implications of In-Car Videos," *Police Quarterly* 5, no. 1 (2002), 25–42.

41. J. Sink, "Obama to Provide Funding for 50,000 Police Body Cameras," *The Hill* (2014), available from http://thehill.com/homenews/administration/225583-obama-to-provide-funding-for-50000-police-body-cameras.

42. M. D. White, *Police Officer Body-Worn Cameras: Assessing the Evidence* (Washington, DC: Office of Community Oriented Policing Services, 2014).

43. National Institute of Justice, "Research on Body-Worn Cameras and Law Enforcement," available from http://www.nij.gov/topics/law-enforcement/technology/pages/body-worn-cameras.aspx; Reaves, *Local Police Departments, 2013*.

44. J. Sanburn, "Los Angeles Plans to Outfit Every Cop With a Camera," *Time* (December 16, 2014), available from http://time.com/3636478/body-cameras-lapd-ferguson/.

45. "Cops See It Differently, Part 2," *This American Life* (February 15, 2015), available from http://www.thisamericanlife.org/radio-archives/episode/548/transcript.

46. J. Stanley, *Police Body-Mounted Cameras: With Right Policies in Place, A Win for All* (ACLU, 2015), available from https://www.aclu.org/police-body-mounted-cameras-right-policies-place-win-all.

47. The Crime Report, "ACLU Phone App Preserves Video of Police Encounters" (*The Crime Report*, May 7, 2015), available from http://www.thecrimereport.org/news/crime-and-justice-news/2015-05-aclu-phone-app-preserves-video-of-police-encounters.

48. R. Grenoble, "Teens Create 'Five-O' App to Help Record Police Brutality," *The Huffington Post* (August 18, 2014), available from http://www.huffingtonpost.com/2014/08/18/teens-police-brutality-app_n_5687934.html.

49. T. Harris, "How Wiretapping Works," *HowStuffWorks.com* (May 8, 2001), available from http://people.howstuffworks.com/wire tapping.htm.

50. Ibid.

51. K. Zetter, "FBI Use of Patriot Act Authority Increased Dramatically in 2008," *Wired* (May 19, 2009), available from http://www.wired.com/threatlevel/2009/05/fbi-use-of-patriot-act-authority-increased-dramatically-in-2008/.

52. M. Farrell, "Obama Signs Patriot Act Extension Without Reforms," *The Christian Science Monitor* (March 1, 2010), available from http://www.csmonitor.com/USA/Politics/2010/0301/Obama-signs-Patriot-Act-extension-without-reforms.

53. R. Singel, "Inside DCSNet, the FBI's Nationwide Eavesdropping Network: Surveillance System Lets FBI Play Back Recordings as They Are Captured, Like TiVo," *ABC News* (August 28, 2007), available from http://www.abcnews.go.com/Technology/story?id=3535528&page=1.

54. Ibid.

55. Ibid.

56. IACP Aviation Committee, "Recommended Guidelines for the Use of Unmanned Aircraft" (2012), available from http://www.theiacp.org/portals/0/pdfs/IACP_UAGuidelines.pdf.

57. IACP, "Technology Policy Framework" (2014), available from http://www.theiacp.org/Portals/0/documents/pdfs/IACP%20Technology%20Policy%20Framework%20January%202014%20Final.pdf.

58. Paterra, "Pa. Police to Watch Schools With Help of Laptops."

59. T. Hughes, "Police Partner With License Plate Readers," *USA Today* (March 4, 2010), 3A.

60. P. D. Schultz, "The Future Is Here: Technology in Police Departments," *The Police Chief* 75, no. 6 (2008), 19–27.

61. Hughes, "Police Partner With License Plate Readers."

62. C. Lum, J. Hibdon, B. Cave, C. S. Koper, and L. Merola, "License Plate Reader (LPR) Police Patrols in Crime Hot Spots: An Experimental Evaluation in Two Adjacent Jurisdictions," *Journal of Experimental Criminology* 7, no. 4 (2011), 321–345.

63. NetworkCameraReviews.com, *What Is an IP Camera?* (2009), available from http://www.networkcamerareviews.com.

64. Connect802, *Understanding Wireless IP Cameras* (n.d.), from http://www.connect802.com/camera_facts.htm.

65. "Drone Use Takes Off on Home Front," *The Wall Street Journal* (April 20, 2012), available from http://www.myfoxdc.com/dpps/news/drone-use-takes-off-on-home-front-dpgonc-20120420-fc_19305791#ixzz1scKWmINg.

66. Ibid.

67. Ibid.

68. P. Repard, "Police Chiefs Groups Offer Drone-Use Policy," *San Diego Union Tribune* (May 20, 2015), available from http://www.utsandiego.com/news/2015/may/20/drones-unmanned-aircraft-iacp-law-enforcement/2/?#article-copy.

69. L. Grossman, "The New Cop on the Beat May Be a Bot," *Time* (April 16, 2014), available from http://time.com/65021/robot-cop/.

70. Electronic Frontier Foundation, "FAA Releases New Drone List—Is Your Town on the Map?" available from https://www.eff.org/deeplinks/2013/02/faa-releases-new-list-drone-authorizations-your-local-law-enforcement-agency-map.

71. R. Boba, *Crime Analysis With Crime Mapping* (Thousand Oaks, CA: Sage, 2009).

72. R. Boba, *Introductory Guide to Crime Analysis and Mapping* (Washington, DC: Community Oriented Policing Services, 2001), available from http://www.policefoundationorg/pdf.introguide.pdf.

73. Boba, *Introductory Guide to Crime Analysis and Mapping*, 19.

74. M. White and T. Wiles, "Jacksonville Sheriff's Office: Mapping With Text Analysis," *Crime Mapping News* 8, no. 1 (2009), 1–5.

75. Ibid.

76. S. Bair, "New Trends in Advanced Crime and Intelligence Analysis: Understanding the Utility and Capability of ATAC in Law Enforcement," *Crime Mapping News* 8, no. 1 (2009), 6–9.

77. National Institute of Justice, *MAPS: Geospatial Tools* (Washington, DC: U.S. Department of Justice, 2009b), available from http://www.ojp.usdoj.gov/nij/maps/tools.htm.

78. V. Furtado, C. Caminha, L. Ayres, and H. Santos, "Open Government and Citizen Participation in Law Enforcement via Crowd Mapping," *Intelligent Systems, IEEE*, 27, no. 4 (2012), 63–69.

79. J. Keyser, "Chicago Police Can Be Recorded at NATO Summit," *Journal Star* (Peoria, April 29, 2012), B7.

80. M. Tarm, "Illinois Supreme Court Deals Final Blow to State's Harsh Eavesdropping Law," *The Huffington Post* (March 20, 2014).

81. Ibid.

82. Worsley School, *Fingerprints* (2001), available from http://www.worsleyschool.net/science/files/finger/prints.html.

83. T. Harris, "How Fingerprint Scanners Work," *HowStuffWorks.com* (n.d.), available from http://www.computer.howstuffworks.com/fingerprint-scanner.htm.

84. A. Winston, "Facial Recognition, Once a Battlefield Tool, Lands in San Diego County" (The Center for Investigative Reporting, November 7, 2013), available from http://cironline.org/reports/facial-recognition-once-battlefield-tool-lands-san-diego-county-5502.

85. Ibid.

86. Federal Bureau of Investigation, "Next Generation Identification (NGI)," available from https://www.fbi.gov/about-us/cjis/fingerprints_biometrics/ngi.

87. P. Moser, *The Vital Role of Forensic Science: Forensics Has Led to Increased Conviction Rates* (January 19, 2008), available from http://forensicscience.suite101.com/article.cfm/the_role_of_forensic_science#ixzz0iveRxHD1.

88. Human Genome Project Information, *DNA Forensics* (Washington, DC: U.S. Department of Energy, Office of Science, June 16, 2009), available from http://www.ornl.gov/sci/techresources/Human_Genome/elsi/forensics.shtml.

89. International Biosciences, *DNA Tests: Impact on Death Row* (2010), available from http://www.ibdna.com/regions/UK/EN/?page=impactOnDeathRow.

90. National Human Genome Research Institute, *DNA Microchip Technology* (2009), available from http://www.genome.gov/10000205.

91. "More Accurate Than DNA? Hand Germs Could ID Criminals" (2011), available from http://gajitz.com/more-accurate-than-dna-hand-germs-could-id-criminals/.

92. Ibid.

93. D. H. Kaye, "Bioethical Objections to DNA Databases for Law Enforcement: Questions and Answers," *Seton Hall Law Review* 31, no. 4 (2001), 936–948.

94. "Bacterial Forensics: Tracing a Suspect From the Microbes on Their Shoes," Phys.org (May 11, 2015).

95. Ibid.

96. S. R. Tridico, C. M. Dáithí, J. Addison, K. P. Kirkbride, and M. Bunce, "Metagenomic Analyses of Bacteria on Human Hairs: A Qualitative Assessment for Applications in Forensic Science," *Investigative Genetics* 5, no. 16 (2014), available from http://www.investigativegenetics.com/content/5/1/16.

97. D. S. Sawicki, "Police Traffic Radar Handbook: A Comprehensive Guide to Speed Measuring Systems," *CopRadar.com* (2009), available from http://www.CopRadar.com.

98. Ibid.

99. *Laser Radar: Lidar, Ladar Facts* (2010), available from http://www.RadarGuns.com.

100. Michigan State Police, *Speed Measurement Devices* (2010), available from http://www.michigan.gov/msp/0,1607,7–123–1593_47090_25002–10134,00.html.

101. Traffic Safety Systems, Inc., *VASCAR-Plus® Home Page* (Richmond, VA: Author, March 30, 2010), available from http://www.vascarplus.com.

102. M. Niederberger, "Police Device Finds Speeders Without Radar," *Pittsburgh Post-Gazette* (September 29, 2008), available March 30, 2010, from http://www.policeone.com/police-products/traffic-enforcement/articles/1738131-Police-device-finds-speeders-without-radar/.

103. Ibid.

104. I. Harris, "How Body Armor Works," *HowStuffWorks.com* (2008), available from http://science.howstuffworks.com/body-armor.htm.

105. National Institute of Justice, *Body Armor* (Washington, DC: U.S. Department of Justice, 2008a), available from http://www.ojp.usdoj.gov/nij/topics/technology/body-armor/welcome.htm.

106. Ibid.

107. D. Tompkins, "Body Armor Safety Initiative: To Protect and Serve . . . Better," *NIJ Journal* 254 (2006), available from http://www.ojp.usdoj.gov/nij/journals/254/body_armor_html.

108. Reaves, *Local Police Departments, 2007*.

109. Y. A. Zakhary, "Ballistic Body Armor: A Chief's Refresher Course," *The Police Chief* 74, no. 12 (2007), 1–7. Retrieved from http://policechiefmagazine.org.

110. K. Bonsor, *How the Future Force Warrior Will Work* (2010), available from http://science.howstuffworks.com/ffw.htm/.

111. J. Jussila, "Future Police Operations and Non-lethal Weapons," *Medicine, Conflict and Survival* 17, no. 3 (2001), 248–259.

112. National Institute of Justice (NIJ), *Types of Less-Lethal Devices* (Washington, DC: U.S. Department of Justice, 2008b), available from http://www.ojp.usdoj.gov/nij/topics/technology/less-lethal/types.htm.

113. G. P. Alpert, M. R. Smith, R. J. Kaminski, L. A. Fridell, J. MacDonald, and B. Kubu, *Police Use of Force, Tasers and Other Less-Lethal Weapons* (Washington, DC: National Institute of Justice, 2011), available from https://www.ncjrs.gov/pdffiles1/nij/232215.pdf

114. NIJ, *Types of Less-Lethal Devices*.

115. M. D. White, J. Ready, C. Riggs, D. M. Dawes, A. Hinz and J. D. Ho, "An Incident-Level Profile of TASER Device Deployments in Arrest-Related Deaths," *Police Quarterly* 16, no. 1 (2012), 85–112.

116. Officer.com, *Talon Net Gun System* (2010), available from http://www.directory.officer.com.

117. J. M. Lakoski, W. B. Murray, and J. M. Kenny, *The Advantages and Limitations of Calmatives for Use as a Non-lethal Technique* (University Park, PA: Pennsylvania State University, 2000), in J. D. Weiss, *Calming Down: Could Sedative Drugs Be a Less-Lethal Option?* (Washington, DC: U.S. Department of Justice, National Institute of Justice, 2008), available from http://www.ojp.usdoj.gov/nij/journals/261/calmatives.htm.

118. A. Achanta, *Non-linear Acoustic Concealed Weapons Detector* (Blacksburg, VA: Luna Innovations, May 2006), available from http://www.stormingmedia.us/05/0520/A052054.html?searchTerms=Non-linear~acoustic~concealed~weapons~detector; N. Wild, *Handheld Concealed Weapons Detector Development. JAYCOR* (March 2003), available from http://www.stormingmedia.us/keywords/infrared_detection.html.

119. R. Nordland, "The Evil Solution," *Newsweek* (December 19, 2008), available from http://www.newsweek.com/id/175980/page/3.

120. Roberts, "Technology Is Playing an Expanding Role in Policing."

## ■ CHAPTER 14

1. J. Sheptycki, "Criminology and the Transnational Condition: A Contribution to International Political Sociology," *International Political Sociology* 1, no. 4 (2007), 391.

2. Ibid.

3. Federal Bureau of Investigation (FBI), *Organized Crime* (Washington, DC: Author, 2010b), available from http://www.fbi.gov/hq/cid/orgcrime/glossary.htm.

4. Ibid.

5. H. Abadinsky, *Organized Crime*, 9th ed. (Belmont, CA: Wadsworth, 2010), 2–5.

6. United Nations, *The Globalization of Crime: A Transnational Organized Crime Threat Assessment* (United Nations Office on Drugs and Crime, 2010).

7. C. M. Renzetti, A. Bush, M. Castellanos, and G. Hunt, "Does Training Make a Difference? An Examination of a Specialized Human Trafficking Training Module for Law Enforcement Officers," *Journal of Crime and Justice* (Advance online publication, 2015). doi: 10.1080/0735648X.2014.997913

8. "Times Topics: Organized Crime," *The New York Times* (June 6, 2012), available from http://topics.nytimes.com/top/reference/timestopics/subjects/o/organized_crime/index.html.

9. R. W. Taylor, E. J. Fritsch, and J. Liederbach, *Digital Crime and Digital Terrorism* (Upper Saddle River, NJ: Prentice Hall Press, 2014).

10. U.S. Department of Justice, "Justice News: Assistant Attorney General Leslie R. Caldwell Delivers Remarks at the Criminal Division's Cybersecurity Industry Roundtable" (April 29, 2015), available from http://www.justice.gov/opa/speech/assistant-attorney-general-leslie-r-caldwell-delivers-remarks-criminal-divisions.

11. J. Helmkamp, J. Ball, and K. Townsend, *Definitional Dilemma: Can and Should There Be a Universal Definition of White Collar Crime?* (Morgantown, WV: National White Collar Crime Center, 1996), 351.

12. Ibid.

13. As cited by E. McFayden Jr., "Global Implications of White Collar Crime," *Social Science Research Network* (January 3, 2010), available from http://ssrn.com/abstract=1530685.

14. As cited in C. Simonsen and J. Spindlove, *Terrorism Today: The Past, the Players, the Future* (Upper Saddle River, NJ: Prentice-Hall, 2000).

15. G. Martin, *Understanding Terrorism*, 2nd ed. (Thousand Oaks, CA: Sage, 2006), 48.

16. FBI Counterterrorism Analysis Section, "Sovereign Citizens: A Growing Domestic Threat to Law Enforcement," *FBI Law Enforcement Bulletin* (September 2011), available from http://www.fbi.gov/stats-services/publications/law-enforcement-bulletin/september-2011/sovereign-citizens.

17. W. Hu, "A Nation Challenged: The Suburbs; Small Towns Find Their Ingenuity Tested by Terrorist Threat," *The New York Times* (November 14, 2001), p. B6.

18. P. Williams, "Getting Rich and Getting Even: Transnational Threats in the Twenty-First Century," pp. 19–63 in S. Einstein and M. Amir (Eds.), *Organized crime: Uncertainties and Dilemmas* (Chicago, IL: Office of International Criminal Justice, 1999), 18.

19. A. Levinson, "Twenty-First Century Crime Goes Global," *Crime & Justice International* 15 (1999), 9–10, 33.

20. L. Shelley, "Crime Victimizes Both Society and Democracy," *Global Issues: Arresting Transnational Crime* (August 6, 2001), p. 2, available from http://usinfo.state.gov/journals/itgic/0801/ijge/gj06.htm.

21. Ibid.

22. S. McHugh, "Intelligence, Terrorism, and the New World Disorder," pp. 57–59 in C. Moors and R. Ward (Eds.), *Terrorism and the New World Disorder* (Chicago, IL: Office of International Criminal Justice, 1998), 57.

23. McHugh, "Intelligence, Terrorism, and the New World Disorder," 57–58.

24. White House, *President Establishes Office of Homeland Security* (October 8, 2001), available from http://www.whitehouse.gov/news/releases/2001/10/20011008.html.

25. U.S. General Accounting Office, *Homeland Security: Key Elements of a Risk Management Approach* (Washington, DC: Government Printing Office, 2001), 3–6.

26. R. Ward, K. Kiernan, and D. Marbrey, *Homeland Security: An Introduction* (Southington, CT: Anderson Publishing, 2006).

27. "U.S. Department of Homeland Security," available from http://www.dhs.gov/xlibrary/assets/dhs-orgchart.pdf.

28. R. Mueller III, "Responding to Terrorism," *FBI Law Enforcement Bulletin* 70 (December 2001), 12–14.

29. J. C. Carter, "Inter-organizational Relationships and Law Enforcement Information Sharing Post 11 September 2001," *Journal of Crime and Justice* (Advance online publication, 2014). doi: 10.1080/0735648X.2014.927786.

30. R. Ward, K. Kiernan, and D. Marbrey, *Homeland Security: An Introduction* (Southington, CT: Anderson Publishing, 2006), 241–258.

31. Racketeer Influenced and Corrupt Organizations ("RICO") Act, 18 U.S.C. §§ 1961–1968.

32. H. Abadinsky, *Organized Crime*, 9th ed. (Belmont, CA: Wadsworth, 2010).

33. Ibid.

34. A. Liptak and J. H. Cushman, "Blocking Parts of Arizona Law, Justices Allow Its Centerpiece," *The New York Times* (June 25, 2012), from http://www.nytimes.com/2012/06/26/us/supreme-court-rejects-part-of-arizona-immigration-law.html?pagewanted_all&_r=0.

35. H. Davies and M. Plotkin, *Protecting Your Community From Terrorism: The Strategies for Local Law Enforcement Series Vol. 5: Partnerships to Promote Homeland Security, Police Executive Research Forum* (Washington, DC: U.S. Department of Justice, Office of Community Oriented Policing Services, 2005).

36. D. Weisburd, B. Hasisi, T. Jonathan, and G. Aviv, "Terrorist Threats and Police Performance," *British Journal of Criminology* 50, no. 4 (2010), 725–747.

37. G. Scaramella and R. Rodriguez, "Local Law Enforcement and Transnational Crime Preparedness," *Illinois Law Enforcement Executive Forum* 4, no. 4 (2004), 169–181.

38. D. Cid, "The Next Worst Thing: Gathering and Analyzing Indicators and Warnings Comprise Crucial Intelligence Techniques," *FBI Law Enforcement Bulletin* (April 2012), available from http://www.fbi.gov/stats-services/publications/law-enforcement-bulletin/april-2012/the-next-worst-thing.

39. M. Cahill Jr., J. Kralik, R. Van Cura, and T. Hazard, "New York State's Counterterrorism Zone 4: A Model of Interagency Cooperation to Fight Terrorism," *Police Chief* 77, no. 2 (February 2010), available from http://www.policechiefmagazine.org/magazine/index.cfm?fuseaction=display&article_id=2012&issue_id=22010.

40. R. Esposito, M. James, and D. Schabner, "COPS: Times Square Car Bomber Got the Wrong Fertilizer," *ABC World News* (May 2, 2010), available from http://abcnews.go.com/WN/times-square-bomb-scare-york-authorities-probe-evidence/story?id=10532755&page=1.

41. As cited in L. O'Brien, "The Evolution of Terrorism Since 9/11," *FBI Law Enforcement Bulletin* (September 2011), available from http://www.fbi.gov/stats-services/publications/law-enforcement-bulletin/september-2011/the-evolution-of-terrorism-since-9–11.

42. T. Hayes, "FBI Sting Nets 24 Arrests in Online Financial Fraud," *USA Today: Technology* (June 27, 2012), p. 3B.

43. S. Rosoff, H. Pontell, and R. Tillman, *Profit Without Honor: White Collar Crime and the Looting of America*, 4th ed. (Upper Saddle River, NJ: Prentice-Hall, 2007).

44. G. Valiante, "Man Arrested in Montreal on Terrorism-Related Charge After His Family Tipped off Police," *The Canadian Press* (December 23, 2014), available from http://news.nationalpost.com/news/canada/man-arrested-in-montreal-on-terrorism-related-charge-after-his-family-tipped-off-police.

45. K. Bohn, "Anarchist Manual, Firearms Found in Motel Room With Ricin," *CNN* (2008), available from http://www.infowars.com/cops-make-ricin-anarchist-connection-in-las-vegas/.

46. U.S. Attorney's Office, "Man Who Formed Terrorist Group That Plotted Attacks on Military and Jewish Facilities Sentenced to 16 Years in Federal Prison," Los Angeles Division (2009), available from https://www.fbi.gov/losangeles/press-releases/2009/la030609ausa.htm.

47. L. Meyers, "Foiling Millennium Attack Was Mostly Luck: Plot to Bomb LAX Thwarted Despite Lack of Warning," *NBC News*. (2004), available from http://www.nbcnews.com/id/4864792/ns/nbc_nightly_news_with_brian_williams/t/foiling-millennium-attack-was-mostly-luck/#.VZnVn9Hn-P8.

48. M. Simon and J. Spellman, "'Tough Woman' Cop Hailed Fort Hood Hero," *CNN* (2009), available from: http://www.cnn.com/2009/CRIME/11/06/fort.hood.munley/index.html.

49. K. Morava, "Trooper Who Arrested Timothy McVeigh Shares Story," *The Shawnee News-Star* (2009), available from http://www.newsstar.com/article/20090225/NEWS/302259941.

50. C. Robinson, "Serial Bomber Eric Robert Rudolph Captured 10 Years Ago Today," Al.com (2013), available from http://blog.al.com/spotnews/2013/05/today_marks_the_10th_anniversa.html.

## ■ CHAPTER 15

1. A. Goldstein, "The Private Arm of the Law," The Washington Post (January 2, 2007), available from http://www.washingtonpost.com.

2. R. Fischer, E. Halibozek, and G. Green, *Introduction to Security*, 8th ed. (Boston, MA: Butterworth-Heinemann, 2008).

3. Ibid.

4. Ibid.

5. Ibid.

6. K. Strom, M. Berzofsky, B. Shook-Sa, K. Barrick, C. Daye, N. Horstmann, and S. Kinsey, *The Private Security Industry: A Review of the Definitions, Available Data Sources, and Paths Moving Forward Literature Review and Secondary Data Analysis* (RTI International and Bureau of Justice Statistics, 2010), available from https://www.ncjrs.gov/pdffiles1/bjs/grants/232781.pdf.

7. M. K. Nalla, *Police: Private Police and Industrial Security—Scope of Security Work, Nature of Security Work, Legal Authority, Public Vis-à-vis Private Police* (2009), available from http://law.jrank.org/pages/1691/Police-Private-Police-Industrial-Security.html.

8. Office of Community Oriented Policing Services (COPS), *National Policy Summit: Building Private Security/Public Policing Partnerships* (Washington, DC: U.S. Department of Justice, 2004), available from http://www.cops.usdoj.gov/.

9. K. Johnson, "Economy Limiting Services of Local Police," *USA Today* (May 17, 2009), available from http://www.usatoday.com/news/nation/2009–05–17-police-closure_N.htm; K. Johnson, "Cities Find Benefits in Mergers of Police," *USA Today* (February 24, 2012), 4A.

10. Johnson, "Cities Find Benefits in Mergers of Police," 2012.

11. H. F. Nasser, "Stop the Anti-white Hatred and Violence," *Cincinnati Post* (June 15, 1993), 9A.

12. Nalla, *Police*.

13. Bureau of Labor Statistics (BLS), "May 2014 National Occupational Employment and Wage Estimates: United States" (2014a), available from http://www.bls.gov/oes/current/oes_nat.htm#33-0000.

14. B. Zalud, "Security Officers: A Matter of Values," *Security: Solutions For Enterprise Security Leaders* 49, no. 2 (2012), 20–28.

15. BLS, "Occupational Employment and Wages, May 2014: 33-9032 Security Guards" (2014b), available from http://www.bls.gov/oes/current/oes339032.htm.

16. R. Fischer, E. Halibozek, and G. Green, *Introduction to Security*, 8th ed. (Boston, MA: Butterworth-Heinemann, 2008).

17. J. R. Bennett, "Police: Going Private," *ISN Security Watch*. (May 18, 2009), available from http://www.isn.ethz.ch/isn/Current-Affairs/Security-Watch/Detail/?lng=en&id=100297.

18. Ibid.

19. S. Rushin, "The Regulation of Private Police." *West Virginia Law Review* 115 (2012), 159–203.

20. BLS, *Occupational Outlook Handbook, 2008–09 Edition: Private Detectives and Investigators* (Washington, DC: U.S. Department of Labor, 2009), available from http://www.bls.gov/oco/ocos157.htm.

21. Zalud, "Security Officers."

22. Rushin, "The Regulation of Private Police."

23. BLS, *Occupational Outlook Handbook, 2012–13 Edition: Private Detectives and Investigators on the Internet* (March 29, 2012), available from http://www.bls.gov/ooh/protective-service/private-detectives-and-investigators.htm.

24. Zalud, "Security Officers."

25. BLS, *Occupational Outlook Handbook, 2008–09 Edition*.

26. BLS, *Occupational Outlook Handbook, 2012–13 Edition*.

27. Ibid.

28. BLS, "Private Detectives and Investigators," *Occupational Outlook Handbook* (July 2015), available from http://www.bls.gov/ooh/protective-service/private-detectives-and-investigators.htm.

29. BLS, *Occupational Outlook Handbook, 2012–13 Edition*.

30. Ibid.

31. Critical Intervention Services, *Threat Management Services/Executive Protection* (2012), available from http://cisworldservices.org/services/ep.html.

32. Nalla, *Police*.

33. BLS, *Occupational Outlook Handbook, 2008–09 Edition*.

34. Rushin, "The Regulation of Private Police."

35. Associated Criminal Justice and Security Consultants LLC, *Evaluation of Basic Training Programs in Law Enforcement, Security and Corrections* (Unpublished research paper, Kaplan University, Fort Lauderdale, FL, June 2005).

36. Strom et al., *The Private Security Industry*.

37. Fischer et al., *Introduction to Security*.

38. A. Goldstein, "The Private Arm of the Law," *The Washington Post*. (January 2, 2007), available from http://www.washingtonpost.com.

39. BLS, *Occupational Outlook Handbook, 2012–13 Edition*.

40. Goldstein, "The Private Arm of the Law."

41. J. Jouvenal, "Private Police Carry Guns and Make Arrests, and Their Ranks Are Swelling," *The Washington Post* (February 28, 2015), available from http://www.washingtonpost.com/local/crime/private-police-carry-guns-and-make-arrests-and-their-ranks-are-swelling/2015/02/28/29f6e02e-8f79-11e4-a900-9960214d4cd7_story.html?hpid=z3

42. Bennett, "Police."

43. Strom et al., *The Private Security Industry*.

44. L. T. Sherman, "LEN Interview: Lawrence Sherman," *Law Enforcement News* 16 (1990), 9–12.

45. Fischer et al., *Introduction to Security*, 60–61.

46. A. Morabito and S. Greenberg, *Engaging the Private Sector to Promote Homeland Security: Law Enforcement-Private Security Partnerships* (Rockville, MD: Bureau of Justice Assistance Clearinghouse, 2005); Fisher et al. 62

47. NYPD Shield, "Commissioner's Message" (2015), available from https://www.nypdshield.org/public/message.aspx.

48. Morabito and Greenberg, *Engaging the Private Sector to Promote Homeland Security*, vii.

49. Fischer et al., *Introduction to Security*.

50. ASIS International, *Press Release: Workplace Security Legislation Supported by ASIS International—Implemented by Department of Justice* (Alexandria, VA: Author, February 7, 2006), available from http://www.asisonline.org.

51. A. Youngs, "The Future of Public/Private Partnerships," *FBI Law Enforcement Bulletin* 73, no. 1 (2004), 7–12.

52. Fisher et al., *Introduction to Security*.

53. COPS, *National Policy Summit*.

54. M. K. Sparrow, "Managing the Boundary Between Public and Private Policing," *New Perspectives in Policing Bulletin* (NCJ 247182) (Washington, DC: U.S. Department of Justice, National Institute of Justice, 2014).

# ■ CHAPTER 16

1. G. Stephens, "Policing the Future: Law Enforcement's New Challenges," *The Futurist* 39, no. 2 (2005), 51–58.
2. Stephens, "Policing the Future," 52.
3. Federal Bureau of Investigation (FBI), "Eight Defendants Charged as Part of an Identity Theft Tax Refund Undercover Operation" (Press Release, 2012), available from www.fbi.gov.
4. E. A. Thibault, L. M. Lynch, and R. B. McBride, *Proactive Police Management*, 7th ed. (Upper Saddle River, NJ: Pearson Education, 2007), 464.
5. P. Zengerle, "Millions More Americans Hit by Government Personnel Data Hack" (Reuters, July 9, 2015), available from http://www.reuters.com/article/2015/07/09/us-cybersecurity-usa-idUSKCN0PJ2M420150709
6. E. Nakashima, "Hacks of OPM Databases Compromised 22.1 Million People, Federal Authorities Say," *The Washington Post* (July 9, 2015), available from http://www.washingtonpost.com/blogs/federal-eye/wp/2015/07/09/hack-of-security-clearance-system-affected-21-5-million-people-federal-authorities-say/.
7. J. M. Ortman and C. E. Guarneri, *United States Population Projections: 2000 to 2050* (2010), available from http://www.census.gov.
8. J. M. Ortman, V. A. Velkoff, and H. Hogan, *An Aging Nation: The Older Population in the United States* (P25-1140) (U.S. Department of Commerce, 2014), available from https://www.census.gov/prod/2014pubs/p25-1140.pdf.
9. C. J. Jensen and B. H. Levin, "The World of 2020: Demographic Shifts, Cultural Change, and Social Challenge," pp. 31–70 in J. A. Shafer (Ed.), *Policing 2020: Exploring the Future of Crime, Community and Policing* (Washington, DC: U.S. Department of Justice, FBI, Police Futurists International, 2007).
10. Ortman and Guarneri, *United States Population Projections*.
11. G. Houde and B. Cox, "Police Feel Sting of Recession: Departments Pare Programs, Purchases to Keep Cops on Streets," *Chicago Tribune* (April 22, 2009), available from http://www.policeone.com/pc_ print.asp?vid=1813441.
12. B. Melekian, "Director's Column," *Community Policing Dispatch* 4, 7 (June 2011), 1–2, available from http://cops.usdoj.gov/html/dispatch/06–2011/DirectorsMessage.asp.
13. R. Colvin, "U.S. Recession Fuels Crime Rise, Police Chiefs Say" (Reuters, January 27, 2009), available from http://www.reuters.com.
14. National Police Research Platform, *Current State of Knowledge About American Policing* (2012), available from http://www.nationalpoliceresearch.org.
15. President's Task Force on 21st Century Policing, "Listening Session: Building Trust and Legitimacy: Literature Review. Comprehensive Law Enforcement Review: Procedural Justice and Legitimacy: SUMMARY" (COPS, U.S. Department of Justice, 2015b), 1, available from http://www.cops.usdoj.gov/pdf/taskforce/Procedural-Justice-and-Legitimacy-LE-Review-Summary.pdf.
16. Ibid.
17. President's Task Force on 21st Century Policing, "Listening Session," 3.
18. President's Task Force on 21st Century Policing, *Final Report of the President's Task Force on 21st Century Policing* (Washington, DC: Office of Community Oriented Policing Services, 2015a), available from http://www.cops.usdoj.gov/pdf/taskforce/TaskForce_FinalReport.pdf.
19. J. Ruderman, "Looking Toward Agencies of the Future: Standard Technology for One Department May Be a Vision of the Future," *Officer.com* (2008), available from http://www.officer.com.
20. G. Wasserman, *Police Technology in the New Economy: Responsible and Sustainable Planning for the Future* (A keynote address at the 36th annual International Association of Chiefs of Police, Law Enforcement Management Training Conference and Technology Exposition, Indianapolis, IN, May 2012), 5, available from www.theiacp.org.
21. J. A. Conser and G. G. Frissora, "The Patrol Function in the Future—One Vision," pp. 173–208 in J. Shafer (Ed.), *Policing 2020: Exploring the Future of Crime, Community and Policing* (Washington, DC: U.S. Department of Justice, FBI, Police Futurist International, 2007).
22. Ibid.
23. Colvin, "U.S. Recession Fuels Crime Rise, Police Chiefs Say."
24. C. Beck and C. McCue, "Predictive Policing: What Can We Learn From Wal-Mart and Amazon About Fighting Crime in a Recession," *The Police Chief* 76(11 (2009), 20–29.
25. Ibid.
26. Portland Police Department, *Predictive Policing* (2012), available from police.portlandmaine.com.
27. NIJ, *Predictive Policing* (2010), available from http://www.nij.gov/topics/lawenforcement.
28. T. Casady, "Predictive Policing," *The Chief's Corner* (November 24, 2009), available from http://lpd304.blogspot.com/2009/11/predictive-policing.html.
29. U.S. Department of Justice, *Solicitation: Predictive Policing Demonstration and Evaluation Program* (Washington, DC: Author, 2009), available from http://www.ncjrs.gov/pdffiles1/nij/s1000877.pdf.
30. Ibid.
31. NIJ.
32. K. K. Koss, "Leveraging Predictive Policing Algorithms to Restore Fourth Amendment Protections in High-Crime Areas in a Post-Wardlow World," *Chi.-Kent. L. Rev.* 90, no. 1 (2015), available from http://scholarship.kentlaw.iit.edu/cklawreview/vol90/iss1/12.
33. Ibid.
34. Ibid.
35. R. F. Vodde, *Andragogical Instruction for Effective Police Training* (Amherst, NY: Cambria Press, 2009), 17.
36. S. Mastrofski, "Community Policing: A Skeptical View," pp. 44–76 in D. Weisburd and A. A. Braga (Eds.), *Police Innovation: Contrasting Perspectives* (New York, NY: Cambridge University Press, 2006).
37. M. J. Cetron and O. Davies, "55 Trends Now Shaping the Future of Policing," *The Proteus Trends Series* 1, no. 1 (2008), 1–200.
38. R. Cox, *Addressing the Shortage of Police Officers. Civilianizing Some Traditional Duties of Sworn Officers* (A Leadership White Paper, Sam Houston State University, Huntsville, TX, 2012), 2, available from digital.Library.shsu.edu.
39. J. Docobo, "Community Policing as the Primary Prevention Strategy for Homeland Security at the Local Law Enforcement Level," *Homeland Security Affairs* 1, no. 1 (2005), 23–30.
40. R. V. Clarke and G. R. Newman, "Police and the Prevention of Terrorism," *Policing* 1, no. 1 (2007), 9–20.
41. "Community Partnership: A Key Ingredient in an Effective Homeland Security Approach," *Community Policing Dispatch* 1, no. 2 (2008), available from cops.usdoj.gov/html/dispatch/February_2008/security.html.
42. CPD, 1.
43. Docobo, "Community Policing as the Primary Prevention Strategy for Homeland Security at the Local Law Enforcement Level."
44. G. L. Kelling and W. J. Bratton, "Policing Terrorism," *Civic Bulletin* 43 (2006), in COPS, "Community Partnerships: A Key Ingredient in an Effective Homeland Security Approach," *Community Policing Dispatch* 1, no. 2 (2008), 1–3.
45. R. Chapman and M. C. Scheider, *Community Policing: Now More Than Ever* (Washington, DC: U.S. Department of Justice, Office of Community Oriented Policing Services, 2008), available from http://www.cops.usdoj.gov.
46. Mastrofski, "Community Policing."
47. C. W. Ortiz, N. J. Hendricks, and N. F. Sugie, "Policing Terrorism: The Response of Local Police Agencies to Homeland Security Concerns," *Criminal Justice Studies: A Critical Journal of Crime, Law and Society* 20, no. 2 (2007), 91–109.
48. G. Tierney, "Intelligence-Led Policing Is a Flexible Tool," *Chronicle Online* (2012), available from http://www.chronicleonline.com.
49. M. Barrett, "The Need for Intelligence-Led Policing," *Domestic Preparedness* (2006), available from www.domesticpreparedness.com.
50. W. Finnegan, "The Terrorism Beat: How Is the NYPD Defending the City?" *New Yorker* 81, no. 21 (July 25, 2005), 58–71, in R. V. Clarke and G. R. Newman, "Police and the Prevention of Terrorism," *Policing* 1, no. 1 (2007), 9–20.
51. Clarke and Newman, "Police and the Prevention of Terrorism."